MASTERING MICROSOFT WORD FOR WINDOWS

Pamela S. Beason

Stephen Guild

John Wiley & Sons

New York   Chichester   Brisbane   Toronto   Singapore

To Marie Beason, with love and respect.—P.B.

To Pat, Darren, and Sue Anne, with love.—S.G.

Editor: Therese A. Zak
Managing Editor: Ruth Greif
Editing, Design, and Production: Impressions, Inc.

Library of Congress Cataloging-in-Publication Data

Beason, Pamela S.
    Mastering Microsoft Word for Windows / Pam Beason and Stephen Guild.
        p.   cm.
    Bibliography: p.
    Includes index.
    ISBN 0-471-50064-X
    1. Microsoft Word for Windows (Computer program)   2. Word processing.   I. Guild, Stephen.   II. Title.
    Z52.5.M523B43   1990
652.553—dc20   89-16493
                                                                                     CIP

Printed in the United States of America

90 91 10 9 8 7 6 5 4 3 2 1

Contents

PART TWO   **REVISING**   *73*

Chapter Four
Editing Your Word Files   *75*

Chapter Five
Working with Multiple Document Windows   106

Chapter Six
Marking Revisions, Comparing Versions, and Annotating   121

PART FOUR   PAGE LAYOUT AND PRINTING *231*

Chapter Fourteen
Perfecting Your Pages *284*

Chapter Fifteen
Adding Page Numbers, Headers and Footers, and Footnotes   *315*

Chapter Sixteen
Printing   *333*

PART FIVE   # WORKING WITH COMPLEX DOCUMENTS *345*

Acknowledgments

We would like to recognize a number of individuals who made the task of writing this book much easier. Teri Zak, our editor at John Wiley & Sons, was a great help at each step along the way. Lynn Brown did a terrific job of editing.

It's never easy to write about a product that's still evolving. However, at Microsoft we found a cooperative and helpful staff who did their best to answer our frequent questions. Melinda French and John Parkey made sure that we received new versions of the program as they became available. Jeff Lemkin helped to coordinate a technical review for us. We would especially like to thank Neil Hoopman, who spent hours poring over our manuscript, correcting technical errors and contributing ideas for easier ways to use Word.

On the home front, we'd like to acknowledge Pat and Mike, who put up with the long hours, many meetings, and our irascibility during the writing of this book. No one could be as happy as they are to see this book in print!

TRADEMARK ACKNOWLEDGMENTS

AutoCAD is a registered trademark of AutoDesk, Incorporated.
Da Vinci Systems is a trademark of Da Vinci Systems Corporation.
DisplayWrite is a trademark, and IBM, Personal System/2, and PC/AT are registered trademarks of International Business Machines Corporation.
Hercules is a registered trademark of Hercules Computer Technology.
LaserJet is a registered trademark of Hewlett-Packard Company.

Lotus and 1-2-3 are registered trademarks of Lotus Development Corporation.

Macintosh is a trademark licensed to Apple Computer, Inc.

Micrografx is a registered trademark, and Windows Draw and Windows Graph are trademarks of Micrographx, Incorporated.

Microsoft Windows is a trademark, and Microsoft, MS-DOS, Multiplan, and the Microsoft logo are registered trademarks of Microsoft Corporation.

MultiMate is a registered trademark of Multimate International Corporation, an Ashton-Tate company.

PackRat is a trademark of Polaris Software.

PageMaker is a registered trademark of Aldus Corporation.

PostScript is a registered trademark of Adobe Systems, Inc.

Quotron is a trademark of Quotron Systems.

Tektronix is a registered trademark of Tektronix, Incorporated.

VideoShow is a trademark of General Parametrics.

WordPerfect is a trademark of WordPerfect Corporation.

WordStar is a registered trademark of MicroPro International Corporation.

Zenographics Mirage is a trademark of Zenographics, Incorporated.

Introduction

Mastering Microsoft Word for Windows is a guide for using Microsoft's newest word processing program. This book shows you how you can take advantage of all the flexibility and sophisticated features that the Word for Windows program offers.

HOW THE BOOK IS ORGANIZED

We have organized this book to follow—as closely as possible—the process most people use to create and produce their documents.

Part I, "Getting Started," looks at some of the basic skills you'll need to use Word.

Part II, "Revising," focuses on the process of editing the text of your documents.

Part III, "Formatting," covers the various aspects of changing the way your document looks.

Part IV, "Page Layout and Printing," details how to add the finishing touches to documents: graphics, tables, page numbers, headers, footers, and footnotes. It also covers how to print out all the elements a Word file can contain.

Part V, "Working with Complex Documents," highlights some of the more sophisticated features of Word. You'll see how to use outlining, add fields, handle calculations, create tables of contents and indexes, set up form letters, and use the document management system.

Part VI, "Customizing Word," gives you tips and tricks about how you can write your own macros and change the Word program to meet your special needs.

Throughout this book, you'll find examples, helpful hints, and speed tips that will make your work with Word easier and more enjoyable.

HOW IS YOUR MACHINE SET UP?

In this book, we assume that your computer and software meet the following requirements:

- IBM Personal System/2 (Model 50 or higher), IBM PC/AT, Compaq computer, or 100% compatible

- 640K or more of memory

- IBM EGA, VGA Hercules graphics card, or other graphics cards compatible with Microsoft Windows version 2.03 or later

- Hard disk or file server (for storing documents)

- A floppy disk drive

- DOS version 3.0 or higher

- Microsoft Windows, version 2.03 or later, or Windows 386

If you're using a special runtime version of Windows, you'll still find this book most useful. However, not all the instructions included here will be valid, because runtime Windows doesn't do everything that the full version of Windows does (such as linking applications, using the Clipboard, using multiple applications, and so forth).

We also assume that you're using all of Word's commands presented on the full menus (rather than the short menus). To use Word's full menus, choose the View Full Menus command.

Part I

GETTING STARTED

Microsoft Word for Windows is a powerful new word processor. Many word processors are available, but Word for Windows is the first product designed specifically for the PC that combines ease of use, graphic representation, and the ability to link Word documents with other Windows-based applications. With Word for Windows, you can do almost any sophisticated word processing task with the ease of use of the Windows environment. This part of the book covers the basic concepts you need to get going with Word for Windows.

In Chapter 1, you'll learn more about the product—its capabilities and flexibility.

Chapter 2 covers the relationship between Word, Windows, and the operating system. You'll learn the basics of using keys and the mouse; using the commands, menus, and dialog boxes; and using Word's on-line help system when you want details on Word's menus and screens.

Chapter 3 deals with Word files. It introduces Word's templates and how you can base documents on them. You'll also discover how to start new documents and save documents in different files and file formats.

## Chapter One

Welcome to Microsoft Word for Windows

Almost as soon as microcomputers became widely available, software developers created a wealth of programs for text processing. Many of them are excellent, giving users the ability to work more efficiently at fast speeds with special features. Yet, most users of word processing programs say they would really like this program or that program "if only. . . ."

Some of these "if onlys" include

- a document display with true WYSIWYG (what you see is what you get)

- the ability to combine text and graphics and to make text "flow" around graphics

- easy exchange of data among different programs and applications

- the ability to easily work with data in rows and columns

- precise positioning of objects on a page

- the ability to view an entire page at a glance

- translation of files into a variety of formats

- customizable key assignments and placement of commands

- the ability to mark revisions, add annotations, and compare different versions of files

- a catalog system that makes it easy to work with a large number of files

■ the ability to easily program the computer to perform repetitious operations

Whereas Macintosh software has offered a few of these features for some time, the PC user has had to settle for more pedestrian products or to use several programs to accomplish what the Macintosh user could do with a single application.

Microsoft's Word for Windows is the first major product to include all the features that users say they would like to have in their "dream" word processor. And it runs in the Microsoft Windows environment, which enables you to use many different applications at once and to share information between applications. Microsoft has designed this new program to respond to the most frequent complaints and wishes of users, especially "power users"—individuals who are doing large, complex jobs. Word for Windows is excellent for these sophisticated applications, but because of its clear graphic design, it is easy for the beginner to learn.

Microsoft Word for Windows provides "compound document processing"—the ability to mix text, pictures, graphics, spreadsheets, and charts in the same file. Mixing various elements in a document—text, pictures, and so on—means that you can produce a finished document using only Word, rather than having to manually cut and paste in those other integral pieces. Just as important is the ability to see what all of these elements will look like together on a printed page. No longer do you have to guess what your final product might look like. Gone is the aggravation of printing a document, then having to adjust it because the pages didn't come out the way you had hoped.

Word is also very flexible. It comes shipped with many "bells and whistles," but you can customize it to meet your specific needs in almost any way you want. In fact, if you wish, you can almost design your own personal word processor with only those commands and functions you want. You can even tailor Word so that it functions differently depending on which document you are working on.

Whereas Word is easy to use for the beginning or occasional user, power users will readily see that Word contains many advanced features that distinguish it from most other word processors. With Word you can use fields not only to create form letters, but to perform calculations; to link documents and spreadsheets; and to create cross-references, indexes, and tables of contents. And you can extend the power of Word by creating programs inside Word using the embedded programming language.

This chapter looks at some of these features of Word for Windows.

THE MANY VIEWS OF WORD

Perhaps Word's greatest achievement is the WYSIWYG—what you see is what you get—interface. In the past, word processing users had to settle for an approximation of what the printed page would look like. Some programs did a better job at this than others, but no one program solved the problem. With Word, you can see on the screen what will actually print out on the page. The printed text will be no wider or longer than what you see on the screen. Graphics and tables appear at their exact place in the document. Character formatting, even type sizes and fonts, appears exactly as it will in the printed document.

Word provides five different ways to look at a document. You can move between different views quickly and easily, and, with the exception of print preview, can edit and revise text and graphics at the same time.

Normal view, the view that you see when you first start Word, is the view you'll use most often. Figure 1–1 shows a sample display of normal view. In normal view, you can see pictures and most formatting, but you can't see headers or footers, page numbers, or footnotes. Using normal view is a fast way to enter and format text.

Page view displays full-size pages with all of the elements in their correct positions, ready for you to add the final touches before printing. You can see text, headers, footers, and footnotes, line numbers,

Figure 1–1.
A Word document in
normal view.

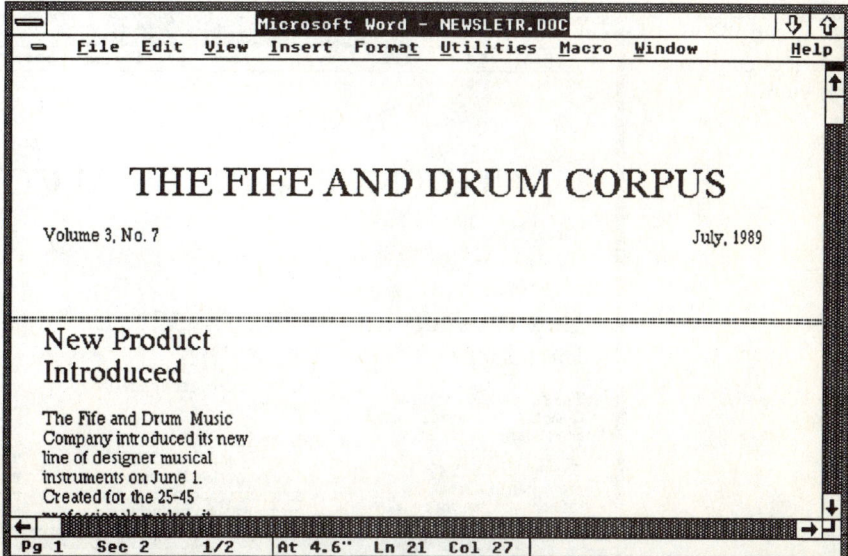

multiple "flowing" columns, and objects assigned to fixed positions. You can't see an entire page at once in page view unless you have a special monitor, but you can easily scroll pages both horizontally and vertically to inspect and edit all the text right up to the edges of the page. Figure 1–2 illustrates page view.

Outline view, shown in Figure 1–3, displays the skeleton structure of your document, which you can use to organize your document and view its structure. Outline view provides an easy way to design large documents, move whole sections around within the document, and create tables of contents and other lists.

Print preview displays a miniature version of entire pages with all text, graphics, multiple columns, tables, headers, and footers in position. You cannot edit text in print preview, but you can move document margins, page breaks, headers and footers, page numbers, and fixed-positioned objects around to add the finishing touches to your pages before printing. Figure 1–4 shows a sample of print preview.

Draft view displays a stripped-down version of the text. Only the most basic formatting shows on the screen—all of the other special features, such as pictures, do not appear. Draft view is designed for fast text entry and fast printing when you want to concentrate on the words in your document, not on the appearance of the pages. See Figure 1–5 for an example of draft view.

You can easily switch among these various views through the menu commands or through special key assignments that you can create.

Figure 1–2.
A Word document in page view.

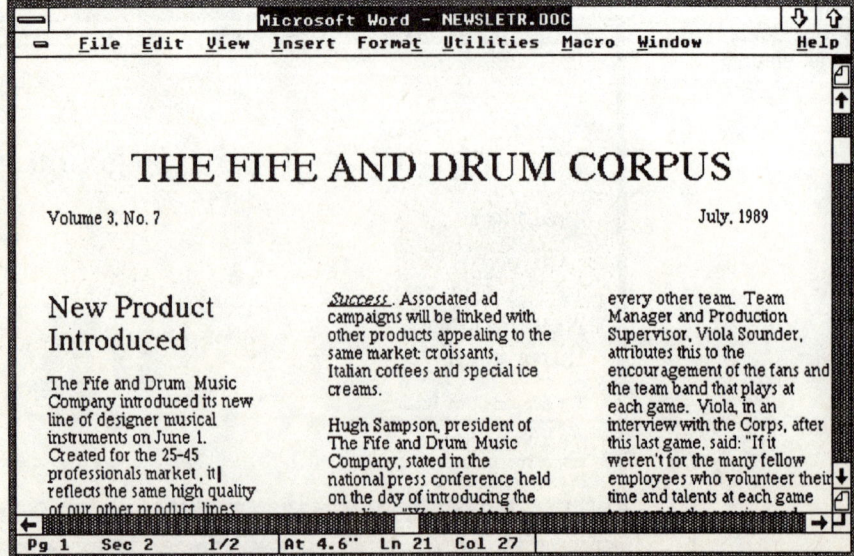

Figure 1–3.
A Word document in outline view.

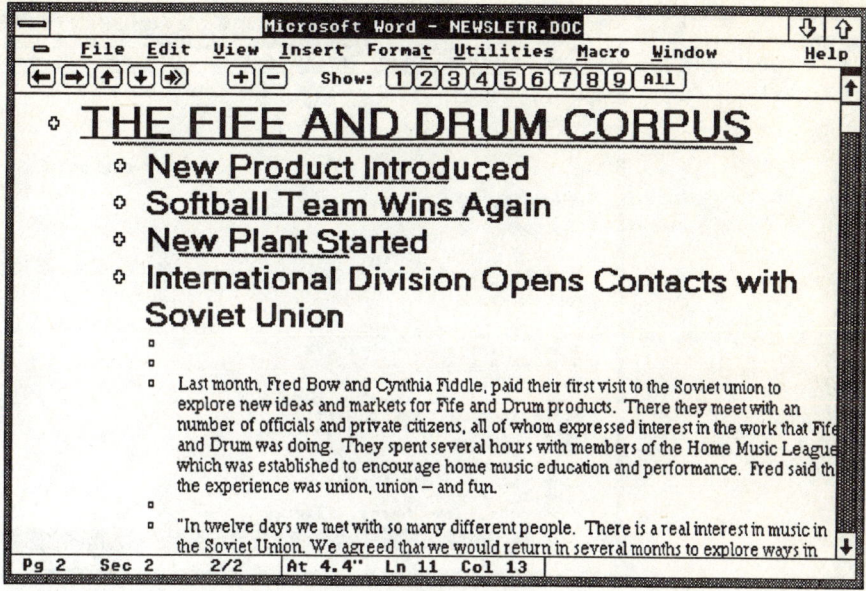

Figure 1–4.
A Word document in print preview view.

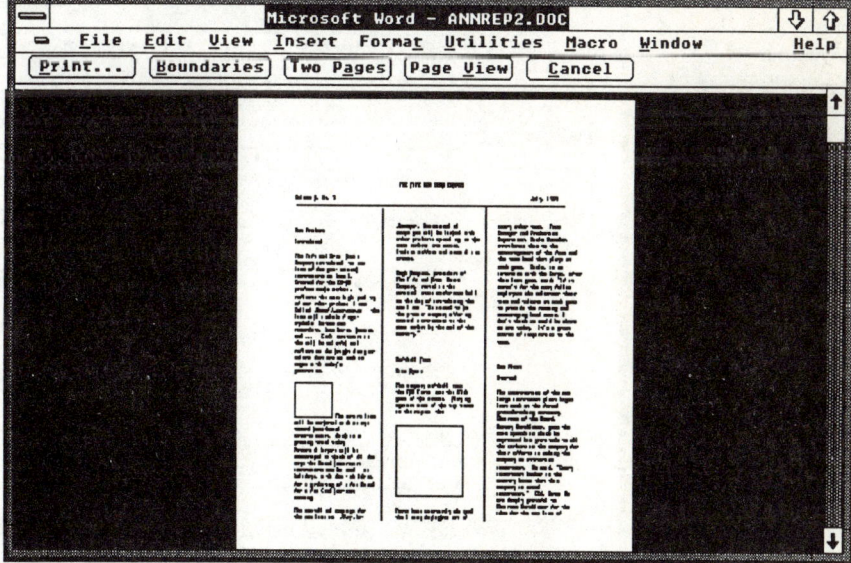

MIXING TEXT AND GRAPHICS

In Word, *picture* is the general term used to describe graphics, scanned pictures, charts, spreadsheets, and imported blocks of text. Word can

Figure 1–5.
A Word document in draft view.

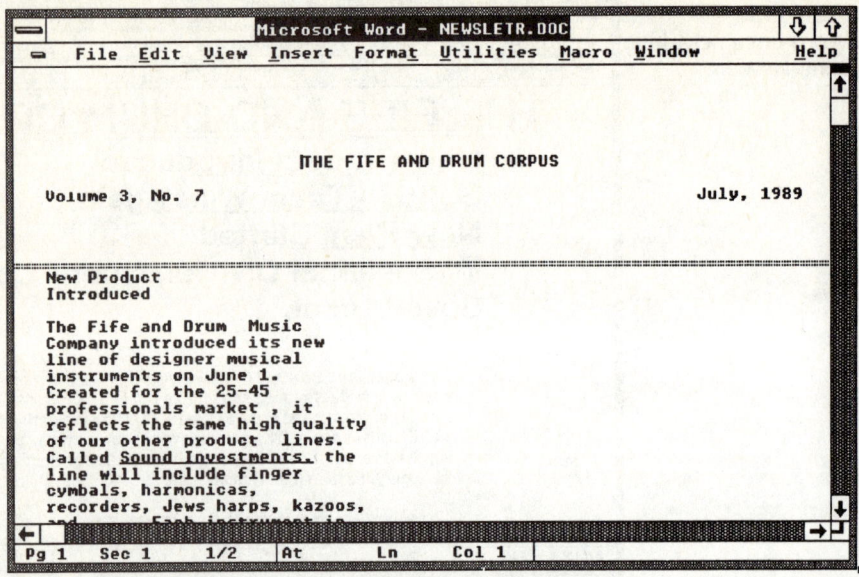

Figure 1–6.
A document containing many of the elements possible in Word: text, a picture, and a spreadsheet-type table.

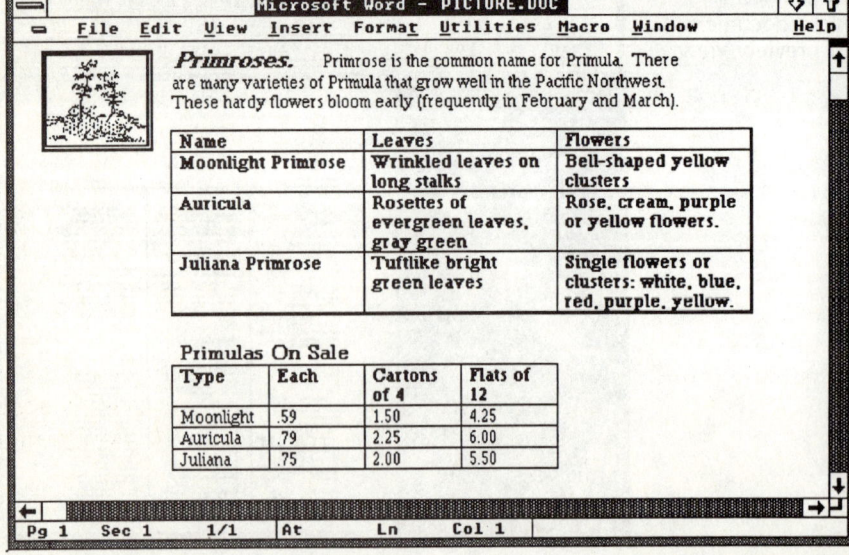

easily mix these diverse elements in the same document, as Figure 1–6 shows. There's no need to paste up artwork. You can import (read in) graphics directly from your graphics software into Word, crop and scale them to fit the space you want, add borders and captions, then position the graphics wherever you want them on the pages. Welcome to desktop publishing!

If you prefer to paste in artwork manually after you print the text, Word makes that easy, too. You can insert graphics frames that reserve just the right amount of space for your art.

START WITH A TEMPLATE

The basic building blocks for Word documents are *templates.* A template is simply a framework or pattern of a document that you can use to base other documents on. If you frequently use documents that share standard text or a standard look, you can put that information into a template, then base your documents on the template to save the time and effort of creating a new document each time.

You may not use the word *template* every day, but odds are that you use the concepts of templates in your daily work. For example, you may have a memo format with the date, addresses, subject, the company logo, and standard text that you use over and over. We've all filled out order forms, which are another type of template. And no doubt you're familiar with the "templates" provided by the IRS—the 1040, W-4, and so on.

Word for Windows expands the power of templates beyond creating forms. You can develop a template that contains *all* of the common elements you use repeatedly, not just text. Word templates can include formatting instructions, macros (miniprograms that tell Word to perform a series of commands at the touch of a key), and even special menu and key assignments that customize Word for your own needs.

Microsoft includes many ready-made, standard templates with Word. Figure 1–7 shows such a template created for memos. Once your taste for templates becomes sophisticated, you can also create your own templates to meet specific needs.

SAVE TEXT, FORMATTING, AND INSTRUCTIONS TO USE AGAIN

With Word for Windows, there's no need to duplicate information or instructions. You can save text and graphics in *glossaries,* save formatting in *styles,* and save programming instructions in *macros.*

Figure 1–7.
A document
template used for
standard memos.

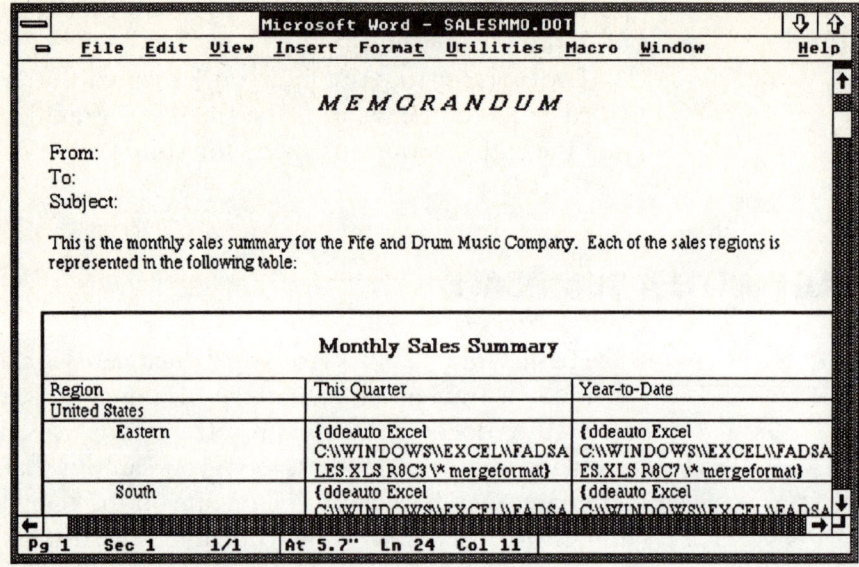

Save Text and Graphics in Glossaries

When you want to reuse a block of characters, there's no need to re-create or copy the same characters over and over. Word can save that text in a glossary. Using a glossary is like renting a safe-deposit box—you can store items in it for safekeeping, then take them out whenever you want. Glossary entries can consist of one word, a sentence, a paragraph, or even whole documents. They can also contain tables, graphics, fields, and all the other elements of a document. You can even construct entire documents by combining glossary entries you've saved. The Edit Glossary dialog box always displays the glossary entries you've saved; a sample dialog box appears in Figure 1–8.

Do It with Styles

If you've used Microsoft Word for the Macintosh or the PC, you may be familiar with styles. Styles are sets of standardized paragraph and character formatting instructions you can apply to any paragraph—or to all paragraphs—in your document. Whenever you change a style, all text formatted with that style changes automatically.

Using styles to format paragraphs saves time and gives your documents a professional, consistent look.

Figure 1–8.
The Edit Glossary dialog box containing glossary entries.

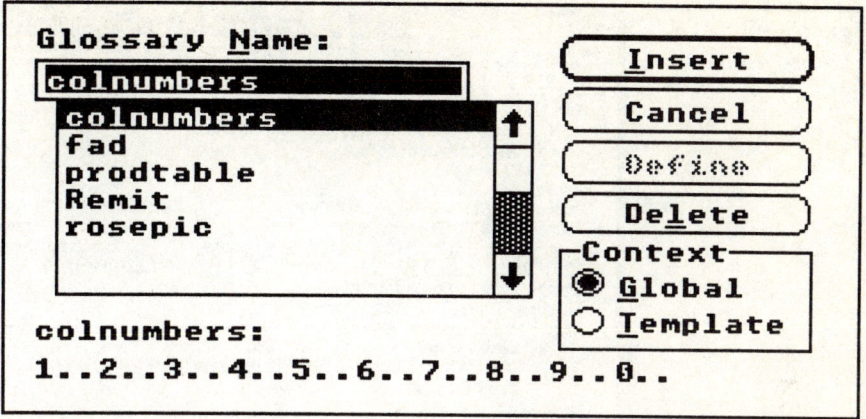

Let Macros Do the Work for You

You can create macros that tell Word to perform a series of operations. In other word-processing programs, macros are hard to learn and complex to store, so only programmers master their use, but now Word makes it simple for anyone to use macros. It's as easy as recording on a video tape—you record the operations and keystrokes you want Word to perform for you. Then just play the macro and watch Word do your repetitious tasks for you in a few seconds!

If you're already familiar with macro languages or if you want to take the time to learn Word's macro language, you can develop a macro script, enter it in text form, and then run it. Figure 1–9 shows a macro script. You can also take one of the many macros provided with Word and adapt it to suit your needs.

LAY OUT YOUR PAGES WITH EASE

Word is more than just a word-processing program. It is also a desktop publishing program that helps you lay out pages easily and see what the pages will look like before they're printed.

Position Text and Graphics Exactly Where You Want Them

When you create documents, often you decide to shift various elements and objects around on the pages. In the past, this has been time-

Figure 1–9.
A macro in the
Macro Edit window.

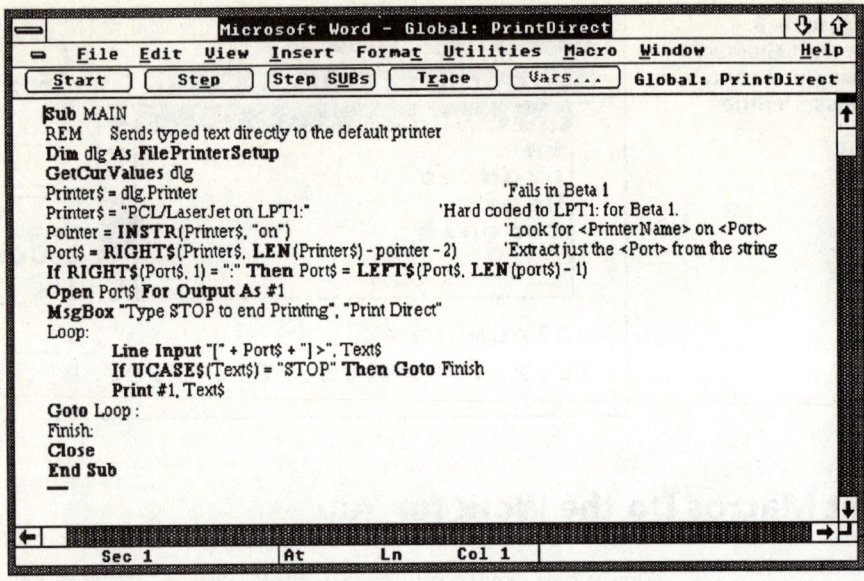

consuming and complicated, and if you made changes later, you usually had to format the pages all over again. Word for Windows makes it easy to position objects—pictures, blocks of text, tables, headers, or footers—exactly where you want them. For example, you can center a graphic on a page, create a sidehead by moving a paragraph into the margin, or position the company logo at the top of the page.

You can use precise measurements (such as 3.5 inches from the top and 2.1 inches from the left) to tell Word where to place an object, or use relative positions (such as Top, Center, and Right) to place objects relative to the document margins, the edges of the page, or within columns. Positioning text or graphics in this way "fixes" the position of the object on a page. When an object has a fixed position, all the other elements of a document adjust to "flow" around the fixed object. If you add or delete information, the surrounding text automatically readjusts, but the fixed object stays exactly where you placed it. Figure 1–10 illustrates a fixed-position graphic.

You can create Word templates that specify positions for text and graphics on the document pages (a report page layout, for instance), and then use the templates to format entire documents.

Add Footnotes

Word makes footnotes much easier to work with. You can create footnotes at the same time you create your document, and because foot-

Figure 1–10.
A document with a fixed-positioned picture.

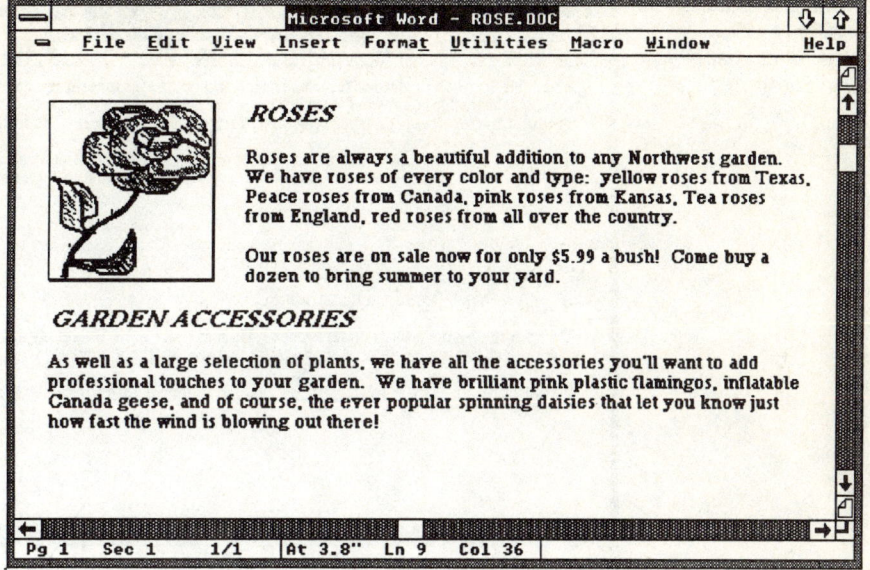

notes appear in a separate window, you can easily review and edit footnote text at any time. You can control whether footnotes print on the same pages as their reference numbers, at the end of sections, or at the end of the entire document. Figure 1–11 presents a technical document that contains footnotes.

Add Headers and Footers

Headers (also called *running heads*) and footers (also called *running feet*) add visual clarity and emphasis to a document. Both elements are easily managed in Word. You can create different headers for even, odd, and first pages. Because headers are also positioned objects, you can move them around in print preview until you get just the look you want.

Put It in a Table

You no longer need to use tabs to format information into rows and columns. Word's new table commands make it easy to set up a table structure, then fill it in later. Or you can create a table from any list of information. Tables in Word don't have to consist of just columns

Figure 1–11.
A technical paper
with footnotes.

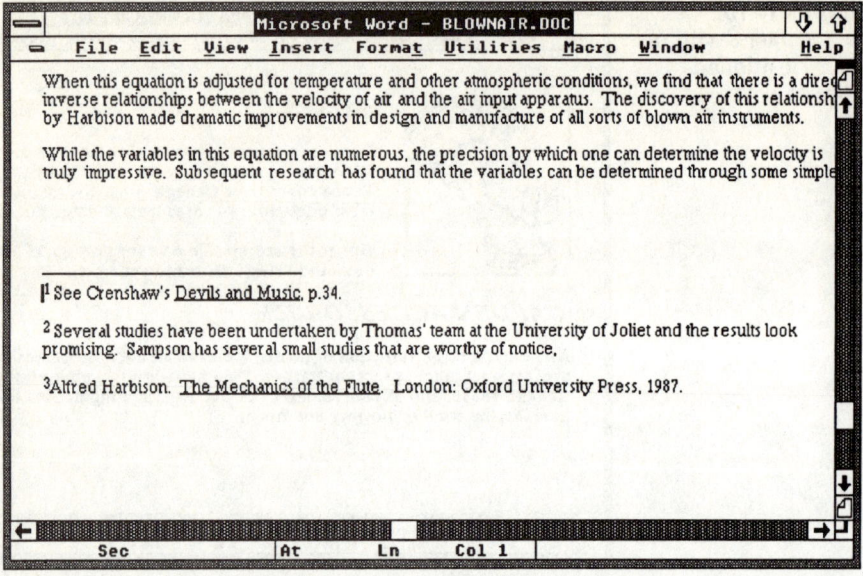

Figure 1–12.
An employee list in a
Word table.

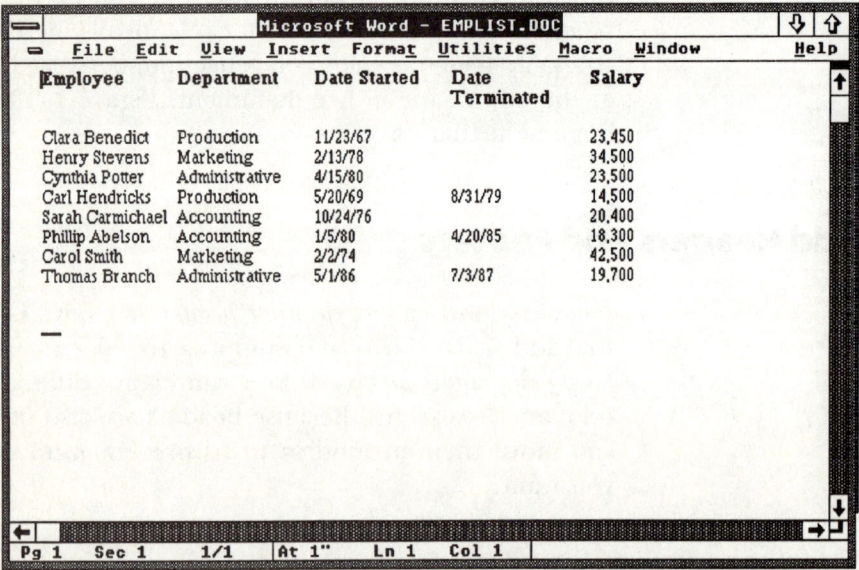

of numbers or words. You can put almost anything into a table, including graphics and paragraphs of text. Word automatically adjusts
rows to make room for the largest object. Figure 1–12 shows a Word
table.

You can set up traditional spreadsheet-type tables and tables of list items, or you can use tables to create side-by-side paragraphs. You can also import information from spreadsheets and other documents and convert that information into a table. Then, if you change your mind later, you can easily convert a table back into regular text.

Word's table formatting is very flexible. You can specify the number of rows and columns in a table, tell Word their width and height, and determine the amount of white space between the items in the columns. You can even merge table cells to create complex arrangements, such as headers spanning several columns. And you can add a variety of borders to individual cells or to the entire table. At last, you can set up a table the way you want it!

Preview Your Pages

Word makes it easy to preview your pages before you print them. The Print Preview command displays one or two pages of your document in a miniature form. You can scroll to see all of the text, graphics, headers and footers, and other elements of your document. Print preview is interactive, too you can reposition a variety of objects on a page and see the results immediately.

DO IT YOUR WAY

Programmers can't anticipate the way every user will interact with the program. We've all run across key assignments or menu commands that don't seem to make sense to us or that we just can't remember. And most of us would like to add or remove something from the screen to make the interface easier to work with. Word for Windows helps you customize the program so that it works the way you want it to.

Customize Menus and Key Assignments

Word is designed so you can make it *your* program. You can modify menus by adding, removing, renaming, and moving commands. You can also modify the actions of keys and add key assignments to speed up those operations you do frequently. If a command or a key assignment doesn't make sense to you, change it!

Display Only What You Want to See

You can adjust the appearance of the Word window—change the menus, display or hide Word's graphics tools (the ruler and the ribbon). You can also choose when to display paragraph marks, tabs, and other special characters that control the way your document looks. You can control the display of the vertical and horizontal scroll bars, so you can hide them if you're not a mouse user. You can look at just what *you* want to display. Figure 1–13 shows the unintimidating displays with which you revise screen and utility settings.

Change How the Program Works

You can customize many aspects of Word's operations. For example, you can determine whether you want your work automatically saved, and if so, how often. You can change the default unit of measurement

Figure 1–13.
The View Preferences and Utilities Customize dialog boxes.

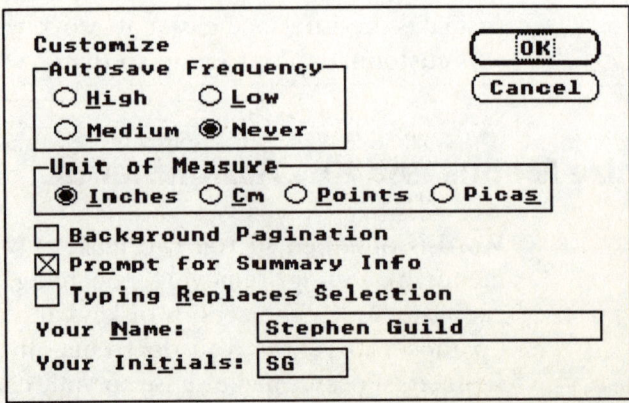

from inches to centimeters or other units. You can change the default tab spacing, the default page formatting, and many other program defaults that control the way your documents look. You can also add or subtract special items from a dictionary, and create whole dictionaries to help you spell check documents containing special terms.

MANAGE DOCUMENTS EASILY

Have you ever tried to find a document when you can't remember the filename? Tried to remember when you first created a document? Ended up with several versions of the same document and wondered which version was current? Word makes it easy to find the answers to all your file management questions.

Find Files with the Document Retrieval System

Word provides a full document management system. You can use Word's document retrieval capabilities to find documents for review, to delete or print several documents at once, or to see the history of a document since its creation. You can search specific drives and directories with the Find File feature to build a list of documents that contain the information you're looking for. Figure 1–14 shows the dialog box for Find File.

You can sort and find particular documents by author, date, title, subject, or by searching for key words in the document's text. You can display and edit a document's *summary information*, a list of information Word maintains for each file. The document retrieval system provides a handy way to keep a list of your most often used documents, as well as a way to locate specific files quickly.

Figure 1–14.
The File Find dialog box.

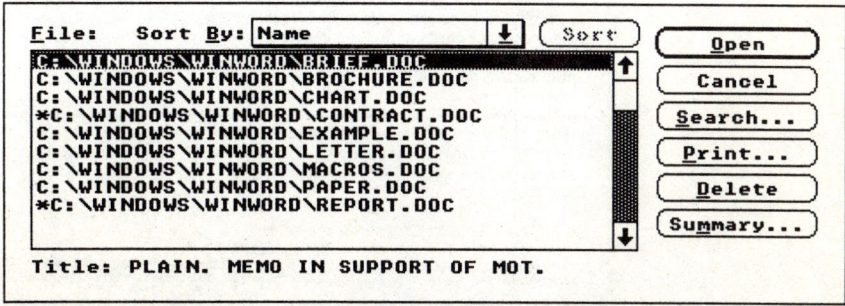

Add Annotations

When your document will be reviewed and edited by several people, Word's annotation capabilities help keep your files straight. Multiple users can add annotations (comments) to a document: Word identifies each annotator's comments with a special code. Annotations are automatically formatted as hidden text, so you can display or hide them at will. As Figure 1–15 shows, displayed annotations appear in a separate area, leaving the document uncluttered for easy reading.

Mark Revisions

When you turn on revision marking, each deletion or addition is clearly indicated, but changes are not made to the file until you approve them. Changes to separate versions of a document can also be easily identified later using Word's capability to compare versions. Figure 1–16 contains samples of revision marks.

HANDLE LONG DOCUMENTS WITH SKILL

Word handles the different elements of long documents easily, helping you to keep all the parts in order and to create tables and lists of reference information.

Figure 1–15.
An annual report
with annotations.

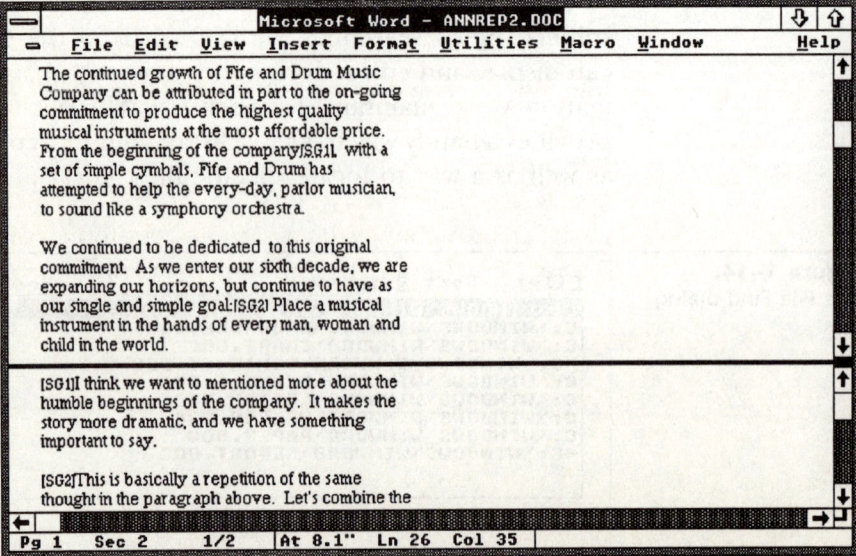

Figure 1–16.
A document with
revision marks.

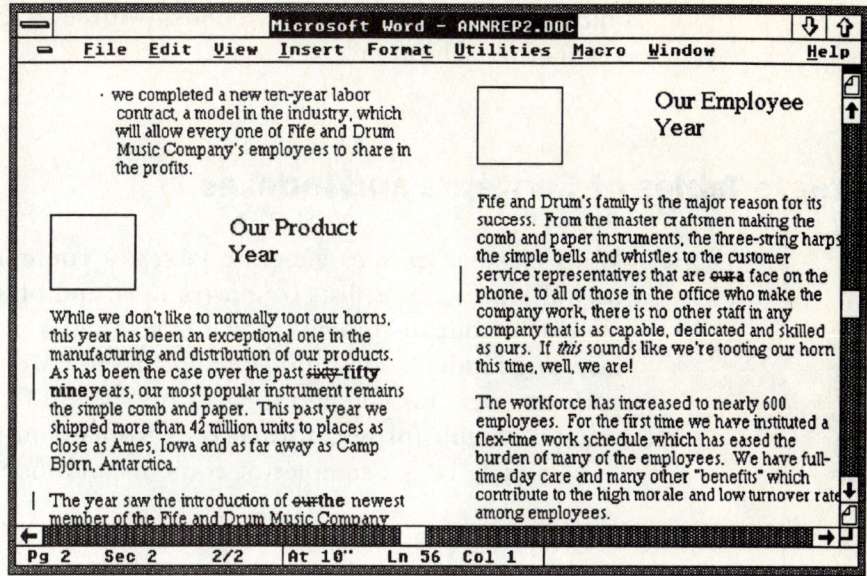

Outline It First

Word's outline view makes it easy to organize, reorganize, and format a complex document. You can use outlining to set up the basic structure of a document before you create it, so you can plan the document thoroughly in advance. Word's outlines aren't separate documents; they're just another way of looking at your document. You can use outlining to view your entire document and to rearrange whole sections. Word's graphic outline tools make it easy to assign levels to headings, to change headings from one level to another, and to display body text or only specific levels of headings.

To travel through a document quickly, you can use outline view to easily see where you want to go and to jump to that exact location. You can move between main topics, subtopics, or even specific portions of text quickly and easily.

Incorporate Dynamic Cross-References

With Word, you can set up cross-references (such as "See Table 3 on page *n*") that Word will update with the correct page numbers before printing your document. This is especially valuable when you are producing a long work—a report, a book—with several chapters or sections related to each other.

Create Tables of Contents and Indexes

Word makes it easy to generate tables of contents, tables of figures, lists of photographs, lists of illustrations, and other lists of items that appear in your documents. You can also quickly develop an index by inserting hidden codes into your documents. Word keeps track of the page numbers for you and formats the tables of contents and indexes using a default (preset) format or a format you specify. See Figures 1–17 and 1–18 for samples of contents and index.

GET IT RIGHT

Once the information is on the pages, you'll want to make sure that the grammar, punctuation, terminology, and hyphenation is as good as it can be. You don't need a dictionary and other reference books—now you can use Word's utilities to check your documents for you.

Figure 1–17.
A table of contents.

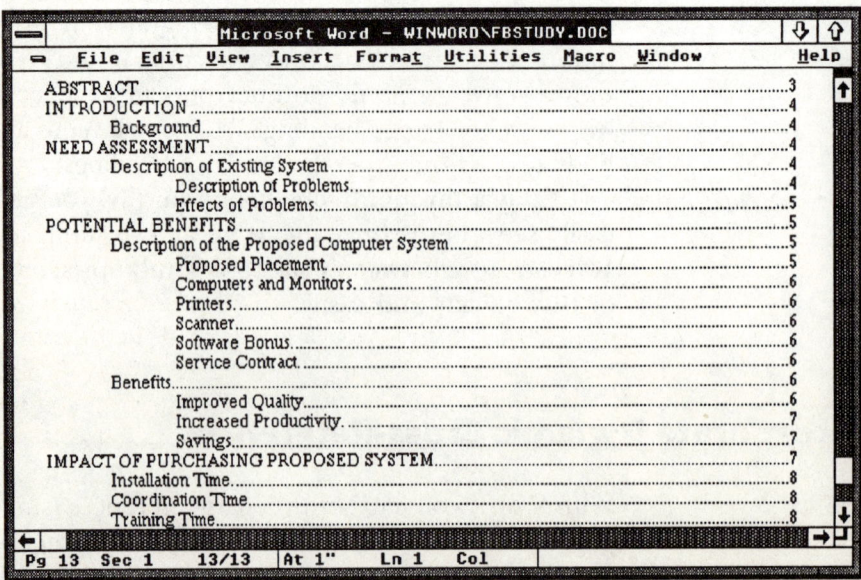

Figure 1–18.
An index.

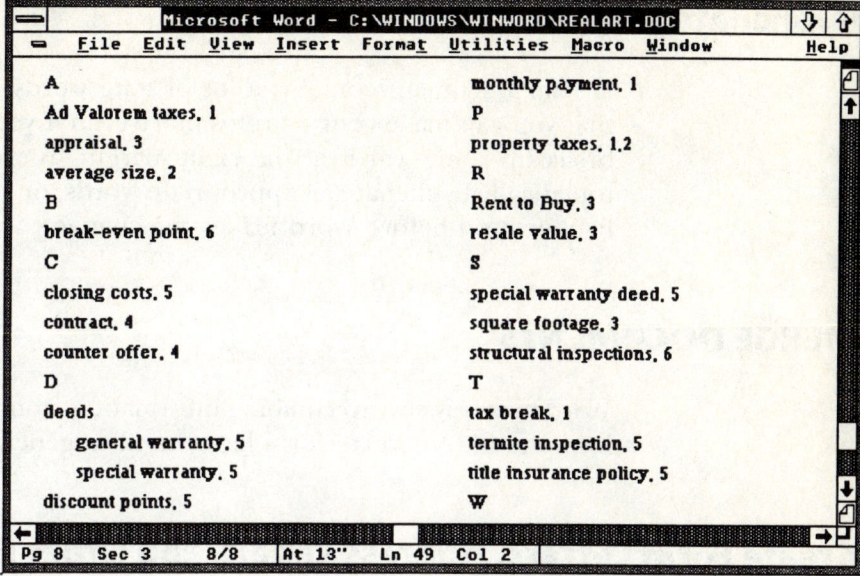

```
━━    ▭      Microsoft Word - C:\WINDOWS\WINWORD\REALART.DOC      ⬇ ⬆
 ━   File   Edit   View   Insert   Format   Utilities   Macro   Window        Help
    A                                      monthly payment, 1                    ◸
    Ad Valorem taxes, 1                    P                                     ⬆
    appraisal, 3                           property taxes, 1,2
    average size, 2                        R
    B                                      Rent to Buy, 3
    break-even point, 6                    resale value, 3
    C                                      S
    closing costs, 5                       special warranty deed, 5
    contract, 4                            square footage, 3
    counter offer, 4                       structural inspections, 6
    D                                      T
    deeds                                  tax break, 1
       general warranty, 5                 termite inspection, 5
       special warranty, 5                 title insurance policy, 5
    discount points, 5                     W                                    ⬇
 ←                                                                           →
  Pg 8   Sec 3    8/8    At 13"   Ln 49   Col 2
```

Check the Spelling

Like its other features, Word's spelling checker is flexible and powerful.
You can check whole documents or just a single word. You can create
special dictionaries that contain uncommon words or special technical
terms. Word checks not only basic arrangements of letters, but also
looks for repeated words, uncommon capitalizations, words whose first
letter should be capitalized, and words in which all letters should be
capitalized.

Find Synonyms and Definitions in Word's Thesaurus

Have you used the same word too many times, or are you unsure of
a term's exact meaning? With Word's thesaurus you can look up synonyms and definitions at any point in the document creation process.
You can browse through the thesaurus and review definitions at your
leisure. You can also select a word in your document or type a new
word and ask Word to display a definition and a list of synonyms for
you to choose from.

Hyphenate Words at Will

If your document contains a lot of long words, you'll soon discover that you can make your margins more even if you use hyphenation to break up some words at the right margin. You can tell Word to automatically hyphenate all appropriate words, or you can approve each hyphenation before Word makes the change.

MERGE DOCUMENTS

Word makes it easy to combine information from various types of files into one file to create form letters and to generate address labels.

Create Form Letters, Address Labels, and Other Forms

Word makes it easy to create form letters, address lists, rosters, phone lists, lists of results, and other documents that combine standard text with variable data. You can print mailing labels using Word's special templates. You can even use data from other applications to create form documents. Figure 1–19 shows a form document in which Word will fill in the fields.

Figure 1–19.
A reply letter that will be merged with a data file.

Link Word Files to Other Applications

You can link Word files to other applications, most notably to Microsoft Excel. These links, which are enabled by Windows' Dynamic Data Exchange (DDE) capability, immediately update information in your Word document whenever a linked file changes. This ensures that your Word document always contains the most up-to-date information. Word's linking feature is especially useful for documents such as sales memos, financial reports, and attendance reports—documents that involve frequent changes and calculations. In Figure 1–20, you can see a Word document in which the financial information has been imported from Excel.

PERFORM CALCULATIONS AND COMPLETE INSTRUCTIONS WITH FIELDS

You can use Word to insert *fields* (special sets of instructions) into your document. Word has myriad field types from which to choose. For example, you can insert fields that tell Word to insert text, graphics,

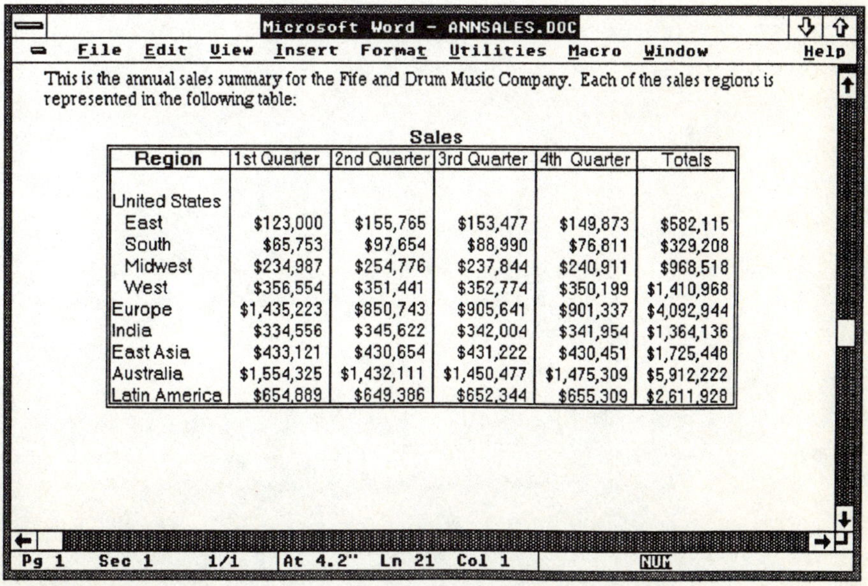

Figure 1–20.
A document linked with a Microsoft Excel document.

Microsoft Word – ANNSALES.DOC

File Edit View Insert Format Utilities Macro Window   Help

This is the annual sales summary for the Fife and Drum Music Company. Each of the sales regions is represented in the following table:

Sales

Region	1st Quarter	2nd Quarter	3rd Quarter	4th Quarter	Totals
United States					
East	$123,000	$155,765	$153,477	$149,873	$582,115
South	$65,753	$97,654	$88,990	$76,811	$329,208
Midwest	$234,987	$254,776	$237,844	$240,911	$968,518
West	$356,554	$351,441	$352,774	$350,199	$1,410,968
Europe	$1,435,223	$850,743	$905,641	$901,337	$4,092,944
India	$334,556	$345,622	$342,004	$341,954	$1,364,136
East Asia	$433,121	$430,654	$431,222	$430,451	$1,725,448
Australia	$1,554,325	$1,432,111	$1,450,477	$1,475,309	$5,912,222
Latin America	$654,889	$649,386	$652,344	$655,309	$2,611,928

Pg 1   Sec 1   1/1   At 4.2"   Ln 21   Col 1   NUM

Figure 1–21.
A technical paper
with an equation
created using a field.

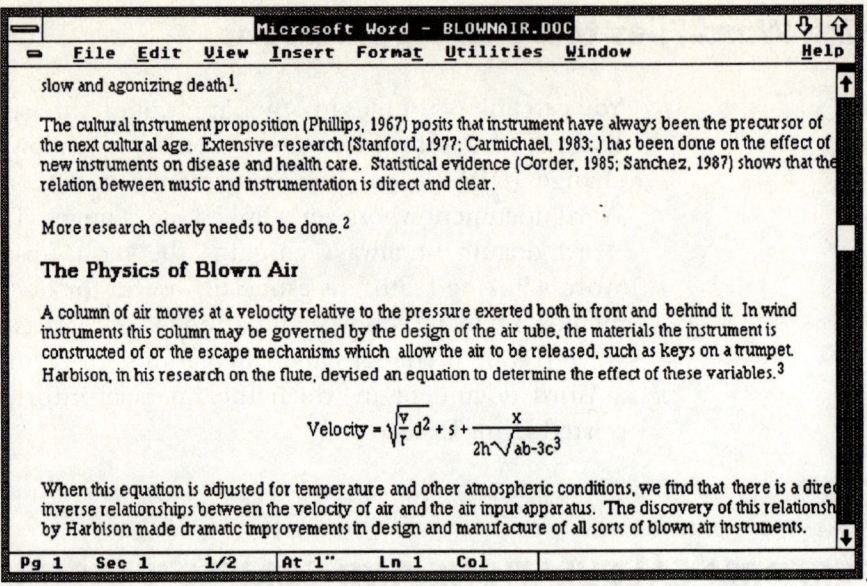

Figure 1–21.
A technical paper
with an equation
created using a field.

slow and agonizing death[1].

The cultural instrument proposition (Phillips, 1967) posits that instrument have always been the precursor of the next cultural age. Extensive research (Stanford, 1977; Carmichael, 1983;) has been done on the effect of new instruments on disease and health care. Statistical evidence (Corder, 1985; Sanchez, 1987) shows that the relation between music and instrumentation is direct and clear.

More research clearly needs to be done.[2]

The Physics of Blown Air

A column of air moves at a velocity relative to the pressure exerted both in front and behind it. In wind instruments this column may be governed by the design of the air tube, the materials the instrument is constructed of or the escape mechanisms which allow the air to be released, such as keys on a trumpet. Harbison, in his research on the flute, devised an equation to determine the effect of these variables.[3]

$$\text{Velocity} = \sqrt{\frac{v}{r}d^2} + s + \frac{x}{2h\sqrt{ab-3c^3}}$$

When this equation is adjusted for temperature and other atmospheric conditions, we find that there is a direct inverse relationships between the velocity of air and the air input apparatus. The discovery of this relationship by Harbison made dramatic improvements in design and manufacture of all sorts of blown air instruments.

numbers, or entire documents before printing. When you activate other types of fields, you can run macros. You can also use fields to create dynamic cross-references to other parts of documents and to develop simple or complex mathematical and scientific equations. Figure 1–21 shows an equation created in a field.

Chapter Two

Learning the Basics

Most word processors share many common elements and procedures, but each has a slightly different approach to easing the task of text processing. To fully use Word's power, you need to know some basic procedures before you can begin to explore the program. This chapter describes the following techniques you need to know to operate Word:

- how to start and quit Word

- how to choose commands and use dialog boxes

- the difference between full menus and short menus

- how to use Word's help system

If you're new to Windows and to Word, you'll want to read this chapter thoroughly before going on.

WORD, WINDOWS, AND THE OPERATING SYSTEM

When you use Word for Windows, you're really dealing with three layers of software, all running at the same time, as illustrated in Figure 2–1.

Word runs on top of Windows, so you can use the Windows Control Panel to control the colors and other aspects of the Word window, and to install fonts and printers. Just like any other Windows application, you can change the size of the Word window, making it larger or smaller or shrinking it to an icon.

Windows runs on top of your operating system (MS-DOS, PC-DOS, or OS/2), which controls the hardware (reading from and writing to

Figure 2–1.
You use three levels
of software when
you run Word for
Windows.

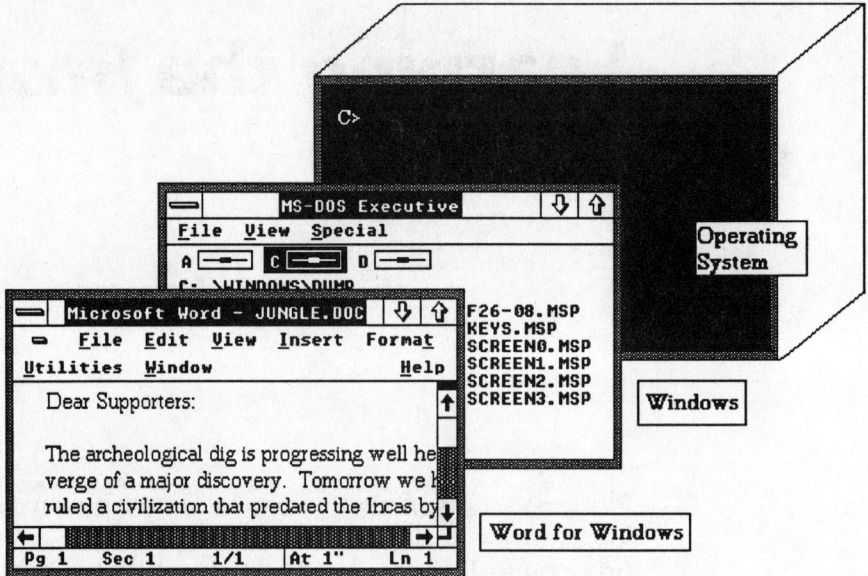

Figure 2–1.
You use three levels of software when you run Word for Windows.

disk, sending information to the printer, and so forth). Because Word and Windows interact with the operating system, you must follow the operating system's naming conventions when you name files created with Word. You should understand the operating system's tree structure and know how to use its pathname conventions when you refer to files in different directories or on different drives. For more information about your operating system, see the manuals that came with your computer.

STARTING WORD

After you've started Windows, you can start Word in three ways.

- Use the arrow keys to highlight WINWORD.EXE in the MS-DOS Executive window, then press Enter; or use the mouse to double-click WINWORD.EXE.

- Use the arrow keys to highlight the name of any file created with Word for Windows (see Figure 2–2), then press Enter; or use the mouse to double-click the name of a Word file. This starts Word and opens the document at the same time.

- Choose the File Run command in the MS-DOS Executive window, type **winword** in the dialog box, then press Enter.

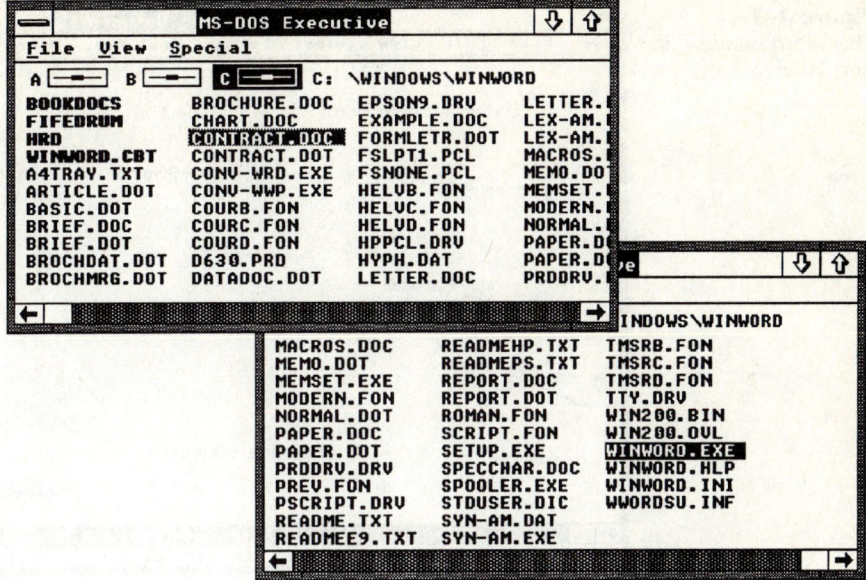

Outside of Windows, you can start Word by typing **winword** at the operating system prompt (usually C>). For this method to work, Windows and Word directories must be on your path (see your operating system manual for more information about paths).

A SURVEY OF THE WORD SCREEN

Word first opens in normal view, the view you'll use most often. Take a look at Figure 2–3, which points out different parts of the Word window in normal view. You'll see these terms used throughout this book.

If you didn't open a specific document when you started Word, you'll notice that the word *Document1* appears in the title bar. This is Word's default name for a new document. You can enter text to create a new document, then save it with the name you want, or you can close this empty document and open another document you've already created.

USING THE MOUSE

Like most Windows applications, you can use the mouse, the keyboard, or a combination of both to choose commands and perform common

Figure 2–3.
The Word window in
normal view.

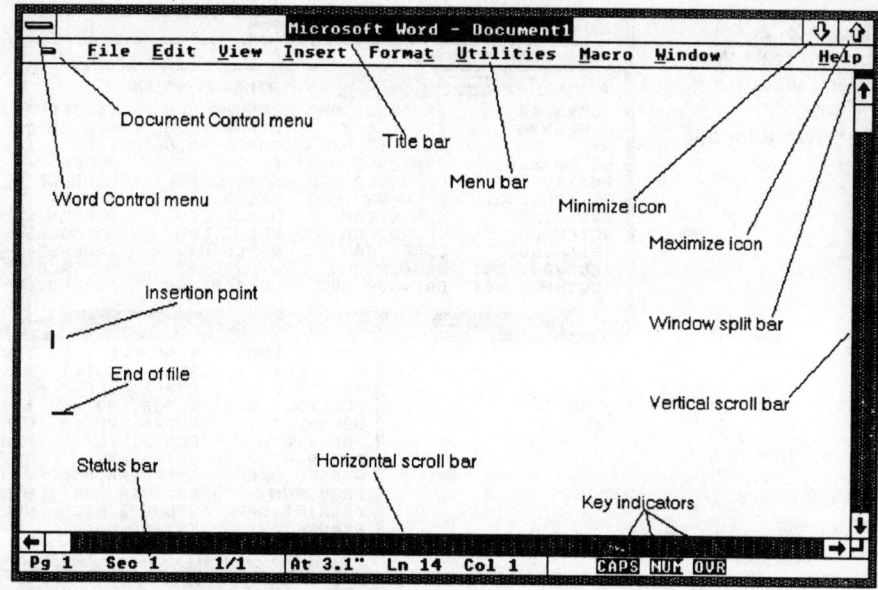

tasks with Word. You may already be familiar with using the mouse,
but just in case you need a reminder, here are the mouse terms used
in this book.

Term	Meaning
Point	Slide the mouse on your desk to move the mouse pointer to a specific location in the Word window.
Click	Quickly press and release the mouse button while the pointer is at a specific location.
	For example, "Click the OK button" means move the mouse pointer to the OK button, then press and release the mouse button. You almost always click the left mouse button; use the right mouse button when you move text or graphics.
Double-click	Quickly press and release the mouse button twice while the pointer is at a specific location.

Drag   Hold down the mouse button while you
                        move the mouse. For example, "Drag the
                        tab icon" means point to the tab icon, then
                        hold down the mouse button while you
                        move the mouse to drag the tab icon to a
                        new location.

The mouse pointer takes on a different shape depending on the
kind of action that is being performed. For instance, it is an outlined
arrow when you're selecting commands from the menu, an hourglass
when Word is saving a file, and a solid black arrow when you're selecting a column in a table.

USING KEYS IN WORD

Because Word is a word-processing program, you'll obviously be using
the keyboard to enter text. As previously mentioned, you can use the
mouse or the keyboard to choose Word commands and perform other
tasks. Usually, it's easiest to use a combination of both keyboard and
mouse techniques, choosing whichever is faster for the task at hand.
However, if you're more comfortable using the keyboard or you don't
have a mouse, you can use the keyboard to do all tasks in Word.

To make sure you won't be confused by the keyboard instructions
in this book, learn the location of these important keys and the names
this book uses for them:

Key name	**Description**
Alt	Marked with the letters *Alt*. Generally used in combination with other keys.
Arrow keys	Marked with arrows pointing left, right, up, and down. Your keyboard has a set of arrow keys on the numeric keypad, and possibly another set as well. Generally used to move the insertion point (cursor) on the screen. In this book, referred to as the Up, Down, Right, and Left arrow keys.
Backspace	Marked with the word *Backspace* and with an arrow pointing left. Generally erases the character to the left.

Control	Marked with the letters *Ctrl* or the word *Control*. Generally used in combination with other keys.
Delete	Marked with the letters *Del* or the word *Delete*. Not the same as the Backspace key. Delete generally deletes selected characters.
Enter	Marked with the word *Enter,* the word *Return,* and/or with a bent arrow indicating that this key creates a new line. Generally used to create a new paragraph or to carry out a command.
Esc	Marked with the letters *Esc,* the word *Escape* or the word *Cancel*. Generally used to cancel an operation.
Function keys	Marked with the letter *F* followed by a number, such as F6 and F10. Most newer keyboards have 12 function keys. Generally used as "shortcut keys," sometimes in combination with other keys.
Insert	Marked with the letters *Ins* or the word *Insert*. Controls the insertion of information.
Numeric keypad	The 10-key pad found at the right side of most keyboards. Generally used to insert numbers (when NumLock is on) or to move the insertion point (when NumLock is off).
Shift	Marked with the word *Shift* and/or with an up arrow. Generally makes letters uppercase.
Tab	Marked with the word *Tab* and/or arrows pointing left and right. Generally inserts a tab character, shifting text to the right.

When this book tells you to press several keys at once, the key combination is shown with a plus sign (+) between the key names. For example,

Ctrl+C

means hold down the Control key while you press the C letter key.

We're using uppercase letters to more clearly show alphabetic keys in key combinations, but you don't need to press Shift to make the letter uppercase—the lowercase letter works just as well.

When you need to press and release keys in sequence, you'll see the key combinations written with commas between the key names. For example,

Alt, F, N

means press and release the Alt key, press and release the F key, and then press and release the N key.

CHOOSING COMMANDS

If you've used a Windows-based program before, you're probably already familiar with choosing commands from menus. This section contains both mouse and keyboard instructions.

In this book, we combine menu names and command names when we refer to commands. For example, when we say "Choose the File Open command," we mean "Pull down the File menu, then choose the Open command."

When a command is dimmed ("grayed") on a menu, that command is not available for use at this time. You cannot choose dimmed commands. Take a look at Figure 2–4; it shows the difference between active and dimmed (inactive) commands.

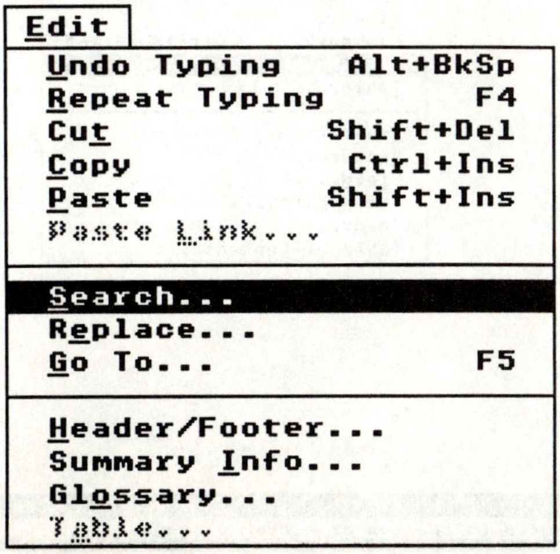

Figure 2–4.
Bold commands are active; dimmed commands are not available.

```
 Edit
 ┌─────────────────────────────┐
 │ Undo Typing      Alt+BkSp   │
 │ Repeat Typing          F4   │
 │ Cut            Shift+Del     │
 │ Copy            Ctrl+Ins     │
 │ Paste          Shift+Ins     │
 │ Paste Link...               │
 ├─────────────────────────────┤
 │ Search...                   │
 │ Replace...                  │
 │ Go To...               F5   │
 ├─────────────────────────────┤
 │ Header/Footer...            │
 │ Summary Info...             │
 │ Glossary...                 │
 │ Table...                    │
 └─────────────────────────────┘
```

Choosing Commands with the Mouse

To choose a command with the mouse:

1. Point to the menu name and hold down the mouse button to pull down the menu.

2. Drag the mouse pointer down the menu until the command you want is highlighted, as shown in Figure 2–5.

3. Release the mouse button.

If you pull down a menu, then decide not to choose a command, just drag the mouse pointer off the menu, then release the button.

Choosing Commands with the Keyboard

To choose a command with the keyboard:

1. Press **Alt**, *Letter* to pull down the menu.
Each menu name has one underlined letter to indicate which letter to use with the Alt key. For example, the letter *F* in the File menu is underlined, so you'd press Alt, F to pull down the

Figure 2–5.
Choosing a command with the mouse.

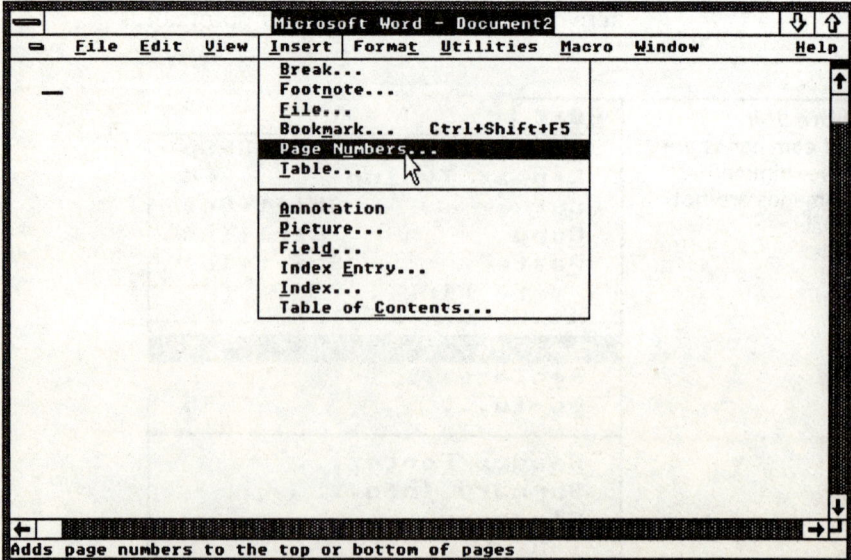

File menu; the letter *T* in the Format menu is underlined, so you'd press Alt, T to pull down the Format menu.

2. Press the underlined letter in the command name. For example, the letter *N* in the New command on the File menu is underlined, so you'd pull down the menu, then press N to choose the New command.

Word has two exceptions to the underlined-letter procedure: the Word Control menu in the Word window's upper left corner, and the Document Control menu in each document window's upper left corner. These menus are represented by icons (pictures) rather than by menu names. The Word Control menu icon is meant to look like the spacebar on the keyboard—this is supposed to remind you that you use Alt, Spacebar to pull down that menu. The Document Control menu icon is meant to look like a hyphen—you use Alt, Hyphen to pull down that menu.

If you pull down a menu, then decide not to choose a command, press the Esc key.

Using Shortcut Keys to Choose Specific Commands

Many commands also have a key combination displayed beside the command name on the menu, as shown in Figure 2–6. When you see a key combination beside a command, that means you can use the key

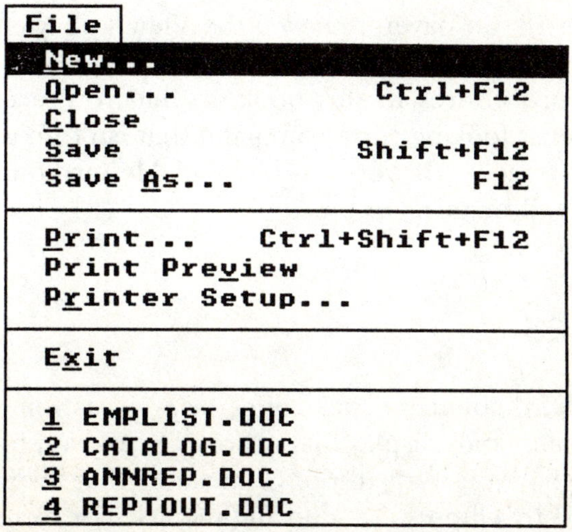

Figure 2–6.
You can choose some Word commands by pressing the key combinations displayed beside the command name on the menu.

```
 File
 New...
 Open...                    Ctrl+F12
 Close
 Save                       Shift+F12
 Save As...                      F12

 Print...        Ctrl+Shift+F12
 Print Preview
 Printer Setup...

 Exit

 1 EMPLIST.DOC
 2 CATALOG.DOC
 3 ANNREP.DOC
 4 REPTOUT.DOC
```

combination to choose the command without first pulling down the menu.

For example, to choose the File Open command from the File menu, you could use the mouse to pull down the menu and highlight the command as described earlier; or press Alt, F, O; or press Ctrl+F12, the shortcut key combination. You'll find that memorizing the shortcut keys for frequently used commands will speed up your work with Word.

ACCESSING ALL OF WORD'S COMMANDS: USING FULL MENUS

Word has two sets of menus: short menus and full menus. Short menus contain a subset of Word's commands, and full menus contain all of Word's commands. When you first start Word, short menus are displayed to make it easier for you to learn. However, most Word users use full menus all the time.

Figure 2–7 shows what Word's menus look like under short menus; Figure 2–8 shows full menus.

To switch to full menus so you can use all of Word's commands:

■ Choose the View Full Menus command.

Although it happens so quickly that you may not notice, Word switches to full menus. When you choose the View Full Menus command, Word adds the Macro menu to the menu bar, as well as adding the full set of Word commands to other menus. If you want to switch back to short menus at some point, you can choose the View Short Menus command.

Note: If you haven't chosen the View Full Menus command, do it now.

The procedures in this book assume you're using full menus. If you're ever looking for a command that isn't on the menu, pull down the View menu. If you see the Full Menus command, choose it to display full menus.

USING DIALOG BOXES

Some Word commands take effect as soon as you choose them. Other Word commands display dialog boxes to ask you for more information about what you want to do. Commands that display dialog boxes are followed by ellipses (...) on the menus. For example, take a look at

Figure 2–7.
Short menus.

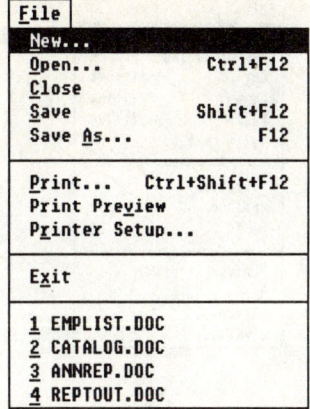

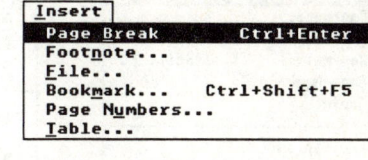

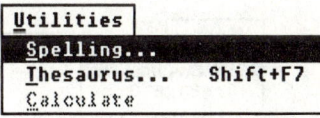

Figure 2–9, which shows how the Format Character command displays a dialog box.

When a dialog box is displayed on the screen, you have to choose an option in the dialog box or close the dialog box before you can choose another command or type text in a document. If you try to do something outside of the dialog box, Word beeps to remind you to close the dialog box first.

Choosing Options in Dialog Boxes

Dialog boxes are filled with options you can choose to affect your document. Word has different types of dialog box options, as shown in Figures 2–10 and 2–11.

Figure 2–8.
Full menus.

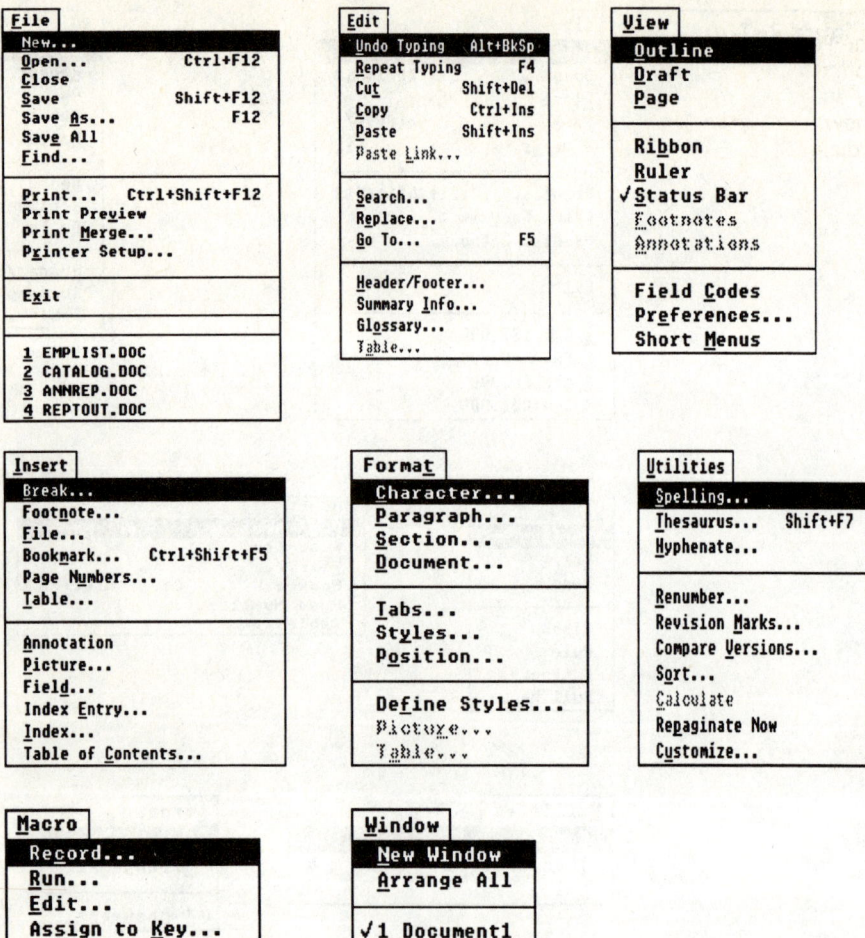

When you open a dialog box for the first time, you'll see that some options are selected, and sometimes you'll see a filename or a measurement in a box. These choices come from Word's *default settings*—the settings Word assumes you'll want to use most of the time. Word's default settings are part of the NORMAL.DOT template.

You can either accept the default settings in a dialog box by leaving them alone, or you can choose new options to affect that particular document. Choosing new options in a dialog box doesn't change the default settings—they'll appear again the next time you choose a command in a new document. (You can, however, control many default settings with the Utilities Customize command.)

Figure 2–9.
The Format Character
command is followed
by an ellipsis to
show that it displays
a dialog box.

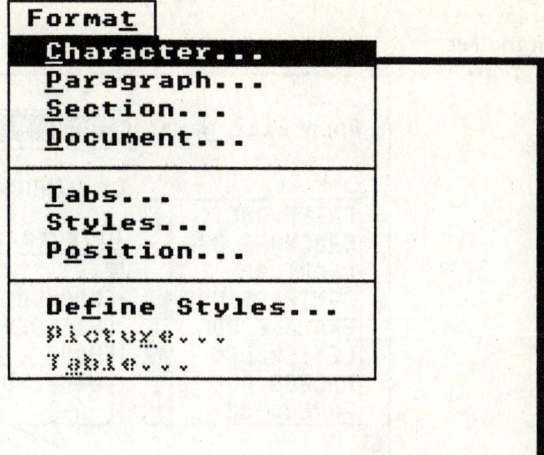

Figure 2–10.
Options in the
Format Character
dialog box.

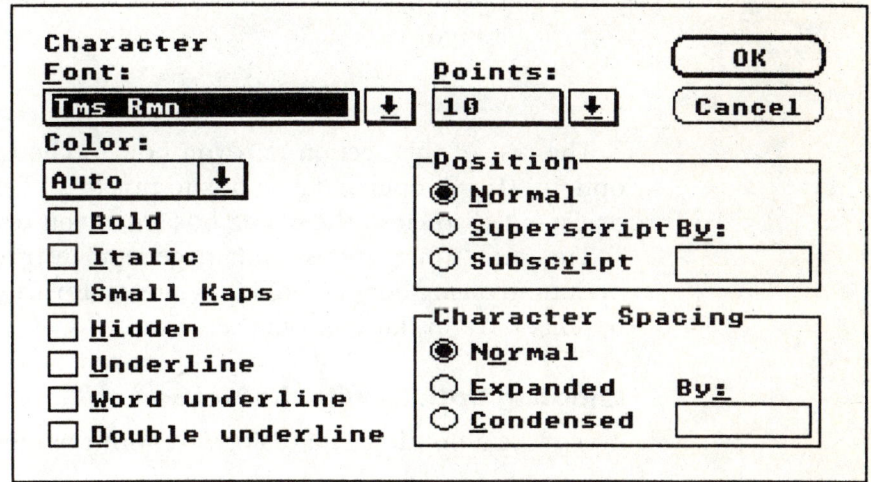

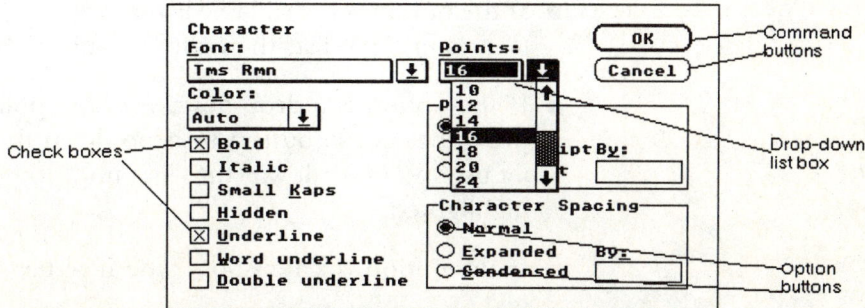

Figure 2–11.
Options in the File
Open dialog box.

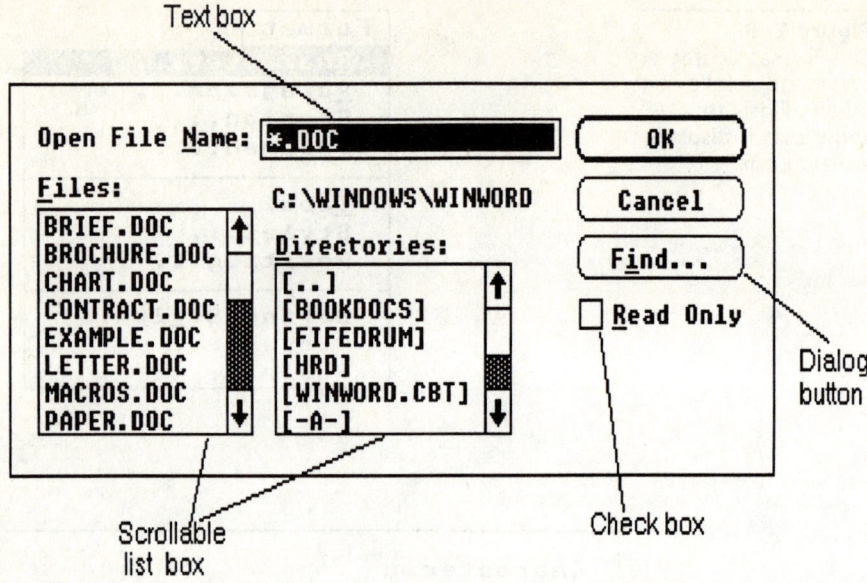

The rest of this section tells you how to choose different types of options. (If you open a dialog box to practice, click the Cancel button or press Esc to close the dialog box when you're finished.)

The next two sections contain general instructions for choosing options in dialog boxes. You'll find more information about how these options work in the following sections.

Choosing Options with the Mouse

To choose an option in a dialog box with the mouse:

1. Click the option.

2. Choose one of the following actions if necessary:

   ■ If the option is a scrollable list box, use the scroll bar if needed to examine the list, then click on a list item to highlight it.

   ■ If the option is a drop-down list box, point to the arrow and press the mouse button to drop down the list, then drag the mouse pointer down the list until the item you want is highlighted.

   ■ If the option is a text box, type new text or edit the existing text.

Choosing Options with the Keyboard

To choose an option in a dialog box with keys:

1. Activate the option using one of the following methods:

   ■ Press **Tab** to move through the options from left to right. **Shift+Tab** moves in the opposite direction.

   ■ Hold down the **Alt** key and press the underlined letter of the option.

2. Choose one of the following actions:

   ■ If the option is a scrollable list box, use the **Up** or **Down arrow** key to highlight an item.

   ■ If the option is a drop-down list box, use the **Up** or **Down arrow** key to display new items. If you want to drop down the list, use **Alt+Down arrow**. When you see the item you want, press **Enter**. (Drop-down list boxes don't "drop down" when used with the keyboard.)

   ■ If the option is a text box, type new text or edit the existing text.

   ■ If the option is a check box, a dialog button or a command button and you've chosen all the options you want in the dialog box, press **Enter**.

Using List Boxes

List boxes display lists of items you can choose from. Word has two types of list boxes: scrollable list boxes and drop-down list boxes, as shown in Figure 2–12. A scrollable list box has a scroll bar you can use to scroll through the list. To scroll one line at a time, click the Up or Down arrow in the scroll bar. To scroll one windowful at a time, click in the gray area above or below the scroll box.

▭ *Keyboard Shortcut*

After the highlight has been moved to a scrollable list box, you can press a letter to jump to the first item in the list beginning with that letter.

For example, if you wanted to select Time from a long list, you could press T to jump to the first item beginning with T. Then you could quickly find Time.

Figure 2–12.
Word has two types of list boxes: drop-down list boxes, as on the left, and scrollable list boxes, like the one on the right.

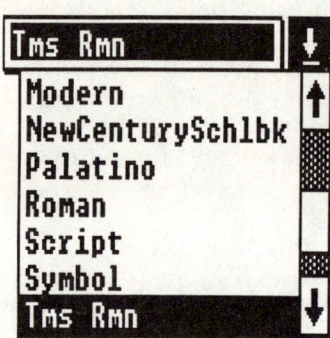

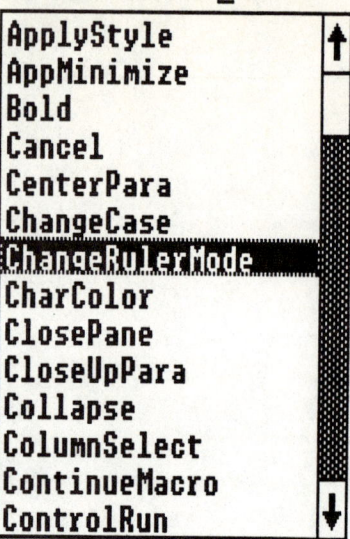

Figure 2–13.
Drop-down list boxes drop down to show the items in the list.

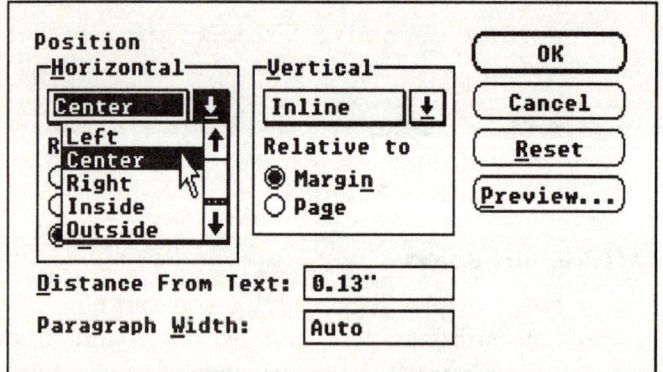

A drop-down list box has a shadow underneath the box and a separate arrow you can click to make the list drop down, as shown in Figure 2–13.

Unlike a scrollable list box, in a drop-down list box you can't see the list of items until you press Alt+Down arrow key or click the arrow to drop down the list. When the list is displayed, choosing from a drop-down list box is just like choosing a command from a menu—just highlight the item you want, then press Enter or release the mouse button.

Text Boxes

You'll use text boxes to type names of items or files and to specify measurements in dialog boxes. You can type new text or edit existing text in a text box, as shown in Figure 2–14. If you type more characters than Word can fit in the box, the text scrolls so you can see what you're typing. You can use the arrow keys to scroll back. Some text boxes are combined with drop-down lists—Microsoft calls these *combo boxes.*

You'll learn more about editing text in Chapter 4, "Editing Your Word Files."

Check Boxes

Word uses check boxes for its options that are *toggles.* A *toggle* is like a switch. You choose the option to "turn it on." To reverse the action of ("turn off") a toggle, you choose the option again.

When you choose a blank check box, an X appears to show that the option is turned on. When you choose a check box containing an X, the X disappears from the box to show that the option is turned off. Figure 2–15 shows check boxes in both states.

Option Buttons

Option buttons come in groups, as shown in Figure 2–16. You can choose only one option button from the same group at any time. When you choose an option button, a solid black circle appears in the button.

Dialog Buttons

Dialog buttons (sometimes called *tunnel buttons*) are—as you've probably guessed—buttons that display another dialog box. Just like commands that display dialog boxes, the names of dialog buttons are fol-

Figure 2–14.
You can type new text or edit the existing text in text boxes.

Figure 2–15.
An X in a check box means the option is turned on; a blank check box means the option is turned off.

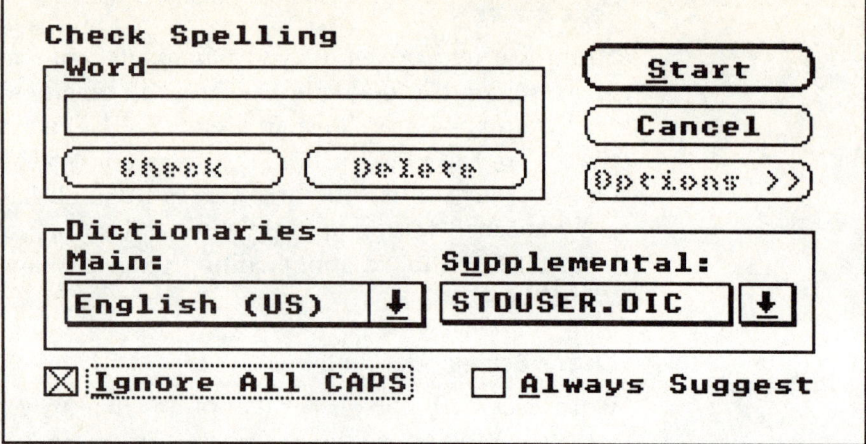

Figure 2–16.
You can select only one option button from the same group.

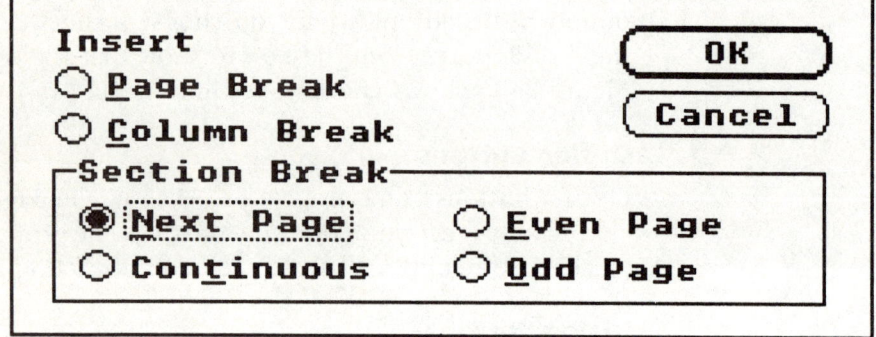

lowed by ellipses (. . .). When you choose a dialog button, another dialog box appears on top of the first one, as shown in Figure 2–17.

Command Buttons

Command buttons are buttons that carry out a command. The most common command buttons in dialog boxes are

OK   Applies the options you've chosen in the dialog box and closes the dialog box. You can always press Enter to choose the OK button.

Figure 2–17.
Clicking the Tabs
dialog button in the
Format Paragraph
dialog box displays
the Tabs dialog box.

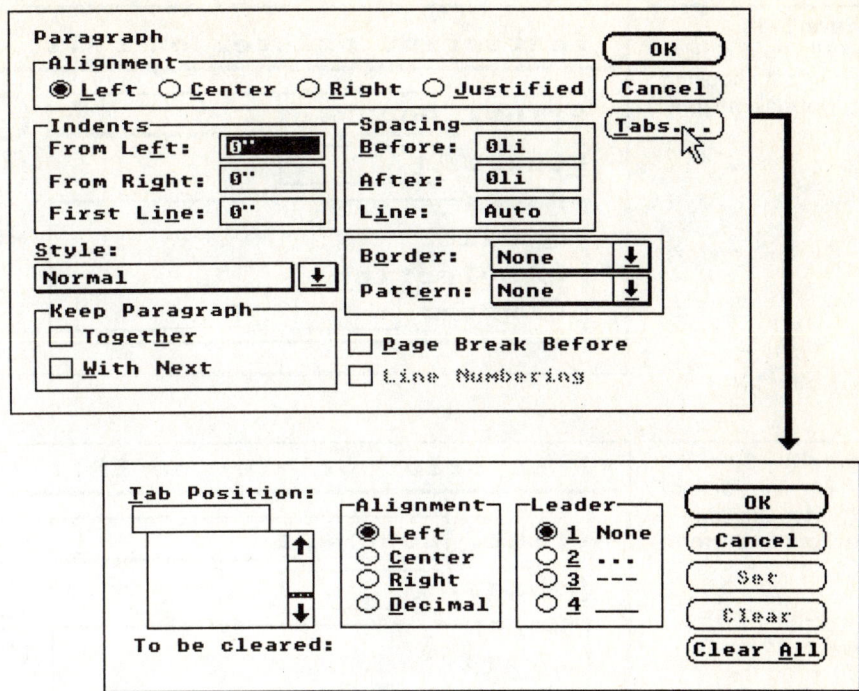

Cancel   Cancels the command and closes the dialog
box without applying options you've chosen
in the dialog box, unless you've already applied them with another button. You can always press Esc to choose the Cancel
button.

If a command button has a heavy border, this means it is the *default
command button*. The default command button (at most times, the OK
button) usually carries out the choices you've made in the dialog box
and closes the dialog box. You can choose the default command button
simply by pressing Enter.

Expandable Dialog Boxes

In some dialog boxes, you'll see a button marked Options... This
button indicates that the dialog box is expandable—it contains additional options that will be displayed only if you choose the Options
button. For example, take a look at the File Print dialog box, shown
in Figure 2–18. If you choose the Options button, the dialog box
expands to display more options, as shown in Figure 2–19.

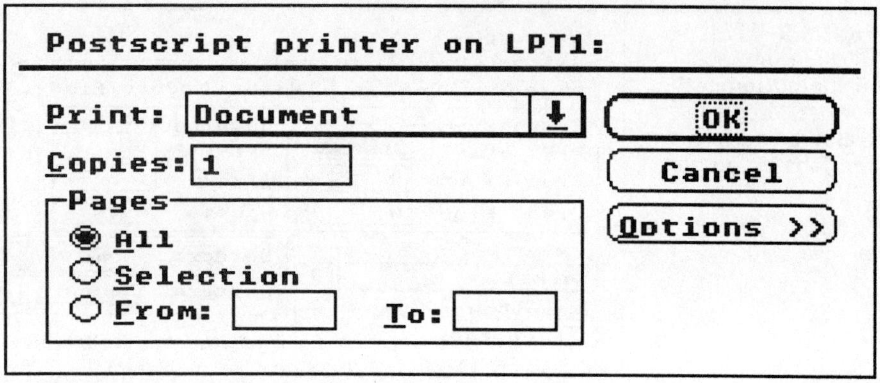

Figure 2–18.
The File Print dialog
box before choosing
the Options button.

```
┌─────────────────────────────────────────────────────────┐
│  Postscript printer on LPT1:                            │
│  ─────────────────────────────                          │
│  Print: │Document              ↓│    ╭──────────╮       │
│                                       │   [OK]   │       │
│  Copies: │1              │            ╰──────────╯       │
│  ┌Pages──────────────────────────╮   ╭──────────╮       │
│  │ ◉ All                         │   │  Cancel  │       │
│  │ ○ Selection                   │   ╰──────────╯       │
│  │ ○ From: │      │   To: │      ││   ╭──────────────╮   │
│  └───────────────────────────────╯   │ Options  >>  │   │
│                                       ╰──────────────╯   │
└─────────────────────────────────────────────────────────┘
```

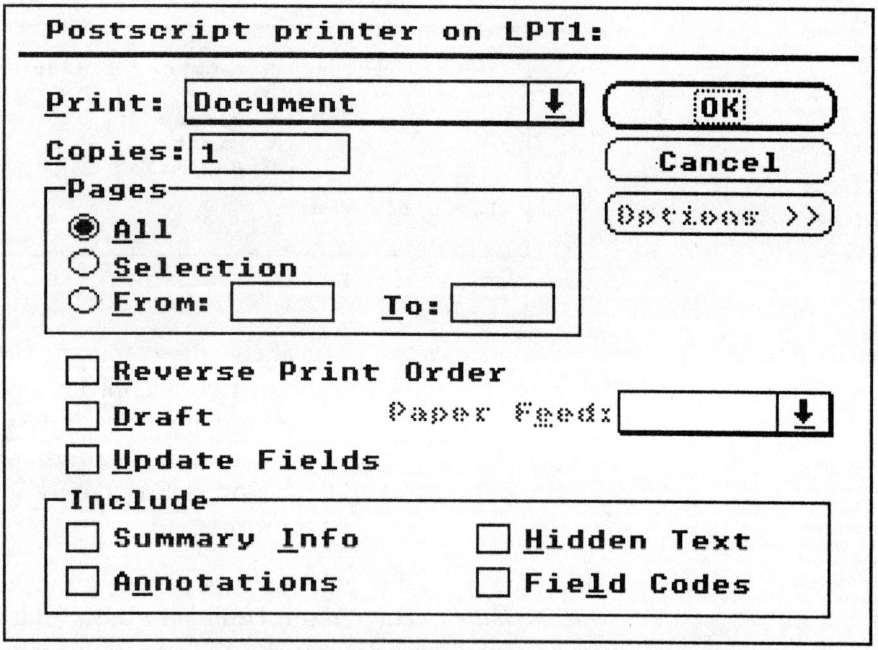

Figure 2–19.
The File Print dialog
box after choosing
the Options button.

```
┌─────────────────────────────────────────────────────────┐
│  Postscript printer on LPT1:                            │
│  ─────────────────────────────                          │
│  Print: │Document              ↓│    ╭──────────╮       │
│                                       │   [OK]   │       │
│  Copies: │1              │            ╰──────────╯       │
│  ┌Pages──────────────────────────╮   ╭──────────╮       │
│  │ ◉ All                         │   │  Cancel  │       │
│  │ ○ Selection                   │   ╰──────────╯       │
│  │ ○ From: │      │   To: │      ││   ╭──────────────╮   │
│  └───────────────────────────────╯   │ Options  >>  │   │
│                                       ╰──────────────╯   │
│  ☐ Reverse Print Order                                  │
│  ☐ Draft          Paper Feed: │           ↓│           │
│  ☐ Update Fields                                        │
│  ┌Include─────────────────────────────────────────────╮ │
│  │ ☐ Summary Info        ☐ Hidden Text               │ │
│  │ ☐ Annotations         ☐ Field Codes               │ │
│  └────────────────────────────────────────────────────╯ │
└─────────────────────────────────────────────────────────┘
```

Closing Dialog Boxes

When Word displays a dialog box, you have to close it before you can
get back to your document. If you try to choose a command or type
something in your document, Word just beeps. You can close a dialog
box in several ways:

To	Do this
Close a dialog box and carry out the command	Click the OK button or press Enter.
Close a dialog box and cancel the command	Click the Cancel button or the Close button or press Esc.

Mouse Speed Tip

In some dialog boxes that contain scrollable list boxes, you can use the mouse to double-click a list item, which selects the list item, chooses the default command button, and closes the dialog box, all at the same time.

Moving Dialog Boxes

If a dialog box is hiding a part of your document that you need to see, use the following procedure to move the dialog box to a new location in the Word window:

1. Press **Alt+F7**.

2. Use the arrow keys to move the dialog box to the new location.

3. Press **Enter** to set the new position of the dialog box or press **Esc** if you change your mind and want to return to the original position.

GETTING HELP

Word has an extensive help system you can use whenever you need more information about commands, a task, or a dialog box option. There's always a minihelp feature available in the status bar displays. If you highlight a command with the mouse or the arrow keys, Word displays a message describing what the command does. At other times, the status bar displays other helpful messages. You can get more extensive help in several ways:

To	Do this
Browse through the help system	Pull down the Help menu, then choose the Using Help command to get instructions about using the help system; or you can choose the Index command to see a list of topics, as shown in Figure 2–20.
Get information about a dialog box option or command	Highlight the command or option with the mouse or the arrow keys, then press F1 to see specific help about that option or command, as shown in Figure 2–21.
Use a mouse pointer to select areas of the window to get more information about	Press **Shift+F1**, then use the mouse help pointer (a question mark shown in Figure 2–22) to click a command or a dialog box option or another area you want to see help about.

Using the Help Menu

The Help menu contains commands that help you find the information you want:

Command	Description
Index	Displays an index of help topics from which you can choose
Keyboard	Displays information about important keys, as well as the list of current key assignments
Active Window	Displays information about the "view" of the active window (normal view, outline view, print preview, page view, draft view)

Figure 2–20.
Choosing from an
index of help topics
displayed with the
Help Index command.

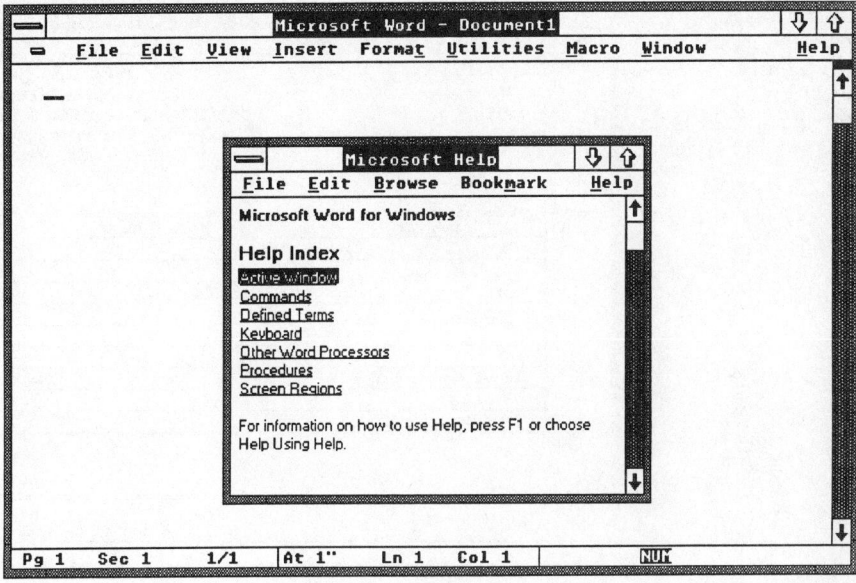

Figure 2–21.
Getting specific help
about a dialog box
option with the F1
key.

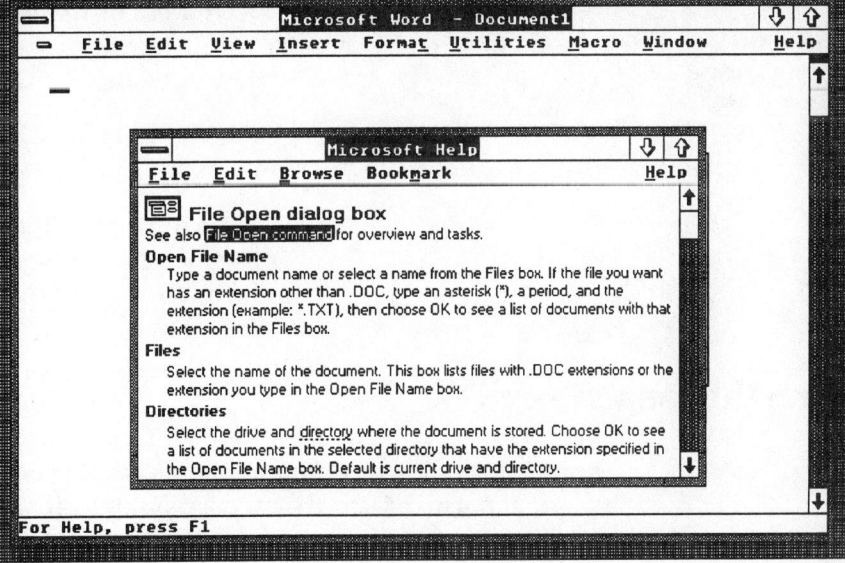

Figure 2–22.
Using the mouse
help pointer
(displayed by
pressing Shift+F1) to
get help.

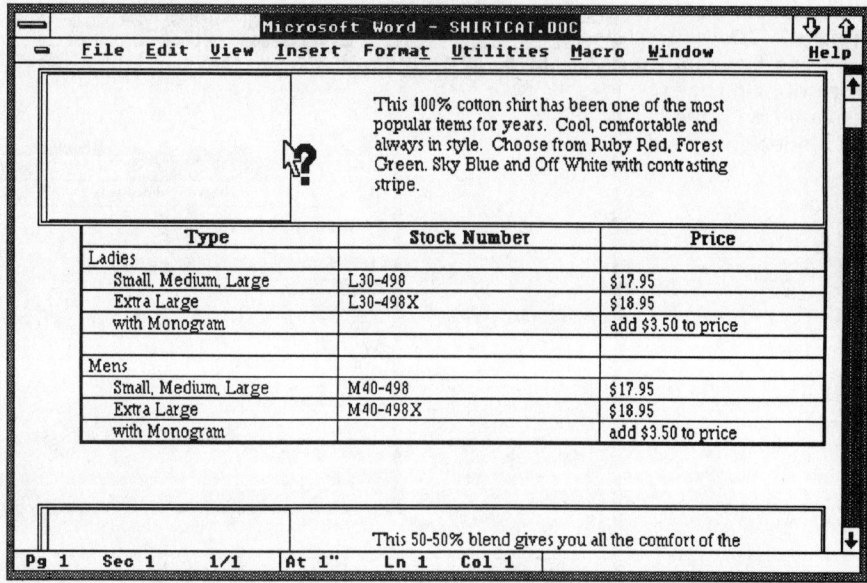

Tutorial	Displays a list of the Word tutorial lessons that you can run (if your computer has sufficient available memory)
Using Help	Displays instructions about how to use the help system
About	Displays Word's version number and information about the disk space and memory available on your computer

Using the Help Window

The Help window is a separate application—you can move it, change
its size, and use the scroll bars to scroll the information in the window,
just like you can manipulate the Word window.

You can scroll through all the help files at your leisure, or you can
use the menus in the Help window to use the help system efficiently.

| **Use this menu** | **To** |
| File | Print a help topic or close the Help window. |

Edit	Copy help information to a Word file.
Browse	Move around within the help files to find the information you're looking for.
Bookmark	Mark a section of help using bookmarks. For more information, see Customizing the Help System in Chapter 26, "Changing Word to Suit You."
Help	Get information about how to use the help system.

Using Definitions and Jump Terms

You also see two types of special items in the Help window: *definitions* and *jump terms,* as shown in Figure 2–23. Definitions have a dotted underline, and jump terms have a normal underline. The mouse pointer becomes a pointing hand when it's on one of these special items. Here's how to use them:

Figure 2–23.
Definitions and jump
terms in the Help
window.

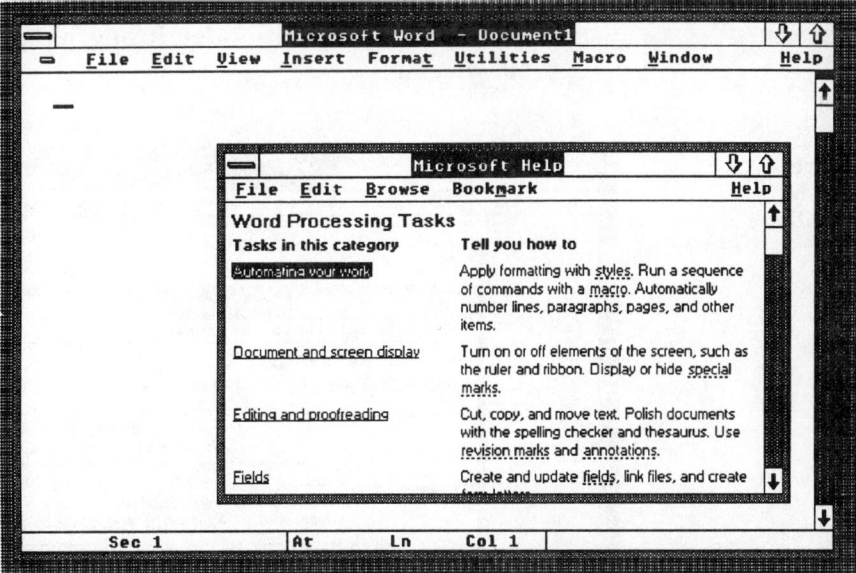

To	Do this
Display a definition	Use the arrow keys to highlight the definition, then hold down the Enter key; or point to the definition, then hold down the mouse button to display a definition window, as shown in Figure 2–24. When you release the Enter key or the mouse button, the definition window disappears.
Jump to a new topic with a jump term	Use the arrow keys to highlight the jump term, then press Enter; or click the jump term to jump to the new topic. To jump back, press the **F9** key or choose the Backtrack command from the Browse menu.

Finding the Right Help Topic

Word's help system is vast, so it sometimes seems overwhelming. You can find the help topic you're looking for in two ways:

■ From the Word window, choose the Help Index command, then scroll through the help index, using jump terms to get to the topic you want.

Figure 2–24.
Displaying a
definition.

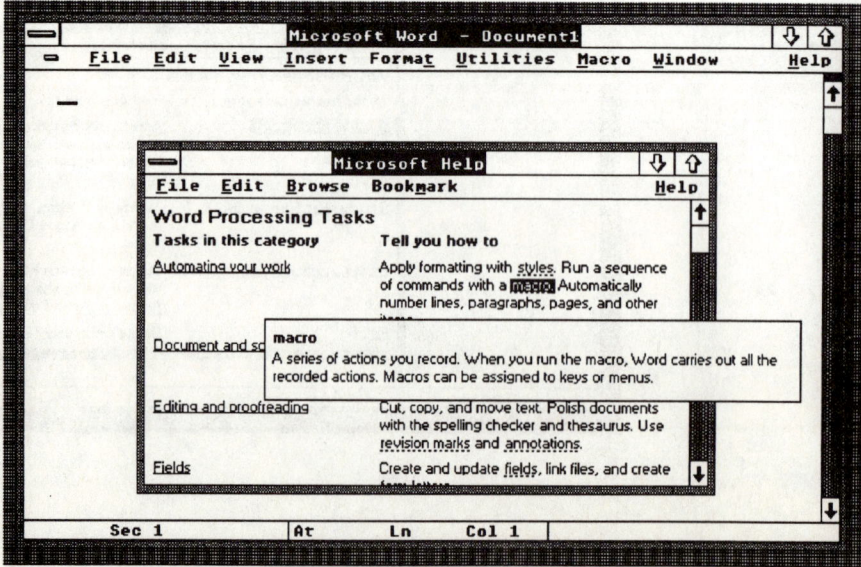

■ In the Help window, choose the Browse Search command, then type the topic you're looking for, or choose Keywords to display a list of help topics you can choose from.

The Browse Search dialog box is shown in Figure 2–25.

Getting Help About Converting from Other Word-Processing Programs

Word's help system contains information to make it easy to convert to Word if you're accustomed to using one of the following word-processing programs:

■ DisplayWrite 4®

■ MultiMate™

■ Wang

■ Microsoft Word (PC Word)

■ WordPerfect®

■ WordStar®

Figure 2–25.
Searching for a help topic with the Browse Search command.

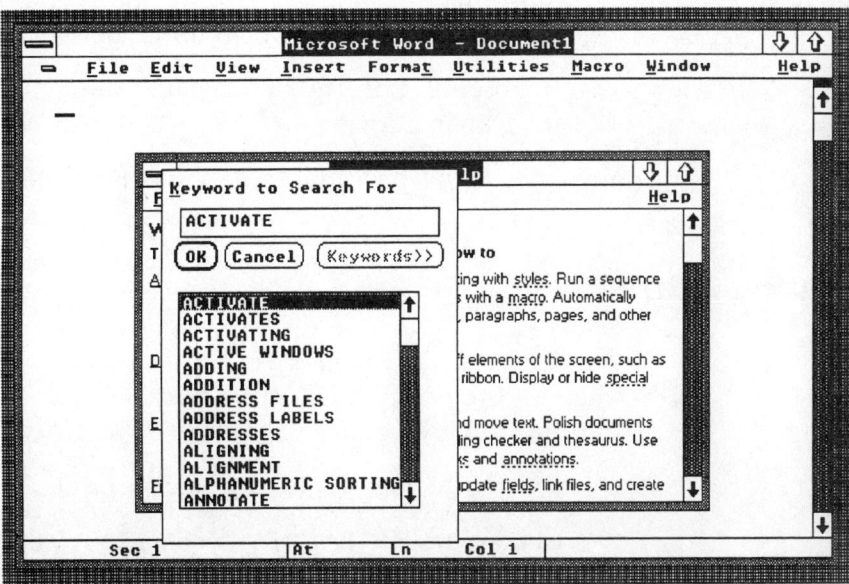

To display help information about another word-processing program:

1. Choose the Help Index command. Word displays a list of topics.

2. Click the Other Word Processors jump term or use the arrow keys to highlight it, then press Enter. Word displays a list of word processors.

3. Use the arrow keys or the mouse to select the word processor you want. Word displays a list of topics for that word-processing program.

4. Use the arrow keys or the mouse to select the topic you want.

Copying Help Topics to a Word File

You might like to copy help topics to a Word file, then edit, format, and print the information using the Word commands.

To copy a help topic to a Word file:

1. In the Help window, display the help topic you want to copy.

2. Choose the Edit Copy command to copy the information to the Clipboard.

3. Move the insertion point to the location in the Word file where you want to insert the help information.

4. Choose the Edit Paste command to insert the information from the Clipboard.

You can use this procedure to copy as many help topics as you like.

Printing Help Topics

You don't have to memorize the instructions you see in the Help window—you can print them for easy reference.

To print a help topic:

1. Display the help topic you want to print.

2. Choose the File Print Topic command. Word sends that topic to the printer.

Figure 2–26.
The Word Help
application reduced
to an icon.

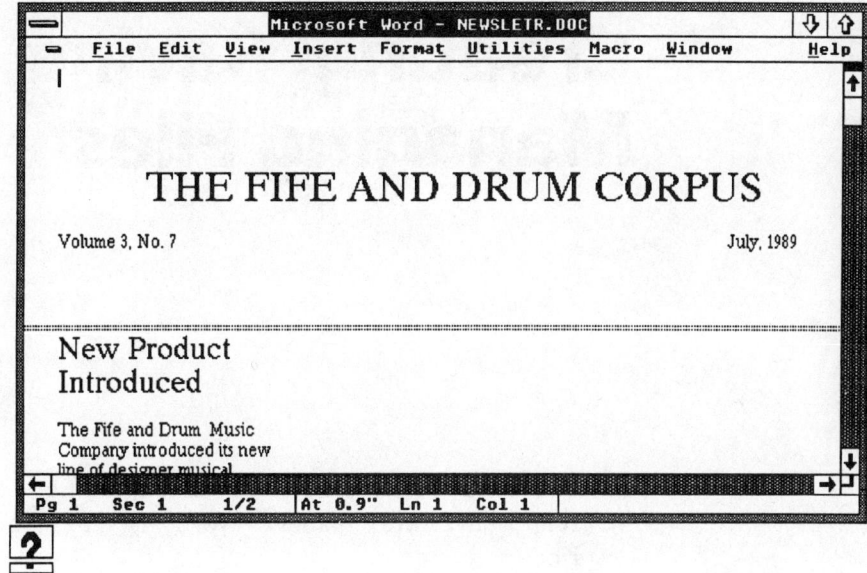

Closing the Help Window

You can leave the Help application open but shrink the Help window
to an icon, just as you do with any other Windows application. The
Help icon is shown in Figure 2–26. Then you can easily double-click
the icon to open it again.

You can also close the Help application to free up the memory and
the screen space. To close the Help application:

- Choose the File Exit command.

QUITTING WORD

You can quit Word using any of the following methods:

- Choose the File Exit command (Alt, F, X).

- Choose the Close command from the Word Control menu (Alt,
  Spacebar, C).

- Double-click the Word Control menu icon.

If you've made any changes that haven't been saved, Word will ask
you if you want to save changes before quitting.

## Chapter Three

Creating, Saving, and Managing Files

Because all Word documents are stored in files, understanding how to create, save, and manage Word files is essential. This chapter describes

- how Word names files.

- using documents and templates in Word.

- entering text.

- opening and saving different files and file formats.

ABOUT DOS FILENAME RULES

When you name a Word file, you must obey the operating system's rules for filenames. If you try to type an invalid filename in Word or any other program running under DOS (MS-DOS or PC-DOS), you'll see a message something like

Not a valid filename

The names of all files you use with DOS must conform to these rules:

- Your filenames must contain no more than eight characters before a period, and no more than three characters in the filename extension after the period. No spaces are allowed in filenames. For example, you could use FILE.MY, INVOICE.601, FOS-TER.LET, LETTER, but not MY FILE (which contains a space) or THISISMINE.DOC (which has too many characters).

- You can't use any of the following characters in a filename:

* (asterisk)

\ (backslash)

: (colon)

, (comma)

. (period)

? (question mark)

; (semicolon)

/ (slash)

HOW WORD NAMES FILES

If you don't specify an extension or a period after the basic filename, Word adds a .DOC extension to a filename. For example, if you tell Word you want a file named *MIKE,* it assumes you want the file named MIKE.DOC. If you want to name a file with no extension, type a period (.) after the basic filename; for example, if you want a file named just MIKE, type

MIKE.

when saving or asking for the file.

When you want Word to find or put a file in a directory or a disk drive that's different from the one you're working in, type a pathname in front of the filename (or choose directories or drive letters in a dialog box, as explained in Opening Existing Files later in this chapter).

For more information about filenames, pathnames, disk drives, and operating system rules, see the operating system manual that came with your computer.

DOCUMENTS AND TEMPLATES

When you use Word, you'll create two basic types of files: *documents* and *templates.* A document is a simple word-processing file: it might be a letter, a chapter from a novel, an outline for a newspaper article, or any other sort of file that contains words.

Every Word document is based on a template. A template is a framework that you can use over and over. Although you may not use the term often, chances are that you're already familiar with the concept of templates. You use a "template" every time you update your company's weekly report, fill out an order form, type a memo using a standard format, and so forth.

In its most basic form, a template is like a sheet of paper you roll into a typewriter or printer. If you want to create a memo, you might insert your company's standard memo form; if you want to send a letter, you insert the company's letterhead stationery. But in Word, templates are more than just standard forms. A Word template can include

- boilerplate text—text that stays the same from document to document

- formatting—instructions that control the look of characters, paragraphs, and documents

- styles—named sets of formatting instructions that you can apply to text to control how a document looks

- glossaries—collections of standard text and graphic items you can paste into a document

- macros—named sets of instructions that perform a sequence of Word commands

The formatting instructions stored in the template control the basic format of all documents based on that template. When you create a template (memo, invoice, inventory form, letter, newsletter, and so on), you can then create new documents based on that template, save them as separate documents, and still keep the template in its original form. You could use a document in the same way, but you would have to be careful not to erase the original document when you saved the new one. When you base your documents on templates, you don't have to worry about this.

An added advantage of templates, especially in situations where more than one person is creating similar documents, is that they can be "locked" so they cannot be changed at all. There are two ways to do this.

- Turn on Lock for Annotations in the File Save As dialog box when you save a template. Although another user can unlock the template by turning off this option, it provides some degree of safety.

■ Use the DOS ATTRIB command outside of Windows to make a file "read-only." For example, to "lock" MEMO.DOT, type this at the operating system prompt:

ATTRIB +R memo.dot

For more information about using the ATTRIB command, see your operating system manual.

Word comes with a standard template, called NORMAL.DOT, that contains all the default settings. Word automatically bases new documents on the NORMAL.DOT template, so you don't really need to concern yourself with creating templates if you don't want to. If you don't like the NORMAL.DOT settings, you can create your own templates to use instead of NORMAL.DOT, or you can change the NORMAL.DOT settings.

If you use a standard format for certain types of documents, such as memos, letters, or invoices, you'll want to create many of your own templates. Templates can even be based on other templates. When you've created and saved your templates, you can base new documents of the same type on a specific template to create documents with the same basic look.

CREATING NEW DOCUMENTS OR TEMPLATES

Word is flexible, enabling you to specify exactly what you want when you create new documents and templates or to change your mind and specify different options when you save a document or template. So don't worry if you don't know exactly what you want when you start a new file; you can always change it later.

If you don't load a document when you start Word, the program opens a new, empty document for you so you can start typing right away. Word labels the document "Document1." When you save the Document1 file later, you give it another name, and Word replaces the name Document1 with the name you assign.

If you have already started Word and opened an existing document, you can use the File New command to open a new, empty document. You can open several new documents during a work session, so Word numbers them (Document2, Document3, and so on) to keep track of how many new documents you've opened.

To create a new document or template:

1. Choose the File New command.

2. Do one of the following:

To	Do this
Create a new document based on the NORMAL.DOT template	Click OK or press **Enter**.
Create a new template	Choose Template in the New box, then click OK or press **Enter**.
Create a new document or template based on a template other than NORMAL.DOT	Choose Document or Template in the New box, then select the name of the template you want to use from the Use Template list, then click OK or press **Enter**.

3. Type and format the text.

4. Save the file.

EXAMPLE: Creating and Using a Memo Template

Say you want to create and use a memo template that includes To, From, Date, and Subject headings like this:

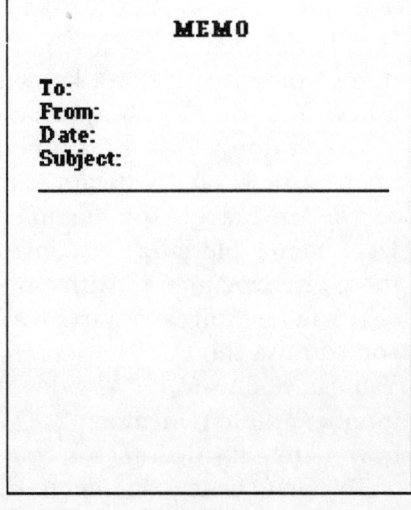

To create the memo template:

1. Choose the File New command.

2. Choose Template in the New box and press **Enter**.

3. Type and format the text for the template.

4. Use the File Save command to save the template as GENMEMO.DOT.

To use the GENMEMO.DOT template when you want to create a memo:

1. Choose the File New command.

2. Select GENMEMO.DOT from the Use Template list and press **Enter**.

3. Make changes and add information to the memo as desired, then save the memo with an appropriate filename (such as MEMO5-17.DOC for a memo created May 17).

ENTERING TEXT

Entering text is easy—just type! You don't need to press Enter when you come to the end of a line. Word automatically begins a new line when the text reaches the right margin. This feature is commonly called *wordwrap*.

To begin a new paragraph, press **Enter**. To back up and erase errors, press the **Backspace** key. You'll learn more about editing in Part II, "Revising."

OPENING EXISTING FILES

Word can open not only existing Word files but also many files created by other programs. Word can open files with the following file formats:

- DCA/RFT: includes DisplayWrite and Display Writer®

- Microsoft Excel BIFF

- Microsoft Windows Write

- Microsoft Word for DOS

- Microsoft Works word processor files

- Microsoft Multiplan® and Multiplan BIFF

- MultiMate (certain versions) and Advantage II

- RTF (Rich Text Format): includes Microsoft Word for the Macintosh

- Text Only (PC-8 with or without line breaks)

- WordPerfect™ (certain versions)

- WordStar® (certain versions)

When you open these files in Word, they become normal Word files. When you save them, they are saved as Word files. (Remember, you're not opening the application program that created the file.)

Word also can import files with ASCII format, but Word doesn't convert the text and line breaks until you save the file in Word's Normal file format.

To open a file:

1. Choose the File Open command. Word displays the dialog box shown in Figure 3–1.

2. Select the name of the file you want to open from the list. The list displays the names of files in the active disk drive and directory. To see names of other files, you may need to do one of the following:

    - To see a list of files on another disk drive, double-click the letter of the disk drive; or type the drive letter followed by a colon (such as A:) in the Open File Name box, then press **Enter**.

    - To see the files in another directory on the same disk, double-

Figure 3–1.
The File Open dialog box.

click the directory names until you see the files you want; or type the directory name in the Open File Name box, then press **Enter**.

3. Click OK or press **Enter** to open the file and close the dialog box.

Mouse Speed Tip

To open a file quickly, double-click the name of the file in the File Open dialog box to select it and close the dialog box at the same time.

If you're using the full version of Windows, you can also start Word and open a Word document at the same time by selecting the document's name in the MS-DOS Executive window.

SAVING WORD FILES

Word doesn't save any of the work you've done until you choose a Save command. To minimize the risk of losing your work, it's wise to save frequently. A good rule of thumb is to save every 15 minutes.

You can use Word's autosave feature, described in Setting Up Word to Save Automatically later in this chapter, to remind you to save your work.

Word has three commands on the File menu that save documents and templates:

Use	To
Save	Name a document the first time you save it and subsequently save the document using the same name.
Save As	Name a document the first time you save it, save a document with a different name or in a different file format, and make a backup copy or do a "fast save."
Save All	Save all documents and templates in one operation.

If you're saving the file for the first time, both the File Save and File Save As commands use the same dialog box, shown in Figure 3–2.

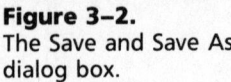

Figure 3–2.
The Save and Save As
dialog box.

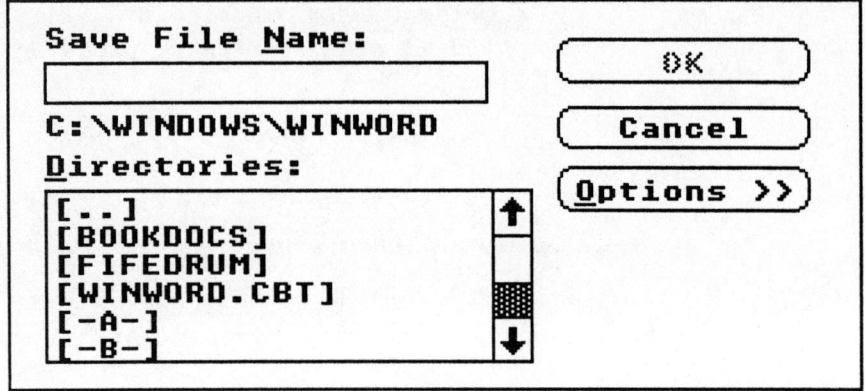

After you've saved your document or template once, the File Save command saves your file without displaying the dialog box. If at any time you decide to save your file with a different name or in a different format, use the File Save As command.

Saving a File for the First Time

To save a document or template for the first time:

1. Choose the File Save command or the File Save As command. Both commands use the same dialog box the first time you save.

2. Type a name for your document in the Save File Name box. If you don't add a filename extension, Word automatically adds .DOC to a document's filename, or .DOT to a template's filename. If you type a name that's already been used for another file, Word asks you if you want to replace that document or template with the document or template you're saving.

3. To choose more options, use the Options button to expand the dialog box, then perform one or both of the following actions:

   ■ To save in a different file format, choose a format from the File Format list. (You can find out more about different formats in Saving in a Different Format later in this chapter.)

   ■ To make a backup copy, turn on the Make Backup option. This option causes Word to automatically save the previous version of every file with the extension .BAK, creating a backup copy you can use if disaster strikes the .DOC or .DOT file. This option stays on until you turn it off.

4. Click Save or press **Enter** to close the dialog box and save your file.

Word displays percentages in the status area as it saves a document, as shown in Figure 3–3.

When Word finishes saving, the status area says 100 percent, then quickly changes to display the number of characters in the file. The filename appears at the top of the window, as shown in Figure 3–4.

Saving an Edited File

To save a document or template in the same file with the same name without opening a dialog box, choose the File Save command. (Because you'll be using this command frequently, you may find it easiest to press the command's assigned key combination, **Shift+F12**.) You won't see a dialog box, but Word displays percentages in the status area as it saves, then displays the number of characters in the file when it's finished saving.

To make saving quicker, turn on the Fast Save option. This option causes Word to save only the portions of the file that have changed.

Figure 3–3.
Word shows the percentage of the file saved in the status area.

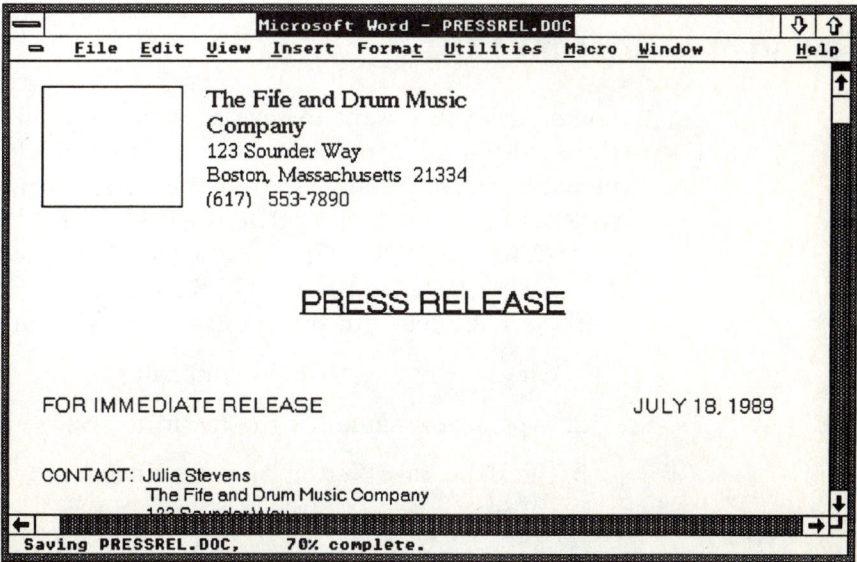

Figure 3–4.
Word displays the
number of characters
in the file and the
filename after it has
saved a document.

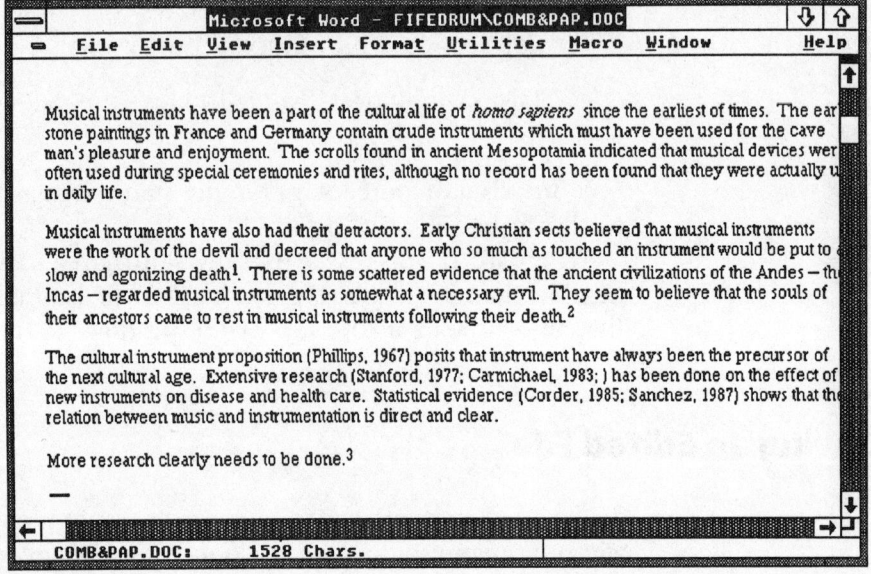

The Fast Save option uses more memory to save a document, so if your system has very little available memory, you may want to avoid this option. This option stays on until you turn it off.

If you want to turn on or off the Fast Save and Create Backup options, choose the File Save As command, choose Options, then change the settings.

Saving in a Different File

Sometimes you'll want to save a version of a document or template with a different name in a different file and leave the original file intact. For example, if you work on billing, you might open a file called APRBILLS.DOC, then update it for May, then save the updated file as MAYBILLS.DOC. Then you'd have both files for your records: APRBILLS.DOC and MAYBILLS.DOC.

To save a document or template in a different file:

1. Choose the File Save As command.

2. Type a new name for the file in the Save File Name box.

3. Click the Save button or press **Enter**.

Word saves the file with the new name and leaves the original file intact.

Saving in a Different Format

Word enables you to save your documents in different file formats so you can use them with other programs. You can save in these formats:

- DCA/RFT (includes DisplayWrite and Display Writer)

- Document Template (a normal Word for Windows template)

- PC Word

- PC Works

- Windows Write

- MultiMate (certain versions) and Advantage II

- Normal (regular Word format)

- RTF (Rich Text Format) (Microsoft word processing format that changes Word formatting into ASCII codes that can be interpreted by other programs that use this format. Includes Microsoft Word for the Macintosh and Microsoft Works for DOS.)

- Text Only, Text + Breaks (ASCII file with or without line breaks)

- Text, Text + Breaks (PC-8) (with or without line breaks)

- WordPerfect (certain versions)

- WordStar (certain versions)

To save a document in a different file format:

1. Choose the File Save As command. Word displays the dialog box shown in Figure 3–5.

2. Choose Options to expand the dialog box.

3. Select a format from the drop-down File Format list (shown in Figure 3–6).

4. Click OK or press **Enter** to save the document and close the dialog box.

Converting Documents into Templates

Perhaps you have written a document in the past that is now used frequently with slight modifications. You can save your existing doc-

Figure 3–5.
The Save As dialog
box.

Figure 3–6.
The File Format drop-
down list.

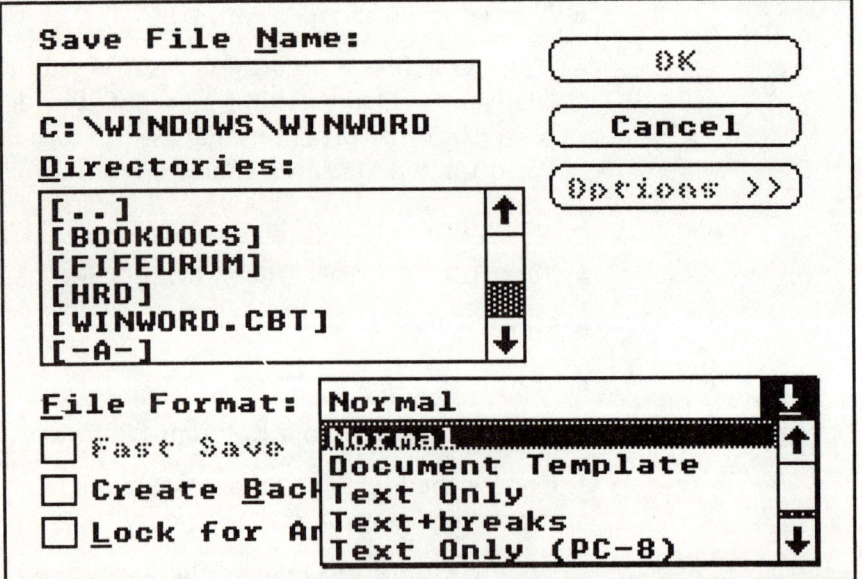

ument as a template with the File Save As command. By converting a
document into a template, you can then use the template to provide
a basic skeleton for similar documents. Then you won't have to worry
about mistakenly saving a new document on top of an existing one
and losing the information in the existing file.

You can also "lock" this new template by turning on Lock for Annotations in the File Save As command or using the DOS ATTRIB
command. (See Documents and Templates in this chapter.)

To convert a document into a template:

1. Choose the File Save As command.

2. Type a template name. Use the .DOT extension or type a base filename and let Word add the .DOT extension.

3. From the File Format drop-down list, select Document Template.

4. Click OK or press **Enter**.

You can make changes in the template at any time just as in any other document. You can also base other templates on this template.

Setting Up Word to Save Automatically

Instead of trying to remember to save frequently, you can set up Word to prompt you to save at regular time intervals. Here's how.

1. Choose the Utilities Customize command. Word displays the dialog box shown in Figure 3–7.

2. In the Autosave Frequency box, choose one of the following options:

Option	Description
High	Displays a save prompt every 10 to 30 minutes

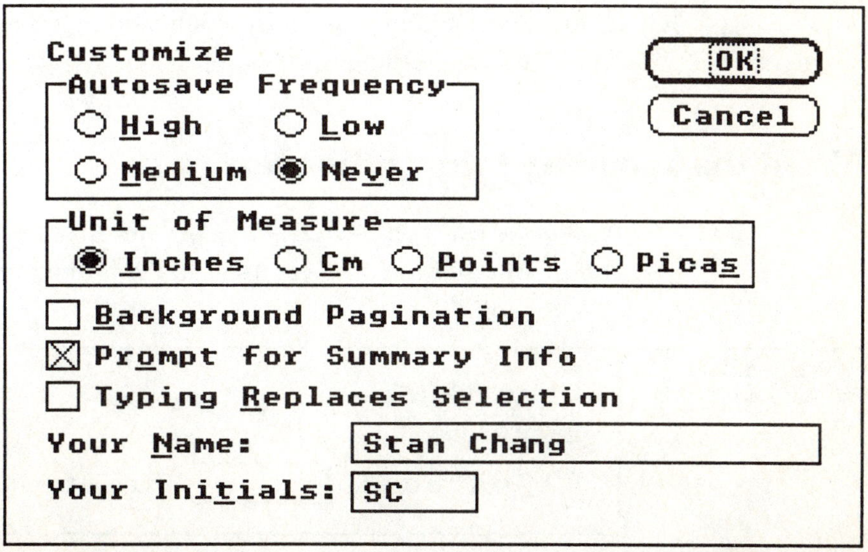

Figure 3–7.
The Utilities Customize dialog box controls the Autosave frequency.

```
Customize                          (  OK  )
┌Autosave Frequency─┐
│ ○ High    ○ Low   │              ( Cancel )
│ ○ Medium  ● Never │
└───────────────────┘
┌Unit of Measure────────────────────────┐
│ ● Inches  ○ Cm  ○ Points  ○ Picas     │
└───────────────────────────────────────┘
☐ Background Pagination
☒ Prompt for Summary Info
☐ Typing Replaces Selection
Your Name:      │Stan Chang            │
Your Initials:  │SC    │
```

| Medium | Displays a save prompt every 20 to 45 minutes |
| Low | Displays a save prompt every 30 to 60 minutes |

3. Click OK or press **Enter**.

When you've set an autosave frequency, Word displays the dialog box shown in Figure 3–8 after a certain length of time has expired. The actual time interval depends on the number of changes you've made to your document: the more changes you've made, the shorter the time interval between the save prompts.

When the Autosave dialog box appears, you can do any of the following:

To	**Do this**
Save the file	Click OK or press **Enter**.
Postpone saving for a while	Choose Postpone, then type a number of minutes in the Minutes box, then click OK or press **Enter**.
Start the time interval over	Click Cancel or press **Esc**. (Example: If the time interval is 20 minutes, this will cause Word to wait another 20 minutes before displaying the Autosave dialog box again.)

If you decide later that you want to turn off the autosave feature, choose the Utilities Customize command again and choose Never in the Autosave Frequency box.

About the Summary Information Box

Whenever you save a document for the first time in Word, you can choose whether to complete items in the Summary Information dialog

Figure 3–8.
The Autosave dialog box.

box (shown in Figure 3–9). This box records information about the file that will help in retrieving the file later. You can indicate the title of the file, the subject, the author, key words, and comments.

Summary information can be used

- to help you recall the contents of and details about a document.

- to help you locate a document.

- to track a document's history.

The Summary Information box provides the information used in Word's document retrieval system, as explained in Chapter 24. You can sort and find documents based on information you enter in the fields of the Summary Information dialog box.

Filling Out the Summary Information Fields

You can type and edit information in the Summary Information dialog box. The File Name box displays the name of the active document. The Directory box indicates where the file is located. (If you want to change either the filename or the directory, use the File Save As command.) You can enter information in the other text boxes as follows:

Field	Type
Title	A descriptive title for the file. For example, you might type "Letter to Dad asking for more money."
Subject	Text describing what the document is about.
Author	The name of the person who created the document.

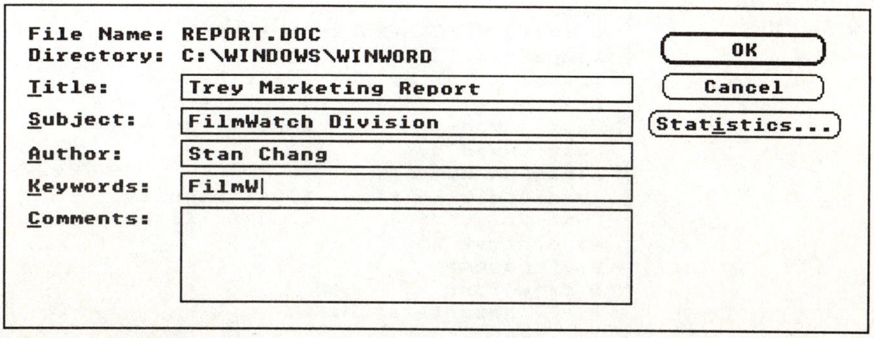

Figure 3–9.
The Summary Information dialog box.

```
File Name: REPORT.DOC
Directory: C:\WINDOWS\WINWORD            (    OK    )
Title:    [Trey Marketing Report     ]   ( Cancel  )
Subject:  [FilmWatch Division         ]  (Statistics...)
Author:   [Stan Chang                 ]
Keywords: [FilmW|                      ]
Comments: [                           ]
          [                           ]
          [                           ]
```

Keywords	Words that tell you something about the document and make it easy to locate the document later. For example, you might want to type the name of the company or the person you're sending the document to.
Comments	Details explaining what the document is about.

You don't have to fill in any of these boxes—you can simply press **Enter** to accept the dialog box as is and get on with your work. If you need to make changes in the dialog box, you can edit text you've typed in the dialog box in the same way you edit regular text in the document window.

Displaying Document Statistics

If you choose the Statistics button in the Summary Information dialog box, Word displays the Statistics window, shown in Figure 3–10. The Statistics window contains data about the document. This data is updated each time a document is saved. You cannot edit any information in the Statistics window.

You can check the statistics of an open document at any time. To display the statistics for the document you're working on:

1. Choose the Edit Summary Info command.

2. Choose Statistics.

3. To update, choose the Update button.

4. Press **Enter** when you're finished reviewing the statistics.

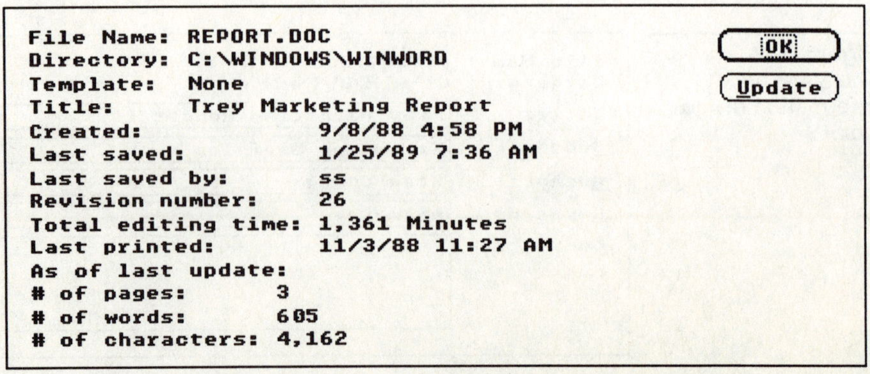

Figure 3–10.
The Statistics window.

```
File Name:  REPORT.DOC                          ( OK )
Directory:  C:\WINDOWS\WINWORD
Template:   None                                (Update)
Title:      Trey Marketing Report
Created:              9/8/88 4:58 PM
Last saved:          1/25/89 7:36 AM
Last saved by:       ss
Revision number:     26
Total editing time:  1,361 Minutes
Last printed:        11/3/88 11:27 AM
As of last update:
# of pages:       3
# of words:       605
# of characters:  4,162
```

Turning Off the Summary Information Display

If you don't always want to fill out the Summary Information fields, you can tell Word not to display the Summary Information box when you save a document. You can still display and add to the summary information any time you want using the Edit Summary Info command.

To turn off the automatic display of the Summary Information dialog box:

1. Choose the Utilities Customize command.

2. Turn off the Prompt for Summary Info option.

3. Click OK or press **Enter**.

Part II

REVISING

Once you have entered text in your document, you'll want to edit, revise, and check spelling and word usage. This part of the book covers these tasks.

In Chapter 4, you'll find out more about selecting text; moving around in your document; cutting, copying, and pasting text; using glossaries; and searching for and replacing text, graphics, and formatting.

One of the important features of Word is the ability to create and use multiple windows. They enable you to compare documents and copy information easily from one file to another. Chapter 5 gives you the details you need to work with several different documents at the same time, as well as techniques for displaying different parts of the same document.

If several users need to work on the same document, you may want to take advantage of Word's revision marking, file comparison, and annotation capabilities. Chapter 6 shows you how.

Word comes with a sophisticated spell checker and a very useful thesaurus. Word can also check the number of characters and words in a document. Chapter 7 explains all of these word-use features.

## Chapter Four

Editing Your Word Files

A document or template is rarely perfect the first time you type the text. You'll usually want to go back and delete text, add new text, or rearrange the sequence in your file. You might also want to copy text from another file or work with multiple windows to view different parts of a long file at the same time. This chapter shows you how to do all these tasks. You'll find out more about

- selecting text.

- moving around the document.

- cutting, copying, and pasting text.

- using glossaries.

- searching for and replacing text, graphics, and formatting.

SCROLLING THROUGH A WORD FILE

If your Word file has more text than will fit in the document window, you need to *scroll* to see all of your file. If you're a mouse user, you'll want to become familiar with clicking on Word's scroll bars to move around within the file. If you like to keep your hands on the keys, you can use the scroll bars as visual guides to tell you where you are in your file, or you might choose to hide one or both scroll bars.

Displaying or Hiding the Scroll Bars

You can control the display of the scroll bars in the Word window. By hiding the scroll bars, you can make the text area of the Word window a little bigger and see more of your file.

To display or hide the scroll bars:

1. Choose the View Preferences command.

2. Turn on or off the Vertical Scroll Bar and the Horizontal Scroll Bar options.

3. Click OK or press **Enter**.

Scrolling with the Mouse

Figure 4–1 shows how to use the scroll bars in normal view. To scroll with the mouse, you use the vertical scroll bar to scroll up or down, or the horizontal scroll bar to scroll right or left (if your text column is wider than the window).

Figure 4–1.
Use the scroll bars to scroll through a file using the mouse.

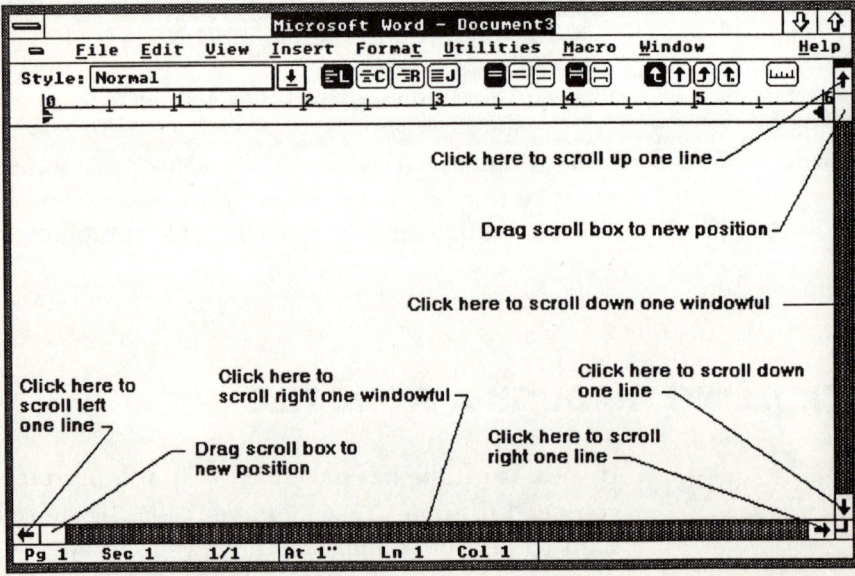

To scroll	Use the mouse to
One line	Click the scroll bar arrow that points toward the location of the text you want to see. For example, click the Down arrow in the scroll bar to see the next line of text at the bottom of the window.
One windowful	Click above or below the scroll box in the vertical scroll bar, or click either side of the scroll box in the horizontal scroll bar toward the location of the text you want to see. For example, click below the scroll box in the vertical scroll bar to see the next windowful of text at the bottom of the window.
To a relative location	Drag the scroll box to a location relative to the text you want to see in the document. For example, drag the scroll box to the middle of the scroll bar to see the middle of your document.

Scrolling with the Keyboard

If you use the keyboard to scroll when the scroll bars are displayed, the scroll boxes move to reflect the position of the text in the window relative to the entire file. For example, if the scroll box is near the bottom of the vertical scroll bar, the text you see in the window is near the end of your file.

Scrolling with keys is the same as moving the insertion point with keys. The next section provides more information on using the keyboard to navigate in files.

MOVING THE INSERTION POINT

The first step in editing is learning to move the insertion point (the cursor that looks a little like an I-beam or a capital I) around in an file. The insertion point moves only within text—you can't position an insertion point just anywhere on a blank screen.

Moving the Insertion Point with the Mouse

To move the insertion point with the mouse:

1. Place the mouse I-beam pointer where you want the insertion point in your text.

2. Click the mouse button to set the insertion point. The blinking insertion point appears. (You may need to move the I-beam pointer to see the insertion point.)

Note that the insertion point and the I-beam mouse pointer are two different objects—you can move the I-beam pointer by rolling the mouse, but the insertion point stays in the same place until you click a new location, as shown in Figure 4–2.

Moving the Insertion Point with Keys

To move the insertion point by pressing keys:

1. Use the arrow keys to move short distances or use the keys on the numeric keypad (with NumLock off) as shown in Figure 4–3.

2. Hold down the **Ctrl** key while you press the number key to get the action listed in italic in Figure 4–3.

Figure 4–2.
The insertion point and the mouse pointer are two different objects.

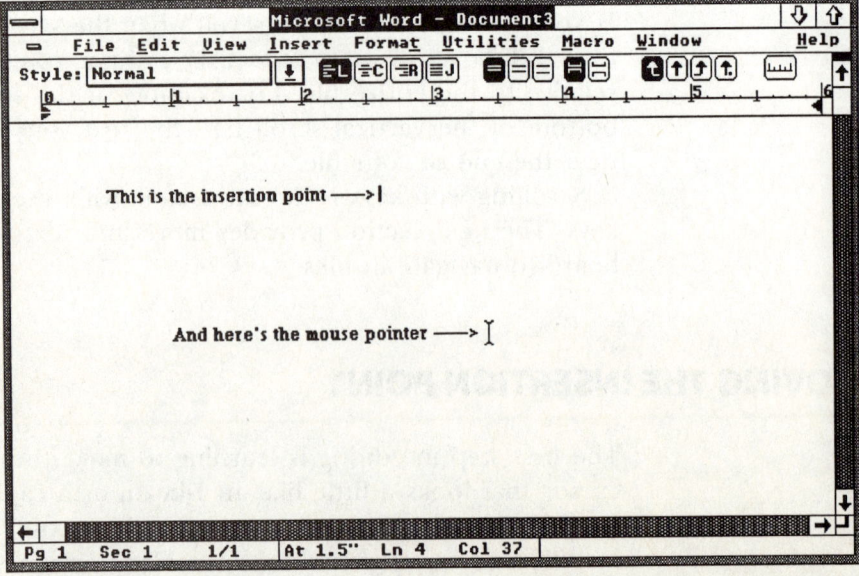

Figure 4–3.
You can use the keys on the numeric keypad to move the insertion point.

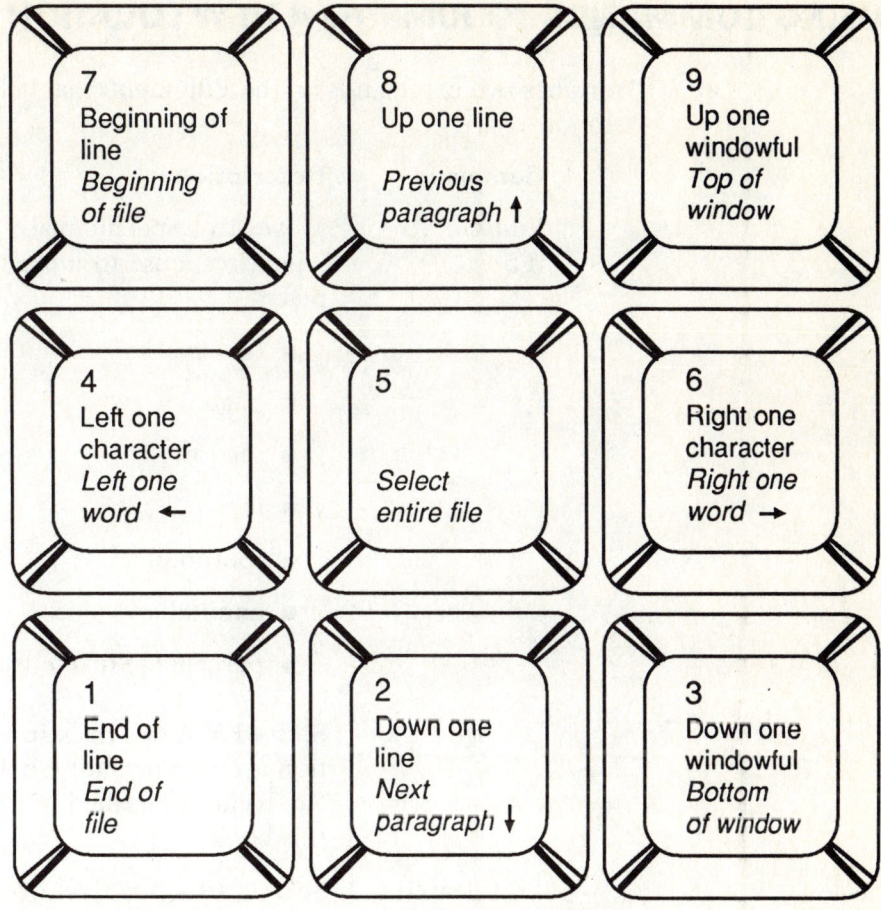

USING THE NUMERIC KEYPAD TO TYPE NUMBERS

You can use the numeric keypad at the right of the keyboard to move the insertion point, as just described, or to type numbers, as with a 10-key calculator. Use the NumLock key to switch between the two uses.

To type numbers:

1. Press the NumLock key. NUM appears in the status bar.

2. Type numbers or symbols on the keypad.

3. Press the NumLock key again to switch back to using the keypad for movement and commands. NUM disappears from the status bar.

USING COMMANDS TO JUMP TO A NEW LOCATION

Word has two commands on the Edit menu that help you jump to new locations:

Command	Description
Edit Go To (F5)	Moves to a specific place in a file. You can type a response to jump to the following places:

- bookmark

- page

- section

- line

- footnote

- annotation

- percentage of file (such as 50 percent)

	Shift+F5 moves back to the previous position after using Edit Go To. Uses of Edit Go To are described in various chapters of this book.
Edit Search	Searches for the next occurrence of a specific word or phrase. You can learn more about searching for text later in this chapter.

SELECTING: TELLING WORD WHERE TO MAKE CHANGES

To change text (edit or format it) in Word:

1. Select the text (using the mouse or keys) that you want to change.

2. Choose a command or use a key combination to change the selected text.

Selecting text highlights the text so you can easily see what you've selected, as shown in Figure 4–4. The commands you choose affect that text as long as it's highlighted.

Figure 4–4.
Selecting text.

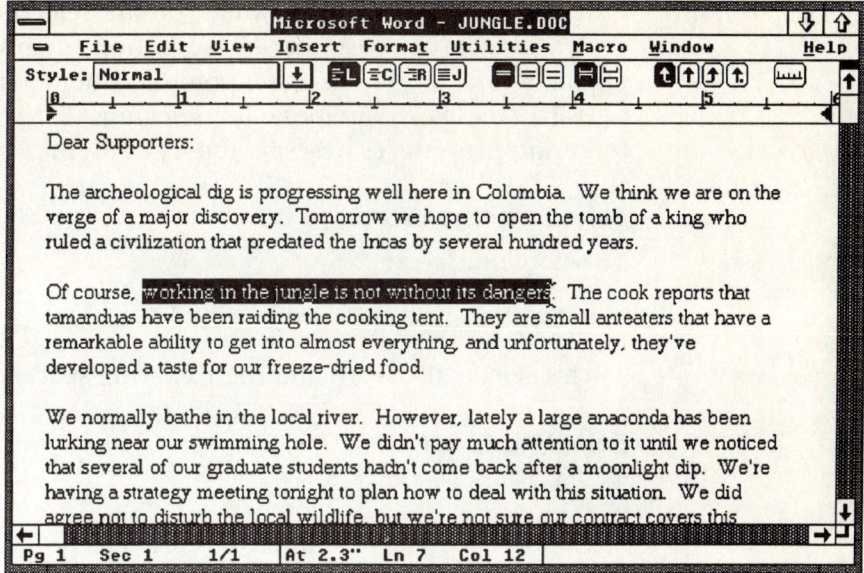

One word of caution about selecting: If you've turned on the Typing Replaces Selection option using the Utilities Customize command, Word *replaces* selected text with any character you type. This means that if you press a key after you've selected text, Word replaces the selected text with the character you typed. If you do this by accident, choose the Edit Undo command to undo the replacement.

Selecting with the Mouse

Here's the basic procedure to select text with the mouse.

1. Set the insertion point at the beginning of the text you want to select.

2. Hold down the mouse button while you move the insertion point to the end of the text you want to select.

3. When all the text you want is highlighted, release the mouse button.

4. Choose the command or press the key combination to change the selected text.

If you change your mind while you are selecting and want to start over again, just release the mouse button, then click to remove the highlight and set the insertion point in a new location.

Word has many variations for selecting text with the mouse. The following procedures describe the most useful variations.

Selecting One Word

To select one word:

■ Double-click the word.

This selects the word and the following space (if any).

Selecting Lines

To select lines of text:

1. Move the mouse pointer into the selection bar to the left of the line you want to select. The mouse pointer becomes an arrow when it's in the selection bar, as shown in Figure 4–5.

2. Click the mouse button to select one line or press the mouse button and drag the mouse pointer down the selection bar until you've selected all the lines you want.

3. Release the mouse button.

Figure 4–5.
Using the selection bar to select text with the mouse.

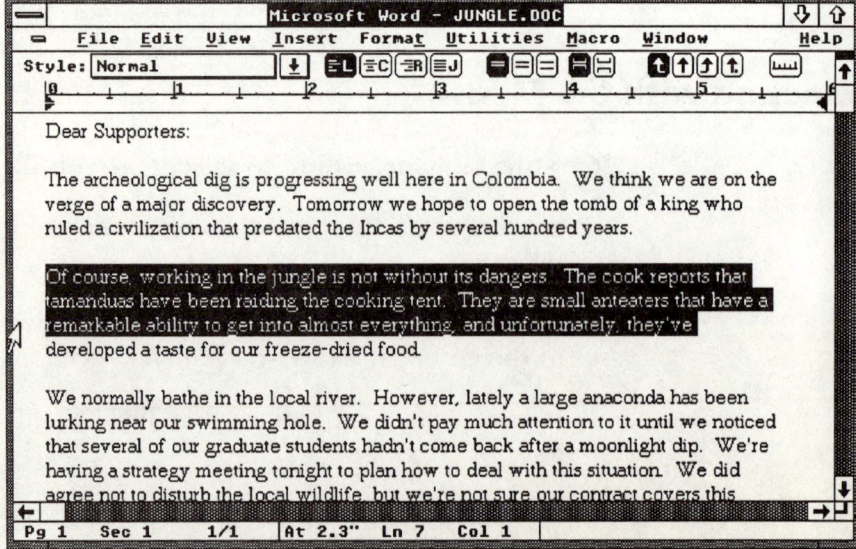

Selecting a Large Amount of Text

To select a large amount of text:

1. Set the insertion point at the beginning of the text you want to select.

2. Move the mouse pointer to the end of the text you want to select. Use the scroll bars if necessary.

3. Hold down the **Shift** key and click the mouse button to set the end point of the selected text. Word highlights the selected text.

It's important that you first press and hold down the Shift key, then click the mouse button; if you don't press the Shift key first, clicking the mouse button moves the insertion point instead of selecting the text.

Selecting Rectangular Blocks of Text

To select a rectangular block of text, such as a column:

1. Set the insertion point at one corner of the rectangle you want to select.

2. Click the right mouse button.

3. Drag to the other corner.

4. Release the mouse button.

Figure 4–6 shows a column selection.

Selecting the Entire File

To select the entire file:

1. Move the mouse pointer into the selection bar.

2. Hold down the **Ctrl** key and double-click the left mouse button.

For information about selecting text in tables, see Chapter 13.

Selecting with Keys

Word has two basic methods you can use to select text with keys. You should choose a command or press a key combination immediately after selecting the text. If you move the insertion point instead, Word removes the highlighting and the text is no longer selected.

Figure 4–6.
Selecting a block of
text.

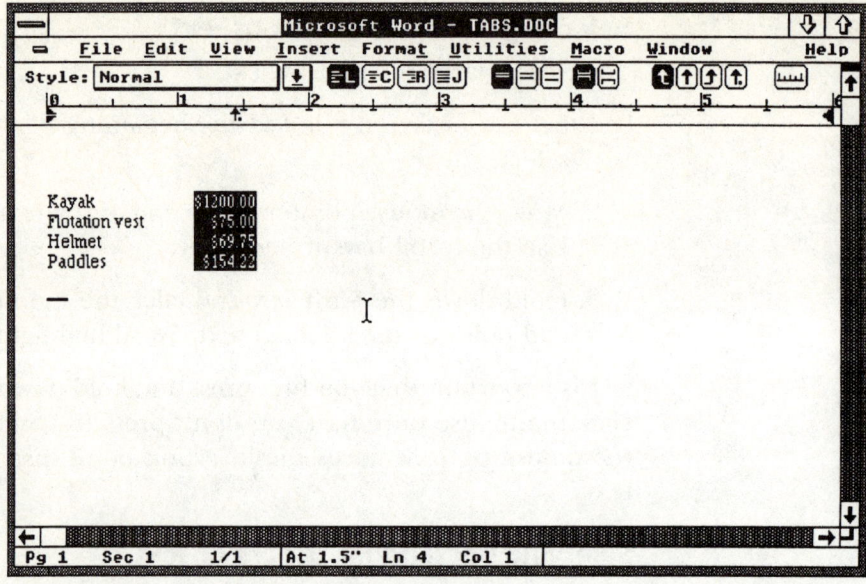

Selecting Short Pieces of Text

To select short pieces of text:

1. Hold down the **Shift** key.

2. Use the keys listed in Figure 4–3 to move the insertion point.

Selecting Long Pieces of Text

To select longer pieces of text:

1. Press **F8** to turn on extend mode. Word displays EXT in the status bar to remind you that you're using extend mode.

2. Move the insertion point until all the text you want to select is highlighted. If you make a mistake and want to start over, press **Esc** to turn off extend mode, then press an arrow key to remove the highlight.

For information about selecting text in tables, see Chapter 13.

Selecting the Entire File

To select the entire file:

■ Press **Ctrl+5** on the numeric keypad.

MAKING INSERTED TEXT REPLACE SELECTED TEXT

By default, Word for Windows inserts new text in front of any selected text. However, if you've used other word-processing programs, you may be accustomed to having inserted text replace selected text. You can set an option to make Word for Windows behave in this way, too.

To make inserted text replace selected text:

1. Choose the Utilities Customize command.

2. Turn on the Typing Replaces Selection option.

3. Click OK or press **Enter**.

When Typing Replaces Selection is turned on, whatever you type replaces *everything* that is selected. Be sure to check selected text before you press a key so you won't accidentally replace text you want to keep. This option stays set from session to session, so use the Utilities Customize command again if you want to change this mode.

TYPING OVER TEXT

You can use Word's overtype mode to type new text, character-by-character, on top of existing text, just as you would on a typewriter.

To use overtype mode:

1. Press the **Insert** key. Word displays OVR in the status bar to remind you that you're using overtype mode.

2. Type over the text.

3. Press the **Insert** key again to turn off overtype mode.

DELETING TEXT

In Word for Windows, deleting text means permanently erasing the text, so be sure this is what you want to do before you delete text.

Deleting text in Word is easy.

1. Select the text.

2. Press the **Delete** key to erase the text.

You can reverse a deletion if you choose the Edit Undo command *immediately* after pressing the Delete key.

If you want to delete text and paste it in somewhere else, you should use the Edit Cut command as described in the following section, Moving Text. If you want to delete text from your file, but save it for later use, you can define it as a *glossary entry*. Then you can use that text again wherever and whenever you want it, or delete it at a later time if you decide not to use it. See Saving Text and Graphics for Repeated Use: Using Glossaries later in this chapter for more information.

MOVING TEXT

When you move text, you'll use the Edit Cut and Edit Paste commands. When you use the Edit Cut command to remove text, Word moves that text to the Clipboard. Text stays in the Clipboard until the next time you copy or "cut" text: The Clipboard always contains the last piece of text or the last graphic you copied or cut. Using the Clipboard is illustrated in Figure 4–7. As long as the text is in the Clipboard, you can move the insertion point to a new location in the same file or to a different file, then paste in the text. (See Chapter 5 for more information about working with multiple files.)

To move text:

1. Select the text you want to move.

Figure 4–7.
The Edit Cut, Edit Copy, and Edit Paste commands use the Clipboard to move text.

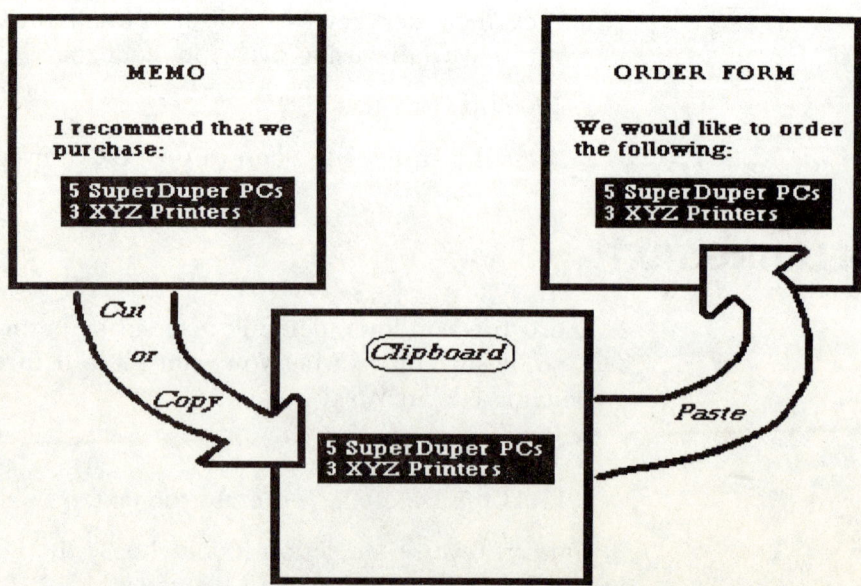

2. Choose the Edit Cut command or press **Shift+Del**. Word removes the selected text from your file and places it in the Clipboard.

3. Place the insertion point where you want to insert the text. If you've chosen the Typing Replaces Selection option and you want the inserted text to replace existing text, select the text you want to replace. Otherwise, make sure no text is selected.

4. Choose the Edit Paste command or press **Shift+Ins**. Word inserts a copy of the text from the Clipboard.

Keyboard Shortcut

You can use the following method to move text or graphics quickly without using the Clipboard.

To move text or graphics with keys:

1. Select the text or graphic you want to move.

2. Press **F2**. The words Move to where? appear in the status bar.

3. Place the insertion point where you want to insert the text.

   If you've turned on the Typing Replaces Selection option and you want the inserted text or graphic to replace existing information, select the information you want to replace. If you don't want to replace information, make sure nothing is selected.

   The insertion point becomes a dotted vertical line, and any selected text is marked with a dotted underline.

4. Press **Enter** to insert the text or graphic.

If you want to delete text but preserve the information that's in the Clipboard, use the **Delete** key to erase selected text without placing it in the Clipboard.

Mouse Shortcut

To move text or graphics using only the mouse:

1. Select the text or graphic you want to move.

2. Point to the place where you want to insert the selected text or graphic.

3. Hold down **Ctrl** and click the right mouse button.

COPYING TEXT

If you've typed a phrase, a paragraph, or even a whole file that you want to use in another location, you can copy that text and paste it in another place without affecting the original text. You can copy text within the same file or to a different file. (See Chapter 5 for more information about working with multiple files.)

To copy text and paste the copy in a new location:

1. Select the text you want to copy.

2. Choose the Edit Copy command or press **Ctrl+Ins**. Word places a copy of the selected text in the Clipboard.

3. Place the insertion point where you want to insert the copy. If you've turned on the Typing Replaces Selection option and you want the copied text to replace existing text, select the text you want to replace. Otherwise, make sure no text is selected.

4. Choose the Edit Paste command or press **Shift+Ins**. Word inserts a copy of the text from the Clipboard.

As long as the text you want is in the Clipboard, you can use the Edit Paste command to insert a copy as many times as you like. If you paste frequently, you may want to get in the habit of pressing the Edit Paste command's shortcut key, **Shift+Ins**, to paste without choosing the command from the menu.

Keyboard Shortcut

You can use the following procedure to copy text or graphics quickly without using the Clipboard.

To copy text or graphics with the keys:

1. Select the text or graphic to copy.

2. Press **Shift+F2**. You'll see the words Copy to where? appear in the status bar.

3. Place the insertion point where you want to insert the copy.

If you've turned on the Typing Replaces Selection option and you want to replace text, select information that you want to replace with the copy. Otherwise, make sure no text is selected.

The insertion point is a dotted line, and a dotted underline appears under any information you select.

4. Press **Enter** to insert the copy.

If you want to use the same text often, you can save that text as a glossary entry and insert it wherever and whenever you like. See Saving Text and Graphics for Repeated Use: Using Glossaries later in this chapter for more information.

Mouse Shortcut

To copy text or graphics with only the mouse:

1. Select the text or graphic to copy.

2. Point to the place where you want to insert the copy.

3. Hold down the **Ctrl** key and the **Shift** key and click the right mouse button.

VIEWING THE CONTENTS OF THE CLIPBOARD

As previously mentioned, when you delete or copy text, Word places that text in the Clipboard. You can check the Clipboard any time you like.

To view the contents of the Clipboard:

1. Choose the Run command from the Word Control menu (**Alt, Spacebar, U**).

2. Choose the Clipboard command.

3. Click OK or press **Enter**. Word opens the Clipboard window to show you the contents of the Clipboard, as shown in Figure 4–8.

To close the Clipboard window:

■ Choose the Close command from the Clipboard Control menu or press **Alt+F4**.

COLLECTING AND INSERTING SEVERAL ITEMS AT ONCE: USING THE SPIKE

Word has a special place to save text and graphics called the *Spike*. The Spike is somewhat like the Clipboard in that you can cut parts of

Figure 4–8.
Checking the
contents of the
Clipboard.

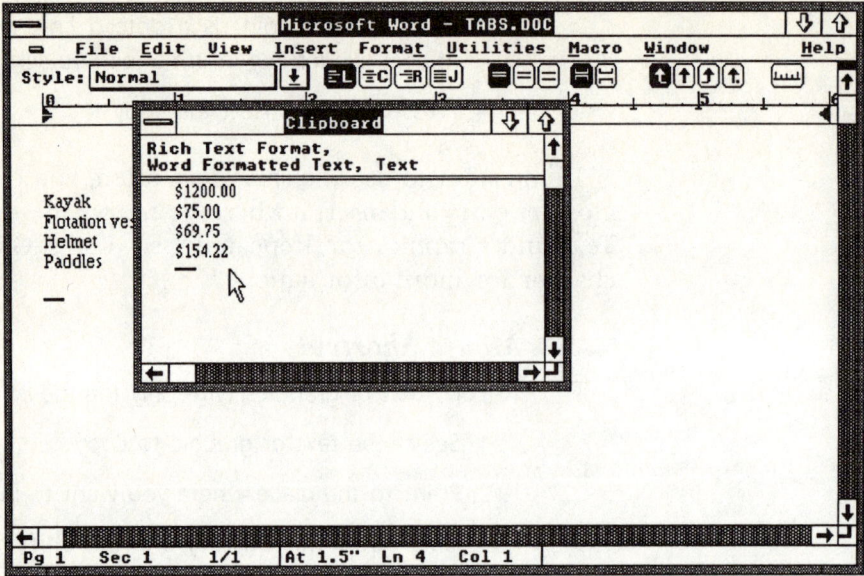

Word files and send those selections to the Spike. However, unlike the Clipboard, each item you put in the Spike is added to items already there, so you can use the Spike to collect a lot of items, then insert them all at once.

For example, you might want to open all your monthly financial reports in sequence, cut the summary paragraph from each monthly report to the Spike, then insert them all at once into your annual report.

To send an item to the Spike:

1. Select the text or graphics you want to send to the Spike.

2. Press **Ctrl**+**F3** to add the selected text or graphics to the Spike. Each item is added to the contents of the Spike.

To insert the contents of the Spike:

1. Move the insertion point to where you want the contents of the Spike.

2. Do one of the following:

   ■ To insert the contents of the Spike and empty the Spike, press **Ctrl**+**Shift**+**F3**.

   or

■ To insert the contents of the Spike, but leave the information in the Spike unchanged, type **spike**, then press **F3**.

UNDOING A CHANGE

Everyone knows that "oh, no!" feeling that you get when you've made a mistake. You've just deleted text you should have kept, moved a phrase to the wrong place, or chosen the wrong command. When this happens to you, don't panic. Word has made allowances for mistakes, and there is practically nothing you can do in Word that can't be undone.

If you realize your mistake immediately after you've made it, you can use Word's Edit Undo command. The Edit Undo command can, in most cases, reverse the last action you took. The wording of the Edit Undo command changes to reflect what you've been doing most recently, as shown in Figure 4–9.

If you've just done something that Word can't undo, the Edit Undo command says Can't Undo. In that case you can probably choose a different command to correct the problem.

To undo the last action:

■ Choose the Edit Undo command or press **Alt**+**Backspace**.

Because Edit Undo is a command you'll use frequently, you may want to get in the habit of using its shortcut key combination, Alt+Backspace, to undo the last action without choosing the command from the menu. If Word can't undo something (like removing the highlight from selected text), it beeps when you press Alt+Backspace.

If you've made a disastrous mistake and Word tells you it Can't undo, consider closing your file without saving it. You'll lose all the changes you've made since the last time you saved it, but that may be more desirable than keeping the file in its altered state.

SAVING TEXT AND GRAPHICS FOR REPEATED USE: USING GLOSSARIES

Do you have an address, a letterhead, or a picture that you'd like to use over and over again in your documents? With Word you can save text and graphics as entries in a *glossary*. Using a glossary is like renting a safety deposit box—you can put the entries you want to keep in it, then open it up and take out the entries any time you like.

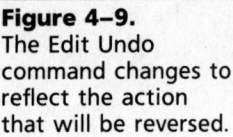

Figure 4–9.
The Edit Undo
command changes to
reflect the action
that will be reversed.

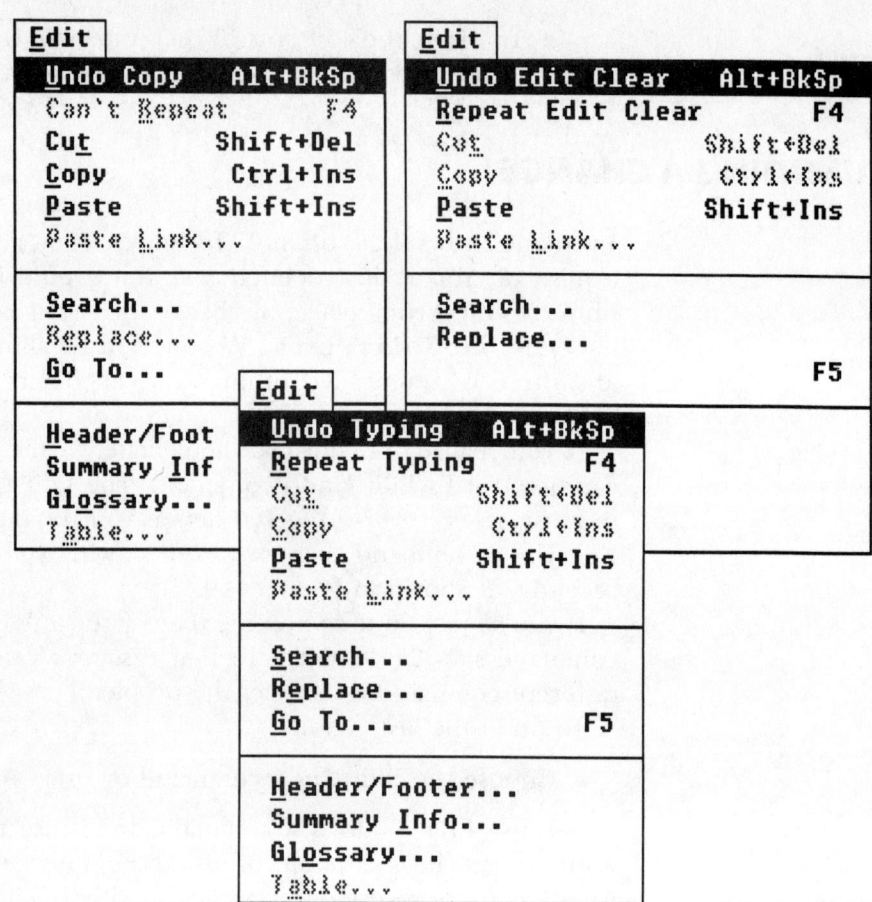

Almost anything can be kept in a glossary, from one character to a whole file. You can even store formatting in glossaries by storing paragraph marks, section marks, and so forth—you'll learn more about that in later sections of this book. Keep in mind, though, that the more information Word has to keep track of, the slower the program runs, so you should only store those entries that you really want to save. You can always delete entries from glossaries, too, if they become too full.

Glossary entries are stored in templates, either in the default template, NORMAL.DOT, or in a special template you've created and attached to the document. Glossary entries in the NORMAL.DOT template are automatically available to all Word documents. If you want to use other glossary entries, base your document on the template that contains them.

Note to experienced Mac Word and PC Word users: Instead of using glossaries to insert fields—such as the time and date, for example—Word for Windows uses the Insert Field command. See Chapter 18 for more information about using fields.

You'll use the Edit Glossary command to work with glossary entries. The Edit Glossary dialog box is shown in Figure 4–10.

Defining Entries in a Glossary

To save text or graphics as a glossary entry:

1. Select the text and/or graphics you want to save.

2. Choose the Edit Glossary command.

3. Type a name for your glossary entry in the Glossary Name box. For example, if you were saving your company logo, you might type **logo**. Glossary entry names can contain up to 31 characters and can include spaces.

4. In the Context box, choose an option:

Global	Saves your entry in the NORMAL.DOT template, making it available to all documents.
Template	Saves your entry in the active template. This option is not available if the active document was created with a template other than NORMAL.DOT.

Figure 4–10.
The Edit Glossary dialog box.

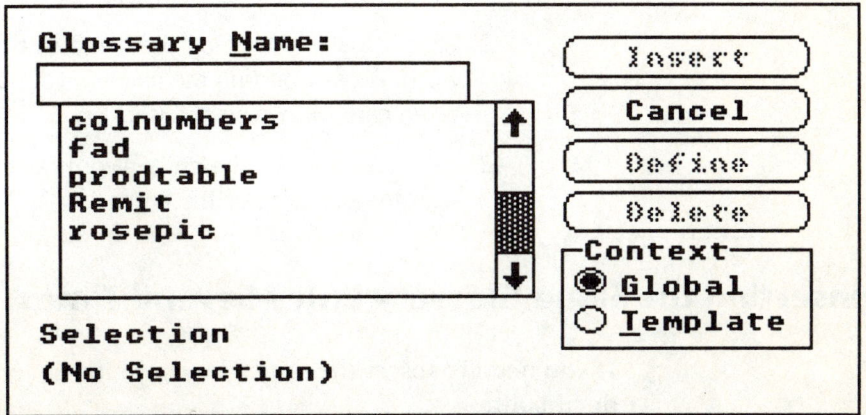

5. Click Define or press **Enter**.

Glossary entries are automatically saved when you save the document and its template.

Inserting Glossary Entries

When you've saved an entry in a glossary attached to a template, you can insert that entry into your documents any time you like.
To insert a glossary entry:

1. If the glossary entry you want to use is in a special template, base your document on that template.

2. Place the insertion point where you want to insert the entry.

3. Choose the Edit Glossary command.

4. Select the name of the entry you want from the Glossary Name list.

5. Choose Insert or press **Enter** to close the dialog box.

Mouse Speed Tip

You can also double-click the glossary entry in the list to select it, insert it, and close the Edit Glossary dialog box at the same time.

Keyboard Shortcut

If you know the name of the glossary entry you want, you can insert it using just the keyboard:

1. Place the insertion point where you want to insert the entry.

2. Type a space, then type the name of the glossary entry. Don't worry about inserting the name in your document—that will be taken care of in the next step.

3. Press **F3** to insert the entry. Word replaces the glossary name with the contents of the entry.

Inserting the Same Glossary Entry Several Times

If you need to insert the same glossary entry several places in the same document:

1. Insert it once.

2. Move the insertion point to the next location.

3. Press **F4** or choose the Edit Repeat command to quickly insert the same entry. (F4 and the Edit Repeat command repeat your last action.)

4. Repeat steps 2 and 3 to insert the same entry as many times as you like.

EXAMPLE: Using a Glossary Entry

Say you frequently use your name and address in letters, so you'd like to save something like the following as a glossary entry:

Dr. Michelle Michaels
3322 Rue Nouvelle
Paris, New Mexico 87022

Here's what you'd do:

1. Type and format the name and address, then select them.

2. Choose the Edit Glossary command and type **address** in the Glossary Name box.

3. Click Define or press **Enter**.

4. Write your letters. At the end of each letter, type **address**, then press **F3** to insert the glossary entry.

Changing a Glossary Entry

You can keep the name of a glossary entry, but change its contents. You might want to do this if you didn't select everything you wanted the entry to contain or if you've decided to change the text or format of the entry.

To change a glossary entry:

1. Change the text or graphics in your file if necessary, then select the information you want the glossary entry to contain.

2. Choose the Edit Glossary command.

3. Select the name of the entry you want to contain the selected information.

4. Choose Define. Word displays this message: `Redefine glossary?`

5. Click Yes or press **Y**. Word replaces the entry's contents with the information you selected in your file.

Deleting a Glossary Entry

You can delete entries you no longer use from a glossary.
To delete a glossary entry:

1. Choose the Edit Glossary command.

2. Select the name of the entry you want to delete from the Glossary Name list.

3. Choose Delete. Word changes the Cancel button to Close.

4. Repeat steps 2 and 3 to delete as many entries as you like.

5. Click Close or press **Enter** to save your changes and close the dialog box.

Printing a Glossary

If you'd like to print a copy of the glossary entries attached to a file, use the following procedure.
To print a glossary:

1. If necessary, open the template file containing the glossary entries you want to print.

2. Choose the File Print command.

3. Choose Glossary from the drop-down Print list, then click OK or press **Enter** to print the glossary.

Word prints glossary entries in alphabetic order. The printed page includes not only the entry names, but also their contents, as shown in Figure 4–11.

Figure 4–11.
A printout of a glossary.

Global Glossaries

    colnumbers

1
2
3
4
5

    fad
The Fife and Drum Company

    flowerpic

    prodtable

Product	Description	Price
Edgers	Plastic and steel	$79.95
Lawnmowers	All steel: Push, electric and riding	$99.99-789.95
Trimmers	Steel and plastic: electric and gas	$59.99-89.95

    Remit
Please remit to the following address:

      Mr. John Cantrell
      345 Forest Avenue
      Olympia, Washington 98504

Attn: Accounts Receivable

SEARCHING FOR AND REPLACING TEXT AND FORMATTING

Word has two commands that search for text:

Edit Search   Searches for the first occurrence of text
you specify.

Edit Replace   Searches for the text you specify and replaces it with the new text you specify.

You can quickly find a word, a phrase, or even a hidden formatting character with these commands, and you can replace occurrences of the text individually or all occurrences all at once.

Word searches from the insertion point to the beginning or end of the file, so be sure the insertion point is where you want the search to start before you choose a command. If you begin the search in the middle of a file, when Word reaches the file's beginning or end it displays a message asking you if you want to continue the search from the beginning of the file.

Searching for Text

Word can search for any character you can type in a file.

To search for text:

1. Choose the Edit Search command. Word displays the dialog box shown in Figure 4–12.

2. Type the text you want to search for in the Search For box. Be sure to type *exactly* the text you want to search for—if you type two spaces between words in a phrase, for example, Word won't find the phrase with just one space between words in your file.

There is *one* case in which you don't have to type exactly the text you want to search for. You can use a question mark (?) to take the place of any character in a word when searching, so when

Figure 4–12.
The Edit Search
dialog box.

```
┌─────────────────────────────────────────────────────────────┐
│  Search For:                                      ┌────────┐  │
│  ┌──────────────────────────────────────────┐     │   OK   │  │
│  └──────────────────────────────────────────┘     └────────┘  │
│                                                   ┌────────┐  │
│  ☐ Whole Word              ┌Direction─┐           │ Cancel │  │
│  ☐ Match Upper/Lowercase   │ ○ Up ◉ Down│          └────────┘  │
│                            └──────────┘                      │
└─────────────────────────────────────────────────────────────┘
```

you want to search for a question mark itself, type a caret (ˆ) before the question mark character, as follows:

To search for	**Type**
Any character in a word	?
	(For example, type **n?w** to find new and now.)
Question mark	ˆ?

3. Choose the following options if desired:

- Turn on Whole Word if you want to find only an entire word rather than part of a word. For example, if you don't choose Whole Word and you type **ear** in the Search For box, Word might find and display matches such as *hear, earth, research,* and so forth, because all these words contain the letters you're searching for.

- Turn on Match Upper/Lowercase if you want Word to pay attention to uppercase and lowercase letters in its search. For example, you might want to search for *United* or *UNITED* but not *united.* If you don't choose Match Upper/Lowercase, Word searches for all occurrences of the letters you type.

4. In the Direction box, choose Up to search from the insertion point to the beginning of the file; choose Down to search to the end.

5. Click OK or press **Enter** to close the dialog box and begin the search. Word highlights the first occurrence of the text or formatting you specified, or, if it reaches the end of the file before finding an occurrence, Word displays a message asking you if you want to search from the other end of the file.

Searching Again for the Same Text

To search again for the same text:

- Press **Shift+F4**.

Word highlights the next occurrence.

Replacing Text

You can replace existing text with new text in one easy step. You can ask Word to make all the changes automatically, or you can approve each change before it's made. You type a word or phrase (up to 255 characters) to search for, and you can replace that word or phrase with text you type or with the contents of the Clipboard.

1. To replace text or formatting in part of your file, select that part. To replace text or formatting in all of your file, make sure nothing's selected.

2. Choose the Edit Replace command. Word displays the dialog box shown in Figure 4–13.

3. Type the text you want to search for in the Search For box.

   or

   If you want to search for the contents of the Clipboard, press **Shift+Ins** to paste the contents into the Search For box.

4. Type the new text you want to replace in the Replace With box.

   or

   To replace with the contents of the Clipboard, press **Shift+Ins** to paste the contents into the Replace With box.

5. Choose the following options if desired:

   - Turn on the Whole Word option if you want Word to search for and replace only a whole word, not just part of a word.

   - Turn on the Match Upper/Lowercase option if you want Word to search for and replace with the exact combination of uppercase and lowercase letters you typed in the dialog box.

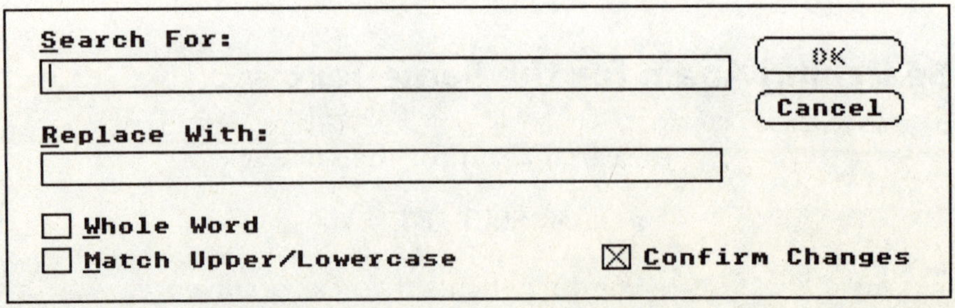

Figure 4–13.
The Edit Replace
dialog box.

Search For:

Replace With:

OK

Cancel

☐ Whole Word
☐ Match Upper/Lowercase   ☒ Confirm Changes

- Turn off Confirm Changes if you want Word to automatically replace all occurrences. If you don't turn off Confirm Changes, Word highlights each occurrence it finds and asks you if you want to replace it—then you can click No or press **N** to go on to the next occurrence, or click Yes or press **Y** to make the change.

6. Click OK or press **Enter**.

If you turned off Confirm Changes, Word makes all the replacements automatically and lists the number of replacements in the status bar. If this number looks suspiciously high, you can choose the Edit Undo command immediately or check your replacements, then use the Edit Replace command again to correct any mistakes.

Helpful Hints

- To enter text faster and with fewer mistakes, substitute a two- or three-character code for long words or phrases that you type often. For example, instead of typing **Hi-Tech Services, Inc.** several times in a memo, just type **hhh**, then use the Edit Replace command later to replace **hhh** with **Hi-Tech Services, Inc**.

  When you choose such a code, be sure to choose a letter or number combination that doesn't occur elsewhere in your file, such as qq, xx, p9, or any character repeated several times: www,]]], \\\, %%, and so forth.

- Use the Clipboard to replace codes with specially formatted text, long segments of text, or even graphics. For example, to repeat a product name that requires special formatting and a registration symbol, such as OpusV®, enter and format the text once, then use a code such as **o5** wherever you want to repeat the product name. When you're finished editing the file, copy the formatted product name to the Clipboard, then replace the code with the contents of the Clipboard by pressing **Shift+Ins** in the Replace With box.

Searching for and Replacing Hidden Formatting Characters and ASCII and ANSI Characters

Characters that control the format of your document, such as tab characters, paragraph marks, page breaks, and so forth, are hidden characters—they don't show when the document is printed. You can, however, display them with the View Preferences command or by pressing **Ctrl+Shift+***. And whether or not these hidden characters are displayed, you can search for them in your Word files.

You can search for and replace a variety of hidden formatting characters:

To search for or replace with	Type
Tab mark	ˆt
Paragraph mark	ˆp
New line (line break) mark	ˆn
Page break or section mark	ˆd
Column break	ˆ14
Optional hyphen	ˆ-
Nonbreaking hyphen	ˆ~
Caret or circumflex	ˆˆ
Clipboard contents	Shift+Ins
Nonbreaking space	ˆs
White space	ˆw
Footnote reference mark	ˆ5
Graphic	ˆ1
Any ASCII or ANSI character	ˆ*nnn* where *nnn* is the ASCII or ANSI code

---

◢ EXAMPLE: Replacing Hidden Formatting Characters

Say you've pressed the Enter key twice at the end of each paragraph in your file: once to end the paragraph, and once to insert a blank line before beginning the next paragraph. Later, you decide to eliminate the blank lines between paragraphs. Instead of deleting each one individually, you can do this:

1. Choose the Edit Replace command.

2. Type **^p^p** in the Search For box to find two sequential paragraph marks.

3. Type **^p** in the Replace With box to replace the two paragraph marks with one paragraph mark.

4. Click OK or press **Enter**.

Searching for and Replacing Formatting

Word can search not only for specific characters, but also for character formatting—such as bold, italic, or small capitals—and for paragraph formatting, such as indents, line spacing, and styles. You'll learn more about character formatting in Chapter 8, and more about paragraph formatting in Chapter 9. You can also type specific text if you want to search for both text and formatting at the same time.

To tell Word what kind of formatting to search for, you use the key combinations that apply character and paragraph formatting.

To search for character or paragraph formatting:

1. Choose the Edit Search or Edit Replace command.

2. If necessary, type the specific text you want to search for and replace in the boxes or use the Delete key to delete text from the boxes.

3. In the boxes, press any of the following key combinations to specify the format you want. You can type several key combinations in succession: Press **Ctrl+B**, then **Ctrl+D**, for example, to find bold text with a double underline. The words Bold, Italic, Underline, and so on, appear beneath the boxes to show you the format you've chosen.

To specify	Type
Bold	Ctrl+B
Italic	Ctrl+I
Underline	Ctrl+U
Double underline	Ctrl+D
Word underline	Ctrl+W

Small capitals	Ctrl+K
Hidden text	Ctrl+H
3-point subscript	Ctrl+equal sign (=)
3-point superscript	Ctrl+plus sign (+)
Font name	Ctrl+F. Repeat until you see the font you want
Point size	Ctrl+P. Repeat until you see the point size you want
Plain text	Ctrl+Spacebar
Color	Ctrl+V. Repeat until you see the color you want
New text	Ctrl+N (only when revision marking is turned on)
Deleted text	Ctrl+Z (only when revision marking is turned on)
Centered paragraph	Ctrl+C
Justified paragraph	Ctrl+J
Left-aligned paragraph	Ctrl+L
Right-aligned paragraph	Ctrl+R
Single-spaced paragraph	Ctrl+1
Double-spaced paragraph	Ctrl+2
1½-spaced paragraph	Ctrl+5
Paragraph with space before	Ctrl+O
Paragraph with no space before	Ctrl+E
Styles	^y*stylename* (do not insert space between the *y* and the style name.) This cannot be used in combination with other formatting key combinations
Default paragraph style	Ctrl+X

Figure 4–14.
Using the Edit
Replace command to
replace underlines
with double-
underlines.

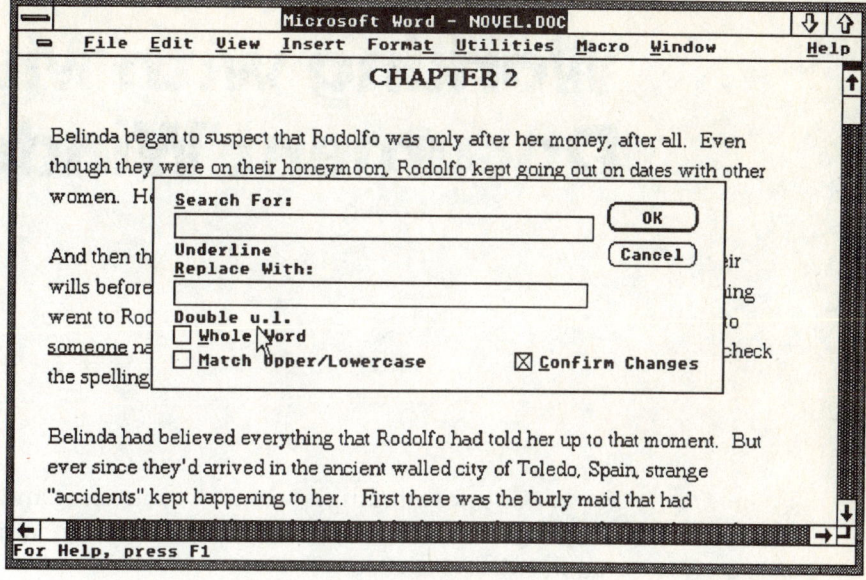

Figure 4–14 illustrates replacing one format with another.

▬▬▬ **EXAMPLE: Replacing Formatting**

Say you've typed a product name (Avalok) in bold throughout your
file to give it emphasis. Later, you decide to change that word to
italic. Instead of changing each occurrence individually, you can do
the following:

1. Choose the Edit Replace command.

2. In the Search For box, type **Avalok**, then press Ctrl+B to find
   the bold word.

3. In the Replace With box, type **Avalok**, then press Ctrl+I to
   change the word from bold to italic.

4. Click OK or press **Enter**.

Chapter Five

Working with Multiple Document Windows

By working with multiple windows, you can handle complex text creation, make extensive edits, and compare documents with ease. This chapter describes

- working with multiple documents at the same time.

- using more than one view of a document.

MICROSOFT WINDOWS AND WORD WINDOWS

One of the main advantages of using Microsoft Windows is that you can work with multiple applications, running each program in its own window, as shown in Figure 5–1. You can use the Windows Clipboard to transfer information between Windows applications. You can also use Windows commands to change the size of the application windows and to rearrange them on the screen.

Like Windows, Word enables you to create multiple windows within the Word window. Each of these windows is called a *document window,* and each can contain a different file. Only one document window can contain the insertion point at a time—the active document window. The active document window displays its own Document Control menu (not to be confused with the Word Control menu, which controls the entire Word window) as well as its own icons and scroll bars, as shown in Figure 5–2. You can move information from one Word file to another using Word's Edit Cut and Edit Paste commands and the Windows Clipboard. You can also move and change the size of each document window.

Figure 5–1.
Using multiple
Windows
applications.

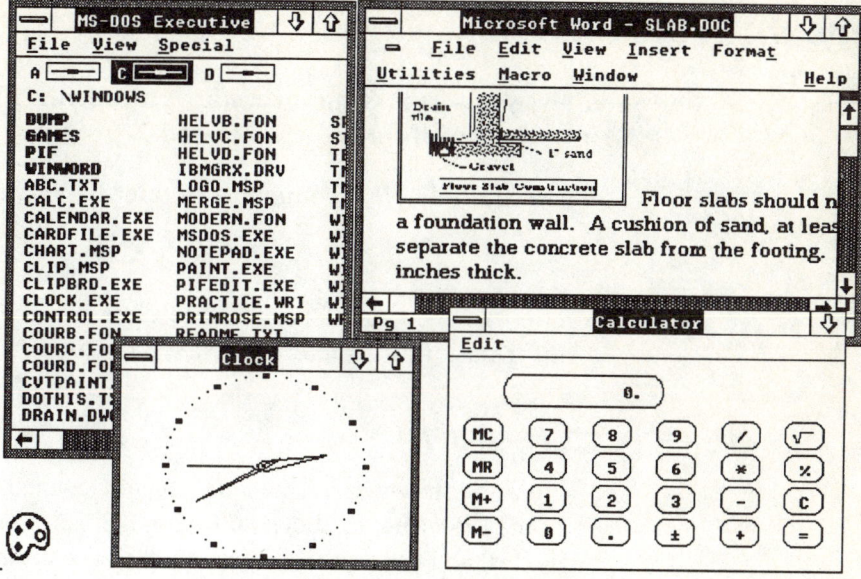

Figure 5–2.
Multiple document
windows in the Word
window.

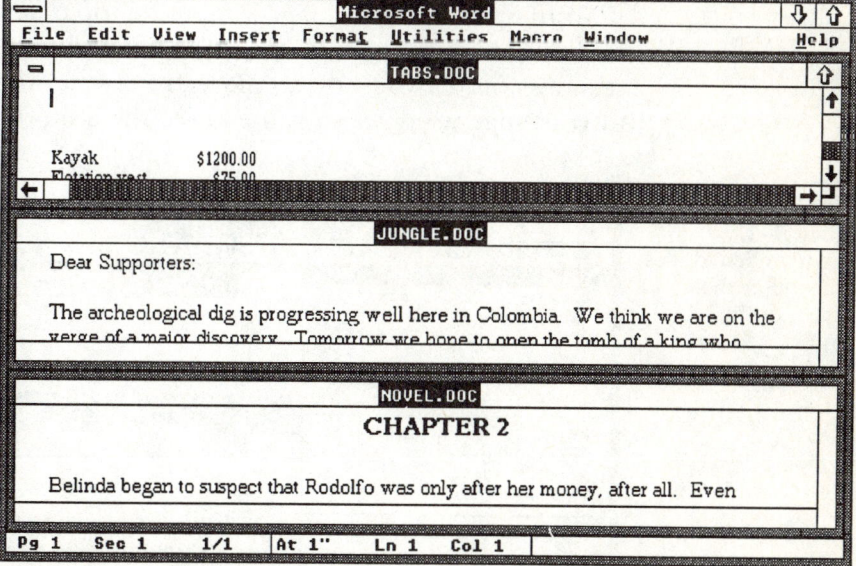

There are many instances when you'll want to have more than one Word file open at a time. You might just want to refer to another document to see what you've written, or you might want to copy or move text between Word files.

OPENING ANOTHER FILE

You always use the same procedure to open a file, whether it's the first or the fourth file you've opened.

■ Use the File New command to open a new, empty file.

or

■ Use the File Open command to open an existing file. (For more information on opening files, see Chapter 3.)

Speed Tip

Word lists several of the most recently opened files at the bottom of the File menu, as shown in Figure 5–3. To quickly open one of these files, you can use the mouse to click the filename from the bottom of the File menu or type the number listed beside the filename.

Word opens a file in a new window on top of any previously opened files. At first, you can't see the other open windows, but the following sections will tell you how to move from window to window and how to rearrange windows so you can see them on the screen.

Figure 5–3.
Recently opened files are listed at the bottom of the File menu.

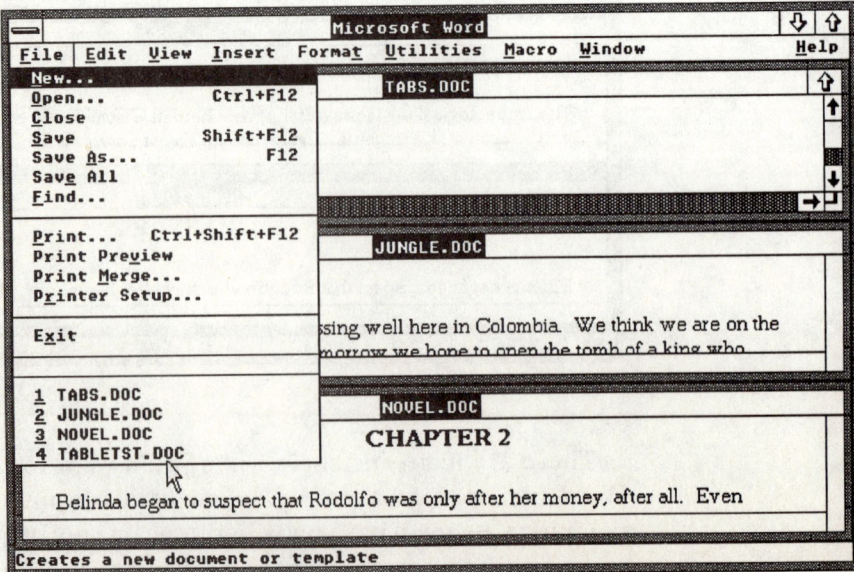

MOVING THE INSERTION POINT BETWEEN WINDOWS

The Window menu lists all the files you have opened. A check mark appears to the left of the file in the active window—the one that contains the insertion point. Figure 5–4 shows an example of how the Window menu might look when multiple files are open.

You can move or copy information from one Word file to another in the following manner:

1. Open both the file containing the information you want to move or copy and the file you want to paste the information into.

2. Move the insertion point to the document window containing the information you want to cut or copy.

3. Use the Edit Cut or Edit Copy command to place the information in the Clipboard.

4. Move the insertion point to the document window containing the file you want to paste the information into.

5. Use the Edit Paste command to paste in the information from the Clipboard.

Figure 5–4.
The Window menu
lists all open files.

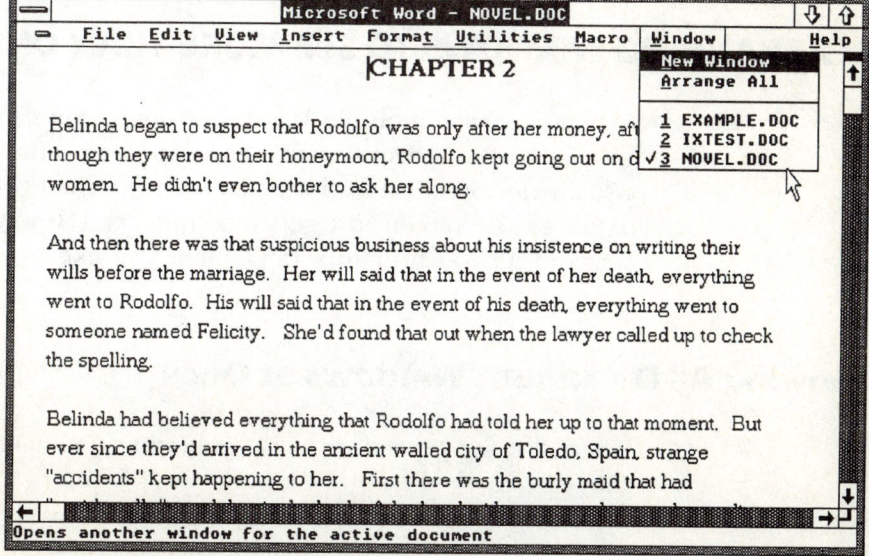

Moving from Window to Window with the Mouse

To move the insertion point to another window with the mouse:

- If the window is hidden, select the name of the file you want to move to from the Window menu. Word places the file you choose on top of other open files.

or

- If you can see the window you want to move to, click anywhere in the window to move the insertion point to it.

Moving from Window to Window with the Keys

To move the insertion point to another window with the keys, use one of the following procedures:

- Press **Ctrl+F6** until the insertion point is in the window you want.

or

1. Press **Alt, W** to display the Window menu.

2. Type the number shown beside the filename.

REARRANGING WINDOWS TO SEE MORE THAN ONE AT A TIME

When you have multiple Word files open, you can change their sizes and positions to display more than one file on the screen at once. It's usually not practical to try to display more than two or three windows at once: The screen just gets too cluttered. However, you can experiment until you find an arrangement you like.

Showing All Document Windows at Once

The following procedure works only when you have two or more Word files open.

To arrange your open document windows so that you can see them all at once:

- Choose the Window Arrange All command.

Word divides the space in the Word window among files, as shown in Figure 5–5.

Changing the Size of Individual Document Windows

The following procedures work only when you have two or more Word files open. Before you can change the size of a window, you may need to choose the Window Arrange All command so that you can see window borders on the screen.

Changing the Size of a Window with the Mouse

To change the size of the active document window with the mouse:

1. Move the mouse pointer to the border you want to move. If you move the pointer to a corner, you can change both the height and the width of the window at once, as shown in Figure 5–6. The pointer becomes a two-headed arrow.

2. Hold down the left mouse button and drag the border to the new position, then release the button.

3. Repeat steps 1 and 2 to move other borders as necessary.

Figure 5–5.
The Window Arrange All command displays up to nine document windows at once.

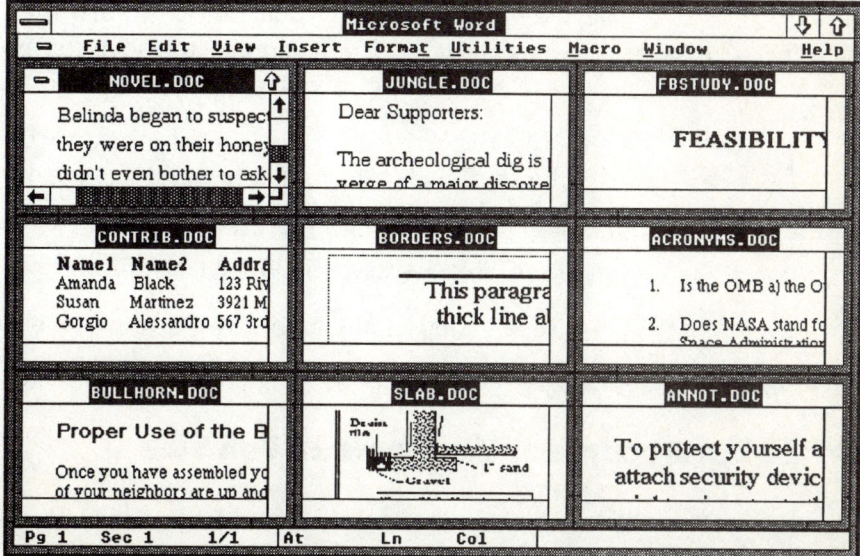

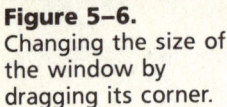

Figure 5–6.
Changing the size of
the window by
dragging its corner.

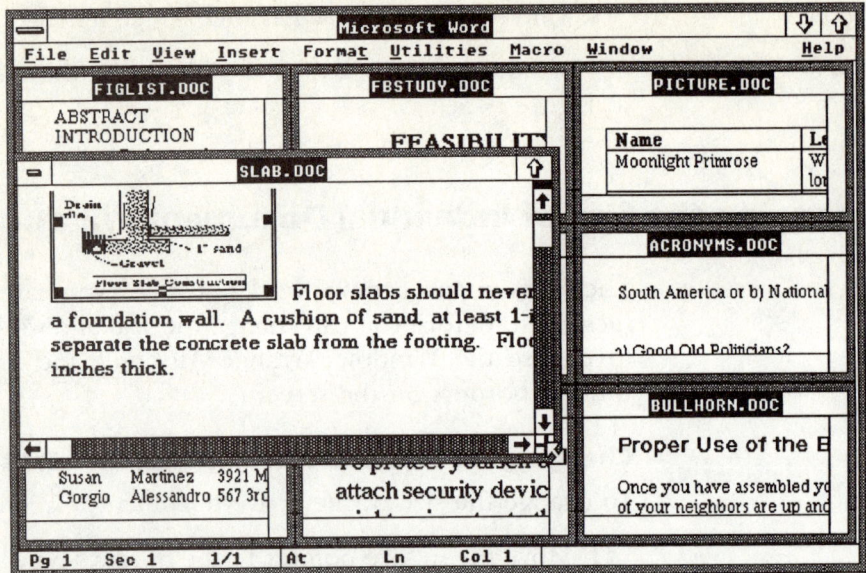

Changing the Size of a Window with the Keys

To change the size of the active document window with keys:

1. Press **Ctrl+F8** or choose the Size command from the Document Control menu (**Alt, Hyphen, S**). Word displays a four-headed arrow in the window, as shown in Figure 5–7.

2. Press the arrow key that points toward the window border you want to move. For example, to move the bottom border, press the Down arrow key. The arrow moves to that border.

3. Press the arrow key that points in the direction you want to move the border. For example, to move the border left, press the Left arrow key until the border is in the position you want.

4. Press **Enter** to set the border at the new position.

5. Repeat steps 1 through 4 to move other borders as necessary.

Returning Document Windows to Full Size

You can return any document window to full size at any time.
To make a document window full-size with the mouse:

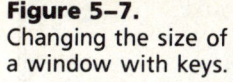

Figure 5–7.
Changing the size of
a window with keys.

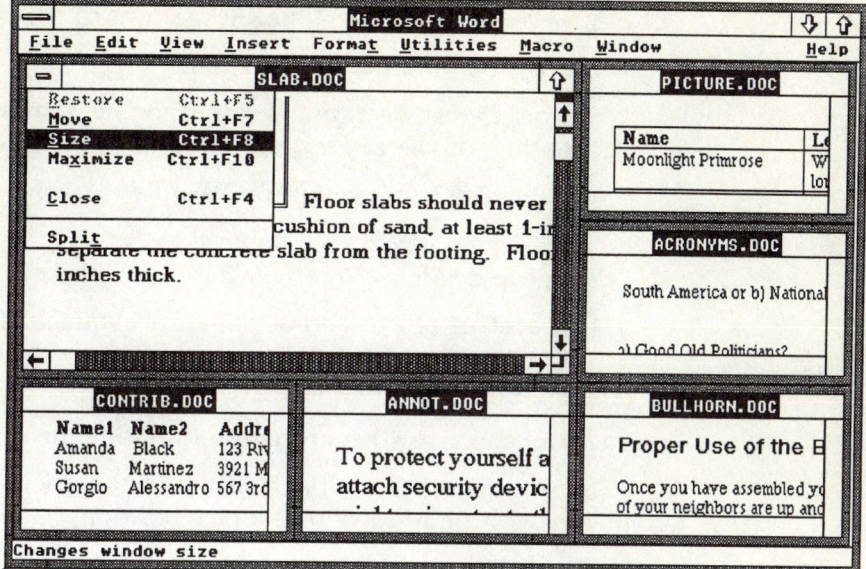

- Click the maximize box (the Up arrow icon) in the document window's upper right corner.

To make a document window full-size with keys:

- Press **Ctrl+F10** or choose the Maximize command from the Document Control menu (**Alt, Hyphen, X**).

Changing Document Windows from Maximum Size to the Previous Size

After you've "maximized" a document window using one of the procedures described in the preceding section, you can use the following procedures to restore the window to its previous size.

To return a document window to its previous size after maximizing:

- Press **Ctrl+F5** or choose the Restore command from the Document Control menu (**Alt, Hyphen, R**).

Moving Document Windows

If you've made an individual document window smaller, you may want to move it to a new location where it won't be covered up by another window.

To move a window to a new location with the mouse:

1. Point to the window's title bar.

2. Drag the window to a new location, as shown in Figure 5–8. An outline of the window moves along with the mouse pointer.

3. Release the mouse button. Word moves the window to the new location.

To move a window to a new location with keys:

1. Press **Ctrl+F7** or choose the Move command from the Document Control menu (**Alt, Hyphen, M**). Word displays a four-headed arrow in the window.

2. Use the arrow keys to move an outline of the window.

3. Press **Enter** to set the position of the document window. Word moves the window to the new position.

Figure 5–9 shows examples of window arrangements you can use.

CLOSING FILES

When you're finished with a file, you can close that file and remove its window from the screen. First, move the insertion point to the window to make it active, then use one of the following procedures:

Figure 5–8.
Dragging a window
to a new location.

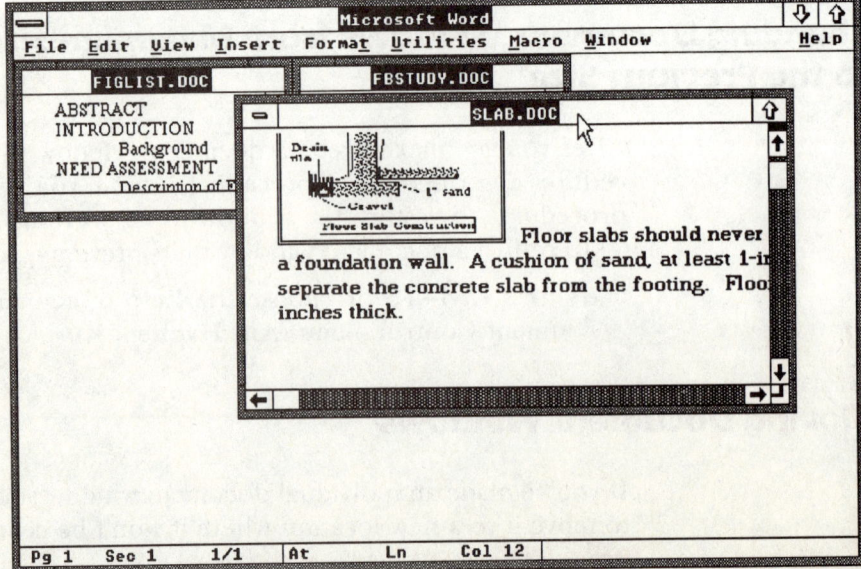

Figure 5–9.
You can arrange
windows in various
ways.

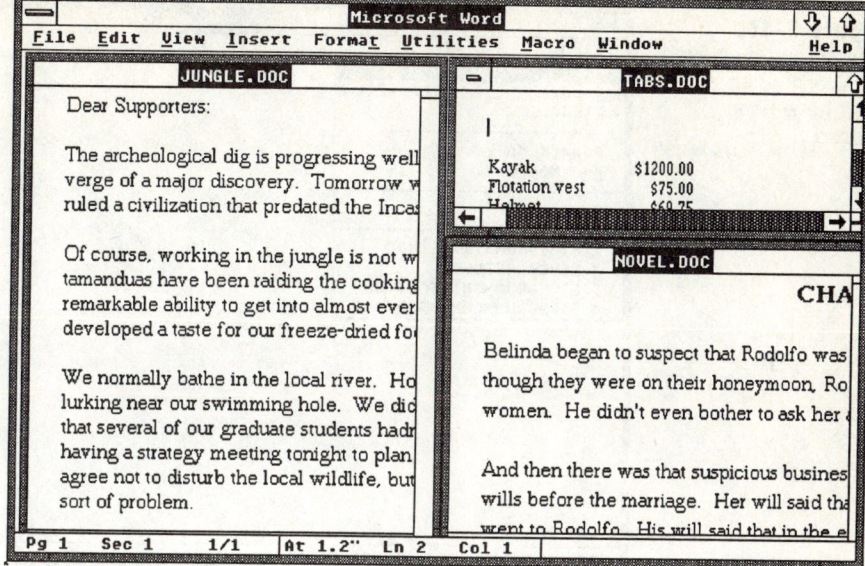

- Double-click the Document Control menu icon in the window's upper left corner.

or

- Press **Alt, Hyphen, C** (this chooses the Document Control Close command).

If you've made any changes since you last saved the file, Word asks you if you want to save the changes before closing the file.

If you close all of the open Word files, you'll see the screen displayed in Figure 5–10. Don't be alarmed because menus are missing and commands have been rearranged on the File menu. You can still use File Open to open a file, File New to create a new file, and File Exit to quit Word.

WORKING WITH TWO OR MORE VIEWS OF THE SAME DOCUMENT

When you're editing a long document, you may wish you could see more than one part of your document at once. For example, you might want to see both the beginning and the end of your document to see if you've used the same phrasing, or view both the location that you

Figure 5–10.
The screen displayed
by Word when all
files have been
closed.

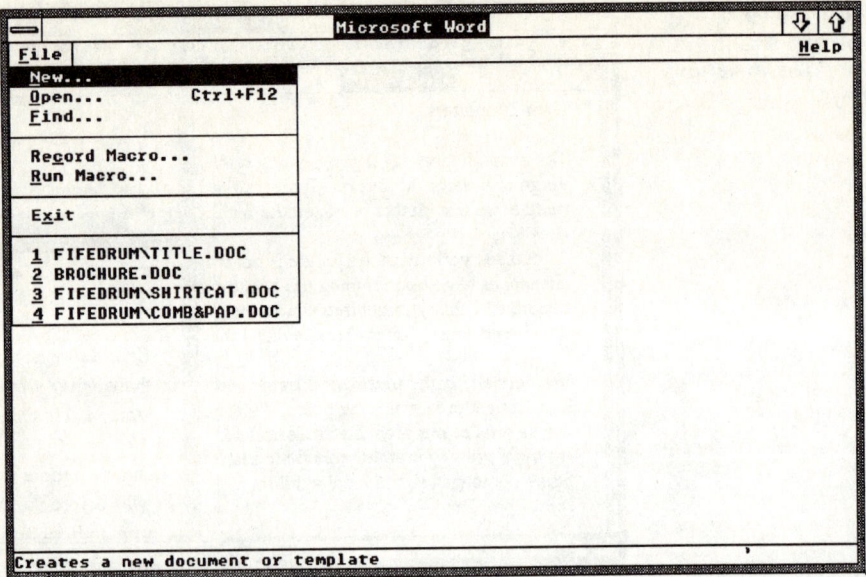

want to delete text from and the location you want to move that text
to. With Word you can use either of two ways to see more than one
view of your document. You can split a document window into two
panes, or you can open another window containing the same
document.

In either case, you'll find having different views of your document
easier than scrolling through a long document. You should also keep
in mind that you're working on the same document, even though you
may see different parts of that document in different windows or panes.
If you make changes to your document using three different windows,
you're still changing just one document.

Splitting the Document Window into Panes

You can split the document window into two panes, one on top of the
other. Each pane has its own scroll bars that you can use to view
different parts of one document at the same time. Unlike document
windows, you can't move panes to a new location or hide one behind
another—panes divide one document window into two parts.

To split a window into panes with the mouse:

1. Point to the split bar (the black rectangle) above the vertical scroll

bar. The mouse pointer becomes a split symbol, as shown in Figure 5–11.

2. Drag the split bar to where you'd like to split the window. You'll see a dotted split line move along with the mouse pointer to show you where the window will split—this is shown in Figure 5–12.

3. Release the mouse button.

◣ *Mouse Speed Tip*

To split a window quickly into half with the mouse, double-click on the split bar above the vertical scroll bar.

To split a window into panes with keys:

1. Choose the Split command from the Document Control menu (**Alt, Hyphen, T**), as shown in Figure 5–13. Word displays a split line across the window with a split icon positioned on the split line.

2. If you want to move the split line, press the arrow key that points in the direction you want to move it. For example, to move the split line down, press the Down arrow key.

3. Press **Enter** to set the split line's position.

Figure 5–11.
The mouse pointer becomes a split icon when on the split bar.

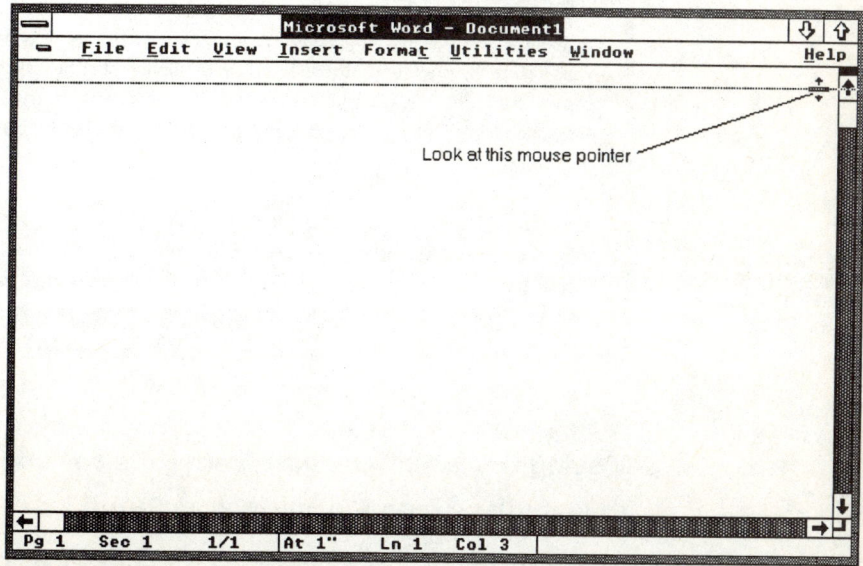

Figure 5–12.
Splitting a window
with the mouse.

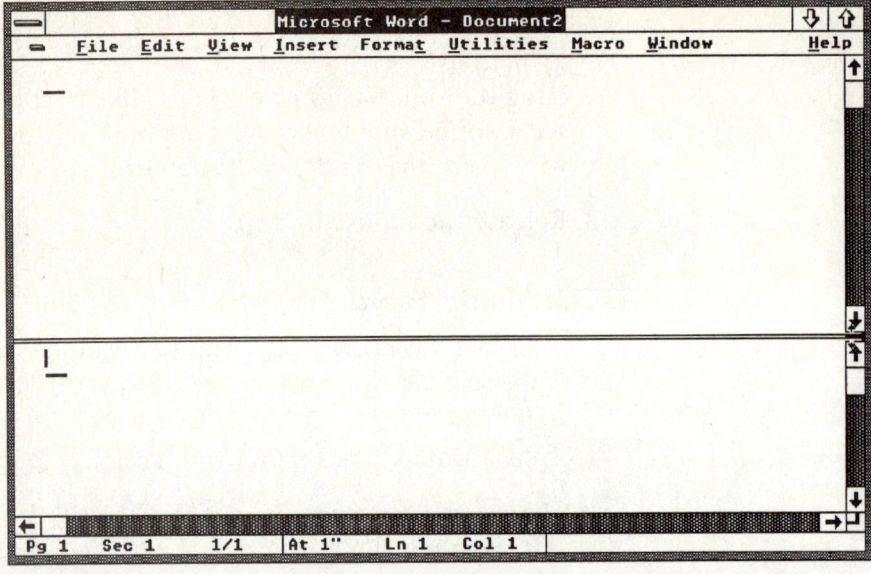

Figure 5–13.
Splitting a window
with keys.

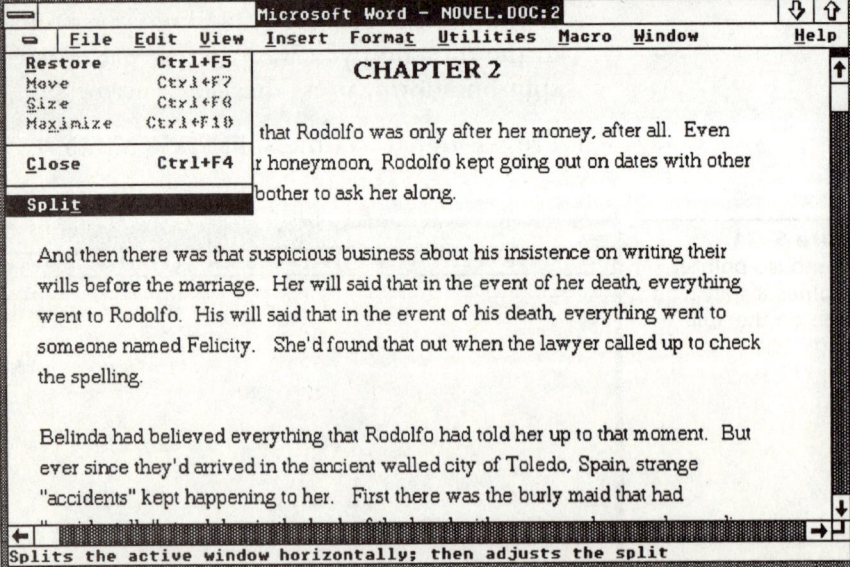

Moving the Insertion Point from Pane to Pane

To move the insertion point back and forth between panes:

- Press **F6** or click the pane you want to move to.

Figure 5–14.
The same document
in two side-by-side
windows.

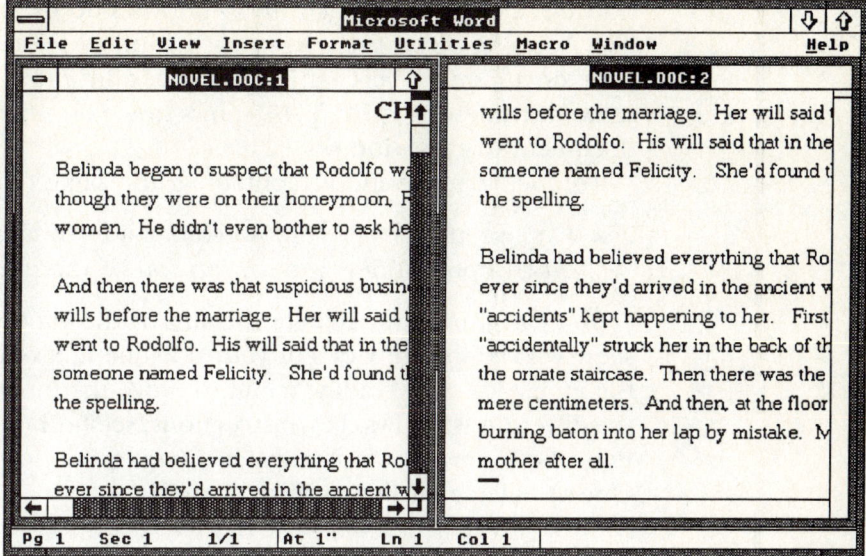

Removing a Window Split

To remove a window split with the mouse:

1. Drag the split bar to the top or bottom of the window.

2. Release the mouse button.

Mouse Speed Tip

> To remove a window split quickly, double-click the split bar.

To remove a window split with keys:

1. Choose the Split command from the Document Control menu
   (**Alt, Hyphen, T**).

2. Press **PgUp** or **PgDn** to move the split line to the window border.

3. Press **Enter** to make the line disappear.

Viewing the Same Document in Two or More Windows

To look at two horizontal views of the same document, you can split
a window as described in the previous section. You're not restricted
to looking at the same document in stacked window panes, however;
you can also open a new window (Figure 5–14) containing the same

document, then rearrange the windows side by side or any way you like. You can scroll the text in each window to see different views of your document. The changes you make in either window affect the same document. Figure 5–14 shows how you might display the same document in two windows.

To open a new window containing the same document:

■ Choose the New Window command from the Window menu. Word opens a new window on top of the previous one.

You can move and change the size of the windows so that you can see several different views of your document at once, and you can use the mouse or the Window menu to move the insertion point between the different windows. For instructions, see both Moving the Insertion Point Between Windows and Rearranging Windows to See More than One at a Time earlier in this chapter.

## Chapter Six

Marking Revisions, Comparing Versions, and Annotating

If you have to review a document before changes can be made, you can use Word's revision marking features to mark additions and corrections to text so they can be approved before the changes are actually made.

If you keep multiple versions of documents, you may want to compare versions and mark the differences. You can use Word's Compare Versions utility to make this a painless process.

To add comments to a document you're reviewing, you can insert comments in the text and format them as hidden text, then remove them later, or you can use Word's annotation features to add annotation marks and comments, compile annotations from several copies, and remove all annotations when the corrections are done.

This chapter shows you how to use all of Word's change-control features to make document management easier. It describes

- uses of revision marks.

- comparisons of two different versions of a document.

- how one or more users can make annotations in a document.

USING REVISION MARKS

When you need to keep track of several versions of a document, you can use revision marks to mark changes in a document before the actual corrections are made. When you turn on revision marking, Word

- marks any new text you insert with a format you specify (such as an underline).

- marks text you delete with the strikethrough format (example: ~~strikethrough~~), but does not delete it from the document.

- if you request it, inserts revision bars in the margin next to each line you change.

Revision marks indicate only changes to the words, not any changes in formatting, such as bold, italic, indents, and so forth. Figure 6–1 shows an example of revision marks in a Word document.

Activating Revision Marking

To begin revision marking:

1. Choose the Utilities Revision Marks command. Word displays the dialog box shown in Figure 6–2.

2. Select the Mark Revisions option.

3. In the Revision Bars box, choose one of the following options:

Option	Action
None	Does not add revision bars.
Left	Inserts revision bars in the left margin next to every line you change.

Figure 6–1.
Marking revisions
with Word.

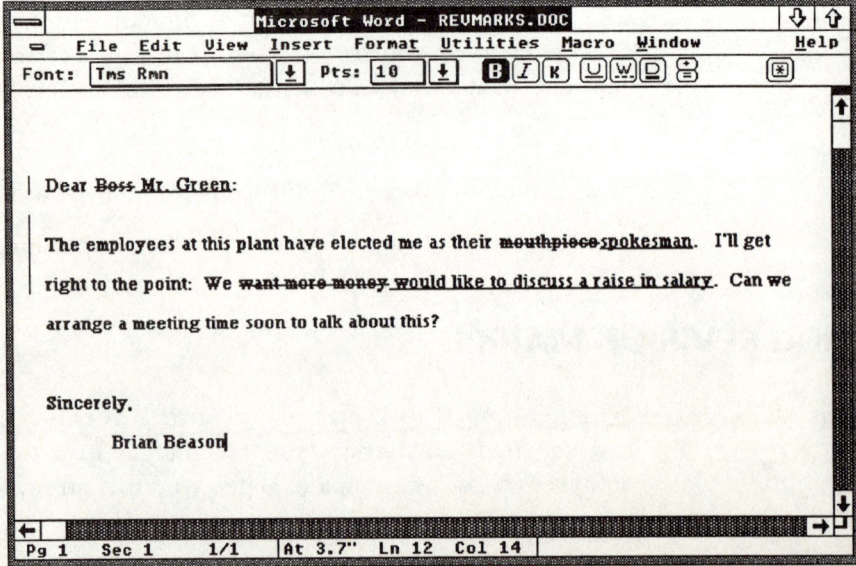

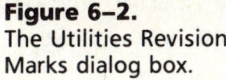

Figure 6–2.
The Utilities Revision
Marks dialog box.

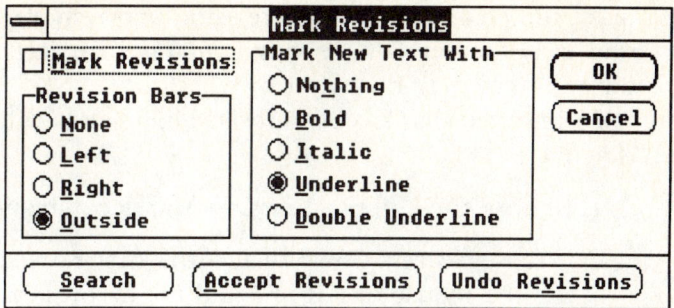

Right	Inserts revision bars in the right margin next to every line you change.
Outside	Inserts revision bars in the right margin on odd-numbered pages and in the left margin on even-numbered pages, next to every line you change.

If your document has multiple columns, Word inserts revision marks beside the column containing the edited line.

4. In the Mark New Text With box, choose the format (Nothing, Bold, Italic, Underline, Double Underline) you want Word to use for any text you add to the document. For example, if you choose Italic, Word formats all inserted text as Italic.

5. Press **Enter** or click the command name. Word displays the letters MRK (Mark Revisions) in the status bar to remind you that revision marking is turned on.

After you have activated revision marking, edit the document. Word marks the revisions according to your instructions. When you're finished editing, you (or someone else) will want to review the changes; then approve the changes and make them individually or all at once, or reject the changes and delete all the revision marks. If you want to accept some changes and reject others, you'll search for the portions of text that have been revised, as described in the following section.

Searching for Revised Text

To review revisions that have been made to a document while revision marking is active, you can use the following procedure. After considering a revision, you can choose to accept the revision as marked and make the change; reject the revision and remove the revision marks; skip over the revision, leaving it marked for later action; or make a different correction of your own.

To find text that has been revised in any way while revision marking is active:

1. Choose the Utilities Revision Marks command.

2. Choose Search. Word selects the first revised line. If necessary, use the mouse or **Alt+F7** and the arrow keys to drag the dialog box out of the way so you can see the revision.

3. Do one of the following:

   ■ To make the change as marked, choose Accept Revisions.

   ■ To reject the change and remove the revision marks from the selected text, choose Undo Revisions.

   ■ To leave the selected text alone and move to the next revision, choose Search again.

   ■ To close the dialog box, click Close or press **Esc**.

Making All Marked Changes

When you have reviewed the changes and accepted them, you can make the changes all at once in part or all of the document.

To make the marked changes:

1. Select the part of your document where you want to make the changes and remove the marks. If you want to select the entire document, hold down the **Ctrl** key and click the left mouse button while the pointer is in the selection bar or press **Ctrl+5** on the numeric keypad.

2. Choose the Utilities Revision Marks command.

3. Choose Accept Revisions. Word does the following:

   ■ Deletes any text marked with the strikethrough character format.

   ■ Removes the special format (italic, for example) you specified from new text to blend it into the other text in your document.

   ■ Removes revision bars from the margins.

4. Click OK or press **Enter** to close the dialog box.

Rejecting All Marked Changes and Removing Revision Marks

To reject the marked changes and remove the revision marks:

1. Select the part of your document where you want to remove the marks. If you want to select the entire document, hold down the **Ctrl** key and click the left mouse button while the pointer is in the selection bar, or press **Ctrl+5** on the numeric keypad.

2. Choose the Format Revision Marks command.

3. Choose Undo Revisions. Word does the following:

   ■ Deletes any text inserted while revision marking was turned on.

   ■ Removes the strikethrough format from all text.

   ■ Removes revision bars from the margins.

4. Click OK or press **Enter** to close the dialog box.

Turning Off Revision Marking

Word continues to mark revisions as long as the Mark Revisions option is active, so when you want to quit marking revisions and return to normal editing, you have to turn the option off.

To deactivate revision marking:

1. Choose the Utilities Revision Marks command.

2. Turn off the Mark Revisions option.

3. Click OK or press **Enter**.

COMPARING VERSIONS

If you work on a document over a long period of time, you may want to save several different versions of that document. You may also end up with several versions of a document if different people work on the same document. Word lets you easily compare two versions of a document and identify the lines that don't match. You open the first file you want to compare and tell Word which file you want to compare to the open file. Then Word adds change bars beside the lines that are different in the open file.

To compare two versions of a document:

1. Open the file to which you want Word to add change bars.

2. Choose the Utilities Compare Versions command.

3. Do one of the following:

   ■ Type the name of the second file you want to compare in the Compare File Name box, including any drive letters or pathnames Word needs to find the file.

   or

   ■ Select the directory containing the file you want to compare from the Directories list, then select the file you want from the Files list.

4. Click OK or press **Enter**. Word compares the two files and adds change bars beside the lines that are different in the open file.

USING ANNOTATIONS

If you want to insert marks and comments into a Word document created by another person, you can use a special form of footnotes called *annotations*. This is one way to review or edit a document on the screen.

Like footnotes, annotations are indicated by reference marks—in this case, the commentator's initials and a number—at specific locations in the document text, as shown in Figure 6–3. These reference marks tell the reader to look for comments at the bottom of the printed page or at the end of the document when viewed on the screen.

Word uses the initials given to Word on that computer during the setup process—these are stored in the WINWORD.INI file. You can use different initials during the annotating process by choosing the Utilities Customize command to change the initials, adding the annotations, then using the Utilities Customize command to change the initials back to the original letters.

Figure 6–3.
Inserting an
annotation.

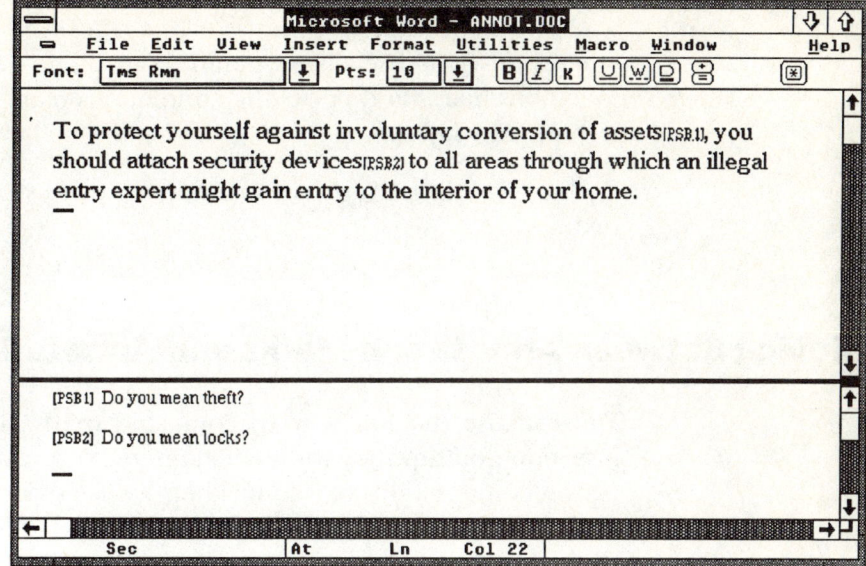

To enter annotations:

1. Move the insertion point to where you want to enter an annotation.

2. Choose the Insert Annotation command. Word inserts a reference mark and moves the insertion point to an annotation pane at the bottom of the screen, as shown in Figure 6–3.

3. Type the annotation text. The text can be any length you want.

4. To insert more annotations, move the insertion point (press **F6**, then use the arrow keys; or point and click with the mouse) to the next place in the document where you want to insert a comment, then repeat steps 1 through 3.

5. When you're through entering annotations, choose the View Annotations command to close the annotations pane.

Viewing Annotations

Annotation marks are formatted as hidden text, so you won't be able to see them unless you either choose View Preferences and turn on the Show Hidden Text option or choose the View Annotations command.

To view annotations:

- Choose the View Annotations command. Word displays annotations marks and opens the annotations pane at the bottom of the Word window.

You can edit and format annotations just as you would any other text.

Moving Between Annotation Marks and Annotation Text

You can use the Edit Go To command or the **F5** key to move the insertion point quickly to the next annotation mark or back and forth between annotation marks and their associated text.

Here's how the command works.

To jump to	Do this
Another annotation mark	1. Choose the Edit Go To command or press **F5**.
	2. Type **a** to jump to the next annotation mark or type **a** followed by the number of the annotation mark you want to jump to (a5 to jump to the fifth annotation mark, for example).
	3. Click OK or press **Enter**.
The annotation mark associated with annotation text	1. Move the insertion point into the annotation text in the annotations pane.
	2. Choose the Edit Go To command or press **F5**.

When the annotations pane is closed, you can also select an annotation mark, then choose the View Annotations command to make Word open the annotations pane and move the insertion point to the text associated with the selected mark.

Deleting Annotations

To delete annotations:

1. Select the annotation mark.

2. Press the **Delete** key. Word automatically deletes both the reference mark and the annotation text.

Locking a File to Add Only Annotations

The author of a document or template can lock that file so that others can add only annotations. This prevents others from making changes to the file.

To lock a file so that others can add only annotations:

1. Choose the File Save As command. Word displays the dialog box shown in Figure 6–4.

2. Choose Options.

3. Turn on the Lock for Annotations option.

4. Click OK or press **Enter**.

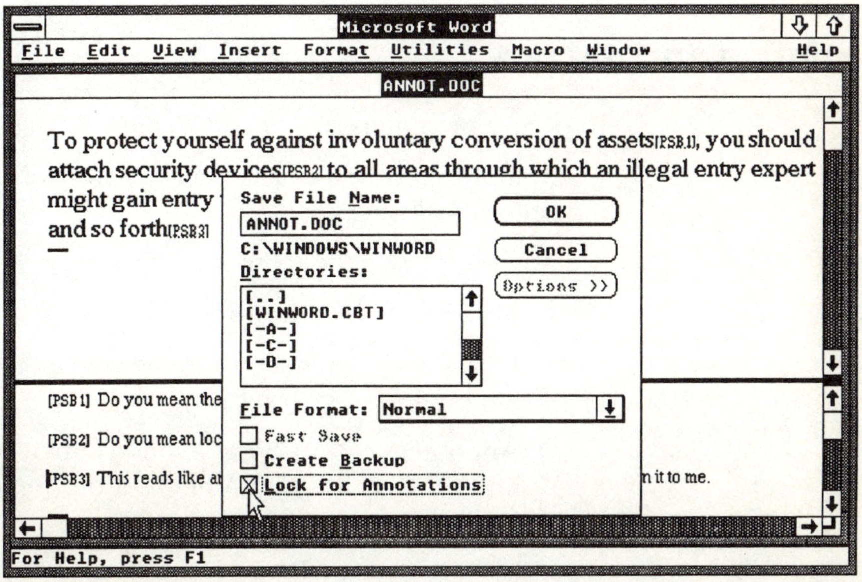

Figure 6–4.
The File Save As dialog box controls locking a document.

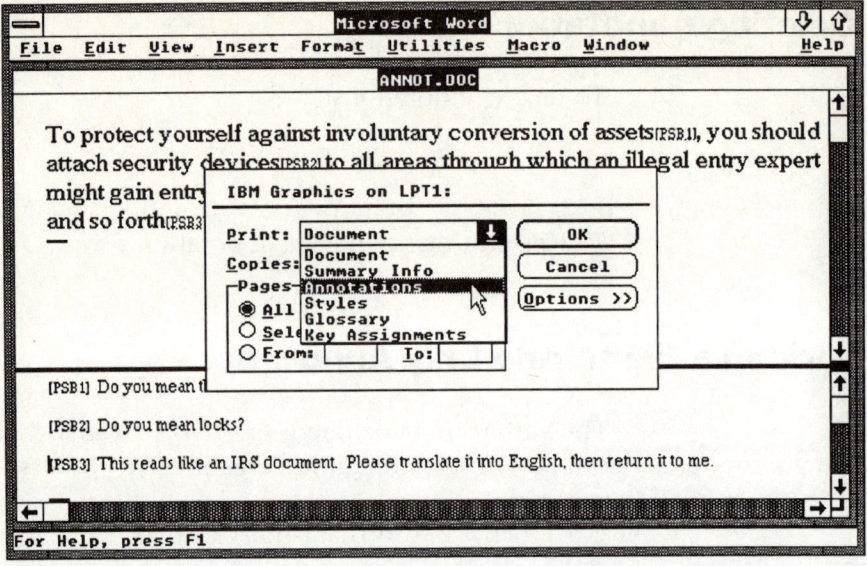

To unlock the file, follow the same procedure, but turn off the Lock for Annotations option.

To determine the author of a Word file, Word compares the initials associated with the file with the initials given to Word during the setup process on a computer. You can check (and change) the author of a file with the Edit Summary Info command.

Printing Annotations

To print annotations:

1. Choose the File Print command. Word displays the dialog box shown in Figure 6–5.

2. Choose one of the following options:

To print	Do this
Only annotations	Choose Annotations from the drop-down Print list.
Annotations and the document	Choose Options, then turn on the Annotations option in the Include box.

3. Click OK or press **Enter**.

## Chapter Seven

Checking Spelling, Usage, and Word Count

After you've finished revising your document, you'll probably want to check the spelling before you pass it along to someone else. If you find that you use one word too frequently, you probably prefer to substitute some synonyms so your writing won't sound too repetitious. And, if you're submitting your masterpiece for publication, your publisher may want to know how many words your document contains. This chapter shows you how to do all of these tasks. It describes

- using Word's spelling checker.

- using the thesaurus.

- counting words and characters automatically.

CHECKING SPELLING

When you've edited your document, you can use Word's built-in spelling checker to check for typing errors and spelling mistakes. Word compares words in your document with words in its main dictionary or in a dictionary you create. Word also checks for repeated words (like *an an*) and for mistakes in capitalization (like *hEre* or *washington*).

Word's spelling checker is relatively sophisticated, but it can't do all your work for you. To test whether a word is spelled correctly, Word's spelling checker compares each word in your document with words in its dictionaries. If there's a match, Word assumes that the word is correct. So if you type *too* when you mean *two*, the spelling checker won't catch that. It also won't tell you whether numbers or single letters surrounded by spaces are wrong, because it has all the letters of the alphabet and all numbers in its main dictionary.

You can check the spelling of

- *the entire document*. Word checks the spelling in a document from the insertion point to the end of the document, so you probably want to move the insertion point to the beginning of the document before you start the checking process.

- *selected text*. You can select a single word or a block of text for Word to check. This is especially handy if you've just added a small portion of new text to a document in which you've already perfected the spelling.

Beginning the Spelling Check

When you use the Utilities Spelling command to invoke the spelling checker, Word doesn't begin checking your text right away. The dialog box gives you an opportunity to choose various options and select dictionaries first. Then, when you're ready to begin, you choose Start.

To begin a spelling check in a document:

1. Move the insertion point or select text if necessary.

2. Choose the Utilities Spelling command. Word loads the main dictionary file and displays the dialog box shown in Figure 7–1. If Word can't find the file, it displays a dialog box asking you to locate the file. If you keep the main dictionary file on a separate disk, insert that disk.

3. If you want to specify more options, choose Options to display the rest of the dialog box, then do the following:

    - If you don't want Word to check words typed in all capital letters, turn on the Ignore All CAPS option. Turning on this feature can save a lot of time if your text is filled with acronyms such as NASA, NYC, and EPA.

    - If you want Word to always suggest alternatives, turn on the Always Suggest option.

    - To open a custom dictionary, choose new dictionaries from the lists. You can find out more about using different dictionaries later in this chapter.

Figure 7–1.
The Utilities Spelling
dialog box.

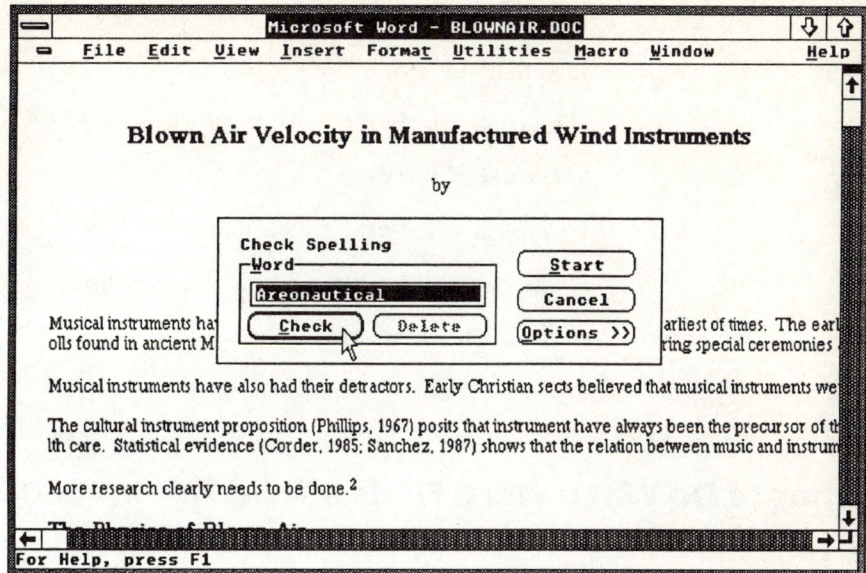

4. Click Start or press **Enter** to begin checking spelling. If the insertion point was not at the beginning of the document, when Word reaches the end of the document, Word asks you if you want to continue the spelling check from the beginning of the document.

If all words in the text match words in the dictionary, Word displays the message Spell check completed in the status bar.

▶ *Keyboard Shortcut*

If you want to use the default settings in the Utilities Spelling dialog box, use the following procedure to quickly check the spelling in your document without choosing a command.

To check spelling quickly:

1. Select text if you want to check only a portion of your document or, if nothing is selected, the word nearest the insertion point is checked.

2. Press **F7**. Word immediately begins checking the spelling.

Checking the Spelling of One Word

You can check the spelling of one word by selecting that word in your document, then using the procedure just described, or you can type a word directly into the Utilities Spelling dialog box to check it.

To select a word and check its spelling:

1. Select the word.

2. Choose the Utilities Spelling command.

3. Choose Check.

To type a word and check its spelling:

1. Choose the Utilities Spelling command.

2. Type the word in the Word box.

3. Choose Check.

What to Do When Word Finds a Term Not in Its Dictionary

When Word finds a term that is not in its dictionary, you see a second dialog box, shown in Figure 7–2, with the unknown word listed in the Not in Dictionary box. The word may not actually be misspelled—this just means that the word does not match anything in Word's dictionary.

When this dialog box appears, you can do any of the following:

■ Correct the spelling by typing the appropriate word in the Change To box and choosing the Change button.

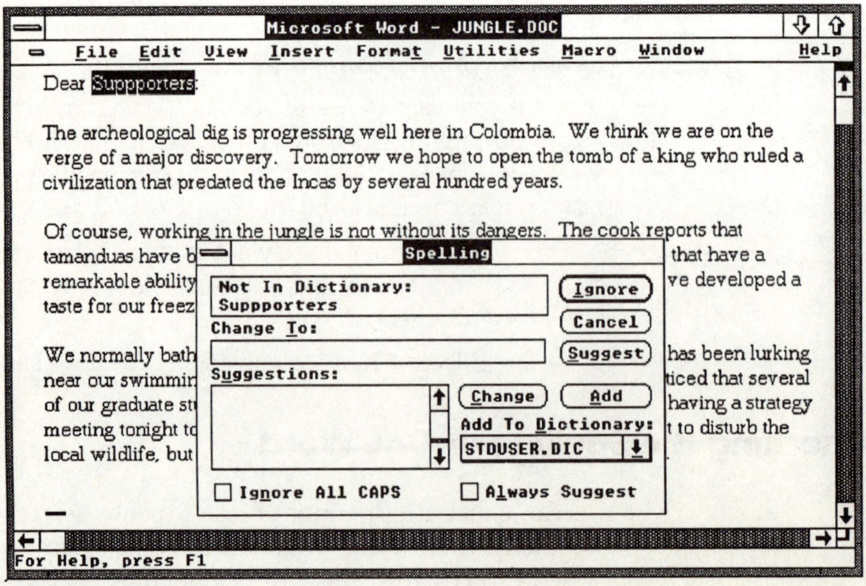

Figure 7–2.
The dialog box Word displays when it can't match a word.

- Ask Word to suggest alternative spellings by choosing the Suggest button if necessary, then selecting a spelling from the Suggestions list and choosing the Change button. Word displays a list of alternatives in the Suggestions list. If Word can't find any alternatives, it displays a message telling you so. If this happens, or if none of the alternatives is correct, type the correct spelling in the Change To box, then choose the Change button.

- Ignore the word and continue checking by choosing Ignore. You'll want to do this when Word displays names of people or places, or specialized terminology that you don't want to save in a dictionary.

- Add the word to a personal dictionary. For example, if your business uses certain terms not normally found in Word's dictionary, you may want to create your own dictionary containing these terms—then you can use that dictionary to check selected documents. See the next section for more information about creating and using your own dictionaries.

You can also turn the Ignore All CAPS and Always Suggest options on or off from this dialog box to affect the rest of the spelling check.

Using Your Own Dictionaries

You can't alter Word's main dictionary, but you can create your own specialized dictionaries and use them as well as the main dictionary to check your documents.

When you choose the Utilities Spelling command, Word opens the main dictionary and a dictionary called STDUSER.DIC. STD-USER.DIC is a personal dictionary Word creates for you—it's empty until you add terms to it. You can use STDUSER.DIC as your personal dictionary, or you can also create other dictionaries, as explained next.

Creating a New Dictionary

To create a new personal dictionary:

1. Choose the Utilities Spelling command.

2. Type the name for your dictionary in the Supplemental box, using a .DIC extension. For example, you might type **MATH.DIC** or **LEGAL.DIC**.

3. Press **Enter**. Word asks you if you want to create a new dictionary.

4. Choose Yes. The name of the new dictionary appears in the Supplemental list. You can add terms to it using the following procedure.

Adding Words to a Personal Dictionary

You may want to add specialized terms that you use frequently to your own personal dictionary. When Word displays a word it hasn't found a match for, you can easily add it to a dictionary so Word won't stop at the same word when you check the next document.

To add a word to a dictionary:

1. If you want to use a dictionary other than STDUSER.DIC, select the dictionary you want from the drop-down Supplemental list. Figure 7–3 illustrates choosing from a list of dictionaries. If only the main dictionary and STDUSER.DIC appear in the list, Word assumes you want to add the term to the STDUSER.DIC dictionary.

2. If the word is misspelled, type the correct spelling in the Change To box.

3. Choose Add to add the term to the selected dictionary.

Word automatically saves changes you make to dictionaries.

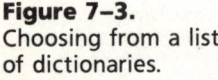

Figure 7–3.
Choosing from a list
of dictionaries.

Microsoft Word – JUNGLE.DOC

File   Edit   View   Insert   Format   Utilities   Macro   Window   Help

Dear Suppporters:

The archeological dig is progressing well here in Colombia. We think we are on the verge of a major discovery. Tomorrow we hope to open the tomb of a king who ruled a civilization that predated the Incas by several hundred years.

Of course, working   Check Spelling   reports that
tamanduas have be   ┌─Word──────────┐   ┌─Start─┐   s that have a
remarkable ability t   │ Dear   │   ┌─Cancel─┐   y've developed a
taste for our freeze   ┌─Check─┐ ┌─Delete─┐ ┌─Options >>─┐

We normally bathe   ┌─Dictionaries───────────┐   a has been lurking
near our swimming   Main: Supplemental: oticed that several
of our graduate stud   ┌English (US)┐ ┌EXOTIC.DIC┐   e having a strategy
meeting tonight to   │   │ STDUSER.DIC   ot to disturb the
local wildlife, but w   ☐ Ignore All CAPS MATH.DIC   n.
                                             EXOTIC.DIC

For Help, press F1

Removing Words from Personal Dictionaries

If you find that you've added a misspelled word to a dictionary, you can easily remove it. (You may have already guessed that the Delete button in the Utilities Spelling dialog box removes a word from a dictionary.)

To delete a word from a dictionary:

1. Choose the Utilities Spelling command.

2. Choose Options, then select the dictionary you want to remove the word from.

3. In the Word box, type the word you want to remove from the dictionary.

4. Choose Check. Word tells you if the word is in the dictionary.

5. Choose Delete. Word deletes the word from its dictionary.

Word automatically saves changes you make to dictionaries.

Renaming Dictionaries

You can rename any personal dictionary, including the STDUSER.DIC directory.

To rename a dictionary:

■ Change the name of the dictionary using the File Rename command in the MS-DOS Executive window or using the MS-DOS Rename command outside of Windows.

Using a Personal Dictionary

Word automatically opens the main dictionary and the dictionary named STDUSER.DIC when you choose the Utilities Spelling command.

To open another dictionary to use in addition to STDUSER.DIC and the main dictionary:

1. Choose the Utilities Spelling command.

2. Choose Options to display the rest of the dialog box.

3. Select the dictionary you want to use from the drop-down Supplemental list.

USING THE THESAURUS

If you use the same word over and over again in your documents, your writing can become monotonous. To introduce some variety, use the thesaurus to look up synonyms for your most commonly used words.

Looking Up Synonyms for a Word

You can select a word in your document to look up synonyms for it, or you can type a word in the Utilities Thesaurus dialog box, then display a list of synonyms. The Thesaurus dialog box also shows definitions for each synonym, so you can choose just the right shade of meaning.

To look up synonyms for a word in your document:

1. Select the word.

2. Choose the Utilities Thesaurus command. The Thesaurus dialog box appears with a list of synonyms for the selected word, as shown in Figure 7–4.

If the word is not in the thesaurus, Word displays the message

Figure 7–4.
The thesaurus lists synonyms for the selected word.

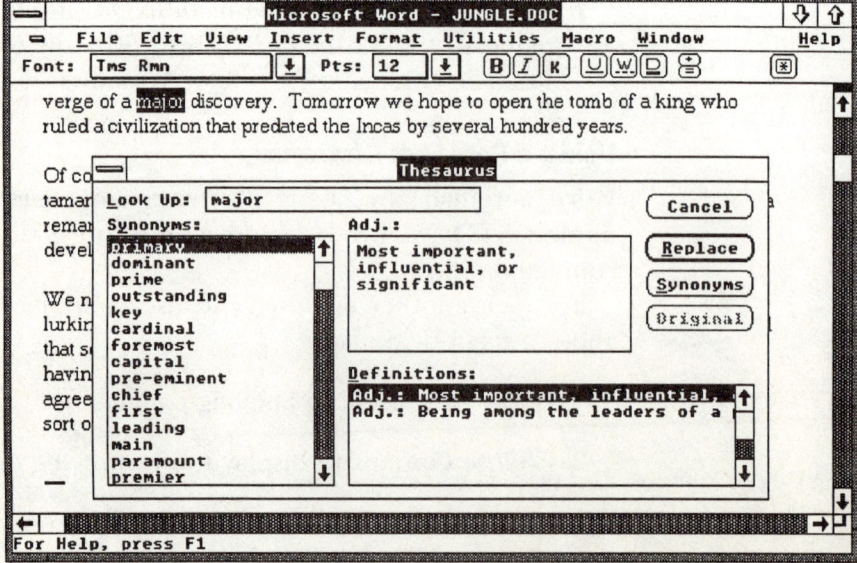

Figure 7-5.
The Statistics dialog
box shows the
number of words and
characters in a
document.

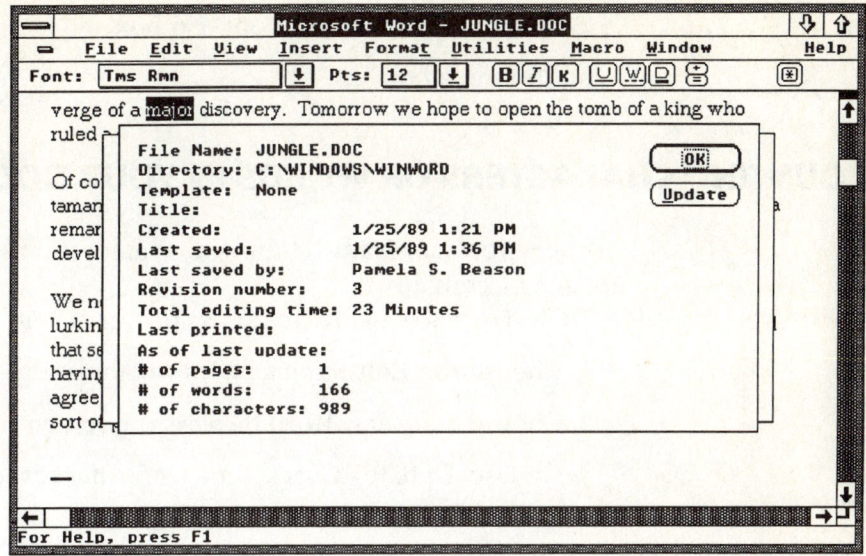

No synonyms at the top of the Thesaurus dialog box. Make sure you've spelled the selected word correctly.

3. Choose one of the following actions:

- To replace the selected word with a synonym, select a word from the Synonyms list, then choose Replace.

- To view definitions for a synonym, select a word from the Synonyms list, then read the definitions in the Definitions list.

- To look up synonyms for a word in the Synonyms list, select the word, then choose Synonyms.

- To go back to the synonym list that was displayed when you chose the command, choose Original.

- To close the Thesaurus dialog box, choose Cancel or press **Esc**.

Finding a Synonym for a Word You Type

To type a word in the Thesaurus dialog box and display synonyms for it:

1. Choose the Utilities Thesaurus command or press **Shift+F7**.

2. Type the word in the Look Up box.

3. Choose Synonyms.

COUNTING CHARACTERS OR WORDS IN YOUR DOCUMENT

At times you may want to know how many characters or words your document contains.

To find out how many characters or words your document contains:

1. Choose the Edit Summary Info command.

2. Choose Statistics. Word displays the screen shown in Figure 7–5.

3. Choose Update. Check the # of characters and # of words fields.

Part III

FORMATTING

To get your document to look just right, you'll use Word's many formatting commands. Word offers four basic types of formatting:

Type	Controls
Character formatting	Bold, italic, underlines, and other styles of type; font types and sizes; spacing between letters; superscripts and subscripts
Paragraph formatting	Indents, alignments, tabs, line spacing, space between paragraphs, and styles
Section formatting	Columns, footnotes, headers, and footers
Document formatting	Margins, page numbers, default tab measurements, facing (mirror-image) page formatting

Chapter 8 discusses the various types of character formatting. You'll learn more about using fonts and point sizes, as well as how to use the ribbon device and the Format Character command to enhance the look of your document.

Formatting paragraphs is covered in Chapter 9. You'll learn how to use the ruler to speed up your paragraph formatting. You'll also see how to format tabs; align paragraphs; change line spacing within and between paragraphs; add boxes, lines, or bars; and control page breaks when they occur in paragraphs.

Word can store formatting instructions as *styles*. When you use styles, you can greatly ease the task of formatting documents and making subsequent changes. Chapter 10 discusses how to define, apply, and change styles. You'll also learn about how styles and templates are related.

In Chapter 11, you'll see how to divide your document into sections and apply special section formats. You'll learn how to create multiple columns and format those columns. You'll find out more about the format options that control the appearance of entire documents.

Chapter Eight

Character Formatting

Character formatting affects the individual letters, numbers, and symbols that you type. You can format one character or every character in your document at one time. This chapter discusses

- information about fonts and point sizes.

- using the ribbon.

- using the Format Character command.

WHAT IS CHARACTER FORMATTING?

Figure 8–1 shows all the formats you can add to characters. You can

- give characters the following formats: bold, italic, single (continuous) underline, word (not spaces) underline, double underline, dotted underline, strikethrough, outline, shadow, small capitals, all capitals, or "hidden."

- make characters superscripts and subscripts, as well as control the amount by which text is raised or lowered from the baseline.

- change fonts and sizes.

- condense or expand spacing between letters and control the amount of space between letters.

The *baseline* mentioned here is the invisible line the letters in a sentence "sit on": the bottoms of characters that don't have descending parts are on the baseline. For example, the letters *w* and *c* sit on

Figure 8–1.
Character formatting.

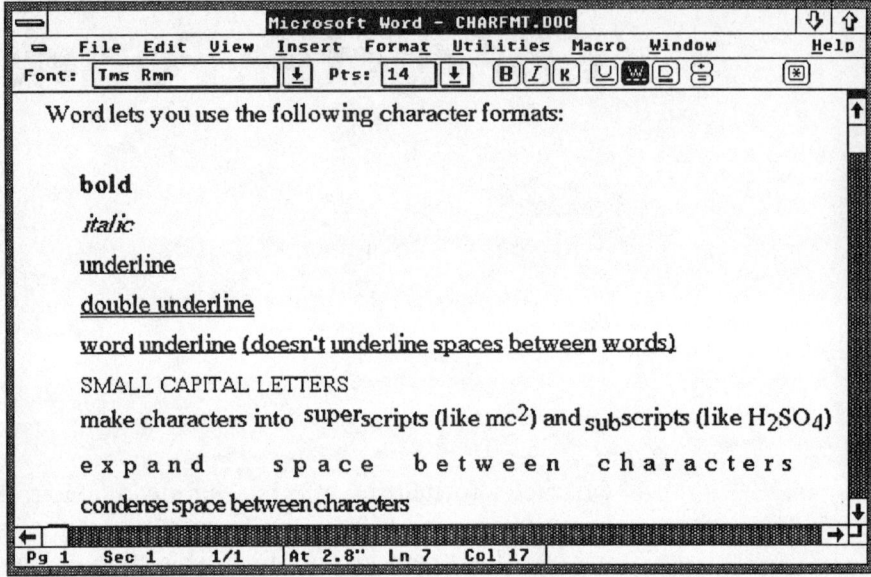

the baseline, whereas *p* and *g* have parts that descend beneath the baseline.

If you have a color monitor, you can also change the color of your text. Note that this changes the color of the text only on your screen—it won't print out in color unless you have your printer set up to produce multiple colors.

ABOUT FONTS AND POINT SIZES

Fonts are families of characters that share a style—very straight and simple, for example, as in a Helvetica font, or very curvy and ornate, as in an Old English font. Figure 8–2 shows a variety of fonts.

Word uses two classes of fonts: *printer fonts,* which come from the printer driver file that Word uses to control your particular printer, and *screen fonts,* which come from Windows. If you want to be sure that the font you see on the computer screen is the same font that will be used when you print your document, choose the View Preferences command and activate the Display as Printed option. This option causes Word to use only printer fonts.

Most fonts for Word are *proportional fonts,* that is, fonts in which the letters are of varying widths. For example, an *M* takes up more

Figure 8–2.
Word enables you to
use a variety of fonts
and point sizes.

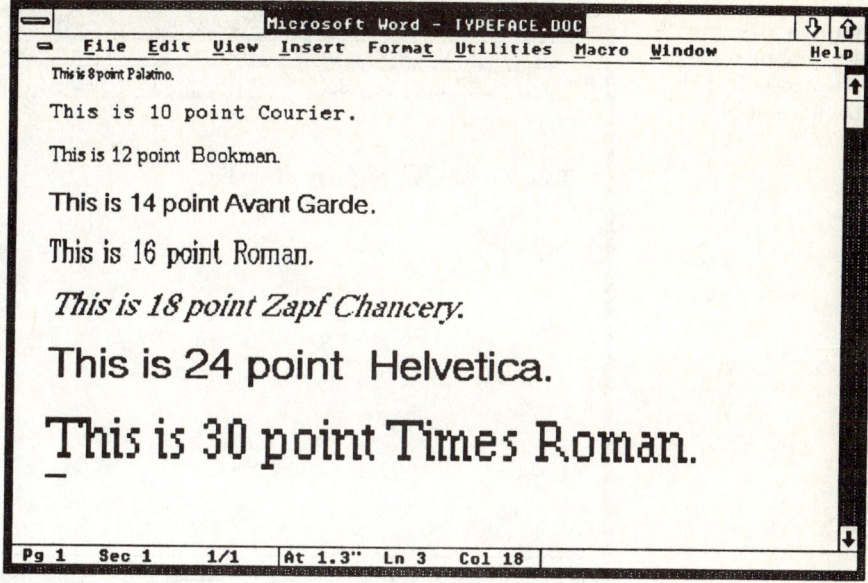

space than an *I* in a proportional font. There are also a few *fixed-width*, or *monospace*, fonts. In these fonts, each character occupies exactly the same amount of space both on the screen and on paper. Generally speaking, you'll want to use proportional fonts for most documents and use fixed-width fonts only when you create text in which characters must line up in rows and columns (as in a computer program listing, for example). You can find out more about fonts available for your printer in the printer manual that comes with Word for Windows.

Fonts come in different sizes, which are measured in points. A point is roughly 1/72 of an inch. Because one font may have different sizes than another, you should always choose a font before you choose the point size for that font.

Word offers two methods to control the way characters look in your document: You can use the ribbon or the Format Character command.

USING THE RIBBON

The *ribbon* (shown in Figure 8–3) is a graphic device that helps you format characters. You can display or remove the ribbon any time you like.

To display the ribbon:

Figure 8–3.
The ribbon formats
characters and shows
the format of
selected text.

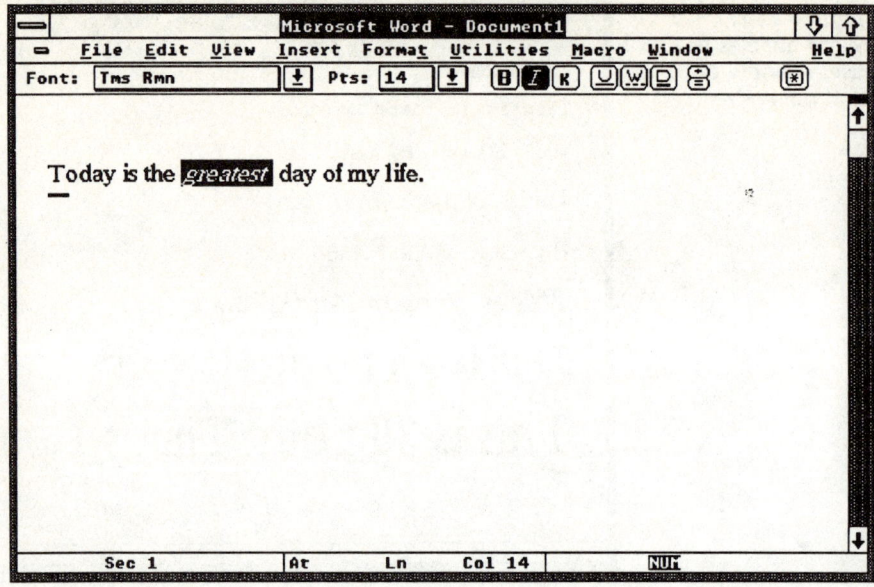

■ Choose the View Ribbon command.

The View Ribbon command is a toggle command, so to remove the
ribbon from your display, you just choose the View Ribbon command
again.

Using the ribbon, you can do the following.

■ Change fonts and point sizes.

■ Add formats to characters for bold, italic, underlines (three
types), and small capitals.

■ Make characters superscripts and subscripts.

■ Display all hidden formatting marks, such as space marks, tab
marks, and paragraph marks, as shown in Figure 8–4.

The ribbon is designed to be used with a mouse. However, even if
you're a die-hard keyboard user, you'll find it's useful to display it,
because the ribbon reflects the format of text you select. For example,
if you select a word in bold 14-point Helvetica type, the Font box
displays Helv, the Points box displays 14, and the bold icon is
highlighted.

Figure 8–4.
A document with all
hidden formatting
marks displayed.

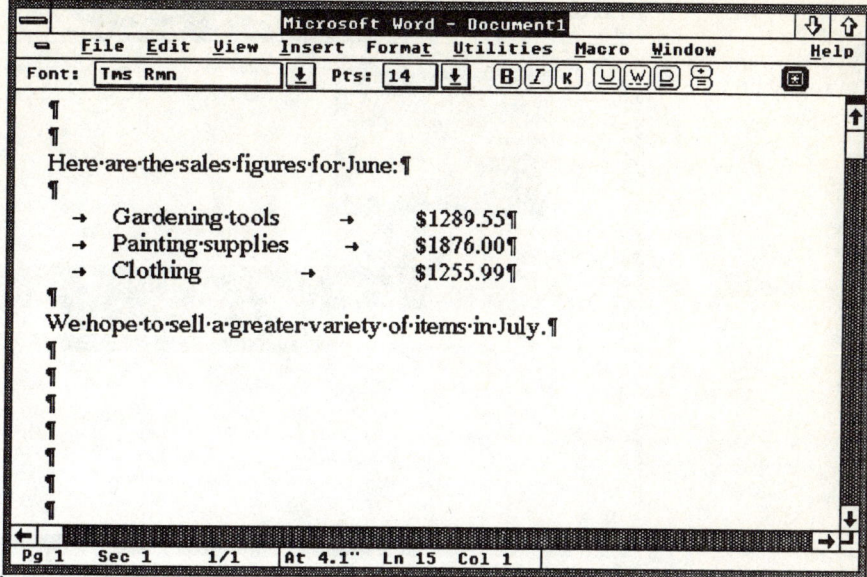

Choosing a New Font or Point Size

To choose a new font or point size with the ribbon:

1. Select the characters you want to change.

2. Choose a new font or point size from the list boxes by doing one of the following:

   ■ Using the mouse, click the arrow beside the Font box or Pts box to drop down the list, then highlight the font or size you want; you can also type the font or point size you want in the Font or Pts box.

   ■ Using keys, press **Ctrl+F** to activate the font box or **Ctrl+P** to activate the point size box, then type the font or point size or use the Down arrow key to highlight the font or size.

Figure 8–5 illustrates selecting a font from the ribbon's Font list.

Choosing Other Character Format Options

To choose a format option from the ribbon:

1. Select the characters you want to change.

Figure 8–5.
Selecting a new font
from the ribbon.

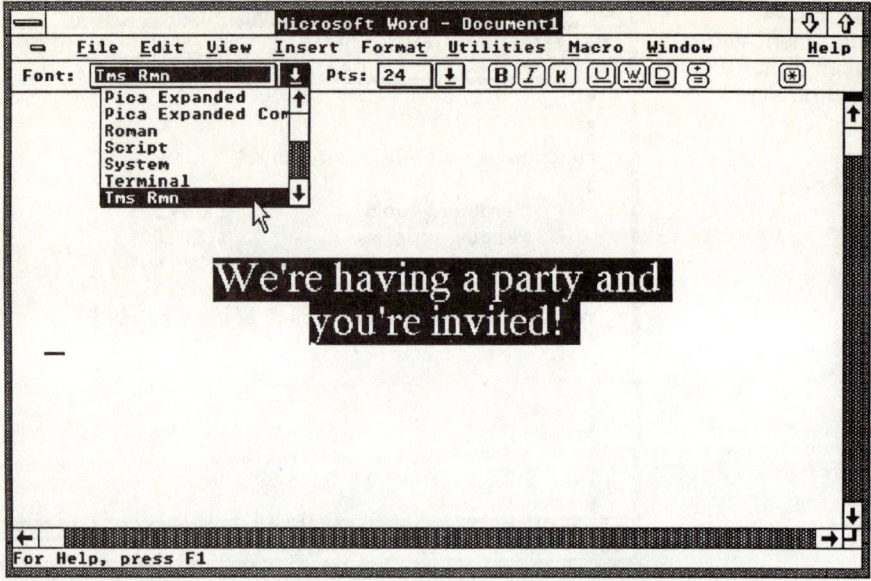

2. Click one of the icons to choose bold, italic, underline, word underline, double underline, superscript, or subscript.

When you apply a format from the ribbon, Word highlights the format's icon. To remove a format (such as bold), just click the icon again.

EXAMPLE: Formatting Characters

Translators Wanted

40 hours per week. Must be fluent in **Spanish**.
Call 999-6207.

To format text like this:

1. Select all of the text.

2. Select the Helvetica font from the ribbon's Font box. (If this font isn't available on your printer, choose another.)

3. Select Translators Wanted.

4. Select 14 from the ribbon's Pts box.

5. Click the underline icon.

6. Click the italic icon.

7. Select Spanish.

8. Click the bold icon.

Displaying Hidden Formatting Characters with the Ribbon

To display space marks (·), paragraph marks (¶), tab characters (→), and other hidden formatting characters with the ribbon:

■ Click the asterisk icon at the right side of the ribbon.

Figure 8–4 shows a document with all the hidden formatting marks displayed.

USING THE FORMAT CHARACTER COMMAND

The Format Character command, whose dialog box is shown in Figure 8–6, helps you to choose all the options you can apply with the ribbon, such as fonts, point size, bold, italic, and underlines, and it also enables you to do a few things you can't do with the ribbon:

■ Format text as hidden text, which is normally used to insert com-

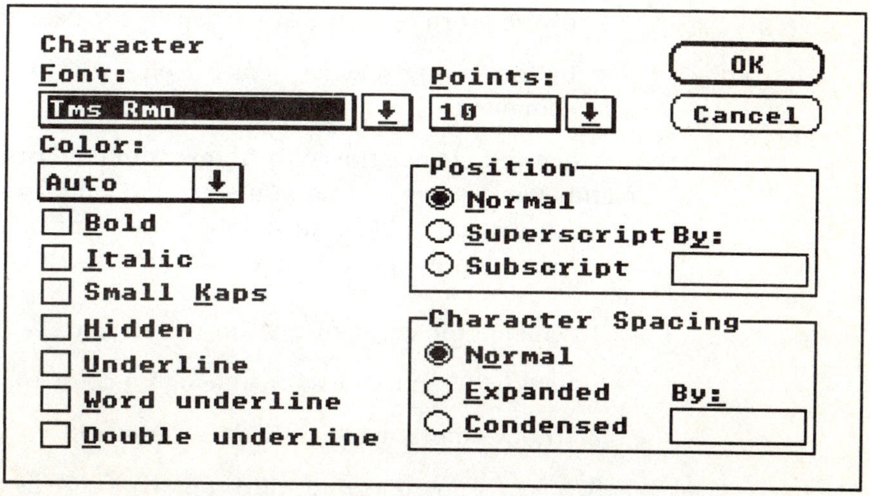

Figure 8–6.
The Format Character dialog box.

ments (annotations) into text. (You can display or hide hidden text with the View Preferences command.)

- Specify the number of points by which to raise or lower text to create a superscript or subscript.

- Expand or compress text by controlling the amount of space between characters.

To format characters with the Format Character command:

1. Select the characters you want to format.

2. Choose the Format Character command.

3. Choose options in the dialog box.

4. Click OK or press **Enter**.

Many of the character formats (such as underlines and bold) are toggles—when you choose one in the Format Character dialog box, an X appears in the accompanying box to show that it's "turned on." To remove a toggle format (such as bold), just choose Format Character and choose the option again; the X disappears.

Changing the Color of Text

You can change the color of text on your monitor in two ways:

- by changing the color of "window text" through the Windows Control Panel, which changes *all* text. (See Changing the Colors of the Word Screen in Chapter 26 for details).

- by formatting selected text in color with the Format Character command.

When you change the color of text with the Format Character command, Word assumes that you want not only to display but also to print in that color. If your printer cannot print in different colors, text formatted in color may not print correctly (or may not print at all).

To change the color of text on the screen:

1. Select the text you want to assign a color to.

2. Choose the Format Character command.

3. Select a color from the drop-down Color list.

4. Click OK or press **Enter** to change the color of the text on the screen.

5. Move the insertion point to remove the highlight and see the color.

Although you see different colors on the screen, your document won't print out in those colors unless your printer is capable of printing in a variety of colors.

Using Hidden Text

Hidden text is so called because you can choose when you to hide or display it. Hidden text is generally used to add annotations or codes, such as PostScript® codes or index codes, to a document.
To display hidden text:

1. Choose the View Preferences command.

2. Turn on the Hidden Text option.

3. Click OK or press **Enter**.

Word displays hidden text with a dotted underline. Regardless of whether it's displayed, hidden text won't print unless you choose the Include Hidden Text option in the File Print dialog box. However, when hidden text is displayed, Word counts it to calculate page breaks. Therefore, if you don't want to include any text formatted as hidden when calculating page breaks, be sure to hide hidden text before choosing any command that causes Word to repaginate, such as the File Print, View Page, or File Print Preview commands.
To hide hidden text:

1. Choose the View Preferences command.

2. Turn off the Hidden Text option.

3. Click OK or press **Enter**. Word erases the hidden text from the screen.

Typing Measurements in the Format Character Dialog Box

You can type measurements in points in the Format Character dialog box (shown in Figure 8–7) to specify a font size, to tell Word how

Figure 8–7.
You can type precise measurements in the Format Character dialog box.

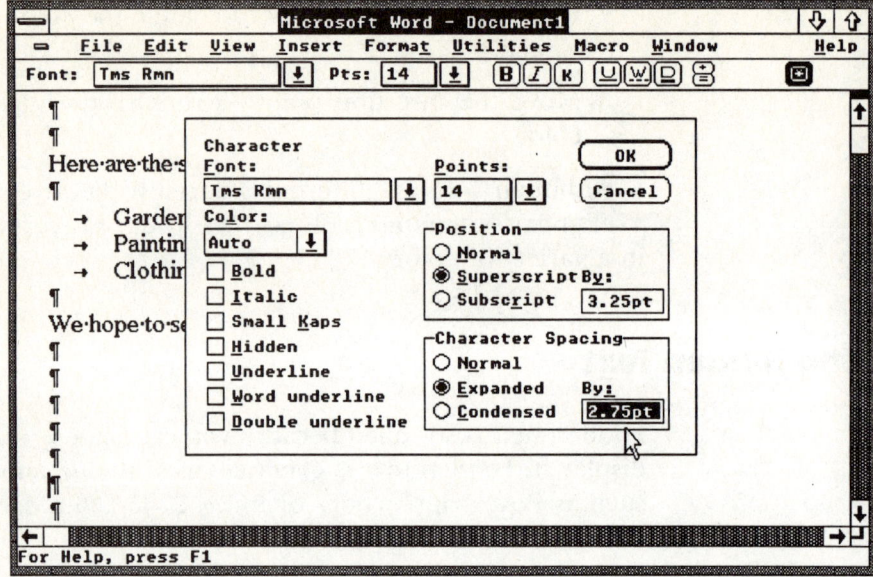

much to raise or lower text for a superscript or subscript, or to specify how much to expand or condense the space between letters in a word.

Creating Superscripts and Subscripts

Word easily creates superscripts (text raised above the baseline) and subscripts (text lowered beneath the baseline). Superscripts are commonly used in mathematical formulas, in trademark and copyright symbols, and as footnote reference marks:

$e = mc^2$

The statue appeared to be an undiscovered Michelangelo.[14]

Subscripts are frequently used in chemical equations:

H_2O

CO_2

You can type a number of points by which to raise or lower selected text in the Position box, or you can let Word use its default measurements to raise a superscript from the baseline by 3 points or to lower a subscript by 3 points. You can type point measurement numbers from .5 to 63.5. Before you get carried away, though, you should be aware that using large numbers for superscripts and subscripts may create uneven line spacing in the paragraph containing the superscript or subscript, because Word determines line spacing based on the character that extends the furthest above or below the baseline in any line.

When formatting superscripts or subscripts, you might also want to choose a point size smaller than the surrounding text.

Expanding or Condensing Text

You can expand text up to 14 points and condense it by up to 1.75 points by choosing the Format Character command and typing a number of points in the Character Spacing By box to change the spacing between characters. You can type measurements in ¼-point increments, such as .75. You might want to expand or condense a few characters, a word, or a sentence to create a special effect in a headline, or just to make the text fit better on a line. Word's default spacing for expanded text is 3 points; for condensed text, 1.5 points. Figure 8–8 shows text that's been expanded and condensed to create special effects.

Keyboard Shortcuts

You can quickly apply character formats to selected text—without using the ribbon or choosing a command—by using the following key combinations:

Bold   Ctrl+B

Italic   Ctrl+I

Figure 8–8.
Expanded and
condensed text.

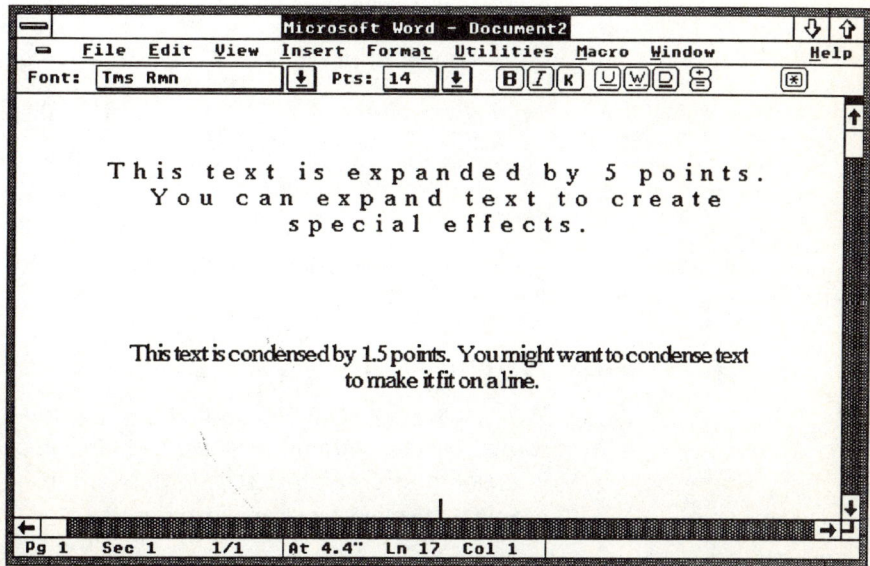

Underline	Ctrl+U
Word underline	Ctrl+W
Double underline	Ctrl+D
Small capitals	Ctrl+K
Change letters to uppercase or lowercase	Shift+F3
Hidden text	Ctrl+H
Strikethrough	Ctrl+Z (can be used only in Edit Search or Edit Replace dialog boxes)
Change font	Press Ctrl+F, then type the font name or press Alt+Down arrow key until you see the font you want, then press Enter
Change point size	Press Ctrl+P, then type the point size or press Alt+Down arrow key until you see the size you want, then press Enter
Next larger point size	Ctrl+F2
Next smaller point size	Ctrl+Shift+F2
3-point superscript	Ctrl+= (equal sign)[1]
2-point subscript	Ctrl+− (hyphen or minus)[1]
Display all characters	Ctrl+Shift+* (asterisk)[1]
Back to plain text	Ctrl+Spacebar

[1]Use the key in the top row, not the key on the numeric keypad at the right of the keyboard.

Helpful Hint

You can specify character formats before you type by choosing the format options with no text selected—this applies the format to the insertion point. Any text typed afterward will have that format. For example, a speed typist might enter

keys can be *faster*

by pressing **Ctrl+B** (for bold), typing **keys**, pressing **Ctrl+Spacebar** (for plain text), typing **can be**, pressing **Ctrl+I** (for italic), then typing **faster**.

INSERTING SPECIAL CHARACTERS

You can add all sorts of characters by typing their special codes. Word provides two sets of special characters:

- the ANSI (American National Standards Institute) character set of 256 characters. The first 128 characters correspond to the letters and symbols on a standard US keyboard (the same as the ASCII character set). The second 128 represent special characters such as letters in foreign alphabets, accents, currency symbols, fractions, or other symbols such as bullets (•).

- the IBM PC extended character set (also known as the extended ASCII set).

You will use different codes depending on which character set you are using. Remember to use the numeric keypad with NumLock turned on. For instance, to make a bullet using the IBM PC Extended Character Set, you would press Alt+249. To make the same bullet using the ANSI character set, you would use Alt+0183.

Some common publishing symbols that can be entered using Alt+0 and a number on the numeric keypad are

Symbol	Keys
Single open quotation mark (')	Alt+0145
Single close quotation mark (')	Alt+0146
Double open quotation mark (")	Alt+0147
Double close quotation mark (")	Alt+0148
Bullet (•)	Alt+0183
Em dash (—)	Alt+0150
En dash (–)	Alt+0151

To add special characters to a Word document:

1. Place the insertion point where you want to insert a special character.

2. If necessary, press the **NumLock** key to turn on NumLock.

3. Hold down the Alt key and press either the IBM PC Extended Character Set code or 0 (zero) and the ANSI Character Set code on the numeric keypad for the character you want.

Special characters may look different in different fonts, so if you don't get just what you're expecting, select the special character and change the font.

SEARCHING FOR AND REPLACING CHARACTER FORMATTING

Word can search for character formatting, such as bold, italic, or small capitals. You can also type specific text if you want to search for both text and formatting at the same time.

To tell Word what kind of formatting to search for, you use the key combinations that apply character formatting.

To search for or replace character formatting:

1. Choose the Edit Search or Edit Replace command.

2. In the text boxes, press any of the following key combinations to specify the format you want. You can press several key combinations in succession: Press **Ctrl+B**, then **Ctrl+D**, for example, to specify bold text with a double underline.

To specify	Type
Bold	Ctrl+B
Italic	Ctrl+I
Underline	Ctrl+U
Double underline	Ctrl+D
Word underline	Ctrl+W
Small capitals	Ctrl+K
Hidden text	Ctrl+H
3-point subscript	Ctrl+equal sign (=)

3-point superscript	Ctrl+plus sign (+)
Font name	Ctrl+F. Repeat until you see the font you want.
Point size	Ctrl+P. Repeat until you see the point size you want.
Plain text	Ctrl+Spacebar
Color	Ctrl+V. Repeat until you see the color you want.

COPYING CHARACTER FORMATTING

If you have a certain combination of character formats you like (such as Bold Italic Helvetica 14), you can use that combination over and over without choosing all those character formatting commands again. Once you have formatted some text the way you want, you can use the mouse to copy that format to new text.

To copy character formatting with the mouse:

1. Format some text the way you want it.

2. Select the next text you want to format.

3. Hold down **Ctrl+Shift**, point to a character that has the format you want to copy, and click the left mouse button.

REPEATING THE LAST CHARACTER FORMATTING ACTION

You can use the F4 key or the Edit Repeat Formatting command to repeat the last character format you used. For example, if you add italic, then add bold to a word, you can use the F4 key to add bold to another word.

To repeat the last character format used:

1. Format a piece of text.

2. Select the next piece of text you want to format in the same way.

3. Press **F4** or choose the Edit Repeat Formatting command.

## Chapter Nine

Paragraph Formatting

Paragraph formatting includes these topics.

- Indenting paragraphs, including left, right, and first line indents
- Aligning paragraphs horizontally
- Setting tabs
- Changing line spacing within and between paragraphs
- Putting borders around paragraphs
- Controlling how page breaks affect paragraphs
- Controlling line numbers in paragraphs

This chapter discusses

- the ruler and how to use it to speed up your paragraph formatting.
- formatting tabs.
- aligning paragraphs.
- changing line spacing within and between paragraphs.
- adding boxes, lines, or bars.
- controlling page breaks when they occur in paragraphs.

In Word, a *paragraph* is anything (even a blank line) that ends with a paragraph mark (¶). You insert a paragraph mark into your document every time you press the Enter key. Paragraph marks are always present, but you can choose when to see them.

DISPLAYING OR REMOVING PARAGRAPH MARKS

To display paragraph marks, do one of the following:

- Choose the View Preferences command and turn on the Paragraph Marks option.

- Press **Ctrl+Shift+*** (asterisk). (Use the asterisk key in the top row, not the multiplication key on the keypad.)

This displays not only paragraph marks (¶), but also marks for tabs (→), spaces (·), and newline characters (↵).

You've probably noticed that when you press Enter to start a new paragraph, the new paragraph takes on the characteristics of the preceding paragraph. This is the default behavior of Word. However, you can change the format of any paragraph at any time. You can format a few paragraphs at a time or format every paragraph in your document simultaneously.

▬▬▬ *Important Point*

Word stores a paragraph's format in the paragraph mark (¶), so if you delete a paragraph mark, you'll lose the formatting attached to the paragraph, and the text will become part of the next paragraph.

To format paragraphs, use the Format Paragraph command or the ruler. If you use the ruler, you'll immediately see your changes in your document. If you use the Format Paragraph command, you'll have to choose OK to see your changes.

SELECTING PARAGRAPHS

The general topic of selecting is explained in Chapter 4, "Editing Your Word Files." Here are a few reminders to make selecting paragraphs easier:

- If you want to format only one paragraph, you don't have to select it—just move the insertion point into the paragraph.

- Drag the mouse pointer in the selection bar to select several paragraphs, as shown in Figure 9–1.

- To quickly select a paragraph, double-click in the selection bar next to any line in the paragraph.

Figure 9–1.
Using the mouse in
the selection bar to
select paragraphs.

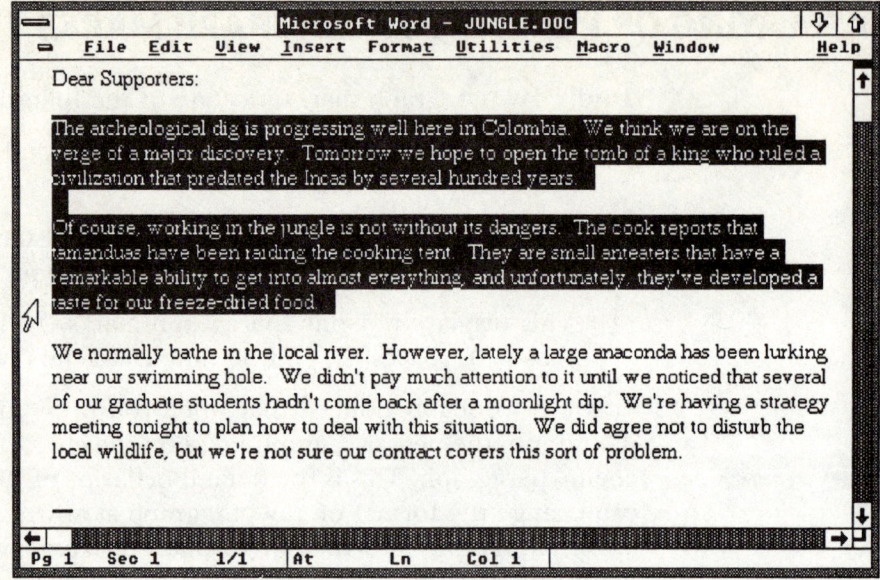

Figure 9–1.
Using the mouse in
the selection bar to
select paragraphs.

- To select every paragraph in the document, press **Ctrl+5** on the numeric keypad or hold down the Control key and click the left mouse button in the selection bar.

USING THE RULER

The ruler is a graphic device you use to format paragraphs and see the results immediately. You can display and use the ruler any time you like.

To display the ruler:

- Choose the View Ruler command or press **Ctrl+Shift+F10**.

The ruler is shown in Figure 9–2.
To hide the ruler:

- Choose the View Ruler command again.

When you use the ruler to format paragraphs, you choose a style from the drop-down list, click an icon to choose an alignment or spacing option, or move markers in the measurement area to set indents and tabs.

The ruler reflects the settings of any paragraphs you have selected. If the selected paragraphs have different settings, icons in the ruler

Figure 9–2.
The ruler formats
paragraphs and
shows the format of
selected paragraphs.

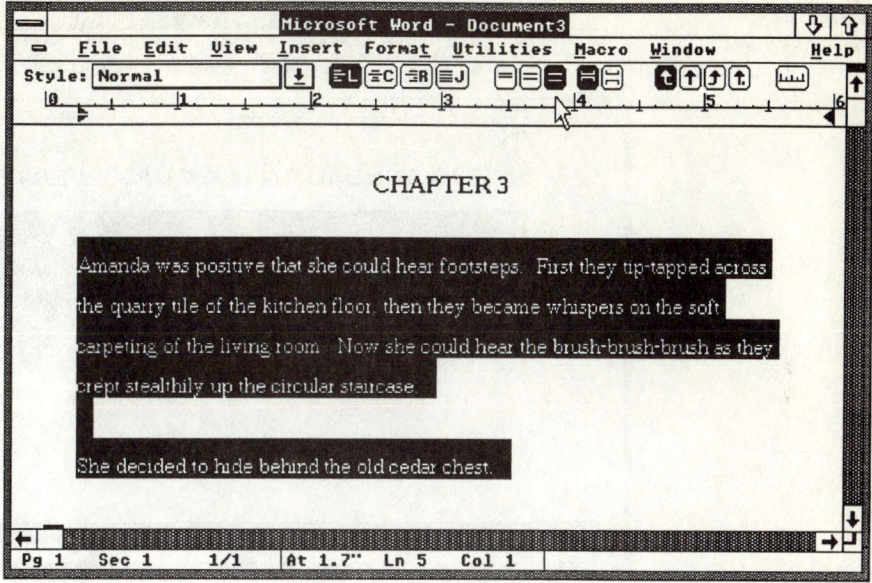

are dimmed to show a mixture of settings. You'll learn how to use the
ruler in the following sections.

Switching Ruler Views

Outside of tables, the ruler has two different views. The first view, the
default mode (shown in Figure 9–3), sets the zero mark at the left
margin, displays the movable indent markers, and is used to format
paragraphs. The other view (shown in Figure 9–4) sets the zero mark
at the left edge of the page and displays movable margin markers ([and
]) (and column markers, if you have multiple columns of text).

To switch between ruler views:

■ Click the ruler view icon (that graphic that looks like a scale or
a comb) at the right side of the ruler.

USING THE FORMAT PARAGRAPH COMMAND

With the Format Paragraph command, you can perform the same
operations you can do with the ruler, and in addition you can perform
these tasks.

Figure 9–3.
This ruler view
formats paragraphs.

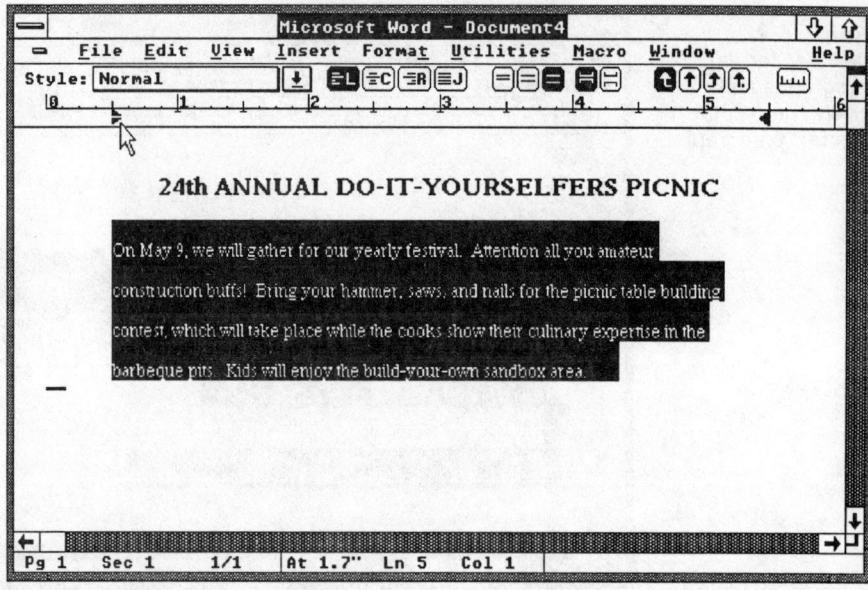

Figure 9–4.
This ruler view marks
the margins.

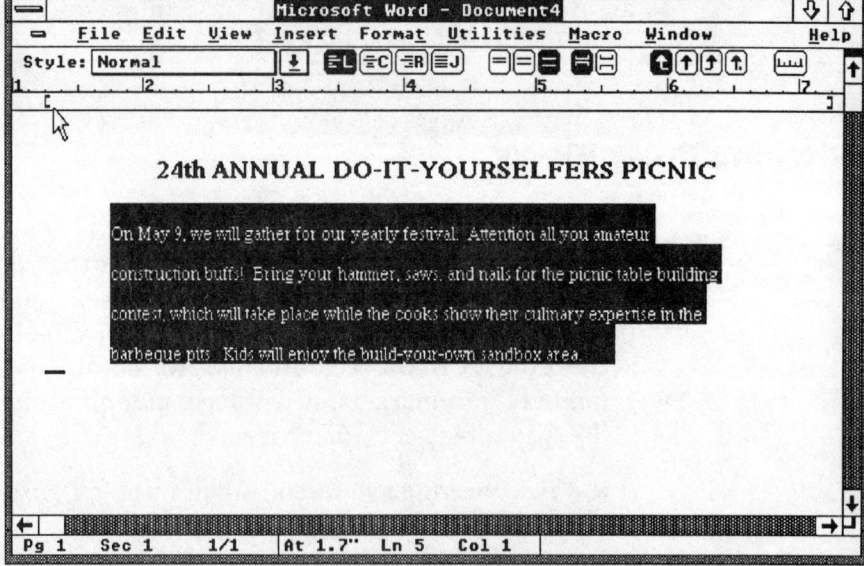

- Type exact measurements for indents, line spacing, and spacing before and after paragraphs.

- Choose options that prevent page breaks within and between paragraphs.

■ Draw borders around paragraphs.

The Format Paragraph dialog box is shown in Figure 9–5.

You'll learn how to use the Format Paragraph command in the following sections.

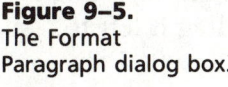 *Helpful Hint*

To keep text aligned in straight columns, always use indent settings or tab settings. If you use spaces, then later change fonts or point sizes, you may find that your text is no longer aligned.

INDENTING PARAGRAPHS

When you indent paragraphs, you set the spacing between the paragraph and the margin, as shown in the following example. You can specify a left indent, a right indent, and a first-line indent, as shown in Figure 9–6.

Indenting Paragraphs with the Ruler

To indent paragraphs using the ruler and a mouse:

1. Select the paragraphs.

2. If the ruler is not displayed, choose the View Ruler command.

Figure 9–5.
The Format
Paragraph dialog box.

```
┌──────────────────────────────────────────────────────┐
│ Paragraph                                             │
│ ┌Alignment──────────────────────────────┐  ( OK )    │
│ │ ◉ Left  ○ Center  ○ Right  ○ Justified │           │
│ └────────────────────────────────────────┘ (Cancel)  │
│ ┌Indents────────────┐ ┌Spacing────────┐  (Tabs...)   │
│ │ From Left:  [0"]  │ │ Before: [01i] │              │
│ │ From Right: [0"]  │ │ After:  [01i] │              │
│ │ First Line: [0"]  │ │ Line:   [Auto]│              │
│ │ Style:            │ Border:  [None] [↓]            │
│ │ [Normal]     [↓]  │ Pattern: [None] [↓]            │
│ │ ┌Keep Paragraph─┐                                  │
│ │ │ ☐ Together    │  ☐ Page Break Before             │
│ │ │ ☐ With Next   │  ☐ Line Numbering                │
│ └───────────────────┘                                │
└──────────────────────────────────────────────────────┘
```

Figure 9–6.
Indents are different
from margins.

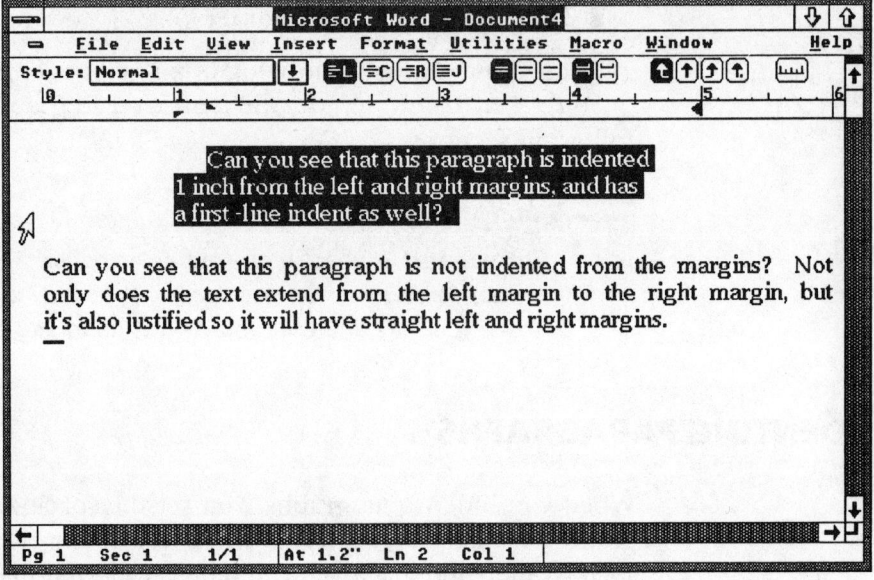

3. Set the indents you want:

Left indent

Drag the ruler's left indent marker (▶) to the position you want. If you want a first-line indent that's different from the left indent, hold down the **Shift** key and drag only the bottom triangle of the marker.

First line
indent

Drag the first-line indent marker (the top triangle of the left indent marker) to the position you want. Drag it right to create a normal first-line indent or drag it left to create a hanging indent. Figure 9–7 illustrates setting a first-line indent.

Right indent

Drag the right indent marker (◀) to the position you want.

EXAMPLE: Setting Paragraph Indents with the Ruler

To saddle a horse:¶

1. Place the saddle blanket on the horse's back.¶

2. Place the saddle on the horse's back, making sure the saddle blanket extends beyond the saddle on all sides.¶

Figure 9–7.
Setting a first-line
indent with the ruler.

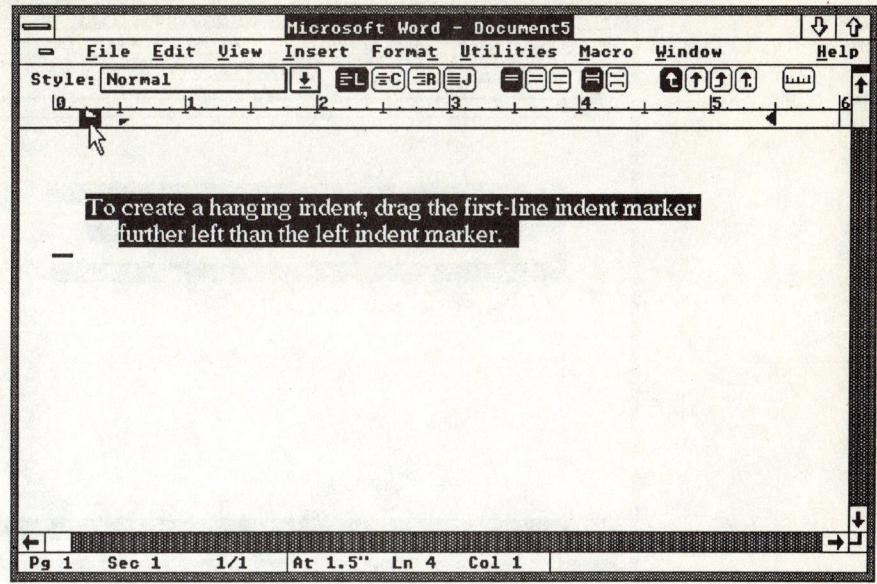

3. Tighten the cinch as far as you can.¶

To duplicate these instructions:

1. Type all text at the left margin—don't try to put spaces before the numbers. Press the **Tab** key after typing a number and a period. Press **Enter** only where you see paragraph marks (¶).

2. Select the three numbered paragraphs.

3. Drag the left indent marker (▶) to ¾ inch and release the mouse button.

4. Hold down the **Shift** key and drag the first line marker (just the top triangle) backwards to ½ inch, then release the mouse button.

You can also indent paragraphs using the ruler and keys:

1. Select the paragraphs.

2. Press **Ctrl+Shift+F10** to activate the ruler. A block cursor appears in the ruler, as shown in Figure 9–8.

3. Use the **Right** and **Left arrow** keys to position the block cursor

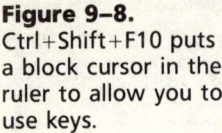

Figure 9–8.
Ctrl+Shift+F10 puts
a block cursor in the
ruler to allow you to
use keys.

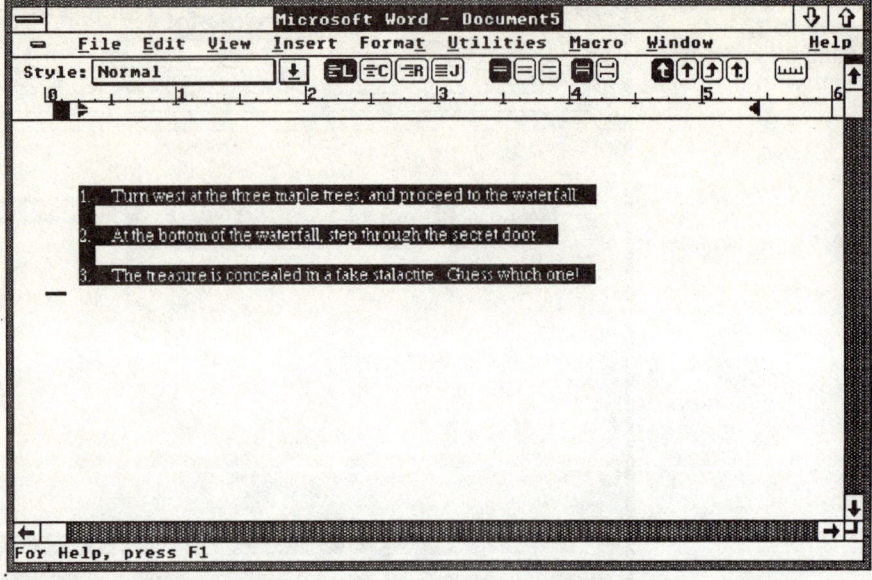

where you want the indent. The indent will be set at the center of the block cursor.

4. Press a key to set the indent:

Left indent   L

Right indent   R

First line   F
indent

Word moves the indent marker to the cursor position.

5. Press **Enter** to return to the document window.

Indenting Paragraphs with the Format Paragraph Command

To set indents with the Format Paragraph command, you type measurements in the indent boxes. These measurements are distances from the margins. For example, if you type 1 in both the From Left and From Right boxes, Word sets a left indent one inch from the left margin, and a right indent one inch from the right margin. Hanging indents (where the first line is farther to the left than the rest of the paragraph) are an exception to the measure-from-the-margin rule. To set a hanging indent you type a negative measurement in the First Line box, measuring backwards from the left indent setting. Figure 9–9 shows an example of setting hanging indents with the Format Paragraph command.

To set indents with the Format Paragraph command:

1. Select the paragraphs you want to indent.

2. Choose the Format Paragraph command.

3. Type measurements in the indent boxes.

4. Click OK or press **Enter**.

Word assumes that the measurements you type are in inches, unless you type cm (for centimeters), pt (for points), or pi (for picas) after the measurement or you've changed the unit of measurement with the Utilities Customize command.

Keyboard Shortcuts

You can use the following key combinations to indent selected paragraphs without using the ruler or a command. When you press one of these, Word sets the indent at the closest tab setting (½ inch if you haven't changed the default settings):

Figure 9–9.
Setting hanging indents with the Format Paragraph command.

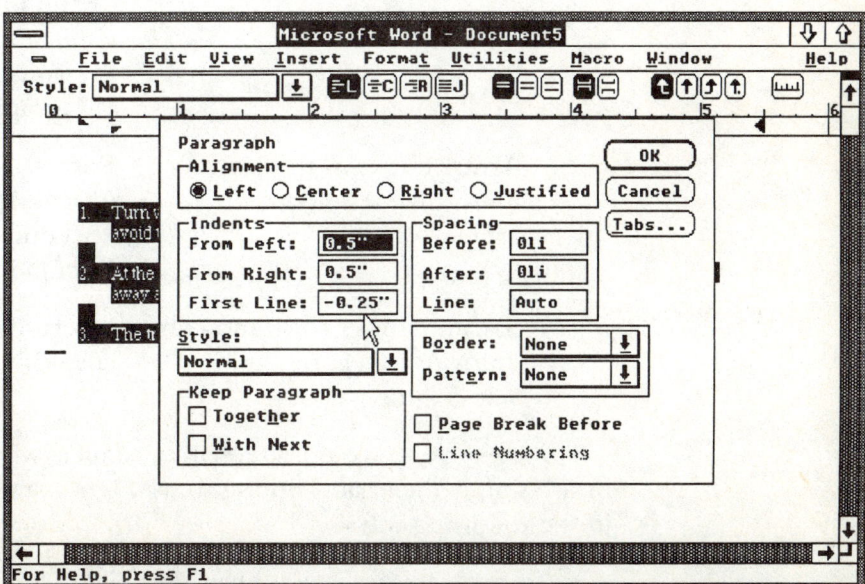

Press	To
Ctrl+N	Shift whole paragraph right.
Ctrl+M	Shift whole paragraph left.
Ctrl+T	Shift all lines except the first line to the right, creating a hanging indent.
Ctrl+G	Shift all lines except the first line to the left.

You can use these key combinations repeatedly to get the indent you want.

WORKING WITH TABS

When your only choices for developing documents were typewriters or primitive word processing software, you had to use tabs to position all text that you didn't want to start at the left margin. With Word, this is no longer necessary. You have many commands at your disposal to accomplish the tasks you used to do with tabs:

To	Use
Indent a paragraph	Indent markers on the ruler or the Format Paragraph command (discussed in the previous section, Indenting Paragraphs)
Arrange text in flowing columns (like a newspaper article)	Format Section command (discussed in Chapter 11, "Section Formatting and Document Formatting"
Set up data in rows and columns or put paragraphs side-by-side	Insert Table command (discussed in Chapter 13)

However, there are still a few circumstances when tabs are important or are simply the easiest option to use. For example, you can use tabs in the following ways.

■ To put data in small tables, like this:

Pythons $105 each

Boas $98 each

■ To align columns of text in special ways, like this:

Decimal Alignment	Centered	Right Alignment
34.112	Fred	92
88.43	Raquel	112
7.9	Sean	13
533.5	Jose Maria	4,299

■ To do simple indents, like this:

His answer to every question was,

"No comment."

■ To put space between numbers or bullets and following text, creating bulleted or numbered lists (often in combination with indents, as shown in the previous section, Indenting Paragraphs), like these:

1. Type the letters.

2. Make copies.

3. Mail the originals.

4. File the copies.

• chairs

• typewriters

• notepads

Displaying Tab Characters

You insert a tab character every time you press the Tab key. Tab characters are bold arrows that point right (→). Tab characters are invisible unless you tell Word to display them.

To display tab characters:

■ Press **Ctrl**+**Shift**+***** (asterisk). (Use the asterisk key in the top row, not the multiplication key on the keypad.) This displays not only tab characters, but also paragraph marks, space marks, and newline characters.

Mouse Speed Tip

To quickly select one tab in text, double-click the tab character (→).

Word has four types of tabs you can choose from the ruler or from the Format Paragraph dialog box. The ruler's tab icons are shown in Figure 9–10. Figure 9–11 shows how text aligned at different tabs would look.

Setting Individual Tabs

You can set tabs for a paragraph before you type the text by placing the insertion point before the paragraph mark on a blank line, then setting the tabs for that paragraph. However, it's usually easier to type your text first, pressing the Tab key wherever you want a tab. Don't be alarmed if your text doesn't line up—that will be taken care of when you set tabs using one of the following procedures.

Figure 9–10.
Tab icons on the ruler.

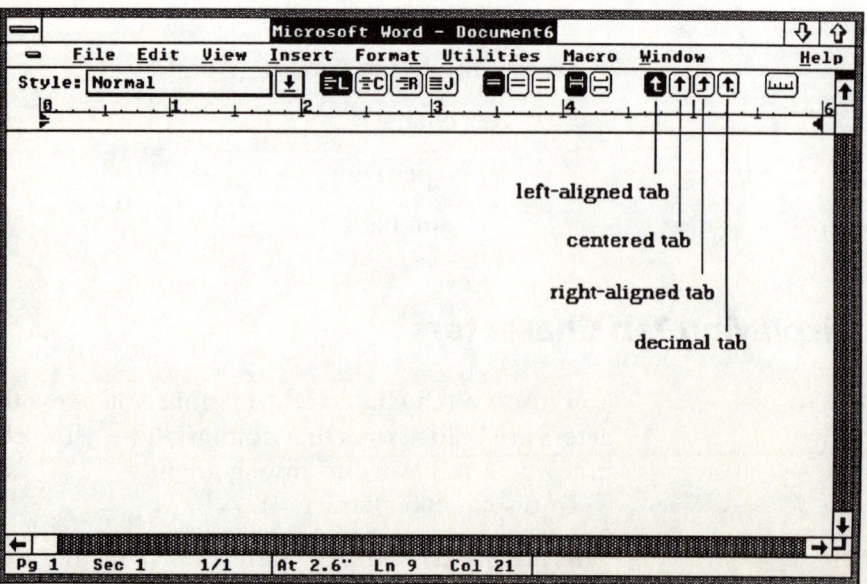

Figure 9–11.
Text aligned at
different types of
tabs.

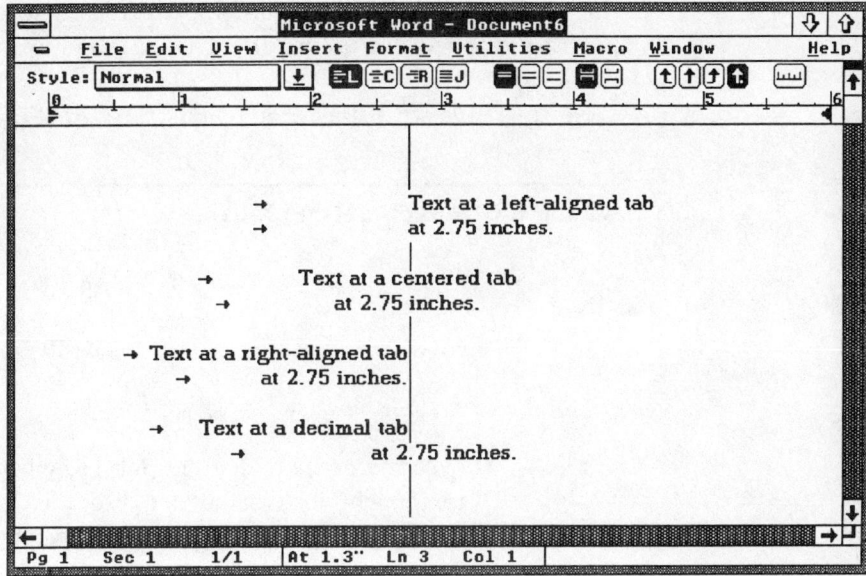

Figure 9–11.
Text aligned at different types of tabs.

Setting Tabs with the Ruler

To set tabs with the ruler using the mouse:

1. Type the text, pressing the **Tab** key where you want tabs.

2. Select the paragraphs containing the tab characters. (Remember, tabs are part of paragraph formatting.)

3. If necessary, choose the View Ruler command or press **Ctrl+Shift+F10** to display the ruler.

4. Choose a tab type by clicking on its icon in the ruler. For example, if you wanted the text at the tab to line up on a decimal point, you'd click the decimal tab icon. Word highlights the icon for the active tab type.

5. Point to the position on the ruler where you want the tab, then click the mouse button. An icon for that tab type appears, and the paragraphs adjust to show the new setting.

6. Repeat steps 4 and 5 for each tab you want to set in the paragraphs.

The first tab icon you set in the ruler controls the location and type of the first tab character in your paragraph, the second tab icon marks the setting for the second tab character, and so on, so you'll need to position one icon in the ruler for each tab character (→) in a selected paragraph.

Setting tabs with the ruler is illustrated in Figure 9–12.

■■■■ **EXAMPLE: Setting Tabs**

24″ × 48″ canvas→ $8.50

Oil Paints→ $59.50

To create this very simple table:

1. Type the text, pressing the **Tab** key where you want a tab. The text might look something like this (assuming you pressed Ctrl+Shift+* to see the tab characters):

    24″ × 48″ canvas→ $8.50

    Oil Paints→ $59.50

2. Select both paragraphs.

3. Click the decimal tab icon on the ruler.

Figure 9–12.
Setting tabs with the ruler.

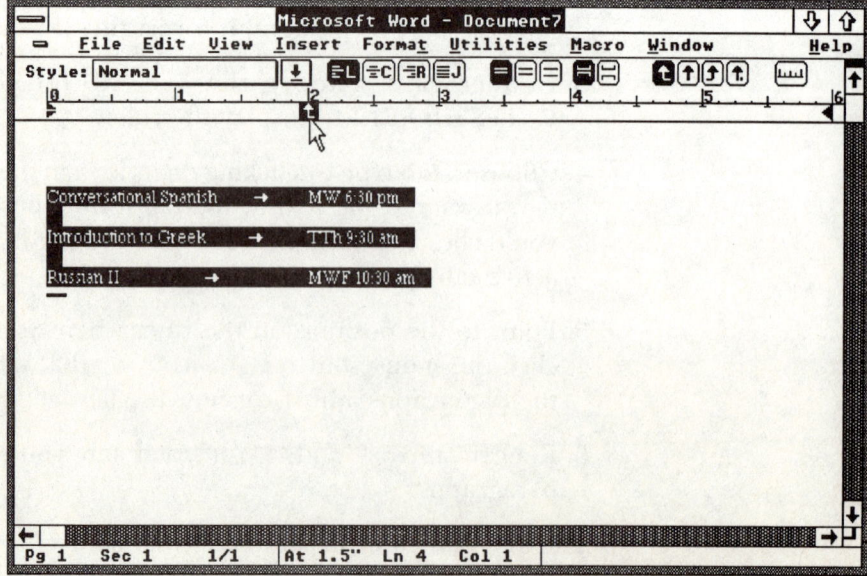

> 4. Drag the tab icon to a position on the ruler to set the tab for the second column.

To set tabs with the ruler using the keys:

1. Type the text, pressing the **Tab** key where you want tabs.

2. Select the paragraphs containing the tab characters. (Remember, tabs are part of paragraph formatting.)

3. Press **Ctrl+Shift+F10** to activate the ruler.

4. Choose a tab type by pressing a number for the type you want, based on the icon's position in the ruler:

Tab type	Press this key in top row
Left	1
Center	2
Right	3
Decimal	4

   Word highlights the icon for that tab type.

5. Use the **Right** or **Left arrow** keys to move the block cursor in the ruler to where you want to insert a tab.

6. Press the **Insert** key. An icon for that tab type appears, and the selected paragraphs adjust to show the new setting.

7. Repeat steps 5 and 6 for each tab you want to set in the paragraphs.

8. Press **Enter** to return to your document.

The first tab icon you set in the ruler marks the location and type of the first tab character in your paragraph, the second tab icon marks the setting for the second tab character, and so forth, so you'll need to position one icon in the ruler for each tab character (→) in a selected paragraph.

Setting Tabs with the Format Tabs Command

You can also use the Format Tabs command to set tabs or see the positions of tabs, as shown in Figure 9–13. You can also get to the

Figure 9–13.
The Format Tabs
dialog box.

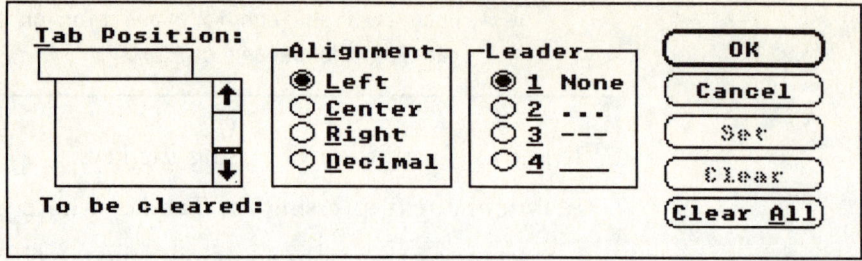

Format Tabs dialog box through the Format Paragraph dialog box:
just choose Tabs after choosing Format Paragraph.

To set tabs with the Format Tabs command:

1. Type the text, pressing the **Tab** key where you want tabs.

2. Select the paragraphs containing the text and tab characters.

3. Choose the Format Tabs command.

4. Type a position in the Tab Position box.

5. Choose a tab type in the Alignment box.

6. Click the Set button to set the tab in the paragraphs.

7. If necessary, repeat steps 4–6 to set more tabs in the paragraphs.

8. Click OK or press **Enter**.

Changing the Default Tab Spacing

Word sets default tab spacing at ½ inch—that's why the insertion point
jumps to the next inch or ½-inch position when you press the Tab
key. As you saw in the previous section, you can set individual tabs
wherever you like. You can also change the default tab spacing to a
new measurement.

To change the default tab spacing:

1. Choose the Format Document command from the Format menu.
   Word displays the dialog box shown in Figure 9–14.

2. Type a measurement in the Default Tab Stops box. For example,
   type .75 if you want to set default tabs every ¾ inch—at .75 inch,
   1.5 inches, 2.25 inches, and so forth.

3. Click OK or press **Enter**.

```
┌──────────────────────────────────────────────────────────────────┐
│ Document                                          ┌────────────┐   │
│ Page Width: │8.5"│      Height: │11"│             │     OK     │   │
│                                                   └────────────┘   │
│ Default Tab Stops: │0.5"│                         ┌────────────┐   │
│ ┌─Margins────────────────────────────────────┐   │   Cancel   │   │
│ │ Top:    │1"│   Left:  │1.25"│  Gutter: │0"│ │   └────────────┘   │
│ │ Bottom: │1"│   Right: │1.25"│  ☐ Mirror Margins                 │
│ └─────────────────────────────────────────────┘                   │
│ ┌─Footnotes──────────────────────────┐  Template                  │
│ │ Print at: │Bottom of Page │↓│        │ │              │ │↓│     │
│ │ Starting Number: │1│                │  ☒ Widow Control           │
│ │ ☒ Restart # Each Section            │  ┌────────────┐            │
│ └────────────────────────────────────┘  │ Set Default│            │
│                                          └────────────┘            │
└──────────────────────────────────────────────────────────────────┘
```

Moving, Deleting, and Changing the Types of Tabs

Moving and deleting tabs is just as easy as setting them. You can use either the ruler or the Format Tabs dialog box to change and rearrange your tabs. If you use the ruler, you'll see the text adjust in the window as soon as you make a change on the ruler. If you use the Format Tabs dialog box, you won't see the text change until you click OK or press Enter.

Deleting Tabs with the Ruler

With the mouse:

1. Select the paragraphs you want to affect.

2. Drag the tab icon off the ruler and release the mouse button. The tab icon will disappear, and the paragraphs will adjust accordingly.

With the keys:

1. If necessary, press **Ctrl+Shift+F10** to put a block cursor in the ruler.

2. Use the **Right** or **Left arrow** keys to move the block cursor on top of the tab you want to delete.

3. Press the **Delete** key.

Changing a Tab's Position

With the mouse:

1. Drag the tab icon to a new position on the ruler.

2. The paragraphs change to reflect the new setting.

With the keys:

1. Press **Ctrl+Shift+F10** to put a block cursor in the ruler.

2. Use the **Right** or **Left arrow** keys to move the block cursor on top of the tab you want to move.

3. Press the **Delete** key.

4. Move the block cursor to the new position.

5. Press the **Insert** key.

Changing the Type of Tab at a Specific Position

With the mouse:

1. Drag the tab icon you no longer want off the ruler.

2. Choose a new type of tab and set it at the same position.

With the keys:

1. Press **Ctrl+Shift+F10** to place a block cursor in the ruler.

2. Use the **Right** or **Left arrow** keys to move the block cursor on top of the tab icon you want to change.

3. Press the **Delete** key.

4. Choose a tab type by pressing a number for the type you want, based on the icon's position in the ruler:

Tab type	Press this key in top row
Left	1
Center	2
Right	3
Decimal	4

Word highlights the icon for that tab type.

5. Press the **Insert** key.

Changing Tabs with the Format Tabs Command

To delete a tab or change the type of tab:

1. Select the paragraphs you want to affect.

2. Choose the Format Tabs command.

3. Type the position of the tab you want to affect in the Tab Position box or select the position from the list.

4. Choose Clear to delete the tab or choose a new tab type in the Alignment box.

5. Click OK or press **Enter**.

To move a tab with the Format Tabs command:

■ Clear the tab at the old position, then set a new tab at the new position.

Filling Tab Spaces with Leader Characters

If you don't want spaces to appear before a tab, you can fill in the tab space with leader characters. For example, you might want to use periods for leader characters in an index, like this:

The Beginning 1

The Middle 99

The End 250

Word has three types of leader characters you can use: periods, hyphens, and underlines.

To fill a tab space with leader characters:

1. Select the paragraphs to be affected.

2. Choose the Format Tabs command.

3. Type the tab's position in the Tab Position box or position the tab icon on the ruler.

4. Choose the option you want in the Leader box. Choose None if you want to remove an existing tab leader.

5. Choose Set.

6. Click OK or press **Enter**.

ALIGNING PARAGRAPHS

Word has four alignment options to determine the placement of text in paragraphs between indents (or between margins, if you haven't set indents).

Figure 9–15 shows how these different paragraph alignments appear.

Aligning Paragraphs with the Ruler

You can choose from four ruler icons that align paragraphs horizontally between indents (or between margins if you haven't set indents), as shown in Figure 9–16.

To align paragraphs with the ruler:

1. Select the paragraphs.

2. Click the ruler icon that represents the alignment you want.

Aligning Paragraphs with the Format Paragraph Command

To align paragraphs with the Format Paragraph command:

1. Select the paragraphs.

Figure 9–15.
Word has four different types of paragraph alignments.

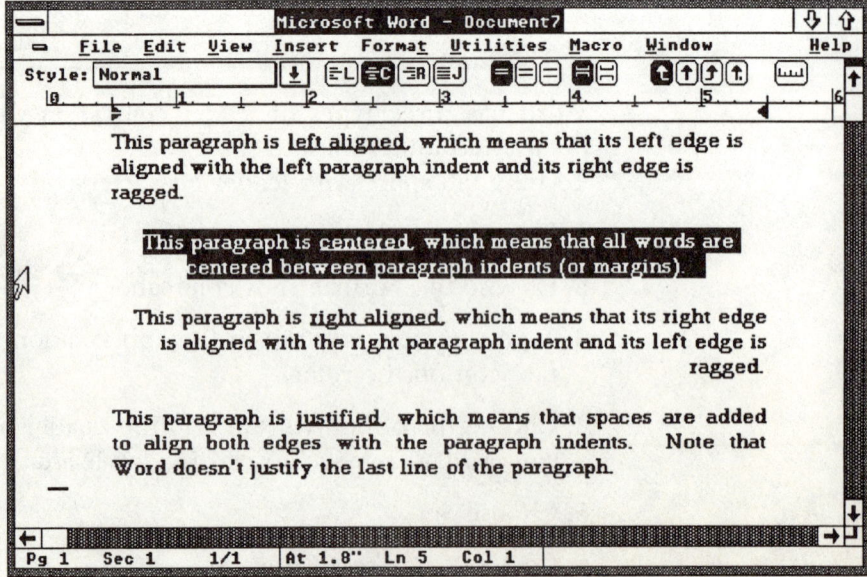

Figure 9–16.
Alignment icons on
the ruler.

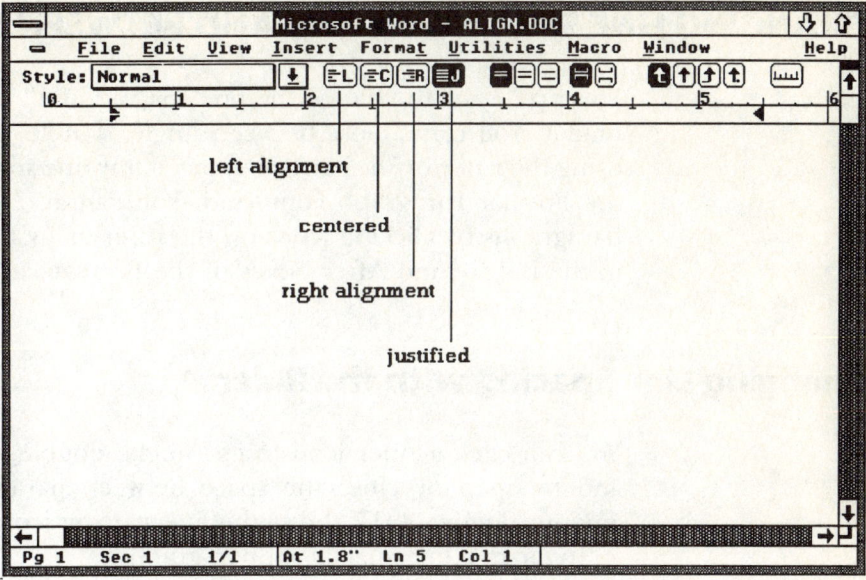

2. Choose the Format Paragraph command.

3. Choose an option in the Alignment box.

4. Click OK or press **Enter**.

Keyboard Shortcuts

You can use the following key combinations to align paragraphs without using the ruler or choosing commands:

Press	To
Ctrl+L	Align text with left indent.
Ctrl+C	Center text.
Ctrl+R	Align text with right indent.
Ctrl+J	Justify text.

When you want to move a paragraph to a completely new position on a page, use the Format Position command to specify its location. For more information, see Positioning Objects Anywhere on a Page in Chapter 14.

CHANGING LINE SPACING WITHIN AND BETWEEN PARAGRAPHS

You may want to change the line spacing in all or part of your document. You can choose between single, double, and 1½ line spacing using the ruler or shortcut keys, or set any line spacing you want using the Format Paragraph command. You can also set spacing between paragraphs by clicking icons on the ruler or by typing measurements in the Before and After boxes of the Format Paragraph command.

Changing Line Spacing with the Ruler

You can click a ruler icon to get single, double, or 1½ line spacing, and to open or close the space between paragraphs by a default amount. Figure 9–17 shows the line spacing icons on the ruler.

To change line spacing in paragraphs:

1. Select the paragraphs.

2. To set the spacing within the paragraphs, click the appropriate ruler icon.

3. To set the spacing before each paragraph, click the appropriate ruler icon.

Figure 9–17.
Line spacing icons on the ruler.

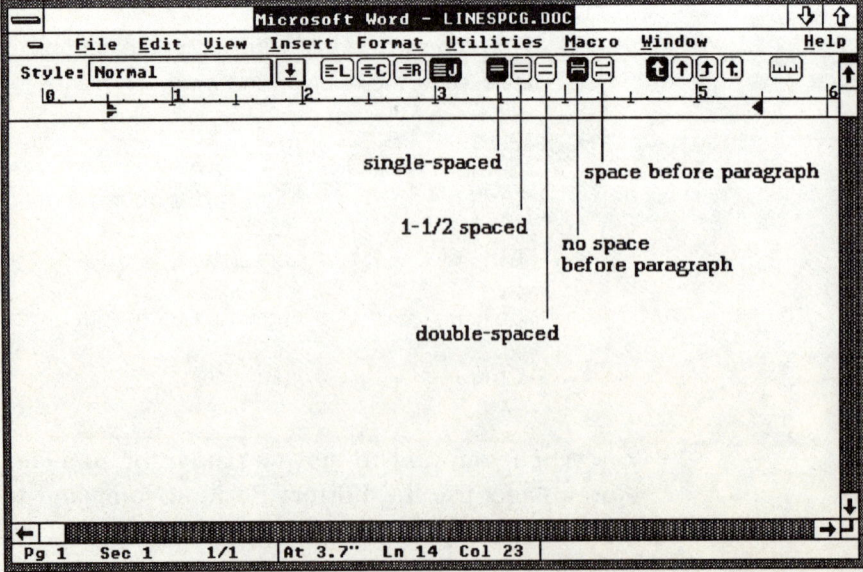

Changing Line Spacing with the Format Paragraph Command

If you want to control the spacing more precisely, you can type measurements in the Before, After, and Line boxes of the Format Paragraph dialog box, as shown in Figure 9–18. To determine the spacing between paragraphs, Word adds the Before measurement of a paragraph to the After measurement of the preceding paragraph. By default, Word measures spacing in lines (li), but you can also specify measurements in other units by typing in for inches, cm for centimeters, pt for points, or pi for picas.

To change line spacing in paragraphs:

1. Select the paragraphs.

2. Choose the Format Paragraph command.

3. To set the spacing within the paragraphs, type a measurement in the Line box.

4. To set the spacing before each paragraph, type a measurement in the Before box.

5. To set the spacing after each paragraph, type a measurement in the After box.

6. Click OK or press **Enter**.

Figure 9–18.
You can type precise line spacing measurements in the Format Paragraph dialog box.

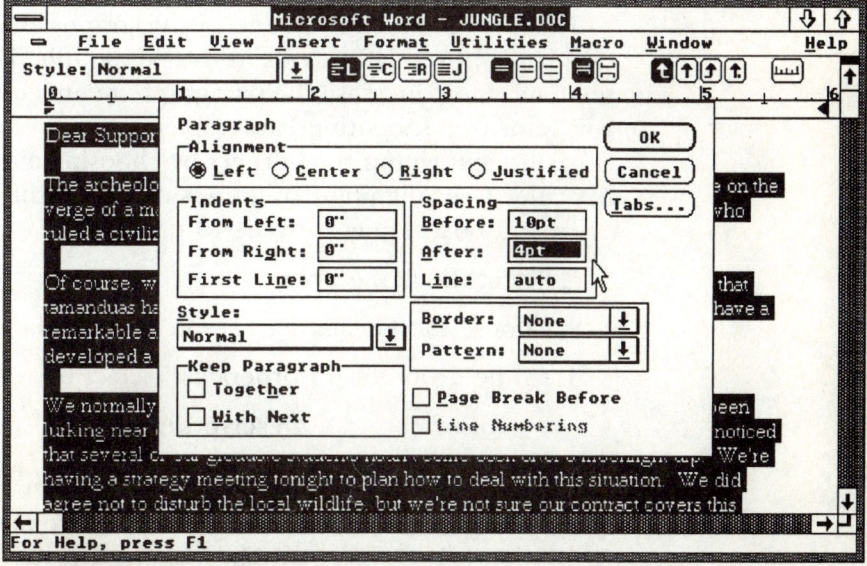

▬ *Keyboard Shortcuts*

You can use the following key combinations to change line spacing in paragraphs without choosing commands or using the ruler. Don't use the number keys on the numeric keypad in these combinations.

Press	To
Ctrl+1	Single-space text
Ctrl+2	Double-space text
Ctrl+5	1½-space text
Ctrl+O	Open spacing before paragraphs (adds 1 line of blank space before the paragraph). Make sure to press the letter *o*, not a zero
Ctrl+E	Eliminate space between paragraphs (deletes any blank space not controlled by paragraph marks in front of the paragraph)

ADDING BOXES, LINES, OR BARS TO PARAGRAPHS

You can draw lines above, below, or beside a paragraph, or you can enclose a paragraph in a box to make it stand out from the rest of your text.

Figure 9–19 shows some examples of what you can do with the border options.

The lines and boxes you add to paragraphs extend from the indents no matter how much text is in the paragraph. Therefore, if the lines seem too long, increase the paragraph indents until you get the effect you want (see Indenting Paragraphs earlier in this chapter). You can align the text within the borders by choosing alignment options from the ruler (see Aligning Paragraphs earlier in this chapter).

To add boxes, lines, or bars to paragraphs:

1. Select the paragraphs.

2. Choose the Format Paragraph command.

3. In the drop-down Borders list, select the option you want:

Option	Description
None	Removes any existing borders
Box	Draws lines on all four sides of the paragraph, forming a box

Figure 9–19.
Paragraphs with a
variety of borders.

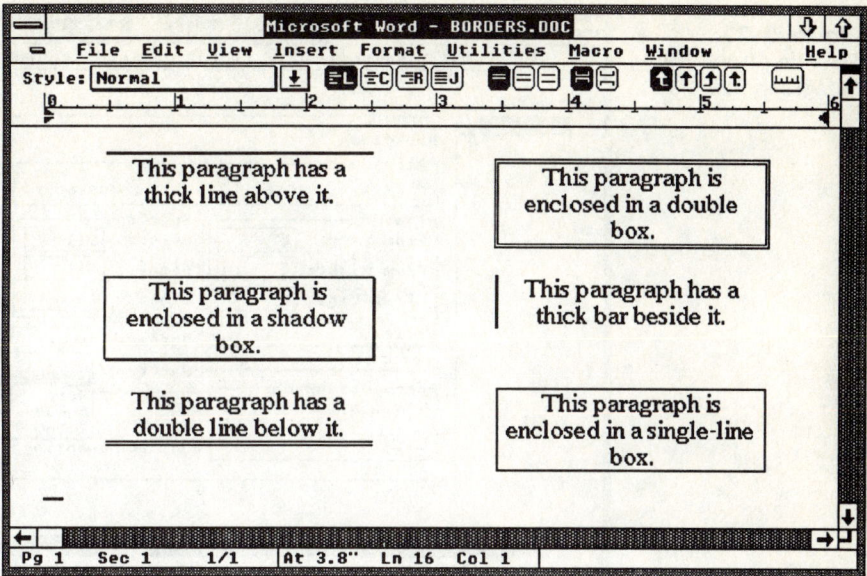

Bar	Draws a bar at the left side of a paragraph, or at the outside edge of a paragraph if you've activated the Mirror Margins option in the Format Document dialog box
Above	Draws a line above the paragraph
Below	Draws a line below the paragraph

Figure 9–20 illustrates selecting options from the Border list.

4. In the drop-down Pattern list, select the line pattern you want to draw lines or boxes with:

Option	**Description**
None	No line is drawn
Single	Draws a line 1 point thick
Thick	Draws a line 2 points thick
Double	Draws two 1-point lines that are two points apart
Shadow	Draws a box with 1-point lines on top and left sides and 2-point lines on bottom and right sides, creating a shadow effect

5. Click OK or press **Enter**.

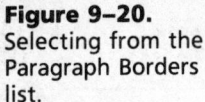
Figure 9–20.
Selecting from the
Paragraph Borders
list.

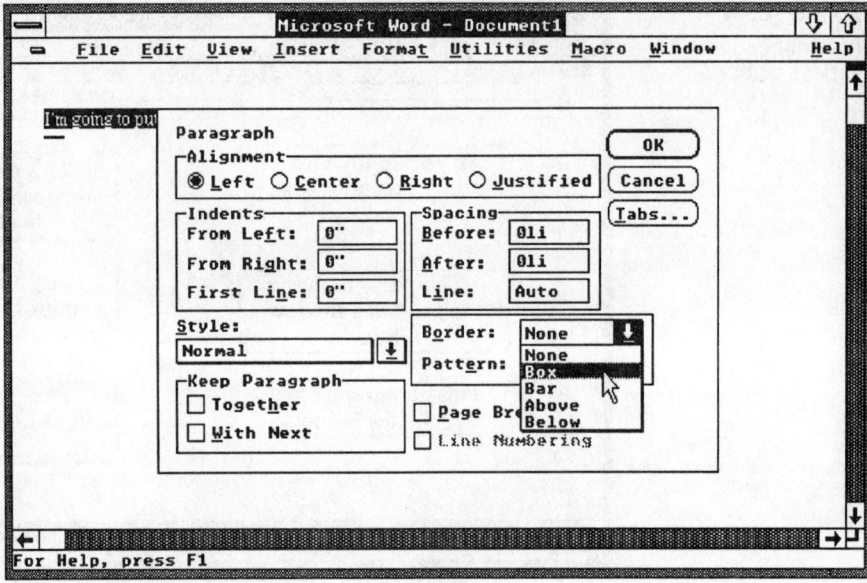

CONTROLLING PAGE BREAKS IN PARAGRAPHS

Sometimes you have a paragraph that absolutely must be kept all on
one page or kept with the next paragraph in order to make sense. You
can control page breaks in paragraphs with the Format Paragraph
command (as shown in Figure 9–21):

1. Select the paragraph(s) you want to affect.

2. Choose the Format Paragraph command.

3. Turn on the options you want in the Keep Paragraph box:

> With Next   Keeps a selected paragraph on the same
> page with the following paragraph (if a
> page break would naturally occur within
> the first paragraph or between the para-
> graphs, Word forces the page to break be-
> fore the first paragraph)

Figure 9–21.
Controlling page
breaks with the
Format Paragraph
command.

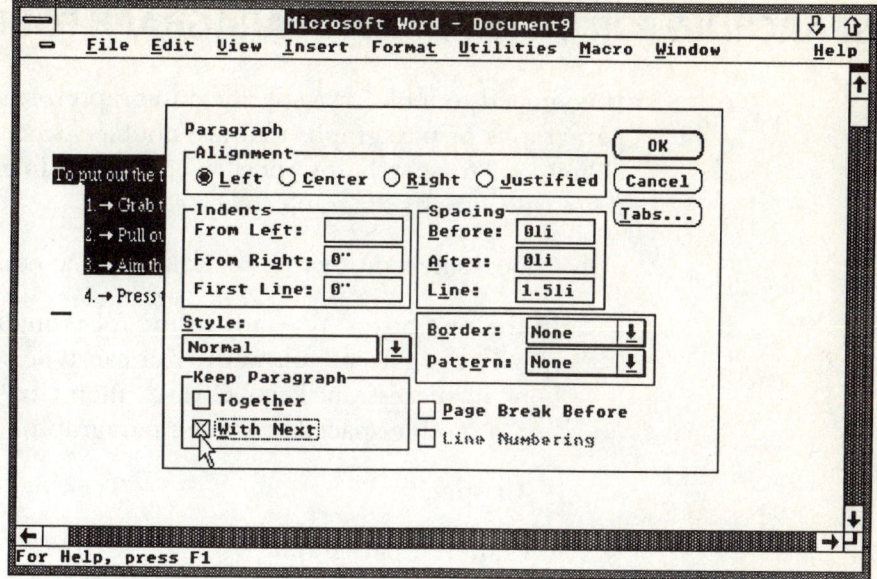

Together | Keeps all lines in a selected paragraph on the same page (if a page break would naturally occur within the paragraph, Word forces the page to break before the paragraph)

If you want to force a page break before each selected paragraph, activate the Page Break Before option.

4. Click OK or press **Enter**.

For more information about controlling page breaks, see Controlling Page Breaks in Chapter 14.

CONTROLLING LINE NUMBERS IN PARAGRAPHS

If you've added line numbers to your document, you can turn off the Line Numbering option in the Format Paragraph dialog box to remove line numbers from selected paragraphs or turn it on to restore line numbers to selected paragraphs. You can't choose this option unless you've added line numbers.

For more information about using line numbers in documents, see Numbering Lines in Chapter 17.

SEARCHING FOR OR REPLACING PARAGRAPH FORMATTING

If you need to look for a specific paragraph format, such as indented paragraphs or paragraphs that are double-spaced, Word helps by enabling you to search for specific paragraph formats and to replace them with other paragraph formats.

1. Choose the Edit Search or Edit Replace command.

2. In the text boxes, type any of the following key combinations to specify the format you want. You can type several key combinations in succession: Press **Ctrl+2**, then **Ctrl+C**, for example, to find a double-spaced, centered paragraph.

To specify	Type
Centered paragraph	Ctrl+C
Justified paragraph	Ctrl+J
Left-aligned paragraph	Ctrl+L
Right-aligned paragraph	Ctrl+R
Single-spaced paragraph	Ctrl+1
Double-spaced paragraph	Ctrl+2
1½-spaced paragraph	Ctrl+5
Paragraph with 1 line of space before (This finds only those paragraphs formatted with Ctrl+O [letter *o*])	Ctrl+O
Paragraph with no space before	Ctrl+E

COPYING PARAGRAPH FORMATTING

You can copy paragraph formatting using four different methods. The first two of these methods work during one editing session with Word. The last two methods save paragraph formatting for later use.

Using the Mouse to Copy Paragraph Formatting

To use the mouse to quickly copy a paragraph format from one place to another:

1. Format a paragraph the way you want it.

2. Select the next paragraph you want to format.

3. Move the mouse pointer into the selection bar next to the paragraph that has the format you want to copy, hold down **Ctrl+Shift**, and click the left mouse button.

Repeating the Last Paragraph Formatting Action

You can use F4 or the Edit Repeat command to repeat the last formatting action you performed on a paragraph. For example, you could double-space a paragraph, then select another paragraph and repeat the double-spacing.

To repeat the last paragraph formatting you did:

1. Format a paragraph the way you want it.

2. Select the next paragraph you want to format the same way.

3. Press **F4** or choose the Edit Repeat Formatting command.

Using the Clipboard to Copy Paragraph Formatting

You can use the Edit Copy and Edit Paste commands to quickly copy paragraph formatting by copying a paragraph mark that contains all the formatting:

1. Select the paragraph mark (¶) of the paragraph whose format you want to copy (press **Ctrl+Shift+*** (asterisk) to see paragraph marks if necessary).

2. Choose the Edit Copy command to copy the paragraph mark to the Clipboard.

3. Do one of the following:

   ■ If you're changing the format of an existing paragraph and you have the Typing Replaces Selection option turned on, select the paragraph mark of the paragraph you want to affect.

■ If you want to insert the paragraph mark, then type new text, move the insertion point to the new location.

4. Choose the Edit Paste command to paste in the copied paragraph mark and its associated formatting. If you selected an existing paragraph mark and you have activated the Typing Replaces Selection option, the copied formatting replaces the old formatting. To type new text, move the insertion point in front of the copied paragraph mark, then type.

Saving a Paragraph Format in a Glossary

If you want to use a certain paragraph format over and over again, you can save the paragraph mark (¶) as a glossary item. Then you can insert it any time you want to replace the format of an existing paragraph or type new text in front of it.

To save a paragraph format in a glossary, then use it to format new text:

1. Select the paragraph mark (¶) of the paragraph whose format you want to copy.

2. Use the Edit Glossary command to define the paragraph mark as a glossary item.

   (See Saving Text and Graphics for Repeated Use: Using Glossaries in Chapter 4 for more information about defining glossary items.)

3. When you want to use that format for new text, use the Edit Glossary command to insert the glossary item. If you selected an existing paragraph mark before inserting the glossary item, the copied formatting will replace the old formatting. If you want to type new text, move the insertion point in front of the copied paragraph mark, then type.

🔲 *Helpful Hint*

You can copy characters along with a formatted paragraph mark (¶) to a glossary for later use.

For example, you might want to copy a bullet character (Alt+249 on the numeric keypad makes a nice one) followed by a tab character and a formatted paragraph mark (•→¶) containing the indent and the tab settings you use for a bulleted list. Then, when you want to start a bulleted list, just use the Edit Glossary command to insert that glossary entry and type the new text in front of the paragraph mark.

Saving Paragraph Formatting as a Style

You can save both paragraph formatting and character formatting as a style in Word—then you can use that style over and over again to format new paragraphs. See Chapter 10, "Combining Character and Paragraph Formatting: Using Styles," for more information about creating and using styles.

## Chapter Ten

Combining Character and Paragraph Formatting: Using Styles

Word offers you a very powerful way to quickly apply both character and paragraph formats to paragraphs by defining and saving these formats as *styles*. Using styles has three advantages:

- When you apply a style, you can apply both character and paragraph formatting in one step to save time.

- You can use the same styles over and over again to give your documents a consistent format.

- If you change a style, Word automatically reformats all text with that style.

This chapter discusses

- how to define, apply, and change styles.

- how styles and templates are related.

WHAT ARE STYLES?

Styles are named sets of formatting instructions that you can use over and over again. Using a style is simple. Say you've formatted a paragraph to look like this:

Chapter 2

The text is bold, the font is New Century Schoolbook, the size is 14 points, the paragraph is indented from the left and right margins, and the text is centered and enclosed in a box. To use this format for all chapter headings, you could define this format as a style named *chapter,* then apply the *chapter* style to all your chapter heading paragraphs to make them look alike.

Using styles can save you a lot of time, because one style can contain a great deal of formatting. Styles can include tab settings, borders, positions fixed with the Format Position command (explained in Chapter 14), and any paragraph and character formats, such as indents, line spacing, fonts, bold, italic, and so forth.

All paragraphs in Word have a style attached to them. If you haven't applied any styles of your own, all paragraphs have Word's default style, the Normal style.

Word has many different routes to approach styles, as shown in Figures 10–1 through 10–3:

Word feature	Description
Format Define Styles command	Defines new styles; changes, deletes, and renames existing styles; merges styles from other files; saves styles in template files
Format Styles command	Applies styles to selected paragraphs and displays the Define Styles dialog box when you choose the Define button
Styles list in the Format Paragraph dialog box	Applies styles to selected paragraphs

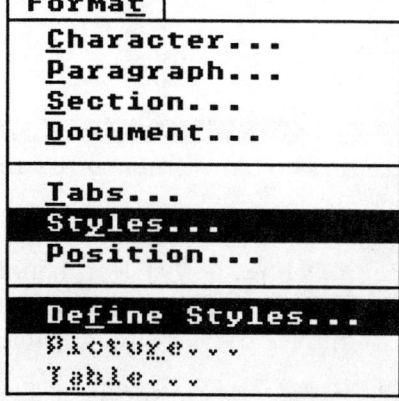

Figure 10–1.
Styles commands on the Format menu.

Figure 10–2.
Styles list in the
Format Paragraph
dialog box.

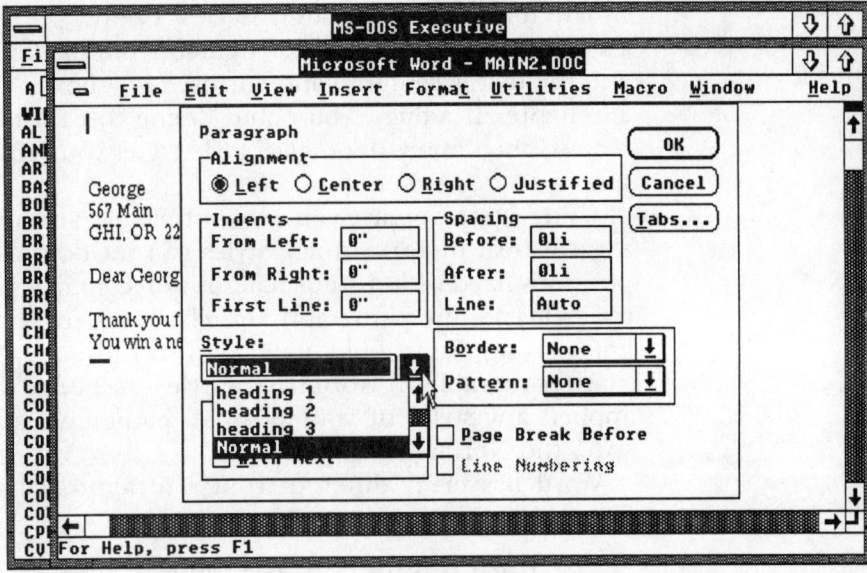

Figure 10–3.
Styles list on the
ruler.

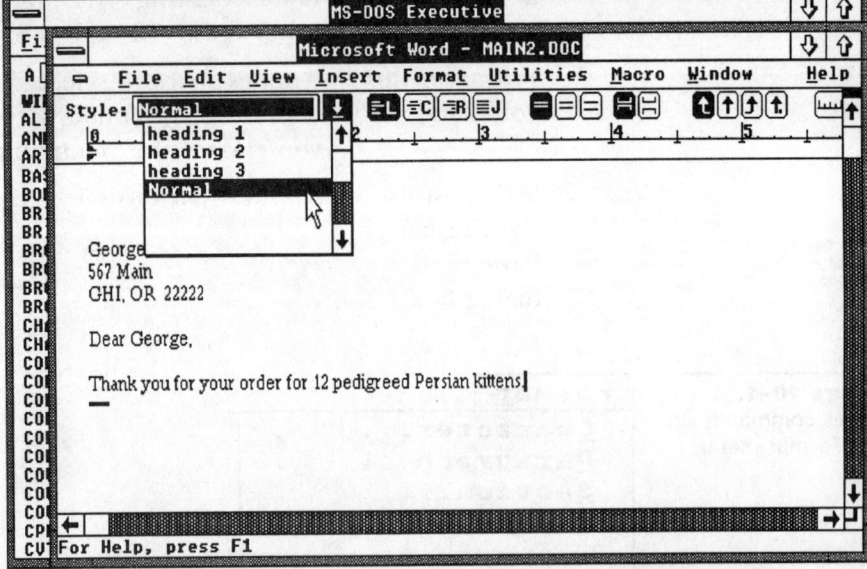

Styles list on the ruler	Defines new styles, changes existing styles, applies styles to selected paragraphs, and saves styles in the document file

Word automatically stores styles in the same file as the active document. You can also store styles in template files, as described in Styles and Templates later in this chapter.

STYLES PROVIDED WITH WORD

If you choose the Format Styles command, you'll see a list of styles in the dialog box, even if you haven't defined any of your own. These styles (shown in the Style Name list of Figure 10–4) are called *automatic styles* and are provided by Microsoft for you to use.

The Normal style is, as already mentioned, Word's default style that all paragraphs have until you apply a different style. You can use the heading automatic styles to format headings from which you can easily create outlines and tables of contents. (For more information, see Using Outlines in Word in Chapter 17 and Creating a Table of Contents in Chapter 19.) Word's automatic styles are stored in the default template file, NORMAL.DOT.

You can change the automatic styles to change the formats Word automatically gives to paragraphs and to headings. You can find out more about that in Changing a Style later in this chapter.

DEFINING A STYLE

The first step in using a style is to identify the format you want to save—to define a style. You can define a style in two ways:

Figure 10–4.
A list of automatic styles in the Format Styles dialog box.

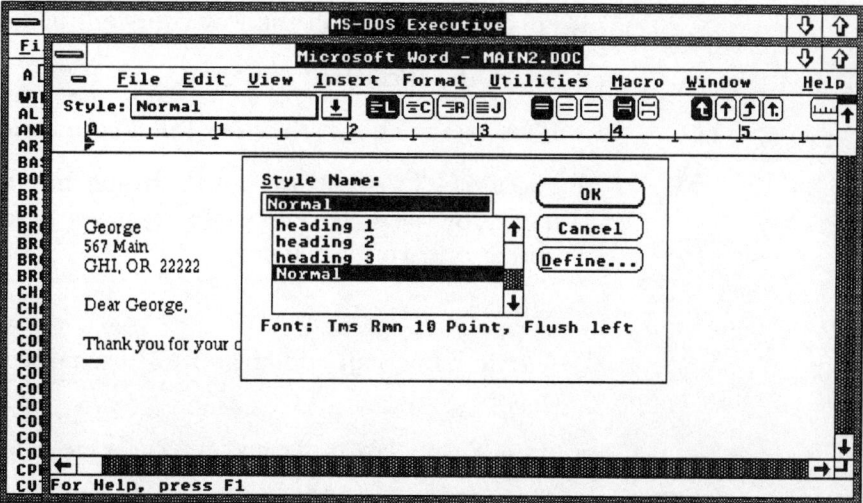

- by recording the formatting of a selected paragraph

- by choosing commands to specify a format

Because recording the formatting of a paragraph is the easiest way to define a style, we'll concentrate on that method first, then move on to defining a style with commands.

Defining a Style by Recording the Formatting of a Paragraph

The easiest way to define a style is to use a formatted paragraph as a model, then assign a name to the style, and save it. You can do this with the ruler or the Format Styles command.

When you format a paragraph to define a style, you can use any combination of character and paragraph format options from the ribbon, the ruler, or the Format Character, Format Paragraph, Format Tabs, and Format Position commands. The only rule is that all characters in the paragraph must have the same character format. You can't format part of the text one way and part another—you can't use half bold and half italic, for example, or different fonts in different words.

Defining a Style with the Ruler and a Formatted Paragraph

To define a style by saving the format of a paragraph using the ruler:

1. Format a paragraph the way you want it.

2. Select the formatted paragraph.

3. If necessary, choose the View Ruler command to display the ruler.

4. Use **Ctrl+S** or the mouse to activate the Style box, then type a name for the style. For example, if you want to save a style for quotations, you can type:

   quote

   A style name can contain up to 20 characters and may include spaces.

5. Press **Enter**. Word displays this message (shown in Figure 10–5):

   `Define style "stylename" based on selection?`

Figure 10–5.
Defining a style with
the ruler.

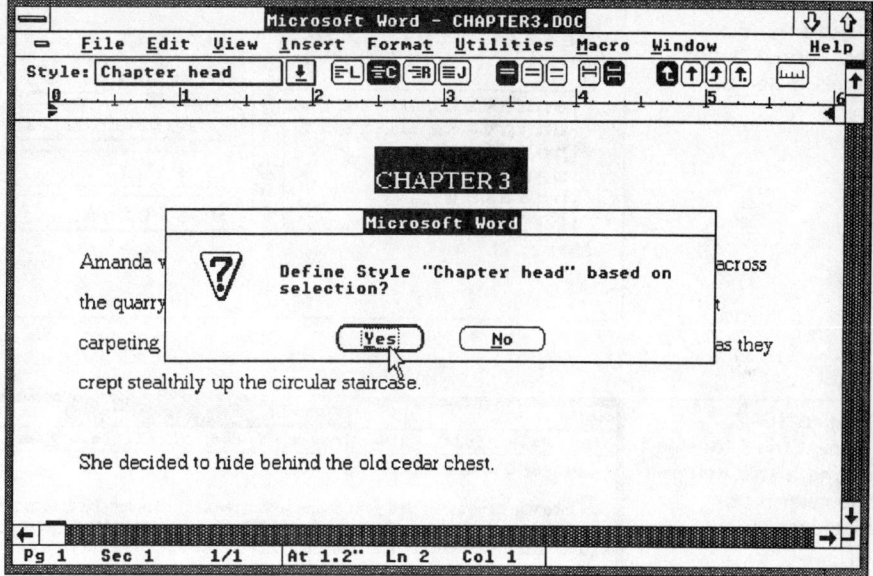

6. Click Yes or press **Y** to define the style.

Word saves the paragraph's format with the name you specify.

Defining a Style with the Format Define Styles Command and a Formatted Paragraph

To define a style by saving the format of a paragraph with the Format Define Styles command:

1. Format a paragraph the way you want it.

2. Select the formatted paragraph.

3. Choose the Format Define Styles command. Word displays the Define Styles dialog box, as shown in Figure 10–6. (You can also display this dialog box by choosing the Format Styles command, then choosing the Define button.) Note the description of the selected paragraph beneath the Style box.

4. Type a name for the new style in the Define Style Name box. For example, you might type:

   chapter heading

   A style name can contain up to 20 characters and may include spaces.

Figure 10–6.
The Format Define
Styles dialog box.

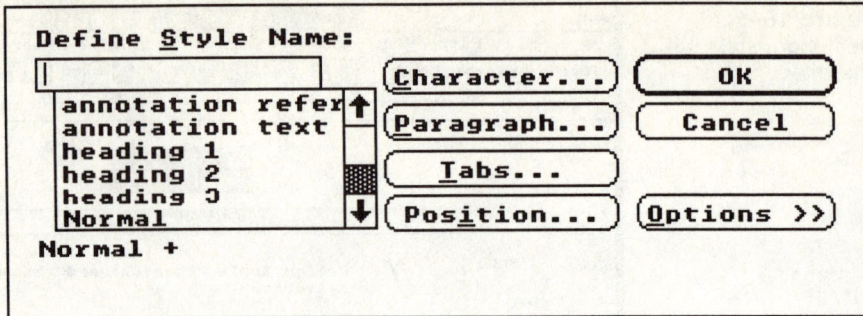

Figure 10–7.
Using Ctrl+S to
define a style when
the ruler is not
displayed.

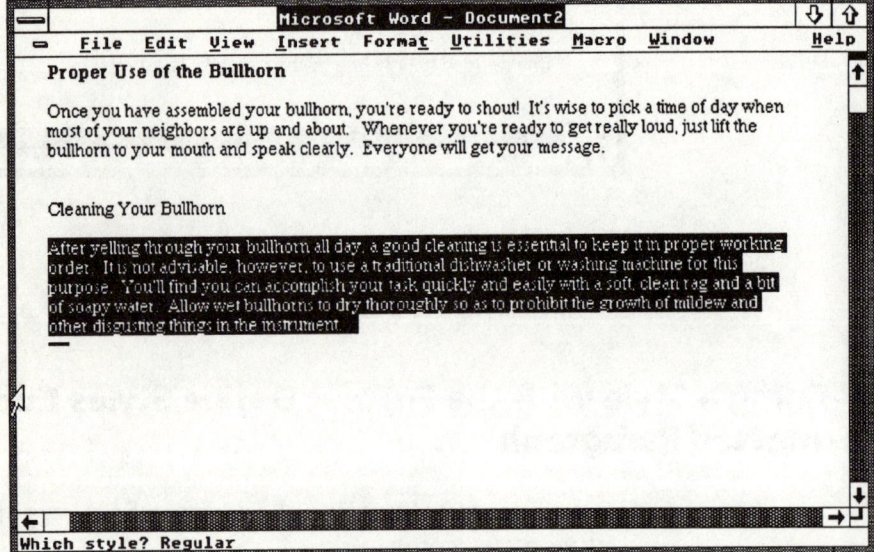

5. Click OK or press **Enter**.

Word saves the paragraph's format as a style that you can apply to other paragraphs.

Keyboard Shortcut

To quickly define a style when the ruler is not displayed:

1. Select a paragraph that has the format you want to save.

2. Press **Ctrl+S**. The message Which style? appears in the status bar, as shown in Figure 10–7. (If the ruler is displayed, **Ctrl+S** activates the style box instead.)

3. Type a name for the style in the status bar.

4. Press **Enter**. Word displays a message asking you whether you want to define the style based on the selected paragraph.

5. Click Yes or press **Y**.

EXAMPLE: Creating a Style

Let's say you want to create a paragraph style for a course catalog. You want the text to be small to fit in the catalog, so the style will specify 10-point type. The style will contain tabs to set the position of the time information and course description "columns," and the description part of the paragraph will "wrap," like this:

Swahili→   MWF 9-10 AM→   Introduction to the
                                       Swahili language. Stu-
                                       dents learn the basics
                                       of Swahili grammar and
                                       pronunciation. No
                                       prerequisites.

To create this style, you'd perform the following steps. (This example assumes that you haven't changed Word's standard margins and that you're using inches as the default measurement.)

1. Type the sample paragraph just shown, pressing the **Tab** key where the arrow (→) is shown. Let the lines wrap naturally—don't try to make anything line up and don't press the Enter key until you reach the end of the paragraph. Your text should look something like this:

    Swahili→   MWF 9-10 AM→   Introduction to the Swa-
    hili language. Students learn the basics of Swahili grammar and
    pronunciation. No prerequisites.

2. Select the paragraph.

3. Choose the Format Character command, type **10** in the Points box, then press **Enter**. This changes the font size to 10 points.

4. Choose the Format Paragraph command, type **4** in the From Left indent box, then type **−4** in the First Line indent box. This creates the hanging indent, wrapping the text in the last "column."

5. Choose Tabs, type **2**, choose Set, then type **4**, then choose Set, then click OK or press **Enter**. This sets left-aligned tabs at 2 inches and at 4 inches.

6. Choose the Format Define Styles command.

7. Type **course catalog** in the Define Style Name box, then click OK or press **Enter**.

You've created the course catalog style. It will be saved in the document file when you save your document.

Defining a Style with Buttons in the Define Styles Dialog Box

You can use buttons in the Format Define Styles dialog box to define a new style without formatting any text first. Here's how:

1. Choose the Format Define Styles command.

2. Type a name for the new style in the Define Style Name box.

3. Choose from the following options to develop the style's formatting:

   ■ If you want to specify character formats, choose Character to display the Format Character dialog box, choose the character format options you want, then press **Enter** to return to the Format Define Styles dialog box.

   ■ If you want to specify paragraph formats, choose Paragraph to display the Format Paragraph dialog box, choose the paragraph format options you want, then press **Enter** to return to the Format Define Styles dialog box.

   ■ If you want to set tabs, choose Tabs to display the Format Tabs dialog box, choose the tab options to set all the tabs, then press **Enter** to return to the Format Define Styles dialog box.

   ■ If you want to specify a position, choose Position to display the Format Position dialog box, choose the position options to specify a fixed position for the style, then press **Enter** to return to the Format Define Styles dialog box.

The description of the style (beneath the list box) changes as you add formats for the style.

4. When the description reflects the formats you want in the style, click OK or press **Enter**.

Basing a New Style on an Existing Style

If you want to use the basic format of one style but not modify the original style, you can base a new style on an existing style.

If you change a style on which other styles are based, all the styles will change to reflect the changes in the base style. For example, if you base a style called Quotation on a style called Sayings, then make the Sayings style bold, the Quotation style will also become bold to reflect the change in its base style.

To base a new style on an existing style:

1. Choose the Format Define Styles command.

2. Type a name for the new style in the Define Style Name box.

3. Choose Options to expand the dialog box, as shown in Figure 10–8.

Figure 10–8.
Basing one style on another.

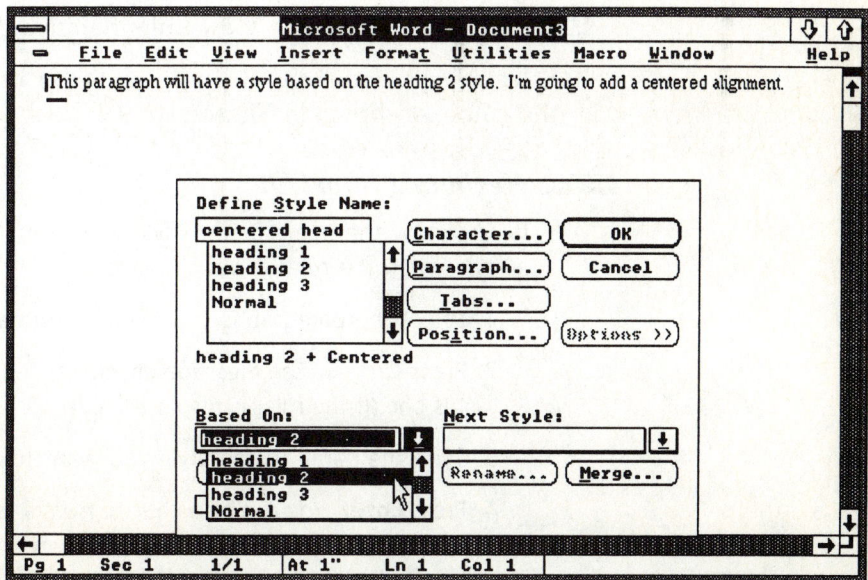

4. In the Based On box, type the name of the style you want to base your new style on or select the style's name from the drop-down list.

5. Choose the Character, Paragraph, Tabs, or Position commands to open dialog boxes and make any changes you want. You can also use the shortcut keys such as **Ctrl+B** for bold, **Ctrl+J** for justified text, **Ctrl+C** for centering, and so forth. The description beneath the list changes as you modify the style.

6. Click OK or press **Enter**.

APPLYING STYLES

Once you've saved a paragraph format as a style, you can apply that format to a paragraph you've already typed, or you can apply it to a paragraph mark before you type the text. You can apply styles with a command or with the ruler.

Applying Styles with the Ruler

To apply styles using the style list on the ruler:

1. Select the paragraphs you want to format.

2. If necessary, choose the View Ruler command to display the ruler.

3. Select a style from the drop-down Styles list at the left side of the ruler, as shown in Figure 10–9.

Keyboard Shortcut

If you know the name of the style you want, you can quickly apply a style when the ruler is not displayed:

1. Select the paragraphs you want to format.

2. Press **Ctrl+S**. The message Which style? will appear in the status bar. (If the ruler is displayed, **Ctrl+S** activates the style box.)

3. Type the name of the style you want to apply.

4. Press **Enter**. You can also choose from a list of styles by pressing **Ctrl+S** twice, then selecting a style in the Format Styles dialog box.

Figure 10–9.
Applying a style with
the ruler.

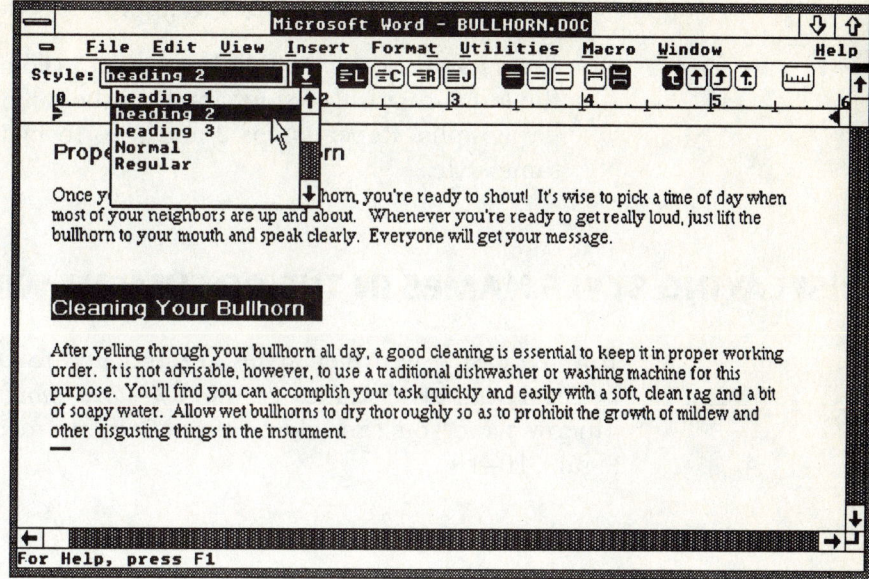

Applying Styles with the Format Styles Command

To apply a style with the Format Styles command:

1. Select the paragraphs you want to format.

2. Choose the Format Styles command.

3. Select the style name from the list.

4. Click OK or press **Enter** to apply the style.

▄▄▄ *Mouse Speed Tip*

To quickly apply a style and close the dialog box at the same time,
double-click the style name in the Format Styles list box.

Applying Styles Repeatedly

If you want to apply the same style several different places in your
document, you can use the **F4** key or the Repeat Styles command on
the Edit menu to speed up the process:

1. Apply the style to the first selection.

2. Select the next paragraphs to apply the style to.

3. Press **F4** or choose the Edit Repeat Styles command. Word repeats the last formatting action, applying the same style to the selected paragraphs. Repeat steps 2 and 3 to format more text with the same style.

DISPLAYING STYLE NAMES IN THE DOCUMENT WINDOW

You can easily see which styles are attached to your text at a glance by displaying style names in the *style area pane,* which is a vertical window pane you can add to the left of the text area, as shown in Figure 10–10.

Opening the Style Area Pane

To display style names in the style area pane:

1. Choose the View Preferences command.

2. In the Style Area Width box, type a measurement to indicate the

Figure 10–10.
Displaying the names of attached styles in the style area window.

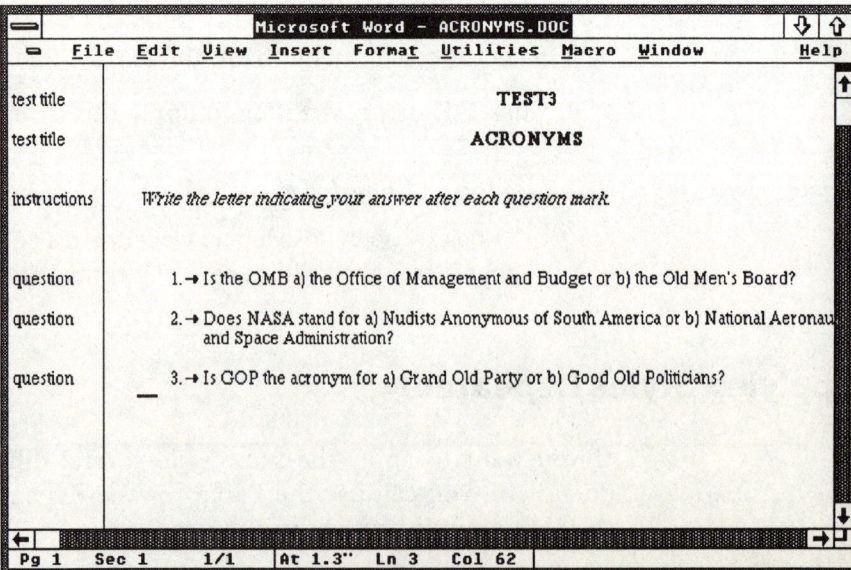

width of the style area (1 inch is a good width to start with—you can always adjust this later).

3. Click OK or press **Enter**. Word opens the style area pane.

Resizing or Closing the Style Area Pane

You can change the size of the style area pane with the keys or with the mouse, or you can close the style area pane, removing style names from the document window.

Changing the Size of the Style Area Pane with Keys

To change the size of the style area pane with the keys:

1. Choose the View Preferences command.

2. In the Style Area Width box, type a new measurement to change the size of the style area. Type zero (**0**) to close the style area.

Changing the Size of the Style Area Pane with the Mouse

To change the size of the style area pane with the mouse:

1. Move the mouse pointer to the style area split line. The pointer changes shape, as shown in Figure 10–11.

2. Drag the split line to the new location. If you want to close the style area pane, drag the split line to the left edge of the document window.

CHANGING A STYLE

You can change any style, including the styles provided with Word—even Word's default Normal style. When you change a style, Word automatically updates every paragraph with that style in your document.

For example, to change the font and point size Word automatically uses for a new document, you can change Word's Normal style. See Example: Changing a Style later in this chapter.

If you change a style on which other styles are based, all the other styles will reflect the changes in the base style. For example, if you base a style called Quotation on a style called Sayings, then make the

Figure 10–11.
Changing the size of
the style area
window with the
mouse.

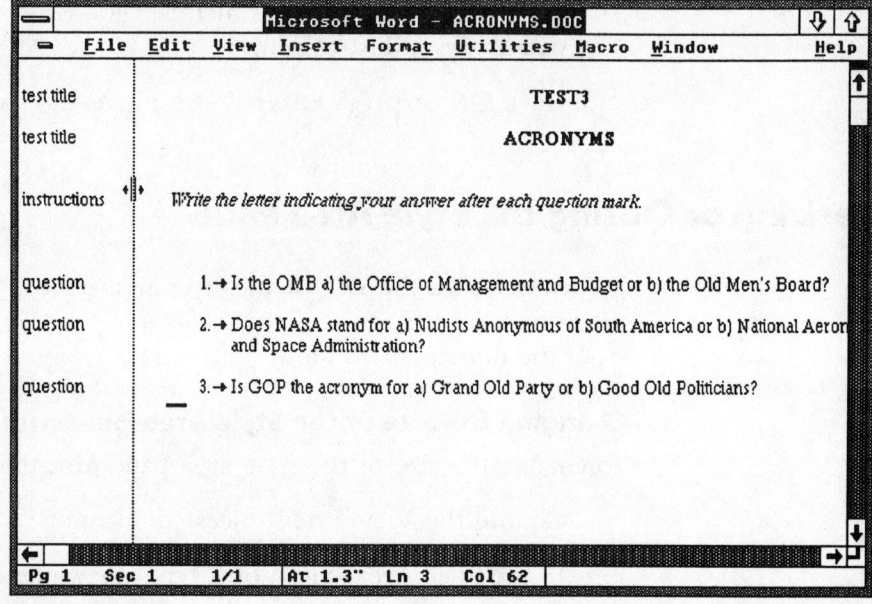

Sayings style bold, the Quotation style will also become bold to reflect the change in its base style.

You can change a style in two ways:

- by changing a paragraph that has the style, then recording the new format with the same style name, using the Format Define Styles command or the Styles list on the ruler

- by changing the style in the Format Define Styles dialog box, using the Character, Paragraph, Tabs, or Position buttons

Because changing a paragraph, then recording the changes with the same style name is the easiest way, we'll concentrate on that first.

Changing a Style by Recording Changes with the Same Style Name

To change a style by recording changes with the same style name:

1. Select a paragraph with the style you want to change.

2. Change the paragraph the way you want to change the style. For example, if you want to add bold to a style, format the paragraph to be bold.

3. Do one of the following:

- If the ruler is displayed, use the mouse or press **Ctrl+S** to activate the Style list, select the name of the style, then press **Enter**.

- Choose the Format Styles command, then select the name of the style from the list, then click OK or press **Enter**.

- If the ruler is not displayed and you know the name of the style, press **Ctrl+S**, type the style name after the `Which style?` message in the status bar, then press **Enter**.

Word displays a message asking you if you want to redefine the style based on the selection.

4. Click Yes or press **Y**.

EXAMPLE: Changing a Style

Let's say you want to change Word's automatic Normal style to use a 12-point Courier font, to have a first-line indent of ½ inch, and add ¼ inch of space after the paragraph so you won't have to use blank paragraphs to separate text paragraphs.

To change the Normal style, you'd perform the following steps.

1. Choose the Format Define Styles command.

2. Select Normal from the Define Style Name list.

3. Choose Character to open the Format Character dialog box.

4. Select Courier from the drop-down Fonts list, select 12 from the drop-down Points list, then click OK or press **Enter** to return to the Format Define Styles dialog box.

5. Choose Paragraph to open the Format Paragraph dialog box.

6. Type **.5**, in the First Line indent box, type **.25** in the Space After box, then click OK or press **Enter** to return to the Format Define Styles dialog box.

7. Click OK or press **Enter** to save the changes and close the dialog box.

All paragraphs with the Normal style or with another style based on the Normal style will change to reflect the new formats.

Changing a Style with Buttons in the Format Define Styles Dialog Box

To change a style by using buttons in the Format Define Styles dialog box:

1. Choose the Format Define Styles command.

2. Select the name of the style you want to change from the list.

3. Choose the Character, Paragraph, Tabs, and Position buttons as necessary, then choose new options in the dialog boxes to change the style. You can also use shortcut keys such as **Ctrl+I** for italic, **Ctrl+R** for right-aligned, **Ctrl+O** for space before, and so forth. The description of the style (beneath the list box) changes as you add and subtract formats from the style.

4. When the style is the way you want it, click OK or press **Enter**. Word changes the format of all paragraphs with that style.

Helpful Hint

If you want to make changes to several styles without closing the Format Define Styles dialog box, choose Options, then choose Define after making changes to a style. When you're through changing styles, click OK or press **Enter** to close the dialog box.

Renaming a Style

There may be times when you want to give a style a name different from the one you originally assigned to it.

To rename a style:

1. Choose the Format Define Styles command.

2. Select the style you want to rename from the list.

3. Choose Options to expand the dialog box.

4. Choose Rename. Another dialog box appears, as shown in Figure 10–12.

5. Type the new name for the style.

Figure 10–12.
Renaming a style.

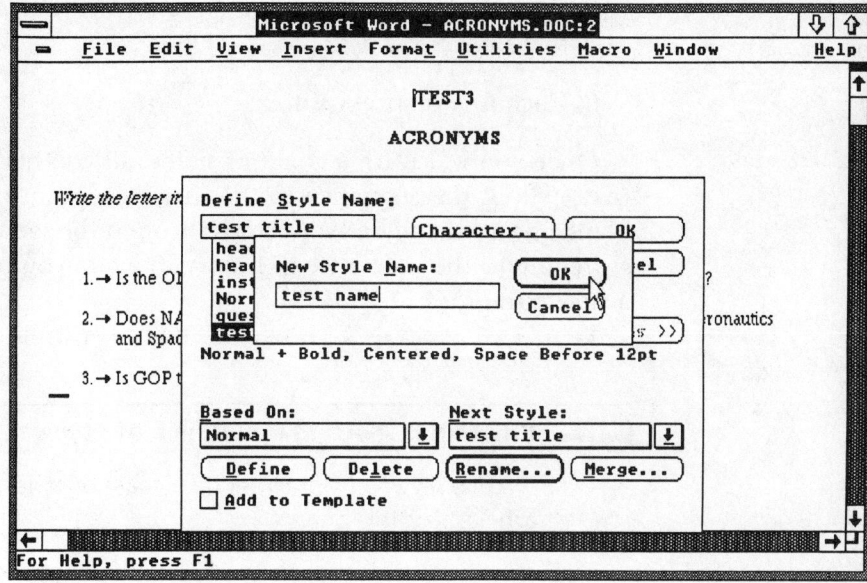

6. Click OK or press **Enter** to return to the Format Define Styles dialog box.

7. Click OK or press **Enter** to close the Format Define Styles dialog box.

SETTING UP A CHAIN OF STYLES TO FORMAT SEQUENTIAL PARAGRAPHS

For certain types of documents, you may develop a sequence of styles that format paragraphs as you type them, using the Next Style option in the Define Styles dialog box. By default, the style name appearing in the Next Style box is the same as the style in the Style box—that's because Word assumes that you probably want to apply the same format to the next paragraph when you press **Enter**.

To set up a chain of styles:

1. Choose the Format Styles command.

2. Choose Define.

3. Select the first style you want from the list.

4. Choose Options.

5. Choose the style you want to use to format the next style from the Next Style list.

6. Click OK or press **Enter**.

Once you've set up a chain of styles, all you have to do is apply the first style in the sequence to the insertion point (make sure it's on a blank line at the time). Word steps through the sequence, automatically switching to the next style in the chain when you press Enter to begin a new paragraph.

Here's an example of how you might set up a chain of styles.

EXAMPLE: Setting Up a Chain of Styles

Let's say you want to set up a chain of styles to format newspaper articles like this one:

Intergalactic Ice Cream Raid?
by *Jan Foster*

The manager of the Calories Galore ice cream shop in Okidoki, Oklahoma, claims to have been visited by a customer from outer space last Saturday night.

Just before closing time, a small orange creature with large ears and long sticky fingers entered the shop, according to Manager Joel Geffs. The 3-foot-high creature sampled several varieties of ice cream, ate a package of napkins, then disappeared into the night.

To set up a chain of styles for a newspaper article like this, you might:

1. Define three styles: One called *Headline,* with the format for the first paragraph; one called *Byline,* with the format for the second paragraph; and one called *Body,* with the format for the body of the article.

2. In the Define Styles dialog box, select the Headline style, choose Options, type **Byline** in the Next Style box, and choose Define.

3. Select the Byline style, type **Body** in the Next Style box, and choose Define.

4. Select the Body style and make sure Body is the name in the Next Style box. This means the Body style will be repeated each time the writer presses Enter.

5. Choose Close to close the dialog box. (If you choose OK, Word applies the style selected in the list to the selected paragraphs in your document.)

When this chain of styles is set up, you can apply the Headline style to the insertion point before typing the first paragraph (the headline), and the byline and body of the article would be automatically formatted. Each time you press Enter, Word applies the next style to the new paragraph.

REMOVING ADDITIONAL FORMATTING FROM STYLED PARAGRAPHS

You can apply any type of formatting after you've attached a style to a paragraph. Formatting added with a Format command overrides the style's formatting, so if you want to see only the style's formatting, you'll have to remove all formatting except for the style.

To remove any formatting you've added to "styled" paragraphs and return the paragraphs to the style's format:

1. Select the paragraphs.

2. Press **Ctrl+X** to remove all formatting added after the style was applied.

RETURNING PARAGRAPHS TO THE NORMAL STYLE

To return paragraphs to the Normal style:

1. Select the paragraphs.

2. Apply the Normal style from the ruler, with the Format Styles command or with the **Ctrl+S** shortcut.

DELETING STYLES

If you've created so many styles that the list in the Format Styles dialog box is getting too long, you should delete the styles you no longer use.

To delete a style you've created:

1. Choose the Format Define Styles command.

2. Choose Options to expand the dialog box.

3. Select the style you want to delete from the list.

4. Choose Delete. Word displays a dialog box asking if you want to delete the style.

5. Click Yes or press **Y**.

6. Repeat steps 3 through 5 to delete all the styles you don't want.

7. Click OK or press **Enter** to close the dialog box.

You can't delete one of Word's automatic styles, such as the Normal style.

USING STYLES FROM ANOTHER DOCUMENT

When you create a style, that style is attached only to the document you're working with at the time. If you're working with one document and decide you want to use the styles you created for another document, you can easily add those styles to the new document.

Note: The incoming styles take precedence, so incoming styles replace any styles that have the same name.

To use styles from another document:

1. Choose the Format Define Styles command.

2. Choose Options to expand the dialog box.

3. Choose Merge. A new dialog box appears, as shown in Figure 10–13.

4. Select a directory and a file name to specify the document containing the styles you want to use. Word displays this message to make sure you know what you're doing: Merge replaces styles with the same name. Continue?

Figure 10–13.
Merging styles from
another document.

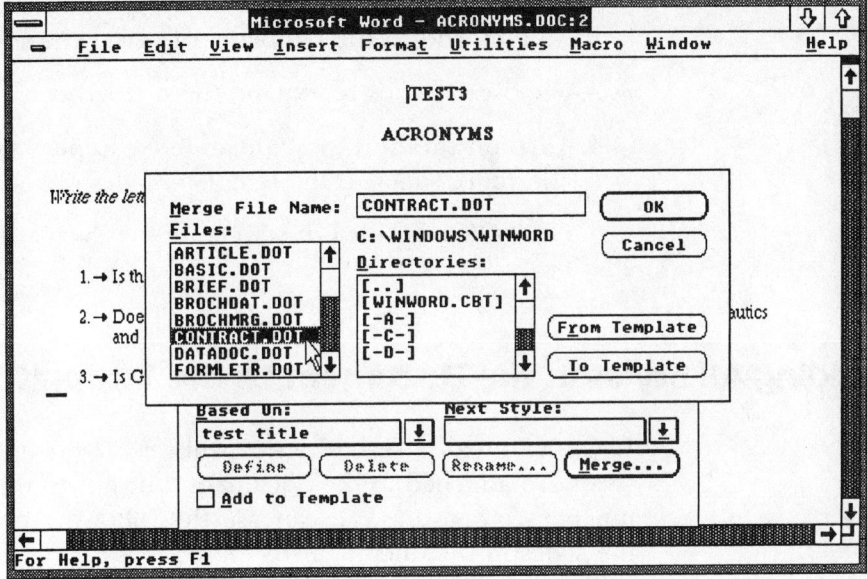

5. Click Yes or press **Y**.

6. Click OK or press **Enter** to close the Format Define Styles dialog box.

STYLES AND TEMPLATES

Styles are automatically saved in the document file that you're working with when you create the styles. You can also tell Word to save styles in the template that your document is based on—this makes the styles available to all documents based on that template. If your document is based on the default NORMAL.DOT template, saving the styles in the template makes those styles available to all Word documents. You can add styles to the template one at a time, or add all styles associated with the document to the template at once.

Adding Individual Styles to the Template

To add individual styles to the template your document is based on:

1. Choose the Format Define Styles command.

2. In the Define Style Name box, type the name of the style you want to add to the template, or select the style from the list.

3. Choose Options to expand the dialog box.

4. Turn on the Add to Template box. Repeat steps 2 through 4 to add more styles to the template if desired.

5. Click OK or press **Enter** to close the Format Define Styles dialog box.

Adding All Styles in the Document to the Template

If you've created several styles while your document is open, those styles are attached to the document, but not to the template the document is based on. You can use the following procedure to add all the styles in the document to the template.

To add all styles attached to the document to the template:

1. Choose the Format Define Styles command.

2. Choose Options to expand the dialog box.

3. Choose Merge.

4. Turn on the To Template option. Word displays this message to make sure you know what you're doing: Merge replaces styles with the same name. Continue?

5. Click Yes or press **Y**.

6. Click OK or press **Enter** to close the Format Define Styles dialog box.

Adding All the Styles in the Template to the Document

Your document may be based on a template that contains many different styles. This makes these styles available to the document, but they are not saved in the document file. If you want to add all these styles to the document file, you can use the following procedure. You might want to do this if you want to base the document on a new template but keep all the styles used in the document.

1. Choose the Format Define Styles command.

Figure 10–14.
Choosing Styles from
the Print list.

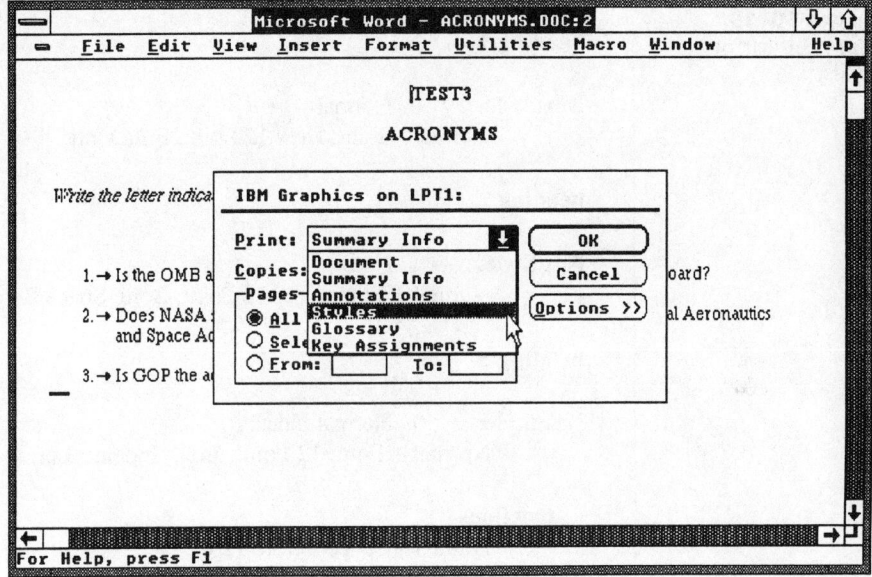

2. Choose Options to expand the dialog box.

3. Choose Merge.

4. Turn on the From Template box. Word displays this message to make sure you know what you're doing: Merge replaces styles with the same name. Continue?

5. Click Yes or press **Y**.

6. Click OK or press **Enter** to close the Format Define Styles dialog box.

PRINTING A LIST OF STYLES

You can print the list of styles attached to a document. Word prints not only the names of the styles, but also their description.

To print a list of styles:

1. Open the document whose styles you want to print.

2. Choose the File Print command.

Figure 10–15.
A printed list of
styles.

heading 1

NextStyle: Normal
                    Normal + Font: Helv 12 Point, Bold Underline, Space Before 12pt

heading 2

NextStyle: Normal
                    Normal + Font: Helv 12 Point, Bold, Space Before 6pt

heading 3

NextStyle: Normal Indent
                    Normal + Font: 12 Point, Bold, Indent: Left 0.25"

instructions
                    Normal + Space Before 12pt

Normal
                    Font: Tms Rmn 10 Point, Flush left

question
                    Normal + Indent: Left 0.5" First -0.25", Space Before 12pt

test title
                    Normal + Bold, Centered, Space Before 12pt

3. Select Styles from the drop-down Print list, as shown in Figure 10–14.

4. Click OK or press **Enter** to begin printing.

Word prints a list of styles similar to those shown in Figure 10–15.

Chapter Eleven

Section Formatting and Document Formatting

In previous chapters, you learned how to format characters and paragraphs. Word documents also contain section and document formats. In this chapter, you'll learn

- how to divide your document into sections and apply special section formats

- how to create multiple columns and format those columns

- how to format entire documents

FORMATTING SECTIONS

When you want part of your document to have a different page layout from the rest, you separate that part into a different *section,* then you format that section. For example, you may want part of your document to be in two columns and part to be in single-column format. Section formatting controls

- headers and footers (sometimes called running heads and running feet)

- the number of columns on a page

- line numbers

- whether footnotes print at the ends of sections

- vertical alignment of text on pages

Figure 11–1 shows a page from a document divided into sections. The first section (containing the headline and wide paragraph) has one column of text. The second section has two columns.

If you don't separate your document into sections, Word considers your document to be one section. You'll probably still want to use some of the section commands to format the entire document.

When you create sections, you'll follow these two steps:

1. Insert a section break to separate the sections.

2. Format the sections.

You use the Insert Break command to insert a section break, and you use the Format Section command to make the sections look the way you want them.

Dividing Your Document into Sections

When you want to begin a new section, you use the Insert Break command to insert a section break, which ends the previous section. Then tell Word where you want the next section to print.

To insert a section break:

1. Place the insertion point where you want to insert a section break.

Figure 11–1.
A document divided
into sections.

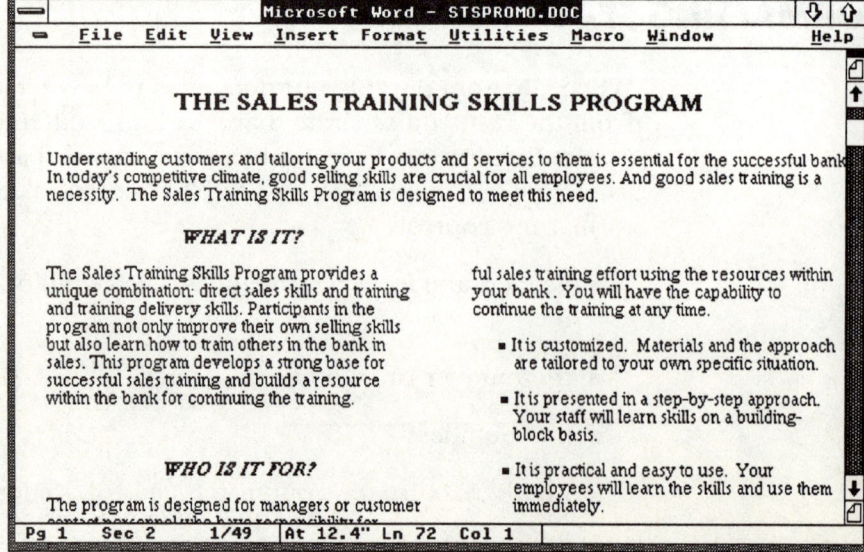

2. Choose the Insert Break command.

3. In the Section Break box, choose one of the following options to specify where you want the next section (the text following the section break) to begin:

Choose	**To start the next section**
Next Page	On the next page.
Continuous	On the same page as the previous section.
Even Page	On the next even-numbered page.
Odd Page	On the next odd-numbered page.

You can always change where a section starts later with the Format Section command, so don't worry about making a final decision at this point.

4. Click OK or press **Enter**. A section break marker (a double dotted line) appears just above the insertion point. You can see a section break marker in Figure 11–2.

Word changes the status area to tell you which section contains the insertion point. For example, the lower left corner of the screen displays something like Pg 1 Sec 2 26/50, indicating that the insertion

Figure 11–2.
A section break marker divides a document into separate sections.

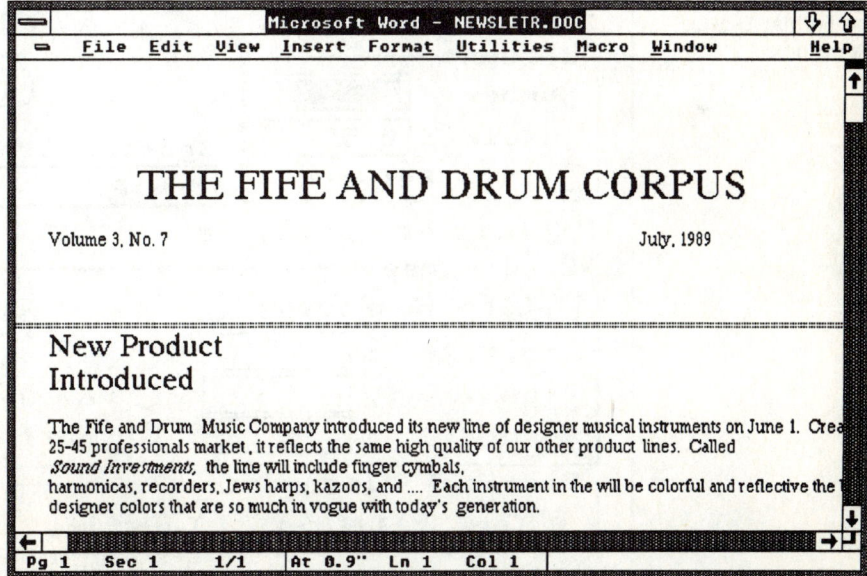

point is on Page 1 of Section 2, on the 26th page of a document that contains 50 pages.

When you have inserted a section break to tell Word where to end one section and begin the next, you're ready to format your sections. All section formatting is controlled by the Format Section dialog box, shown in Figure 11–3.

The options you choose in the Format Section dialog box affect the section that the insertion point is in at the time. If you don't separate your text into sections, Word considers your document to be one section—in that case, the options you choose apply to your entire document.

▅▅▅▟ *Mouse Speed Tip*

You can quickly open the Format Section dialog box by double-clicking on the section break marker (the double dotted line). The dialog box that appears controls the format of the text preceding the marker.

Formatting Text in Columns

In word processing, the term *column* means any text in which lines are "stacked" on top of one another. Microsoft Word for Windows enables

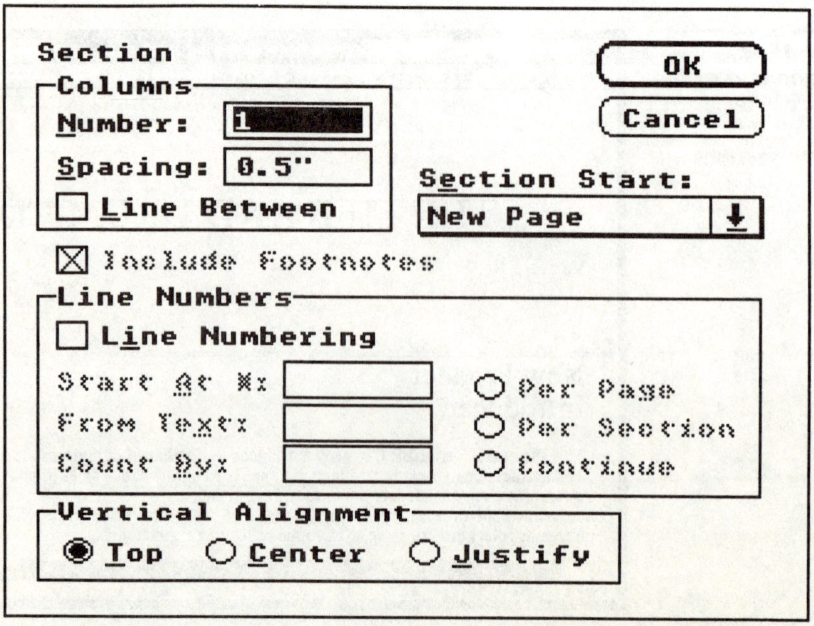

Figure 11–3.
The Format Section
dialog box.

you to create several types of columns. You can use the Format Section command to set up columns of equal width in which the text "flows" from the bottom of one column to the top of the next, as in a newspaper (these are sometimes called "snaking columns"). This section shows you how to work with flowing columns of text. If you want to create different types of columns, use one of the following commands:

To create	Use
Items arranged in rows and columns or side-by-side text in columns of unequal widths	The Insert Table command (described in Chapter 13).
Very small tables of simple text	Tabs on the ruler or the Format Paragraph command (described in Chapter 9).

Planning for Columns

When you plan for columns, keep in mind that you're working with a limited amount of space—the width of your page. Be sure to calculate spacing for

■ left and right margins and gutters

■ all columns

■ space between columns

Figure 11–4 illustrates a way to lay out space for columns.

Changing the Number of Columns

Although you can set the number of columns before you type the text in a section, you'll generally find it easier to type all your information, then place it in columns. This technique makes it easier to see how the column width and the space between columns looks on the pages.

To change the number of columns:

1. Move the insertion point into the section you want to change. If your document is not divided into sections, the entire document is affected.

2. Choose the Format Section command.

3. In the Column Number box, type the number of columns you want.

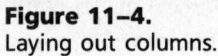

Figure 11–4.
Laying out columns.

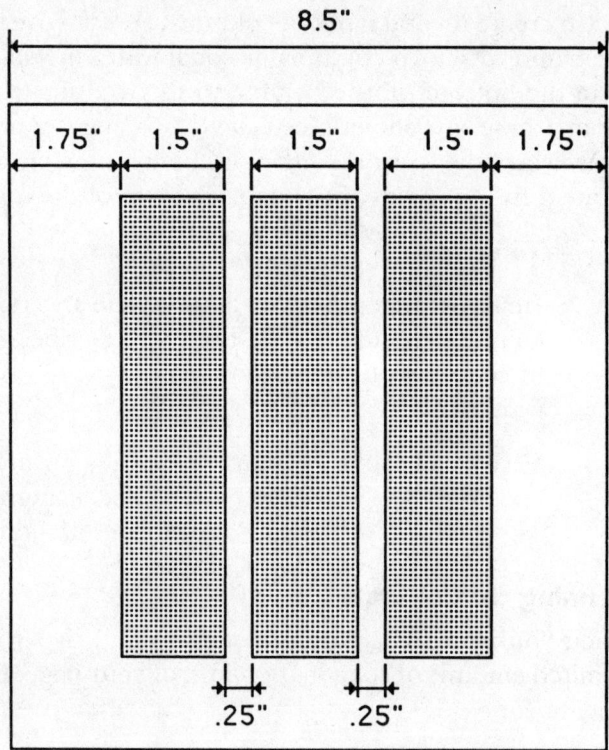

4. If you want to change the default spacing between columns, type a new measurement in the Spacing box. For example, if you want ¼ inch of white space between columns, type **.25**.

5. Click OK or press **Enter**.

Don't panic if you only see one column of text on the screen after you've specified two or more. You can't see multiple columns in normal view. You have to switch to page view or print preview for that. Figures 11–5 and 11–6 show columns in page view and print preview.

To switch to page view:

■ Choose the View Page command.

To switch to print preview:

■ Choose the File Print Preview command.

When you use multiple columns in a document, you'll probably find it easier to edit and format text in page view, where you can see changes to columns more easily. You can learn more about working in page view or print preview in Chapter 14.

Figure 11–5.
Multiple columns in page view.

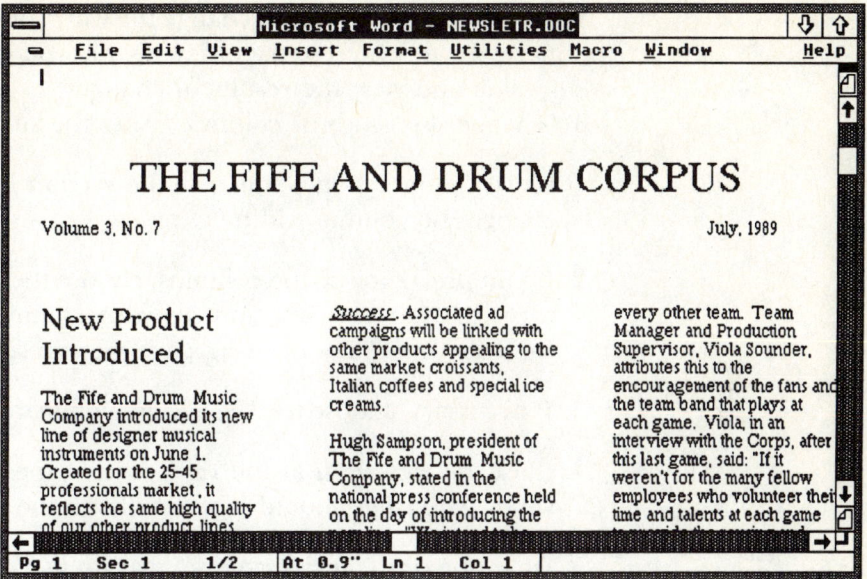

Figure 11–6.
Multiple columns in print preview.

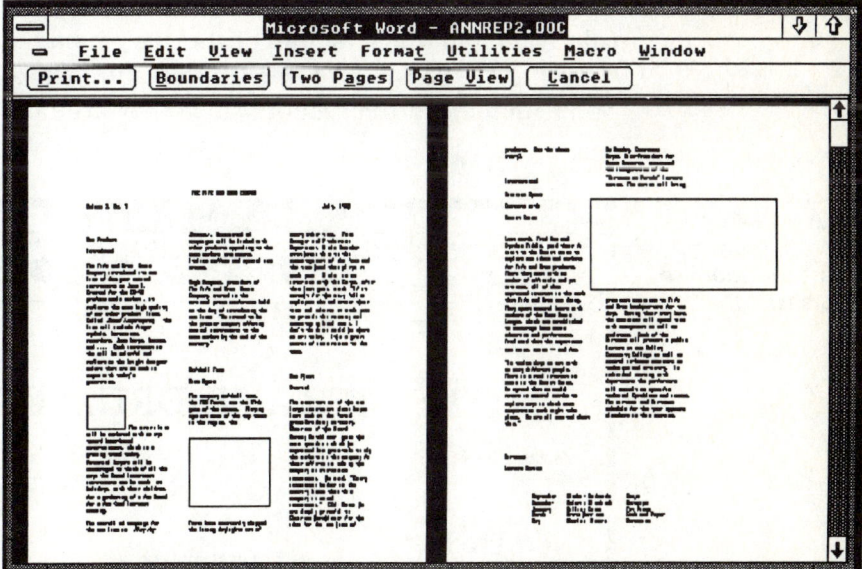

Changing the Width of Columns

You can change the widths of flowing columns by changing the document margins and the space between columns, or you can change the width of columns with the ruler, which is much simpler.

Before you use the ruler to change the width of columns in a section, you may want to switch to page view so that you can see your columns side by side and view the results of changes.

To change the width of columns using the ruler:

1. Move the insertion point into the section in which you want to change the column width.

2. If you prefer to see the columns, choose the View Page command to switch to page view and see your columns side by side. (You can learn more about using page view in Chapter 14.)

3. If necessary, choose the View Ruler command to display the ruler.

4. Click the view icon at the right side of the ruler to switch ruler views. The ruler should look similar to the one in Figure 11–7.

5. Drag one of the inside column margin markers to a new location to change the width of the columns.

You can also change the width of columns by switching to the other ruler view and dragging one of the margin markers to a new position.

Changing the width of one column automatically changes the width of all columns in the section, since they are flowing columns.

Figure 11–7.
Using the ruler to adjust the width of columns.

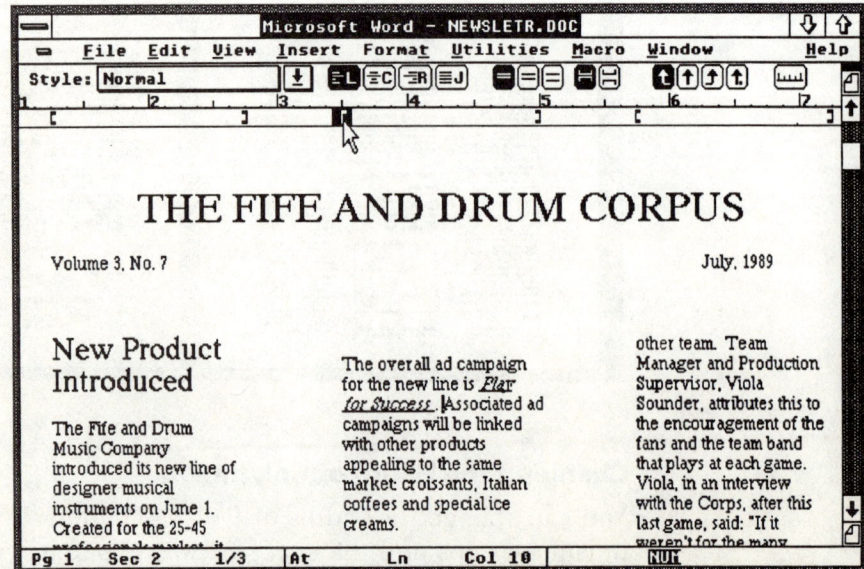

Adding Lines Between Columns

To add a line between columns:

1. Move the insertion point into the section in which you want to add lines between columns.

2. Choose the Format Section command.

3. Turn on the Line Between option.

4. Click OK or press **Enter**.

Figure 11–8 shows an example of lines drawn between columns.

Changing Column Breaks

Word automatically breaks a column when the text reaches the bottom margin on the page and starts the new column at the top margin. If Word's automatic column breaks don't meet your needs, you can insert your own column break marker wherever you want in normal view or in page view.

To insert a column break:

1. Place the insertion point where you want the column break.

2. Do one of the following:

Figure 11–8.
Lines between
columns.

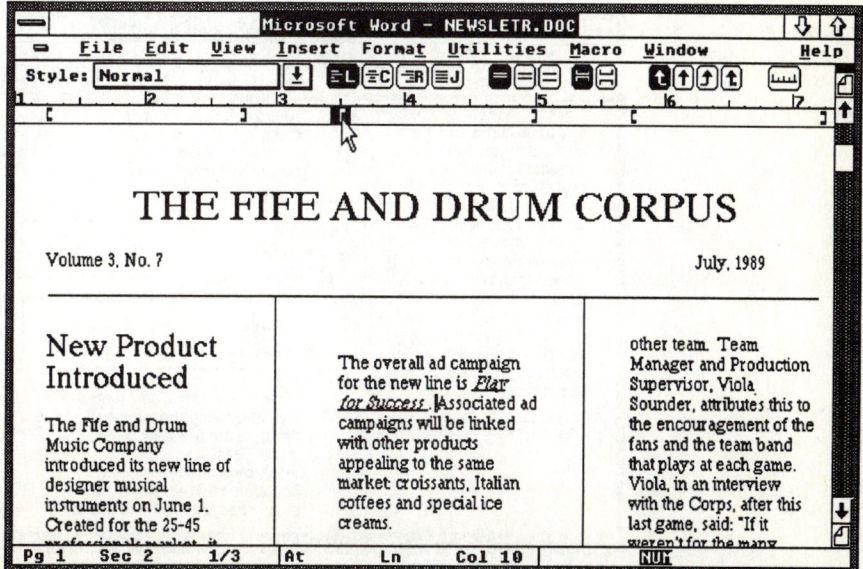

- Press **Ctrl+Shift+Enter**.

or

- Choose the Insert Break command, choose the Column Break option (as shown in Figure 11–9), then click OK or press **Enter**.

Word inserts a column break marker (a dotted line the width of the column).

4. Click OK or press **Enter**.

To delete a column break you've inserted:

1. Move the mouse pointer into the selection bar next to the column break marker and click to select it or use the direction keys to move the insertion point onto the mark.

2. Press the **Delete** key.

Setting the Vertical Alignment of Text in a Section

You can use the Format Section command to control how Word positions text vertically on a page. You can also position text this way by

Figure 11–9.
Inserting a column break.

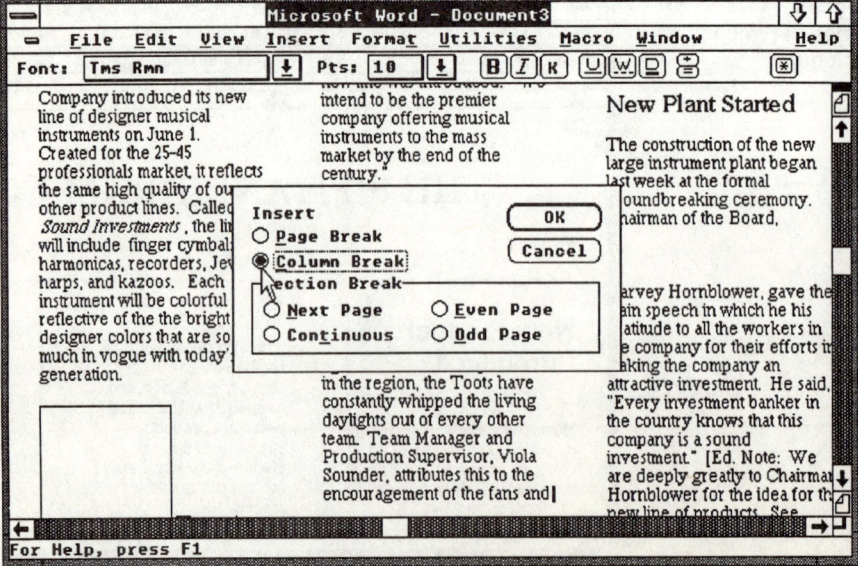

adding blank space before and after lines of text, but if you use the Format Section command, Word centers it for you.

This option is especially useful for creating title pages where you want to center the text vertically as well as horizontally. Figure 11–10 shows a title page in which the text has been centered vertically by placing it in a separate section and choosing centered vertical alignment with the Format Section command.

To specify the vertical alignment of text in a section:

1. Move the insertion point into the section that you want to affect.

2. Choose the Format Section command.

3. In the Vertical Alignment box, choose one of the following options:

Option	Description
Top	Aligns the first line of text with the top margin (just like any normal page).
Center	Centers the lines on a page between the top and bottom margins.
Justify	Adds space between paragraphs to align the first line of text with the top margin and the bottom line of text with the bottom margin.

4. Click OK or press **Enter**.

You may need to insert page breaks or adjust the Section Start settings to control the amount of text on a page and use these options effectively.

Adding Other Section Formats

Although headers, footers, footnote positions, and page numbers are controlled by the Format Section command, they are also affected by other commands, so they deserve chapters of their own. You'll find more information about these subjects in the following sections:

To find out about	See
Headers and footers	Adding Headers or Footers in Chapter 15.

Figure 11–10.
A title page section
with center vertical
alignment.

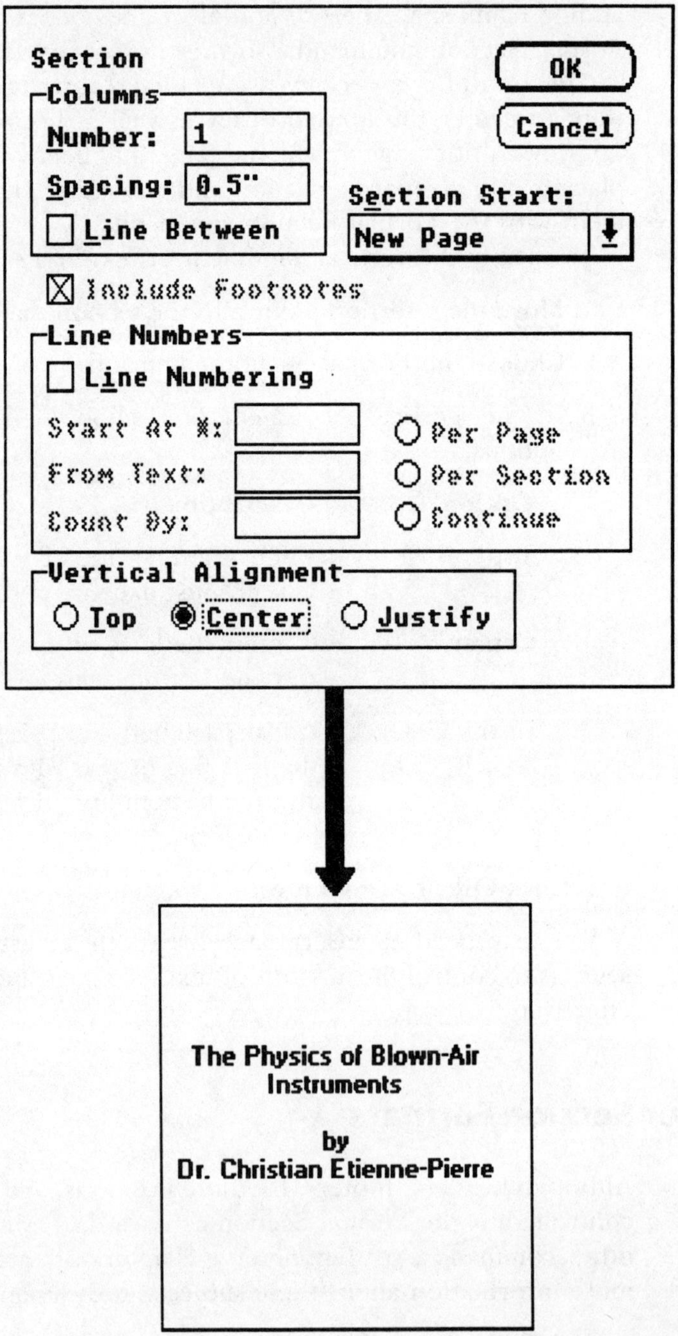

Section
┌─**Columns**─────────────────┐
Number: `1`

Spacing: `0.5"`

☐ **L**ine Between   **Section Start:**

`New Page` `↓`

☒ **I**nclude Footnotes

┌─**Line Numbers**────────────────────┐
☐ **L**ine Numbering

Start At %: `          `   ○ Per **P**age

From Text: `          `   ○ Per **S**ection

Count By: `          `   ○ **C**ontinue

┌─**Vertical Alignment**──────────────┐
○ **T**op   ◉ **Center**   ○ **J**ustify

[**OK**]

[**Cancel**]

The Physics of Blown-Air
Instruments

by
Dr. Christian Etienne-Pierre

Footnotes	Adding Footnotes in Chapter 15.
Page numbers	Adding Page Numbers in Chapter 15.
Line numbering	Numbering Lines in Chapter 17.

Reuniting Sections by Deleting Section Breaks

You can always delete a section break and unite sections again. Just like a paragraph mark, a section break contains the formatting for a section. So when you delete a section break, you remove all the formatting associated with it, and the text becomes part of the following section. To delete a section break and unite sections:

1. Select the section break marker.

2. Press the **Delete** key.

Copying Section Formats

You can copy the section break marker and its associated formatting to another location by using the Edit Copy and Edit Paste commands, or you can copy and save it by using the Edit Glossary command to save it as a glossary item (see Chapter 4 for more information about moving text and using glossaries).

For example, if you've set up a section with three columns, lines between columns, and ¾″ white space between columns, you could copy the section break marker containing that format, then insert it at the end of text you want to format in the same way, creating an identical section.

FORMATTING DOCUMENTS

The title of this section may sound strange to you, because you're always formatting part of a document, such as a word, a paragraph, or a section. However, when you make changes that affect all of your document, that's called document formatting, and you do it with the

Format Document command. Figure 11–11 shows the Format Document dialog box.

Document formatting controls

- top, bottom, right, left, and gutter margins

- default spacing for tabs

- position of footnotes and the starting footnote number

- prevention of page breaks that leave one line of a paragraph on a page (*widow* prevention)

- page width and height

Because most of these options can be addressed more effectively in other sections, you'll find discussions of them in this book, as follows:

To learn about	See
Changing margins	Changing Margins in Chapter 14.
Setting up facing pages	Creating Mirrored Margins on Facing Pages in Chapter 14.
Creating different headers for even and odd pages	Adding Headers and Footers in Chapter 15.
Specifying the starting page number of the document	Adding Page Numbers in Chapter 15.
Specifying the starting line number of the document	Numbering Lines in Chapter 17.

Figure 11–11.
The Format
Document dialog
box.

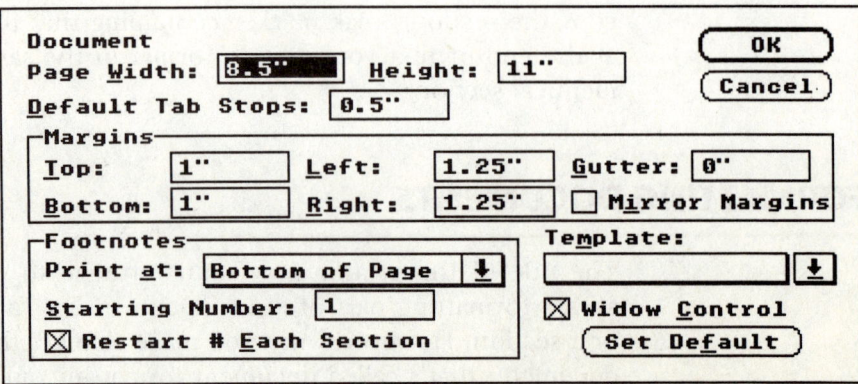

Setting the default measurement for tabs	Working with Tabs in Chapter 9.
Specifying the position and starting number for footnotes	Adding Footnotes in Chapter 15.
Preventing Word from leaving one line of a paragraph on a page (preventing *widows*)	Controlling Page Breaks in Chapter 14.

Creating a Default Document Format

Every time Word displays a new document, it applies its default document format to that document. This default format includes

Page width	8.5″
Page height	11″
Default tab stops	.5″
Top and bottom margins	1″
Right and left margins	1.25″
Gutter margin	None
Mirror margins	Off
Footnote position	Bottom of page
Footnote starting number	1
Restart footnote numbers in each section	On
Widow control	On

To use different settings for the default document format:

1. Choose the Format Document command, then choose options in the dialog box to specify the default format you want.

2. Choose Set Default.

3. Click OK or press **Enter**.

Word records the document format in the NORMAL.DOT file. Unless you revise the format again, it is the default format for all new documents based on the NORMAL.DOT template.

Part IV

PAGE LAYOUT AND PRINTING

After you perfect the text, you're ready to add the finishing touches and print. This part of the book shows you how to perfect your documents so that they'll end up looking great when you print them.

Chapter 12 shows you how to incorporate graphics into your Word files. You'll learn how to change their size, add frames, and add captions. And when you just want to save space to paste in a picture later, you'll also see how to do that.

Chapter 13 introduces a very important feature of Word—tables. You can put anything into a table—numbers, text, graphics, fields. You'll see how to use tables to easily create complex page layouts.

Chapter 14 details how to work with two of Word's views—print preview and page view. You'll learn how to adjust margins, move page breaks, and view your pages in different ways. In this chapter, you'll also see how to control where page breaks occur and how to use hyphenation to perfect your pages.

Headers and footers are often added right before printing to give documents a polished appearance. For technical documents, footnotes are often a finishing touch. Chapter 15 shows you how to add these elements to your files. You'll also be introduced to one of Word's most important features, the Format Position command, which you use to fix the position of a paragraph on the page and to "flow" text around it.

No document is "done" until it's printed. Chapter 16 answers your common printing questions. You'll learn how to print different parts of your document and how to control the features of your printer. And if you run into trouble, you'll find troubleshooting tips at the end of the chapter.

## Chapter Twelve

Adding Pictures to Word Files

Word uses the general term *picture* to mean graphics, drawings, charts, photographs, or any visual element that you can't create with Word. Word makes it easy to incorporate pictures into your documents and templates. You can insert, format, and position pictures in Word files, adding captions or other text, and making text flow around the picture if you like.

You can create a picture by drawing in a variety of graphics programs, by scanning a photograph, or by capturing part of a chart or spreadsheet as a picture. Then you can paste the graphic into your Word document wherever you want it—even in tables and in headers and footers, if you like. You can change the picture's size and position, manipulating the page layout to suit your needs.

This chapter discusses

- inserting graphics files into Word files
- inserting parts of graphics files from the Windows Clipboard
- inserting blank frames as placeholders for pictures
- scaling and cropping pictures
- adding borders and other formatting
- adding captions and other text
- positioning pictures and making text flow around them

INSERTING A PICTURE

You can add a picture to a Word file in two ways:

- by inserting a graphics file created with a compatible graphics program.

■ by using the Windows Clipboard to paste in any part of a picture created in a Windows-based graphics program (such as Microsoft Paint).

If you're going to paste in artwork manually, you can also reserve just the right amount of space for art by inserting a picture frame as a placeholder.

Inserting an Entire Graphics File

In your Word file you can insert entire graphics files that are saved as TIFF (Tagged Image File Format) files. TIFF is a format that many graphics programs use. In addition to TIFF files, Word can translate the following graphics formats:

■ AutoCAD® ADI ASCII or binary

■ CGM

■ HPGL

■ Lotus® .PIC

■ Micrografx Windows Draw!™

■ Tektronix 4014 vector mode

■ VideoShow NAPLPS

■ Zenographics Mirage IMA

Word doesn't actually insert a picture into a Word file, but instead inserts an IMPORT field that establishes a link to the graphics file. Word uses the path in this field to find the file.

To insert an entire graphics file:

1. Place the insertion point at the place where you want the picture to appear.

2. Choose the Insert Picture command. Word displays the dialog box shown in Figure 12–1.

3. In the Picture File Name box, type the name of the graphic file, including any path and drive names Word needs to find the file, or type a new extension (*.PIC, for example), then select the file from the Directory and Files lists.

Figure 12–1.
The Insert Picture
dialog box.

Figure 12–2.
A field that inserts a
picture into a Word
file.

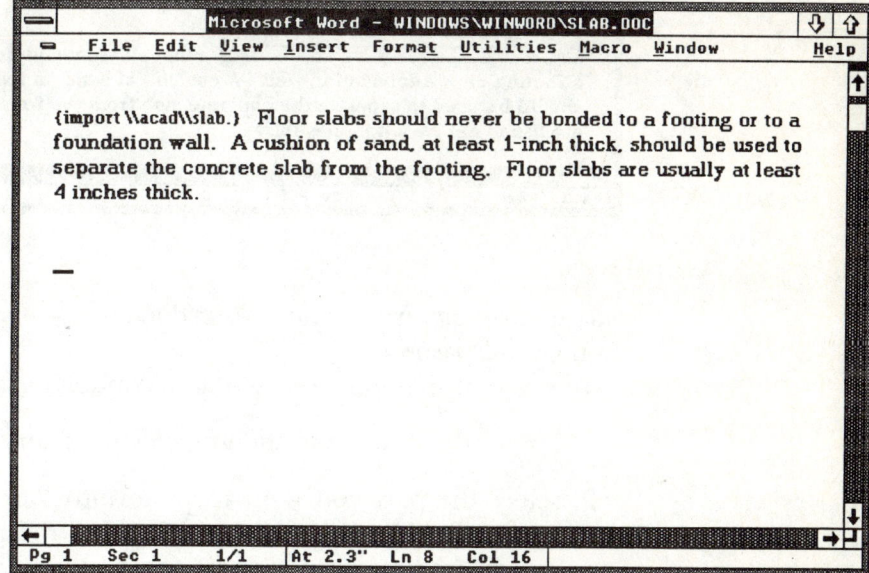

4. Click OK or press **Enter**. Word inserts an IMPORT field similar to the one shown in Figure 12–2.

5. To see the picture, place the insertion point in the field, press **F9** to update the field, then press **Shift+F9** to switch the field view (the same as choosing the View Field Codes command). Figure 12–3 shows the picture created by the IMPORT field shown in Figure 12–2.

Pasting in a Picture from a Windows-Based Graphics Program

If you use a Windows-based graphics program (such as Microsoft Paint) to draw a picture, you can use the Windows Clipboard to copy all or

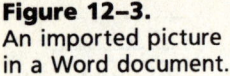

Figure 12–3.
An imported picture
in a Word document.

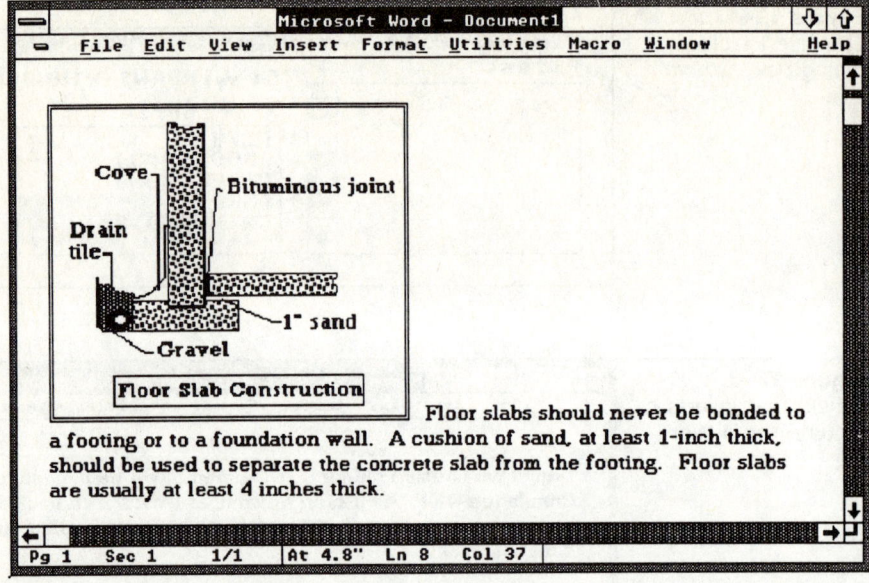

part of that picture to your Word document—it's a simple matter of cutting and pasting.

To paste in a graphic created in a Windows graphics program:

1. Create the graphic in the graphics program.

2. Select the part you want to paste into Word, then choose the program's Edit Copy command to put the picture in the Clipboard. For best results, select only what you want. Don't include white space around the picture—you can always add white space later with Word.

3. Move to your document in the Word window.

4. Place the insertion point where you want to insert the picture. Most of the time you'll want to insert a picture into a blank paragraph (immediately before a paragraph mark [¶])—this makes it easier to change its size and position.

5. Choose the Edit Paste command. Word inserts the picture, as shown in Figure 12–4.

The shape and size of the picture may appear somewhat different from the original dimensions in the graphics program, because Word adjusts the size according to the type of printer you are

Figure 12–4.
A picture pasted
from the Clipboard
into a Word
document.

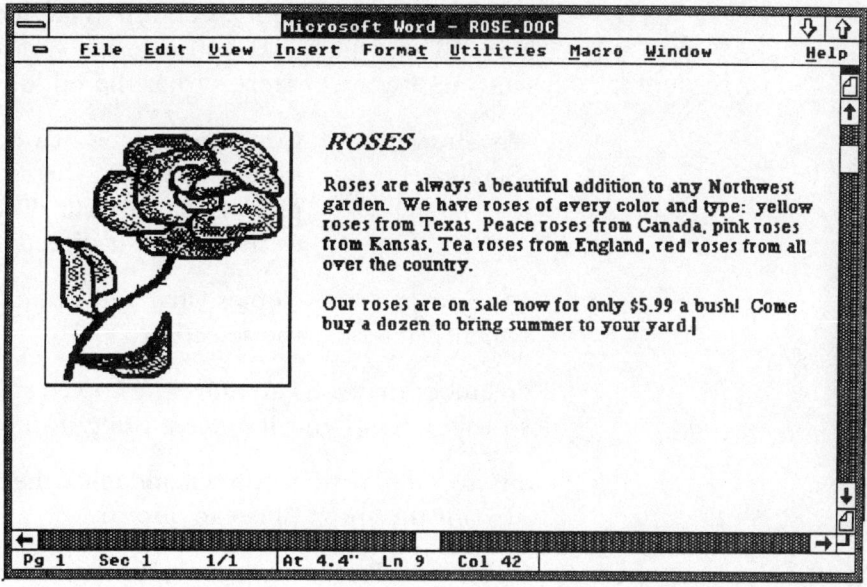

using. Don't worry about this—you can always change the dimensions later with Word.

Pasting in Charts and Spreadsheets from Microsoft Excel

You can easily use the Clipboard to paste spreadsheets and charts from Microsoft Excel for Windows to your Word documents. This procedure transforms the copied information into a picture—this is different than linking information in a spreadsheet or chart with a Word document. (See Chapter 22, "Using Information from Other Files," for more on creating links between files.)

Pasting in a Spreadsheet from Microsoft Excel as a Picture

To paste a spreadsheet from Microsoft Excel into a Word document as a picture:

1. In Microsoft Excel, display the spreadsheet and select the cells you want to copy. If you don't want the column and row headings or the gridlines to appear, choose the Options Display command and turn these off.

2. Hold down the **Shift** key and choose the Edit Copy Picture command. (Holding down the Shift keys changes the usual Copy com-

mand to Copy Picture.) Excel displays a dialog box, as shown in Figure 12–5, which asks you to make choices about the spreadsheet's appearance. Here's what the options mean.

As Shown on Screen
Copies exactly what you see on the screen. (When you print the chart from Word, the picture may appear different than if you were to print it directly from Excel.)

As Shown when Printed
Copies what you would see if you printed the selection.

Remember that you can move the copied spreadsheet to a graphics program and edit it *before* pasting it into Word.

3. Move to your Word document and place the insertion point where you want the spreadsheet to appear.

4. Use the Edit Paste command to paste in the spreadsheet. Figure 12–6 shows how a sample Excel spreadsheet appears.

Pasting in a Chart from Excel as a Picture

To paste a chart from Microsoft Excel into a Word document:

1. In Excel, display the chart you want to copy.

Figure 12–5.
The Excel Edit Copy Picture dialog box for spreadsheets.

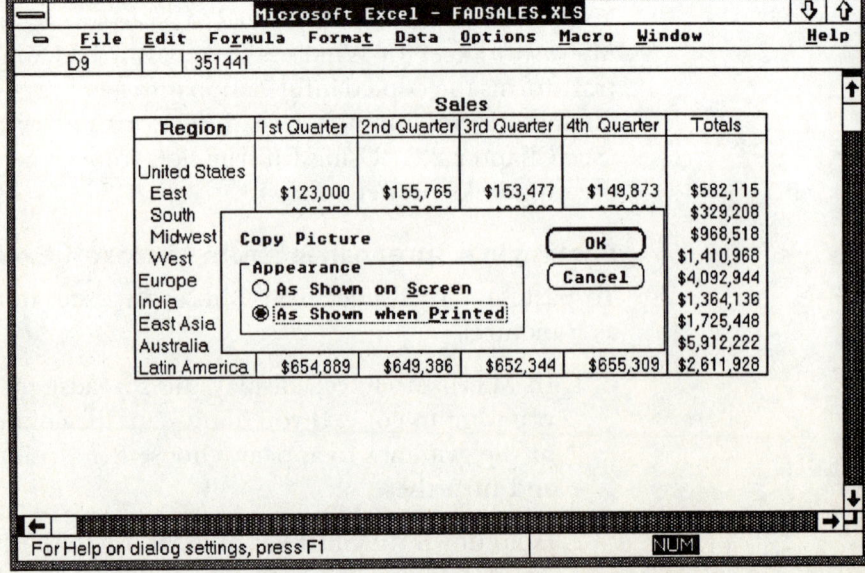

Microsoft Excel - FADSALES.XLS						
File	Edit	Fo**r**mula	Format	**D**ata	**O**ptions	Macro	**W**indow	**Help**
D9	351441						

Sales

Region	1st Quarter	2nd Quarter	3rd Quarter	4th Quarter	Totals
United States					
East	$123,000	$155,765	$153,477	$149,873	$582,115
South					$329,208
Midwest					$968,518
West					$1,410,968
Europe					$4,092,944
India					$1,364,136
East Asia					$1,725,448
Australia					$5,912,222
Latin America	$654,889	$649,386	$652,344	$655,309	$2,611,928

Copy Picture

Appearance
○ As Shown on **S**creen
◉ As Shown when **P**rinted

OK
Cancel

For Help on dialog settings, press F1   NUM

Figure 12–6.
Part of an Excel
spreadsheet copied
as a graphic and
pasted into a Word
document.

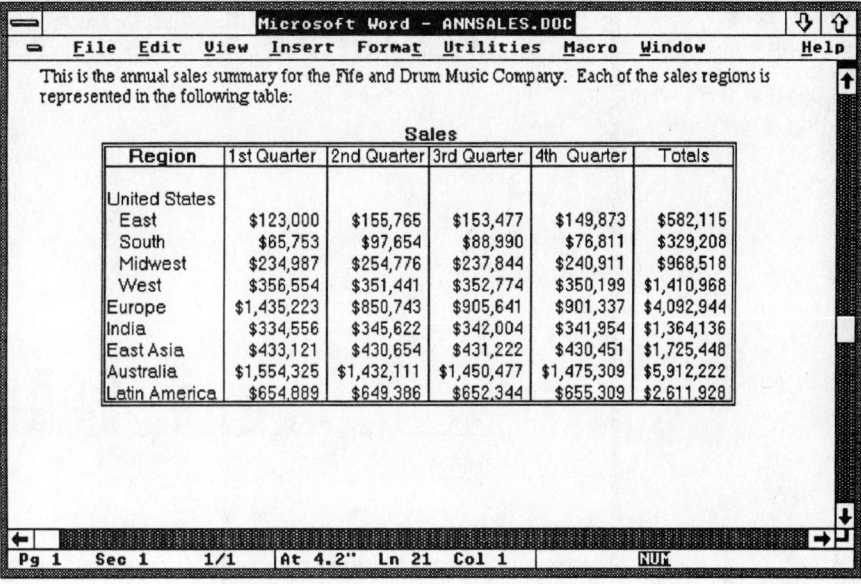

Figure 12–7.
The Excel Chart
Select Chart
command.

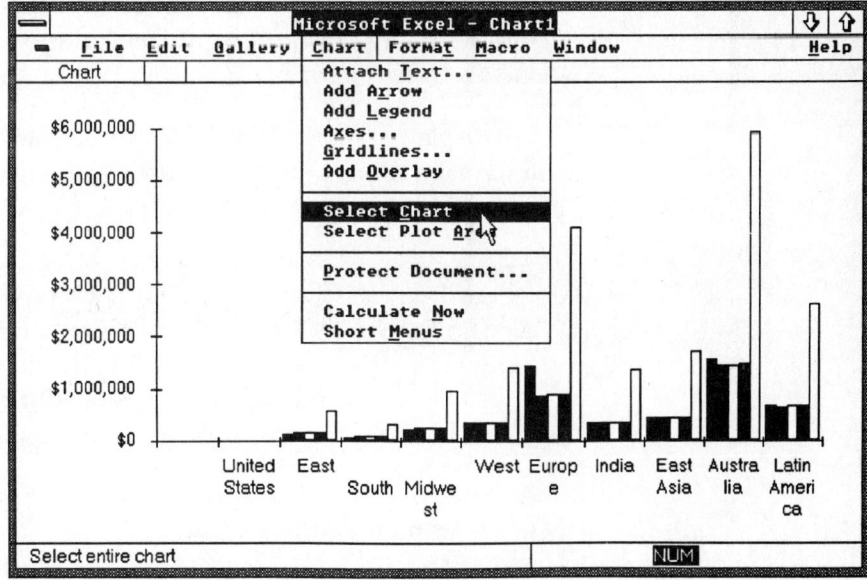

2. Select the chart with the Chart Select Chart command, as shown
   in Figure 12–7. The chart will appear as the sample does in Figure
   12–8.

Figure 12–8.
Selecting a chart in
Microsoft Excel in
preparation for
pasting into Word.

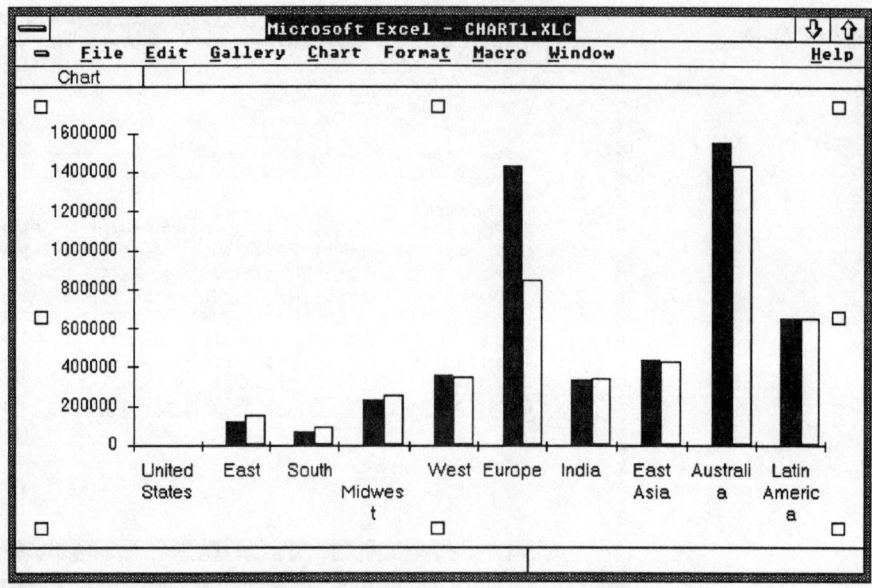

3. Hold down the **Shift** key and choose the Edit Copy Picture command. (Holding down the Shift key changes the usual Copy command to Copy Picture.)

   Excel displays a dialog box, as shown in Figure 12–9, which asks you to make choices about the spreadsheet's appearance and size. Here's what the options mean.

   Appearance

   As Shown on   Copies exactly what you see on the screen.
   Screen   (When you print the chart from Word, the
                         picture may appear different than if you
                         were to print it directly from Excel.)

   As Shown   Copies what you would see if you printed
   when Printed   the selection.

   Size

   As Shown on   Copies the chart in the same size as it is
   Screen   displayed. You can change the size of the
                         resulting picture by changing the size of
                         the window before copying the chart.

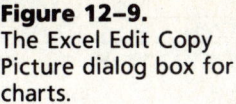

Figure 12–9.
The Excel Edit Copy
Picture dialog box for
charts.

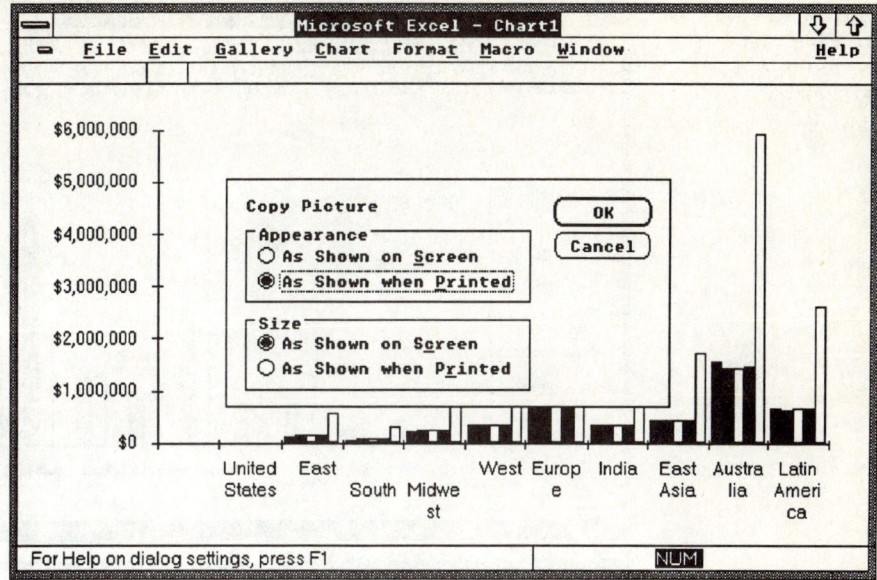

| As Shown when Printed | Copies the chart in the size you would see if you printed the chart. The picture varies, depending on the shape of the window and the kind of printer you have. |

If you want to edit the chart with a graphics program before pasting it into Word, choose the As Shown on Screen option to make sure the chart will fit in the graphics program window.

4. Move to your Word document and place the insertion point where you want the chart to appear.

5. Use the Edit Paste command to paste in the chart. Figure 12–10 shows an Excel chart in a Word document.

USING FRAMES TO RESERVE SPACE FOR PICTURES

If you want to reserve a blank space so you can manually paste a picture there, you can insert an empty frame into your document. You can change the frame's size and position to reserve just the right amount of space.

To insert a picture frame into your document:

1. Place the insertion point where you want to insert the frame.

Figure 12–10.
An Excel chart
pasted in a Word
document.

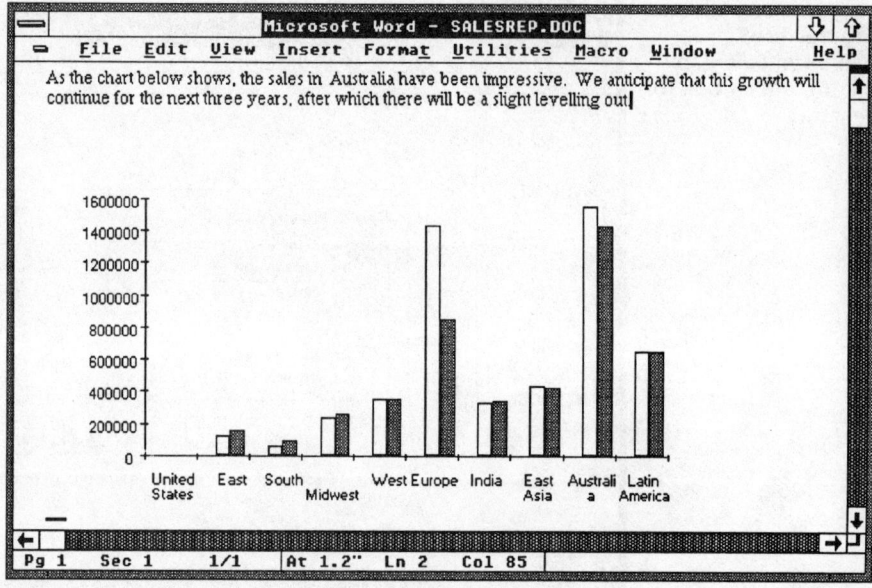

Figure 12–11.
Picture frames in a
Word document.

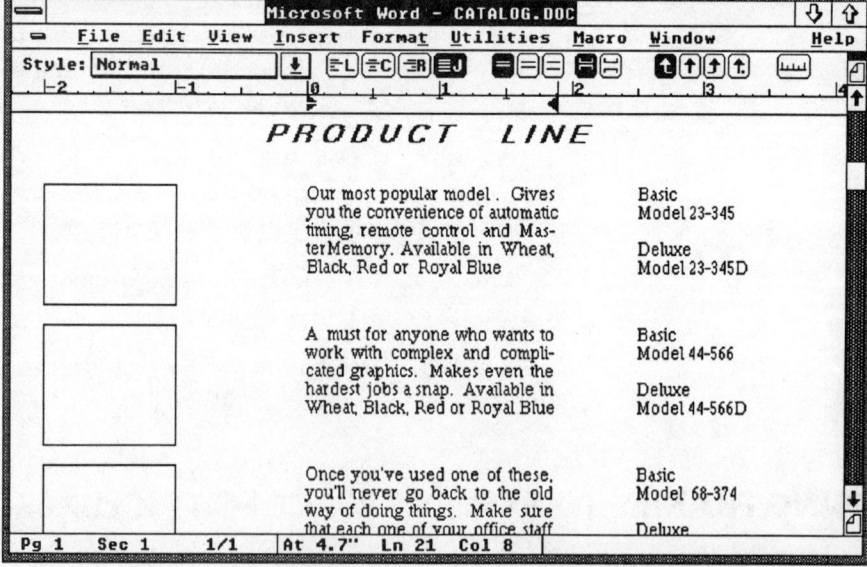

2. Choose the Insert Picture command.

3. Turn on the New Picture option. Word inserts a 1-inch by 1-inch
   picture frame (shown in Figure 12–11). You can later choose

other types of frames, as described in Adding or Changing Picture Frames later in this chapter.

🖾 *Helpful Hint*

Inserting and formatting a picture frame is a great way to add check boxes to forms and other documents. This way you give readers a place to select an item with an X or a check mark.

CHANGING THE SIZE OF PICTURES AND PICTURE FRAMES

You can use Word commands to change the size of the picture or frame. You can change the size of pictures in two ways:

- Scaling: changing the relative size of the picture while you retain the entire picture. Scaling works like using a reduction feature on a copy machine—it shrinks the picture.

- Cropping: cutting out portions of the picture to focus on one area.

Scaling a Picture or Frame

To scale (change the size of) a picture or picture frame with the mouse in normal view or page view:

1. Click the picture or empty frame to select it. Small black square "handles" appear at the edges of the picture or frame, as shown in the upper square of Figure 12–12.

2. Point to the handle on the side you want to move.

3. Hold down **Shift** and drag the handle to a new position. **Note:** Be sure to hold down the Shift key; otherwise, you'll cut off (crop) parts of the picture. An outline of the picture moves with the mouse pointer. Word redraws the picture or frame when you release the mouse button. The percentage of the original size of the picture appears in the status bar and changes as you move the mouse, as shown in Figure 12–13.

To change the size of a picture or picture frame with a command in normal view or in page view:

Figure 12–12.
Word adds handles
when you select a
picture.

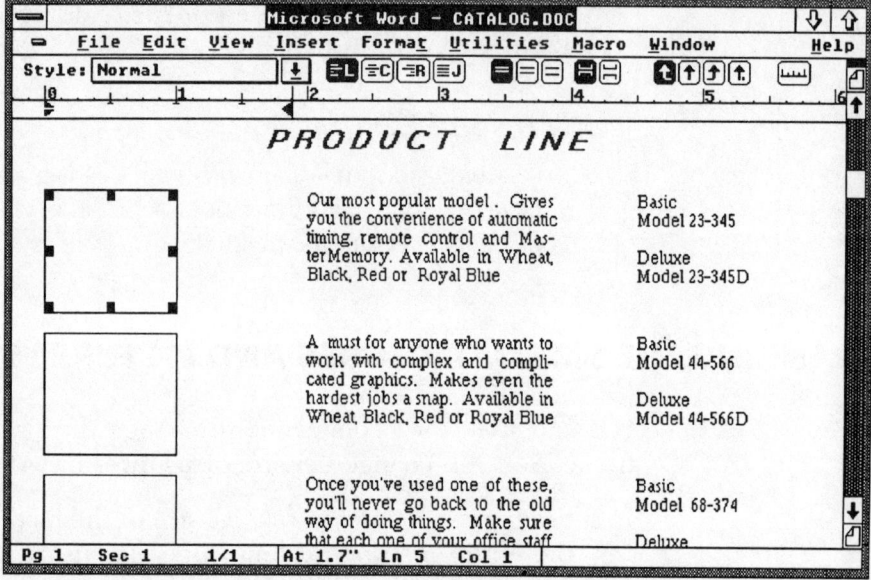

Figure 12–13.
Dragging a picture
frame to a new size.

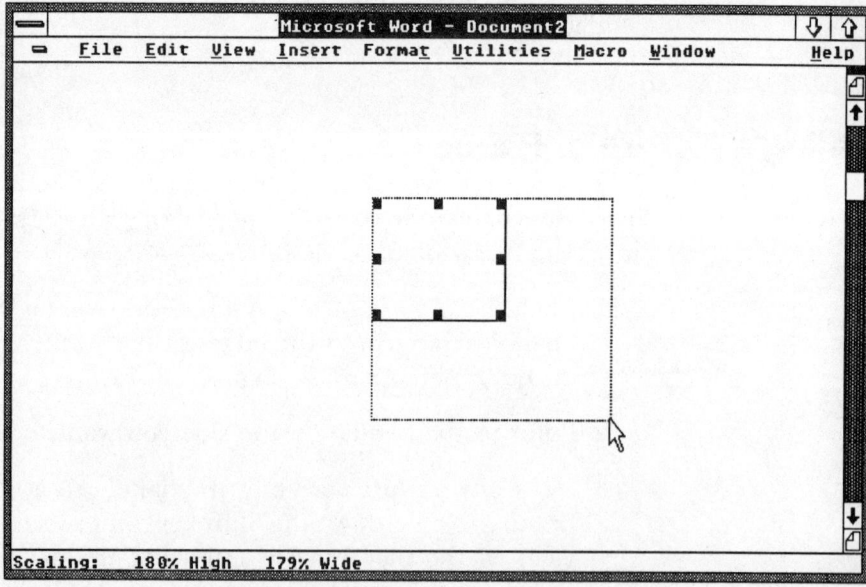

1. Place the insertion point in the picture or empty frame to select
   it. Handles appear around the picture.

2. Choose the Format Picture command. Word displays the dialog box shown in Figure 12–14.

3. Type scaling percentages in the Height % and Width % boxes. 100% equals the original size of the picture. If you want to make the picture 50 percent taller, type **150** in the Height % box. If you want to make the picture 25 percent narrower, type **75** in the Width % box.

4. Click OK or press **Enter**. Word redraws the picture at the new percentages.

Cropping a Picture

When you want to cut out a portion of a picture rather than just change its size, you'll crop the picture.

To crop a picture with the mouse:

1. Select the picture. Word draws handles at the edges of the picture.

2. Drag the handles to change the size of the picture frame until the picture is cropped the way you want it. An outline of the picture moves as you move the mouse pointer. Word redraws the picture when you release the mouse button.

Figure 12–14.
Changing the size of a picture by typing percentages in the Format Picture dialog box.

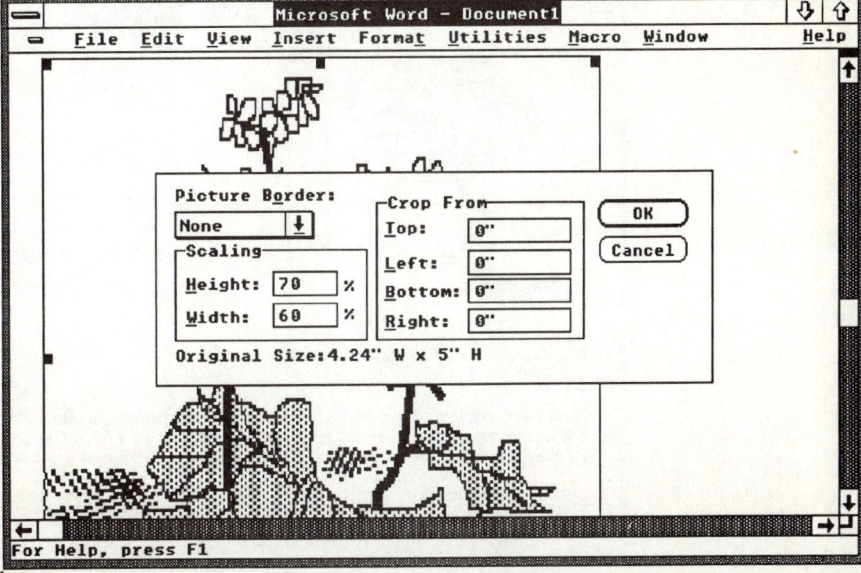

Figure 12–15 illustrates cropping a picture.
To crop a picture using a command:

1. Select the picture. Word draws handles around the edges of the picture.

2. Choose the Format Picture command. Word displays the Format Picture dialog box (shown in Figure 12–16).

3. Type decimal cropping measurements in the Top, Left, Bottom, and Right boxes. For example, if you want to take $1/10$ of an inch off the Right side, type **.10in** or **.10″** in the Right box.

4. Click OK or press **Enter**. Word redraws the picture according to your instructions.

Returning Pictures and Frames to Their Original Sizes

To return a picture or frame to its original size:

1. Select the picture or frame.

2. Choose the Format Picture command.

3. Type **100** in the Height % and Width % boxes.

Figure 12–15.
Cropping a picture
with the mouse.

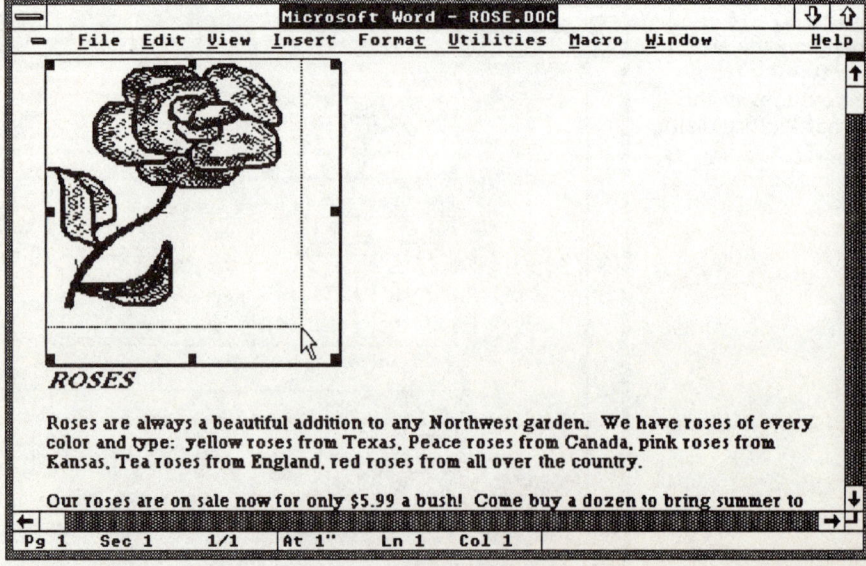

Figure 12–16.
Typing cropping
measurements in the
Format Picture dialog
box.

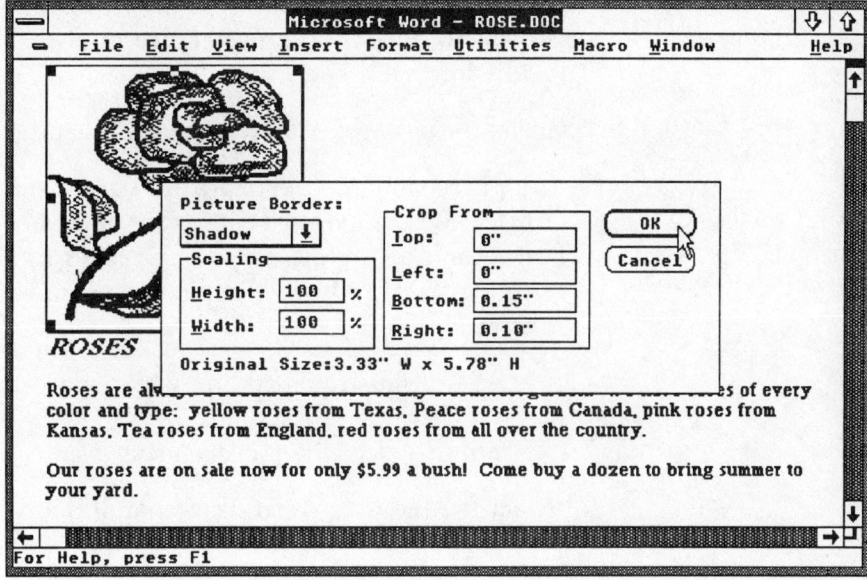

4. Type **0** in all the cropping boxes.

5. Click OK or press **Enter**.

⬛▬▶ *Helpful Hint*

If you have many pictures in a Word document, Word can become very slow, because the program has to redraw each picture when the screen changes.

To speed up using Word, you can control when pictures are displayed fully or as empty boxes. When you want to speed up Word and you don't need to see the pictures, choose the View Preferences command and turn off the Pictures option. When you need to see the pictures, use View Preferences again to turn the option back on.

You can also switch to draft view, where pictures are displayed as empty boxes, if you want to concentrate on text and not on page formatting.

ADDING WHITE SPACE AROUND PICTURES

You can use the Format Picture command to add white space between pictures and their frames if you've inserted the picture using the Windows Clipboard.

To add white space around pictures, you'll follow the same basic procedure you'd use to crop a picture in normal view or page view.

To add white space with the mouse:

1. Select the picture. Word draws handles at the edges of the picture.

2. Drag the handles to expand the size of the picture frame until you see the amount of white space you want around the picture. An outline of the picture frame moves as you move the mouse pointer. Word redraws the picture when you release the mouse button.

Figure 12–17 illustrates adding white space to a picture with the mouse.

To add white space to a picture using a command:

1. Select the picture. Word draws handles around the edges of the picture.

2. Choose the Format Picture command. Word displays the Format Picture dialog box (shown in Figure 12–18).

3. Type negative decimal measurements in the Top, Left, Bottom, and Right boxes. For example, if you want to add 2/10 of an inch of white space on all sides, you'd type **.2in** in all four boxes.

Figure 12–17.
Adding white space to a picture with the mouse.

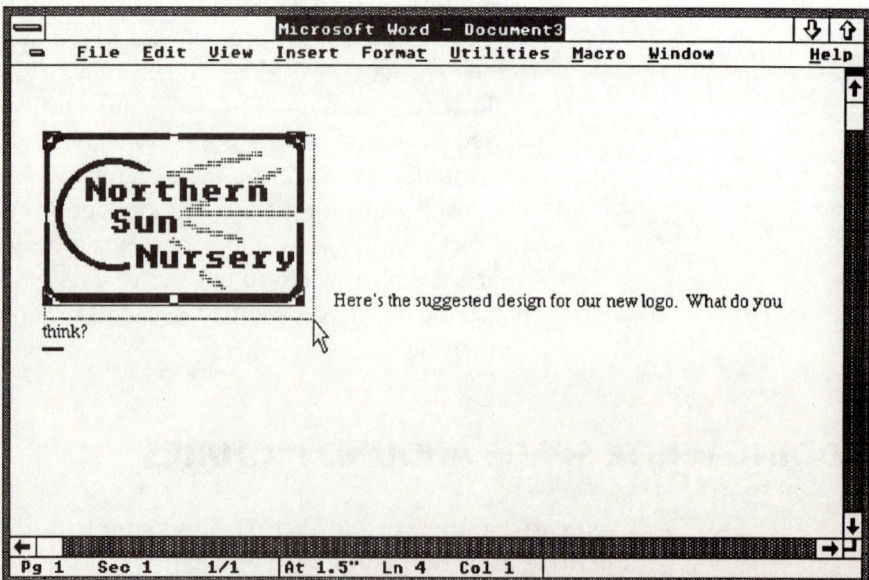

Figure 12–18.
Typing negative
measurements in the
Format Picture dialog
box to add white
space around a
picture.

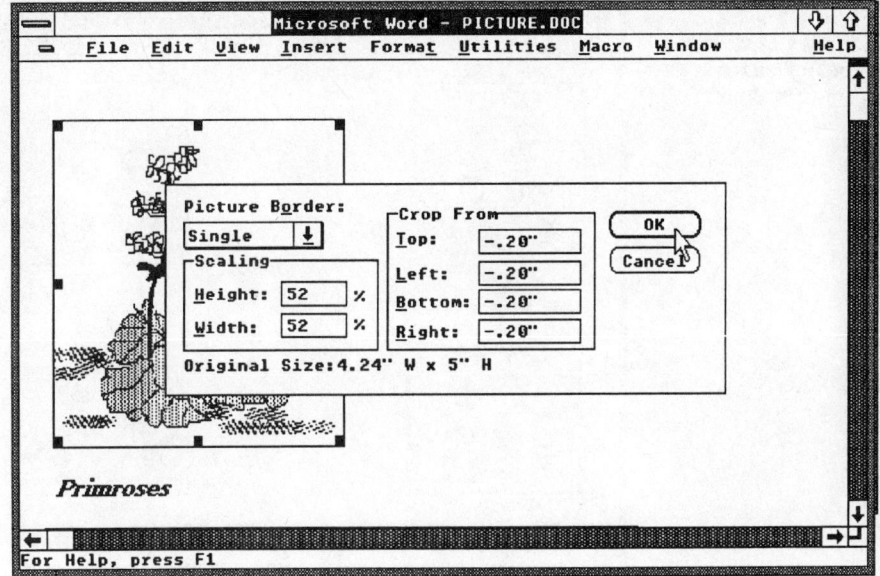

4. Click OK or press **Enter**. Word redraws the picture according to your instructions.

ADDING OR CHANGING PICTURE FRAMES

Pictures inserted from the Windows Clipboard have invisible frames around them. You can choose from various types of frames to set off the picture, as shown in Figure 12–19. You can also choose various types of frames when you've inserted picture frames as placeholders.

To choose a new type of frame:

1. Select the picture or frame. Word draws handles at the edges of it.

2. Choose the Format Picture command.

3. From the Picture Border drop-down list, select a new type of frame. Select none if you want to make the frame invisible.

4. Click OK or press **Enter**.

POSITIONING PICTURES AND FRAMES

In Word, paragraphs can have two kinds of positions: free-floating and fixed. Paragraphs with free-floating positions move as changes are

Figure 12–19.
Samples of various
types of picture
frames in Word.

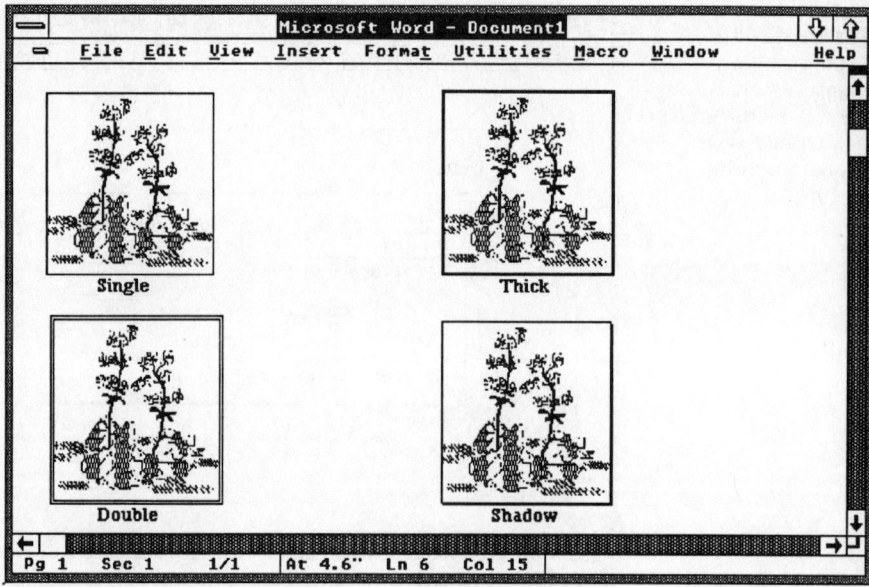

Figure 12–20.
Text flows around a
graphics paragraph
with a fixed position.

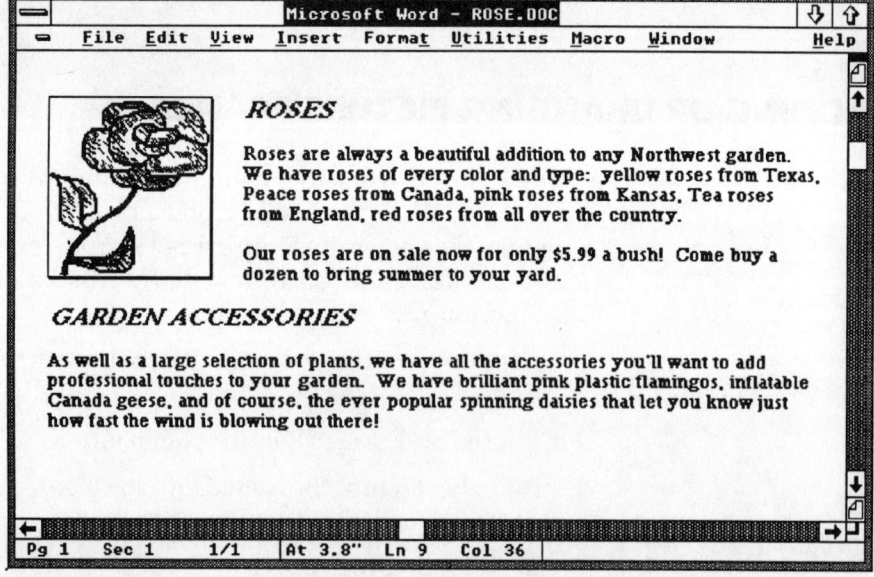

made to the text. Paragraphs with fixed positions stay in their assigned
positions, and surrounding free-floating text automatically flows
around the positioned paragraphs, as shown in Figure 12–20. You

can't see the proper positions of text using the normal view—you have to switch to print preview or page view for that.

Word considers a frame or a picture inserted from the Clipboard to be one character. If you inserted the picture or frame immediately before a paragraph mark (¶), the picture or the frame is the only character in that paragraph. You can precisely position a picture paragraph on a page using precise measurements or relative positions (top, bottom, center, for example) with the Format Position command. See Positioning Objects Anywhere on a Page in Chapter 14 for more information about using the Format Position command.

When you've used the Format Position command to fix the position of a picture, that picture (oddly enough) becomes a movable object in print preview. This means you can use a mouse to change a paragraph's position by dragging the picture to a new location on the print preview screen. See Moving Page Breaks, Headers, Footers, and Fixed-Positioned Objects in Print Preview in Chapter 14 for more information. To arrange pictures side-by-side with text or other pictures, you might want to create a table. See Chapter 13 for more information.

◆ *Helpful Hint*

If you have a picture that you want to use over and over again, such as a business logo, you can save that picture along with its attached formatting as a glossary entry, then insert it into your documents whenever you need it.

For more information on using glossary entries, see Saving Text and Pictures for Repeated Use: Using Glossaries in Chapter 4.

PICTURES AS CHARACTERS

Word considers a picture to be a single character, so it places the bottom of the picture frame on the baseline for text characters, in effect creating a very tall line, just as Word would for a large font size. Because a picture is a character, you can use the Format Character command to make a picture a superscript or subscript, offsetting it from the baseline. And, because they're characters, you can put several pictures on the same line.

COPYING, MOVING, AND DELETING PICTURES

A picture is a character, so you copy it, move it, and delete it just like any other character:

1. Select the picture.

2. Do one of the following:

To	Do this
Copy the picture	Use the Edit Copy and Edit Paste commands
Move the picture	Use the Edit Cut and Edit Paste commands
Delete the picture	Press the **Delete** key

USING WORD TEXT IN OTHER WINDOWS FILES

Word is not a graphics program, but there may be times when you want to create text with Word and paste it into another file created with a Microsoft Windows application. For example, you might want to paste several paragraphs of Word text into a Microsoft Paint file, as shown in Figure 12–21.

To copy Word text:

1. Display the Word document and select the text you want to copy.

Figure 12–21.
Word text pasted into a Microsoft Paint file.

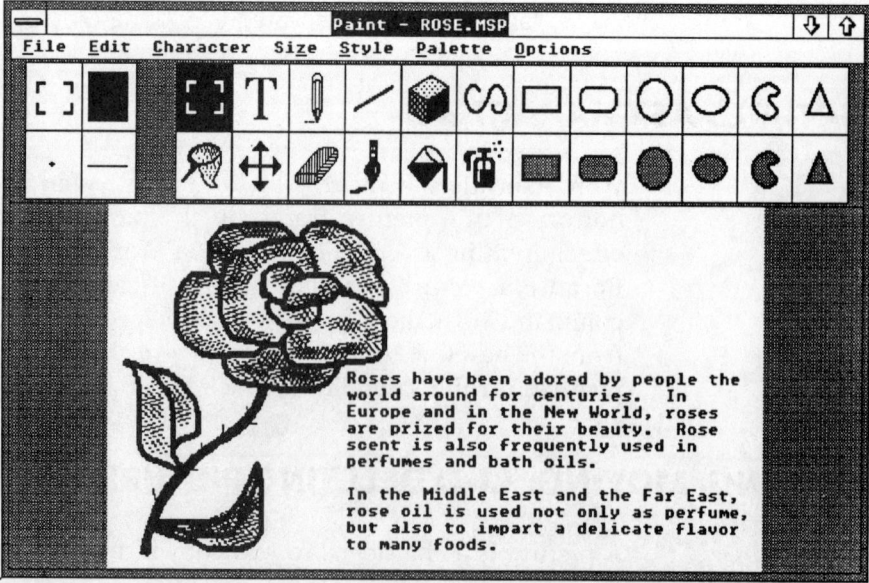

Figure 12–22.
A picture with a
caption.

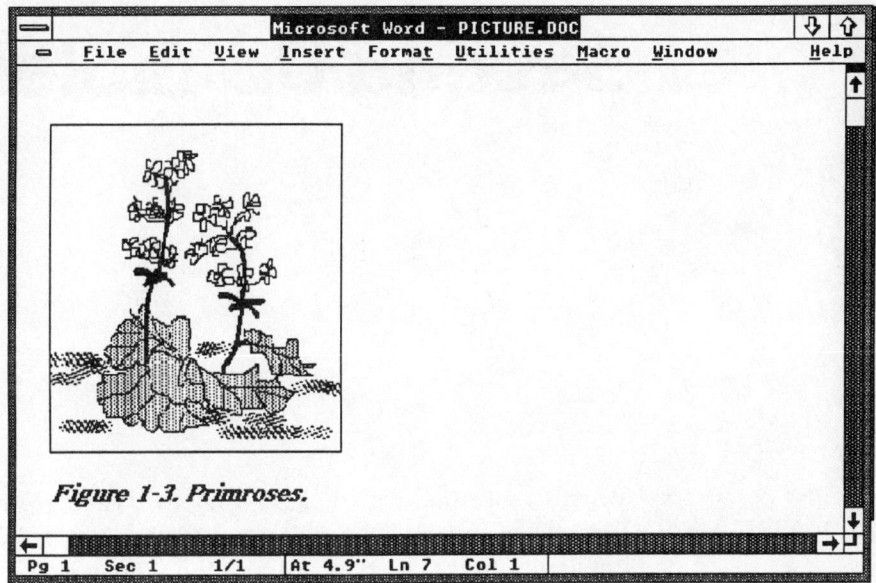

2. Choose the Edit Copy command to copy the text to the Clipboard.

3. Switch to the other Windows application.

4. Choose the Edit Paste command.

ADDING A CAPTION TO A PICTURE

You may want to add a caption to a picture and make sure it stays with the picture. Figure 12–22 shows a picture with a caption.

To add a caption:

1. Place the insertion point immediately after the picture (but in front of the paragraph mark, if there's one nearby).

2. Press **Shift+Enter** to enter a newline character. This begins a new line but keeps the picture and the paragraph in the same paragraph.

3. Type the text of the caption.

You can format the caption just as you would format any characters. Keep in mind that if you use the Format Paragraph command, you'll change the format of the picture as well as the caption because they're in the same paragraph.

## Chapter Thirteen

Setting Up Tables

Word's table features make it easy to structure, edit, and format information you want to arrange in rows and columns. To add visual impact to tables, you can add graphics, change the column widths, and indent and align rows in a variety of ways. You can also fix the position of the entire table on a page and make text flow around the table. You can add various types of borders to tables, drawing lines around individual cells or around all the cells in the table.

This chapter discusses

- creating a blank table

- creating a table from selected text

- entering text, pictures, and graphics in a table

- formatting and editing tables

USES FOR TABLES

You're probably used to thinking of a table as just rows and columns of numbers. But in Word, you can put almost anything in a table: text, numbers, and graphics. Take a look at Figures 13–1 through 13–3; all were created as tables in Word.

You can create a blank table by specifying the rows and columns first and filling in the cells later, or you can create a table by selecting information you've typed or imported from another file, then formatting the selected text as a table. You can control the width of each column in a table and the minimum height of rows, or you can let Word set up the table for you. Word automatically divides the space

Figure 13–1.
Side-by-side paragraphs in a table.

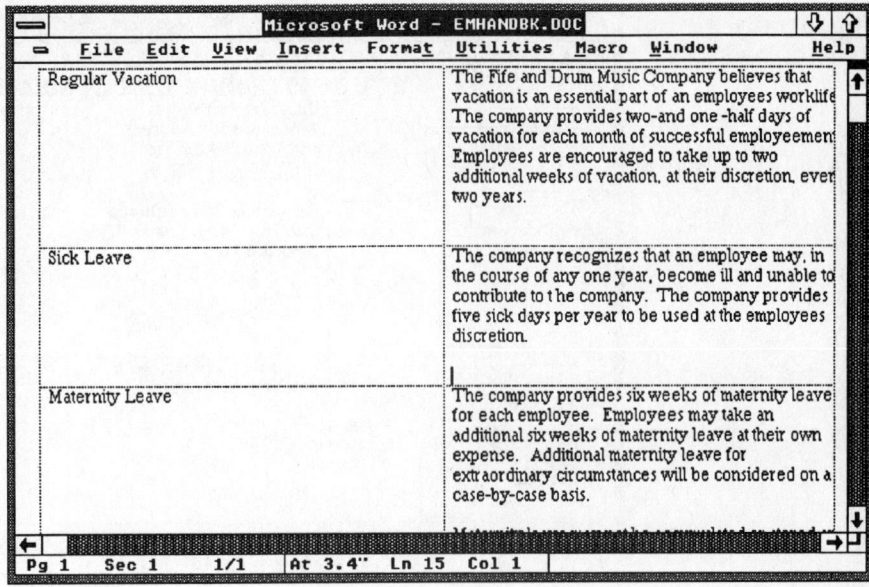

Figure 13–2.
A spreadsheet in a table.

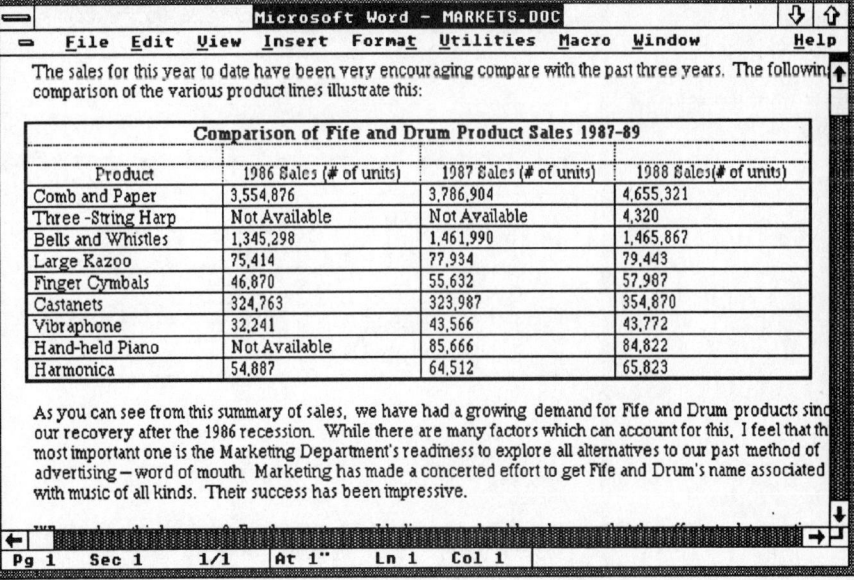

between margins into equal columns and determines the height of rows by measuring the highest cell in each row.

By putting a list into a table (as shown in Figure 13–4), you can easily sort the list using the data in any table column as the sorting

Figure 13-3.
Graphics in a table.

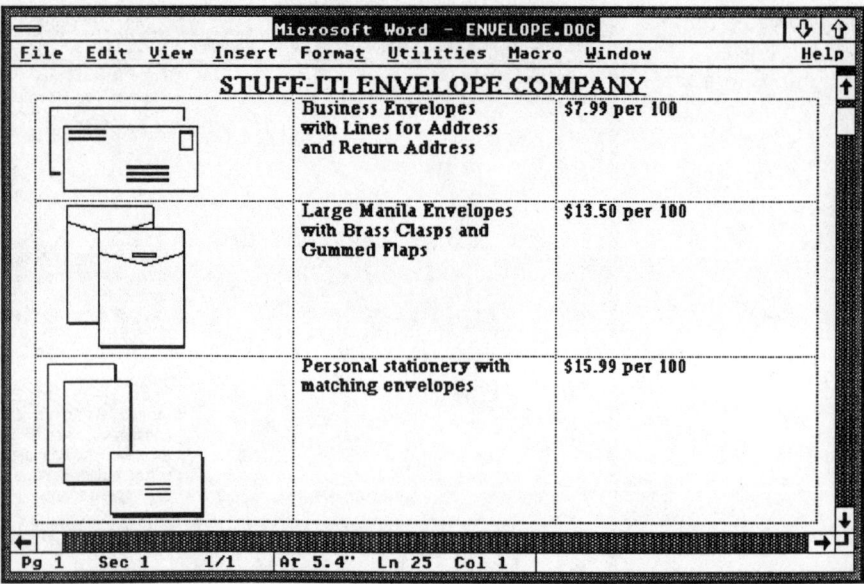

Figure 13-4.
Complex lists of
information can be
easily manipulated in
Word tables.

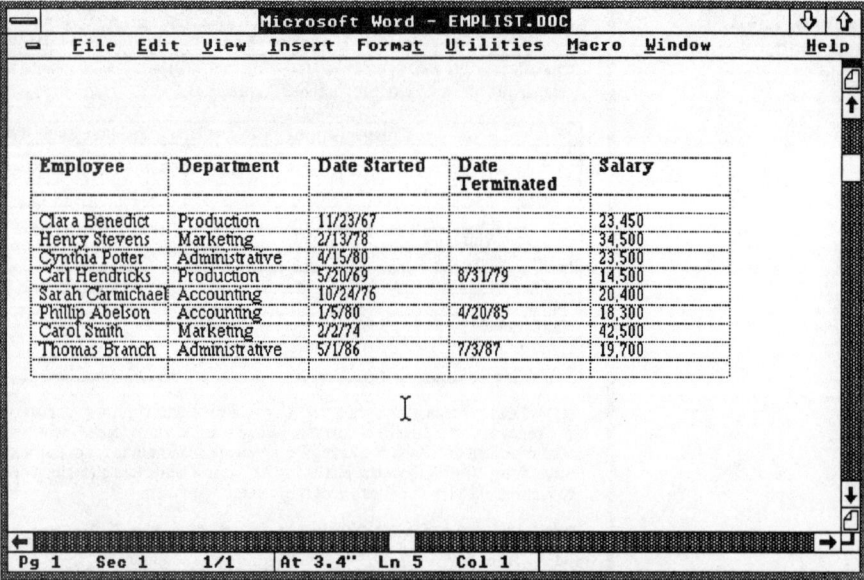

key. This means you can create and manipulate complex lists of information, such as customer address lists for form letters. See Sorting Lists in Alphabetic or Numeric Order in Chapter 23 for more information.

INSERTING A BLANK TABLE

Word inserts a table at the insertion point. Word automatically divides the space between margins into equal columns, or, if the insertion point is in a narrow column (as on a two-column page), Word divides up the text space in that column only. If you want to insert a table into a document that's divided up into columns, but you want the table to occupy the full width between page margins, you create a separate section for your table. (See Formatting Sections in Chapter 11 for more information about dividing a document into sections.)

To insert a blank table into your document:

1. Place the insertion point where you want to insert a table. Make sure no text is selected in your document.

2. Choose the Insert Table command. Word displays the dialog box shown in Figure 13–5.

3. Type the number of columns you want in the Number of Columns box.

4. Type the number of rows you want in the Number of Rows box.

5. Word automatically sets the initial column width, based on the space between margins and the number of columns. You can make the columns narrower by typing a new measurement in the Initial Col Width box. However, you can always change the column width later, so in most cases you'll want to leave this option alone. To specify different widths for different columns, go on to the next step.

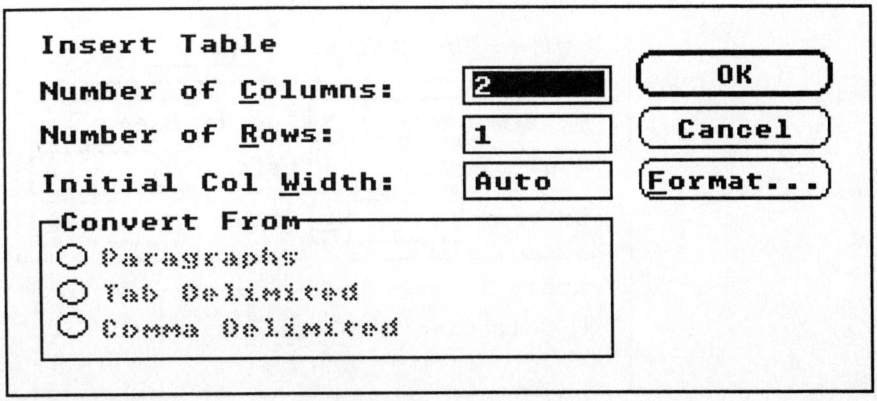

Figure 13–5.
The Insert Table
dialog box.

Insert Table

Number of **C**olumns: [2   ]   (OK)

Number of **R**ows: [1   ]   (Cancel)

Initial Col **W**idth: [Auto   ]   ([Format...])

-Convert From-
  O Paragraphs
  O Tab Delimited
  O Comma Delimited

6. If you want to specify a variety of column widths, align or indent rows, or draw borders around cells at this time, choose Format. Word displays the Format Table dialog box (shown in Figure 13–6). See Adjusting the Width of Columns, Indenting Rows, Aligning Rows, and Adding Borders to a Table later in this chapter for instructions on completing these tasks.

You can always change or add formatting to a table, so you can ignore the format if you like until you fill in the table cells.

7. Click OK or press **Enter** to close the dialog box and draw the table.

Figure 13–7 shows a blank, unformatted table that would be inserted by typing the number of rows and columns, then choosing OK to accept the rest of the default settings in the Insert Table dialog box. Figure 13–8 shows a blank table that has borders added by choosing options in the Format Table dialog box.

DISPLAYING OR REMOVING TABLE GRIDLINES AND CELL TEXT MARKERS

When you create a table, you'll see *gridlines* outlining the table cells. These dotted lines are especially helpful when you haven't added bor-

Figure 13–6.
The Format Table
dialog box.

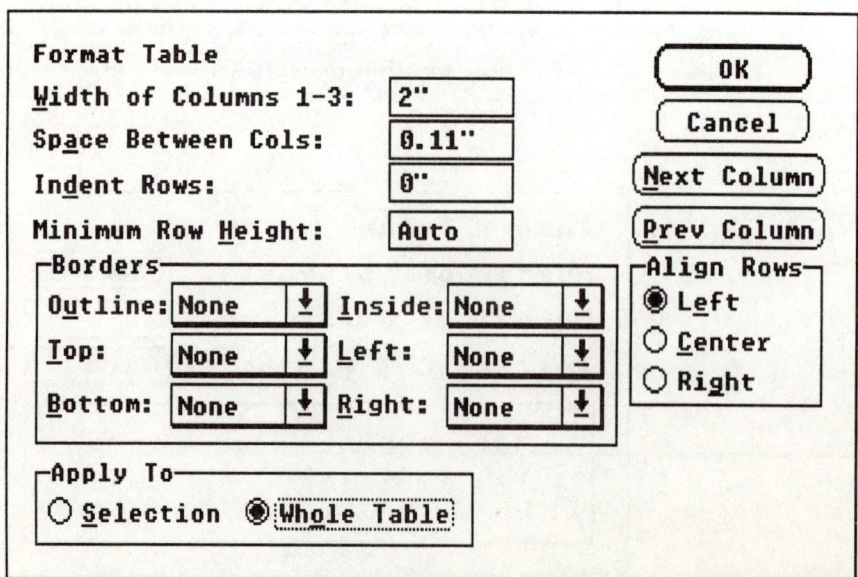

Figure 13–7.
A blank, unformatted
table.

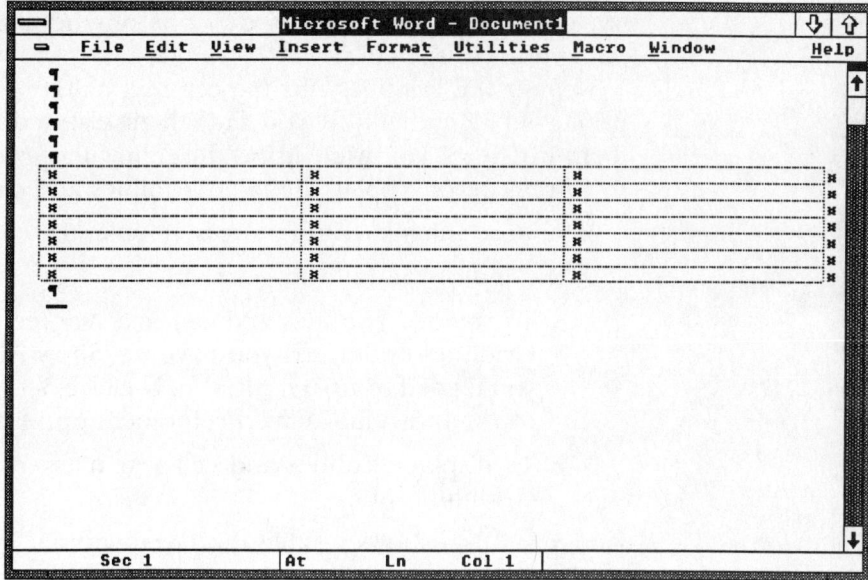

Figure 13–8.
A blank table with
borders added.

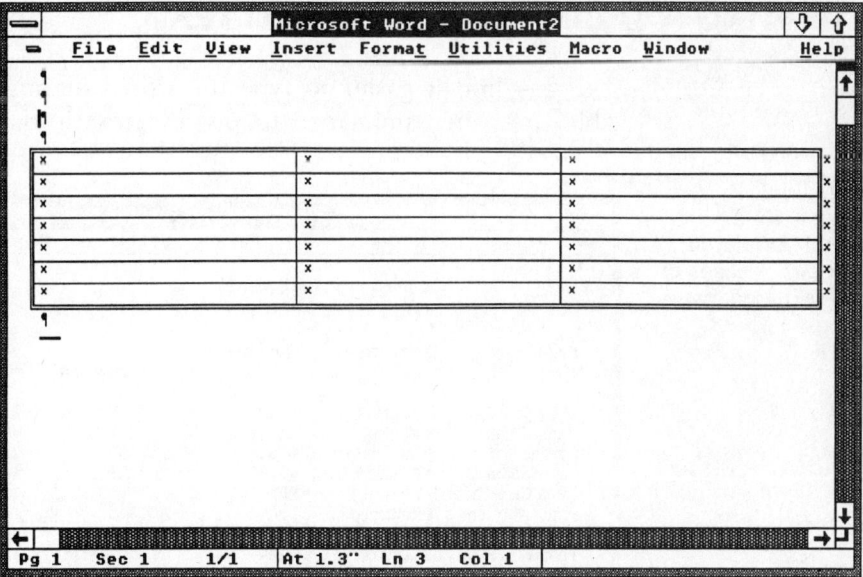

ders to a table. You'll also see *cell text markers*—special characters that
mark the end of text in a cell. The cell text markers are some form
of an *x*—the character used depends on the font used in the cell, and

the position of the markers depends on the alignment assigned to paragraphs in the cells.

Neither the gridlines nor the cell text markers will print when you print your document. If you find them distracting, you can remove them whenever you want using the following procedure.

To remove or display the table gridlines and cell text markers:

1. Choose the View Preferences command.
2. Do one of the following:
   - To remove gridlines and cell text markers, turn off the Table Gridlines option. (If you have the Show All option turned on, you'll need to turn it off, too, because Show All overrides most of the individual View Preferences options.)
   - To display gridlines and cell text markers, turn on the Table Gridlines option.

Figure 13–9 shows a table displayed without gridlines or cell text markers. Figure 13–10 shows a table displayed with both gridlines and cell text markers.

CREATING A TABLE FROM SELECTED TEXT

You may find it easier to type the words or numbers you want in a table first, then tell Word to put the text into a table. Most often,

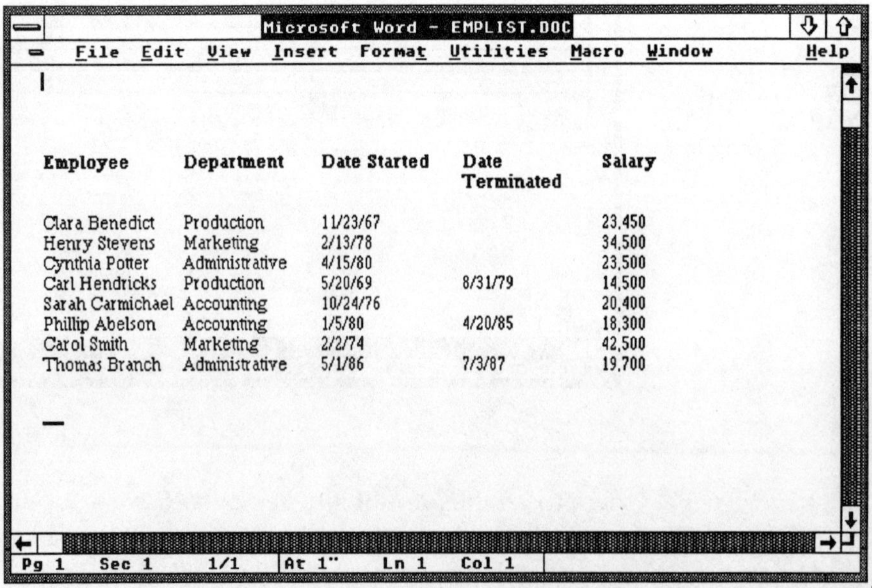
Microsoft Word - EMPLIST.DOC
File Edit View Insert Format Utilities Macro Window Help
Employee Department Date Started Date Terminated Salary
Clara Benedict Production 11/23/67 23,450
Henry Stevens Marketing 2/13/78 34,500
Cynthia Potter Administrative 4/15/80 23,500
Carl Hendricks Production 5/20/69 8/31/79 14,500
Sarah Carmichael Accounting 10/24/76 20,400
Phillip Abelson Accounting 1/5/80 4/20/85 18,300
Carol Smith Marketing 2/2/74 42,500
Thomas Branch Administrative 5/1/86 7/3/87 19,700
Pg 1 Sec 1 1/1 At 1" Ln 1 Col 1

Figure 13–9. A table displayed without gridlines or cell text markers.

Figure 13-10.
A table displayed
with gridlines and
cell text markers.

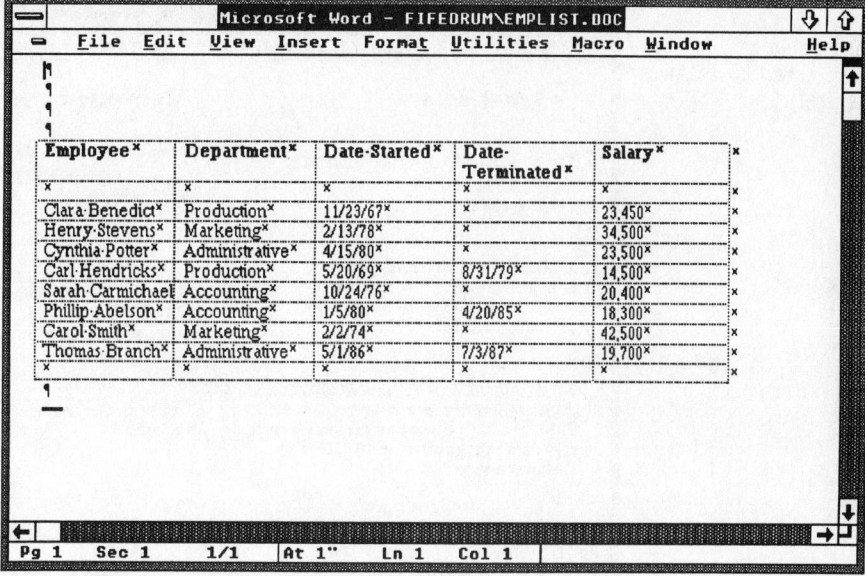

you'll probably want to separate items with commas or tabs and press Enter to end each row with a paragraph mark. Don't try to align columns by adding extra tabs or spaces and don't use commas to separate thousands in numbers—your table won't come out right. Word reads each comma or tab as a separator (*delimiter*) between columns. If you have two commas or two tabs next to each other, you'll end up with a blank cell in that spot.

You can also put whole paragraphs of text into table cells. Take a look at Figure 13-11 to see how these different options work.

You can also import information from another file to a Word table and even link that information to its source file so that Word can automatically update the Word table. (For more information about linking data in a Word file to another file, see Chapter 22, "Using Information from Other Files.")

If you use data from another file, you must be sure that the information to put into cells in a table is separated by commas, tabs, or paragraph marks—those are the only separators that Word understands. Also, make sure that there are no extra commas, tabs, or paragraph marks, because each comma or tab causes Word to insert one column.

To create a table from selected text:

1. Type the words or numbers you want to put into a table, or import that information from another file.

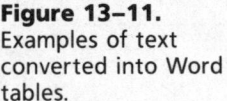

Figure 13–11.
Examples of text
converted into Word
tables.

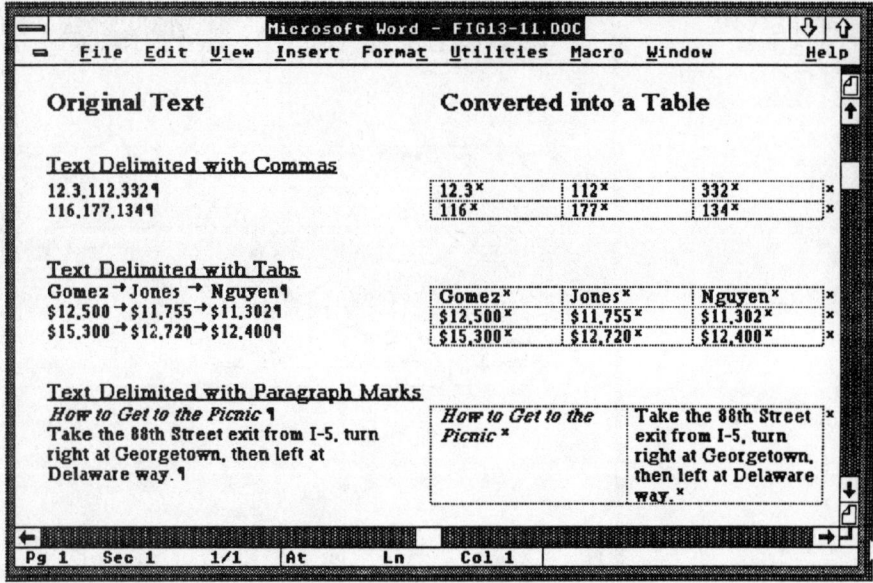

2. Select the text for the table.

3. Choose the Insert Table command. Word fills in the Number of Columns and Number of Rows boxes, based on the selected text.

4. If necessary, type a new measurement in the Initial Col Width box. Word calculates a default column width (Auto), which is based on the space between document margins and the number of columns.

You can always change the column width later, so in most cases you'll want to leave this option alone. To specify different widths for different columns, go on to the next step.

5. Make sure that the option selected in the Convert From box matches the selected text. In other words, if your items are separated by commas, the Comma Delimited option should be selected.

6. If you want to specify individual column widths, align or indent rows, or draw borders around cells at this time, choose Format. See Adjusting the Width of Columns, Indenting Rows, Aligning Rows, and Adding Borders to a Table later in this chapter for

instructions on completing these tasks. You can always change or add formatting to a table, so you can ignore the format until later if you like.

7. Click OK or press **Enter** to close the dialog box and draw the table.

▭ *Helpful Hint*

If you've inserted a table as the first item in your file, and you now want to insert new information in front of the table, here's how to do it:

1. Place the insertion point in the first cell in the table.

2. Press **Ctrl+Shift+Enter**. Word inserts a paragraph mark in front of the table.

3. Place the insertion point in front of the new paragraph mark and type or paste in text.

ENTERING INFORMATION IN TABLE CELLS

All of Word's editing commands work in tables just as they do in the rest of your document, so you enter, edit, and format text and graphics in a table in the same way as you would anywhere else. The only difference is that the text in a table is contained in individual cells, so you have to move the insertion point to the cell you want to affect before you can enter or edit text in that cell.

Moving the Insertion Point in Tables

To move the insertion point to a cell with the mouse:

■ Click the cell you want to work in.

To move the insertion point to a cell with the keyboard, choose from the following list.

To move	Use
Right one cell	Tab
Left one cell	Shift+Tab
To first cell in current row	Alt+Home

To last cell in current row	Alt+End
To top cell in current column	Alt+PgUp
To bottom cell in current column	Alt+PgDn

To move the insertion point within a cell, use the arrow keys or point and click with the mouse, just as you would outside of a table.

Inserting or Editing Text or Graphics

When the insertion point is in a cell, just type, choose commands to paste in text or graphics, or edit text as you would normally do, with one exception:

■ To enter a tab character in a table cell, press **Ctrl+Tab**.

Word wraps the text you type when it reaches the cell margin to maintain the width of the column and adjusts the height of the row as you add new text. Pressing Enter adds a new paragraph to the cell and increases the height of all cells in the row.

Selecting in Tables

A table has an invisible selection bar at the top of each column and at the left side of each cell, as shown in Figure 13–12. When the mouse pointer is in the selection bar at the top of a column, it becomes a downward-pointing arrow. When the mouse pointer is in the selection bar at the left side of a cell, it becomes a slanted arrow, just as it does at the side of paragraphs in regular text.

Selecting text in a table cell is generally the same as selecting text anywhere in a document, with the following exception: You can't select individual lines of text by clicking in the selection bar to the left of a line—in tables, this selects the contents of the cell. To select lines, drag the mouse to highlight the text; or set the insertion point, move to the end of the text, press the **Shift** key, then click the mouse button.

When you select a cell, you select all the text in that cell—then you can choose editing or formatting commands to change the text. For example, you could select a column of cells and make all the text in those cells bold. Here's how selecting cells works in Word:

Figure 13–12.
Selection bars in a table.

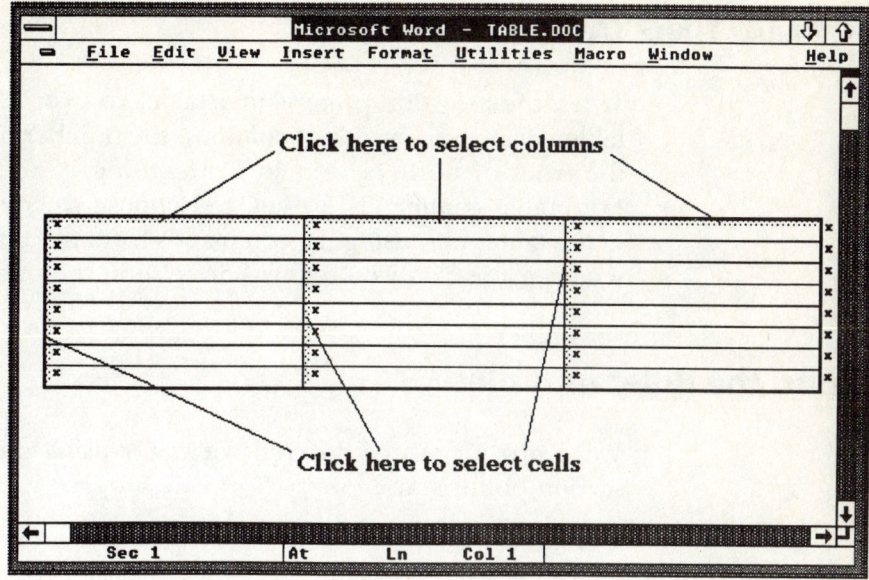

To select	With mouse	With keys
One cell	Click the selection bar in the cell	Press the Tab key
Group of cells	Drag to highlight the cells	Hold down the Shift key and use arrow keys to highlight the cells
Column of cells	Click the selection bar above the column	Hold down the Shift key and use the Up and Down arrow keys to highlight cells
Row of cells	Double-click the selection bar of any cell in the row	Hold down the Shift key and use the Tab key to highlight the cells
Entire table	Click the left mouse button in the top left cell and drag to the bottom right corner of the table	Hold down the Alt key and press 5 on the numeric keypad (with NumLock off)

FORMATTING TABLES

When the insertion point is in a table, you can choose to format the table—change the width of columns, the number of rows and columns, the types of borders, and so forth—using Word's Format Table and Edit Table commands; or you can choose to edit or format the text in the table cells, using the commands from the Edit menu and Format menu just as you would anywhere else in the document.

Using the Ruler in Tables

Word provides three different views for using the ruler when the insertion point is in a table:

- indent view

- column view

- margin view

When you choose the View Ruler command, the ruler first displays indent markers for the paragraph containing the insertion point, as shown in Figure 13–13. You can use this ruler view to format paragraphs just as you would outside of a table, adding indents, alignments,

Figure 13–13.
This view of the ruler enables you to format paragraphs in table cells.

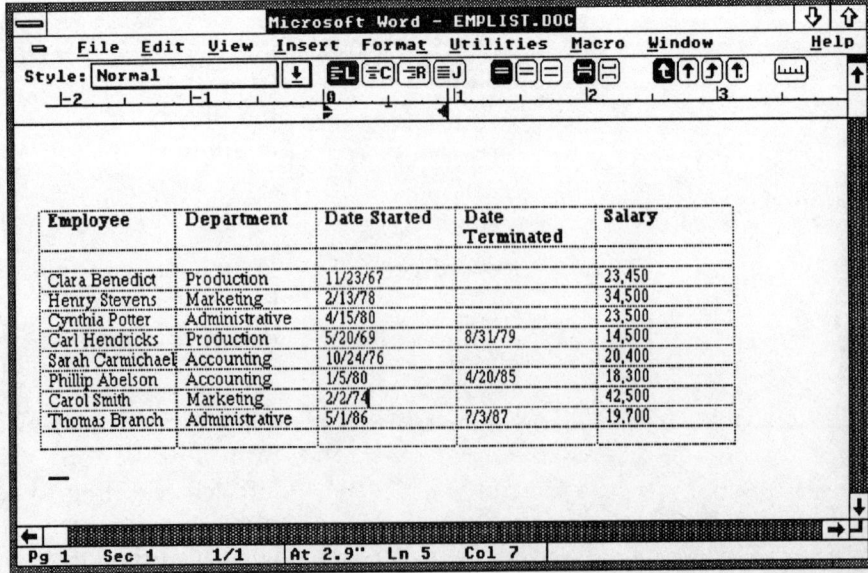

Employee	Department	Date Started	Date Terminated	Salary
Clara Benedict	Production	11/23/67		23,450
Henry Stevens	Marketing	2/13/78		34,500
Cynthia Potter	Administrative	4/15/80		23,500
Carl Hendricks	Production	5/20/69	8/31/79	14,500
Sarah Carmichael	Accounting	10/24/76		20,400
Phillip Abelson	Accounting	1/5/80	4/20/85	18,300
Carol Smith	Marketing	2/2/74		42,500
Thomas Branch	Administrative	5/1/86	7/3/87	19,700

line spacing, and styles to paragraphs. See Chapter 9 for more information about formatting paragraphs.

If you click the ruler view icon (the icon on the right that looks like a small scale or comb), the ruler displays column markers for the row containing the insertion point, as shown in Figure 13–14. In this view, you can drag the left indent marker to indent selected rows in the table or drag a column marker to make cells wider or narrower. These tasks are explained in Indenting Rows and in Adjusting the Widths of Columns later in this chapter.

If you click the ruler view icon again, Word displays margin markers, as shown in Figure 13–15. You can drag the markers to change the margins of the entire document.

Formatting Paragraphs in Table Cells

Here are a few facts you should keep in mind when formatting paragraphs in table cells:

■ Indenting and aligning paragraphs: Paragraphs in cells are indented and aligned relative to the cell margins. For example, justifying a paragraph in a cell aligns the text with the margins of the cell that contains it.

Figure 13–14.
View of the ruler you use to indent rows and change the width of columns in a table.

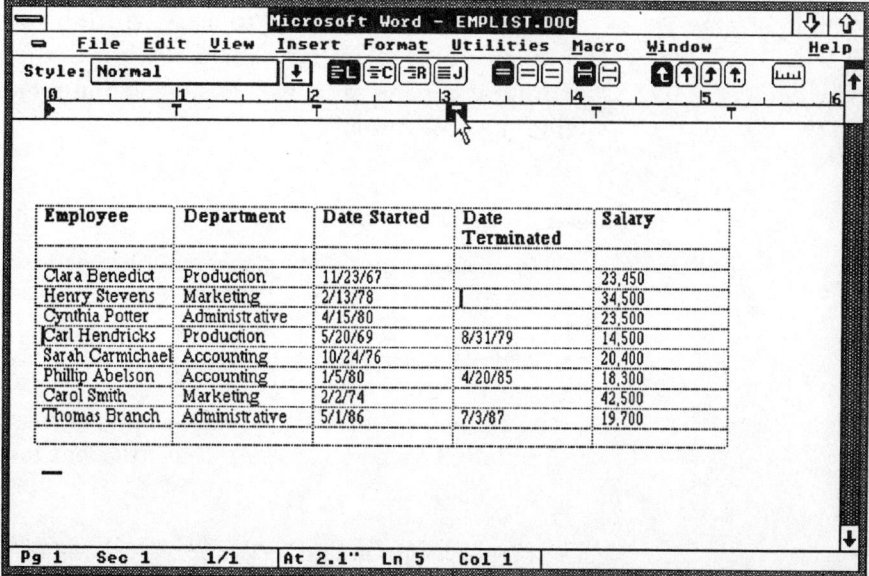

Figure 13–15.
View of the ruler you
use to change
margins in the entire
document.

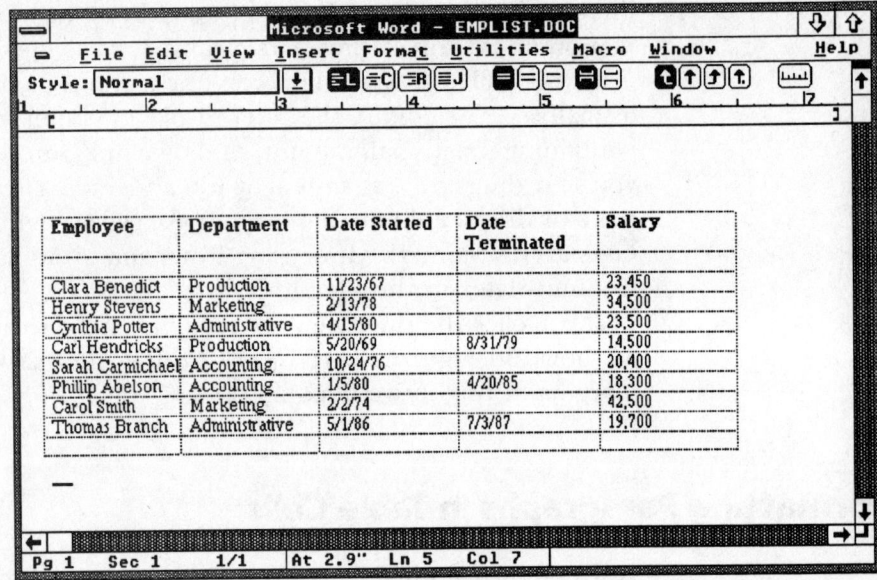

- Setting tabs in tables: You can set tabs in tables to align or set spacing of text, and you can even use tabs to create minitables within table cells.

- To align columns of numbers containing decimal points, select the column, then set a decimal tab to align the numbers in the column. There's no need to use Ctrl+Tab to insert tab characters in the cells; just setting a decimal tab with the ruler or the Format Paragraph command will make the numbers in a table column line up on decimal points.

Helpful Hint

To include more white space around your text in tables, you can do the following:

- Add blank lines before and after paragraphs by pressing Enter.

- Use the ruler or the Format Paragraph command to put space before and after paragraphs in a cell or to indent the paragraphs from the cell margins.

- Type a measurement in the Space Between Cells box in the Format Table dialog box to put more space between the text in table cells.

Adjusting the Width of Columns

You can specify different widths for columns before or after you insert a table. You can change the width of any column using the Width of Columns box in the Format Table dialog box.

To specify different widths for columns:

1. Do one of the following:

   ■ If you're inserting a table for the first time, choose the Insert Table command, type the number of columns and rows, then choose Format to open the Format Table dialog box.

   ■ If you're changing the width of columns in an existing table, select the columns, then choose the Format Table command.

2. Choose Next Column or Prev Column until you see the number of the column you want to change at the top left of the dialog box (Width of Column n). For example, if you want to change the width of the third column, make sure this says Width of Column 3.

3. Type a measurement for that column. Word assumes measurements are in inches unless you use an abbreviation (such as *cm* for centimeters) or unless you've changed the default unit of measurement with the Utilities Customize command.

4. Repeat steps 2 and 3 until you've changed the width of all columns you want to affect.

5. Click OK or press **Enter** to close the dialog box and redraw the table.

Figure 13–16 illustrates changing the width of a column with the Format Table command.

You can also change the width of columns in an existing table with the ruler and the mouse:

1. Select the column(s) whose width you want to change.

2. If necessary, choose the View Ruler command.

3. Click the ruler view icon to see column markers on the ruler.

4. Drag the column markers to a new location to widen or narrow the selected columns, as shown in Figure 13–17.

Figure 13–16.
Changing the width
of a column with the
Format Table
command.

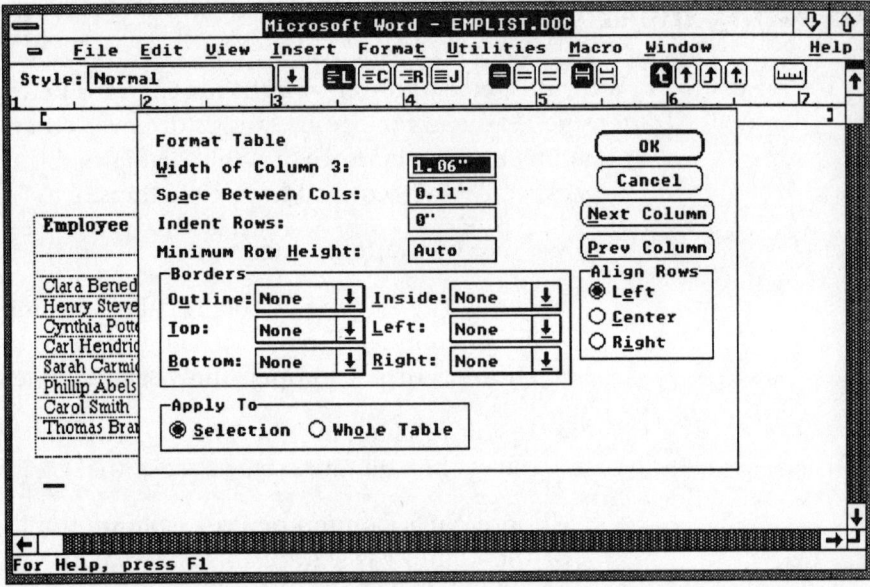

Figure 13–17.
Changing the width
of columns with the
ruler.

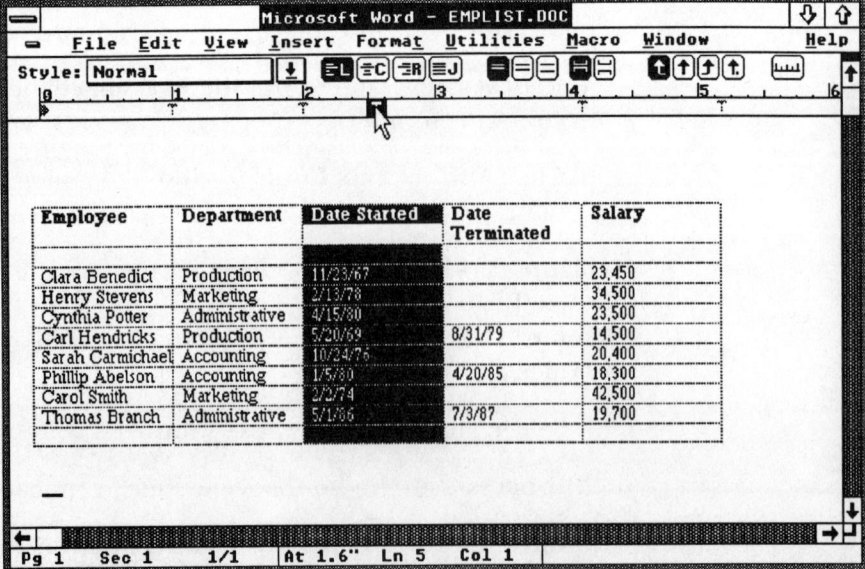

Indenting Rows

You can use the Format Table command or the ruler to indent rows in a table, repositioning the entire table or just a few rows. Rows are indented from the left margin of the document. Figure 13–18 shows an example of a table with indented rows.

To indent rows with the Format Table command:

1. Do one of the following:

   ■ To indent rows as you create a table, choose Format in the Insert Table dialog box to display the Format Table dialog box.

   ■ To indent rows in an existing table, select the rows to indent, then choose the Format Table command.

2. Type a measurement in the Indent Rows box to indent rows from the left margin. For example, type **.5** to indent rows ½ inch.

3. In the Apply To box, choose Selection to indent only selected rows or choose Whole Table to indent the whole table.

4. Click OK or press **Enter** to close the dialog box and redraw the table.

Figure 13–18.
A table with
indented rows.

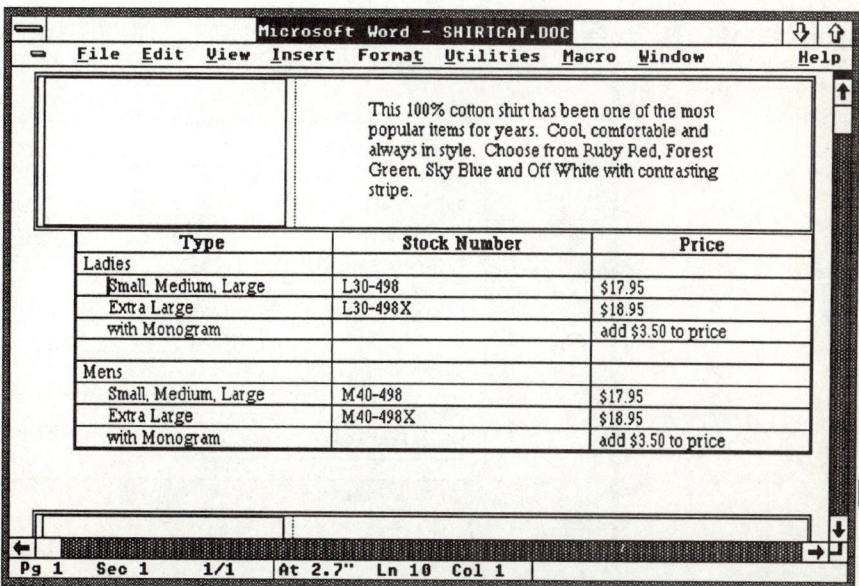

Type	Stock Number	Price
Ladies		
Small, Medium, Large	L30-498	$17.95
Extra Large	L30-498X	$18.95
with Monogram		add $3.50 to price
Mens		
Small, Medium, Large	M40-498	$17.95
Extra Large	M40-498X	$18.95
with Monogram		add $3.50 to price

This 100% cotton shirt has been one of the most popular items for years. Cool, comfortable and always in style. Choose from Ruby Red, Forest Green, Sky Blue and Off White with contrasting stripe.

Figure 13–19 illustrates indenting rows with the Format Table command.

To indent rows using the ruler:

1. Select the rows you want to indent.

2. If necessary, choose the View Ruler command.

3. Click the ruler view icon to see column markers and a left indent marker, as shown in Figure 13–20.

4. Drag the left indent marker to a new position.

Aligning Rows

You can align table rows with the left or right document margin, or you can center rows between the two margins. Figure 13–21 shows tables with different row alignments.

To align rows in a table:

1. Do one of the following:

   ■ To align rows as you create a table, choose Format in the Insert Table dialog box to display the Format Table dialog box.

Figure 13–19.
Indenting rows with the Format Table command.

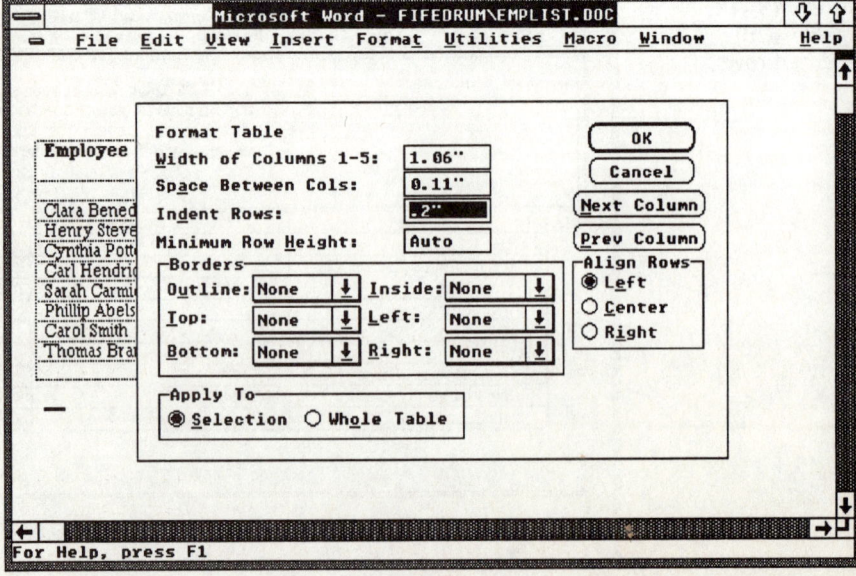

Figure 13–20.
Indenting rows with
the ruler.

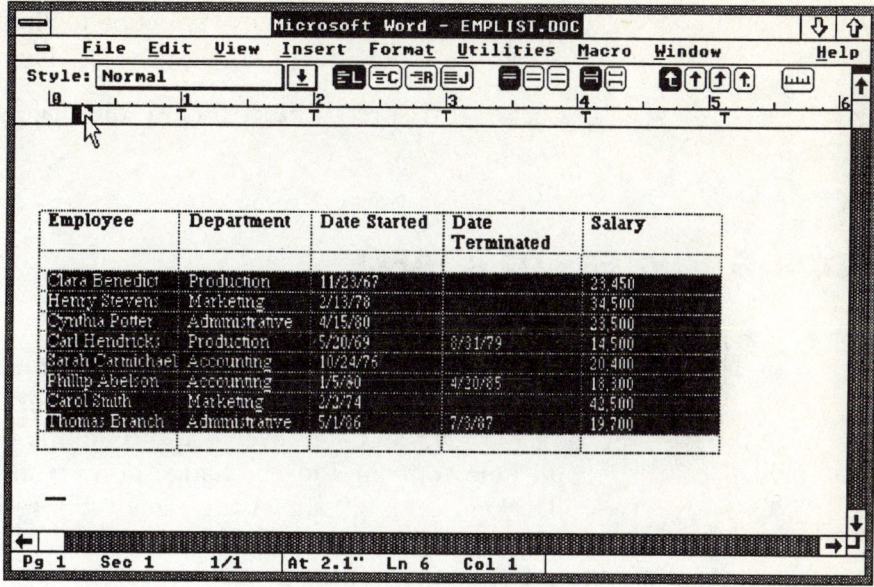

Figure 13–21.
Tables with different
row alignments.

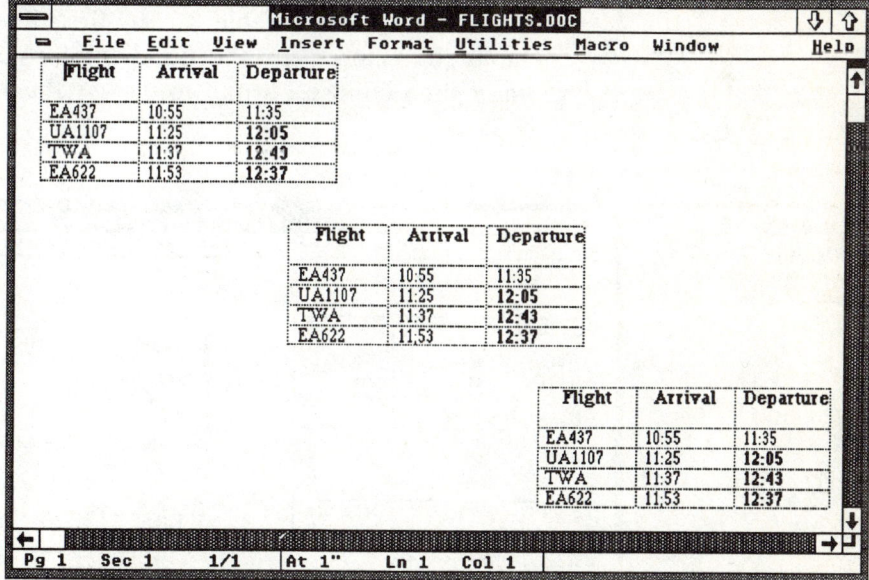

■ To align rows in an existing table, select the rows to indent,
then choose the Format Table command.

2. Choose Left, Center, or Right in the Align Rows box.

3. In the Apply To box, choose Selection to align only selected rows, or choose Whole Table to align the whole table.

4. Click OK or press **Enter** to close the dialog box and make the change.

ADDING BORDERS TO A TABLE

You can add borders of different thicknesses around individual cells, groups of cells, or whole tables. You might want to insert lines between rows and columns, just between columns, or just around the outside of the table. Or you might even want to outline just one cell to make it stand out. You can add or change borders around cells any time you like. Figure 13–22 shows the same table with different types of borders.

To add borders to cells or change borders around cells in a table:

1. Do one of the following:

■ If you're inserting a table for the first time, choose the Insert Table command, type the number of columns and rows you want, then choose Format to display the Format Table dialog box.

Figure 13–22.
Tables with a variety of borders.

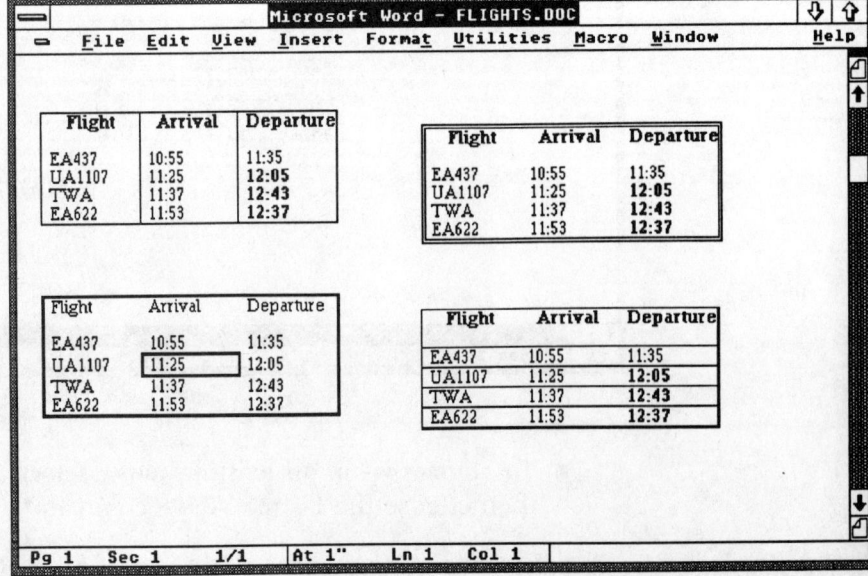

■ If you're adding borders to or changing borders in an existing table, select the cells you want to affect, then choose the Format Table command.

2. Choose the option that controls the position of the border you want to add:

Choose	**If you want to draw a line**
Outline	Around the outside of the selected cells.
Inside	Between all of the selected cells.
Top	At the top edge of the selected cells.
Bottom	At the bottom edge of the selected cells.
Left	At the left edge of the selected cells.
Right	At the right edge of the selected cells.

4. From the drop-down list, choose the type of line you want at that location:

■ Single

■ Thick

■ Double

■ Shadow (only in the Outline box)

Figure 13–23 illustrates selecting a line type for an outside border around one cell.

5. If necessary, repeat steps 3 and 4 to choose different lines for different locations.

6. In the Apply To box, choose Selection to add borders to only the selected cells, or choose Whole Table to add borders to the whole table.

7. Click OK or press **Enter** to redraw the table.

To remove borders that you've added to a table, just select the cells you want to affect, choose the appropriate position option in the Format Table dialog box, then select None from the drop-down list.

Figure 13–23.
Selecting a line type
for a border around a
cell.

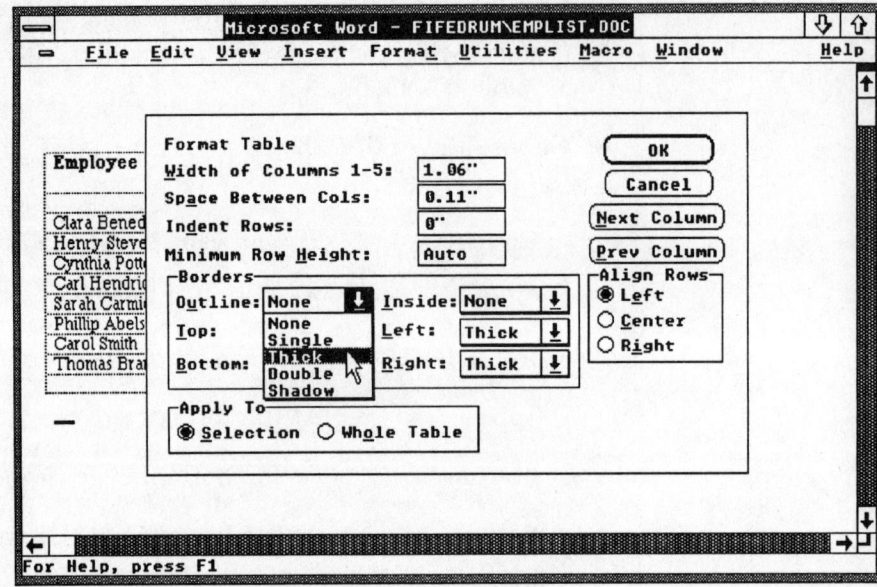

PRECISELY POSITIONING A TABLE ON A PAGE

If you want to move a table to a specific location on a page (like 2″ from left margin and 3″ from the top margin, for example), select the entire table, then use the Format Position command. When you use the Format Position command, the surrounding text automatically adjusts to "flow" around the positioned table. For more information about using the Format Position command, see Positioning Objects Anywhere on a Page in Chapter 14. Figure 13–24 shows a table that's been positioned in this way.

REARRANGING TABLE CELLS

When you add, delete, or merge cells in a Word table, you use the Edit Table command to rearrange the cells. The Edit Table dialog box is shown in Figure 13–25.

Merging Table Cells

Sometimes you may want to have one wide cell over two or more narrower ones, as shown in Figure 13–26.

Figure 13–24.
A table positioned with the Format Position command. Note the way surrounding text flows around the table.

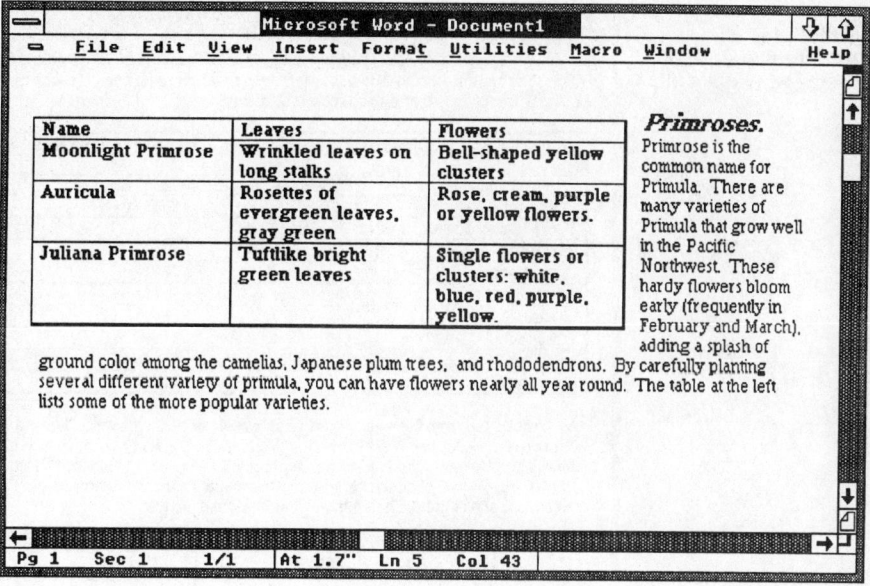

Figure 13–25.
The Edit Table dialog box.

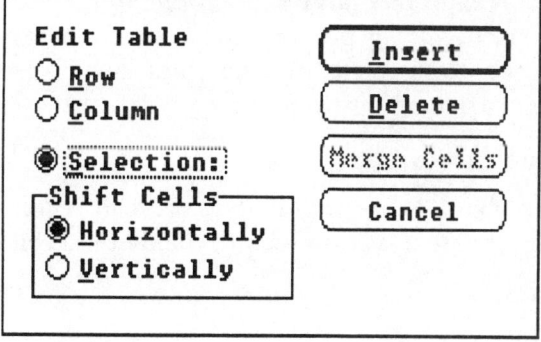

To create this effect, you merge two or more table cells in a row—this "dissolves" the boundaries of adjoining cells to create one wide cell.

To merge table cells:

1. Select the cells you want to merge. The cells must be in the same row. Word cannot merge cells stacked on top of each other in a column.

2. Choose the Edit Table command.

3. Choose Merge Cells. Word dissolves the boundaries between cells

Figure 13–26.
You can merge cells
to create wider cells.

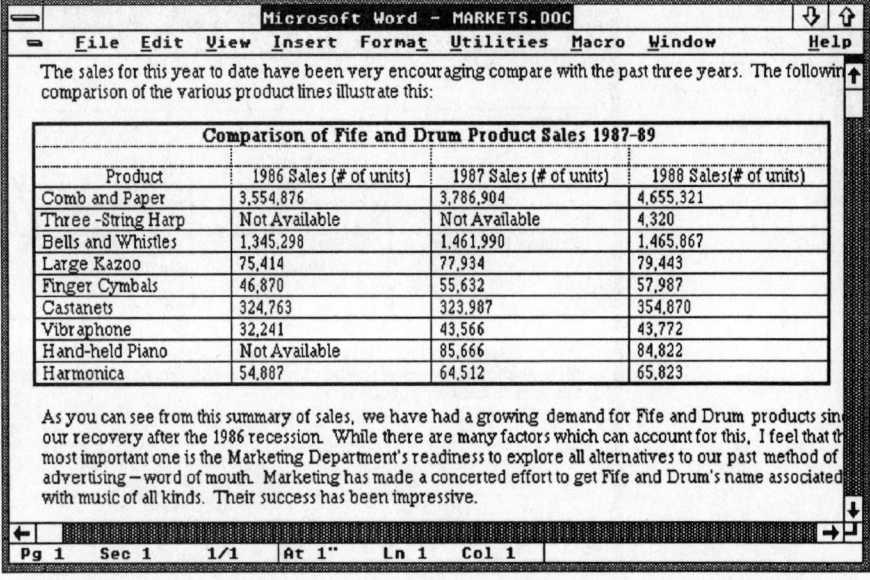

and creates one large cell. (If the Merge Cells button is dimmed, close the dialog box and make sure that you have selected only adjacent table cells in a row, not any stacked cells, and not any text surrounding the table.)

4. Click OK or press **Enter**.

If you change your mind later, you can reverse the process as discussed in the next section to split the merged cell into individual cells.

Splitting Merged Cells

To split a merged table cell back into individual cells:

1. Select the merged cell.

2. Choose the Edit Table command.

3. Choose Split Cells.

4. Click OK or press **Enter**.

> ◣ *Helpful Hint*

If you think you might use a certain table format—five rows and three columns with thin vertical lines dividing columns and a shadow outline around the whole table, for example—create and format an empty table, then save that table as a glossary entry that you can use over and over.

For more information about using glossaries, see Saving Text and Graphics for Later Use: Using Glossaries in Chapter 4.

Adding Rows or Columns to Tables

To add a row or column to a table:

1. Move the insertion point into the row or column before which you want to insert a new row or column. If you want to add a column to the right side of a table, click to the right of the table to move the insertion point there.

   If you want to insert more than one row or column, select the number of rows or columns you want to insert. For example, to insert three rows, select three rows in your table. The new rows or columns will be inserted in front of the first selected row or column.

2. Choose the Edit Table command.

3. Choose the Row option to add rows, or choose the Column option to add columns.

4. Choose Insert. Word redraws the table with new rows or columns.

▭ *Helpful Hint*

To quickly add a row at the bottom of the table, move the insertion point into the last cell in the last row, then press the **Tab** key.

Deleting Rows or Columns from Tables

If you just want to delete the text in a row or column of cells, select the cells, then choose the Edit Cut command. The following procedure removes whole rows and columns, as well as the text in those columns, from a table.

To delete rows or columns from a table:

1. Select the rows or columns you want to delete.

2. Choose the Edit Table command.

3. Choose Delete. Word redraws the table.

To delete an entire table, select all the cells, choose the Edit Table command, choose the Selection option, then choose Delete.

Splitting One Table into Two

If you want to split one table into two tables, you can do it this way:

1. Place the insertion point in the cell before which you want to split the table.

2. Press **Ctrl+Shift+Enter**. Word inserts a paragraph mark, separating the table into two.

COPYING AND MOVING THE CONTENTS OF CELLS

You can copy or move the contents of cells within the same table or between tables with the Edit Copy, Edit Cut, and Edit Paste Cells commands.

When pasting cells, Word pastes in the same number of cells in the same pattern. In other words, if you copy a block of cells arranged in two columns and three rows, Word will paste the contents of those cells in two columns and three rows, beginning with the cell containing the insertion point and replacing any information in the paste area. If the paste area doesn't contain enough cells to hold the copied cells, Word displays a message telling you the areas are different shapes.

To copy or move the contents of table cells:

1. Select the cells whose contents you want to copy.

2. Choose the Edit Copy command (to copy the contents of the cells) or the Edit Cut command (to delete the contents of the cells).

3. Select the cells you want to paste the contents into or place the insertion point in the first cell you want to paste into (the upper left cell of the paste area).

4. Choose the Edit Paste Cells command.

You can also paste table cells outside a table—in that case, Word creates a new table with the dimensions and format of the pasted cells.

CALCULATING IN TABLES

You can include fields that will automatically perform calculations in your table. Just as in a spreadsheet, you can refer to specific cells or to ranges of cells in a Word table by inserting a field and specifying the row and column numbers like this: [R*n*C*n*]. For example, a cell in the first row and the first column is [R1C1]. To specify a range of cells, you separate the cell references with a colon ([r1c1:r5c3]). You must enclose the references in square brackets. Figure 13–27 shows a table that uses fields to calculate.

You can also use the Utilities Calculate command to calculate selected numbers and display the result in the status bar. You can then paste in the result if you like.

For more information about all types of calculations, see Chapter 20, "Performing Calculations."

CONVERTING A TABLE INTO NORMAL TEXT

Just as you can convert normal text into a table, you can reverse the process and convert a table into normal text.

Figure 13–27.
Using fields to
calculate in tables.

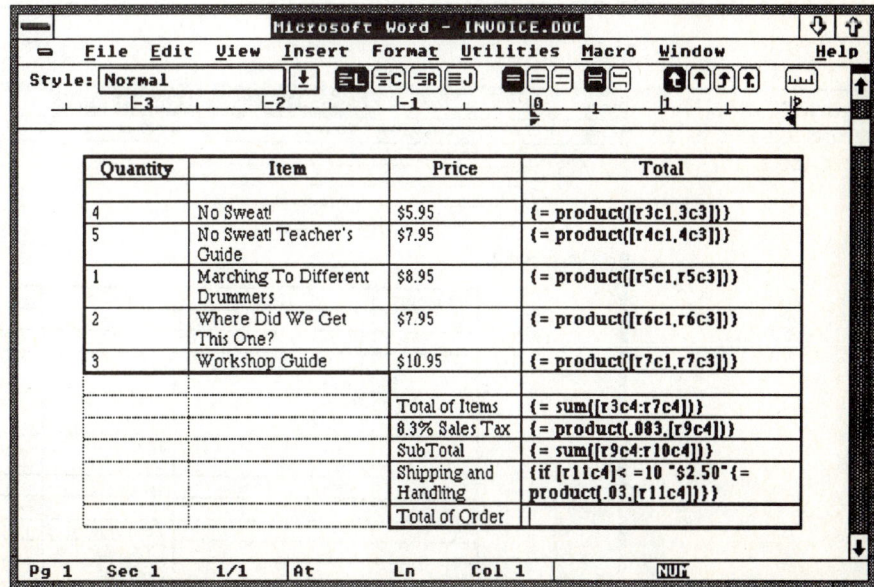

To convert a table into normal text:

1. Select the table.

2. Choose the Insert Table to Text command. (The Insert Table command becomes the Insert Table to Text command.) Word displays the dialog box shown in Figure 13–28.

3. Select an option to pick the character you want to separate the contents of each cell:

   ■ Paragraphs (paragraph marks)

   ■ Tab Delimited

   ■ Comma Delimited

4. Click OK or press **Enter**.

Figure 13–28.
The Insert Table to
Text dialog box.

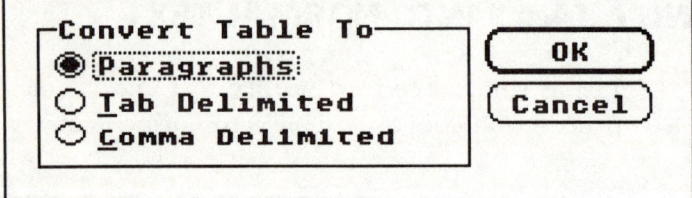

Figure 13–29.
A form created as a
Word table.

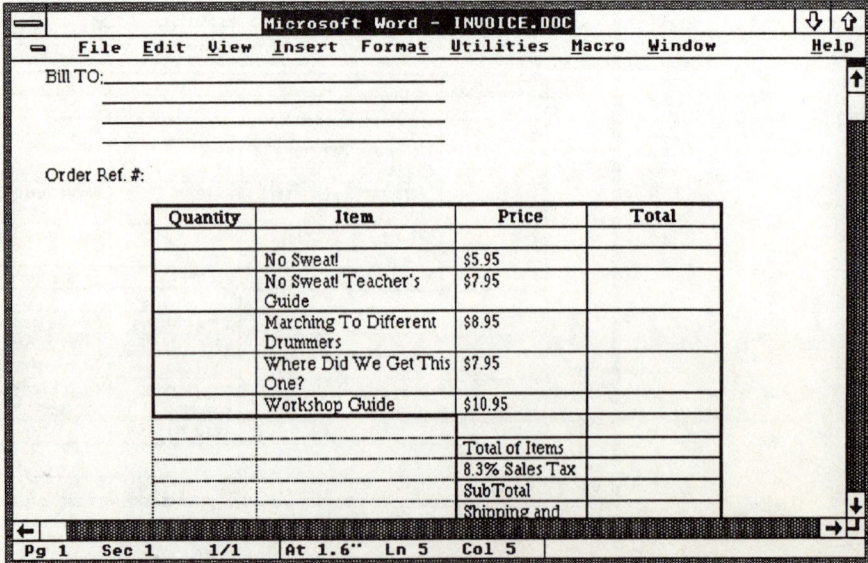

USING TABLES TO CREATE FORMS

You can use Word's table features to create elaborate forms, as shown in Figure 13–29. Remember that you can format characters and paragraphs in tables any way you like, adding borders, italics, underlines, and more. You can use special fonts and graphics to create check boxes and special effects, and you can even add instructions formatted as hidden text.

## Chapter Fourteen

Perfecting Your Pages

When you've finished editing and formatting your document, you'll want to see the finished pages before you print them. This chapter shows you how to use Word's print preview and page view features to check and change page layouts. You'll also learn how to control page breaks and how to use hyphenation to make your pages look better.

USING PRINT PREVIEW AND PAGE VIEW

Generally speaking, it's most efficient to enter, edit, and format your text in normal view—Word's default view that you see when you first start Word. But you can't see some parts of a document in normal view, like headers and footers, page numbers, footnotes, multiple columns, and the correct positions of some objects on a page. To see these elements, you can switch to page view or print preview.

Using Print Preview

When you want to see what a document looks like before you print, switch to print preview (shown in Figure 14–1), the view that shows you a miniature version of your pages. For best results, make sure the Word window is full size when you use print preview.

You can use the mouse in print preview to change margins, page breaks, and column breaks, and position page numbers, headers, and footers for your document. You can also use the mouse to move any object you positioned with the Format Position command.

Figure 14–1.
Print preview shows
entire pages.

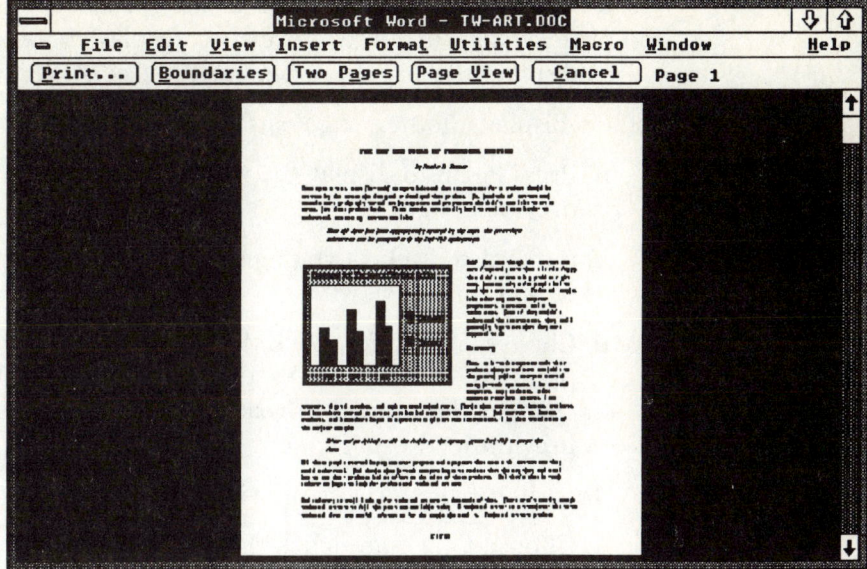

You can't edit or format text in print preview because the text is too small—to see a full-size page with all the text in place, you use page view, as described later in this chapter.

Switching to and from Print Preview

To switch to print preview from normal view or from page view:

■ Choose the File Print Preview command.

To switch to page view from print preview:

■ Choose Page View (press V or click the button at the top of the print preview screen).

To switch to normal view from print preview:

■ Choose Cancel (press Esc or click the button at the top of the print preview screen).

Viewing Pages in Print Preview

When you first switch to print preview, Word displays a one-page view of the page containing the insertion point. You can flip back and forth through all the pages in your document, and you can also display just one page at a time.

To display another page with the mouse:

- Click below the scroll box in the vertical scroll bar to display the next page or click above it to display the previous page. Word displays the page numbers at the top of the window.

To display another page with keys:

- Press PgDn to display the next page or press PgUp to display the previous page.

You can also display two pages at a time. To switch from a one-page view to a two-page view:

- Choose Two Pages (click the button at the top of the window or press A). Word redraws the window to display two pages and changes the button to read One Page. Figure 14–2 shows print preview in two-page view.

To switch from a two-page view to a one-page view:

- Choose One Page (click the button at the top of the window or press A). Word redraws the window to display one page and changes the button to read Two Pages.

Moving Margins in Print Preview

You can use the mouse to change the position of margins in print preview. Changing the margins on one page in print preview changes margins throughout the document.

Figure 14–2.
Two-page view in
print preview.

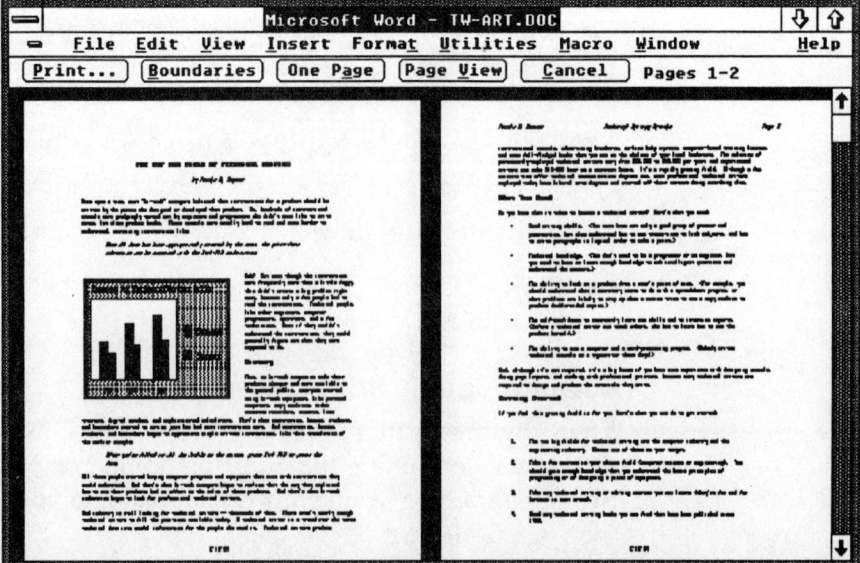

To move a margin in print preview with the mouse:

1. Click the Boundaries button at the top of the window to display text boundary lines. Word displays dotted lines, as shown in Figure 14–3.

2. Point to the black rectangle attached to the margin line you want to move. The mouse pointer becomes a cross-hair (a thin cross) symbol, as shown in Figure 14–3.

3. Drag the margin line to a new position. Word changes the position numbers at the top of the window as you move the margin line.

4. Release the mouse button, then click outside of the page diagram. Word redraws the pages using the new margin measurement.

To move a margin in print preview with keys:

1. Press B (to choose the Boundaries button) to display text boundary lines. Word displays dotted lines, as shown in Figure 14–3.

2. Press the Tab key until the margin line you want to move is highlighted.

3. Use the direction keys to move the margin line.

4. Press the Tab key to set the new position.

Figure 14–3.
Moving the top margin in print preview.

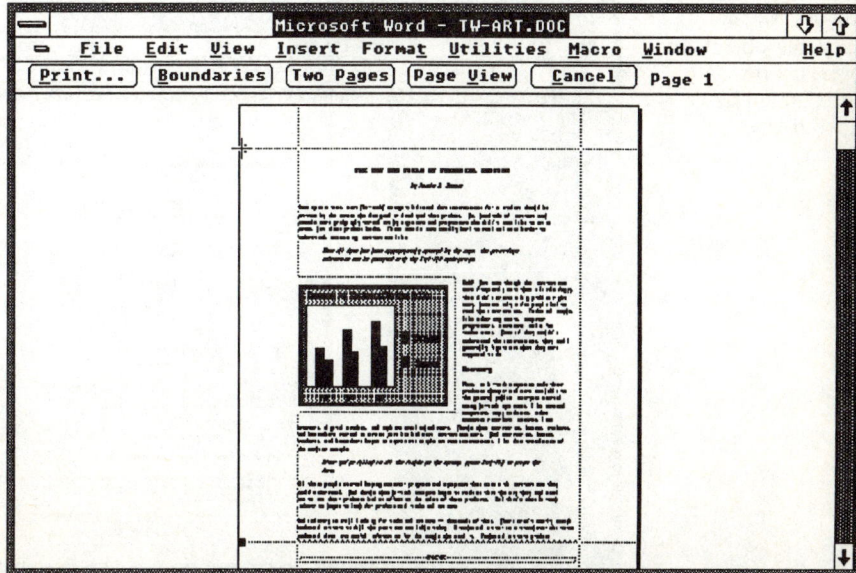

Moving Page Breaks, Headers, Footers, Page Numbers, and Positioned Objects in Print Preview

When you choose the Boundaries button in print preview, Word draws dotted lines around the following movable objects: page breaks, headers, footers, page numbers, and all objects positioned with the Format Position command (fixed-positioned objects). Figure 14–4 shows movable objects in the print preview window. For more information about positioning objects, see Positioning Objects Anywhere on a Page later in this chapter.

Note: Don't confuse the page break marker in print preview with the bottom margin marker. It's sometimes hard to see, but the page break marker is always positioned above the margin marker and extends only the width of the text area. The margin markers extend to the edges of the page. If you move a margin marker, the margins will be changed on all pages throughout your document.

To move a page break, header, footer, page number, or any positioned object with the mouse:

1. If necessary, click the Boundaries button at the top of the Print Preview window, then click a page to draw lines around movable objects.

2. Point to the object you want to move. The mouse pointer becomes a cross-hair (a thin cross) symbol. If a picture or text has not

Figure 14–4.
Movable objects in print preview are surrounded by dotted lines.

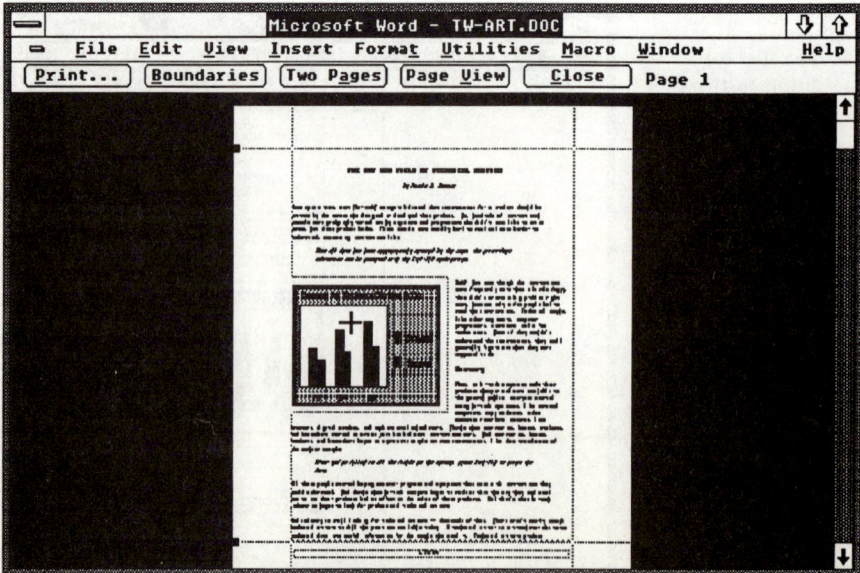

been previously positioned using the Format Position command, the cross-hair symbol won't appear.

3. Drag the object to a new position. Word changes the position numbers at the top of the window as you move the object.

4. Release the mouse button, then click outside of the page diagram. Word redraws the pages. Moving a header, footer, or page number on one page changes the position of those objects on all pages of the document. Moving a page break causes Word to recalculate the breaks on the following pages.

To move a page break, header, footer, page number, or any positioned object with the keys:

1. If necessary, press B to draw boundary lines around movable objects.

2. Press the Tab key until the object you want to move is highlighted.

3. Use the arrow keys to move the object to a new position. Word changes the position numbers at the top of the window as you move the object.

4. Press the Tab key to set the new position. Word redraws the pages. Moving a header, footer, or page number on one page changes the position of those objects on all pages of the document. Moving a page break causes the following pages to be recalculated.

Printing from Print Preview

Once you've made sure all your pages look the way you want, you usually want to print them.

To print from print preview:

1. Choose Print (press P or click the Print button at the top of the window). Word opens the Print dialog box, just as it would if you chose the File Print command.

2. Choose options in the dialog box if necessary, then click OK or press Enter to print.

For more information about printing, see Chapter 16, "Printing."

Using Page View

When you want to see a full-size preview version of your document, you should switch to page view, shown in Figure 14–5.

Figure 14–5.
Page view displays a full-size view of your document with all elements in place.

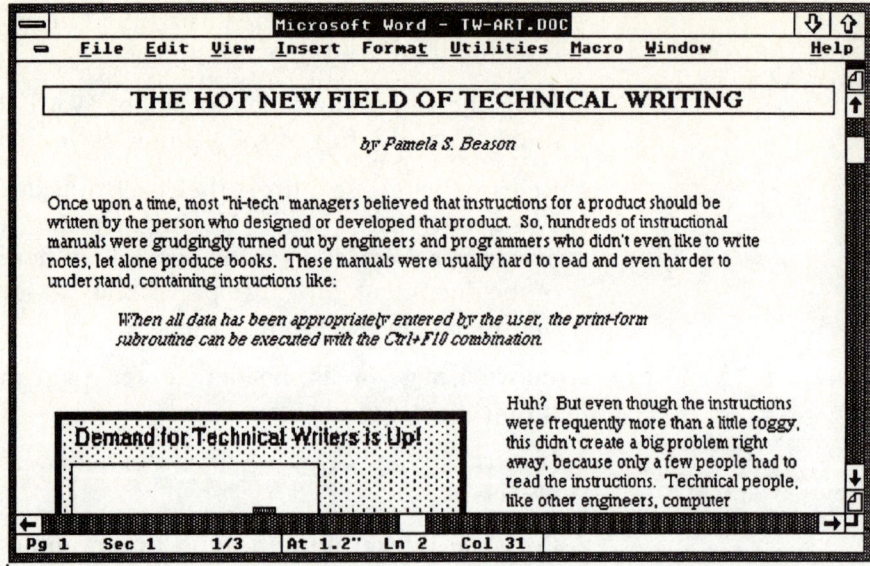

Page view shows you text and formatting you can't see in normal view: multiple columns, page numbers, headers, footers, footnotes, and positioned objects (objects you positioned with the Format Position command). Everything on the page looks just like it will when you print it.

All of Word's editing and formatting commands are available in page view. You can add new text and graphics here, too. You're probably thinking, "Why shouldn't I use page view all the time?" The answer is—you can, but it's not really practical to do so. The drawback to using page view is that Word works more slowly in page view than in normal view. Also, you can't use many commands that open a separate window on the screen, such as a style area, a footnote pane, and so forth. So, you may want to do some editing and formatting in page view to polish your document's appearance, but you'll probably want to do most work in normal view to maximize Word's performance.

Switching to and from Page View

To switch to page view from normal view:

■ Choose the View Page command.

The View Page command is a *toggle command*—when page view is "on," a check mark appears beside the command. To turn page view "off," you choose the command again to remove the check mark. So, to switch to normal view from page view:

- Choose the View Page command.

To switch to page view from print preview:

- Choose Page View (type **V** or click the Page View button at the top of the print preview screen).

To switch from page view to print preview:

- Choose the File Print Preview command.

Displaying Different Pages in Page View

In page view, pages look different than they do in normal view. Word displays the pages as they'll look when you print them, with all of the elements—page numbers, headers, footers, multiple columns, and so on—in their proper positions. And if you scroll to the top or the side of a page in page view, you'll see the edge of the paper, as shown in Figure 14–6.

To move to a specific page, you can use the Edit Go To command to jump to that page, as described in Jumping to a Specific Page later in this chapter.

If you want to scroll from page to page, click the page icons at the top or bottom of the vertical scroll bar:

- To display the next page, click the page icon at the bottom of the scroll bar.

Figure 14–6.
You can see the edges of pages in page view.

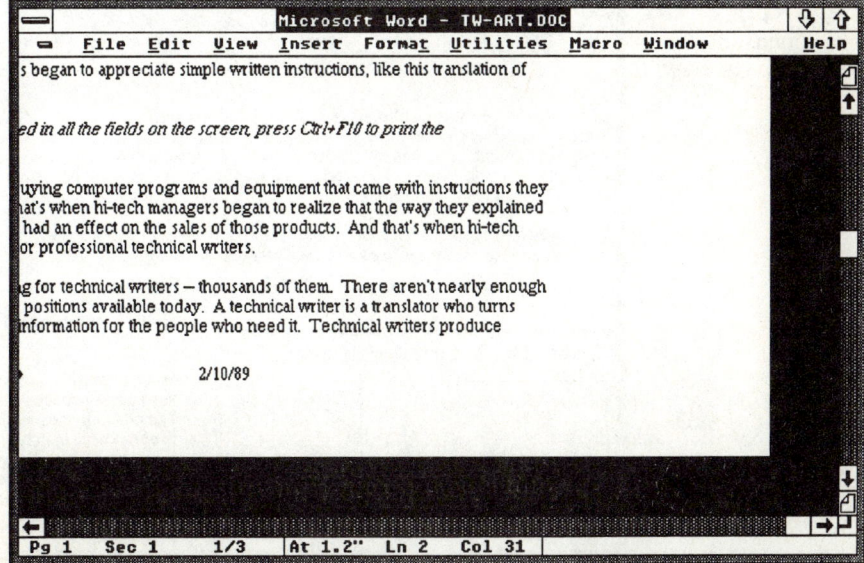

■ To display the previous page, click the page icon at the top of the scroll bar.

Displaying or Removing Text Boundaries

To make it easier to see movable objects in page view, Word draws dotted rectangles called *text boundaries* around the text, as shown in Figure 14–7. You can remove or display text boundaries any time you like.

To display or remove text boundaries in page view:

1. Choose the View Preferences command.

2. Turn on the Text Boundaries option to display the dotted lines or turn off the option to remove text boundaries. (If you have the Show All option turned on, you'll also need to turn it off to remove text boundaries, because Show All overrides most of the individual View Preferences options.)

3. Click OK or press **Enter**.

Using the Ruler in Page View

You can use the ruler in page view just like you do in normal view. The ruler shows the settings of the selected paragraphs.

You can use the ruler to change the alignment, line spacing, and indents of any paragraph, including paragraphs you've positioned with

Figure 14–7.
Text boundaries drawn in page view.

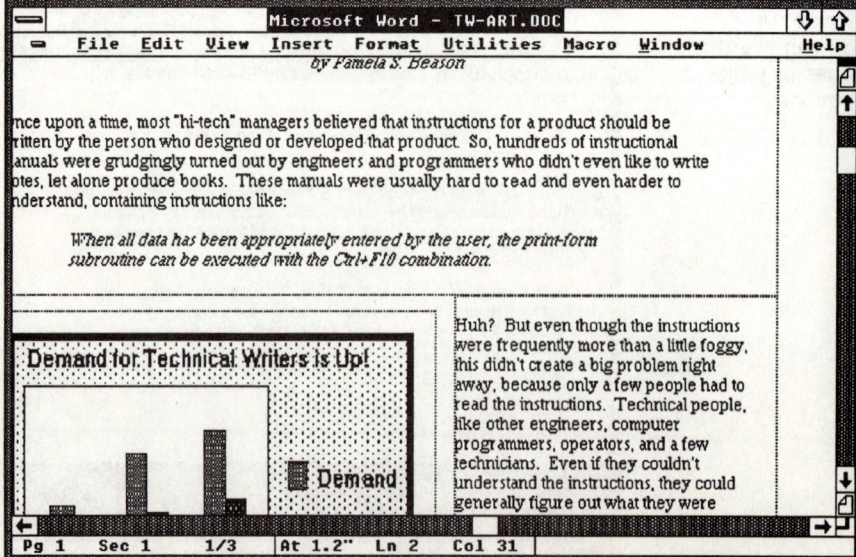

the Format Position command. Because positioned paragraphs may be side by side, you must be careful to move the insertion point into the paragraph you want to adjust before changing settings on the ruler. Figure 14–8 shows how the ruler reflects the settings of a positioned paragraph.

For more information about using the ruler to format paragraphs, see Chapter 9, "Paragraph Formatting."

POSITIONING OBJECTS ANYWHERE ON A PAGE

You can use the Format Position command to tell Word exactly where to position paragraphs on a page. Because paragraphs can contain not only text but graphics and tables too, this means you can move almost anything anywhere on a page. Want that graphic placed 3″ from the top of the page and 2″ from the left margin? You can specify exactly those measurements. You can provide both horizontal and vertical positions; tell Word to align paragraphs with columns, margins, or page edges; and specify paragraph widths. You can also move more than one paragraph as a unit. This means you can extend paragraphs into margins, position paragraphs side-by-side, put a paragraph into the center of a page, and precisely control page layout.

Figure 14–8.
Using the ruler in page view to indent a fixed-positioned paragraph.

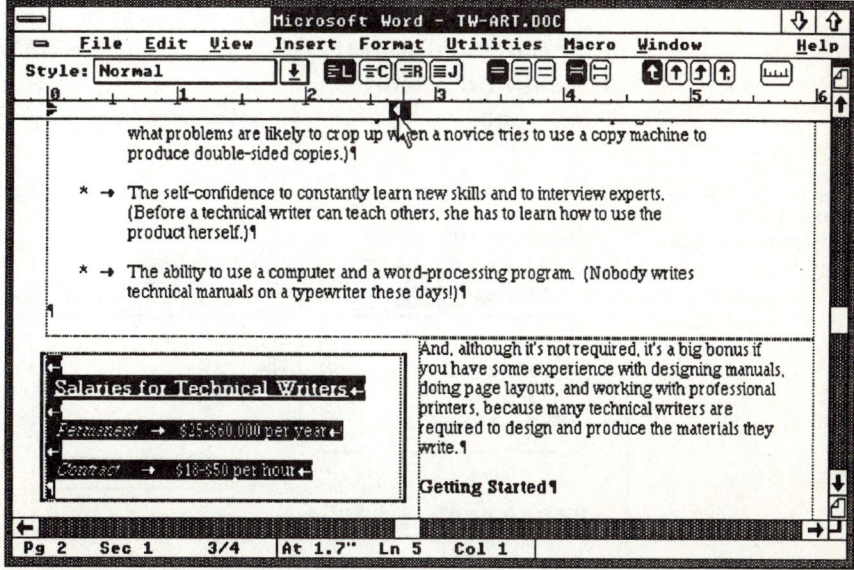

When you use the Format Position command to position a paragraph, Word automatically adjusts surrounding text to "flow" around the positioned paragraph, provided that there is sufficient room. Paragraphs positioned with the Format Position command also become movable objects in print preview, so you can use the mouse to change their locations if you want. Page layout couldn't get much easier!

Specific Positions Versus Relative Positions

Two types of positions are shown in the Format Position dialog box (shown in Figure 14–9):

- specific positions (exact measurements from the top and left margins or page edges).

- relative positions (left, right, inside, outside, center, top, and bottom positions, relative to margins or page edges). (The Inside and Outside options are appropriate only when you've turned on Mirror Margins in the Format Document dialog box to create facing pages.)

When you want to be specific, you type measurements in the Horizontal and Vertical boxes. To indicate the measurements, specify inches, centimeters, points, or picas using the abbreviations **in**, **cm**, **pt**, and **pi**. If you don't use one of these abbreviations, Word assumes the measurement is in inches, unless you've changed the default unit of measurement with the Utilities Customize command. Type a measurement in the Horizontal box, then choose whether that measurement is relative to the left column margin (if you're working with

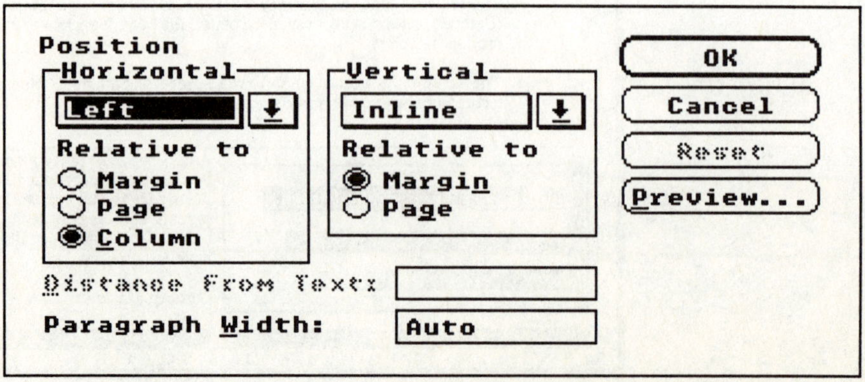

Figure 14–9.
The Format Position dialog box.

columns), the left document margin, or the left edge of the page. Next, type a measurement in the Vertical box, then choose whether that measurement is relative to the top margin or the top edge of the page.

When you want to specify a relative position, move to the Horizontal box and use the mouse of the **Down arrow** key to choose a left, right, center, inside, or outside position from the list. Then choose whether that position is relative to the column, the document margins, or the edges of the page. Next, move to the Vertical box and choose a top, center, bottom, or in-line (original) position from the list. Then choose whether that position is relative to the margins or page edges.

You can also mix specific and relative positions. For example, you might type **8cm** in the Horizontal box and choose Center from the Vertical list.

Setting Up a Paragraph for Positioning

Using the Format Position command draws an invisible boundary around a paragraph. Within this boundary, Word keeps any paragraph formats that affect the paragraph. This means that a paragraph's line spacing, indents, and alignment move with the paragraph. Because this can make positioning paragraphs confusing, you may want to remove space-before and space-after formats, as well as indents, from paragraphs before positioning them with the Format Position command.

If you want text to wrap around a paragraph after you've fixed its position, you may have to change the fixed paragraph's width to create enough room for wrapping text beside the fixed paragraph. The easiest way to change a paragraph's width is to type a measurement (such as **2.5″**) in the Paragraph Width box of the Format Position dialog box.

How Word Calculates Positions

When you type a precise measurement (such as **.5in**) in the Horizontal box of the Format Position command, Word measures from the left column edge, left margin, or left page edge (depending on which option you choose beneath the Horizontal box) and the left paragraph edge. When you type a precise measurement in the Vertical box, Word measures from the top page edge or top margin (whichever you choose beneath the Vertical box) to the top of the paragraph. For example, if you type **2in** in the Horizontal box and **3in** in the Vertical box and choose Margin beneath both boxes, Word places 2 inches between the left margin and the left paragraph edge and 3 inches between the top margin and the top paragraph edge.

When you choose a relative position (Top, Center, Left, and so forth) from the Horizontal or Vertical list, Word measures between the relative page position you choose (the column, margin, or page edge options beneath the Horizontal and Vertical boxes) and the closest edge of the paragraph. For example, Word will align the bottom edge of the paragraph with the bottom margin.

General Procedure

You can position more than one paragraph at a time by selecting several consecutive paragraphs before you choose the Format Position command.

To fix the position of a paragraph:

1. Select the paragraph to position.

2. Choose the Format Position command. Word displays the Format Position dialog box.

3. If you want to specify a precise horizontal position, type a measurement in the Horizontal box. For example, if you want to position the left edge of the paragraph ½ inch from the left edge of the page, type **.5in** in the Horizontal box.

   If you want to specify a relative position, use the mouse to pull down the Horizontal list and select a position or press the **Down arrow** key until you see the option you want. For example, if you want to align the right edge of the paragraph with the right margin, select Right.

4. Choose whether the horizontal position relates to the column, the margins, or the page edges. For example, to position a paragraph ½ inch from the left edge of the page, you'd type **.5in** in the Horizontal box and choose Page beneath the Horizontal box.

5. If you want to specify a vertical measurement from the top page edge or from the top margin, type a measurement in the Vertical box. For example, to position the top edge of the paragraph 2 inches down from the top margin, type **2in** here.

If you want to specify a relative position, use the mouse to pull down the Vertical list and select a position or press the **Down arrow** key until you see the option you want. For example, to position a paragraph at the bottom of the page, select Bottom.

6. Choose whether the vertical position relates to the margins or the page edges. For example, to position the top edge of the paragraph 2 inches from the top margin, type **2in** in the Vertical box and choose Margin beneath the Vertical box.

7. Change the measurement in the Paragraph Width box if you want to change the width of the paragraph. (If you want text to wrap around your fixed paragraph, you may need to do this.) For example, if you want to make the paragraph 2 inches wide, type **2in** here. Type **Auto** if you want to return the paragraph to its original width.

8. Click OK or press **Enter**.

Figure 14–10 illustrates positioning a paragraph with the Format Position command.

Figures 14–11 and 14–12 show boxed paragraphs positioned with the Format Position command.

You can't see the true placements of positioned objects in normal view. To do that, you have to switch to page view or print preview, as discussed earlier in this chapter.

Figure 14–10.
Fixing the position of a paragraph.

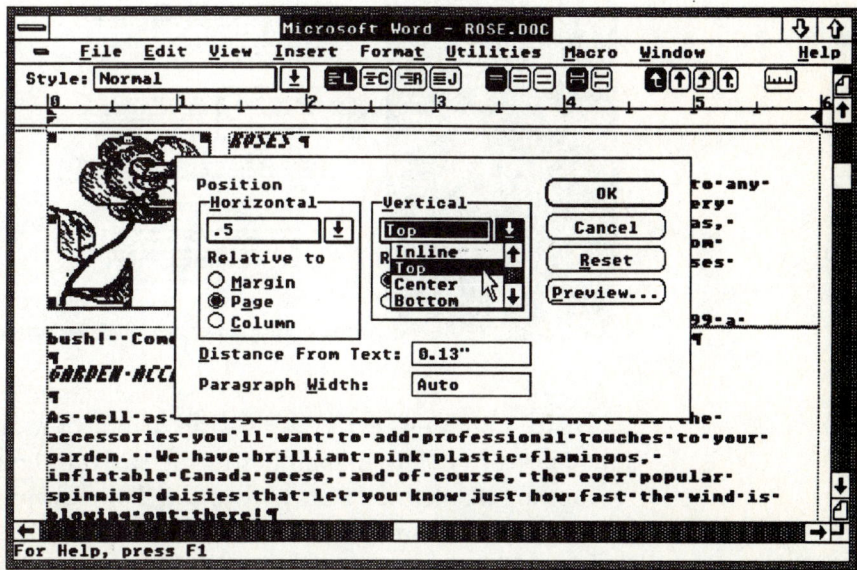

Figure 14–11.
A boxed paragraph
centered with the
Format Position
command
(Horizontal = Center,
relative to Page;
Vertical = Center,
relative to Page;
Width = 2.5 in).

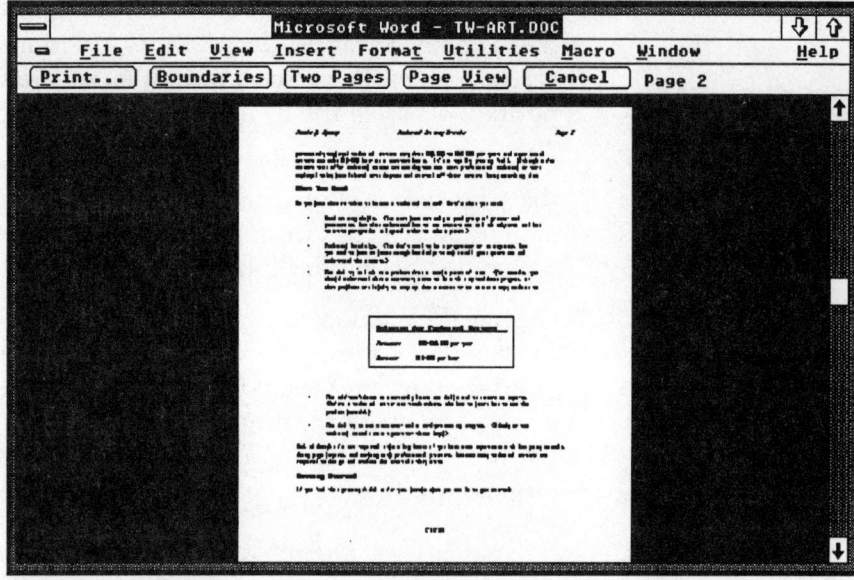

Figure 14–12.
A sidebar paragraph
positioned with the
Format Position
command
(Horizontal = .5 in,
relative to Page;
Vertical = Center,
relative to Page;
Width = 2.5 in).

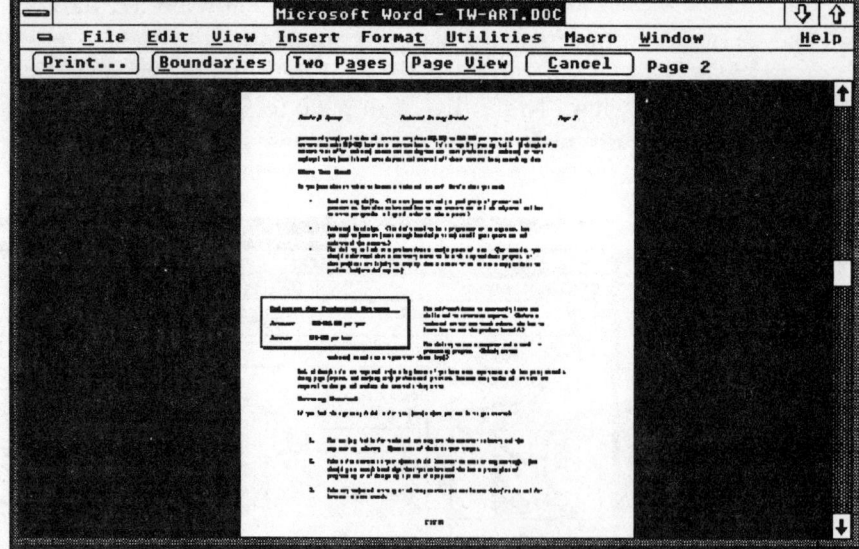

If surrounding text doesn't wrap around the fixed paragraph, you
may need to delete blank lines in the surrounding text (Word may be
wrapping blank lines around your fixed paragraph) or make your fixed
paragraph narrower by choosing the Format Position command again
and typing a narrower width in the Paragraph Width box.

You may want to add a border around fixed paragraphs with the Borders option of the Format Paragraph dialog box. See Adding Boxes, Lines, or Bars to Paragraphs in Chapter 9 for more information on adding borders.

EXAMPLE: Positioning a Quotation Paragraph

Say you'd like to position a boxed quotation paragraph 3 inches from the top of the page, center it horizontally, and make it 2 inches wide.

Here's how you'd do it:

1. Type all of the text on the page, and add the border around the quotation paragraph you want to position.

2. Select the quotation paragraph.

3. Choose the Format Position command.

4. From the Horizontal drop-down list, select Center.

5. Beneath the Horizontal box, choose Page.

6. In the Vertical box, type **3in**.

7. Beneath the Vertical box, choose Page.

8. In the Paragraph Width box, type **2in**.

9. Click OK or press **Enter**.

To see the paragraph in the correct position, switch to page view or print preview.

Positioning the Same Object on Every Page

If you'd like to position a paragraph of text or a graphic—such as a company logo—on every page of your entire document, you can apply the Format Position command to a header or footer. This sounds strange, but a header or footer appears on every page (or just on even or odd pages, if you set them up that way with the Format Document command), can contain any type of formatted text or graphics, and can be positioned anywhere with the Format Position command.

━━━▶ **EXAMPLE: Positioning the Same Object on Every Page**

Suppose you want to position the company logo at the left edge of every page and center it vertically, as shown in Figure 14–13. This is what you would do:

1. Copy the logo to the Clipboard.

2. Choose the Edit Header/Footer command.

3. Select Footer.

4. Paste the logo in the footer window.

5. Select the footer paragraph.

6. Choose the Format Position command.

7. Select Left from the drop-down Horizontal list, then choose Page from the related options below.

8. Select Center from the drop-down Vertical list, then choose Page from the related options below.

9. Click OK or press **Enter**.

10. Change to page view or print preview if you want to see your new positioned object.

Figure 14–13.
A graphic "footer" positioned with the Format Position command appears in the same place on every page (shown in print preview).

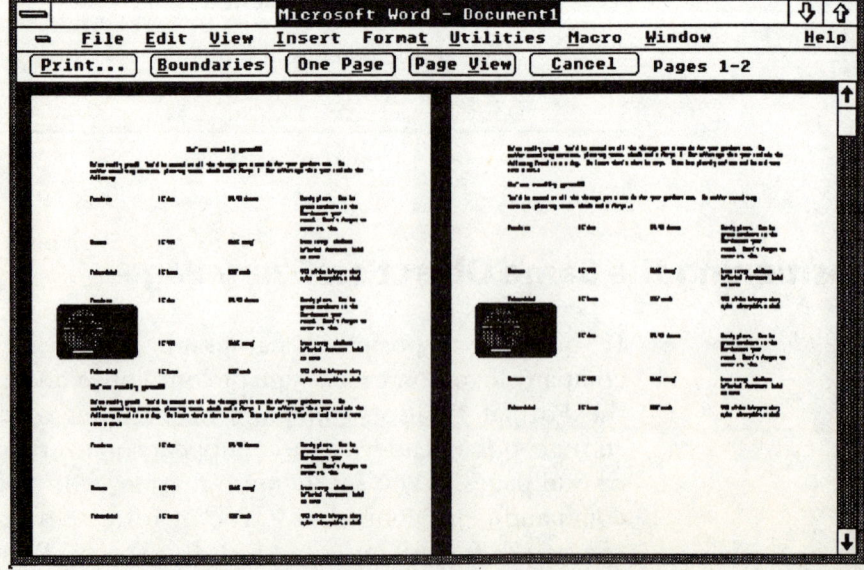

You might want to use this technique to create a template file or a glossary item you can use over and over again.

Returning a Paragraph to Its Original Position

If you decide that you no longer want to fix the position of a paragraph:

1. Select the positioned paragraph.

2. Choose the Format Position command.

3. Choose Reset.

4. Click OK or press **Enter**.

Word returns the paragraph to its original position.

CONTROLLING WHEN WORD REPAGINATES

By default, Word calculates page breaks only when it needs to—when it needs to make a table of contents or an index, display pages in page view or print preview, or print a document, for example. However, you can choose to repaginate whenever you want to see page breaks or count pages, and you can also choose to have Word repaginate automatically as you work.

Repaginating on Demand

To calculate pages on demand:

- Choose the Utilities Repaginate Now command. Word calculates the page breaks. When it's finished, you can scroll through your document, noting the page break marks (dotted lines) and the page numbers displayed in the status bar.

For information about changing page breaks, see Controlling Page Breaks later in this chapter.

Repaginating Automatically as You Work

You can use the following procedure to tell Word to recalculate pages automatically as you work:

1. Choose the Utilities Customize command.

2. Turn on the Background Pagination option.

3. Click OK or press **Enter**.

Word will adjust page breaks whenever there's a pause between typing or choosing commands. This option does slow down Word somewhat, so if you find the program is too slow, follow this procedure again to turn Background Pagination off.

How Hidden Text Affects Pagination

If you are displaying text you've formatted as hidden at the time Word repaginates, the hidden text will affect the pagination. If you don't plan to print hidden text, choose the View Preferences command and turn off the Hidden Text option before choosing any command that causes Word to repaginate.

JUMPING TO A SPECIFIC PAGE

When you have paginated your document and you know the page number you want to go to, you can quickly jump to that page using one of the following procedures:

1. Press **F5**. Word displays the words Go To: in the status bar.

2. Type the page number you want to jump to. If you have more than one section, type **P** followed by the page number, then **S** followed by the section number. For example, type **P5S2** to specify page 5 in section 2.

3. Press **Enter**.

or

1. Choose the Edit Go To command. Word displays the dialog box shown in Figure 14–14.

2. Type the page number in the dialog box. If you have more than one section, type **P** followed by the page number, then **S** followed by the section number. For example, type **P5S2** to specify page 5 in section 2.

3. Click OK or press **Enter**. Word displays the page you specified.

Figure 14–14.
The Edit Go To dialog box.

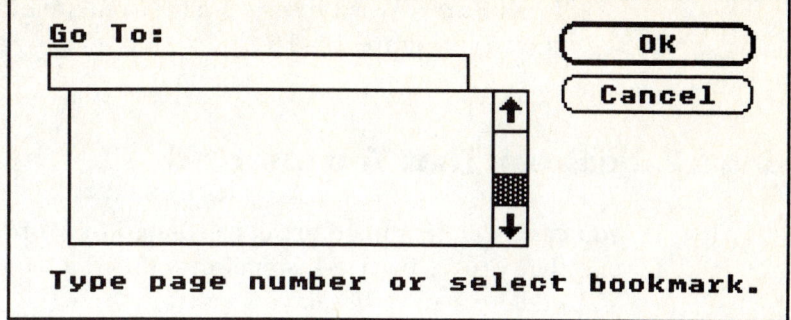

Figure 14–15.
The Insert Break dialog box.

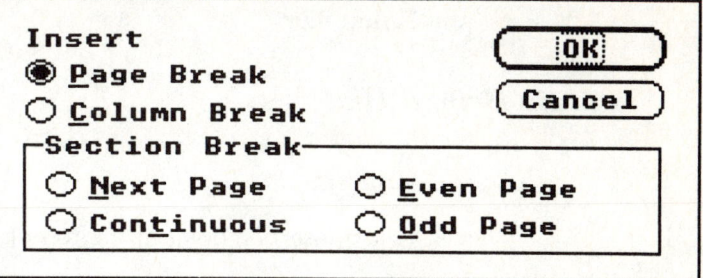

CONTROLLING PAGE BREAKS

You can control how Word breaks your document into pages by inserting your own page breaks, by choosing options that prevent page breaks within or between paragraphs, or by dragging a page break marker to a new position using print preview.

Inserting a Page Break

To insert your own page break, use one of the following procedures:

1. Place the insertion point where you want to insert a page break.

2. Press **Ctrl+Enter**.

or

1. Choose the Insert Break command. Word displays the dialog box shown in Figure 14–15. Note that the Page Break option is already chosen.

2. Press **Enter**. Word inserts a page break marker—a dotted line, as shown in Figure 14–16.

Deleting a Page Break That You Inserted

You can't delete a page break calculated by Word, but you can delete one that you've inserted (sometimes called a *manual page break*).

To delete a page break you inserted:

1. In normal view, select the page break marker.

2. Press the **Delete** key.

Helpful Hint

Here's a way to quickly remove all the page breaks you've inserted from a document:

1. Place the insertion point at the top of the document.

2. Choose the Edit Replace command.

3. In the Search For box, type **^d** (the ASCII code for a page break character). (**Note:** Make sure to type the caret character: this

Figure 14–16.
Pressing Ctrl+Enter or choosing the Insert Break command inserts a page break marker.

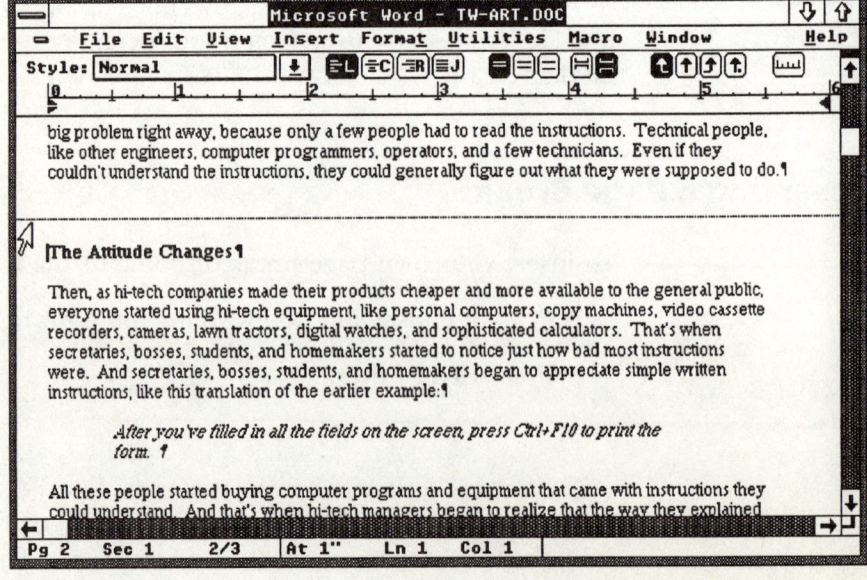

```
┌──────────────────────────────────────────────────────────────────┐
│ ▭           Microsoft Word - TW-ART.DOC                    ⇩ ⇧ │
│ ▭   File   Edit   View   Insert   Format   Utilities   Macro   Window          Help │
│ Style: Normal          ↧  ≡L ≡C ≡R ≡J  ≡ ≡ ≡  ⊟ ⊟  ⬆⬆⬆⬆  ⌷  ⬆ │
│ |0 . . . |1 . . . |2 . . . |3 . . . |4 . . . |5 . . . |6 │
│ big problem right away, because only a few people had to read the instructions. Technical people, │
│ like other engineers, computer programmers, operators, and a few technicians. Even if they │
│ couldn't understand the instructions, they could generally figure out what they were supposed to do.¶ │
│ - - - - - - - - - - - - - - - - - - - - - - - - - - - - - - - - - - - - - - - - │
│ ✎  |The Attitude Changes¶ │
│                                                                      │
│ Then, as hi-tech companies made their products cheaper and more available to the general public, │
│ everyone started using hi-tech equipment, like personal computers, copy machines, video cassette │
│ recorders, cameras, lawn tractors, digital watches, and sophisticated calculators. That's when │
│ secretaries, bosses, students, and homemakers started to notice just how bad most instructions │
│ were. And secretaries, bosses, students, and homemakers began to appreciate simple written │
│ instructions, like this translation of the earlier example:¶ │
│                                                                      │
│      After you've filled in all the fields on the screen, press Ctrl+F10 to print the │
│      form. ¶ │
│                                                                      │
│ All these people started buying computer programs and equipment that came with instructions they │
│ could understand. And that's when hi-tech managers began to realize that the way they explained │
│ ← →                                                                  ↓ │
│ Pg 2    Sec 1    2/3   At 1"   Ln 1   Col 1 │
└──────────────────────────────────────────────────────────────────┘
```

doesn't stand for pressing the Ctrl key as it does in many other programs.)

4. Make sure the Replace With box is blank. (If there are characters in the box, select the contents and press the **Delete** key.)

5. Turn off the Confirm Changes option.

6. Click OK or press **Enter**.

Controlling Page Breaks Within and Between Paragraphs

You can make sure that Word doesn't split one paragraph between pages or doesn't split up related paragraphs. You can also tell Word to put a page break before a specific paragraph to make sure it comes at the top of a page.

To control page breaks within or between paragraphs:

1. Select the paragraphs to control page breaks in.

2. Choose the Format Paragraph command.

3. Choose the appropriate option:

Page Break Before	Inserts a page break immediately before the paragraph
Keep Paragraph Together	Keeps the entire paragraph together—if a page break would normally occur within the paragraph, Word inserts the page break before the paragraph
Keep Paragraph With Next	Prevents a page break between the selected paragraph and the following paragraph

4. Click OK or press **Enter**.

Controlling Widows

By default, Word automatically prevents *widows*—single lines of text separated from their accompanying paragraphs. However, you can change the setting any time you like.

To prevent or allow widows:

1. Choose the Format Document command. Word displays the dialog box shown in Figure 14–17.

2. Turn on or turn off the Widow Control option.

3. Click OK or press **Enter**.

CHANGING MARGINS

Margins are the white space between your text and the edges of your page. Word uses the following margins by default:

Top	1 inch
Bottom	1 inch
Right	1.25 inches
Left	1.25 inches
Gutter	0 inches

A *gutter margin* is the space reserved for binding pages in a notebook or cover, as shown in Figure 14–18.

If you have formatted your document to have facing pages by choosing the Mirror Margins option in the Format Document dialog box, you'll have inside and outside margins rather than right or left margins.

The amount of space available for text on a page is, of course, affected by the size of the page and the horizontal or vertical orientation of the paper. If you're using pages that are not 8½ × 11 inches or if you've changed the paper orientation, use the Format Document

Figure 14–17.
The Format
Document command
controls widows.

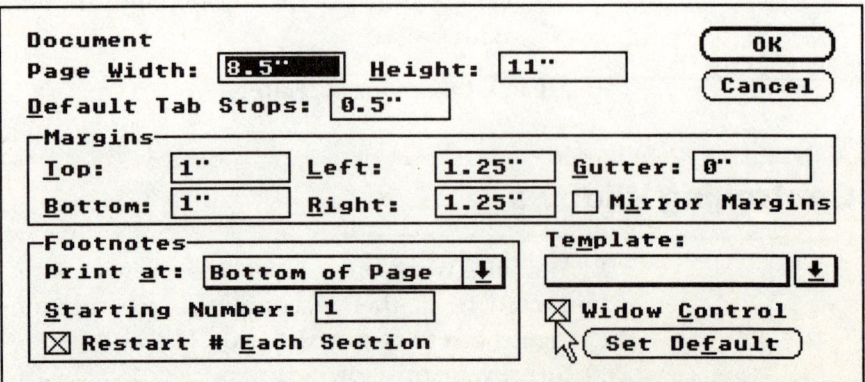

Figure 14–18.
A page with a gutter
margin.

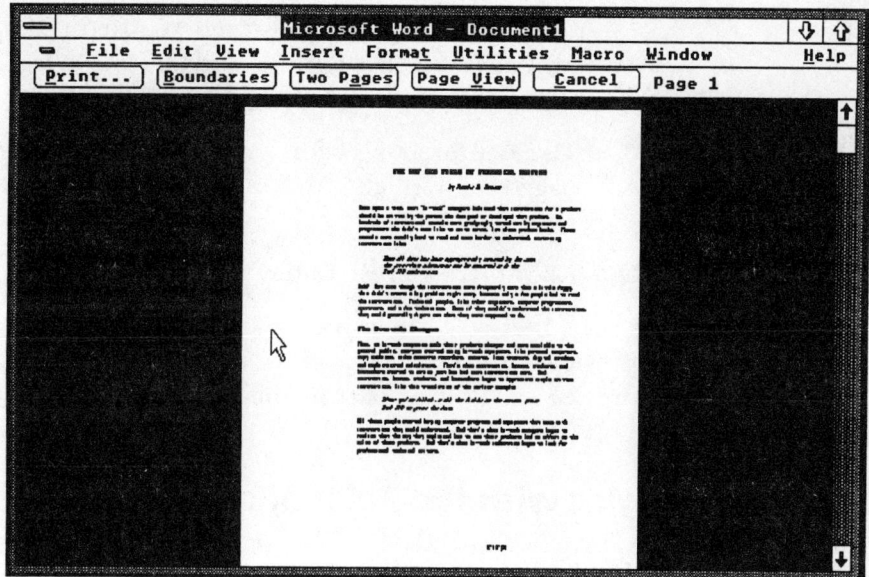

command to specify a new page size or the File Printer Setup command
to specify the paper orientation so that Word displays pages accurately.

When you change margins, it affects every page in your document,
even though you can only see one or two pages at a time. If you want
one page to have more white space around the text than other pages,
you have to indent the paragraphs on that page (see Indenting Paragraphs in Chapter 9) or keep that page in a separate file.

You can change the margins for your document three different ways:

- by typing new settings in the Format Document dialog box

- by dragging the margin markers on the ruler

- by dragging the margin lines in print preview (discussed earlier
  in this chapter)

Changing Margins with the Format Document Command

To change the margins in your document with the Format Document
command:

1. Choose the Format Document command.

2. Type new measurements in the Top, Bottom, Left, Right, and

Gutter boxes. If you've turned on Mirror Margins to format facing pages, you'll see Inside and Outside margin boxes rather than Right or Left boxes.

The Gutter box is for specifying extra space on the inside of pages for binding. You don't need to have a gutter margin in your document.

3. Click OK or press **Enter**.

The best way to see your margins is to switch to page view or print preview. You can learn more about working in page view or print preview in the first part of this chapter.

Changing Margins with the Ruler and the Mouse

To change margins by dragging the ruler's margin markers with the mouse:

1. If necessary, choose the View Ruler command to display the ruler.

2. If necessary, click the Ruler View icon (that graphic that looks like a tiny scale or comb at the right) on the ruler to set the zero mark at the left edge of the paper and display margin markers. The ruler should look like Figure 14–19.

Figure 14–19.
Changing margins
with the ruler.

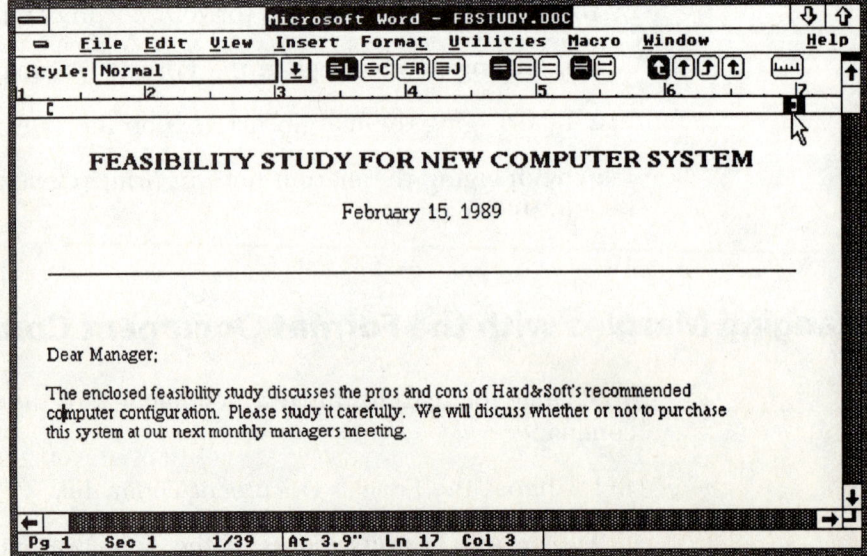

3. Drag the margin markers to the position you want. The text throughout your document adjusts to reflect the new margins.

Creating Mirrored Margins on Facing Pages

If your document will be printed double-sided (on both the fronts and backs of pages), you'll want to format your pages so that the margins mirror each other. Formatting your pages as mirror images does the following:

- Makes inside and outside margins mirror each other

- Places gutter margins (if any) at the inside of pages

- If you've added bars to paragraphs, places bars at the outside edge of paragraphs (the left edge of paragraphs on even pages, and at the right edge of paragraphs on odd pages)

Look at Figures 14–20 and 14–21 to see the difference between regular pages and pages with mirrored margins.

The Mirror Margins option does not cause headers or page numbers to mirror each other. If you want to create different headers or different page number positions for even and odd pages, turn on the

Figure 14–20.
Pages with regular margins.

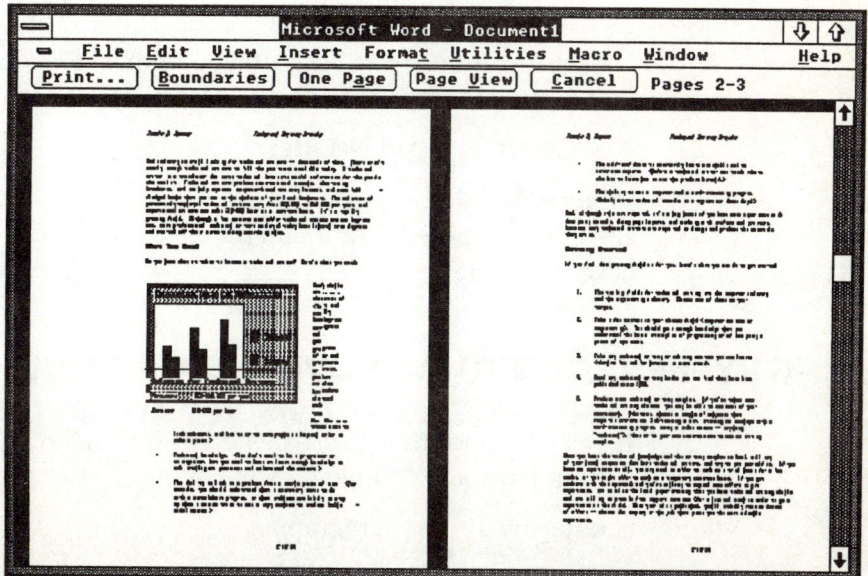

Figure 14–21.
Pages with mirrored
margins.

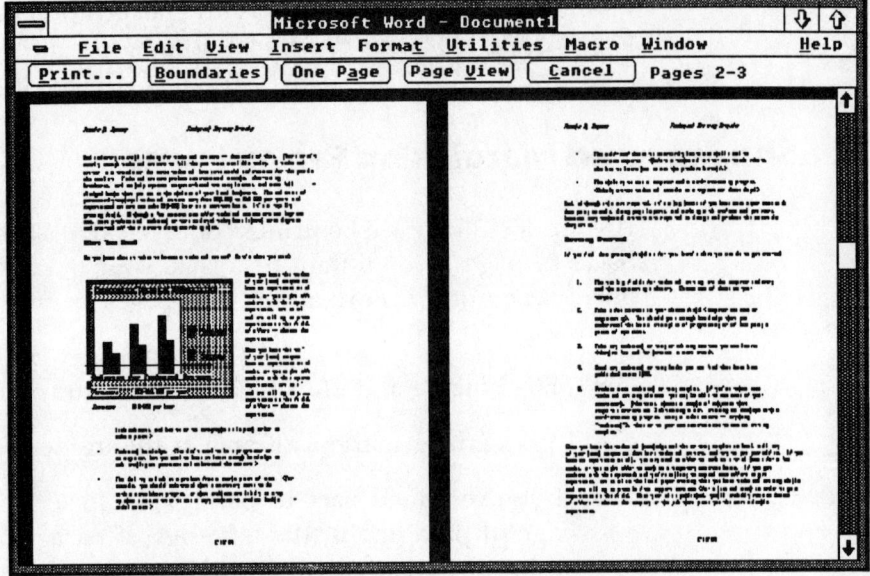

Odd/Even Headers option, and see Adding Headers and Footers in
Chapter 15 for more information about creating headers and footers.
To make margins mirror each other on facing pages:

1. Choose the Format Document command.

2. Turn on the Mirror Margins option. Word changes the Right and
   Left Margin boxes in the dialog box to Inside and Outside.

3. If you want to add a gutter margin, type a measurement in the
   Gutter box.

4. Click OK or press **Enter**.

Note: Word always makes even-numbered pages left-hand pages,
and odd-numbered right-hand pages, so page 1 of your document may
have no facing page.

USING HYPHENATION TO IMPROVE THE APPEARANCE OF PAGES

If your paragraphs are left-aligned or right-aligned and you think one
margin looks too "ragged," you can

- justify all the paragraphs

- hyphenate words to help fill the lines

To justify paragraphs (make the left and right sides even), Word adds enough spaces between words to fill up the lines. This can put big gaps in your text and make your pages look as though they're filled with "holes." You can fill these "holes" by using a combination of justified paragraphs and hyphenated words.

You may also choose to keep left or right alignment, but use hyphenation to make the other margin less ragged. See how adding even one hyphen makes the right side of a paragraph more even in the example below:

> She could hear the intruder coming up the stairs, creeping as silently as possible. From her cramped position behind the mahogany door, Angelina saw his shadow, barely visible in the gloom, approaching her bedroom. He clutched a revolver in his hand.

> She could hear the intruder coming up the stairs, creeping as silently as possible. From her cramped position behind the mahogany door, Angelina saw his shadow, barely visible in the gloom, approaching her bedroom. He clutched a revolver in his hand.

For more information on aligning paragraphs, see Aligning Paragraphs in Chapter 9.

Using the Hyphenate Command

You can always press the hyphen key to add a hyphen to a word, but if you later add text or change margins or indents, the hyphen remains in the word even though the word may no longer be at the end of a line. A safer way to hyphenate is to have Word suggest where to put hyphens throughout your document, or just in selected text. Word inserts *optional hyphens* that are removed if the word is later relocated. This also saves you the trouble of using a dictionary to determine where to break a word.

Word begins hyphenating at the insertion point, so you may want to move the insertion point to the beginning of your document before you choose the Utilities Hyphenate command. You can have Word hyphenate all the appropriate words in your document or selection automatically, or you can approve or reject each hyphenation Word proposes. You can also change the "hot zone"—the space measured from the end of the line within which Word will try to hyphenate words.

To have Word hyphenate all appropriate words automatically:

1. If you don't select anything, Word hyphenates the entire document. To hyphenate only part of your document, select the text you want to hyphenate.

2. Choose the Utilities Hyphenate command. Word displays the dialog box shown in Figure 14–22.

3. If you want Word to hyphenate capitalized words (which may be headings), turn on the Hyphenate Caps option.

4. If desired, type a new measurement in the Hot Zone box.

5. Turn off the Confirm option.

6. Click OK or press **Enter**.

To have Word ask for confirmation before hyphenating a word:

1. To hyphenate only part of your document, select the text you want to hyphenate. If you don't select anything, Word hyphenates the entire document.

2. Choose the Utilities Hyphenate command.

3. If you want Word to hyphenate capitalized words (which may be headings), turn on the Hyphenate Caps option.

4. If desired, type a new measurement in the Hot Zone box.

5. Turn on the Confirm option.

6. Click OK or press **Enter**.

7. When Word displays a word as shown in Figure 14–23, type **Y** or click Yes to approve the hyphenation, or type **N** or click No to skip that word and move on to the next.

If you need to interrupt the hyphenation process, press **Esc** or click Cancel.

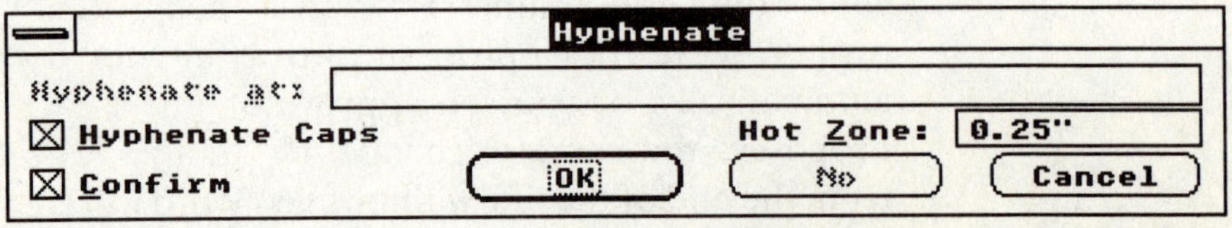

Figure 14–22.
The Utilities Hyphenate dialog box.

Figure 14–23.
The dialog box Word
displays for you to
confirm a
hyphenation.

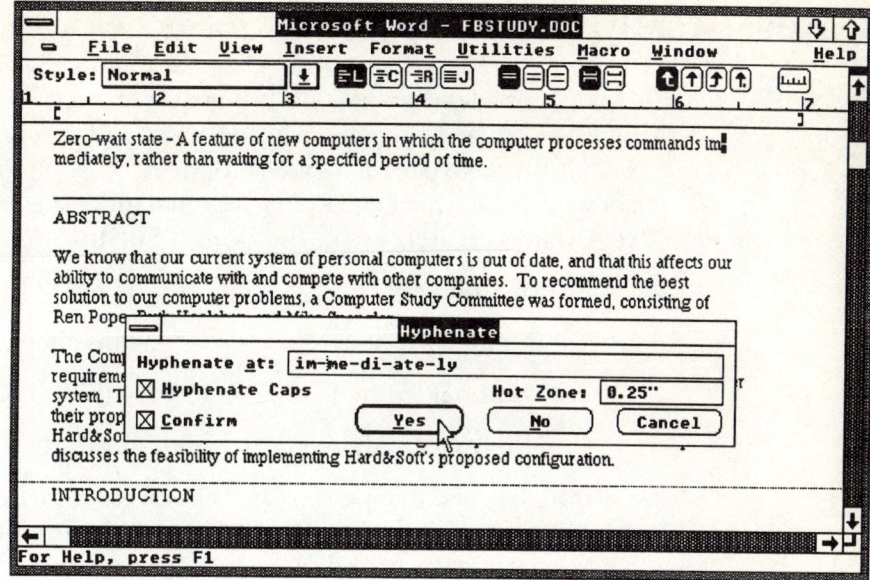

Typing Optional Hyphens

If you don't want to use the Utilities Hyphenate command but you
want to insert hyphens that will be removed if the word is not at the
end of a line, you can insert optional hyphens to divide words at the
ends of lines.

To insert an optional hyphen:

■ Press **Ctrl**+- (hyphen).

Using Nonbreaking Hyphens to Keep Words Together

If you don't care whether Word breaks up strings of words connected
with hyphens, you can just insert normal hyphens wherever you want
them.

If you have a string of words connected by hyphens that you don't
want Word to break up at the end of a line—such as seventy-five,
Stratford-upon-Avon, and ill-fated—you can use nonbreaking hyphens
instead of regular hyphens to keep the words together on a line.

To insert a nonbreaking hyphen:

■ Press **Ctrl**+**Shift**+- (hyphen).

Searching for Hyphens

If you've added hyphens and then you change the margins or delete or add text, you may need to go back and delete hyphens. You can search for all types of hyphens in Word. Just choose the Edit Search command (or the Edit Replace command), then type the character you want to search for in the Search For box:

To find	Type
Regular hyphen	- (hyphen).
Optional hyphen	^- (Shift+6, hyphen).
Nonbreaking hyphen	^~ (Shift+6, tilde).

Note: Be sure to type the caret characters (created by holding down the Shift key while you press the 6 key at the top of the main keypad). These carets are not used as symbols for the Ctrl key, as they sometimes are in other programs.

USING NONBREAKING SPACES TO KEEP WORDS TOGETHER

If you have two or more words that you don't want Word to break up at the end of a line—such as Jane Doe, New York, Grand Prix—you can use nonbreaking spaces instead of regular spaces to keep the words together on a line.

To insert a nonbreaking space:

■ Press **Ctrl+Shift+Spacebar**.

You'll see a caret (^) above each nonbreaking space if you've pressed Ctrl+Shift+* or chosen the View Preferences Show All option to display hidden formatting characters.

Adding Page Numbers, Headers and Footers, and Footnotes

This chapter shows you how to add the finishing touches to your document or template. You'll learn how to

- add page numbers

- add headers and footers

- add footnotes

ADDING PAGE NUMBERS

Word doesn't add page numbers to your file unless you say so—then you can specify exactly where and how you want the page numbers to be printed. Word has two commands that affect page numbers:

Command	Use
Insert Page Numbers	Adds only page numbers to tops or bottoms of pages
Edit Header/ Footer	Adds text, time, and date as well as page numbers to the top (header) or bottom (footer) of each page (you choose among Roman numerals, letters, or Arabic numbers); adds character and paragraph formatting

Note: You cannot use the Insert Page Numbers command *and* the Edit Header/Footer command to add page numbers to your file.

When you add page numbers to a file, Word adds a {page} field that is updated with the correct number when you print.

To add only page numbers with the Insert Page Numbers command:

1. Move the insertion point into the section you want to affect. If your file isn't divided into sections, your choices will affect the entire document.

2. Choose the Insert Page Numbers command. Word displays the dialog box shown in Figure 15–1.

3. Choose a Top or Bottom vertical position in the Page Number Position box.

4. Choose a Left, Center, or Right horizontal position in the Page Number Position box.

5. Click OK or press **Enter**. If you've already added a header or footer to the section, Word asks you if you want to replace the header or footer with the page number.

You won't see page numbers in normal view—you have to switch to page view or print preview. In page view, you'll see the {page} field if you've toggled the View Field Codes command off and if hidden formatting characters are not displayed. If these two conditions are reversed, you'll see the actual page numbers in page view. In print preview, you'll always see the page numbers (shown in Figure 15–2), although you may need a magnifying glass to identify them. See Using Print Preview and Page View in Chapter 14 for more information.

ADDING HEADERS OR FOOTERS

When you want to print text at the top of each page, you add a *header* (also known as a *running head*). When you want to print text at the bottom of each page, you add a *footer* (or *running foot*). In Word,

Figure 15–1.
The Insert Page Numbers command controls the position of page numbers.

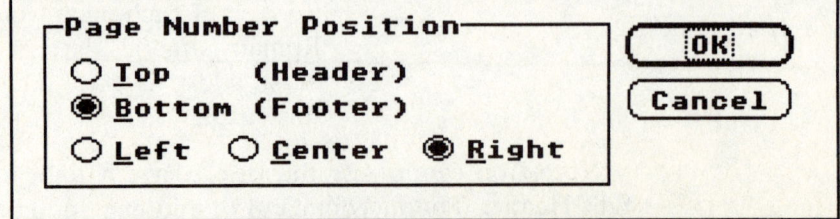

Figure 15–2.
Page numbers in
print preview.

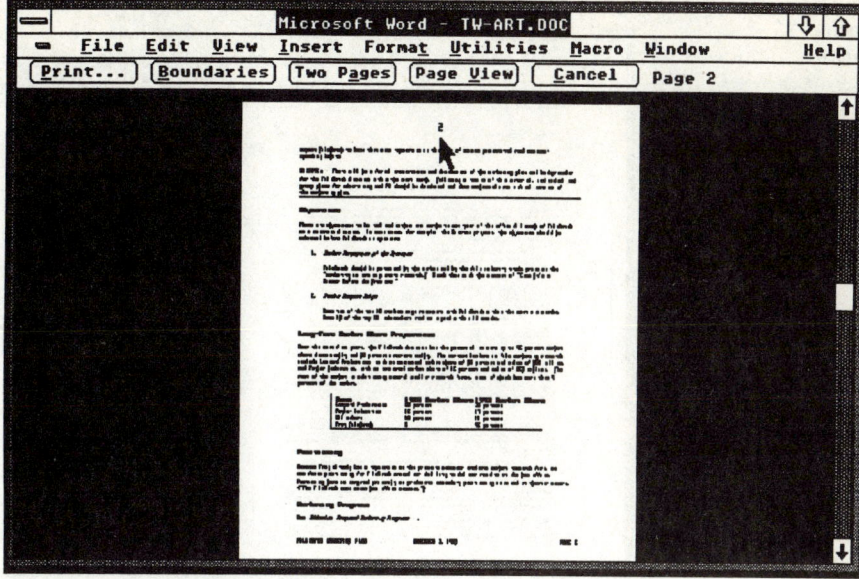

headers and footers belong to sections, but you can use the same headers or footers throughout your document or create different headers and footers if your document is divided into sections. Headers and footers can contain date, time, and page number fields that Word fills in when you print the document. You can see headers and footers in print preview or in page view, as shown in Figures 15–3 and 15–4.

Adding a header or footer involves two steps:

1. Choose options in the Edit Header/Footer dialog box and select a name from the list to tell Word exactly what kind of header or footer you want to set up.

2. Type and format the text you want to appear in the header or footer.

You must repeat this process for each header and footer.

Setting Up a Header or Footer

Word has many options you can choose for a header or footer. For example, instead of having the same header and footer on each page, you may want to create different headers or footers for even and odd pages in your document, as shown in Figure 15–5.

Figure 15–3.
Headers and footers in print preview.

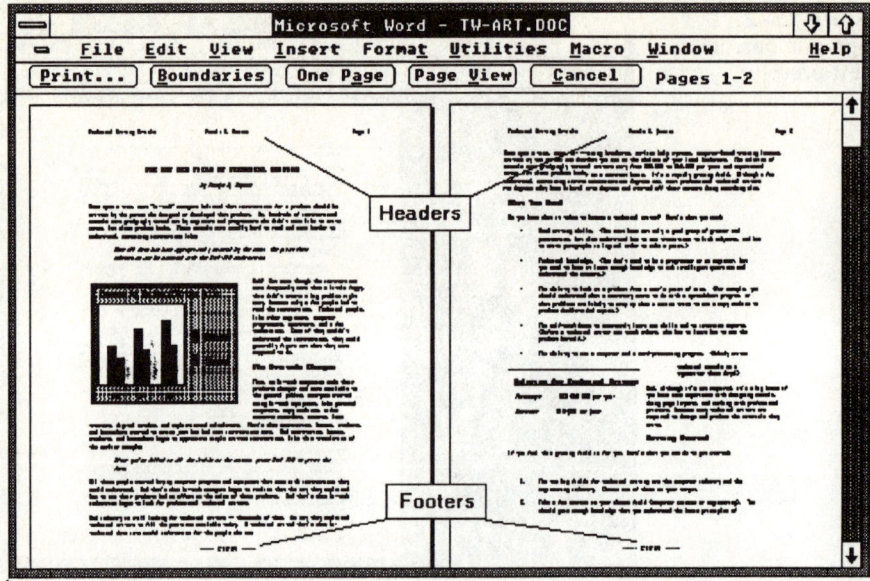

Figure 15–4.
A header in page view.

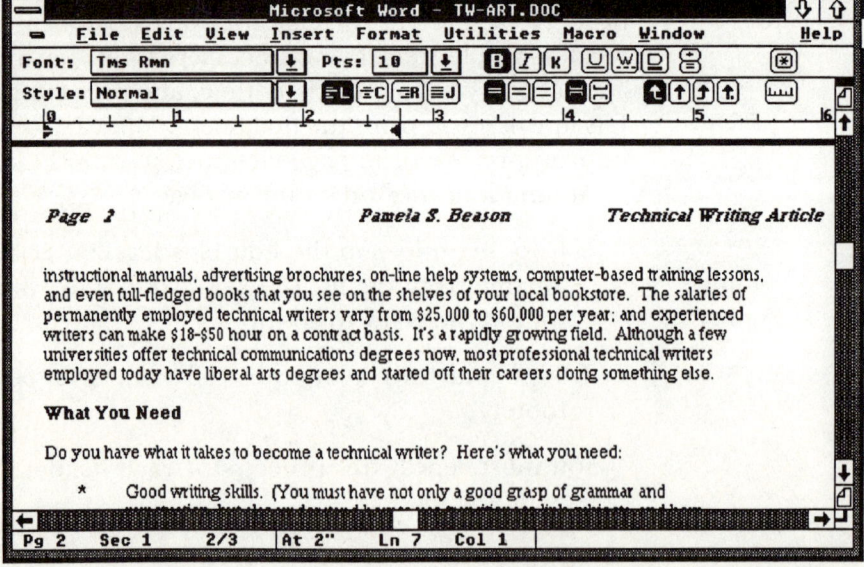

You can also create a unique header or footer just for the first page of a section. If you don't want a header or footer to appear on the first page of a section, specify a unique first-page header or footer, but don't type any text for that header or footer.

Figure 15–5.
Word can create different headers and footers for even and odd pages.

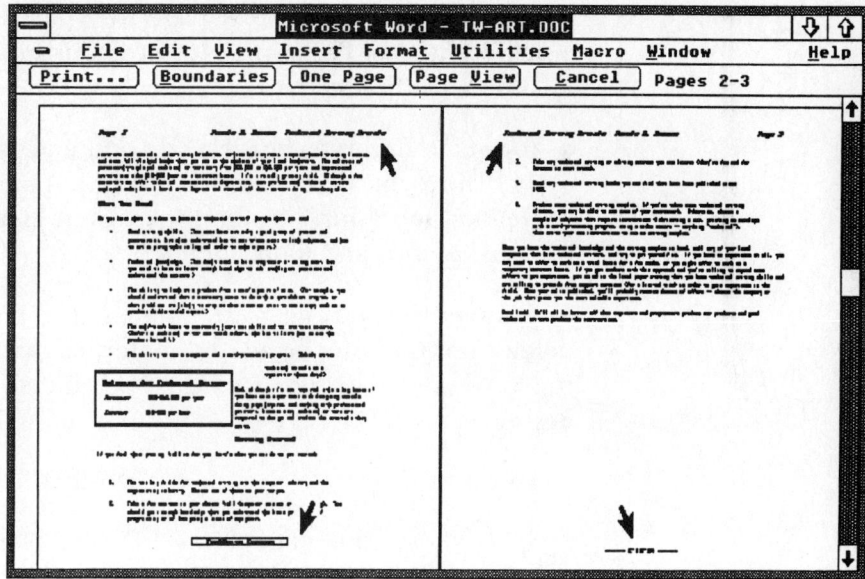

Figure 15–6.
The Edit Header/ Footer dialog box.

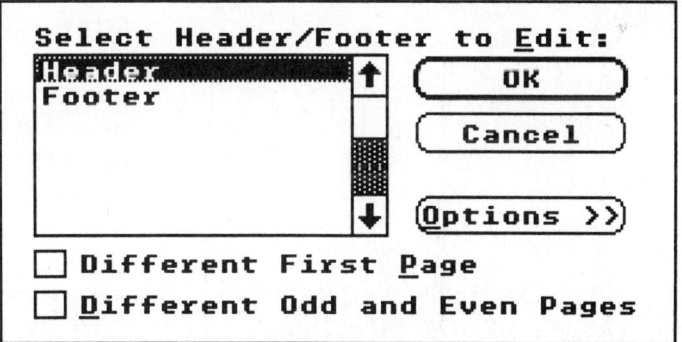

By default, Word uses Arabic numerals (1, 2, 3, and so forth) for page numbers in headers, but you can choose to use Roman numerals or letters instead. All of these options are controlled by the Edit Header/Footer command, whose dialog box is shown in Figure 15–6.

To set up a header or footer:

1. If necessary, switch to normal view, then move the insertion point into the section you want to affect. If your document is not divided into sections, Word adds headers or footers to the entire document.

2. If you want different headers and footers for specific pages, choose one or both of the following options:

- To create a different first page for your section, turn on the Different First Page option. Word adds First Header and First Footer to the list.

- To create different headers for odd and even pages, turn on the Different Odd and Even Pages option. Word changes Header and Footer in the list to Even Header, Odd Header, Even Footer, and Odd Footer.

3. To change the starting page number, the number type, or the default position of a header or footer, choose Options to display the rest of the dialog box, then set the following options as desired:

To do this	Do this
Specify a starting page number for the section	Type a page number in the Page Numbers: Start At box.
To change the number type	Use the mouse or the **Down arrow** key to choose a different type of number (Arabic, uppercase or lowercase Roman numerals, or uppercase or lowercase letters) from the list in the Page Numbers: Format box.
Set a new position for the header in the top margin	Type a decimal measurement (such as **.75in**) in the Distance From Edge: Header box.
Set a new position for the footer in the bottom margin	Type a decimal measurement (such as **.75in**) in the Distance From Edge: Footer box.

4. From the list, select the header or footer you want to create. (You can create only one type of header or footer at a time.)

5. Click OK or press **Enter**. Word opens a separate pane at the bottom of the document window and moves the insertion point into that pane, as shown in Figure 15–7.

Figure 15–7.
Word opens a
header/footer pane
at the bottom of the
window.

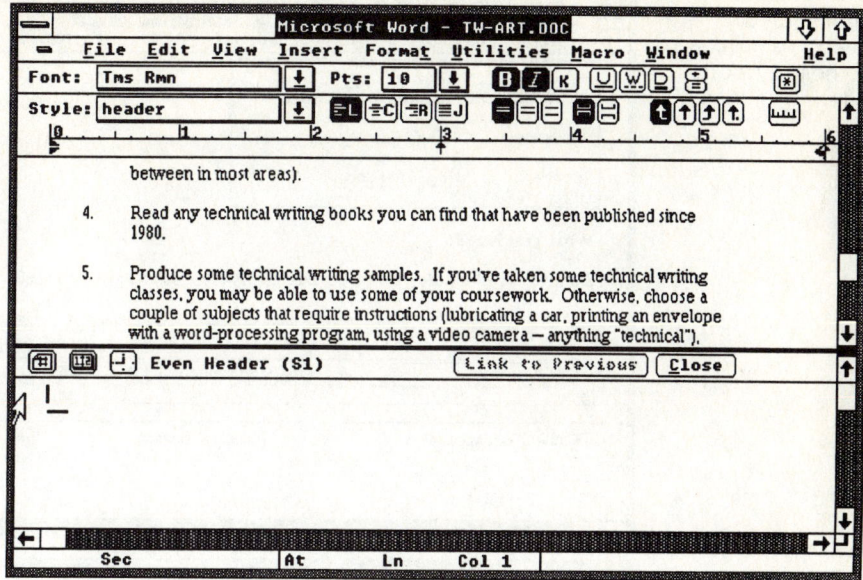

Typing and Formatting a Header or Footer

After you've told Word where you want the header or footer, you're ready to type and format text to create the header or footer. Headers and footers can contain just a couple of characters, whole paragraphs of text, graphics—anything you can put in your document you can put in a header or footer. You can also add page number, date, and time fields to your text—Word updates these fields when it prints your document. If your document is divided into sections and you want the same header or footer to appear throughout your document, you just choose the Link to Previous option to copy the header or footer from the previous section.

Creating a New Header or Footer

To create a header or footer in the header/footer pane:

1. Type or edit the text you want to appear in the header or footer, as shown in Figure 15–8.

2. To add page numbers, the date of printing, or the time of printing to your header or footer, position the insertion point, then do the following:

Figure 15–8.
Creating a header in
the header/footer
pane.

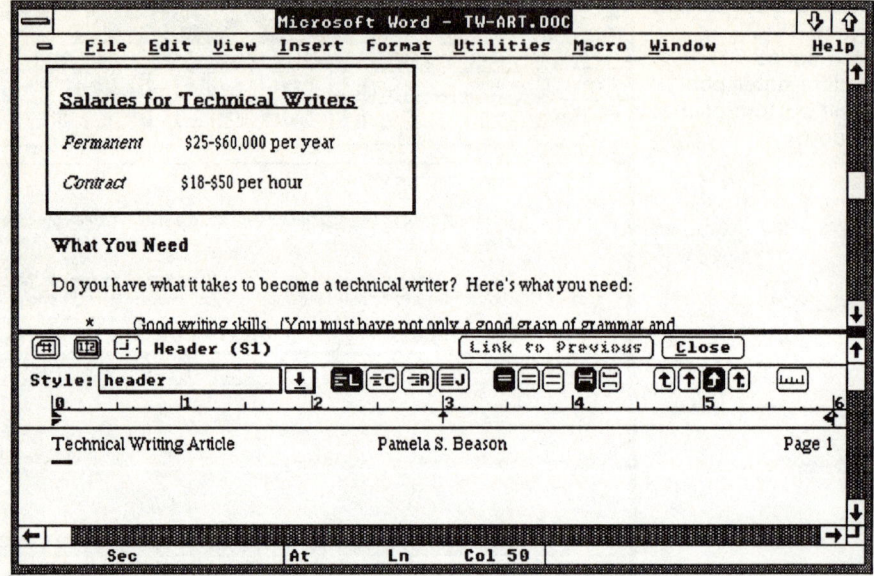

To add	Do this
Page numbers	Click the number sign icon (the leftmost icon) or press **Shift+F10**, then type **P**.
Date of printing	Click the date icon (the middle icon) or press **Shift+F10**, then type **D**.
Time of printing	Click the time icon (the clock icon) or press **Shift+F10**, then type **T**.

Word adds a field that will be updated when you print your file.

Note: If you want to add a specific date or time to your header or footer, just type the date or time you want.

3. Format the text as desired. You can use the ruler and the Format commands to format headers and footers, choosing different alignments, borders, or character formatting such as bold or italic.

Word automatically attaches a default style named Header to headers, and a default style named Footer to footers, but you can apply different styles if you like. You can also modify the Header and Footer styles with the Format Define Styles command. (See Changing Styles in Chapter 10 for more information about modifying styles.)

4. To close the header/footer pane, click the Close button or press **Shift+F10** and type **C**.

Don't panic if you don't see your header or footer in the document. You can't see headers or footers in normal view—you have to switch to page view or print preview for that. You can learn more about working in page view or print preview in Chapter 14.

Copying the Header or Footer from the Previous Section

If you're adding a header or footer to a section and you want the header or footer to be identical to the header or footer in the previous section:

1. In the header/footer pane, click the Link to Previous button or press **Shift+F10**, then type **L**. Word displays the header or footer of the previous section.

2. To close the header/footer pane, click the Close button or press **Shift+F10** and type **C**.

If the Link to Previous button is dimmed, your document is not divided into sections, or there is no header or footer in the previous section.

Editing and Formatting Existing Headers or Footers

All of Word's editing and formatting commands affect headers and footers just as they affect other text in a document. You can edit headers and footers in a separate pane in normal view or change the text on the page in page view.

To change headers or footers in normal view:

1. Move the insertion point into the section you want to affect. If your document is not divided into sections, your changes will affect headers or footers in the entire document.

2. Choose the Edit Header/Footer command.

3. Select the header or footer you want to change from the list.

4. Click OK or press **Enter**. Word opens the header/footer pane at the bottom of the document window and displays the header or footer you selected.

5. Edit or format the text as desired. To remove a header or footer, simply delete all its text.

6. To close the header/footer pane, click the Close button or press **Shift+F10** and type **C**.

When you edit or format a header or footer in page view, you change the text on one page, and Word changes the rest of the section to match.

To change a header or footer in page view:

1. If necessary, choose the View Page command to switch to page view.

2. Move the insertion point to the header or footer you want to change.

3. Edit or format the header or footer as desired. To add fields for page numbers, date, or time of printing in page view, press **Ctrl+F9** to enclose the insertion point in field braces, then type **page**, **date**, or **time** within the braces to specify the type of field you want at that location.

ADDING FOOTNOTES

Word has four commands that affect footnotes:

Command	Action
Insert Footnote	Inserts footnotes
View Footnotes	Displays footnotes in a footnote pane at the bottom of the document window in normal view or scrolls to footnotes in page view
Format Document	Prints footnotes at the bottom of a page, at the end of the text on a page, at the ends of sections, or at the end of the document
Format Section	Prevents footnotes from printing at the end of a section

You'll learn more about these commands and functions in this section.

Inserting Footnotes

Every footnote has two parts, as shown in Figure 15–9: the footnote reference (that little number or mark in text that tells you to look for a footnote), and the footnote text.

To insert a footnote:

1. Place the insertion point where you want the footnote reference (usually a superscripted number) to appear.

2. Choose the Insert Footnote command.

3. Do one of the following:

   ■ If you want an automatically numbered footnote, click OK or press **Enter**.

   ■ If you don't want Word to automatically number your footnotes, type the character you want to use instead in the Footnote Reference Mark box. For example, if you want to mark your footnote with an asterisk, type * in the Footnote Reference Mark box, then click OK or press **Enter**.

Word inserts a footnote reference mark and opens the footnote pane at the bottom of the document window in normal view; Word scrolls to the footnote area in page view.

Figure 15–9.
The parts of a footnote.

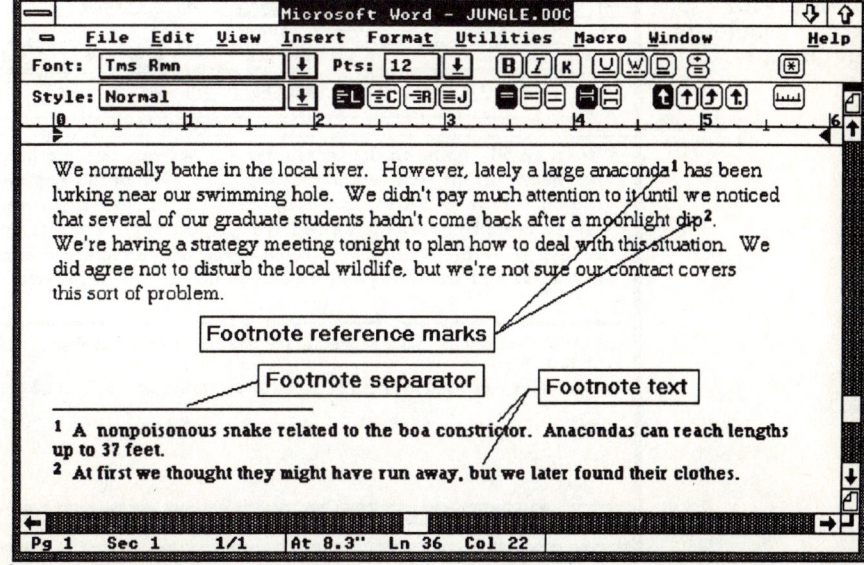

Word automatically attaches a default style named Footnote Ref to the footnote reference mark. You can modify this style (see Changing Styles in Chapter 10 for details).

4. Type and format the text for your footnote. You can use the ruler and the Format commands to format footnotes. Word automatically attaches a default style named Footnote Text to the footnote text, but you can apply a different style if you like. You can also modify the Footnote Text style with the Format Define Styles command. (See Chapter 10 for more information about changing styles.)

5. To add more footnotes, press **F6** or click the document if you're using normal view, then repeat steps 1 through 4 to add more footnotes to the document.

6. When you're finished adding footnotes in normal view, close the footnote pane by dragging the split line (between the two vertical scroll bars) to the bottom of the document window or by choosing the View Footnotes command.

Figure 15–10 illustrates adding footnotes to a document using normal view.

To separate footnotes from text on a page, Word uses a 2-inch line as a *footnote separator*. If the text of a footnote is long and must continue

Figure 15–10.
Adding footnotes to a document.

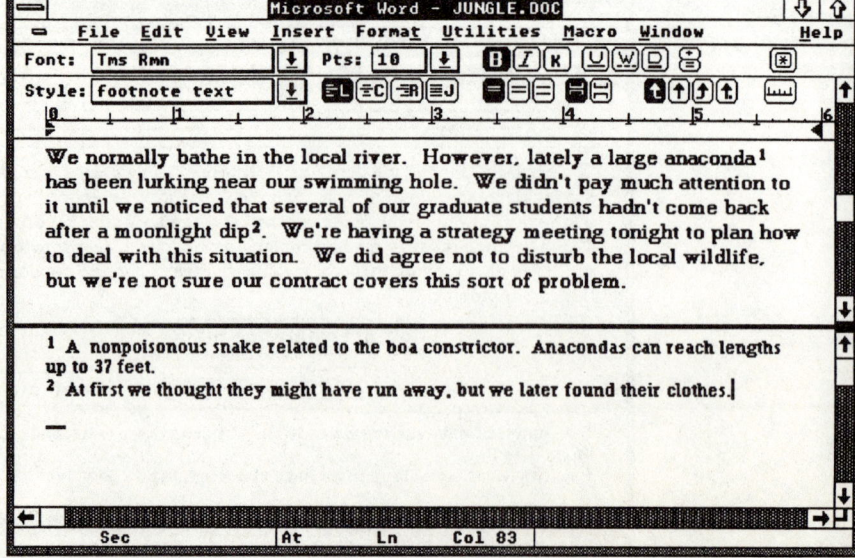

on the next page, Word uses a margin-to-margin line as the *continuing separator,* the mark that separates a continued footnote from following text. You can edit these separator characters if you like, and you can also add a notice (a *continuation notice*) to tell readers that a footnote is continued on the next page. Figure 15–11 shows how a continued footnote might look at the bottom of a page.

Jumping to Footnotes

You can use the F5 key or the Edit Go To command to jump to the footnote reference mark you want. If the footnote window is open at the bottom of the screen in normal view, the text scrolls to display the text of the selected reference mark.

To jump to a footnote reference mark, use one of the following procedures:

1. Press **F5**. Word displays Go To: in the status bar.

2. Type **f** to jump to the next reference mark or type **f** followed by a footnote number to jump to a specific footnote reference mark (such as f7 to jump to the seventh reference mark).

3. Press **Enter**.

Figure 15–11.
Footnote separator characters.

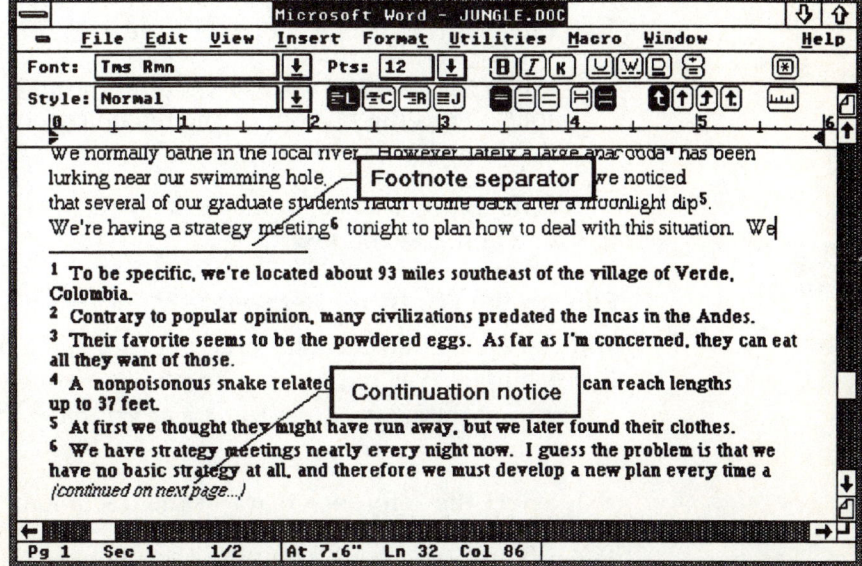

or

1. Choose the Edit Go To command.

2. In the dialog box, type **f** to jump to the next reference mark or type **f** followed by a footnote number to jump to a specific footnote reference mark (f7 to jump to the seventh reference mark, for example).

3. Click OK or press **Enter**.

Editing Footnotes

You can change three aspects of a footnote:

- the footnote text

- the reference mark

- the separator characters and continuation indicators

Editing Footnote Text

To edit the text of a footnote in normal view:

1. Choose the View Footnotes command to display the footnote pane at the bottom of the document window.

2. In the footnote pane, scroll to the footnote text you want to edit.

3. Edit the text in the footnote pane.

4. When you're finished, close the footnote pane by dragging the split line to the bottom of the document window or by choosing the View Footnotes command.

To edit the text of a footnote in page view, simply scroll to the footnote and edit the text.

Editing the Footnote Reference Mark

You can change a footnote reference character that you've specified. For example, you might want to change from an ampersand to an asterisk, or change to an automatically numbered footnote.

To edit a footnote reference mark:

1. Select the reference mark in the document.

2. Choose the Insert Footnote command.

3. If you want to specify a new character, type the new character in the Footnote Reference Mark box. If you want to change to an automatically numbered reference, choose the Auto-numbered Reference option.

4. Click OK or press **Enter**.

If you change to an automatically numbered reference, Word renumbers footnotes throughout the document.

Editing the Footnote Separator Characters

To change the footnote separator, the continuing separator, or the continuation notice:

1. Choose the Insert Footnote command.

2. Choose the element you want to change: Separator, Cont. Separator, or Cont. Notice. Word displays the character in a footnote pane at the bottom of the screen, as shown in Figure 15–12.

3. Delete the existing character or text.

4. Type the new character or text you want to use.

5. When you're finished, close the pane by dragging the split line to the bottom of the document window or by choosing the View Footnotes command.

Figure 15–12.
Changing the footnote separator.

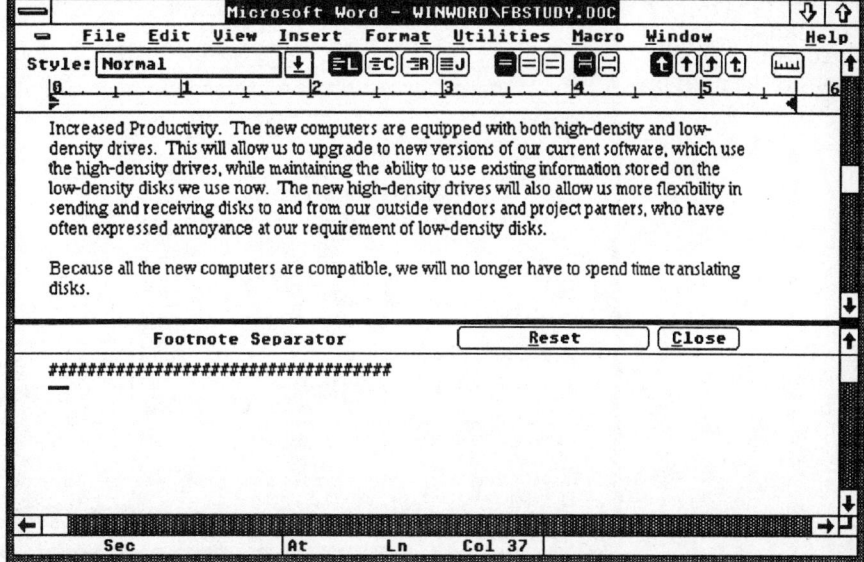

Controlling Position and Numbering of Footnotes

To control the position and numbering of footnote text in the document:

1. Choose the Format Document command. Word displays the dialog box shown in Figure 15–13.

2. Select one of the following options from the drop-down Print At list in the Footnotes box.

Option	Positions footnotes
Bottom of Page	In the same position at the bottom of the page, no matter where the text ends on a page.
Beneath Text	Directly beneath the text, wherever it ends on the page.
End of Section	At the end of each section containing footnote references, unless the Include Footnotes option is turned off in a section.
End of Document	At the end of the entire document.

Figure 15–13.
The Format Document command controls the position of footnotes.

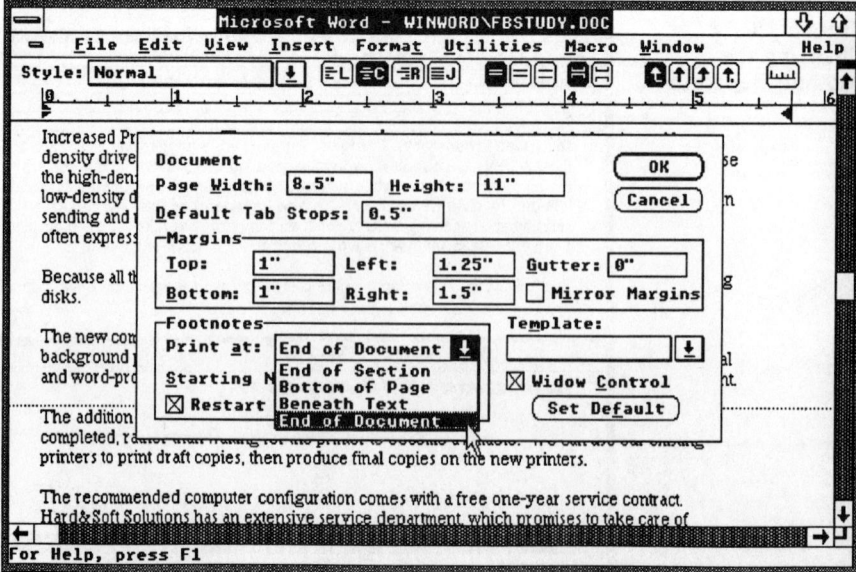

3. To start footnotes at a number other than 1, type that number in the Footnotes: Starting Number box.

4. If you want to start footnote numbers at 1 in each section of your document, turn on the Restart # Each Section option. If you want footnote numbers to be continuous from section to section, turn off this option. (If your document is not divided into sections, this option has no effect.)

5. Click OK or press **Enter**.

Preventing Footnotes from Printing at the End of Specific Sections

If the document is divided into sections and you've chosen the End of Section option in the Document dialog box, but you don't want footnotes to print at the end of a particular section, complete the following procedure. This situation may occur when you've used section formatting to give parts of the document a different look, but the text of the document is not logically divided into those sections.

To prevent footnotes from printing at the end of a section:

1. Move the insertion point into the section at whose end you don't want to print footnotes.

2. Choose the Format Section command. Word displays the dialog box shown in Figure 15–14.

3. Turn off the Include Footnotes option.

4. Click OK or press **Enter**. Word will print the footnotes at the end of the next section in which the Include Footnotes option is active.

Deleting Footnotes

To delete a footnote:

- Delete the footnote reference mark. Word automatically deletes the footnote text and renumbers footnotes as appropriate.

Figure 15–14.
The Format Section command controls whether footnotes print at the end of a section.

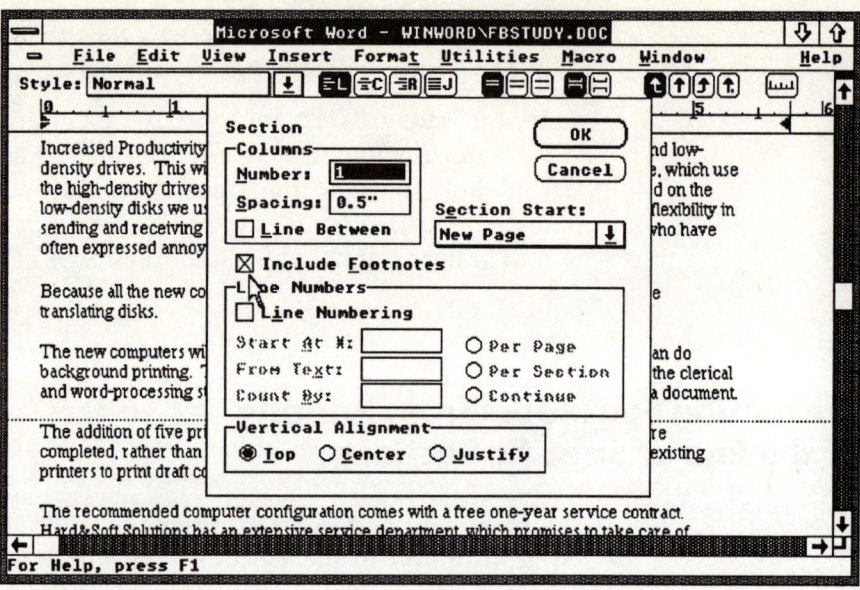

## Chapter Sixteen

Printing

When you're finished editing and formatting, you'll want to print all or part of your file. You can also print other items associated with your file, such as the glossary, the summary information sheet, annotations, styles, and so forth. The instructions in this chapter show you how to effectively use your printer with Word and how to check for problems when something goes wrong.

ABOUT .DRV FILES

What's a .DRV file? .DRV is the extension Windows and Word use for printer driver files. You must use the appropriate printer driver file installed for your printer before you can print from Word. Chances are that you already installed the appropriate printer driver when you installed Windows. If you don't have the proper printer driver installed, you can install it using the Control Panel, as described later in this chapter. If you're uncertain about which .DRV file is appropriate for your printer or about the capabilities of your printer, see the printer manual that came with Word.

PREPARING TO PRINT

Before you print, you may want to complete these preprinting tasks:

- Choose the File Printer Setup command and check the printer selection, then use the Setup button in the dialog box to check paper size, and orientation options to make sure they're right.

- Choose the Format Document command and check the page height and width.

- Choose the View Preferences command and turn on the Display as Printed option so Word displays the file in the document window just as the file will be printed.

- Check pages using print preview and page view.

BASIC PRINTING

To print a Word file:

1. If necessary, open the document or template you want to print. Word prints the file that contains the insertion point.

2. Choose the File Print command. Word displays the dialog box shown in Figure 16–1. The text at the top of the dialog box indicates the printer Word will use. If this text says None, you need to install a printer, as explained later in this chapter.

3. If your file contains fields that should be updated before printing, choose Options to expand the dialog box, then turn on the Update Fields option.

4. Click OK or press **Enter**.

Don't be alarmed if printing doesn't begin instantly—Word takes a few seconds to format pages and communicate with the printer, then your file should start to print. If it doesn't, read What if It Doesn't Print? later in this chapter for suggestions about how to find the problem.

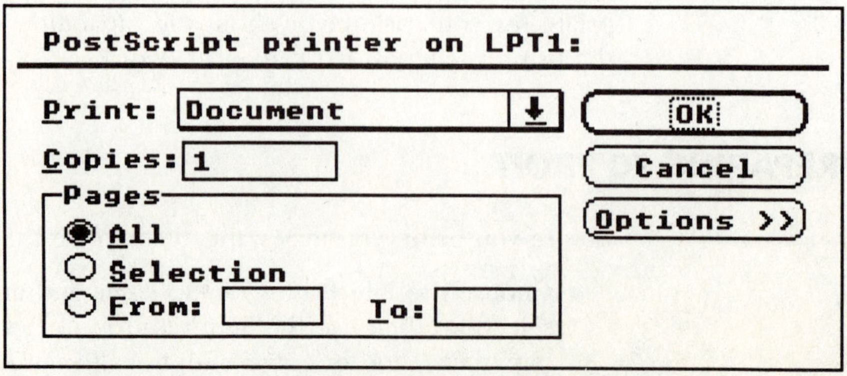

Figure 16–1.
The File Print dialog box.

```
 ┌─────────────────────────────────────────────────────────┐
 │  PostScript printer on LPT1:                            │
 │  ─────────────────────────────────────────              │
 │                                                          │
 │  Print: │Document            │ ↓│   ┌──────────┐         │
 │                                     │    OK    │         │
 │  Copies:│1                   │     └──────────┘         │
 │  ┌─Pages──────────────────────┐   ┌──────────┐          │
 │  │ ◉ All                      │   │  Cancel  │          │
 │  │ ○ Selection                │   └──────────┘          │
 │  │ ○ From: │      │  To: │    ││  │Options >>│          │
 │  └────────────────────────────┘   └──────────┘          │
 └─────────────────────────────────────────────────────────┘
```

PRINTING MORE THAN ONE COPY

To print more than one copy of your document:

1. Choose the File Print command. Word displays the dialog box shown in Figure 16–1.

2. Type the number of copies you want in the Copies box.

3. Click OK or press **Enter**.

CANCELLING PRINTING

If you need to cancel printing at any time:

■ Press **Esc**.

The printer may not stop immediately, because it continues to print whatever is in its memory until it receives the Stop! message from Word. If the paper is jammed or another emergency situation has developed, press the "on-line" printer button (if your printer has one) to take the printer "off line," or, in the case of dire emergencies, turn off the printer. (Turning off some printers causes them to lose information, and you'll have to send your file to it again to restart.)

CONTROLLING THE PAPER FEED TO THE PRINTER

The File Print command controls from where and when paper enters the printer.

1. Choose the File Print command.

2. Choose Options to expand the dialog box. The expanded dialog box is shown in Figure 16–2.

3. From the Paper Feed drop-down list, select the appropriate option:

Option	Description
Manual	The printer stops at the end of every page. Depending on which printer you're using, Word may display a message asking you to press Y when you've inserted another piece of paper.

```
┌─────────────────────────────────────────────────────────┐
│  PostScript Printer on LPT1:                            │
│ ────────────────────────────────────────────────────── │
│  Print: │Document          │ ↓│  ╭─────────────╮       │
│                                  │     OK      │        │
│  Copies:│1                │      ╰─────────────╯       │
│  ┌Pages──────────────────┐      ╭─────────────╮        │
│  │ ◉ All                 │      │   Cancel    │        │
│  │ ○ Selection           │      ╰─────────────╯        │
│  │ ○ From: │      │  To: │      │ ╭─────────────╮      │
│  └───────────────────────┘      │Options  >>  │       │
│                                   ╰─────────────╯       │
│     ☐ Reverse Print Order                              │
│     ☐ Draft         Paper Feed: │            │ ↓│     │
│     ☐ Update Fields                                    │
│     ┌Include───────────────────────────────────┐      │
│     │ ☐ Summary Info     ☐ Hidden Text         │      │
│     │ ☐ Annotations      ☐ Field Codes         │      │
│     └──────────────────────────────────────────┘      │
└─────────────────────────────────────────────────────────┘
```

Auto	The printer feeds paper in automatically until it reaches the end of the document.
Bin 1	The printer gets paper from bin 1.
Bin 2	The printer gets paper from bin 2.
Bin 3	The printer gets paper from bin 3.
Mixed	The printer gets paper from bin 1 for the first page and gets paper from bin 2 for all following pages.

3. Click OK or press **Enter**.

CHANGING PRINTERS

When you used Word's Setup program, you told Word what kind of printer you're using. Word displays the dialog boxes appropriate for that printer. If you have installed several printers during the Setup process, you can use Word's File Printer Setup command to switch to a different printer. If you need to install a new printer, see the next section.

To switch to a different printer:

1. Choose the File Printer Setup command. Word displays the dialog box shown in Figure 16–3.

2. From the Printer list, select a printer description.

3. Choose Setup. Word displays the Setup dialog box. This dialog box contains different options according to the type of printer. Figure 16–4 shows a dialog box for a PostScript printer.

4. Select options in the dialog box.

5. Click OK or press **Enter**.

Figure 16–3.
The File Printer Setup dialog box.

Figure 16–4.
The dialog box Word displays for a PostScript printer.

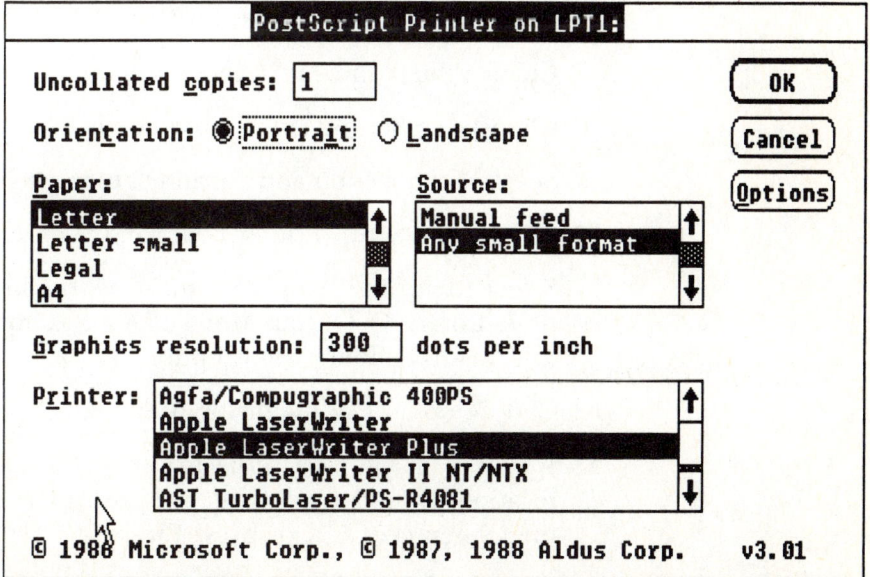

INSTALLING A NEW PRINTER

If you forgot to install a printer during the Setup process or you obtained a new printer since installing Word, you can use the following process to install a new printer. Word typically comes with two printer disks. Before you begin this procedure, make sure you have the printer disks at hand.

1. Choose the Run command from the Word Control menu (**Alt, Spacebar, U**).

2. Choose Control Panel, then click OK or press **Enter**.

3. Insert a printer disk in the A: drive.

4. Choose the Installation Add New Printer command and choose OK.

5. Scroll through the list of printers to find your specific brand and model. If you can't find it, press **Esc**, then replace the disk in drive A: with the other printer disk, then go back to step 4. If you can't find your printer, consult Word's printer manual for advice on which printer to choose.

6. Select the printer from the list, then click Add or press **Enter**. A dialog box appears, asking whether you want to copy the driver file to your Windows directory.

7. Change the pathname if necessary, then click Yes or press **Enter**.

8. Choose the Setup Connections command.

9. Select a connection and a printer, then click OK or press **Enter**.

10. Choose the Setup Printer command.

11. Select the printer you'll use most of the time, then click OK or press **Enter**. An Output Mode dialog box appears, asking you for information about output options.

12. Choose options in the dialog box, then click OK or press **Enter**.

13. If you're installing a serial printer, choose the Setup Communications command, choose the appropriate communications settings, then click OK or press **Enter**.

14. Press **Alt+F4** or double-click the Control Panel Control menu to close the Control Panel.

PRINTING PART OF YOUR DOCUMENT

You can use the File Print command to tell Word to print a range of pages or to print only the text you have selected at the time.

To print only part of your document:

1. If you want to print only a selection, select the part of your document you want to print.

2. Choose the File Print command.

3. In the Pages box, choose an option to tell Word what you want to print:

To print	Do this
Selected text only	Choose Selection.
Certain pages	In the From box, type the number of the first page you want to print, then move to the To box and type the number of the last page you want to print. For example, to print pages 5 through 10 you'd type **5** in the From box and **10** in the To box. You can specify pages in sections like this: **P3S2** (page 3 in section 2).

4. Click OK or press **Enter**.

PRINTING ENVELOPES

If your printer carriage is wide enough or supports an envelope-feed mode, you can print envelopes with Word. The method you use to print envelopes depends on the type of printer you have. You can create a template for your envelopes using procedures described under Envelopes in the Word *User's Reference*.

You may need to experiment somewhat to find a method that works for your printer. To print envelopes, complete these tasks:

1. Choose the Format Document command and adjust the Page Width and Height boxes in the Format Document command to match the height and width of the envelope.

2. Use the Format Position command to position the addresses within the envelope area.

3. Set the paper orientation to Landscape (vertical) or Portrait (horizontal), according to whether you're inserting the envelope vertically or horizontally. On most laser printers, it's best to set the orientation to Landscape and insert the envelope "short end" first.

4. Use the File Print command to print the envelope.

PRINTING GLOSSARIES, STYLE SHEETS, SUMMARY SHEETS, AND KEY ASSIGNMENTS

You can use the File Print command to print the following items: a summary information sheet containing information you entered about the file, a glossary, a style sheet, and a list of key assignments.

You can decide whether to print these items in addition to the document or to print only these items.

Printing Summary Sheets, Annotations, Hidden Text, or Field Codes with the Document

To print any of these items at the same time as you print your document:

1. Open the document or template you want to print.

2. Choose the File Print command.

3. Choose Options to expand the dialog box.

4. In the Include box, turn on the options to mark the items you want to print along with the document:

Choose	To print
Summary Info	The summary information sheet.
Annotations	The text of annotations (if any).
Hidden text	Text formatted as hidden (if any).
Field Codes	The codes contained in fields (if any) instead of the field results.

5. Click OK or press **Enter**. Word prints the document or template text first, then prints annotations and/or summary information (if you marked the choice) on separate pages.

Printing Only Glossaries, Style Sheets, Summary Sheets, or Key Assignments

To print one of these items:

1. Open the document or template containing the items you want to print.

2. Choose the File Print command.

3. From the Print drop-down list (shown in Figure 16–5), choose the item you want to print:

Choose	To print
Summary Info	The summary information sheet.
Annotations	The text of annotations (if any).
Styles	The styles contained in the document or template.

Figure 16–5.
Selecting an option from the Print list in the File Print dialog box.

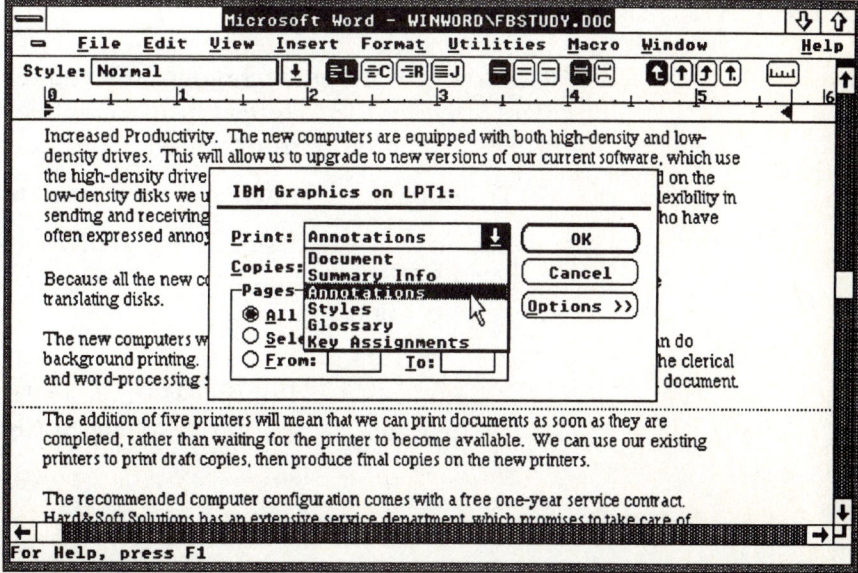

Glossary	The glossary entries from the template and from NORMAL.DOT.
Key assignments	The names of macros and commands, their key assignments for the template, and the description text.

4. Click OK or press **Enter**.

PRINTING A DRAFT COPY

When you don't care about the document's layout, page breaks, or anything else except the words, you can print a draft copy of your document. Printing a draft copy is fast, because Word doesn't print graphics, use microspace justification, or perform other time-consuming printing tasks. For draft copies Word prints an empty frame where a graphic belongs.

To print a draft copy:

1. Choose the File Print command.

2. Choose Options to display the rest of the dialog box.

3. Turn on the Draft option.

4. Click OK or press **Enter**.

PRINTING SEVERAL FILES AT ONCE

Word offers two different techniques you can use to print several files, one right after another. Here are the techniques you can choose from and where to find more information about how to use them:

Technique	For more information, see
Use an INCLUDE field to chain files together	Using INCLUDE Fields in Chapter 22
Print all marked files from the document retrieval window	Printing Documents Using the Document Retrieval System in Chapter 24

PRINTING PAGES IN REVERSE ORDER

If your printer stacks the pages face up as they emerge, you may want to print the pages in your file in reverse order to save yourself the work of shuffling the pages into the correct order.

To tell Word to print in reverse order:

1. Choose the File Print command.

2. Choose Options to display the rest of the dialog box.

3. Turn on the Reverse Print Order option.

4. Click OK or press **Enter**.

WHAT IF IT DOESN'T PRINT?

If Word displays a message saying that your document is printing, but the printer is just sitting there silently, don't lose your temper right away. It takes Word a few seconds to format pages and communicate with the printer. The length of time required depends on the length of your document and the speed of your computer. However, if you've waited a moment or two and it still isn't printing or Word has displayed an error message, go through the steps in the following checklist. We can't foresee all the problems, but if you complete all the steps in the checklist in order, the odds are good that you'll find and fix your problem along the way.

1. Make sure the printer is plugged in and turned on.

2. Make sure the printer cable is securely plugged into the correct printer and the computer ports.

3. Make sure the printer buttons (such as on-line and ready) are "on" if they should be.

4. Make sure there's paper positioned properly in the printer.

5. Make sure all parts of the printer (covers, ribbon or cartridge, paper trays, and so on) are in place.

6. Choose the File Print command and check the settings to make sure they're right.

7. Turn the printer off, wait a few seconds, then turn it back on and try to print again using the File Print command.

8. If you're using PostScript codes in your document, create another copy of the document, remove the PostScript codes, and try printing the copy. An error in a PostScript code can cause a document not to print.

9. Make sure the printer "connections" shown on the Control Panel are set to the correct port.

10. Check the Word printer manual to make sure that the driver file that's installed is the correct one for your brand and model of printer.

If you're an experienced MS-DOS user, you might also want to check the "TEMP" environment variable, which is typically set in the AUTOEXEC.BAT file with a statement such as **SET TEMP**=**c:**. If this line is not present or sets an invalid path, fix it and restart your computer.

If you've gone through every step in this list and your document still doesn't print, call your printer manufacturer or call the Microsoft Product Support number.

Part V

WORKING WITH COMPLEX DOCUMENTS

Complex documents require special techniques. In this part of the book, you'll learn how to use a few of Word's features that are designed for the user who works with a variety of sophisticated documents.

Chapter 17 concentrates on working with long documents. You'll be introduced to Word's outline view screen with all of its functions, and you'll also learn how to number lines and paragraphs for easy reference.

Chapter 18 shows the general aspects of working with Word's powerful fields. You can use fields to perform calculations, to import other files, and to add different kinds of information to your document. This chapter introduces you to the various types of fields, how to insert fields, how to format the results, and how to update fields to keep them current.

Frequently, the last two steps for long documents are to add a table of contents and an index. Chapter 19 shows you how to use Word to generate them for your document. You'll also see how you can use these features to create lists of tables and figures.

Word isn't a spreadsheet program, but Word can do some pretty advanced calculations. Chapter 20 shows you how to calculate with Word's Utilities Calculate command and how to calculate with fields.

When you need to refer to a portion of text or to a graphic, you can attach a Word bookmark to it. Then you can cross-reference the bookmarked portion, import it into other files, use it in calculations, and make other tasks easier. Chapter 21 details how to use bookmarks.

Two of the advantages of using Windows are the ability to import information from other applications and the feature that links applications so that the information they share is automatically updated. Chapter 22 shows you how to use Word's import and linking features.

If you're running a business that does mass mailings, you'll want to use Word's print merge capabilities. Chapter 23 shows you how to create the files you'll need, how to merge them, and how to create address labels.

The more files you have, the more you need Word's document retrieval system. Chapter 24 illustrates how to find the files you want and how to print or delete groups of files.

## Chapter Seventeen

Working with Long Documents

When you're creating a long document, such as a screenplay for Hollywood or a proposal for the office, Word helps you develop special techniques for keeping track of all the text.

Word has built in a number of features to help you work with long documents, including

- outline view

- numbering paragraphs and lines

- bookmark names assignable to parts of documents

- jumping to specific locations with the Edit Go To command

This chapter shows you how to effectively handle long documents and keep both Word and your computer operating at maximum efficiency.

USING OUTLINES IN WORD

Outlining is one way to organize long documents. A Word outline is not a separate document—Word's outline view is another way to view your document. Take a look at Figure 17–1, which shows a document created in outline view, and Figure 17–2, which shows the same document in normal view. Whether you are the kind of person who takes the time to organize a document well beforehand, or one who simply writes and then reorganizes the pieces afterwards, you'll find outlining in Word can help you produce a complex document more easily.

Figure 17–1.
A document created in outline view.

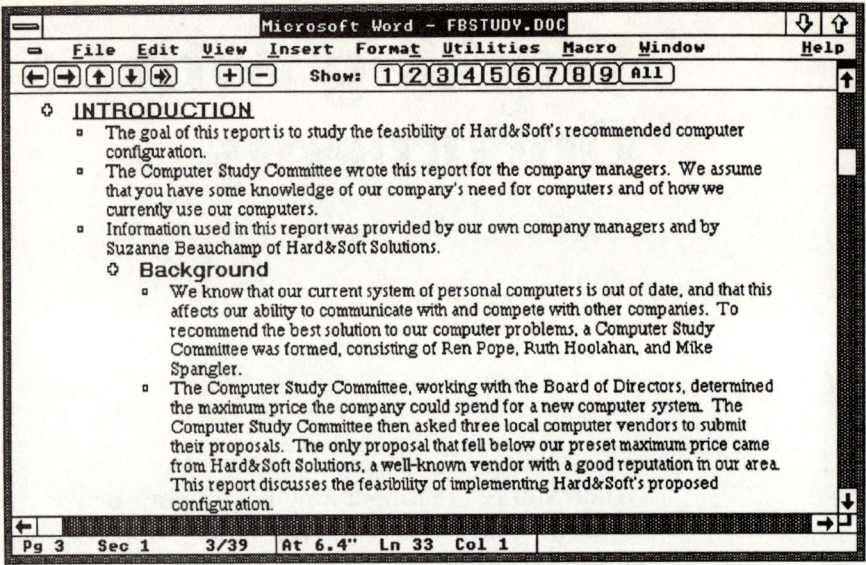

Figure 17–2.
The same document in normal view.

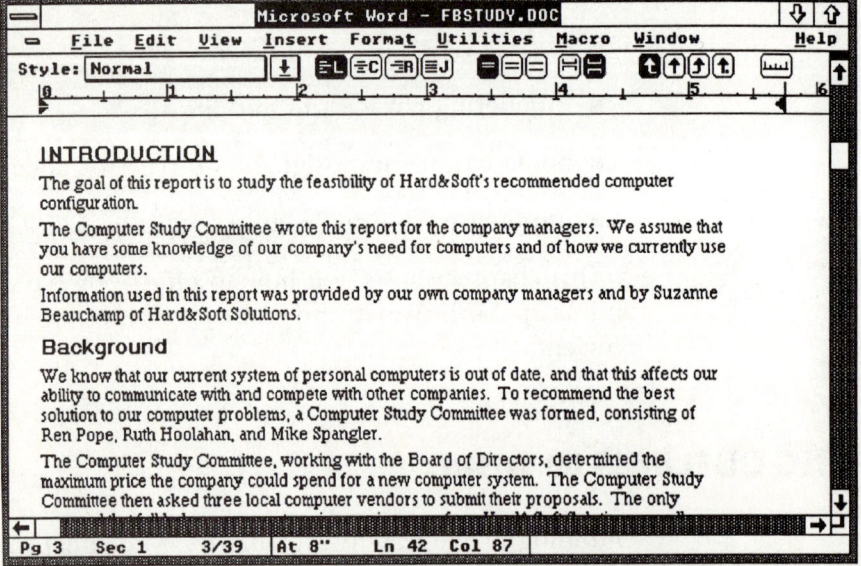

Outlining can be used with any type of document. However, it's most helpful when you use it with longer and more complex documents. Documents that have a number of topic headings and subheadings, such as a contract or a research report, are good candidates for outlining.

SWITCHING TO AND FROM OUTLINE VIEW

To switch to outline view from normal view:

- Choose the View Outline command. Word puts a check mark next to the command and displays outline view, shown in Figure 17–3.

If you're using a mouse, you can click icons at the top of the screen to assign heading levels and arrange your outline.

To switch back to normal view:

- Choose the View Outline command. Word removes the check mark from the command and displays normal view.

CREATING AN OUTLINE

The easiest way to use Word's outlining feature is to create an outline before you type the text for your document. In outline view, the text in your document falls into two categories: headings and body text. Headings are the titles of sections and are arranged according to levels that indicate their relative importance in the document. Paragraphs in a section are the body text.

Figure 17–3.
Outline view with no document displayed.

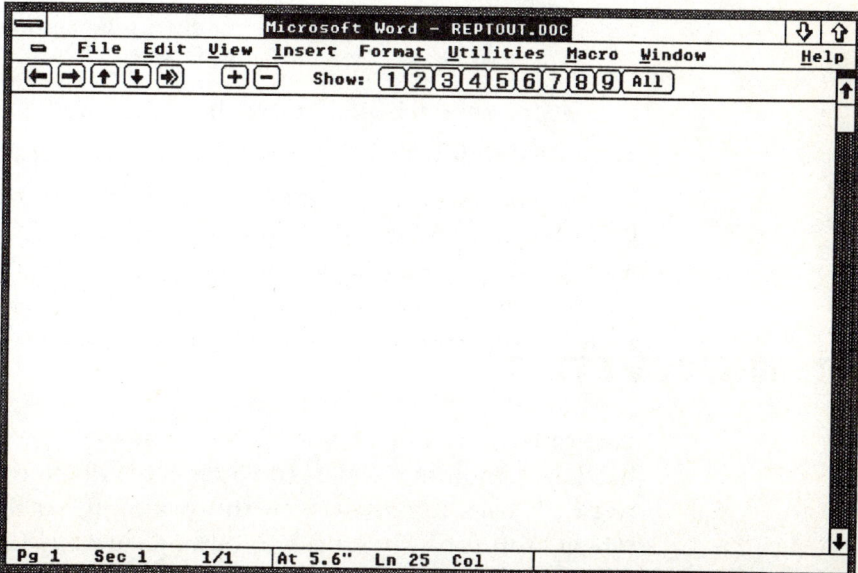

When you create an outline in outline view, Word assigns outline styles to your text. These styles are named Heading 1 through Heading 9, and are part of Word's default style sheet. One advantage of using these Heading styles is that Word can easily create a table of contents by collecting paragraphs with heading styles. (For more information about styles and how to apply them or change them, see Chapter 10. For information about creating a table of contents, see Chapter 19, "Creating Tables of Contents and Indexes.")

A Word outline can include up to nine levels of headings, plus *body text*—the paragraphs, graphics, and so on, that are not headings and that make up the majority of your document. Word marks headings with hollow plus signs and rectangles and marks body text with hollow squares.

To create an outline:

1. Choose the View Outline command. Word displays outline view, as shown in Figure 17–3.

2. Type the outline heading paragraphs, assigning levels as you type:

   ■ To make a paragraph one level lower than the preceding paragraph, click the right arrow icon at the top of the screen, drag the heading marker (the hollow plus sign or rectangle) to the right or press **Alt+Shift+Right arrow**.

   ■ To make a paragraph one level higher than the preceding paragraph, click the left arrow icon at the top of the screen, drag the heading marker (the hollow plus sign or rectangle) to the left or press **Alt+Shift+Left arrow**.

   ■ To make the paragraph the same level as the preceding paragraph, just type the text.

You can always change the heading levels and rearrange the outline later. You'll learn how to do that in the following section. Figure 17–4 illustrates creating an outline.

ENTERING BODY TEXT

You can enter or edit the body of your document (all text except headings) in outline view, but you'll generally find it more convenient to switch back to normal view to work on the main text of your document. You can switch back to outline view any time you want to see the structure of the document.

Figure 17–4.
Creating an outline.

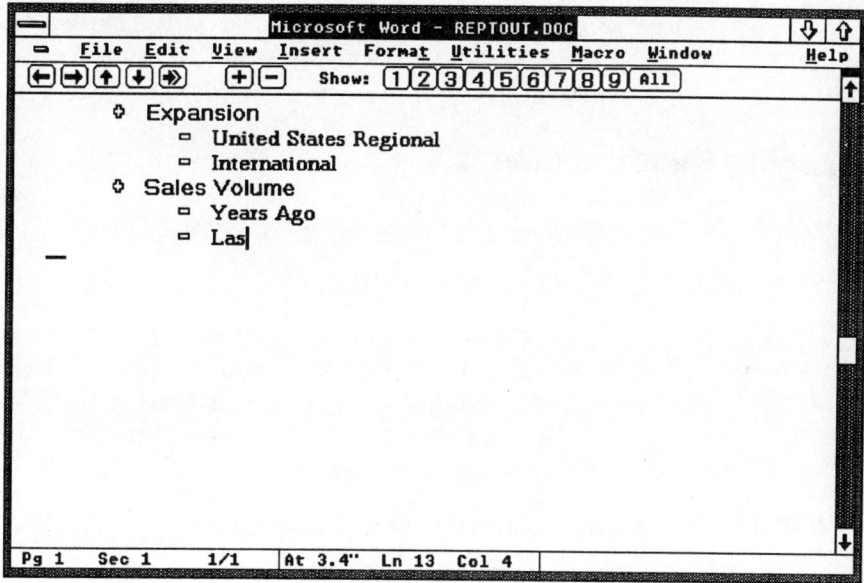

To enter body text:

1. Choose the View Outline command to switch back to normal view.

2. Type the body text.

EDITING AN OUTLINE

You can always edit the text, change the levels of headings in your document, or rearrange your headings in outline view. Just remember—when you edit an outline, you're editing the entire document, not just a separate outline file.

Selecting in Outline View

Selecting text in outline view is much like selecting in normal view, with the following exceptions:

■ You can select text within a single paragraph, but if you extend the selection between two paragraphs, both paragraphs are selected automatically.

■ If you double-click beside a heading while the pointer is in the selection bar, the heading and all subtext are selected.

Changing Heading Levels

To demote a heading to the next lower level:

1. Select the heading.

2. Click the right arrow icon at the top of the screen, drag the heading marker to the right, or press **Alt+Shift+Right arrow**. Word indents the text and assigns it the Heading style for the next lower level. You can repeat this step several times to demote a heading several levels.

To demote a heading to body text:

1. Select the heading.

2. Click the shadowed right arrow icon at the top of the screen, or press **Alt+Shift+5** on the numeric keypad (NumLock off). Word indents the text, draws a hollow square next to it, and assigns it the Normal style from the default style sheet.

To promote body text to a heading or promote a heading to the next higher level:

1. Select the body text or heading.

2. Click the left arrow icon at the top of the screen, drag the heading marker to the left, or press **Alt+Shift+Left arrow**. Word shifts the text left and assigns it the Heading style for the next higher level. You can repeat this step several times to promote a heading several levels.

VIEWING DIFFERENT HEADING LEVELS IN YOUR OUTLINE

You can collapse or expand all or part of an outline to view different levels of text. Collapsing and expanding doesn't remove text from or add text to a document—it just displays or hides specific levels of headings on the outline view screen. Figure 17–5 shows some collapsed outline headings.

To collapse or expand all the subheadings and body text beneath a specific heading:

Figure 17–5.
You can expand and
collapse an outline to
show only the
heading levels you
want.

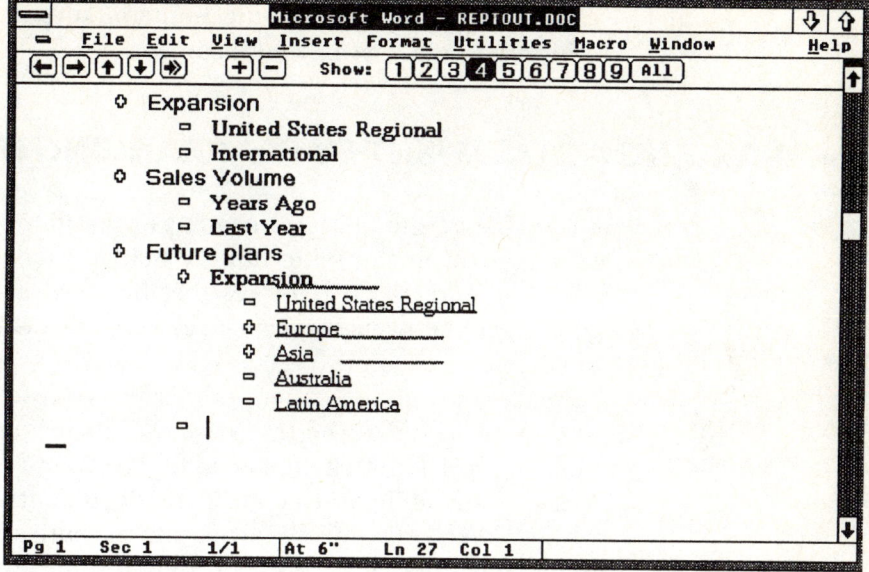

1. Select the heading whose subheadings and body text you want to collapse or expand.

2. Collapse or expand the text with either the mouse or keys.

   ■ To collapse the text, double-click the heading marker or press the minus key on the numeric keypad. Word draws a dotted gray line to indicate that a heading has hidden text beneath it.

   ■ To expand the text, double-click the heading marker or press the plus key on the numeric keypad.

   ■ To show only the first line of body text, press **Alt+Shift+F**.

To display specific levels of your outline:

■ Click a level number icon at the top of the outline view screen or hold down the **Alt** and the **Shift** keys while you press a number key in the top row of the main keypad to indicate the level number you want. Word hides all headings and text beneath that level. For example, click 3 or press **Alt+Shift+3** to see only levels 1 through 3.

To display all levels of your outline:

■ Click the All icon at the top of the outline view screen or press the multiply key (*) on the numeric keypad. Word displays all headings and text in the document.

REARRANGING A DOCUMENT BY REARRANGING ITS OUTLINE

You can change the order of headings in outline view and rearrange your document at the same time. When you move a heading whose text is collapsed, Word relocates that heading, all of its subordinate headings, and all of its associated text in your document as well as in outline view.

To make rearranging easier and faster, collapse text beneath headings to make sure that the text stays with its headings. Moving text in outline view does not change heading levels.

At any time while you create your document—when you outline, enter body text, or complete formatting the entire document—you can reorganize the document's structure easily and quickly.

To move headings and rearrange your document:

1. Select the paragraphs you want to move.

2. Select either the body text or the headings. You can move body text by itself to a different location. However, when you move a heading, Word automatically moves all of the subheadings and collapsed text beneath that heading.

3. Move the text to where you want it.

   ■ To move the selected text a short distance, click the up or down arrow icon at the top of the screen, or press the up or down arrow keys until the text is where you want it.

   ■ To move the selected text a sizable distance in a long outline, use the Edit Cut and Edit Paste commands. (See Chapter 4, "Editing Your Word Files," for more information about cutting and pasting text.)

▰▰ *Mouse Shortcut*

You can use the mouse to change heading levels and to move headings within the document window:

1. Select the marker in front of the heading you want to promote, demote, or move to a new location.

2. Hold down the left mouse button. When you begin to move the

mouse, a thin dotted line appears, as shown in Figure 17–6. If you move the mouse right or left, a vertical line appears to enable you to promote or demote the heading. If you move the mouse up or down, a horizontal line appears to enable you to relocate the heading.

3. Drag the line to the new position.

4. Release the mouse button to set the new heading position.

DISPLAYING NONOUTLINE TEXT IN OUTLINE VIEW

If you didn't use outline view to create an outline, you can still display your document in outline view. This won't be of much use to you unless you have formatted your headings using Word's Heading styles from the default style sheet, or unless you want to reformat your headings using these styles. Word uses the Heading styles to keep track of the levels of text in an outline. If your text contains no Heading styles, Word can't distinguish between the levels of text.

Word displays all nonoutline text as body text in outline view, as shown in Figure 17–7.

Figure 17–6.
Changing heading
levels in the
document window
with a mouse.

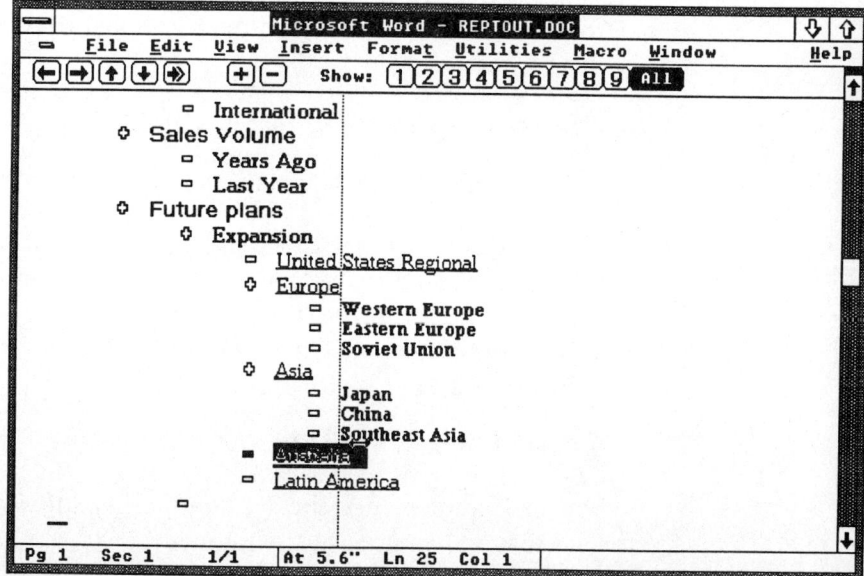

Figure 17–7.
Nonoutline text in
outline view.

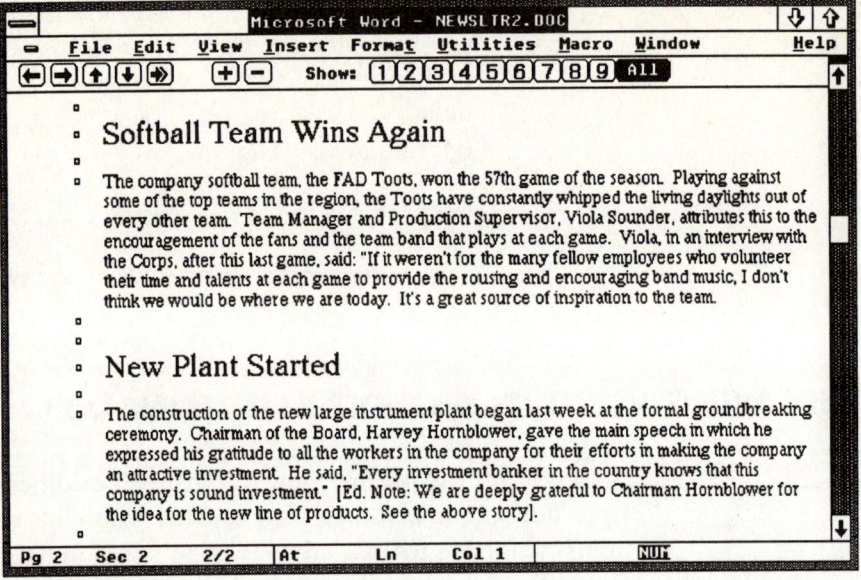

Converting a Document into an Outline

To turn your document into an outline, you can use the procedures described earlier in Editing an Outline to change heading levels. This causes Word to replace the styles assigned to your text with the Heading styles from the default style sheet.

You could also create an outline by applying styles to your headings in this way:

1. Select the paragraph you want to be an outline heading.

2. Press **Ctrl+S**. Word displays the words `Which style?` in the status bar.

3. Type the heading style you want. For example, if you want to make the selected text a first-level heading, you'd type **heading 1**. If you want to make it a second-level heading, you'd type **heading 2**, and so forth.

4. Press **Enter** to apply the style.

You may want to use the F4 key or the Edit Repeat command to format several headings at the same level without having to retype the style name.

USING OUTLINE VIEW TO NAVIGATE THROUGH A LONG DOCUMENT

You can use outline view as a tool to get around in a large document in which the headings have the Heading styles (attached through outlining or with style commands). You simply collapse the text beneath headings to see the structure of your document, then select the appropriate heading in the outline, expand the text, and begin work. You can expand and collapse the document as many times as you wish and make as many changes as you wish. If you want to refer to a particular section, copy words or phrases, or check for terms or other data, you can locate the section quickly if you know its heading. You don't need to remember page numbers or scroll through a long document.

To use an outline to travel quickly through a long document that contains Heading styles:

1. If you're working in normal view, choose the View Outline command.

2. Collapse the outline to its major headings by clicking 1 or 2 at the top of the outline view screen or by pressing **Alt+Shift+1** or **Alt+Shift+2**.

   - If a heading's text is displayed and you want to move it, select any subheadings and associated text to move the entire section at once.

   - If a heading's text is collapsed, select just the heading. Word moves collapsed text with its associated headings.

3. Select the heading you want to move the insertion point to.

4. Choose the View Outline command to switch back to normal view.

NUMBERING OUTLINE HEADINGS

You can use the Utilities Renumber command to number headings in outline view. (You can also use this command to number all paragraphs in your document—see Numbering Paragraphs later in this chapter for more information.) This command inserts fields that are updated on printing. By default, Word numbers outlines using the scheme described in *The Chicago Manual of Style* (University of Chicago Press), as shown in Figure 17–8.

You can also choose to use a legal numbering format, as shown in Figure 17–9.

Figure 17–8.
Outline headings numbered with a traditional outline number format.

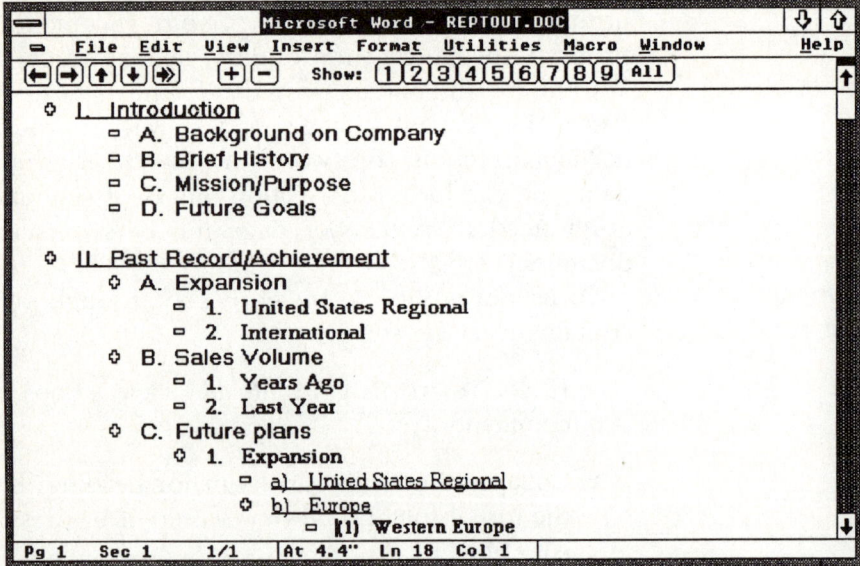

Figure 17–9.
Outline headings numbered with a legal format.

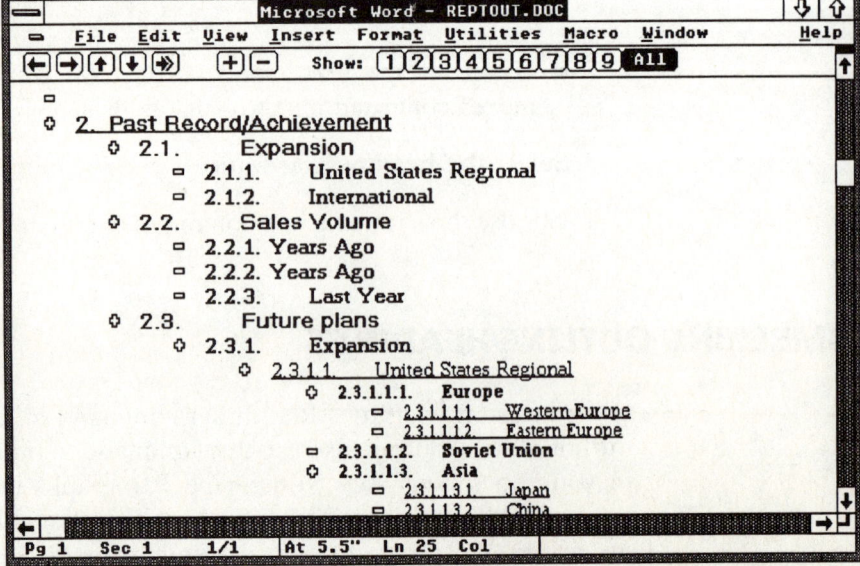

To number outline headings:

1. If necessary, choose the View Outline command to switch to outline view.

2. Display only the headings you want to number. (Word numbers *all* headings and body text displayed on the screen, so be sure to collapse headings to hide any paragraphs you don't want numbered.)

3. Choose the Utilities Renumber command.

4. Do one of the following:

   ■ To number the displayed headings with the traditional outline format, select Outline from the Format list.

   ■ To number the displayed headings with the legal format, select Legal from the Format list.

5. Click OK or press **Enter**. Word inserts number fields and tab characters in front of the displayed paragraphs, as shown in Figure 17–10. You'll see the numbers when you choose the View Field Codes command or when you print the document.

Figure 17–10.
Outline headings with number fields inserted with the Utilities Renumber command fields.

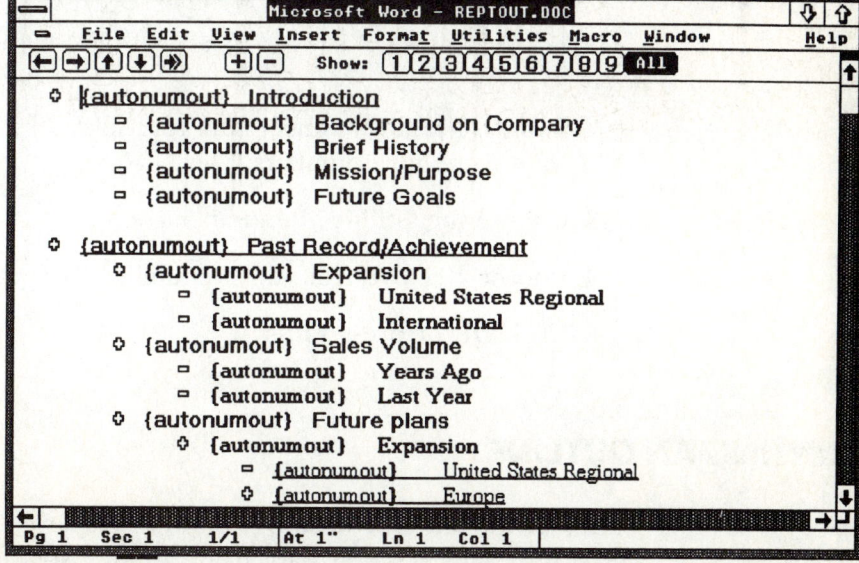

Updating Heading Numbers

To update heading numbers after you've added text to or deleted text from your outline:

1. If necessary, choose the View Outline command to switch to outline view.

2. Collapse headings as necessary to display only the levels of headings you want to number.

3. Choose the Utilities Renumber command.

4. Do one of the following:

   ■ To renumber the headings with the traditional outline format, select Outline from the Format list.

   ■ To renumber the headings with the legal format, select Legal from the Format list.

5. Click OK or press **Enter**.

Removing Heading Numbers

To remove numbers from headings:

1. If necessary, choose the View Outline command to switch to outline view.

2. Expand headings as necessary to display all the levels of text you want to remove numbers from.

3. Choose the Utilities Renumber command.

4. Choose Remove from the Renumber Paragraphs box.

5. Click OK or press **Enter**.

PRINTING AN OUTLINE

Word prints only the headings that are displayed in outline view, so make sure all levels you want to print are displayed.

To print an outline:

1. Expand or collapse headings as necessary to display the levels of text you want to print.

2. Use the File Print command to print your outline.

NUMBERING PARAGRAPHS

One way to keep track of text positions in long documents is by numbering paragraphs. You can use a variety of number formats in your document for easy reference.

If you created an outline for your document in outline view, or if you indented subordinate text in your document, Word can recognize subordinate paragraphs of text and can number them according to outline headings or the amount of indentation. (See Numbering Outline Headings earlier in this chapter for more information.) If you didn't use outline headings or indent subordinate paragraphs, Word assumes all your paragraphs are at the same level and numbers paragraphs sequentially. Word numbers only those paragraphs that contain text, not those that create blank lines.

You can also insert and format a number, then ask Word to use your formatted number as an example for numbering paragraphs. (See Creating Your Own Number Format later in this section to find out how.)

About Automatic and Manual Numbering

When you number paragraphs in Word, you can choose between automatic numbering and manual numbering. To number automatically, Word inserts fields at the beginning of each paragraph, and Word automatically updates these fields to keep the numbers in order when you add or delete paragraphs. To number manually, Word inserts numbers at the beginning of selected paragraphs. If you add or delete paragraphs that have manual numbers, you need to update the numbers to keep them in order. Generally speaking, you'll want to use manual numbers only when you want to number just a few paragraphs in your document or when you want to create your own number format.

Numbering Paragraphs with Automatic Numbers

To number paragraphs with automatic numbers:

1. If you want to number only part of your document, select the paragraphs you want to number. To number all paragraphs in the document, make sure nothing is selected.

2. Choose the Utilities Renumber command. Word displays the dialog box shown in Figure 17–11.

3. If you want to start at a number other than 1, type that number in the Start At box.

4. Choose one of the following:

   ■ If your headings are formatted with outline styles or indented, select Outline from the Format list to get traditional outline numbering (I, A, 1, a) or select Legal to get legal numbering (1, 1.1, 1.1.1, 1.1.1.1).

   ■ If your headings are not formatted with outline styles or indented, select Sequence from the Format list to have Word number your paragraphs sequentially (1, 2, 3, . . .).

5. Click OK or press **Enter**. Word inserts number fields and tab characters at the beginning of the paragraphs. When you print

Figure 17–11.
The Utilities Renumber dialog box.

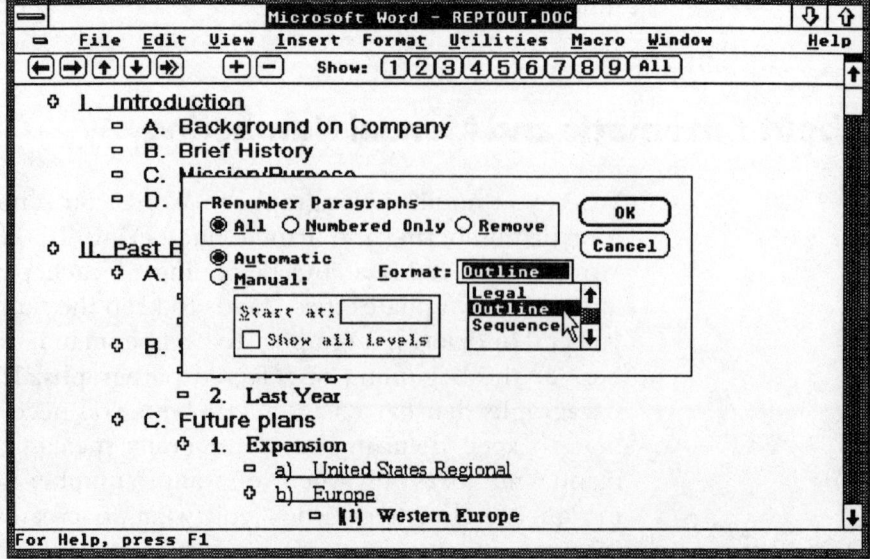

your document or choose the View Field Codes command, you'll see the numbers.

Numbering Paragraphs with Manual Numbers

To number paragraphs with manual numbers:

1. Select the paragraphs you want to number.

2. Choose the Utilities Renumber command.

3. If necessary, choose Manual.

4. If you want to start at a number other than 1, type that number in the Start At box.

5. Select Sequence from the Format list to have Word number your paragraphs sequentially (1, 2, 3, . . .).

6. Click OK or press **Enter**.

Creating Your Own Number Format

You can create your own number format. Word attempts to duplicate the format you type. The results, however, depend on how accurately Word can interpret what you want. (Remember that you can use the Edit Undo command if you don't want to keep the results.) Figure 17–12 illustrates creating a number format.

To create your own number format:

1. In front of the first paragraph you want to number, type and format a paragraph number the way you want. Make sure to put a space or a tab character between your number and the following text.

2. Select all the paragraphs you want to number.

3. Choose the Utilities Renumber command.

4. Choose All in the Renumber Paragraphs box.

5. Make sure that the Manual option is selected and that Learn is selected from the Format list.

6. Click OK or press **Enter** to number your paragraphs.

Figure 17–12.
Creating a number format.

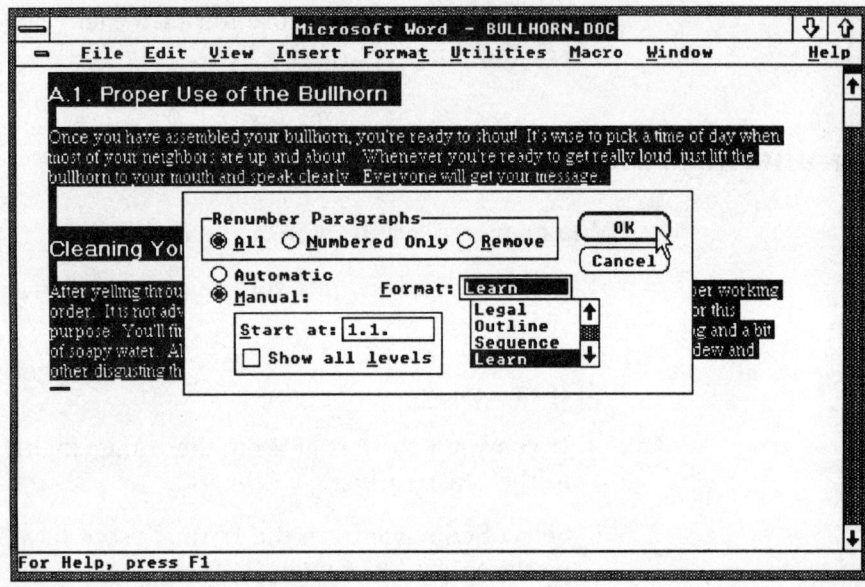

Numbering Nonsequential Paragraphs

There may be some times when you want to number only a paragraph here and there, leaving paragraphs in between unnumbered. To number selected paragraphs:

1. Type a number and a space in front of each of the paragraphs you want to number. You can use the same number and space over and over again, so you might want to type a **1** and a space, then copy and paste the number and space in front of every paragraph you are numbering.

2. Make sure no text is selected in your document, then choose the Utilities Renumber command.

3. Choose Numbered Only in the Renumber Paragraph box.

4. Choose any other options you want in the dialog box, then click OK or press **Enter**.

Updating Paragraph Numbers

To update paragraph numbers:

1. If only a portion of your document has manual paragraph num-

bers, select that portion. Otherwise, make sure nothing is selected.

2. If you've numbered nonsequential paragraphs with the Numbered Only option in the Renumber Paragraph box, choose Numbered Only again.

3. Click OK or press **Enter**.

Removing Paragraph Numbers

To remove numbers from paragraphs in your document:

1. Select the paragraphs to remove numbers from.

2. Choose the Utilities Renumber command.

3. Choose Remove in the Renumber Paragraphs box.

4. Click OK or press **Enter**.

NUMBERING LINES

You can add line numbers to your document when you need to count lines at a glance or to make text easier to refer to on a page. Line numbers are commonly used in legal documents and military specifications.

When you use line numbering in Word, you assign numbers to each line of text in a document. The numbers appear only when the document is printed or when you choose the File Print Preview command. You can decide how many lines you want to number—each line, every other line, or every fifth line, for example. You can also turn off line numbering in selected paragraphs, such as headings and figures.

Adding Line Numbers to a Document

To add line numbers:

1. Select the section(s) you want to add line numbers to.

2. Choose the Format Section command. Word displays the dialog box shown in Figure 17–13.

Figure 17–13.
The Format Section
command controls
line numbering.

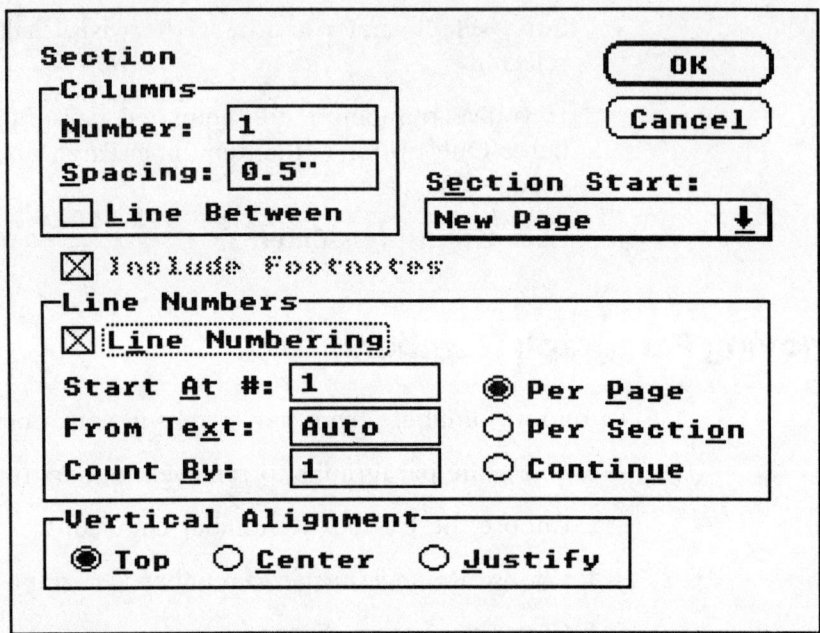

Figure 17–13.
The Format Section command controls line numbering.

3. Turn on the Line Numbering option in the Line Numbers box.

4. You can choose from the following options:

If you want to	Do this
Start at a line other than 1	Type the starting number in the Start At box.
Change the distance between the text and the line numbers (default = .25 inch for single-column sections or .13 for multiple-column sections)	Type a new measurement in the From Text box.
Print line numbers at intervals (every third or fifth line, for example)	Type the interval you want in the Count By box (for example, type **5** to print a number beside every fifth line).

5. To determine when line numbering starts over, choose one of the following options:

Choose	To
Per Page	Start each page with line number 1.

Per Section	Starts each section with line number 1.
Continue	Numbers each line in sequence throughout the document.

6. Click OK or press **Enter**.

If you don't see line numbers in your document after you've specified them, don't panic. You can't see line numbers in normal view. You have to print your document or switch to print preview to see them. Figure 17–14 shows line numbers in print preview. For more information about using print preview, see Chapter 14, "Perfecting Your Pages."

Removing Line Numbers

You can remove line numbers from all or part of a document.

To remove line numbers from an entire document:

1. Select the section(s) you want to remove line numbers from.

2. Choose the Format Section command.

3. Turn off the Line Numbering option.

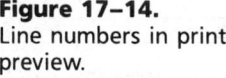

Figure 17–14.
Line numbers in print preview.

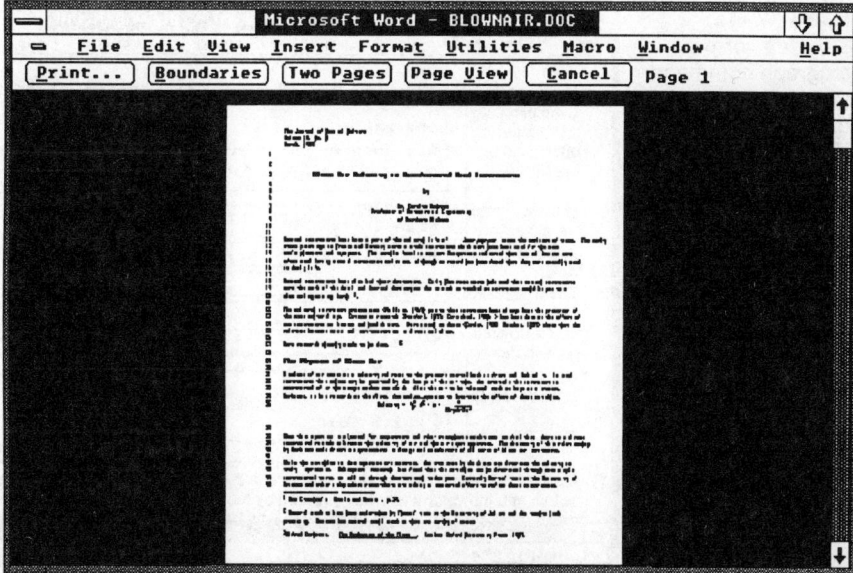

To remove line numbering from selected paragraphs in a document:

1. Select the paragraphs to remove line numbers from.

2. Choose the Format Paragraph command. Word displays the dialog box shown in Figure 17–15.

3. Turn off the Line Numbering option.

Jumping to a Specific Line Number

Once you have added line numbers, you can use the Edit Go To command to jump to a specific line number, as shown in Figure 17–16.
To jump to a line number:

1. Press **F5**. Word displays Go To: in the message line.

2. Do one of the following:

To	Do this
Jump to a line number in the current page or section	Type **l** (lowercase L) followed by the line number (example: **l5** for line 5).

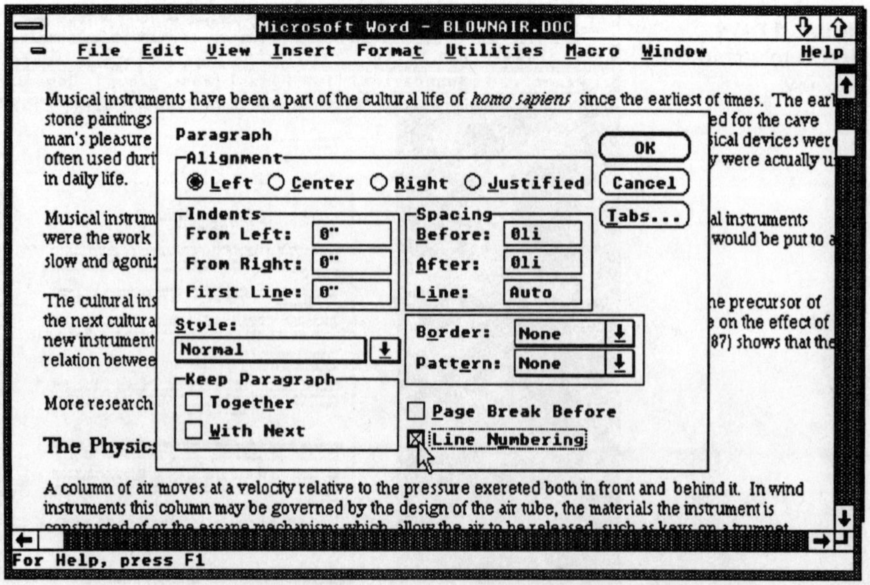

Figure 17–15.
Using the Format Paragraph command to remove line numbers from selected paragraphs.

Figure 17–16.
Using the Edit Go To command to find a numbered line.

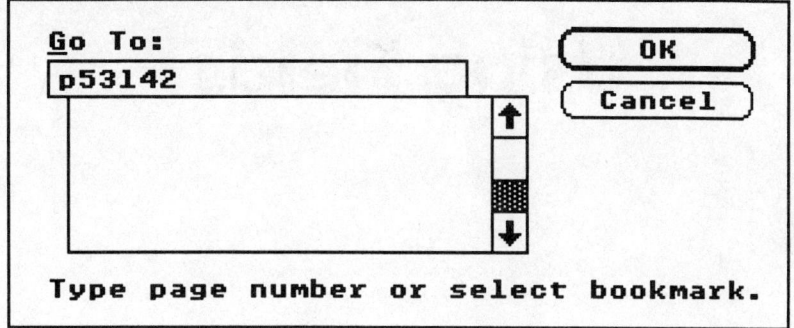

Go To:

p53l42

OK

Cancel

Type page number or select bookmark.

Jump to a line number on a different page or in a different section	Type **s** for section or **p** for page, followed by the page or section number, then type **l** (lowercase L) followed by a line number (example: **p2l10** for page 2, line 10, or **s3l20** for section 3, line 20).
Jump to a relative line number	Type **l** (lowercase L) followed by a plus (+) or minus (−) sign and a number (example: **l–10** to jump down 10 lines, or **l–10** to jump up 10 lines).

3. Click OK or press **Enter**.

## Chapter Eighteen

Using Fields

If you have worked with form letters and other documents that use information in fields, you're already familiar with how fields can speed and simplify your work.

A *field* is a special set of codes that instruct Word to insert information into a document. You can insert almost anything—text, pictures, tables, charts, indexes, tables of contents, numbers, dates, times, page numbers—into your document. Some common uses of fields are to

- merge large amounts of data into a standard format.

- create cross-references to another part of the document.

- include information from other parts of the document as well as from other documents.

- assemble indexes and tables of contents.

This chapter describes the following general information about fields:

- what a field contains

- how to insert a field

- how to format and edit fields

- how to link and update fields

For more information about specific uses of fields, refer to the Word Reference manual or use this list to find what you want in this book:

For more details about	See
Creating cross-references	Chapter 21, "Using Bookmarks"
Creating tables of contents and indexes	Chapter 19, "Creating Tables of Contents, Lists, and Indexes"
Calculating with fields	Chapter 20, "Performing Calculations"
Linking Word files with other files	Chapter 22, "Using Information from Other Files"
Merging files to create form letters and address labels	Chapter 23, "Creating Form Letters and Address Labels: Using Print Merge"

CONTENTS OF FIELDS

Fields typically consist of three parts:

- *field characters*—the symbols { and }—that Word inserts to show the beginning and end of the field. The symbols look similar to braces, but they are not the same as the brace characters on your keyboard.

- the *field type*, which is a name identifying the action you want the field to perform. The field type is the first item in the field after the beginning field character. A field type can consist of a field name (such as ASK, INCLUDE, QUOTE), an equal sign (=), or a bookmark name.

- *instructions*, which describe how you want the action performed. Instructions can consist of arguments, bookmark names, expressions, text, and switches.

Figure 18–1 shows an annotated example of a field.

INSERTING FIELDS

You can insert fields into Word documents with the Insert Field command or with the **Ctrl+F9** key combination.

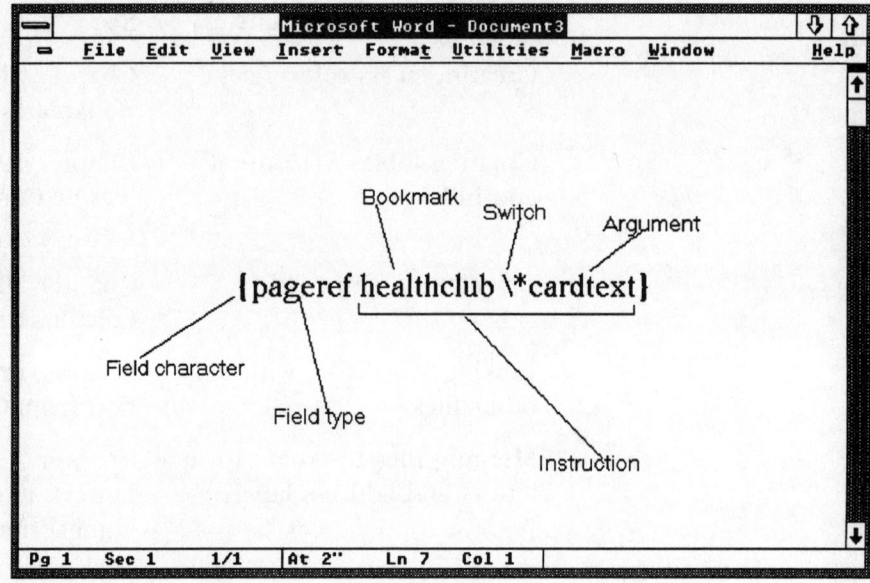

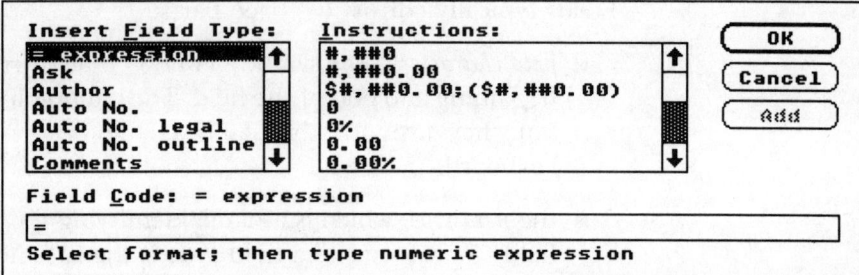

To insert a field with the Insert Field command:

1. Place the insertion point where you want the field to appear.

2. Choose the Insert Field command. Word displays the dialog box shown in Figure 18–2.

3. Select a field type from the Insert Field Type list. Word displays the text for that field type in the Field Code box.

4. If you want to change the format of the result, select formatting instructions from the Instructions list, then choose Add.

5. Type any additional instructions (such as mathematical expressions) needed in the Field Code box.

6. Click OK or press **Enter** to insert the field.

7. Press **F9** to update the field.

To insert a field with keys:

1. Press **Ctrl**+**F9** to enclose the insertion point with the field characters.

2. Type the field type and its instructions.

3. When you have finished typing and formatting the field, press **F9** to update the field.

4. Press a direction key to move the insertion point out of the field.

You can also type the contents of the field first, select them, then press **Ctrl**+**F9** to add field brackets.

DISPLAYING CODES OR RESULTS IN FIELDS

You can display fields in two ways:

- show field codes: field types and instructions

- show results: the visible text or graphics produced by the field codes

Figure 18–3 shows two windows displaying the same document. In the top window, the field displays its field codes; in the bottom window, the field displays its results.

You can switch from displaying codes to displaying results and back again by selecting the field, then pressing **Shift**+**F9** or choosing the View Field Codes command. The View Field Codes command is a toggle command: when a check mark appears beside the command on the menu, Word displays field codes. When you choose the command again, the check mark disappears, and Word displays the results of fields.

Some Word fields do not have a visible result, but instead initiate an action. The XE (Index Entry), TC (TOC Entry), and RD (Referenced Document) fields are a few of these. When you display field results, these fields "disappear," although the field codes are still in the document.

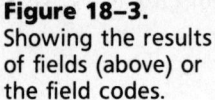

Figure 18–3.
Showing the results
of fields (above) or
the field codes.

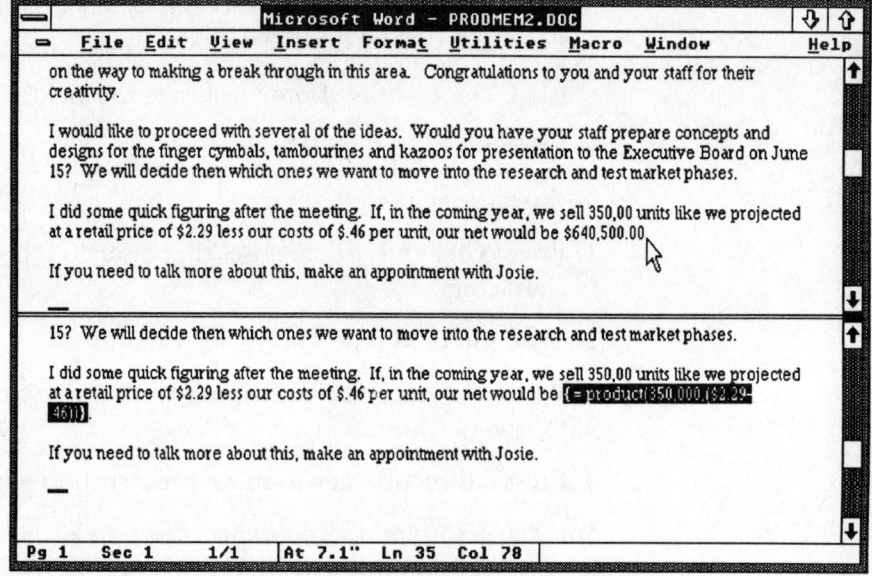

Some fields are automatically formatted as hidden text, so you may need to choose View Preferences and turn on the Hidden Text option to see the fields at all.

When you print a document, Word prints the results of all the document's fields unless you specifically tell Word to print the codes, as explained in the following section.

PRINTING FIELD CODES

If you want to print a document that contains fields but want to print the field codes rather than the results, do this:

1. Choose the File Print command.

2. Choose Options to expand the dialog box.

3. Turn on the Field Codes option.

4. Click OK or press **Enter** to begin printing.

EDITING AND DELETING FIELDS

Once you have inserted a field in your document, you can edit and delete the field like any other text. You can select text in a field the same way you select normal text, but if you select either the beginning or closing field character, Word automatically selects the entire field.

To edit a field:

1. Position the insertion point in the field.

2. If the result is shown, press **Shift+F9** to see the field codes.

3. Edit the text of the field as desired.

4. With the insertion point still in the field, press **F9** to update the field.

5. Press **Shift+F9** to check the results.

To delete a field:

1. Select the entire field, including the field characters.

2. Delete the text as you would any other text.

INCLUDING FIELD INSTRUCTIONS

A field's instructions contain one or more *arguments*. Arguments can be mathematical expressions, bookmark names, text, or graphics that make an action or effect of a field more specific. Here are some rules that govern the use of arguments in field instructions:

- Surround an argument consisting of several words with quotation marks (").

  Example: {quote "The 12th Man Phenomenon"}

- When an argument contains quotation marks, each quotation mark should be preceded by a backslash (\). This tells Word to print the quotation marks.

  Example: {quote "The 12th \"Man\" Phenomenon"}

- When an argument contains a backslash that you want to appear in the result, type another backslash in front of the argument's backslash (\\). This tells Word to print one backslash at that position.

  Example: {quote "Using the Root Directory Symbol (\\)"}

FORMATTING THE RESULTS OF FIELDS

The results of fields can be formatted like any other text using Word's Edit and Format commands. However, if you want Word to always format a field's results in a specific way even if you update the field several times, you should include instructions in the field to tell Word what to do. There are three basic types of formatting that you can control by adding instructions to fields:

- character formatting (specifying bold, italic, uppercase, lowercase, and so on)

- number formatting (specifying the number of digits, whether or not to include zeros, arabic or roman numerals, and so on)

- date or time formatting (specifying different ways of displaying dates or times)

Adding Character Formats

You can tell Word to add character formats to the results of fields by formatting the first character (after the opening field character) of a field and adding a *charformat switch. For example, to make the result of your field italic, you'd make the first character of your field italic and add a *charformat switch to the field, like this:

The time is now {*time* *charformat}.

This field would yield the result

The time is now *11:00*.

To control whether results are displayed in uppercase or lowercase letters, you'll want to use a * formatting switch from the following list:

Switch	To
*upper	Convert all characters in field's result to uppercase.

Example:

Field: {quote *upper "warning!"}
Result: WARNING!

*lower   Convert all characters in field's result to lowercase.

         Example:

         Field: {quote *lower "Little Mousie"}
         Result: little mousie

*firstcap   Convert the first word in the field's result to an initial capital letter.

         Example:

         Field: {quote *firstcap "we, the people"}
         Result: We, the people

*caps   Convert all words in the field's result to initial capital letters.

         Example:

         Field: {quote *caps "we, the people"}
         Result: We, The People

If you've already expended a lot of time and energy formatting the results of a field, you can tell Word to copy that format when you update the text by editing the field's codes to add the *mergeformat switch. This tells Word to use the format of the previous result, word for word, for the new result. For example, suppose you have created a field that inserts a list you've marked with a bookmark name, like this:

{include Saleslist}

This field inserts a list of names, like this:

Fleming - $500, Kavinski - $1200, Nguyen - $850, O'Conner - $610, MacDougal - $750, Best - $490

Say you've formatted the list (the results of the field) to look like this:

Fleming - $500, Kavinski - $1200, Nguyen - $850, O'Conner - $610, MacDougal - $750, Best - $490

Suppose that now you need to update the figures, but you don't want to redo the formatting. You could edit the field codes to add the *mergeformat switch, like this:

{include *mergeformat Saleslist}

This causes Word to copy the format from the previous results.

Formatting Numerical Results

Because a number can have many different formats, you can include instructions in a field to tell Word exactly what you want. To choose between different types of numbers, you use the * switch, followed by one of the following arguments:

Switch	Description
*arabic	Converts numbers in the field's result to the arabic cardinal form (if used in a header or footer, this switch overrides the number format setting in the Edit Header/Footer dialog box).

Example:

Field: {= *arabic 7 + 20}
Result: 27

*ordinal	Converts numbers in the field's result to ordinal form.

Example:

Field: {= *ordinal 7 + 20}
Result: 27th

*roman	Converts numbers in the field's result to roman numerals (the case of the first character of "roman" determines whether the roman numerals will be uppercase or lowercase, such as Roman for I, III, V, roman for i, iii, v).

Example:

Field: {= *Roman 7 + 20}
Result: XXVII

*alphabetic	Converts the field's number result to the corresponding alphabetic characters (matching the case of the first character of "alphabetic," such as Alphabetic for A, B, C, alphabetic for a, b, c).

Examples:

Field: {= *alphabetic 7 + 20}
Result: bg

Field: {= *Alphabetic 7 + 20}
Result: BG

*cardtext   Converts the field's result to cardinal text (an initial capital is the default; if you want any other case, use a case conversion switch).

Example:

Field: {= *cardtext 7 + 20}
Result: Twenty-Seven

*ordtext   Converts numbers in the field's result to ordinal text form (an initial capital is the default; if you want any other case, use a case conversion switch).

Example:

Field: {= *ordtext 1500 + 500}
Result: Two Thousandth

*hex   Converts numbers in the field's result to hexadecimal form.

Example:

Field: {= *hex 31 + 16}
Result: 2F

*dollartext   Converts numbers in the field's result to cardinal text, inserts *and,* and displays fractions as arabic numerals over 100.

Example:

Field: {= *dollartext 3.45 + 15.67} Dollars
Result: Nineteen and 12/100 Dollars

When you want to further specify the format for a number, you can use a \# switch followed by a "numeric picture" to tell Word just how you want the resulting number to look. The following list shows arguments you can use to create your numeric pictures. In the examples, the field consists of an initial bookmark named "sales" followed by the \# switch and a numeric picture. The "sales" bookmark is attached to the input data, and the result is determined by the numeric picture in the field.

Argument	Description
# (number sign)	Holds a place for a digit. If the result contains more digits than your example, Word rounds the result to match. If the result is zero, Word inserts a space.

Example:

Field: {sales \# $##.00}
Input Data: **4.5**
Result: $4.50

0 (zero)	Holds a place for a digit. If the result contains fewer digits than in your example, Word places a zero in that space. If the result contains more digits than your example, Word rounds the number to match.

Example:

Field: {sales \# $00.00}
Input Data: **4.5**
Result: $04.50

x	Holds a place for a digit to the left of the decimal point but truncates the result if it includes more numbers than your example.

Example:

Field: {sales \# x#.00}
Input Data: **123.11**
Result: 23.11

, (thousands separator)	Displays a thousands separator when the numeric picture switch has a # or zero on each side of the separator. The number must be large enough to require a thousands separator.

Examples:

Field: {sales \# #,##0}
Input Data: **454**
Result: 454

Input Data: **76341**
Result: 76,341

− (negative sign) Displays a minus sign if the number is negative. If a number is positive or zero, displays a space.

Examples:

Field: {sales \# -#0}
Input Data: **−43**
Result: -43

Field: {sales \# -#0}
Input Data: **43**
Result: -43

+ (plus sign) Displays a plus sign if the number is positive; displays a minus sign if the number is negative; displays a space if the number is zero.

Examples:

Field: {sales \# +#0.00}
Input Data: **73**
Result: 73.00

Field: {sales \# +#0.00}
Input Data: **−73**
Result: -73.00

Field: {sales \# +#0.00}
Input Data: **0**
Result: 0

positive; negative Displays the number using the positive picture if the number is positive or zero or the negative picture if the number is negative.

Examples:

Field: {sales \# $#0.00;($#0.00)}
Input Data: **0**
Result: $0.00

Field: {sales \# $#0.00;($#0.00)}
Input Data: **43.95**
Result: $43.95

Field: {sales \# $#0.00;($#0.00)}
Input Data: −**29.90**
Result: ($29.90)

positive; Displays the number using the positive picture
negative; if the number is positive; the negative pic-
zero   ture if the number is negative; or the zero
           picture if the number is zero.

Examples:

Field: {sales \# $#0.00;($#0.00);'-0-'"}
Input Data: −**99.95**
Result: ($99.95)

Field: {sales \# $#0.00;($#0.00);'-0-'"}
Input Data: **0**
Result: -0-

Formatting Dates and Times

You can use the following switches to tell Word how to format and display a date or time. The field names {date} and {time} tell Word to use the current date or time from your computer's clock.

Switch	Description
month	Displays a month in one of four formats using the uppercase letter *M* (the number of *M*'s determines the format)/

Examples:

Field: {date \@ "M}
Result range: 1 through 12

Field: {date \@ "MM}
Result range: 01 through 12

Field: {date \@ "MMM}
Result range: Jan through Dec

Field: {date \@ "MMMM}
Result range: January through December

day   Displays the date or day in one of four for-
               mats using the letter *D* (can be uppercase or
               lowercase).

               Examples:

               Field: {date \@ "d}
               Result range: 1 through 31

               Field: {date \@ "dd}
               Result range: 01 through 31

               Field: {date \@ "ddd}
               Result range: Mon through Sun

               Field: {date \@ "dddd}
               Result range: Monday through Sunday

year   Displays the year in one of two formats, using
               the letter *Y* (can be uppercase or lowercase).

               Examples:

               Field: {date \@ "yy}
               Result range: 00 through 99

               Field: {date \@ "yyyy}
               Result range: 1900 through 2040

hours   Displays the time in one of four formats using
               the letter *h* or *H* (*h* means a 12-hour clock; *H*
               means a 24-hour clock).

               Examples:

               Field: {time \@ "h}
               Result range: 1 through 12

               Field: {time \@ "hh}
               Result range: 01 through 12

               Field: {time \@ "H}
               Result range: 0 through 23

               Field: {time \@ "HH}
               Result range: 00 through 23

minutes   Displays the minutes in one of two formats
               using the letter *m* (*m* must be lowercase).

Examples:

Field: {time \@ "m}
Result range: 0 through 59

Field: {time \@ "mm}
Result range: 00 through 59

am/pm   Displays the time in one of four morning or afternoon formats (set the formats in the Control Panel).

Examples:

Field: {time \@ "h:mm AM/PM}
Result: 12:00 AM through 11:59 PM

Field: {time \@ "h:mm am/pm}
Result: 12:00 am through 11:59 pm

Field: {time \@ "h:mm A/P}
Result: 12:00 A through 11:59 P

Field: {time \@ "h:mm a/p}
Result: 12:00 a through 11:59 p

JUMPING TO FIELDS

When your document contains a number of fields, you may want to move from one field to another while you are revising or editing.

To quickly jump to fields, you can use these keys:

- To jump to the next field, press **F11** or **Alt+F1**

- To jump to the previous field, press **Shift+F11** or **Alt+Shift+F1**

LINKING AND UNLINKING FIELDS

You can link fields with files created by other applications to include information from those files in your Word document. To do this, you'll use Windows' Direct Data Exchange (DDE) technology. You must have Windows available on your computer and must have applications that accept DDE.

You can create two kinds of links:

- Regular links, which do not automatically update information in the Word document.

- Auto Update links, which automatically update the Word document when you save, close, or open a Word document.

Creating Regular Links

To create a regular link:

1. Open the file containing the information you want to link with Word.

2. Select the information you want to copy.

3. Choose the Edit Copy command to copy the information to the Clipboard.

4. Switch to Word.

5. Place the insertion point where you want to paste the copied information.

6. Choose the Edit Paste Link command. (If this command is "gray" on the menu, the odds are that the information was copied from an application that does not support DDE—in that case, you can't link.)

7. Turn off the Automatic Update box in the dialog box (this is the default setting).

8. Click OK or press **Enter**.

Instead of copying the text to the Clipboard, you can also use the Insert Field command:

1. In Word, place the insertion point where you want the linked information to appear.

2. Choose the Insert Field command.

3. In the Field Code text box, type the field codes for the link you want using the following format:

dde *app-name filename place-reference*

Be sure to type a pathname, if necessary, in front of the *filename*. For example, type

dde excel c:\\windows\\excel\\jansales.xls r1c1:r4c2

to import information from the specified area of the JAN-SALES.XLS file in the \WINDOWS\EXCEL directory.

Creating Automatic Update Links

To create a link that Word will automatically update:

1. Open the file containing the information you want to link with Word.

2. Select the information you want to copy.

3. Choose the Edit Copy command to copy the information to the Clipboard.

4. Switch to Word.

5. Place the insertion point where you want to paste the copied information.

6. Choose the Edit Paste Link command.

7. Turn on the Automatic Update box if it's not already on.

8. Click OK or press **Enter**.

Instead of copying the text to the Clipboard, you can also use the Insert Field command.

1. In Word, position the insertion point where you want the linked information to appear.

2. Choose the Insert Field command.

3. Type in the field codes for the link you want using the following format:

   `ddeauto app-name filename place-reference`

   Add a pathname, if necessary, before the `filename`. For example, type

   ddeauto excel c:\\windows\\excel\\annrept.xls r1c1:r4c2

   to import information, which is automatically updated, from the specified area of the ANNREPT.XLS file in the \WIN-DOWS\EXCEL directory.

Unlinking Fields

Fields can be unlinked at any time. To unlink a field:

1. Select the field.

2. Press **Ctrl+Shift+F9**.

LOCKING AND UNLOCKING FIELDS

When several people are working with the same documents and you want to prevent inadvertent changes to fields in those documents, you can lock the fields. When you've locked fields, they cannot be changed unless you unlock them first.

To lock a field:

1. Select the field.

2. Press **Ctrl+F11**.

To unlock a field:

1. Select the field.

2. Press **Ctrl+Shift+F11**.

You can also prevent the result of a field from being updated by including a lock result switch (\!) in a field, like this:

```
{= sales _ commissions \!}
```

UPDATING FIELDS

You can update fields directly by selecting the field (or the whole document), then pressing **F9**. F9 does not affect fields that don't produce visible results, such as

- DATA
- NEXTIF
- NEXT
- RD (Referenced Document)
- SET

Figure 18–4.
A nested field.

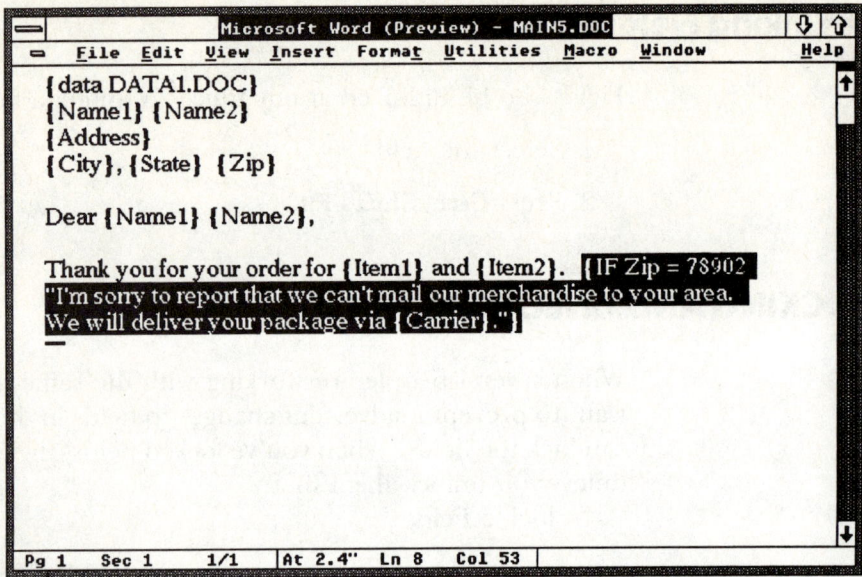

- SKIPIF

- TC (Table-of-Contents Entry)

- XE (Index Entry)

If text you've selected contains ASK fields, Word displays dialog boxes requesting information to update the ASK fields.

Some fields are also updated when you use the File Print, File Print Merge, or Utilities Repaginate Now commands. To be sure that all fields are updated when you print the document, choose Options in the File Print dialog box, then turn on the Update Fields option before printing.

NESTING FIELDS

You can give Word complicated instructions by nesting fields—making one field dependent on another enclosed field. Fields can be nested up to 20 fields deep. (Figure 18–4 shows a nested field.) For example, you might include an IF field within another to create a nested field that tells Word that both conditions must be met before a result is printed.

## Chapter Nineteen

Creating Tables of Contents, Lists, and Indexes

Two final steps in finishing a long document are creating a table of contents for the front of the document and creating an index for the back. This chapter shows you how to

- create a table of contents from outline entries.

- create a table of contents from fields.

- add index entries to your file.

- collect index entries to create an index.

- compile a list of figures, tables, or other items.

CREATING A TABLE OF CONTENTS

When you finish writing and formatting a long document, you usually add a table of contents so readers can see the document's structure at a glance and know where to find the information they're looking for. Figure 19–1 shows a table of contents created by Word.

If you used Word's outlining feature to create an outline for your document, or you formatted your headings using Word's Heading 1 through 9 paragraph styles, you can create a table of contents from your document's outline—that's by far the easiest way. (For more information about outlining, see Chapter 17.) If you didn't use the heading level styles or outlining to create your headings, you'll insert fields into your document to create a table of contents.

Figure 19–1.
A table of contents
created by Word.

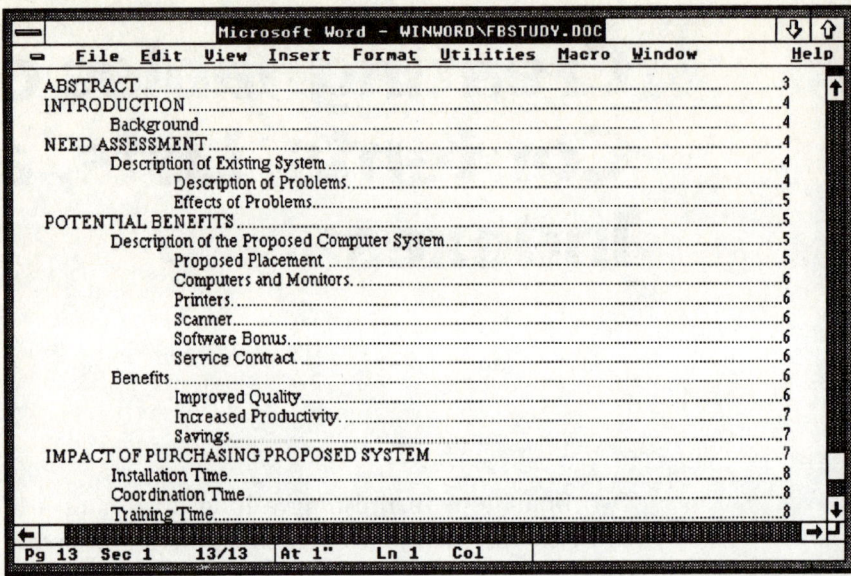

Figure 19–2.
The Insert Table of
Contents dialog box.

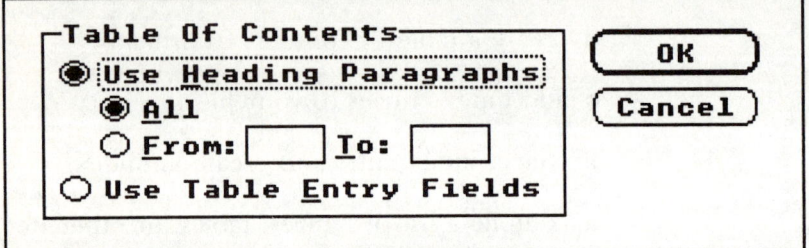

Creating a Table of Contents from Headings with Assigned Levels

If you've used Word's outlining feature or Word's Heading 1 through Heading 9 styles to assign levels to your headings, you can use the following procedure to create a table of contents:

1. Place the insertion point where you want the table of contents to appear (usually at the front of your document).

2. Choose the Insert Table of Contents command. Word displays the dialog box shown in Figure 19–2.

3. Choose the Use Heading Paragraphs option.

4. If you want to use only certain heading levels in your table of contents, type the beginning level number in the From box and the ending level number in the To box. For example, if you want the table of contents to contain only heading levels 1 and 2, type **1** in the From box and **2** in the To box.

5. Click OK or press **Enter**. Word collects the headings from your document and formats them into a table of contents. If your document is long, this process may take a few moments.

The table of contents is inserted into a TOC field. You can edit and format the text in the table of contents just as you would edit and format any other text, and you can update the field when you make changes in your document. See Updating a Table of Contents or a List later in this chapter for more information.

Creating a Table of Contents from Fields

If you don't have your headings formatted with outline level styles, you can create a table of contents by inserting TC fields in front of your headings, then collecting all the TC fields. The TC fields are formatted as hidden text, so they won't print unless you specifically tell Word to print hidden text.

When you have inserted all the TC codes you need and you're ready to compile the table of contents, Word collects all the TC fields along with their associated page numbers. Be sure to put each TC field as close as possible to the information it references to ensure that it ends up on the right page.

Inserting Fields to Mark Table-of-Contents Entries

To insert a TC field to mark a table-of-contents entry:

1. Place the insertion point close to the information you want to reference.

2. Choose the Insert Field command. Word displays the dialog box shown in Figure 19–3.

3. From the Field Type list, select TC. Be sure that you select TC, *not* TOC. A TC field creates a table-of-contents entry, whereas a TOC field creates the actual table of contents.

4. In the Field Code box, type a space after tc, then type a quotation

Figure 19–3.
Creating a table-of-contents entry in the Insert Field dialog box.

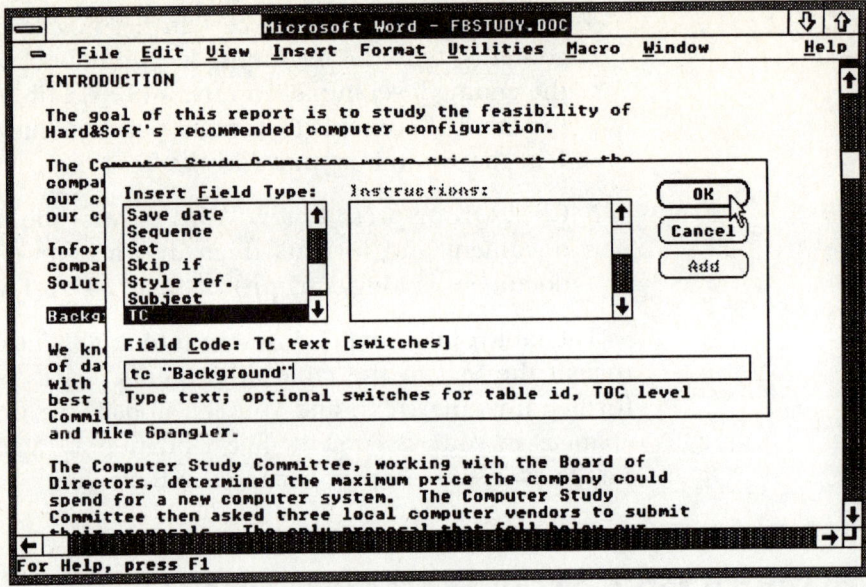

mark ("), then type the text you want to use as an entry in the table of contents, followed by a quotation mark ("), like this:

tc "Starting the Compressor"

5. If you want your entry to be other than a level 1 entry, type a space, then type **\l** (backslash lowercase L) followed by a level number. For example, the following entry creates a level 2 table-of-contents entry, which would be indented beneath the preceding entry:

tc "Starting the Compressor" \l2

6. Click OK or press **Enter**. Word inserts a TC field similar to the one shown in Figure 19–4. The field is automatically formatted as hidden text, so if you want to see it, you may need to choose View Preferences and turn on the Hidden Text option.

▬▬▶ *Keyboard Shortcut*

When you're familiar with the appearance of TC fields, you can enter them more quickly this way:

1. If necessary, choose View Preferences and turn on the Hidden Text option.

Figure 19–4.
A table-of-contents entry in a TC field.

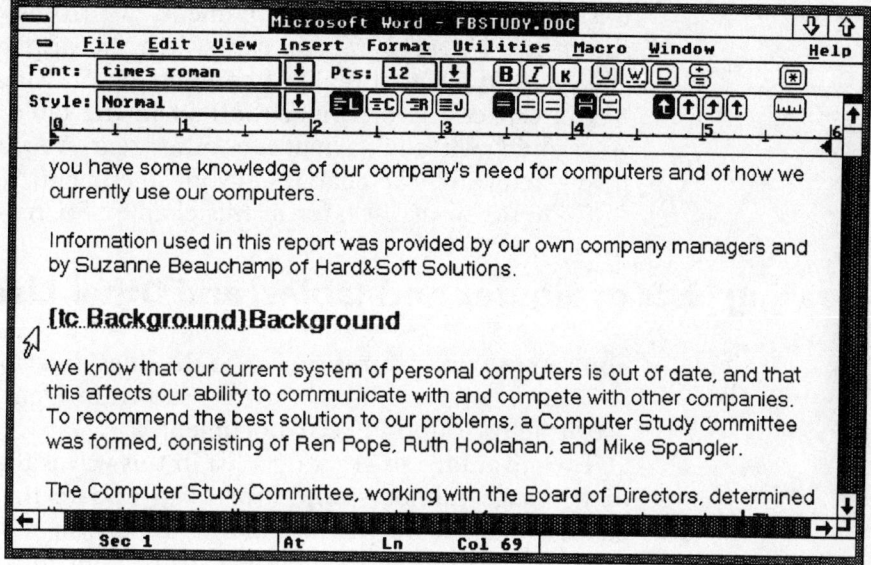

2. Place the insertion point where you want to insert a table-of-contents entry field.

3. Press **Ctrl+F9**. Word surrounds the insertion point with field characters ({ }).

4. Type the **tc** code, a space, and your entry enclosed in quotation marks (for example, {tc "Climbing Mount Rainier"}.

Repeat steps 2–4 to insert more table-of-contents entries.

Compiling a Table of Contents from Fields

When you've finished inserting TC fields in your document, you're ready to create the table of contents.

To create a table of contents:

1. Place the insertion point where you want the table of contents to appear (usually at the front of your document).

2. Choose the Insert Table of Contents command. Word displays the dialog box shown in Figure 19–2.

3. Choose the Use Table Entry Fields option.

4. Click OK or press **Enter**.

Word collects the TC fields from your document and formats them into a table of contents. Depending on how long your document is, this process may take a few moments. Word inserts a TOC field, as shown in Figure 19–5. You can switch the display between the field codes and the actual table of contents by pressing **Shift+F9**.

You can edit and format the text in the table of contents just as you would edit and format any other text. You can also update the field when you make changes in your document. See Updating a Table of Contents or a List later in this chapter for more information.

Creating Lists of Figures and Tables, and Other Lists

You can use procedures similar to the ones described in the preceding sections to create a list of figures (shown in Figure 19–6) or another list of items found in your document.

The advantage to creating a list in this way is that Word keeps track of the page numbers, and Word can update this list whenever you change the document, just like it updates a table of contents (see Updating a Table of Contents or a List later in this chapter).

You can create a list in two ways:

- You can assign a Heading level style to the list items throughout your document.

  or

- You can insert TC fields with special switches to mark each list item.

Figure 19–5.
A table of contents field.

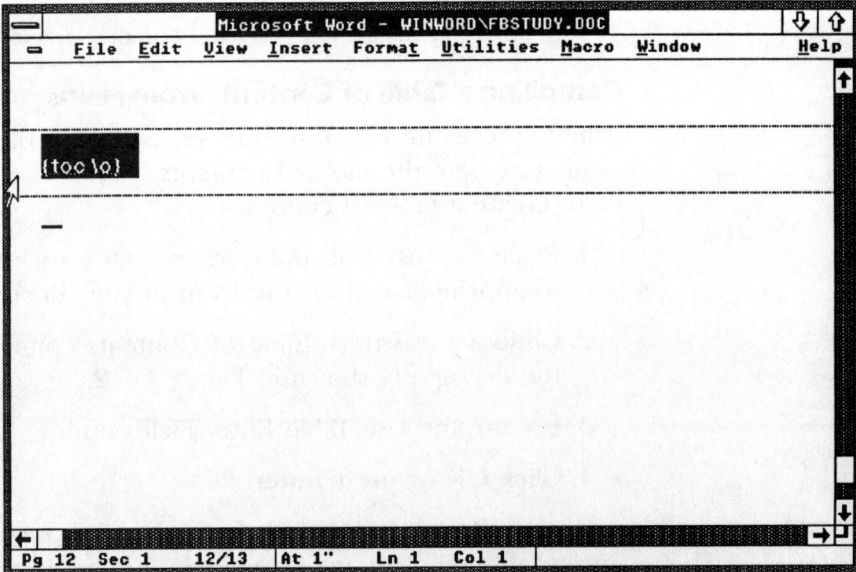

Figure 19–6.
A list of figures
created by Word.

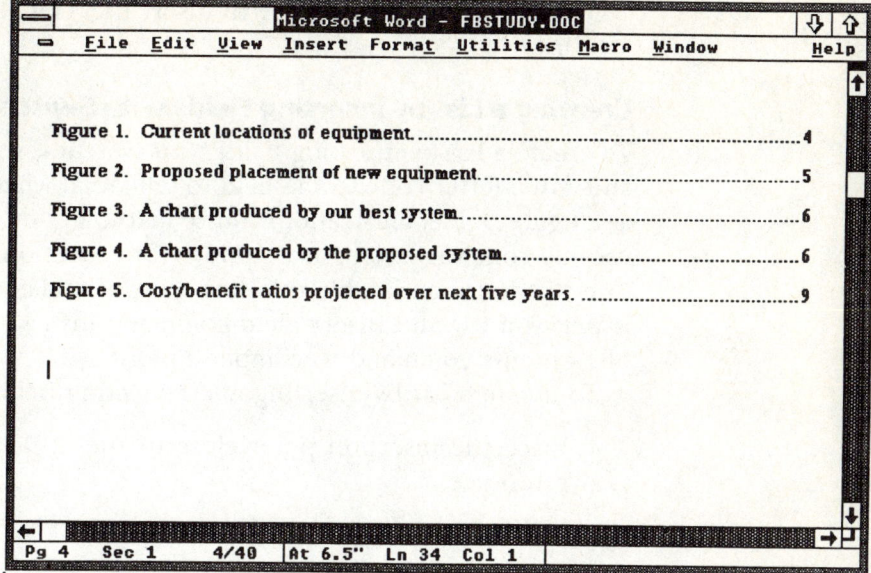

Creating a List by Assigning Heading Styles

Word has nine heading styles you can use to format your text. Word uses these heading styles to create outlines and to distinguish headings for tables of contents. Most of the time, you'll only use a few of the heading levels for actual headings in your text (for example, Headings 1–3). You can assign remaining heading level styles to table titles, figure captions, photo descriptions—to any items you want to collect into a list. For example, you might want to assign the Heading 7 style to all table titles and the Heading 8 style to figure captions. For more information about using styles, see Chapter 10.

To create a list by assigning heading styles to items:

1. Assign heading styles to all items using the Format Styles command. (Remember, you can select text and press **F4** to repeat the action after you've used the command once.)

2. Choose the Insert Table of Contents command.

3. Choose the Use Heading Paragraphs option.

4. In the From and To boxes, type the heading level you want to collect. For example, if you've assigned the Heading 8 style to all figure captions and you want to create a list of figures, type **8** in both boxes.

5. Click OK or press **Enter** to insert the TOC field containing the list.

Creating a List by Inserting Fields with Switches

To create a list by inserting fields with switches, you'll add a \f switch and a one-letter code to the field to tell Word what kind of item (such as a figure, table, illustration) you're marking. For example, you might use an f code to mark figure captions for collection into a list of figures or a t code to mark table titles for a list of tables. Another difference is that you use the Insert Field command instead of the Insert Table of Contents command to compile the list.

To create a list by inserting and collecting fields:

1. Place the insertion point close to the information you want to reference.

2. Choose the Insert Field command.

3. From the Field Type list, select TC.

4. In the Field Code box, type a space after tc, then type the text you want in quotation marks (""), then type a space followed by \f and a space, then type a one-letter code to indicate the type of item. For example, here's a code for a figure, followed by a code for a table.

   tc **"Figure 1-1. Pentagon Floor Plan." \f f**

   tc **"Table 3-2. First Quarter Sales by Region." \f t**

5. Click OK or press **Enter**. Word inserts a TC field similar to the one shown in Figure 19–7.

6. Repeat steps 1–5 to mark all items you want to collect into a list.

7. Place the insertion point where you want to insert the list (usually near the beginning of the document).

8. Choose the Insert Field command.

9. From the Field Type list, select TOC.

10. In the Field Code box, type a space after toc, then type the \f switch, another space, then the one-letter code you used to mark your items. For example, if you used f as your one-letter code, fill out the Field Code box to look like this:

    toc **\f f**

Figure 19–7.
A TC field that marks
a table title for
collection into a list.

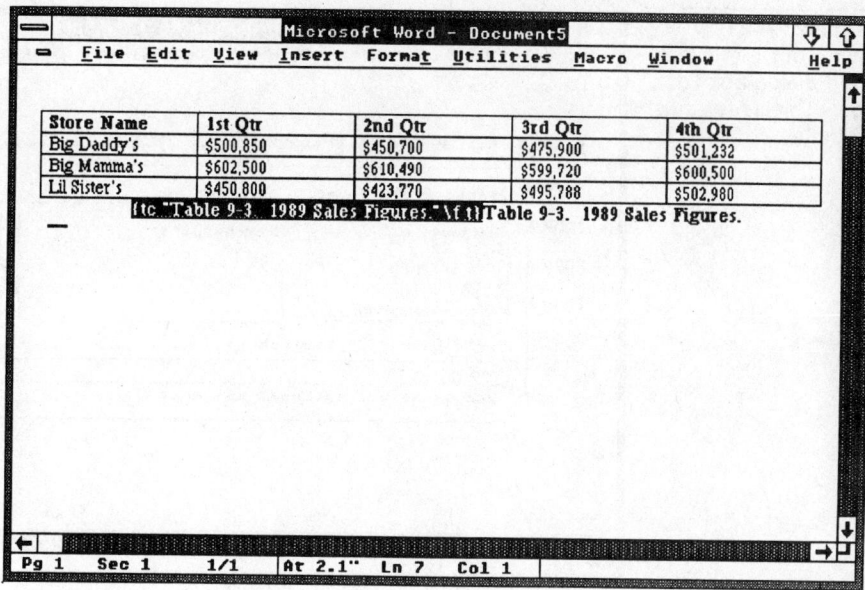

or if you used t as your one-letter code, you'd fill out the box like this:

toc \f t

Figure 19–8 illustrates filling out the Insert Field dialog box to collect fields in this way.

11. Click OK or press **Enter** to gather all the fields and insert a list field.

12. Press **F9** to update the field, then press **Shift+F9** to see the results.

Creating a Table of Contents or a List from Several Files

If you have several files that you want to put together to create one long document, you can use the following process to make Word create a table of contents or a list for the entire document. Keep in mind that the more files you have to work with, the more memory Word needs for this process.

1. Open each file and do the following:

■ Assign heading styles or insert TC fields to mark all table-of-contents or list entries.

Figure 19–8.
Filling out the Insert
Field dialog box to
collect fields for a list
of tables.

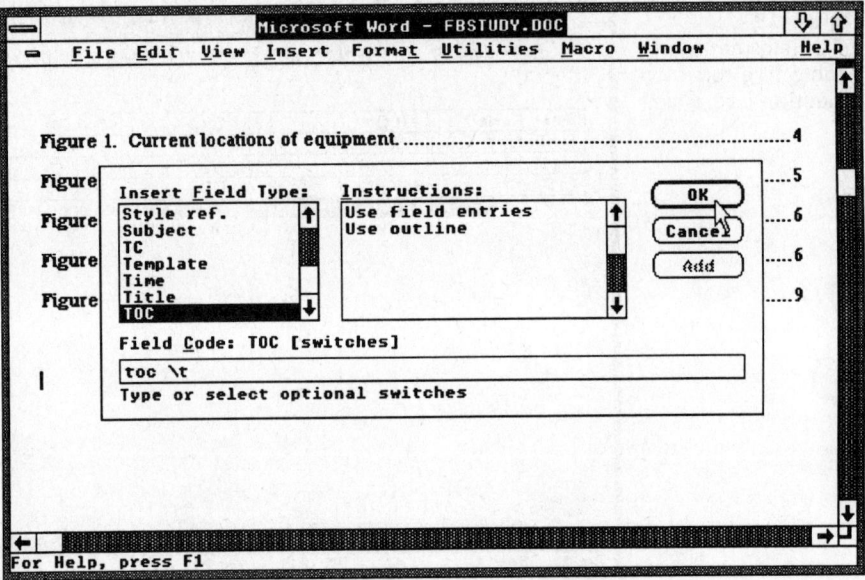

- If necessary, use the Utilities Repaginate Now command to paginate the file, note the ending page number, open the next file in the sequence, and use the Edit Header/Footer command (Options button) to set the starting page number to make page numbers sequential.

- Save all the files.

2. Use the File New command to open a new document.

3. Using the Insert Field command, insert one RD (Referenced Document) field for each file from which you want to collect table-of-contents entries or list entries. For example, if your files were named "Part1," "Part2," and "Part3," you'd insert RD fields like this:

{**rd part1**}

{**rd part2**}

{**rd part3**}

RD fields are formatted as hidden text, so you may need to use the View Preferences command and turn on the Hidden Text option to see them.

4. Place the insertion point at the end of the document on a new line after all the RD fields.

5. Use the Insert Table of Contents command as described in Creating a Table of Contents or a List earlier in this chapter to create the table of contents or list. Your file should look something like Figure 19–9.

6. Save the document. Be sure to update the index field (select it and press **F9**) whenever you've changed one of the files associated with the index.

Updating a Table of Contents or a List

When you change the document, Word doesn't automatically update a table of contents or any list. If you've made changes to your document, you need to compile the table of contents and lists again to make sure they have the correct page numbers and include all appropriate items.

Tables of contents and lists are contained within fields, so you'll use the same process you'd use to update any field.

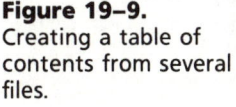

Figure 19–9.
Creating a table of contents from several files.

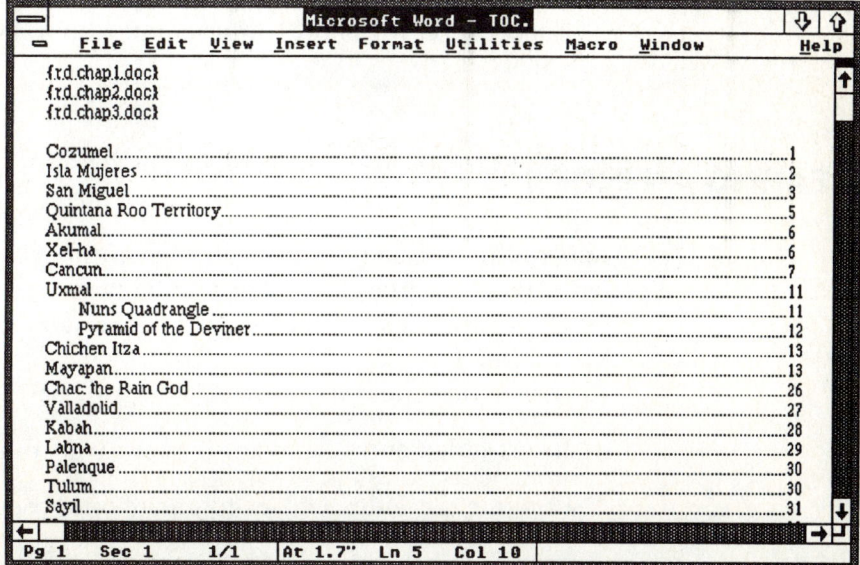

To update a table of contents or a list:

1. Place the insertion point anywhere within the TOC field you want to update.

2. Press **F9** to update the field.

Formatting Tables of Contents and Lists with Styles

Word uses several styles from its default style sheet to format a table of contents or a list created with the Insert Table of Contents command. You can alter the table of contents by selecting and changing each line, or you can change the styles Word uses for each level—this changes all lines at that level in one fell swoop.

Word uses the TOC Level 1 style to format first level headings in a table of contents or a list, TOC Level 2 to format second-level headings, and so forth. Even if you don't want to change the styles, you can use the Format Styles command to apply the correct level style to lines in the table or list.

To change the styles used in the table of contents or list:

1. Choose the Format Define Styles command.

2. Select the name of the TOC style you want to change.

3. Change the style as desired. If necessary, see Changing Styles in Chapter 10 for more information about using and changing styles.

CREATING AN INDEX

When you're finished writing and formatting a long document such as your PhD dissertation or that feasibility study for the office, you'll want to add an index to make it easier for readers to look up important information.

To create an index with Word, follow two basic steps:

1. Insert index entry fields throughout your document.

2. Compile the index entries to create and insert an index.

Figure 19–10 shows an index created with Word.

Figure 19–10.
An index created
with Word.

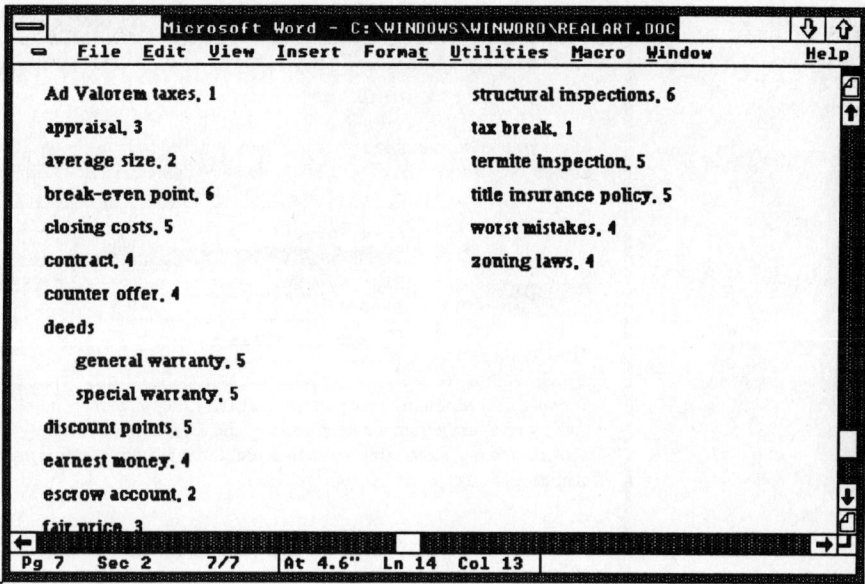

Figure 19–10.
An index created
with Word.

Inserting Index Entry Fields

You'll put index entry fields (XE fields) on each page whose number you want to appear in the index.

You can designate existing text on a page as an index entry (as shown in Figure 19–11), or you can type new text for an index entry (as shown in Figure 19–12). Either way, you insert an index entry field that is formatted as hidden text—these fields won't appear in your document when printed. You may need to choose the View Preferences command and turn on the Hidden Text option to see these fields on the screen.

To insert index entry fields:

1. Do one of the following:

   ■ If your document contains text you want to use as an index entry, select that text.

   or

   ■ If you want to type an index entry, place the insertion point next to the text the entry references.

2. Choose the Insert Index Entry command.

Figure 19–11.
Designating existing text as an index entry.

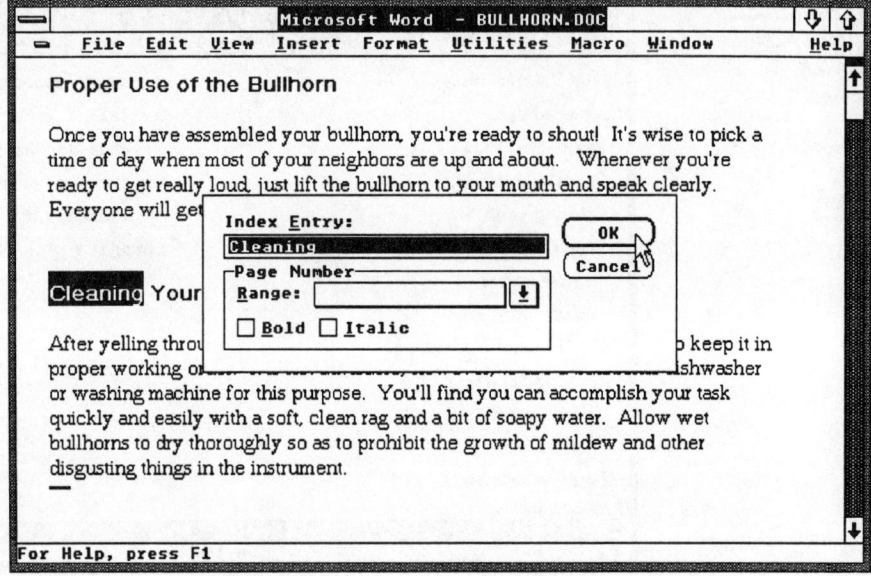

Figure 19–12.
Typing new text for an index entry in the Insert Index Entry dialog box.

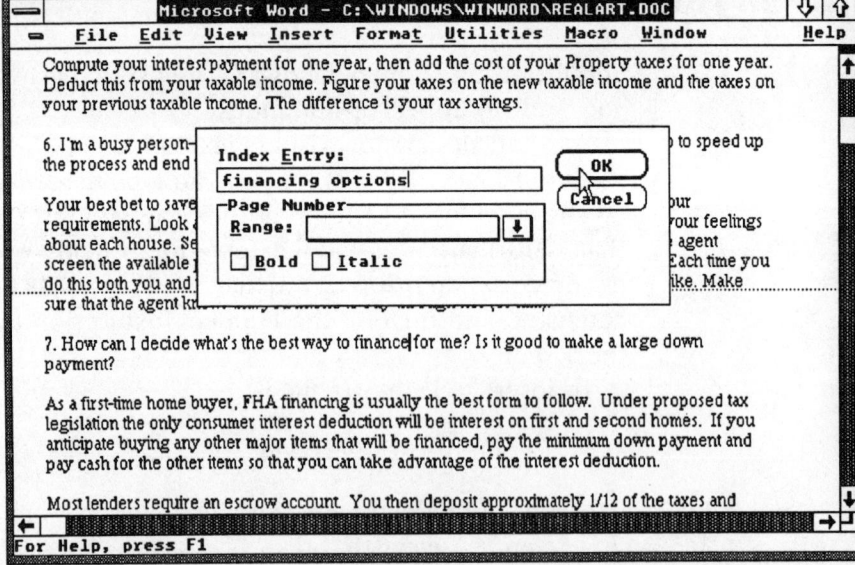

3. In the Index Entry box, do one of the following:

- Edit the existing text as appropriate.

or

- Type new text, enclosed in double quotation marks, for the index entry.

4. Click OK or press **Enter**. Word inserts a field containing the index entry, shown in Figure 19–13.

5. Repeat steps 1–4 to insert all the index entry fields you need.

Indicating Subentries for the Index

Indexes usually have at least two levels of entries: main entries and subentries, like this:

Arctic Circle, 17
Bears
   black, 93
   grizzlies, 112, 119
   polar, 87-89

To indicate a main entry, follow the instructions in the previous section, Inserting Index Entry Fields.

Figure 19–13.
An index entry field.

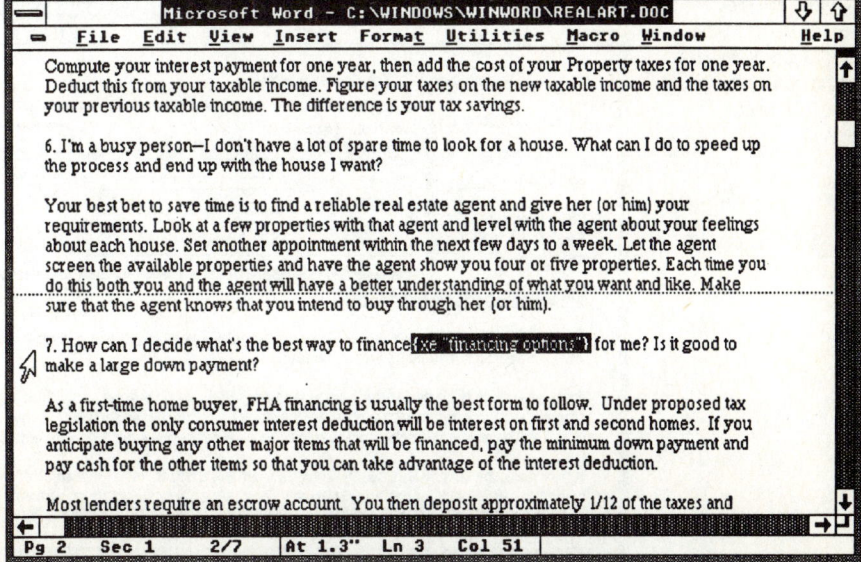

To indicate a subentry, type a colon (:) between the main entry and the subentry in the Index Entry box, like this:

Bears:black

You can use colons to mark the entry and multiple levels of subentries, like this:

Bears:black:sightings

Selecting Entries That Contain a Colon

If you want to use an entry in a document that contains a colon, such as "Africa: The Hungry Continent," don't worry about Word interpreting this as a subentry code. Just do this:

1. Select the text.

2. Choose the Insert Index Entry command.

   In the Index Entry box, notice that Word automatically adds a backslash in front of the colon, as shown in Figure 19–14. The backslash tells Word that the following colon is just ordinary text, not a code character.

3. Click OK or press **Enter**.

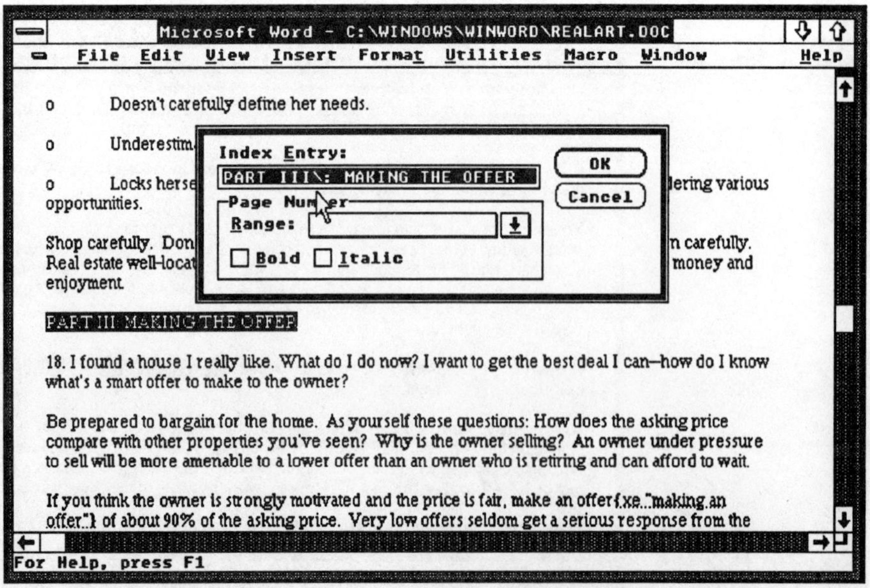

Figure 19–14.
Word automatically inserts backslashes before colons in selected text.

Marking an Index Entry That Spans Several Pages

When the subject of your index entry spans several pages, you may want to indicate a range of pages in an index entry, such as "Huckleberries, 49-51." To do this, you could insert entries on each page, then edit the index later, or you can use the following procedure:

1. Select all the paragraphs in your document that refer to your entry. For example, if your index entry is going to be about huckleberries, you'd select all the text about huckleberries.

2. Choose the Insert Bookmark command.

3. Type a name in the Bookmark Name box. For example, you might type **Hberries**.

4. Click OK or press **Enter**. This assigns a bookmark name to the selected text.

5. Choose the Insert Index Entry command.

6. In the Index Entry box, type the text for the entry as you want it to appear in the index.

7. From the Range drop-down list, select the bookmark name.

8. Click OK or press **Enter**.

Word keeps track of the page range the "bookmarked" text spans. For more information about bookmarks, see Chapter 21.

Marking Cross-References in Index Entries

Sometimes you may want to use a cross-reference instead of a page number in an index, like this:

```
Pachyderm, See Elephant.
```

To use text cross-references instead of page numbers, follow these steps:

1. Select text if necessary.

2. Choose the Insert Index Entry command.

3. In the Index Entry box, type the text for the entry (enclosed in quotation marks), then type a **t** switch (for text), then type the text you want to appear in quotation marks, like this:

```
Pachyderm \t "See Elephant"
```

4. Click OK or press **Enter** to insert the field.

Making Page Numbers Bold or Italic

You can always edit and format an index after you compile it to change the format of the page numbers. You can also use the following procedure to format page numbers when you insert index entries.

1. Select text if necessary.

2. Choose the Insert Index Entry command.

3. In the Page Number box, choose between the following options:

   ■ If you want to make page numbers bold, turn on the Bold option.

   ■ If you want to make page numbers italic, turn on the Italic option.

4. Click OK or press **Enter** to insert the index entry field.

When you compile the index, Word formats the page numbers as specified.

Keyboard Shortcut

When you're familiar with the appearance of XE (index entry) fields, you can enter them more quickly this way:

1. If necessary, choose View Preferences and turn on the Hidden Text option.

2. Place the insertion point where you want to insert an index entry field.

3. Press **Ctrl+F9**. Word surrounds the insertion point with field characters ({ }).

4. Type the **xe** code, a space, your entry enclosed in quotation marks, and any switches you might want (\b for bold page numbers or \i for italic page numbers, for example). Your field might look something like this: {xe "Volcanos:Mt. Saint Helens" \b}.

Repeat steps 2–4 to insert more index entries.

Compiling Index Entry Fields to Create the Index

When you've inserted index entry fields throughout your document, you're ready to create the final index. You can choose to create a *normal index,* where the subentries are indented, like this:

Ponies
   Shetland, 34
   Welsh, 53

or a *run-in index,* where subentries continue on the same line after main entries, separated by semicolons, like this:

Ponies: Shetland, 34; Welsh, 53

If you want to put space or print a letter between letter groups in an index, you can also choose a *heading separator,* the character that separates one letter group from another.

To compile the index:

1. Choose the Insert Index command. Word displays the dialog box shown in Figure 19–15.

2. In the Insert box, choose one of the following options:

Choose	To do this
Normal Index	Indent subentries.
Run-in Index	Print subentries on the same line as main entries.

3. In the Heading Separator box, choose one of the following options:

Choose	To do this
None	Continue from one letter group to another with no space or separator characters between.

Figure 19–15.
The Insert Index
dialog box.

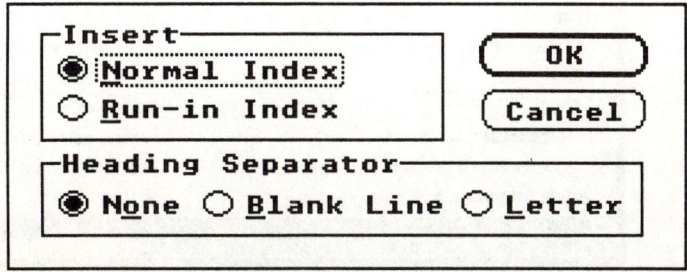

Blank line	Place a blank line between letter groups.
Letter	Place a letter between letter groups, as shown in Figure 19–16.

4. Click OK or press **Enter** to compile the index. Word inserts an index field, as shown in Figure 19–17.

5. With the insertion point still in the field, press **F9** to update the field.

To see the index, press **Shift**+**F9** or print the index.

An existing index is not automatically updated when you add or change material, so if you make changes to your document after compiling an index, you'll have to update the index to be sure it's accurate. See Updating an Index later in this chapter for instructions.

Formatting the Index with Switches

You can format an index any way you want after you've compiled it, but your formatting is wiped out if you update the index after applying the formatting. You can also add switches to the index field to control the appearance and contents of the index. Figure 19–18 shows an index field in which switches specify that the index should contain only the letters A–D.

Figure 19–16.
An index with letter groups separated by letter heading separators.

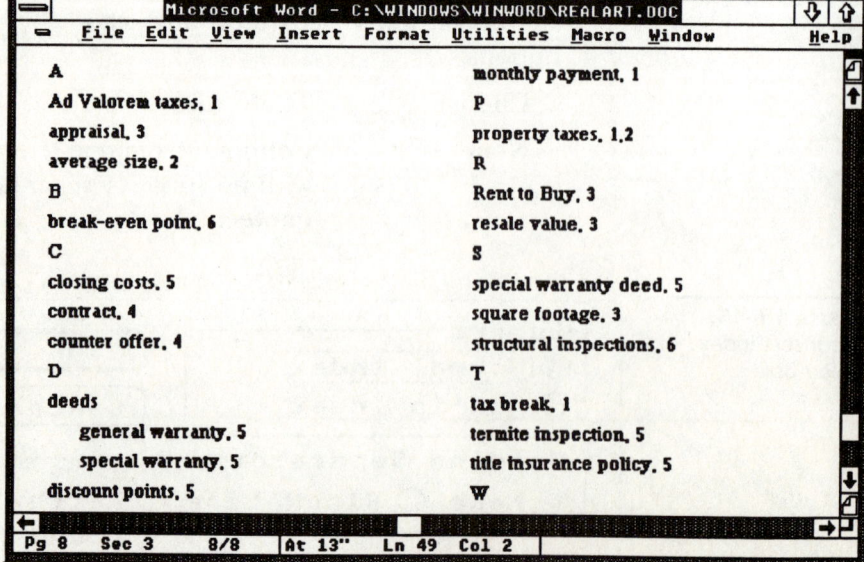

Figure 19–17.
An index field.

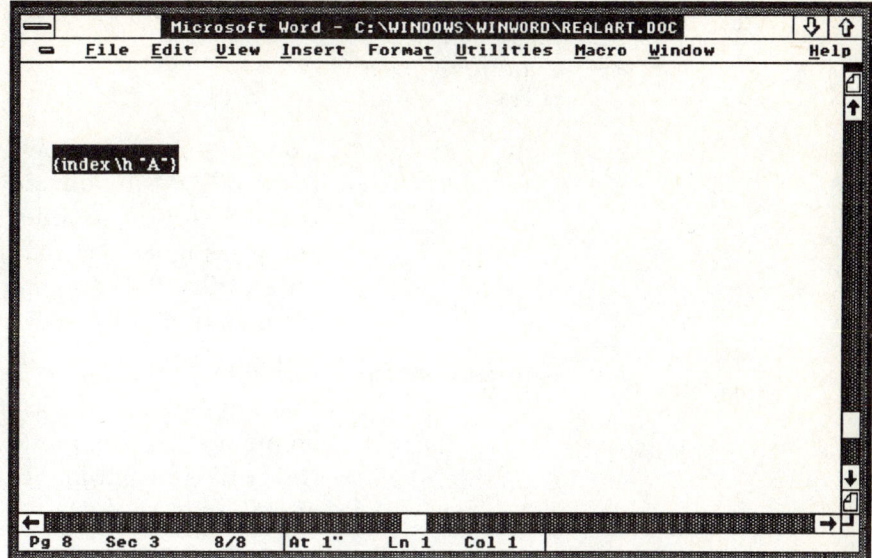

Figure 19–18.
Formatting an index
by inserting switches
in the field.

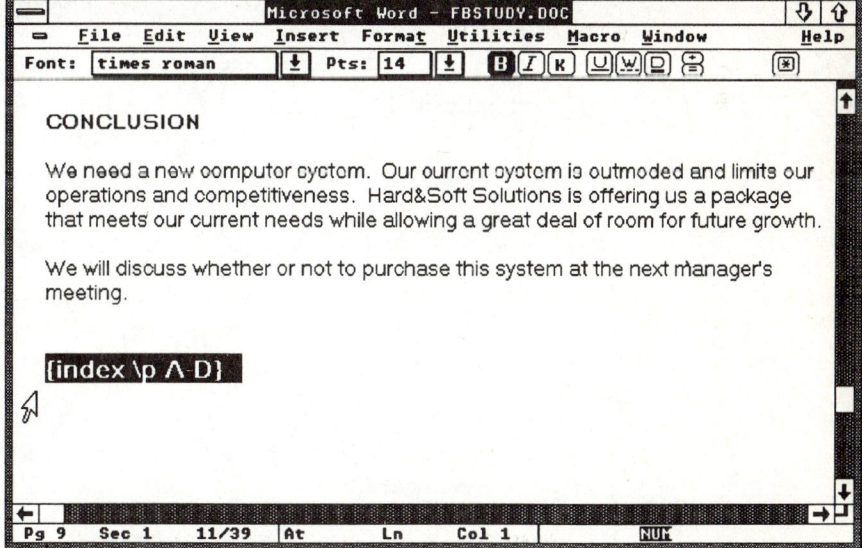

To format an index with switches:

1. Compile and insert the index, as described in the previous section.

2. Place the insertion point before the ending field character of the
   index field (}).

3. Type a space, then type any of the following switches and arguments to format the index:

Type	To do this
\b *bookmarkname*	Compile the index only from "bookmarked" text in your document. For example, if you want to index only text to which you've assigned the Exotica bookmark, type **\b Exotica**. (See Chapter 21 for more information about bookmarks).
\p *letter-letter*	Compile an index only from main entries that begin with the specified letters. For example, to create an index containing only the entries beginning with the letters A, B, and C, type **\p A-C**.
\e *"characters"*	Specify characters between the index entry and the following page number. For example, if you want three periods between the entry and the page number, type **\e** "...".
\g *"characters"*	Specify characters between page numbers in a range. For example, if you want to insert the word *to* surrounded by spaces between page ranges (for example, "4 to 6"), type **\g** "to".
\h *"characters"*	Specify characters that separate letter groups in the index. For example, if you want to put three asterisks between letter groups, type **\h** "* * *".

These are some of the more useful switches that format indexes. To see a complete listing, check the section on indexing in the *Word User's Reference* manual.

Creating One Index from Several Files

If you have inserted index entry fields in several files that compose one long document, you can use the following process to make Word create an index for the entire document. Keep in mind that the more files you have to work with, the more memory Word needs for this process.

1. Insert index entry fields to mark index entries in all the files.

2. Move to the first file in the sequence and use the Utilities Re-paginate Now command to paginate the file, note the ending page number, open the next file in the sequence, and use the Edit Header/Footer command (Options button) to set the starting page number. Repeat this process for all files in the sequence. This makes page numbers sequential.

3. Save all the files.

4. Use the File New command to open a new document.

5. Using the Insert Field command, insert one RD (Referenced Doc-ument) field for each file from which you want to collect index entries. For example, if your files were named PART1, PART2, and PART3, you'd insert RD fields like this:

   {**rd part1**}

   {**rd part2**}

   {**rd part3**}

6. Place the insertion point at the end of the document, on a new line after all the RD fields.

7. Use the Insert Index command as described in Compiling an Index earlier in this chapter to create the index.

Formatting Indexes with Styles

Word uses several styles from its default style sheet to format an index created with the Insert Index command. You can alter the index by selecting and changing each line, or you can change the styles Word uses for each index level—this changes all lines at that level in one fell swoop.

Word uses the Index 1 style to format first-level entries in an index, Index 2 to format second-level entries, and so forth. You might want to change the indents, the tab settings, or some other aspect of an index level.

You can also change the Index Heading style, which Word uses to format the characters (if any) that separate the letter groups in an index. For example, you might want to make the letters italic, or change the font or point size.

To change the styles used in the index:

1. Choose the Format Define Styles command.

2. Select the name of the Index style you want to change.

3. Change the style as desired. If necessary, see Changing a Style in Chapter 10 for more information about using and changing styles.

Updating an Index

When you change the document, Word doesn't automatically update an index. If you've made changes to your document, you need to compile the index again to make sure it has the correct page numbers and includes all appropriate items.

The index is contained within a field, so you'll use the same process you'd use to update any field.

To update an index:

1. Place the insertion point anywhere within the index.

2. Press **F9** to update the field.

## Chapter Twenty

Performing Calculations

To perform a calculation, you don't need to switch to another program. Word can sum columns or lines; perform simple addition, subtraction, multiplication, and division; and handle more complex calculations, including those using formulas. This chapter shows you how to use these Word features. It describes:

- how to calculate with the Utilities Calculate command.

- how to calculate with fields.

PERFORMING CALCULATIONS

Although Word is not a spreadsheet program, you can use it to perform calculations. You can use Word's calculating features to quickly check your arithmetic, or to include calculations in your documents. For example, Word can solve mathematical expressions like these:

$$267 + 433 + 188.3 \qquad\qquad 10555 - 290 * 3/15$$

$$
\begin{array}{r}
99.45 \\
13.22 \\
\underline{(19.13)}
\end{array}
\qquad\qquad
\begin{array}{r}
\$19{,}300.55 \\
\underline{* \ 75\%}
\end{array}
$$

$$
\begin{array}{r}
13300021 \\
-899 \\
\underline{-206}
\end{array}
\qquad\qquad a^3
$$

$$\$237.96 + 18\% \qquad\qquad \sqrt{4}$$

CALCULATING WITH THE UTILITIES CALCULATE COMMAND

When Word calculates using the Utilities Calculate command, it displays the result in the status bar at the bottom of the screen. You can then paste this result into your document. However, if you include these results in your document, keep this in mind: Word cannot automatically update the results of the Utilities Calculate command, so if you change a number in your expression, you'll have to recalculate, then paste in a new result.

To sum columns of numbers with the Utilities Calculate command, you don't have to type a plus sign operator (+) in front of the number. Word assumes you want to add the numbers unless you surround a number with parentheses to indicate subtraction or include another operator in front of a number.

When you use the Utilities Calculate command, Word calculates numbers in order from left to right and from top to bottom. You can't use parentheses to group numbers, because Word associates parentheses only with negative numbers. Word also ignores most characters associated with numbers, such as $ and #. However, if you include a comma in a number in your calculation, Word includes a comma in the result.

To perform a calculation with the Utilities Calculate command:

1. Type the numbers you want to calculate in a line or column. The following lists the symbols that indicate math operations:

To	Symbol	Example	Result
Add	+ or no operator	1+234 or 1 234	235
Subtract	− or parentheses around number	56−1 or 56 (1)	55
Multiply	*	12*23	276
Divide	/	3/56	0.05
Calculate Percentage	%	200*25%	50

Multiply by Power	^ (1 or more)	10^2	100
Calculate Square Root	^0.5	9^0.5	3
Calculate Cube Root	^(1/3)	10^(1/3)	2.15

2. Select all the numbers to calculate.

3. Choose the Utilities Calculate command. The result appears in the status bar, as shown in Figure 20–1.

4. If you want to paste the result into your document, position the insertion point, then choose the Edit Paste command.

EXAMPLE: Perform a Quick In-line Calculation and Show Only the Results

Before calculation:

On orders of more than $1000.00, you'll receive a 5% discount (for example, if your order totals $3200.00, we'll subtract <u>$3200 * 5%!</u>).

After calculation:

On orders of more than $1000.00, you'll receive a 5% discount (for example, if your order totals $3200.00, we'll subtract <u>$160.00!</u>).

Figure 20–1.
The Utilities Calculate command displays results in the status bar.

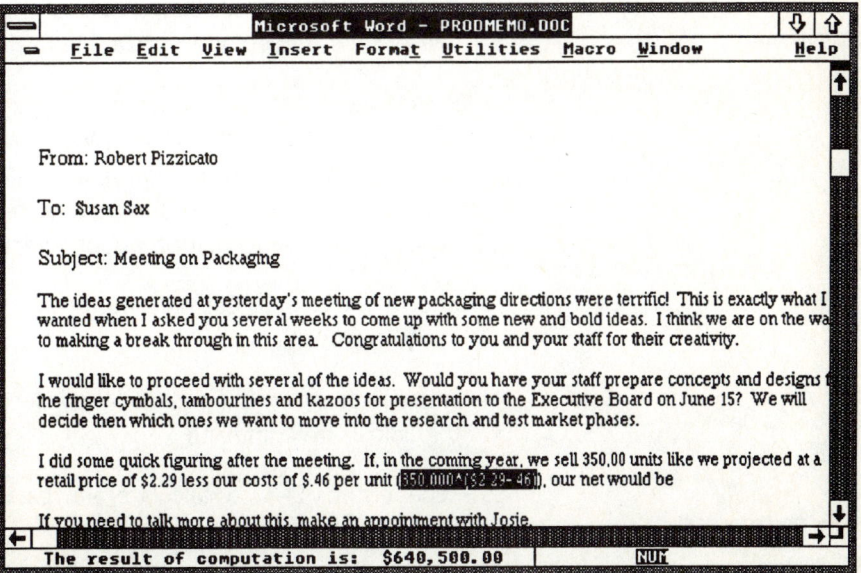

To calculate an in-line expression like the one underlined here:

1. If necessary, choose the Utilities Customize command and turn on the Typing Replaces Selection option. This way you can replace selected text with the contents of the scrap.

2. Select the numbers to calculate. In this example, you'd select 3200*5%.

3. Choose the Utilities Calculate command. Word displays the results in the status bar.

4. To replace the expression (which is still selected) with the result, choose the Edit Paste command.

EXAMPLE: Setting Up a Simple Spreadsheet

Stores	Quarter 1	Quarter 2
San Francisco	212,531.53	315,233.15
Atlanta	144,599.22	140,288.33
Bangor	98,930.93	98,500.62
	[column sum]	[column sum]

To set up a spreadsheet like this and have Word calculate the results:

1. Create a table or set up paragraphs with tabs, then enter the data. Be sure to leave space to paste in the results (create an extra row in tables or an extra line in regular paragraphs).

2. Select one column of numbers. (If your data is in paragraphs with tabs, see Selecting: Telling Word Where to Make Changes in Chapter 4 for information about selecting rectangular portions of text. If the data is in a table, see Selecting in Tables in Chapter 13 for information about selecting cells in tables.)

3. Choose the Utilities Calculate command. Word displays the result in the status bar.

4. To paste in the result, position the insertion point, then choose the Edit Paste command.

5. Repeat steps 2–4 to calculate and paste in the results of the other column.

USING FIELDS TO CALCULATE

When you want Word to calculate automatically, you can use calculating fields in your documents. For example, if you insert a {=2+3} field into your document, Word prints 5 at that location when you print your document. You can use simple expressions or very complex formulas in fields, sum columns or rows in tables, and use bookmark names to reference specific areas to calculate (see Chapter 21 for more information). You can also include switches in fields to format the results or choose options in the Insert Field dialog box. Chapter 18 provides general information about using fields in Word.

Figure 20–2 shows a document that contains several calculating fields.

Here are the basic instructions for inserting a calculating field.

1. Press **Ctrl+F9** to enclose the insertion point with a pair of field characters ({ }).

2. Type an equal sign (=), followed by the expression you want to calculate, between the field characters.

3. With the insertion point still in the field, press **F9** to update the field.

4. To see the results, press **Shift+F9**.

Figure 20–2.
A Word document with calculating fields.

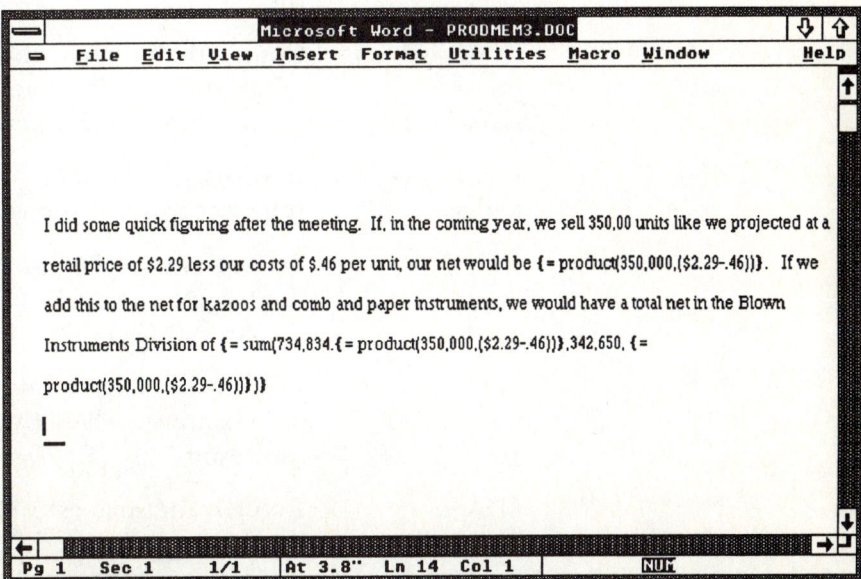

You can also use the Insert Field command to insert the "= expression" field type. With this field you can choose an option in the dialog box to format the results. See Chapter 18 for more information about using the Insert Field command.

Using Mathematical Functions in Fields

To use a mathematical function (or any other text) in Word fields, you must begin the field with an equal sign (=) to let Word know that this is a calculation. You can select among the following mathematical functions in Word:

Function	Description
ABS *(expression)*	Returns the absolute value of the expression. Example: {=ABS (-15)} yields the result 15.
AND *(logical1, logical2)*	Returns 1 if all arguments are true; returns 0 if any arguments are false. Example: {=AND (2+3=5, 3-1=2)} yields the result 1; {=AND (5+3=8, 4-4=1)} yields the result 0.
AVERAGE *(expression1, expression2)*	Returns the average value of the arguments. Example: {=AVERAGE (1,3,5)} yields the result 3.
COUNT *(value1, value2,...)*	Counts the number of arguments in a list of arguments. Example: {=COUNT (10,23,4.4,9,1.253)} yields the result 5.
DEFINED *(value)*	Returns 1 if the value is evaluated successfully; returns 0 if the result is an error.
INT *(expression)*	Truncates the value of the expression to the largest integer less than the value. Example: {=INT (7.53)} yields the result 7.
MAX *(expression1, expression2)*	Returns the largest value in the argument list. Example: {=MAX (3,22,51,6,49)} yields the result 51.
MIN *(expression1, expression2)*	Returns the smallest value in the argument list. Example: {=MIN (3,22,51,6,49)} yields the result 3.

MOD
(*expression1,*
expression2)

Returns the remainder (modules) after dividing *expression1* by *expression2*, and gives the result the same sign as *expression2*. Example: {=MOD (10,4)} yields the result 2.

NOT (*logical*)

Reverses the value of *logical*: if *logical* is FALSE, returns 1; if *logical* is TRUE, returns 0. Example: {=NOT (2+2=4)} yields the result 0.

OR (*logical1,*
logical2)

Returns 1 if any value in the list is TRUE; returns 0 if all values are false. Example: {=OR (1+1=2,2+2=5)} yields the result 1; {=OR (1+1=3,2+2=5)} yields the result 0.

PRODUCT
(*expression1,*
expression2)

Multiplies all numbers in the argument list and returns the product. Example: {=PRODUCT (2,3,5)} yields the result 30.

ROUND
(*expression,*
number-of-
digits)

Rounds the expression to the number-of-digits. Example: {=ROUND (42.149,1)} yields the result 42.1.

SIGN
(*expression*)

Returns 1 if the expression is a positive number, 0 if the expression is 0, and -1 if the expression is negative. Example: {=SIGN (-100)} yields the result -1.

SUM
(*expression1,*
expression2)

Adds all numbers in the argument list and returns the sum. Example: {=SUM (30,50,1)} yields the result 81.

Using Fields to Calculate in Tables

When using fields to calculate in a Word table, you can refer to cells just like you would in a spreadsheet program. To refer to a cell, you use the following syntax: [R*n*C*n*], where R stands for row and C stands for column. (The letters *R* and *C* can be either uppercase or lowercase.) For example, to refer to the cell in the first row and in the first column, you'd type either [r1c1] or [R1C1]. To refer to a range of cells, you separate the cell references with a colon (:). For example, to refer to the cells in rows 1 through 3 in column 1, you'd type [r1c1:r3c1]. All cell references must be enclosed in square brackets. Be sure to use an equal sign (=) to begin any field that includes cell references like this.

You can use all of the mathematical functions described in the previous section in table cells. Figure 20–3 shows a spreadsheet-type table that includes calculating fields.

Using Formulas in Fields

You can insert formula codes into a field when you want to include a mathematical statement or expression in your document. To print a formula, you need to use one of the following printers:

- an HP LaserJet® printer with 512K or more of memory

- a PostScript printer

- a printer with a PostScript-compatible Symbol font

Before using a formula in your document, you should check to make sure your printer meets these requirements.

To create a formula, you insert formula codes in an EQ field. Formulas can be quite complex—see the following section, Formatting a Formula, to get a better idea of what you can put in a formula.

To create a formula:

Figure 20–3.
A Word table that includes calculating fields.

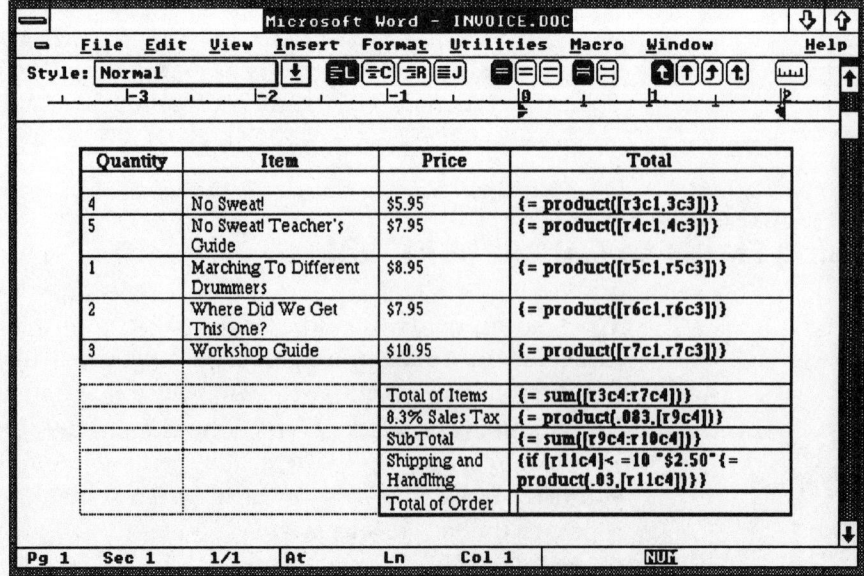

1. Place the insertion point where you want to insert the formula.

2. Choose the Insert Field command.

3. Select Formulas from the Insert Field Type list. After you select Formulas, Word displays formula items in the Instructions list.

4. Select the item you want from the Instructions list, then choose Add to add the appropriate code to the text box. For example, if you wanted to build a fraction, you'd select Fraction.

   Word adds the appropriate code and other characters (if appropriate) to the text box. For example, when you add Fraction, Word adds \F (,) to the text box.

5. Type any necessary numbers or letters in the text box. For example, if you wanted to display the fraction ⅚, you'd type **5** and **6** in the appropriate spots in the Field Code box so the fractions area would look like this: \F (5,6).

6. If necessary, reposition the insertion point in the Field Code box, then repeat steps 4 and 5. Continue until you have built the formula you want.

7. Click OK or press **Enter** to insert the formula field into your document.

8. To view the formula, press **Shift I F9** to turn off the display of field codes.

You could also press **Ctrl+F9** to enclose the insertion point in field characters, then type the appropriate codes and arguments to create the formula you want.

Formatting a Formula

You control the formatting for a formula using special switches and arguments that are included within the field. Each of these switches and arguments has various options that control the formula. Consult the Formula section of your *User's Reference* and the EQ Field section of the *Technical Reference* for exact information on these options.

Switch	Name and description
\a	Array. Formats and displays a two-dimensional array

\b	Bracket. Brackets a single element
\d	Displace. Controls the horizontal placement of the next character
\f	Fraction. Formats a fraction
\i	Integral. Creates an integral from three elements
\l	List. Creates a list of values separated by commas
\o	Overstrike. Places an element on top of the previous element
\r	Radical. Displays a radical
\s	Subscript. Sets the position of the elements as either subscript or superscript
\x	Box. Draws a box around a single element

Helpful Hint

When inserting complex formulas, you might want to split your document window into two panes, using one pane to view the field codes for the formulas and the other pane to view the resulting formulas.

1. Split the document window using one of the following methods:

   ■ Choose the Document Control Split command and press **Enter**.

   or

   ■ Use the mouse to point to the split bar (the black rectangle above the vertical scroll bar), drag the split line to the center of the window, then release the mouse button.

2. In one pane, choose the View Field Codes command (if necessary) to remove the check mark beside the command name. When the check mark is gone, the pane displays results instead of field codes.

3. In the other pane, make sure the View Field Codes command is "turned on" (a check mark appears beside the command name). This pane displays the field codes.

Figure 20–4 shows a formula field in both panes.

Figure 20–4.
Creating a formula with the document window split and set to show both results and field codes.

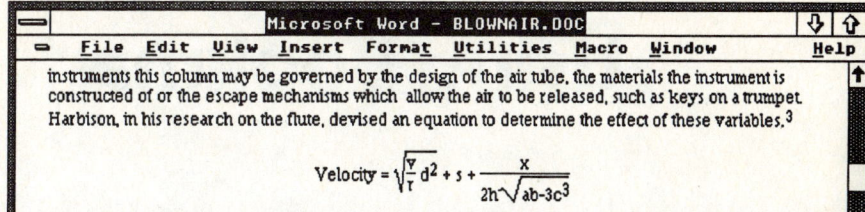

```
┌────────────────────────────────────────────────────────────────────┐
│ ▭        Microsoft Word - BLOWNAIR.DOC                    ⇩  ⇧      │
│ ⊟   File   Edit   View   Insert   Format   Utilities   Macro   Window        Help │
├────────────────────────────────────────────────────────────────────┤
```

instruments this column may be governed by the design of the air tube, the materials the instrument is constructed of or the escape mechanisms which allow the air to be released, such as keys on a trumpet. Harbison, in his research on the flute, devised an equation to determine the effect of these variables.[3]

$$\text{Velocity} = \sqrt{\frac{v}{r}\, d^2} + s + \frac{x}{2h\sqrt{ab-3c^3}}$$

When this equation is adjusted for temperature and other atmospheric conditions, we find that there is a direct inverse relationships between the velocity of air and the air input apparatus. The discovery of this relationship by Harbison made dramatic improvements in design and manufacture of all sorts of blown air instruments.

A column of air moves at a velocity relative to the pressure exerted both in front and behind it. In wind instruments this column may be governed by the design of the air tube, the materials the instrument is constructed of or the escape mechanisms which allow the air to be released, such as keys on a trumpet. Harbison, in his research on the flute, devised an equation to determine the effect of these variables.[3]

Velocity = { eq \r(\f(v,r) d\s(2)) + s + \f(x,2h\r(ab-3c\s(3))) }

When this equation is adjusted for temperature and other atmospheric conditions, we find that there is a direct inverse relationships between the velocity of air and the air input apparatus. The discovery of this relationship by Harbison made dramatic improvements in design and manufacture of all sorts of blown air instruments.

While the variables in this equation are numerous, the precision by which one can determine the velocity is

```
├────────────────────────────────────────────────────────────────────┤
│ Pg 1    Sec 1    1/2    At 6.9"   Ln 36   Col 1                     │
└────────────────────────────────────────────────────────────────────┘
```

## Chapter Twenty-One

Using Bookmarks

In Word, bookmarks are not slips of paper you use to mark your place in a manuscript. Word's bookmarks are names that you attach to selected text. For example, you might want to name a section of a report "Sales_by_Region," or a section of your great American novel "Dramatic_Climax." A bookmark can mark anything—it might be a list of illustrations, a picture and its caption, a paragraph, or several pages of text.

Once you've attached a bookmark name to a piece of text or to a picture, you can use that bookmark name to quickly move the insertion point to that spot, to include that text or picture in another document, to set up a cross-reference that Word automatically updates, or to perform calculations. If you're accustomed to working with spreadsheets, you'll find that using bookmarks in Word is much like using named ranges in a spreadsheet program.

This chapter shows you how to work with bookmarks.

CREATING A BOOKMARK

To create a bookmark, you name a selected piece of text. A bookmark name can be up to 20 characters long, must begin with a letter, and can contain letters, numbers, and underscore characters (_). A bookmark name cannot contain spaces or punctuation. Here are some examples of bookmark names: Epilog, Buying_List, Calendar_89, Mtg_Minutes.

Each bookmark name must be unique within a document. If you've already created several bookmarks within the document, you can check the list in the Insert Bookmark dialog box to make sure that you don't duplicate a name you've already used.

To create a bookmark:

1. Select the part of your document you want to name. Be sure to select the entire part, especially if you want to use bookmarks to insert the text in other documents.

2. Choose the Insert Bookmark command. Word displays the dialog box shown in Figure 21–1.

3. Type a name for your bookmark.

4. Click OK or press **Enter**.

That's all there is to it! Don't expect to see any changes in the Word window—bookmarks are invisible. Word uses the first and the last characters of the selected text to mark the beginning and end of the bookmark. If you later delete one of these characters, Word moves the beginning or end of the bookmark to the next letter within the bookmark.

To see what a bookmark contains, use the procedure described in the next section, Jumping to a Bookmark.

Figure 21–1.
Attaching a bookmark name to selected text with the Insert Bookmark command.

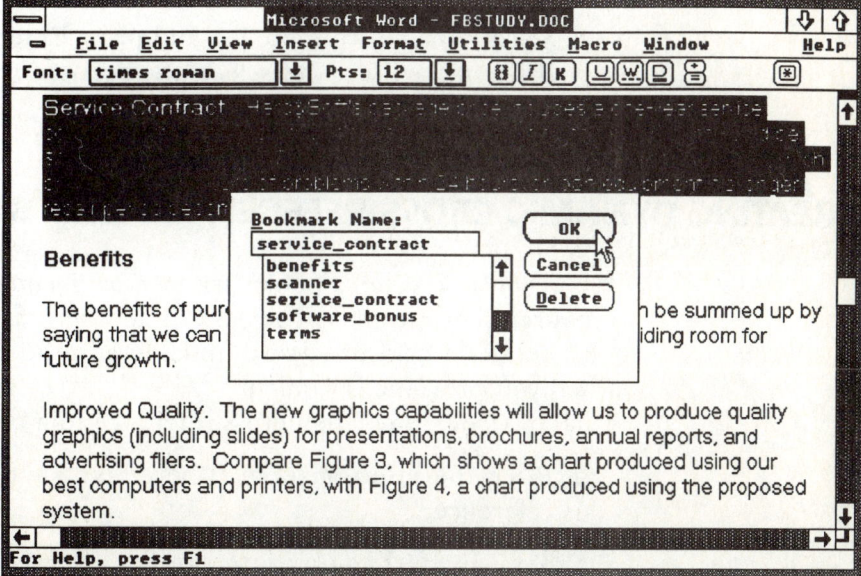

You can assign more than one bookmark name to the same text, so you can have bookmarks within bookmarks within bookmarks, if you like.

▬ *Keyboard Shortcut*

If you're sure the bookmark name you want to use hasn't been used before in your document, you can attach a bookmark without choosing a command, like this:

1. Select the text or graphic you want to attach a bookmark to.

2. Press **Ctrl+Shift+F5**. Word displays Insert bookmark: in the status bar.

3. Type the bookmark name.

4. Press **Enter**.

JUMPING TO A BOOKMARK

One big convenience associated with using bookmarks is that you can tell Word to move the insertion point to a bookmark.

To jump to a bookmark:

1. Choose the Edit Go To command. Word displays a list of bookmarks used in the document, as shown in Figure 21–2.

2. Select a name from the list and press **Enter** or double-click the name in the list. Word selects the portion of your document that has the bookmark assigned to it.

CREATING DYNAMIC CROSS-REFERENCES WITH BOOKMARKS

When you've created a bookmark in your document, you can insert a cross-reference to that bookmark in another part of your document. This creates a field that Word updates with the correct page number when you print the document.

Here's how to create a cross-reference to a bookmark:

1. Place the insertion point where you want to insert the cross-reference.

2. Type any text you want to precede the page number.

Figure 21–2.
Jumping to a
bookmark with the
Edit Go To command.

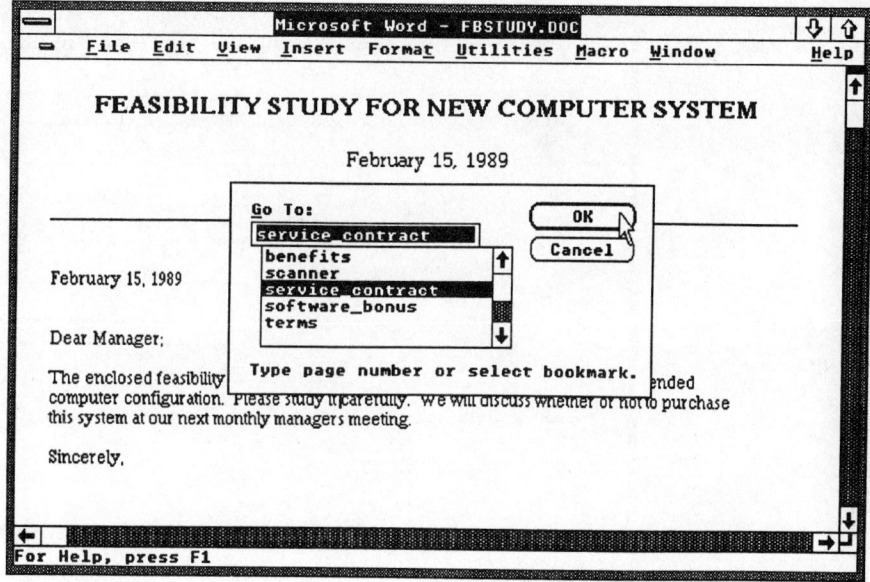

3. Choose the Insert Field command.

4. Select Page ref. from the Insert Field Type list.
   Word inserts page ref in the Field Code box and displays a list
   of bookmarks in the Instructions box.

5. Select the bookmark name you want from the Instructions box
   and choose Add. Word inserts the bookmark name after page
   ref. in the Field Code box, as shown in Figure 21–3.

6. Click OK or press **Enter**. Word inserts a field (as shown in Figure
   21–4) to be updated with the correct page number when the
   document is printed.

EXAMPLE: **Using a Bookmark to Create a Dynamic
Cross-Reference**

Say that you want to create a cross-reference (such as "See Table
3 on page *n*") for Word to update with the correct page number
before each printing. Here's what you'd do.

1. Use the Insert Bookmark command to attach a bookmark named
   Table_three to Table 3.

2. Place the insertion point where you want to insert the cross-
   reference.

Figure 21–3.
Inserting a cross-reference to a bookmark named Table_3.

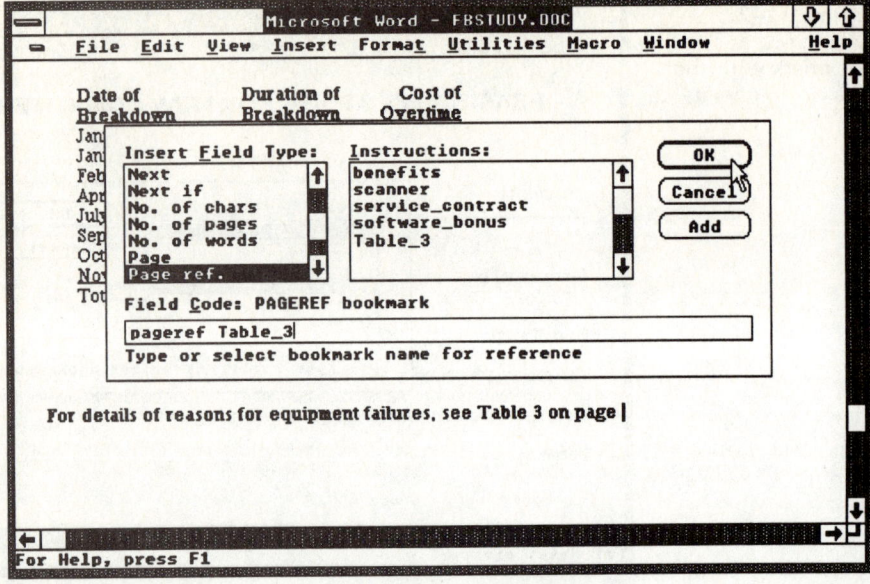

Figure 21–4.
A dynamic cross-reference field that Word updates with the correct page number whenever the document is printed.

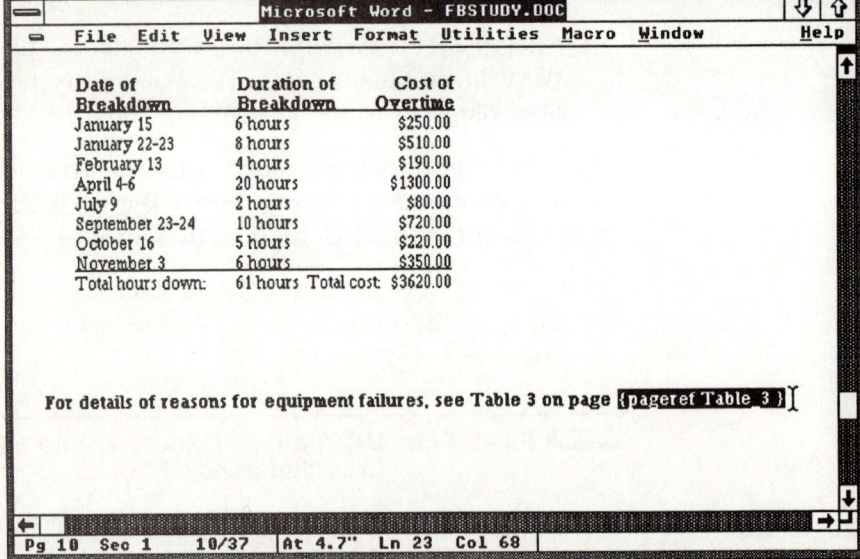

3. Type **See Table 3 on page** followed by a space.

4. Choose the Insert Field command.

5. Select Page ref. from the Insert Field Type list.

6. Select Table_3 from the Instructions box, then choose Add.

7. Click OK or press **Enter** to insert the field. The sentence in your document should now look like this (assuming that you haven't turned off field codes with the View Field Codes command):

See Table 3 on {pageref Table_3}

Now Word automatically inserts the correct page number when you print the file.

USING BOOKMARKS IN CALCULATIONS

You can use bookmarks to simplify calculations that change frequently. When you use bookmark names in a field, Word updates the result automatically whenever there's a change to the "bookmarked" text. The following example shows you one way to use bookmarks in calculations.

EXAMPLE: Using Bookmarks in Calculations

Say that you've created a monthly balance sheet template containing a table like the one here. Each month, you plan to fill in the cells with the appropriate expense and income figures and to sum the columns using the fields in the last row.

Income		Expenses	
Paychecks		Rent	
Interest		Groceries	
Dividends		Utilities	
Income=	{=sum([r2c2:r4c2])}	Expenses=	{=sum([r2c4:r4c4])}

When you fill in the balance sheet, the fields total your income and your expenses for the month. To make this template also figure your net monthly income, you could do this:

1. Select the field that calculates the total income—
{=sum([r2c2:r4c2])}.

2. Use the Insert Bookmark command to attach a bookmark named Total_income to it.

3. Select the field that calculates the total expenses—
   {=sum([r2c4:r4c4])}.

4. Use the Insert Bookmark command to attach a bookmark named
   Total_expenses to the field.

5. Type the following line after the table in the template file:

   Net income = {= Total_income − Total_expenses}

6. Save the file.

Presto! Now Word automatically calculates your net monthly income using the bookmarks. You can use the template over and over
again, changing the figures, and the calculations always are correct.

You can use bookmarks to perform simple or complicated equations,
both inside and outside of tables. See Chapter 18 if you need more
information about using fields.

IMPORTING BOOKMARKED TEXT OR GRAPHICS FROM ANOTHER FILE

You might want to attach a bookmark to a section of text or to a
graphic that you'd like to use in another file. Then you can use a field
to import that "bookmarked" text or graphics from the other file.
Here's how:

1. Move the insertion point to where you want to insert the field
   that imports the text or graphic.

2. Press **Ctrl+F9** to surround the insertion point with field
   characters.

3. Type **include**, then press the **Spacebar** to insert a space.

4. Type the filename, a space, then the bookmark name to identify
   the bookmarked text or graphic you want to insert, as shown in
   Figure 21–5. If the file that includes the bookmark is not in the
   same directory as the file you're inserting this field into, be sure
   to include a pathname so Word can find the file and be sure to
   double the backslashes (a rule for fields). For example, if the
   bookmark file was contained in the \LIST directory on drive B,
   you'd type: **b:\\LIST** *filename bookmarkname*.

Figure 21–5.
A field that inserts bookmarked text from another document whenever this document is printed.

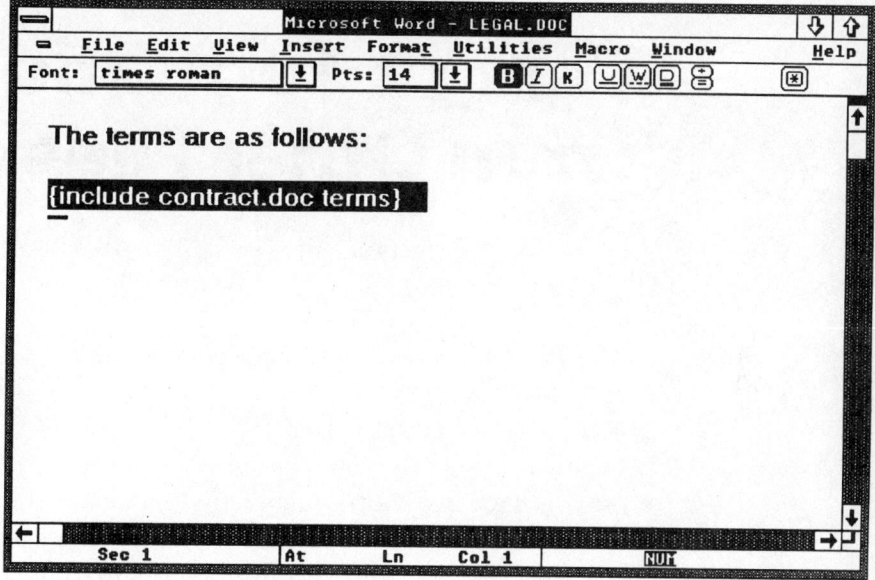

Word inserts the bookmarked information from the other file when you display the results of fields using the View Field Codes command or when you print the document.

EXAMPLE: Using a Bookmark to Insert Text from Another Document

Say that you've created a file named ORDER.DOC that contains an order form and that you've attached a bookmark named Order_form to the order form text. Now you'd like to insert that order form into a letter file that's in the same directory. Here's what you'd do.

1. In the letter file, move the insertion point to the place you'd like to insert the order form.

2. Press **Ctrl+F9** to surround the insertion point with field braces.

3. Type **include**, a space, then type **ORDER.DOC Order_form**. Your field should now look like this:

   {include ORDER.DOC Order_form}

Word automatically inserts the bookmarked text when you update and display field results or when you print the letter file. You can change the bookmarked text in the ORDER.DOC file as often as you like—this field ensures that Word inserts the most current order form.

## Chapter Twenty-Two

Using Information from Other Files

Do you have two Word documents that share the same information? Or do you want to copy data from a spreadsheet into your Word document? If you find yourself constantly copying the same information from one file to another, you need to know about the various ways in which Word can share information between files.

You can include all or part of the text and graphics from one Word document in another Word document. Also, you can import any part of a spreadsheet from Microsoft's Excel or Multiplan spreadsheet programs, or from Lotus® 1-2-3®. You can also link your Word file to a file created with an application that uses Dynamic Data Exchange (DDE)—this means you can update the information automatically in your Word document whenever the information changes in the other file.

This chapter describes how to use information from other files in your Word documents. It covers

- using the Clipboard to copy from one file to another.

- using the Insert File command.

- using the INCLUDE field.

- linking Word files with Excel files and with other Windows applications.

All methods of inserting information from other files use fields to accomplish their tasks. For general information about working with fields, see Chapter 18.

THE MANY METHODS OF COPYING INFORMATION FROM OTHER FILES

You can copy information from other files into Word files in the following ways:

- Use the Edit Copy and Edit Paste commands to copy and paste information from the Clipboard.

- Use the Insert File command to include part or all of one Word file in another Word file.

- Use an INCLUDE field to include part or all of a file in a Word file.

- Link files from other applications to Word using the Edit Paste Link command.

- Use the Insert Picture command or create your own IMPORT field to place a bit-mapped graphic in a Word file.

The method you choose depends on the type of information you want to import. You must be using Windows applications to use the Edit Cut and Edit Paste commands and to link files. To link files, the other application must support DDE. If you are in doubt about your Windows application's ability to support DDE, check the application's documentation.

If you are importing pictures into your Word document you should see Chapter 12, "Adding Pictures to Word Files."

COPYING INFORMATION FROM ANOTHER FILE WITH THE CLIPBOARD

To copy information to a Word document from another Windows application using the Clipboard:

1. Open the file you want to copy from.

2. Select the information to copy. Figure 22–1 illustrates selecting text in a Microsoft Excel spreadsheet.

3. Choose the Edit Copy command to copy the information to the Clipboard.

Figure 22–1.
Marking a selection in another application to copy to the Clipboard.

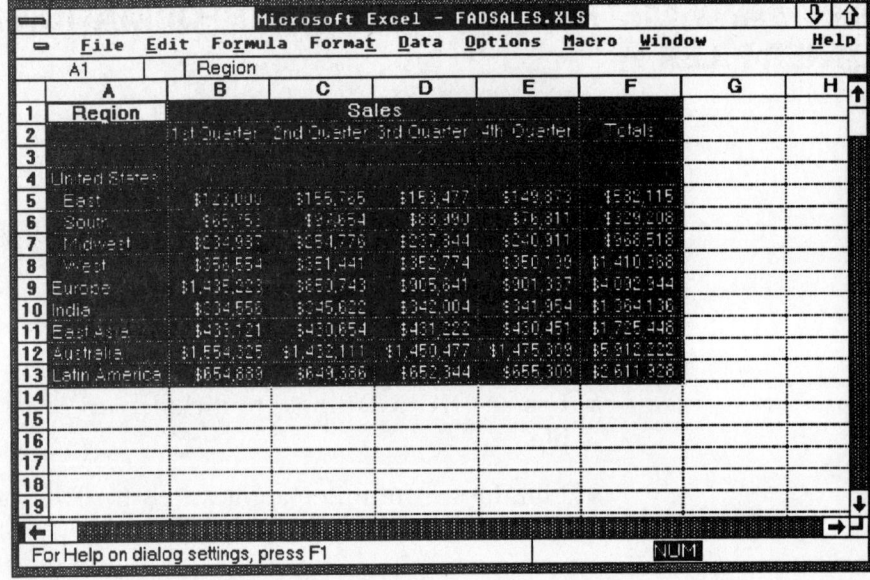

4. Switch to the Word document you want to paste the information into.

5. Place the insertion point where you want to paste the information.

6. Choose the Edit Paste command to paste in the information. Figure 22–2 shows spreadsheet information that's been pasted in and formatted into a Word table.

USING THE INSERT FILE COMMAND TO INSERT ALL OR PARTS OF FILES

You can insert the contents of an entire file, or just a part of a file, using the Insert File command. (You can also use the INCLUDE field to do this. See Using INCLUDE Fields later in this chapter.)

When you use the Insert File command, you can specify whether to import either another Word file or a file in any of the following formats:

- DCA/RFT: includes DisplayWrite and DisplayWriter

- Microsoft Excel BIFF

- Microsoft Windows Write

Figure 22–2.
The same information pasted in a Word file.

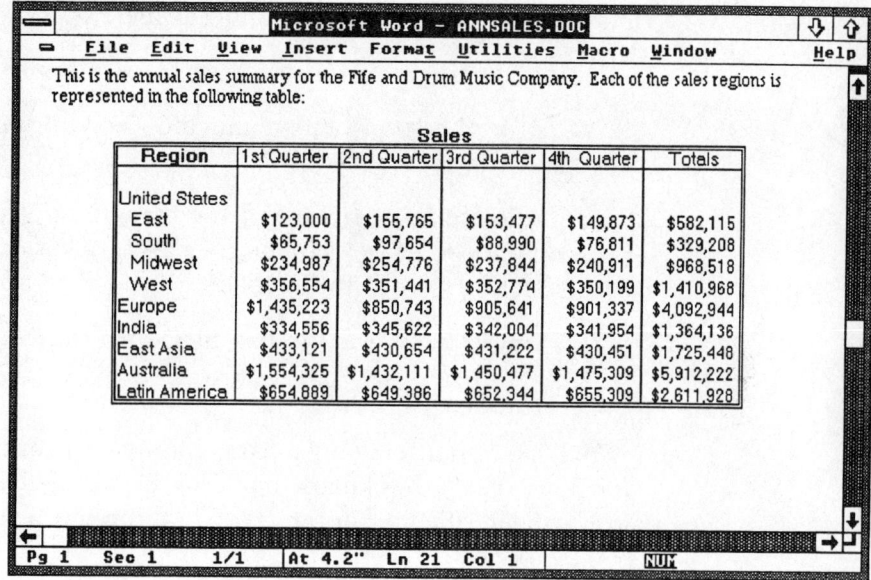

	Sales				
Region	1st Quarter	2nd Quarter	3rd Quarter	4th Quarter	Totals
United States					
East	$123,000	$155,765	$153,477	$149,873	$582,115
South	$65,753	$97,654	$88,990	$76,811	$329,208
Midwest	$234,987	$254,776	$237,844	$240,911	$968,518
West	$356,554	$351,441	$352,774	$350,199	$1,410,968
Europe	$1,435,223	$850,743	$905,641	$901,337	$4,092,944
India	$334,556	$345,622	$342,004	$341,954	$1,364,136
East Asia	$433,121	$430,654	$431,222	$430,451	$1,725,448
Australia	$1,554,325	$1,432,111	$1,450,477	$1,475,309	$5,912,222
Latin America	$654,889	$649,386	$652,344	$655,309	$2,611,928

This is the annual sales summary for the Fife and Drum Music Company. Each of the sales regions is represented in the following table:

Microsoft Word — ANNSALES.DOC
File Edit View Insert Format Utilities Macro Window Help
Pg 1 Sec 1 1/1 At 4.2" Ln 21 Col 1 NUM

- Microsoft Word for DOS

- Microsoft Works word processing files

- Microsoft Multiplan and Multiplan BIFF

- MultiMate (certain versions) and Advantage II

- RTF (Rich Text Format): includes Microsoft Word for the Macintosh

- Text Only (PC-8 with or without line breaks)

- WordPerfect (certain versions)

- WordStar (certain versions)

If you want to link the Word document with the other file, you can turn on the Link option in the Insert File dialog box. When files are linked, Word inserts an INCLUDE field that you can update periodically, asking Word to get the information again when it changes in the other file. Word uses the pathname in the INCLUDE field to find the file, so if you move the file you have to link it again.

When files are not linked, Word only merges the contents of the file (or the portion you specify), rather than creating automatic updates. Press the **F9** key with the insertion point in the field to update the field when necessary.

To insert a whole file into another file:

1. Position the insertion point where you want the file inserted.

2. Choose the Insert File command. Word displays the dialog box shown in Figure 22–3.

3. Type or select the name of the file you want to insert. If the file you want to insert is in another drive or directory, type the pathname in front of the filename.

4. If you want to link the two files, turn on the Link option.

5. Click OK or press **Enter**.

You can also insert only a part of a file into another file. To do this, you must use a bookmark name or a specified range of cells in a spreadsheet. (See Chapter 21 for more information about using bookmarks.)

To insert part of a file in another file:

1. Place the insertion point where you want the file inserted.

2. Choose the Insert File command.

3. Type or select the name of the file you want to insert. If the file you want to insert is in another drive or directory, type in the pathname.

4. In the Range box, type the bookmark name or the cell references for the part of the file you want to include.

5. If you want to link the two files, turn on the Link option box.

6. Click OK or press **Enter**.

Figure 22–3.
The Insert File dialog box.

USING IMPORT FIELDS TO INSERT PICTURES

You can use an IMPORT field to insert TIFFs (Tagged Image Format Files) in a Word document. When you import TIFFs, Word inserts the file's contents in a picture frame. The easiest way to be sure that you use the correct format with the IMPORT field is to use the Insert Picture command, which inserts an IMPORT field for you. For more information on importing pictures to Word documents, see Chapter 12, "Adding Pictures to Word Files."

USING INCLUDE FIELDS

You can use an INCLUDE field to insert almost any type of file into a Word document.

The INCLUDE field tells Word to insert the entire contents or a specific portion of a file in your document. When you insert part of a file, you use a bookmark to specify the part you want. (For more information about using bookmarks, see Chapter 21.) You can use many INCLUDE fields in a single Word document.

To insert the contents of a file in a Word file using an INCLUDE field:

1. Press **Ctrl+F9** to enclose the insertion point in field brackets.

2. Type **include**, then a space, followed by the filename and—if you're inserting part of the file—a space and a bookmark name. For example, to insert the entire file named BILLS.89, you'd type **include bills.89**. If you're inserting a bookmarked section named January from the BILLS.89 file, you'd type **include bills.89 january**.

When you want to see the results of this field, press **Shift+F9** to turn off field codes, then press **F9** to update the field.

When you use the INCLUDE field to insert files that have different formats from Word's, you may need to use a \c switch and a file-type argument in the field instructions. The \c switch must be used with the following formats:

File format	Type this after the filename
DCA/RTF	\c "DCA (RFT)"
WordPerfect 4.1	\c "WordPerfect 4.1"
WordPerfect 4.2	\c "WordPerfect 4.2"
WordPerfect 5.0	\c "WordPerfect 5.0"

MultiMate 3.3,	\c "MultiMate 3.3"
MultiMate Advantage,	\c "MultiMate Advantage"
and MultiMate Advantage II	\c "MultiMate Adv II"
WordStar 3.3	\c "WordStar 3.3"
WordStar 3.45	\c "WordStar 3.45"
WordStar 4.0	\c "WordStar 4.0"

For example, if you want to include a WordPerfect 5.0 file, you'd insert a field that would look something like {include CHAPTER.DOC \c "WordPerfect 5.0"}.

Word can recognize and read the following formats without using the \c switch:

- Text

- Text with line breaks (PC-8)

- RTF

- BIFF (Excel)

- Microsoft Windows Write

- Microsoft Word 4.0 or 5.0

- Microsoft Works word processor files

- Multiplan

- WKS and WK1 (Lotus)

CREATING LINKS WITH WINDOWS APPLICATIONS

You can link your Word file with files created by other Windows applications, such as Excel. Then you can update the linked information in your Word file when you change the linked file using the other application. For example, you might want to paste part of an Excel spreadsheet into your Word document, then update the Word document when you update the Excel spreadsheet. This section shows you how to create a link and how to update linked information.

Linking with Microsoft Excel

To link information in a Microsoft Excel file with your Word document:

1. Open the Excel file.

2. Select the text or chart you want to copy.

3. Choose the Edit Copy command to copy the data you want to link to the Clipboard.

4. Switch to Word and open the file in which you want to insert the Excel information.

5. Position the insertion point, then choose the Edit Paste Link command as shown in Figure 22–4.

6. If you want to automatically update your Word file, turn on Auto Update. If you do not turn on Auto Update, you have to update the INCLUDE field using the F9 key each time data changes.

7. Click OK or press **Enter**.

Word uses the pathname in the INCLUDE field to find the linked file, so if you move the file, link it again.

Linking with Other Windows Applications

To create a link with another Windows application:

1. In Word, position the insertion point where you want the linked information to appear.

Figure 22–4.
The Edit Paste Link command.

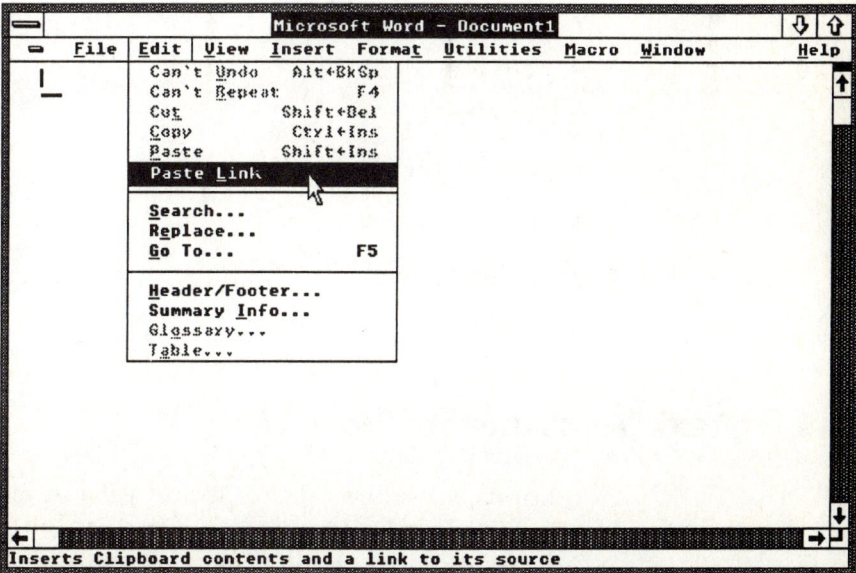

2. Press **Ctrl**+**F9** to enclose the insertion point in field brackets.

3. Type the field codes for the link you want:

- To insert a field to update with F9, type:

   dde *app-name file-name* [*place-reference*]

   Example: {dde c:\\windows\\excel\\jansales.xls R3C2:R7C4}

- To insert a field for Word to automatically update, type:

   ddeauto *app-name file-name* [*place-reference*]

   Example: {ddeauto c:\\windows\\excel\\jansales.xls R3C2:R7C4}

Be sure to specify the directory and drive name if the source files are in a different drive and directory. The pathname includes double backslashes (\\) because you need to double backslashes in pathnames within fields (otherwise, Word interprets the argument as a switch).

Some other applications that support linking with Word through DDE include

- Micrografx Windows Graph Plus

- Polaris PackRat

- Quotron

- Dynacom

- COMPETE!

- HALO DPE

- MailPlus

- Da Vinci eMail

- ASCII-Pro

Linking Text from Another Word File

You normally use the Edit Copy and Paste commands to copy information between two Word files, as described in Moving Text in Chapter 4. You should use the following procedure only if you want to link information in one document to another. For example, if you want to include a list of products and prices in a brochure you're creating, you could copy that list from your main product file and link the two Word files. This way, when the prices change in the main product file they are updated in the brochure file as well.

You can insert part of another Word file by naming the area or the entire file you want to link with a bookmark.

To insert and link text from another Word file:

1. Open the Word file that contains the text you want to copy.

2. Select the text you want or the entire file.

3. Choose the Insert Bookmark command and name the bookmark.

4. Open the Word file into which you want to insert the copy.

5. Position the insertion point where you want the text to appear.

6. Follow the procedure for importing bookmarks as described in Importing Bookmarked Text or Graphics from Another File in Chapter 21.

Word uses the pathname in the field to find the linked file, so if you move the file, link it again.

FORMATTING INFORMATION FROM ANOTHER FILE

You can use all of Word's commands to format text imported with a field, just as if it were any other type of text. However, keep this in mind: when you update the text, Word overwrites any formats you've applied, unless they're paragraph formats or styles attached to the last imported paragraph.

Here are some specific rules to keep in mind about formatting when you use the INCLUDE field:

■ The information inserted from the source file maintains its styles and character formatting if the information ends with a paragraph mark. (Remember, paragraph marks contain a paragraph's formatting instructions.) When the inserted text doesn't contain a paragraph mark, the contents assume the formatting of the receiving file.

■ If the inserted text ends in a section mark, the information retains the section formatting from the original file. (Remember, section marks contain a section's formatting instructions.) When the inserted information doesn't contain a section mark, the information assumes the section formatting of the receiving file.

Unfortunately, when you import spreadsheet information, it loses any character or paragraph formatting it had in the spreadsheet file. You can use the commands in Word's Format menu to add formats—bold, italic, indents, borders, and so on—to the imported information. You can also edit the information if you don't want to update it later. (Updating overwrites any changes you've made.)

UPDATING IMPORTED TEXT

The whole point of linking information in a Word file with another file is to be able to update the information in the Word file to match the source file. To update linked information in your Word file after changing the linked file:

1. Move the insertion point into the field in your Word document.

2. Press **F9** to update the information.

If a source application is not running when you update a linked field, Word asks you if you want to start the source application. You can choose not to start the application, and any previous changes will still be made in Word.

BREAKING LINKS

If you no longer want your Word file to be linked to another file, you can break links in this way:

1. Move the insertion point into the linked field.

2. Press **Ctrl+Shift+F9**.

Chapter Twenty-Three

Creating Form Letters and Address Labels: Print Merge

You can use Word to create form letters, invoices, and other merged documents using a list of names, addresses, and other information you supply.

To create form letters and other form documents, you follow three basic steps:

1. Create a *data document* containing the names, addresses, and other variable information to insert into the main document.

2. Create a *main document* containing the text that remains the same and fields that contain the names, addresses, and other variable information.

3. Use the File Print Merge command to print the individual forms.

Figure 23–1 shows a very simple data document and main document and the resulting form letters.

You'll learn how to create these two documents and how to merge them together in this chapter. You'll also learn how to create address labels and how to sort lists of data.

CREATING A DATA DOCUMENT

It really doesn't matter whether you create the main or data document first for a form letter, but it's easier to understand how the two documents are related if you create the data document first.

A data document contains two elements, as shown in Figure 23–2:

■ A row of field names, called a *header record*

Figure 23–1.
To create form letters, you create a data document and a main document and merge them together.

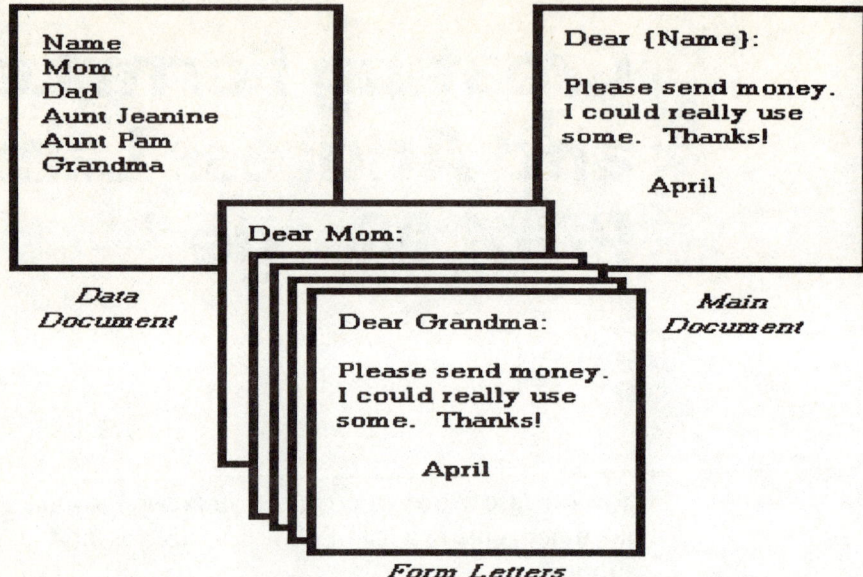

Figure 23–2.
A data document with a header record followed by data records.

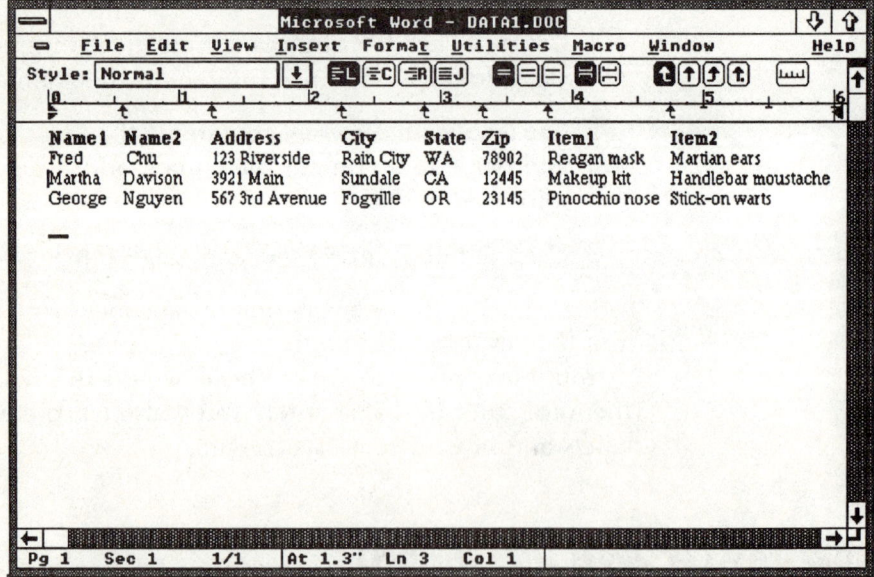

■ Data records containing field entries in the same order as the header record

You can put your records into paragraphs, separating the items with tabs, like this:

Name	Address	City	State	Zip
Jones	123 Main	Bedford	ID	99122
Gonzalez	345 First	Seaside	CA	99133
Kazorski	9125 W. 63rd	Dustbowl	TX	77932

or with commas, like this:

Name,Address,City,State,Zip

Jones,123 Main,Bedford,ID,99122
Gonzalez,345 First,Seaside,CA,99133
Kazorski,9125 W. 63rd,Dustbowl,TX,77932

Outside of tables, each record must be a separate paragraph, with no blank lines between records. If the field entries are so long that the lines in a record wrap, that's okay—Word assumes entries all belong to the same record until it reaches the paragraph mark.

If each record can fit into one table row, you can also put your records into a table, as shown in Figure 23–3. In a table, Word assumes that all the information in a cell is the data for that field in the record and that each row is a separate record. Don't worry if the text wraps within the cells. (For more information about working with tables, see Chapter 13.)

Figure 23–3.
A data document
formatted as a table.

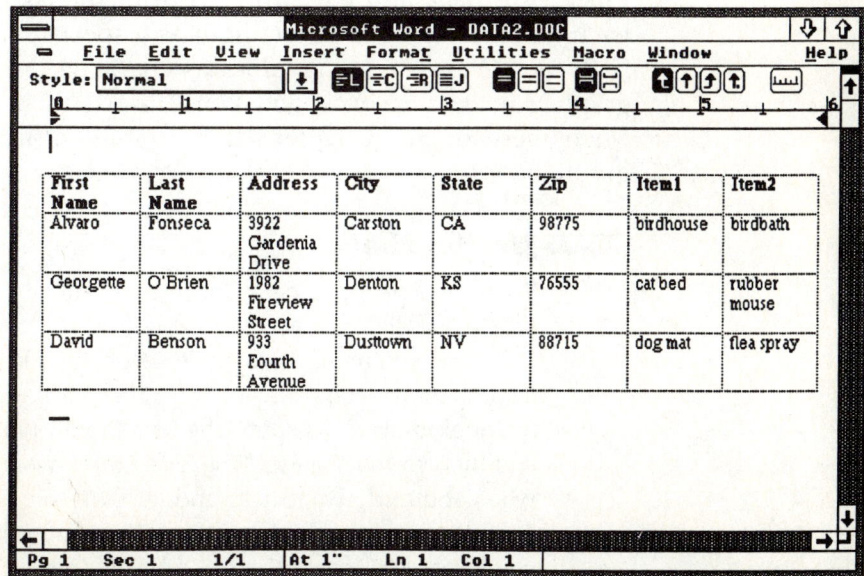

To create a data document:

1. Type the header record, separating the field names with commas or tabs outside of a table or placing each field into a separate cell in a table. The header record must be the first paragraph or row in the data document.

2. Type the data records, separating the items with commas or tabs outside of tables or placing them into table cells, just like the header record. Put the record entries in the same order as their names in the header record.

If a field in a record is blank, be sure to put in a separator character (a comma or tab outside of tables, or a blank cell in a table) as a placeholder to indicate a blank item. Because Word counts the separator characters (or table cells) to find items in each record, this process keeps the items in order.

If an entry in a data record contains commas or tab marks, enclose that entry in quotation marks (" "). For example, if a customer name is U&I, Inc., enclose the customer name in quotation marks: "U&I, Inc." The quotation marks prevent Word from interpreting a character in a field as a separator character between items.

If an entry in a data record contains actual quotation marks (") or backslashes (\), precede the quotation mark or backslash with a backslash (\). For example, if you want to print Ying\Yang, type this: **Ying\\Yang**; if you want to print `"Mark's Place"`, type **\"Mark's Place\"**. A backslash tells Word to print the character following the backslash instead of interpreting it as a special character.

Because Word treats graphics as characters, you can also include graphics in data records, and Word inserts them in the form letters when merged. See Chapter 12 for more information about using graphics.

Helpful Hint

When you set up a data document, separate first and last names, articles (a, an, the), and titles (Mr., Ms., Dr.) into different columns. This gives you more flexibility in sorting and in including information in your form letters.

For example, if you put "The Sofa Store" in a Company_name field and then sorted the list, "The Sofa Store" would end up with the *T*s, when you really want it to end up with the *S*s. By placing *The* in a separate column, your list stays in the appropriate order. Likewise, if you insert *Mr. Franco Giovi* in a Name item, you don't have the flexibility of using only his first or last name in your form letters, and you can't sort your records according to last name only.

As well as creating data documents with Word, you can import information from other applications to use in data documents. The fields in imported information must be separated by tabs or commas, or placed into a table so that Word can separate data among fields correctly. See Chapter 22 for more about using information from other files.

CREATING A MAIN DOCUMENT

A main document contains two elements:

- the standard text, which remains the same in each letter

- fields that tell Word where to find the variable information to insert into the main document from the data document

You can enter and format the standard text of a main document just like any other Word document.

All fields in the main document must be enclosed in special field characters, { }. You can't use the brace keys on the keyboard to insert these. Instead, to insert a field:

1. Press **Ctrl+F9** to enclose the insertion point in field characters.

2. Type the text you want in the field between the field characters.

To create a main document:

1. Begin the letter with a field containing a DATA instruction and the name of your data document file. For example, if the data document was named LIST.DOC, the DATA instruction field would be:

   {**data list.doc**}

   The DATA instruction field must be the first paragraph in your document—it tells Word where to find information to insert into the fields. If the data document is not in the same directory as the main document, include a pathname with double backslashes, so it has the format {data \\windows\\datadocs\\list.doc}.

2. Type and format the standard text.

3. Insert a field wherever you want Word to insert information from your data document. For example, insert the field {**Last_Name**} where you want the name in the data document's Last_Name field to be inserted from a record.

Figure 23–4 shows a main document.

> ### *Helpful Hint*
>
> To make sure that the field names you've used in your data document match the field names in your main document, use the File Open command to open both files, then use the Window Arrange All command to arrange the windows so you can view both files simultaneously, as shown in Figure 23–5. See Chapter 5 for more information about splitting windows.

Formatting Fields in the Main Document

If you want the information that you're inserting in the field to be formatted a certain way, format the first character of the field in your main document and use the *charformat switch in the field.

Formatting the records in the data document has no effect, because Word doesn't keep that formatting when it merges the information

Figure 23–4.
A sample main
document.

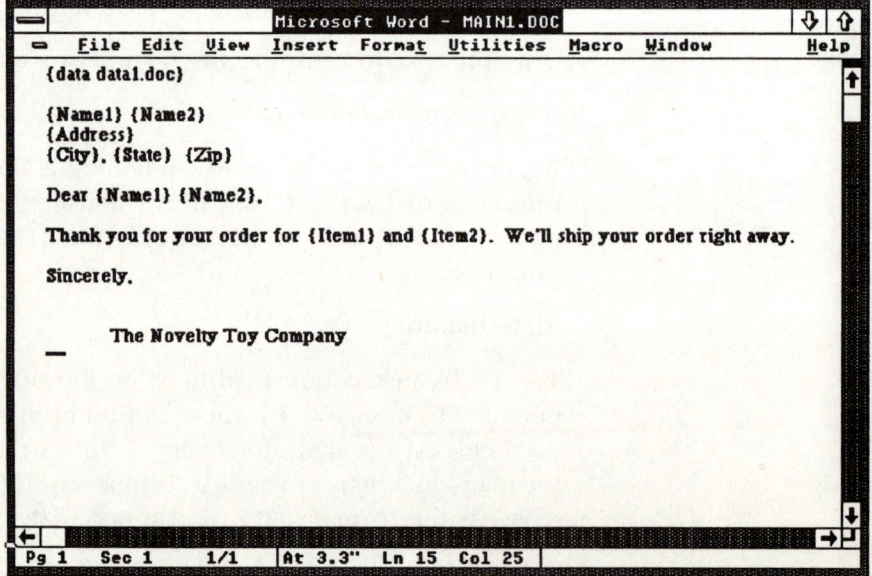

Figure 23–5.
Using two windows makes it easier to compare field names in data and main documents.

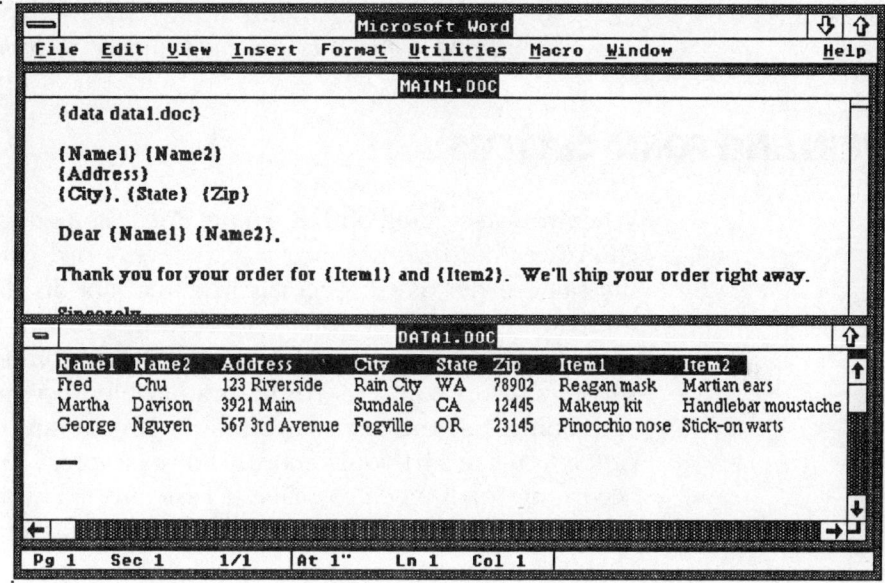

with the form letters. The *charformat switch tells Word to copy the character format from the first character in the field after the opening field character ({).

For example, if you want the customer's last name to appear in italic in the form letters, italicize the first character of Last_Name field in your main document and add the *charformat switch, like this:

Dear Ms. {**Last_Name *charformat**}

Controlling Blank Lines

For every paragraph mark you insert in your main document, Word inserts a paragraph mark in the form letter. This causes Word to create blank lines at the beginning of form letters where you have the DATA instruction and perhaps other instructions ending with paragraph marks. If this creates gaps in your form letters that you don't want, you can do one of the following:

- Place the DATA instruction on the same line with the next instructions, like this:

   {**DATA NURSORDS.DOC**}{**First_Name**} {**Last_Name**}

- Format the DATA instruction (and SET and ASK instructions, too, if you're using them) along with their paragraph marks as hidden text using the Format Character command.

PRINTING FORM LETTERS

When you've created both the main document and the data document, you're ready to print your form letters. Word prints form letters in the same order as the records in your data document. If you don't want to print a letter for every record, you can specify a range of record numbers with the File Print Merge command. You can also sort records or copy records to another file to create a data document containing only the records you want. If you want to print in a certain order, you can sort your records. For example, you might want to sort according to zip code to make it easier to mail the letters. For more information about sorting, see Sorting Data Records later in this chapter.

It may take a few practice runs to successfully print exactly the form letters you want, especially if your main document includes a lot of IF clauses. To avoid wasting paper and printing time, you might want to save your form letters in a file (as described in Saving Form Letters in a File later in this chapter). Then you can check the results before you print.

To print form letters:

1. Open the main document. Make sure the data document is on the same disk and in the same directory as the main document or that you've specified the correct pathname in the DATA instruction at the top of the document.

2. Choose the File Print Merge command. Word displays the dialog box shown in Figure 23–6.

3. If you don't want to print form letters for all the records in the data document, type record numbers in the From and To boxes

Figure 23–6.
The Print Merge
dialog box.

to specify a range of records. For example, type **5** in the From box and type **10** in the To box to print records 5–10 or type **3** in the From box and **3** in the To box to print only record 3.

4. Click the Print button to begin printing.

Two problems can crop up when you merge print:

■ If Word can't find the data document, it displays an error message. Make sure the DATA instruction is the first paragraph in the main document and that the filename in the DATA instruction is the same as that of the data document, including any drive names or pathnames Word needs to find the file.

■ If Word can't match a field name in the main document with a field name in the data document, it prints an error message instead of the record entry in the form letter. Make sure the field name as typed in the main document is *exactly* the same as the field name in the header record of the data document.

Canceling Printing

To cancel printing:

■ Press **Esc** to interrupt the merge process.

SAVING FORM LETTERS IN A FILE

If you don't want to print your form letters directly from your data document, you can save all the letters in a file. This way you can test your merge instructions without wasting paper. It also means you can edit and format the letters and put off printing until it's convenient.

To save form letters in a file:

1. Open the main document. Make sure the data document is on the same disk and in the same directory as the main document.

2. Choose the File Print Merge command.

3. If you don't want to create form letters for all the records in the data document, type record numbers in the From and To boxes to specify a range of records. For example, type **5** in the From box and type **10** in the To box to print records 5–10 or type **3** in the From box and **3** in the To box to print only record 3.

4. Click the New Document button. Word creates a new document called Form Letters*n* and enters the form letters in it, as shown in Figure 23–7. The letters are separated by section marks.

5. When Word finishes creating the form letters, save the Form Letters document (Word asks you for a filename) if you want to keep it. (Or, if the merge wasn't perfect, you can close the file without saving it, throwing away the form letters.)

6. When you're ready to print the form letters, use the File Print command.

CREATING A DOCUMENT THAT ASKS YOU FOR INFORMATION

You can use the ASK instruction to create a main document that asks you for the information to put into fields immediately before printing a form letter.

The basic form of the ASK instruction is

{ask *field_name* "*text*"}

where *field_name* is the name of the field to fill with the information you type, and the "*text*" is the information you want Word to print

Figure 23–7.
By saving form letters in a file you can see the results before you print.

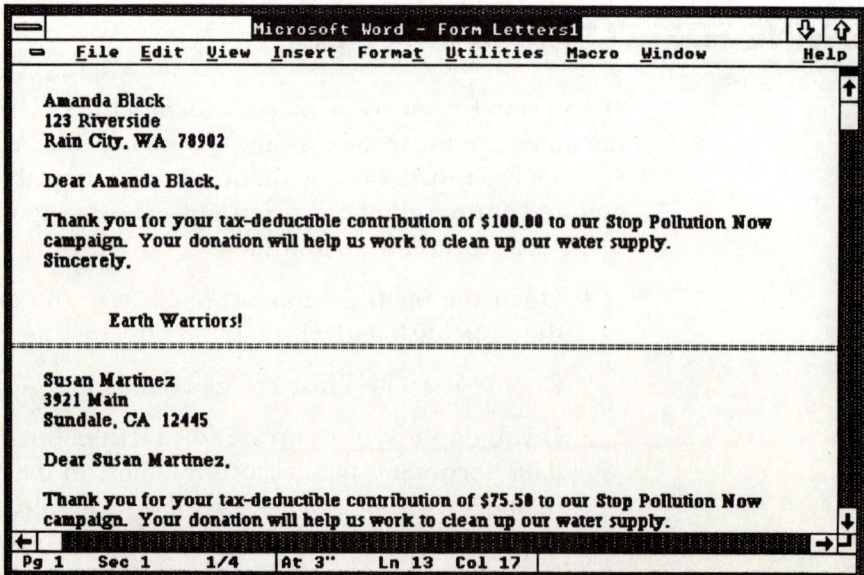

in a dialog box as a prompt. Figure 23–8 shows how a main document uses an ASK instruction to fill in its Grand_Prize field.

You can also use multiple ASK instructions to fill in all fields, eliminating the need for a data document. Figure 23–9 shows a main document that uses only ASK instructions to fill in its fields.

Figure 23–8.
If you use the ASK instruction, Word prompts you for information to enter in the fields.

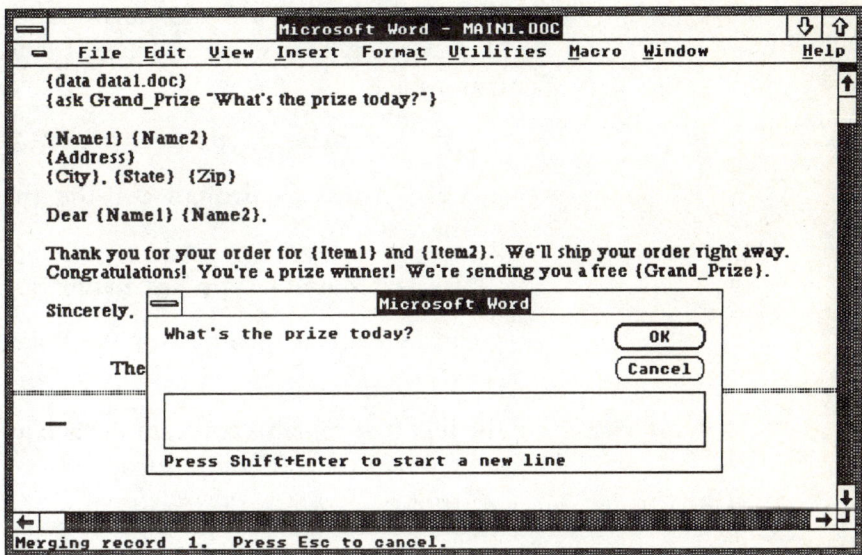

Figure 23–9.
A document that uses ASK to fill in all fields.

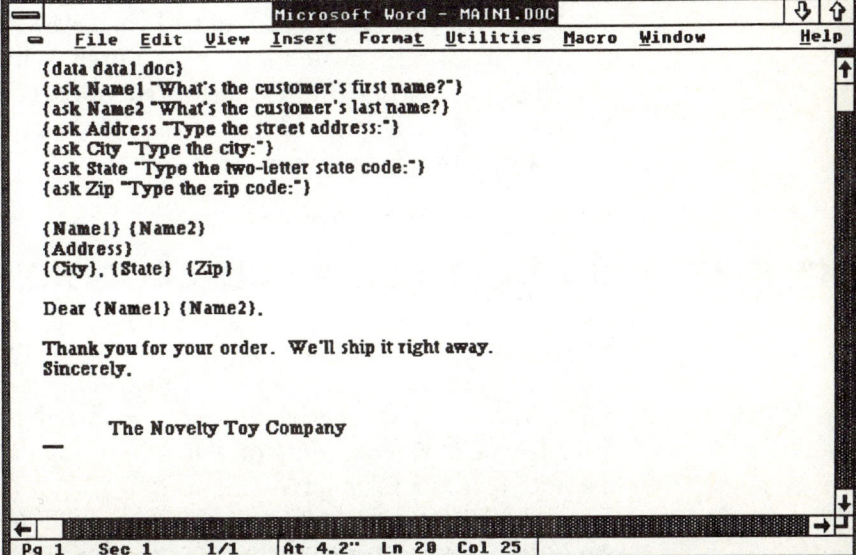

To create and use a main document that asks you for information:

1. Type fields containing ASK instructions at the beginning of the main document, using the following guidelines:

   ■ Put the ASK instructions after the DATA instruction if you're merging information from a data document.

   ■ If you want Word to use your answers to fill in the specified field in all form letters, type \o after the text in the ASK field. For example,

   > {ask first_prize "Type first prize:" \o}

   causes Word to prompt for the first prize only once, whereas

   > {ask last_name "Type last name:"}

   causes Word to prompt for the last name for each form letter.

2. Type the text that remains constant in each letter and insert fields that will contain the variable information.

3. Choose the Print Merge command.

4. Choose Print to print the form letters or choose New Document to save the form letters in a file.

5. When Word displays the text in each ASK instruction, type the information requested and press **Enter**. When Word has filled in all of the fields with the ASK instructions, it creates the first form letter, then (if you didn't use the \o switch) it displays the ASK instructions for the next form letter.

INCLUDING IF CLAUSES FOR VARIABLE CONDITIONS

If you want to print a field's contents in a form letter only when certain conditions are met, you can use IF instructions.

You can use several variations of IF instructions when you want Word to check the contents of a field in your data document before inserting text in a form letter. Figure 23–10 shows a sample document that uses several types of IF instructions. These instructions are explained in greater detail in the following sections.

Figure 23–10.
IF instructions in a
main document.

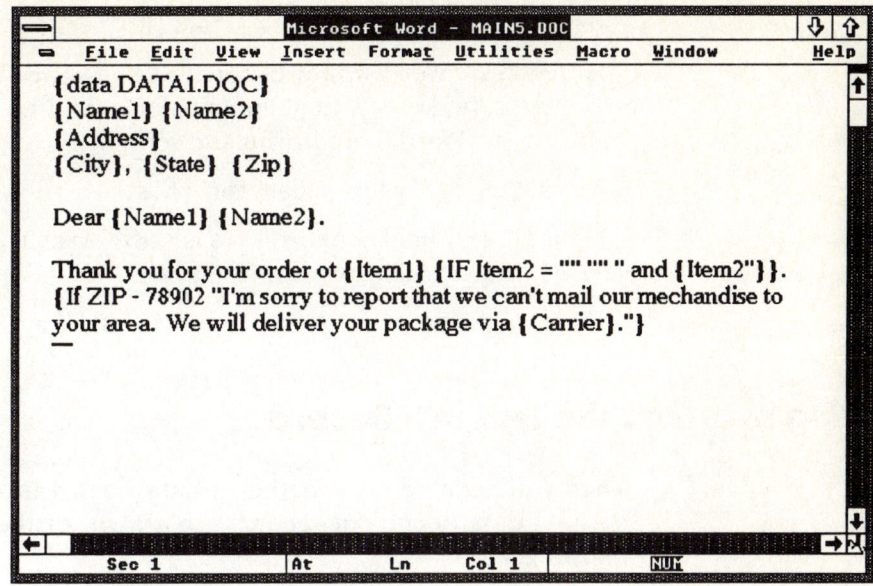

You can use an IF clause in three ways:

- to test whether a field exists in the data document

- to test whether text in a field matches text you specify in the IF clause

- to test whether numbers in a field match numbers you specify in the IF clause

Testing for Empty Fields

When you want to see whether a field is empty or contains text in a data document record, you use a form of the IF clause that looks like the following:

{if *field_name* = "" "" "*text to print*"}

Each set of quotation marks means "no text." Here's an example of when you might use this type of IF clause: You're using print merge to mail confirmation of orders and you don't know if one or two items have been ordered, so you tell Word "if there's text in the {Item2} item, print that text here." To do this, use an IF clause in your main document that looks like this:

Thank you for your order for {Item1}{if Item2 = "" "" " and {Item2}"}.

Here's how Word would deal with this clause. When Word checks a record, if the {Item1} field contains skis and there's nothing in the {Item2} item, Word would print the sentence

Thank you for your order for skis.

If the {Item1} field contains skis and the {Item2} field contains kayak paddles, Word would print the sentence

Thank you for your order for skis and kayak paddles.

Using IF to Test the Text in a Record

When you want to see whether a data record field contains specific text in a data document record, use a form of the IF clause like the following:

{if *field_name* = "*text to match*" "*text to print*"}

Be sure to place the "*text to match*" in double quotation marks. For example, when you use print merge to mail confirmation of orders and want to include a sentence only if the customer has ordered a certain item, you can tell Word if the {Item1} field contains "snowshoes," print "We're sorry to inform you that we cannot ship snowshoes until October 1st." You'd do this with an IF clause in your main document that might look something like this:

Thank you for your order for {Item1}. {if Item1 = "snowshoes" "We're sorry to inform you that we cannot ship snowshoes until October 1st."}

Here's how Word would deal with this clause. When Word checks a record, if the {Item1} field contains water skis, Word prints

Thank you for your order for water skis.

If the {Item1} field contains snowshoes, Word prints

Thank you for your order for snowshoes. We're sorry to inform you that we cannot ship snowshoes until October 1st.

Using IF to Test Numbers in a Record

To check whether a data record field contains a specific number in a data document record, use a form of the IF clause like the following:

{if *field_name* = *number* "*text to print*"}

You can also use the following symbols in place of the equal sign to test for numbers:

Comparison	Symbol to type
greater than	>
less than	<
not equal to	<>
greater than or equal to	>=
less than or equal to	<=

For example, when you're using print merge to mail confirmation of orders and want to include a sentence only if the customer has ordered a certain item, you might want to tell Word if the {Number1} field contains a number greater than or equal to 12, print "You qualify for our Baker's Dozen bonus—with each order of 12 or more, we give you an extra one free!" You'd do this with an IF clause in your main document like that in sentence two here:

Thank you for your order for {Number1} {Item1}. {if Number1 >= 12 "You qualify for our Baker's Dozen bonus--with each order of 12 or more, we give you an extra one free!"}

When Word deals with this clause, it checks a record; if the {Number1} field contains 6 and the {Item1} field contains footballs, Word prints

Thank you for your order for 6 footballs.

If the {Number1} field contains 12 and the {Item1} field contains footballs, Word prints

Thank you for your order for 12 footballs. You qualify for our Baker's Dozen bonus--with each order of 12 or more, we give you an extra one free!

Adding an "Else" Clause

The IF clauses described in the preceding sections instruct Word to print something only if a field matches certain conditions. There may be occasions when you want Word to print one phrase if one condition is met and print another phrase if the condition is not met. In that case, you'd use an IF clause in the following general form:

```
{if field = data "text to print if true" "text to print if
false"}
```

For example, you might want to tell Word if the {State} field in the data record is equal to OK, print "The shipping fee is $3.50."; otherwise, print "The shipping fee is $4.00." To do this, you'd write an IF statement like this:

```
{if State = "OK" "The shipping fee is $3.50." "The shipping
fee is $4.00."}
```

To deal with this clause, Word checks a record; if the {State} field contains any text but OK, Word prints

```
The shipping fee is $4.00.
```

If the {State} field contains OK, Word prints

```
The shipping fee is $3.50.
```

Nesting IF Instructions

When you want to test a field to see if it meets several conditions, you can nest IF instructions, like this:

```
{if field_name = first text or number {if field_name = sec-
ond text or number "text to print"}}
```

For example, you might want to tell Word if the {Number1} field is less than 10 and if the {Item1} field contains horse halters, print "You must order a minimum of 10 horse halters." You'd write an IF statement like this:

```
{If Number1 <10 {if Item1 = "horse halters" "You must order
a minimum of 10 horse halters."}}
```

To deal with this clause, Word checks a record; if the {Number1} field contains 10 or any greater number, Word simply skips the rest of the IF clause and adds nothing to the form letter.

If the {Number1} field contains a number less than 10, Word checks the {Item1} field. If {Item1} does not contain horse halters, Word adds nothing to the form letter.

If the {Number1} field contains a number less than 10 and {Item1} contains `horse halters`, Word prints the following phrase in the form letter:

```
You must order a minimum of 10 horse halters.
```

PRINTING SELECTED RECORDS IN A DATA DOCUMENT

If you want to print form letters only if records in your data document meet certain conditions, you can use a SKIPIF instruction, like this:

```
{skipif field_name = "text" or number}
```

You can also use math symbols other than an equal sign—such as <, >, <>, and so on—to specify the condition in the SKIPIF clause. A SKIPIF instruction should be the second paragraph in your main document, right after the DATA instruction field. This instruction tells Word to go on to the next record if the specified field does not meet the condition.

For example, you might want to print letters for those records that contain only the 98126 zip code. To do this, you'd write a SKIPIF instruction similar to

```
{skipif Zip <> 98126}
```

This tells Word to check the {Zip} field in each data record. If the field does not contain (is not equal to) 98126, Word goes on to the next record in the data document. If the record's {Zip} field contains 98126, Word prints a form letter using the information in that record.

SUPPLYING INFORMATION FOR A FIELD

If you want to supply information for a field in your main document instead of merging it in from the data document, you can use a SET instruction. You might want to keep only a mailing list in the data document, and put the other variable information in your main document. For example, say you are using print merge to produce requests for donations for a nonprofit organization. You can type information for Word to put into a field in the form letters in a SET instruction at the top of the main document, as shown in Figure 23–11.

You can use combinations of SET and ASK instructions in a main document to create form letters without using a data document.

Figure 23–11.
This SET instruction
supplies information
for a field in the
main document.

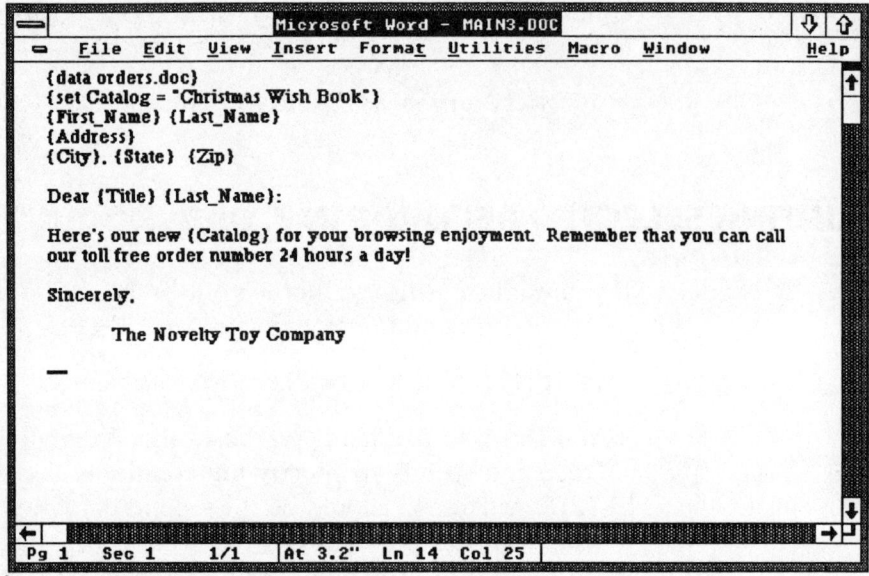

```
{data orders.doc}
{set Catalog = "Christmas Wish Book"}
{First_Name} {Last_Name}
{Address}
{City}, {State}  {Zip}

Dear {Title} {Last_Name}:

Here's our new {Catalog} for your browsing enjoyment.  Remember that you can call
our toll free order number 24 hours a day!

Sincerely,

        The Novelty Toy Company
```

INSERTING ANOTHER DOCUMENT

When you want to insert another document into a form letter, you can use the INCLUDE instruction. The basic form of the INCLUDE instruction is

{include *filename*}

You can use the INCLUDE instruction anywhere in your main document that you want to include another document. For example, if you are soliciting magazine subscriptions, you can keep your subscription form in a separate file and type an instruction like the following where you want to insert the form:

{**include SUBSCRIP.FRM**}

You can combine the INCLUDE statement with an IF clause to test the value of a field before you insert a document, like this:

{**if Contribution > 100 {include GOLDCLUB.DOC}}**

If the file you want to include is in a different directory or on a different drive, be sure to include a pathname with double backslashes: {**include a:\\FORMS\\GOLDCLUB.DOC}**. You can also use the IN-CLUDE instruction to merge specific parts of other documents, as described in Chapter 21, "Using Bookmarks."

MERGING MULTIPLE RECORDS INTO ONE DOCUMENT

Normally, Word prints one form for each record in a data file. However, there may be times when you want Word to print the information from all records on one copy of the form document. To do this, you insert a NEXT instruction ({next}) whenever you want Word to go on to the next record.

The most common usage of the NEXT instruction is to create a sheet of address labels. This use of the NEXT instruction is shown in Figure 23–12.

CREATING ADDRESS LABELS

You can use the processes described in the previous section, Merging Multiple Records into One Document, to create address labels by setting up a main document as an address label document. The tricky aspect of creating an address label document is to space addresses appropriately so that they print correctly on a sheet of stick-on labels. The basic idea is to create rows and columns of addresses that match the positions of the labels on the sheet. You can set tabs to create a table of addresses, like this:

Figure 23–12.
Using a NEXT instruction to merge multiple records into one document.

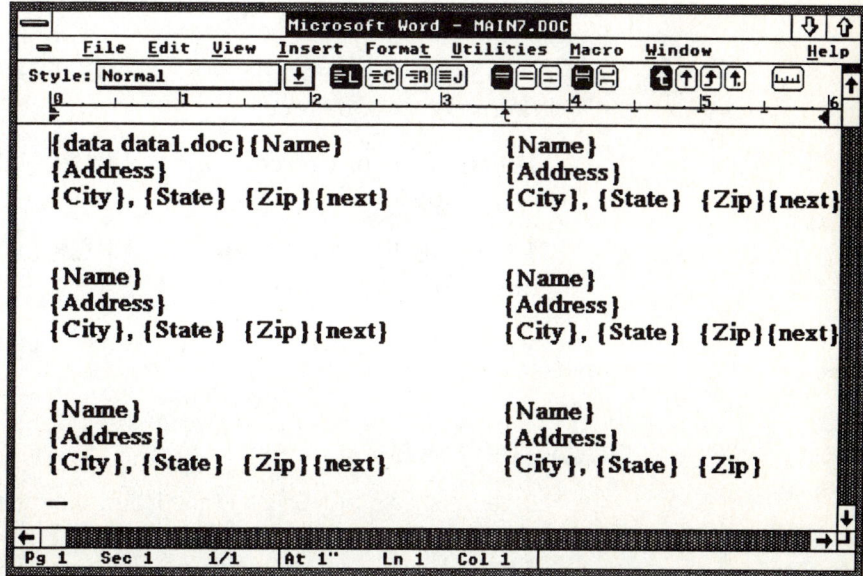

Name1	Name5
Address1	Address5
Name2	Name6
Address2	Address6
Name3	Name7
Address3	Address7
Name4	Name8
Address4	Address8

Using Templates to Create Address Labels

Word includes five document templates to create address labels. To use one of them:

1. Choose the File New command.

2. Select the template for the labels you want to print.

If you want to print	Use
1-inch labels in two columns, one sheet at a time	LBL2COL.DOT.
1-inch labels in three columns, one sheet at a time	LBL3COL.DOT.
1-inch labels in a single column, continuous feed	LBL1COLT.DOT.
1-inch labels in two columns, continuous feed	LBL2COLT.DOT.
1-inch labels in three columns, continuous feed	LBL3COLT.DOT.

The Word *User's Reference* also has some suggestions for printing labels.

▭ *Helpful Hint*

Because sheets of labels and the labels themselves vary in size, you'll probably need to experiment a little to create perfect labels. To avoid wasting expensive sheets of labels, do one of the following:

- Draw a grid that matches the label sheet, make copies, then use these as test sheets to see whether the labels print within the gridlines.

   or

- Print the labels on plain paper, then hold the paper up to a light source with the label sheet behind it to check their alignment.

Sorting Data Records

When you have a list of names or numbers, such as a mailing list, you don't have to arrange them yourself—you can use Word to sort the list.

In tables or in columns separated by tabs, you can choose to use any column or row as a sorting key. Word rearranges all rows in the table based on the sorting-key column. For example, in the following table, you might choose to do an alphabetic sort based on the first column of names, or you might choose to do a numeric sort based on the second column of salary figures:

NAME	SALARY
Gorgios	54,500
Alessandro	51,350
Callahan	52,448
Foster	67,112

Sorting Outside of Tables

To sort a list in which the items are separated by tab characters or commas:

1. If the items are separated by tab characters, position the insertion point at the beginning of the column you want to use as a sorting key, press **Ctrl+Shift+F8** to turn on Column Select mode, then select the column.

2. Choose the Utilities Sort command.

3. Choose the following options from the dialog box:

To	Do this
Sort in ascending order (A–Z or 1–9)	Choose Ascending in the Sort Order box.
Sort in descending order (Z–A or 9–1)	Choose Descending in the Sort Order box.
Sort alphabetically	Select Alphanumeric from the Key Type list.
Sort numerically	Select Numeric from the Key Type list.
Sort by date items	Select Date from the Key Type list.
Specify the separator character used in the records	Choose Tab or Comma.
Specify the field to use as a sorting key when items are separated by commas and you want to sort using a field other than the first field as a sorting key	In the Field Number box, type the number of the field in the list (for example, type **3** to use third field as the sorting key.
To rearrange only the items in the selected column, leaving all other items in the same position (you will rarely, if ever, use this option)	Turn on the Sort Only Column option.
To make uppercase letters precede lowercase letters	Turn on the Case Selection option.

4. Click OK or press **Enter**. Figure 23–13 illustrates sorting a list outside of a table.

You can also sort whole paragraphs of data, such as a list of names in which each line ends with a paragraph mark, like this:

Johnson, Bill¶

Baker, Holly¶

Chung, Samson¶

Figure 23–13.
A list sorted outside
of a table.

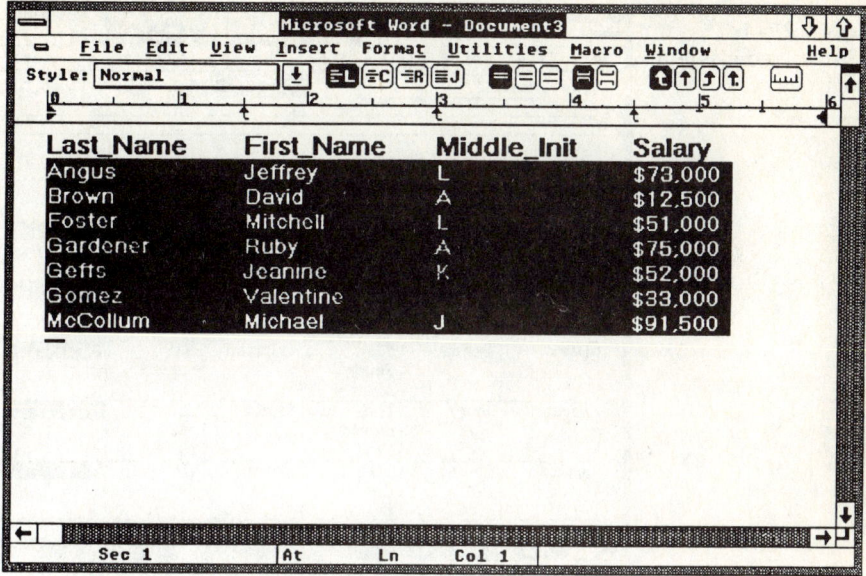

When sorting paragraphs of information, Word uses the first character in the paragraph to put the items in order.

If you don't like the results of your sort, choose the Edit Undo command immediately.

Sorting in Tables

To sort a list in a table:

1. Select the column to use as a sorting key.

2. Choose the Utilities Sort command.

3. Choose the following options from the dialog box:

To	Do this
Sort in ascending order (A–Z or 1–9)	Choose Ascending in the Sort Order box.
Sort in descending order (Z–A or 9–1)	Choose Descending in the Sort Order box.
Sort alphabetically	Select Alphanumeric from the Key Type list.

Figure 23-14.
A list sorted inside a table.

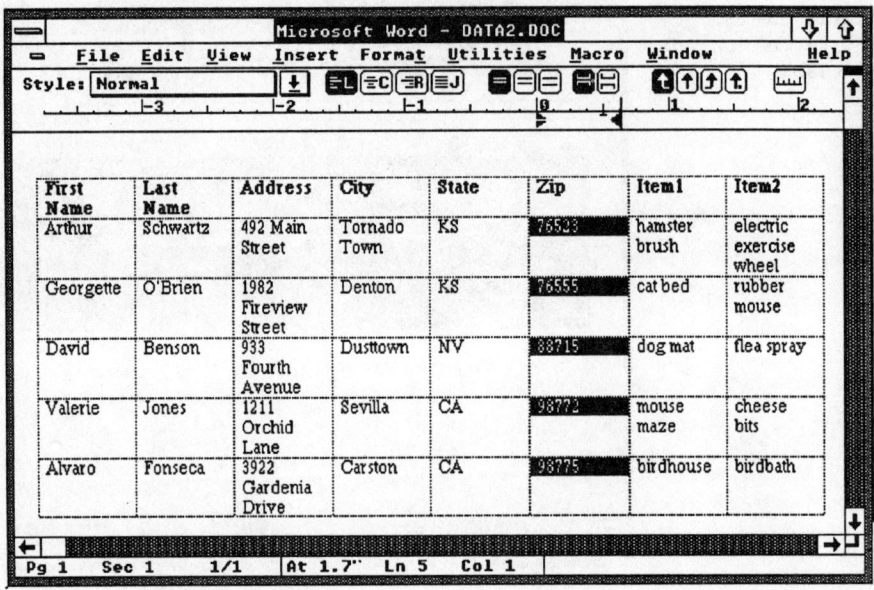

First Name	Last Name	Address	City	State	Zip	Item1	Item2
Arthur	Schwartz	492 Main Street	Tornado Town	KS	76533	hamster brush	electric exercise wheel
Georgette	O'Brien	1982 Fireview Street	Denton	KS	76555	cat bed	rubber mouse
David	Benson	933 Fourth Avenue	Dusttown	NV	88715	dog mat	flea spray
Valerie	Jones	1211 Orchid Lane	Sevilla	CA	98772	mouse maze	cheese bits
Alvaro	Fonseca	3922 Gardenia Drive	Carston	CA	98775	birdhouse	birdbath

Sort numerically	Select Numeric from the Key Type list.
Sort by date fields	Select Date from the Key Type list.
To rearrange only the items in the selected column, leaving all other items in the same position (you will rarely, if ever, use this option)	Turn on the Sort Only Column option.
To make uppercase letters precede lowercase letters	Turn on the Case Selection option.

4. Click OK or press **Enter**. Figure 23-14 illustrates sorting a list in a table.

If you don't like the results, choose the Edit Undo command immediately.

## Chapter Twenty-Four

Using the Document Retrieval System

Word has a very sophisticated document retrieval system to keep track of all of your documents. You can easily locate a specific document or quickly list a series of documents that deal with the same subject, have the same author, were created on the same day, or that share almost any common element you can think of.

For example, say you produce a number of documents dealing with varied subjects in your advertising business. When you need to locate all documents about client presentations, you can't remember all the filenames. Say you also need to find all of the documents written by a single person in the company, as well as all of those written by an individual before a certain date. Using the searching and sorting features of Word's document retrieval system, you can easily list all the appropriate documents.

You can use the document retrieval system to

- locate documents by telling Word to look for text, author's name, creation date, last revision date, or other criteria you can specify.

- print or delete a group of documents with one command.

- sort a list of files according to creation or revision dates, author's or operator's name, or file size.

This chapter shows you how to use the document retrieval system.

HOW THE DOCUMENT RETRIEVAL SYSTEM WORKS

When you want to locate one or more documents, you use the File Find command, which displays the dialog box shown in Figure 24–1.

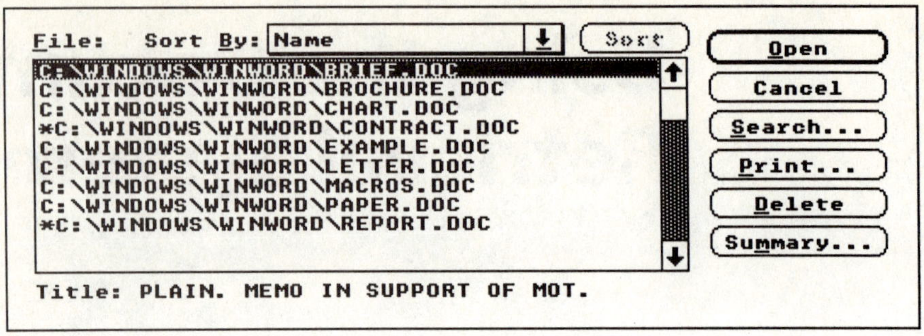

Figure 24–1.
The File Find dialog box is the key to Word's document retrieval system.

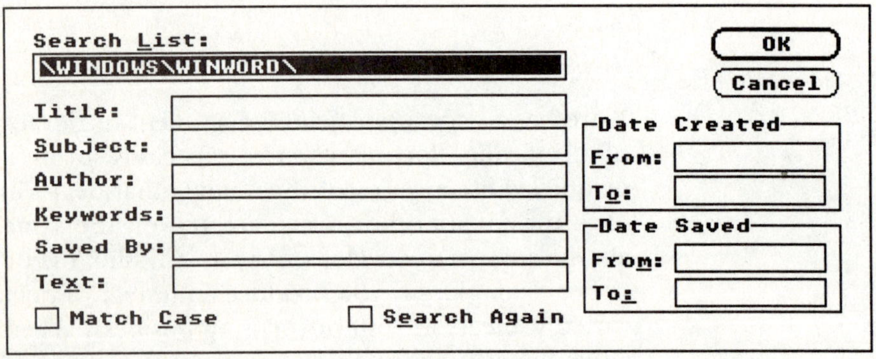

```
File:   Sort By: Name              ↓    ( Sort )      ( Open )
C:\WINDOWS\WINWORD\BRIEF.DOC          ↑          ( Cancel )
C:\WINDOWS\WINWORD\BROCHURE.DOC
C:\WINDOWS\WINWORD\CHART.DOC                     ( Search... )
*C:\WINDOWS\WINWORD\CONTRACT.DOC
C:\WINDOWS\WINWORD\EXAMPLE.DOC                   ( Print... )
C:\WINDOWS\WINWORD\LETTER.DOC
C:\WINDOWS\WINWORD\MACROS.DOC                    ( Delete )
C:\WINDOWS\WINWORD\PAPER.DOC
*C:\WINDOWS\WINWORD\REPORT.DOC                   ( Summary... )
                                      ↓

Title: PLAIN. MEMO IN SUPPORT OF MOT.
```

Figure 24–2.
The Search dialog box.

```
Search List:                                    ( OK )
\WINDOWS\WINWORD\                                ( Cancel )

Title:   [_____]     ┌─Date Created─┐
Subject: [_____]     From: [_____]
Author:  [_____]     To:   [_____]
Keywords:[_____]
Saved By:[_____]     ┌─Date Saved───┐
Text:    [_____]     From: [_____]
☐ Match Case    ☐ Search Again  To:   [_____]
```

The first time you use the File Find command, Word makes a list of all files with .DOC extensions in all directories on the active drive. It may take Word a while to collect the entire list, so be patient. When you use the File Find command again, Word quickly lists files from the previous search.

Word initially lists directories and files in alphabetic order, but you can sort the list any way you want. See Sorting the List of Files later in this chapter for more information.

SEARCHING FOR DOCUMENTS

To search for a single document or a list of documents, you use the Search button in the File Find dialog box to specify a path to search and to tell Word what you're looking for: a certain author, revision date, key words or phrases. Word displays the dialog box shown in Figure 24–2 for you to enter your search criteria.

Word compares text you type in the Title, Subject, Author, Keywords, and Saved By boxes with the same information in a document's

Summary Information dialog box. So if you didn't fill out these fields in the Summary Information dialog boxes, you can't use them as search criteria. See Filling Out Summary Information Dialog Boxes later in this chapter for more information about filling out that dialog box.

You can use the following symbols to set up your search criteria.

Symbol	Meaning	Example
?	Any one character	part?.doc means search for file-names that begin with *part* followed by a single character, and end with the .DOC extension (part1.doc, part3.doc, parts.doc)
*	Any number of characters	Jon* means search for any word beginning with *Jon* followed by any number of characters (Jonathan, Jones, Jonson)
^	Treat next character as text	^? means search for a question mark, ^* means search for an asterisk, ^^ means search for a caret character (^)
& or space	AND	Juanita Smith or Juanita&Smith means search for documents that contain both *Juanita* and *Smith*
, (comma)	OR	Coffee, Chocolate means search for documents that contain either *Coffee* or *Chocolate*
~ (tilde)	NOT	Data~Database means search for *Data,* not for *Database*

Word searches for documents that match *all* the information in the dialog box. In other words, if you type **\COOKBKS,\ARTICLES** in the Search List box, type **Nguyen** in the Author box, and type **Vietnamese cooking** in the Text box, Word lists only those documents in the \COOKBKS and \ARTICLES directories that were written by Nguyen and that also contain the words *Vietnamese cooking* within the text. So before you tell Word to begin searching, make sure that all the text in the dialog box is correct.

Note: Word may not find specific text (words you type in the Text box) in files that were saved using the Fast Save option of the File Save command. Word displays an asterisk before the names of files saved with the Fast Save format in the File Find dialog box.

To search for documents:

1. Choose the File Find command.

2. Choose Search.

3. Type the information you want to search for. You can fill in as many boxes as you like.

Box	Type
Search List	One or more drive letters and directories to search, separated by commas, like this: c:\Word\Legal,b:\Word\Invoices
Title Subject Author Keywords Saved By	Text used in the Title, Subject, Author, Keywords, or Saved By boxes of the document's Summary Information dialog box or Statistics box
Text	Any text used in the file
Date Created From	The earliest creation date to search for; leave blank to list all files created before the "To" date
Date Created To	The latest creation date to search for; leave blank to list all files created after the "From" date
Date Saved From	The earliest save date to search for; leave blank to list all files saved before the "To" date
Date Saved To	The latest save date to search for; leave blank to list all files saved after the "From" date

4. If you filled in the Text box and you want Word to search for the exact combination of upper and lowercase letters you typed there, turn on the Match Case option. Turn this option off if you want Word to match only the letters, not the case.

5. Choose Search. Word closes the Search dialog box and looks for documents that match the criteria you typed in the dialog box. While searching, Word displays a message box that tells you how many documents are being searched and how many match the criteria. Then Word displays a list of documents that match that criteria in the File Find dialog box, as shown in Figure 24–3.

You can select documents from the list and open them, print them, delete them, or review their summary information sheets. See the appropriate section later in this chapter for instructions on how to do these tasks.

SORTING THE LIST OF FILES

You can choose the order for the list of files in the File Find dialog box by sorting the list.

To sort the list of files:

1. In the File Find dialog box, select an option from the Sort By drop-down list (shown in Figure 24–4):

Option	Description
Name	Sorts alphabetically by filename, from A to Z
Author	Sorts alphabetically by author's name, from A to Z

Figure 24–3.
Word displays a list of documents that match the search criteria.

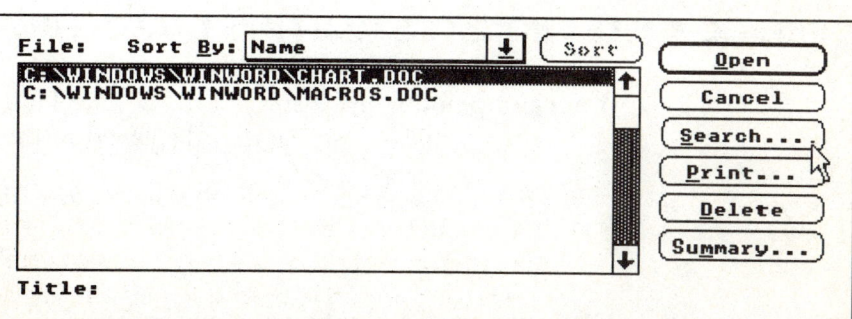

Figure 24–4.
The option selected
in the Sort By drop-
down list controls
the order of the list.

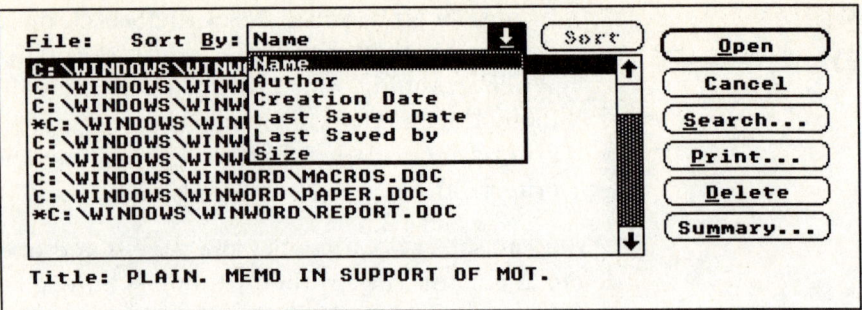

Creation Date	Sorts chronologically by creation date, beginning with the file created most recently
Last Saved Date	Sorts chronologically by save date, beginning with the file saved most recently
Last Saved by	Sorts alphabetically by person's name, from A to Z
Size	Sorts numerically by file size, beginning with the smallest file

2. Choose Sort.

The selected Sort By option affects the message Word displays at the bottom of the dialog box. When you select a file in the list, the message gives appropriate information about the file: the file's size if you sorted by Size, the file's author if you sorted by Author, the file's creation date if you sorted by Creation Date, and so forth.

OPENING A FILE FROM THE FILE FIND DIALOG BOX

You can open any file displayed in the File Find list.

To open a file whose name is displayed in the File Find list:

■ Highlight the filename in the dialog box, then press **Enter**.

or

■ Double-click the filename in the list.

PRINTING DOCUMENTS USING THE DOCUMENT RETRIEVAL SYSTEM

You can print several documents, several Summary Information dialog boxes, or both Summary Information dialog boxes and documents at once using the document retrieval system.

To print documents whose names are displayed in the File Find dialog box:

1. Choose the File Find command.

2. If necessary, use the Search function to display a list of appropriate documents as described in Searching for Documents earlier in this chapter.

3. Select the files you want to print. To select several, hold down the **Shift** key and click the filenames, as shown in Figure 24–5.

4. Choose Print. Word displays the File Print dialog box.

5. Do one of the following:

   ■ To print only the document(s), click OK or press **Enter**.

   or

   ■ To print both the summary information and the document(s), choose Options, turn on the Summary Info option in the Include box, then click OK or press **Enter**.

DELETING DOCUMENTS USING THE DOCUMENT RETRIEVAL SYSTEM

If you have a lot of old files to remove from your system, you can use the document retrieval system to select multiple files and delete them with one command.

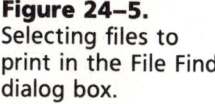

Figure 24–5.
Selecting files to print in the File Find dialog box.

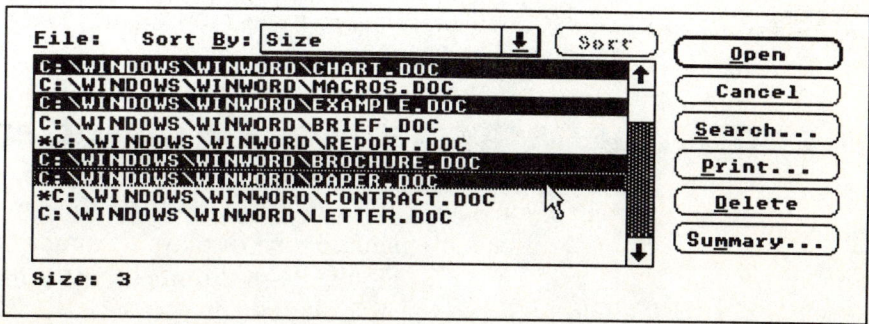

To delete documents whose names are displayed in the File Find dialog box:

1. Choose the File Find command.

2. If necessary, use the Search function to display a list of appropriate documents, as described in Searching for Documents earlier in this chapter.

3. Select the documents you want to delete. To select more than one, hold down the **Shift** key and click the document names.

4. Choose Delete. Just to be sure that you mean it, Word displays a message asking whether you want to delete the files.

5. Click Yes or type **Y**. Word erases the files and removes the names from the list.

DISPLAYING SUMMARY INFORMATION FOR FILES IN THE FILE FIND DIALOG BOX

To display summary information about a document whose name is displayed in the File Find dialog box:

1. Choose the File Find command.

2. If necessary, use the Search function to display a list of appropriate documents, as described in Searching for Documents earlier in this chapter.

3. Select the document's name in the list.

4. Choose Summary. Word displays the Summary Information dialog box on top of the File Find dialog box.

5. When you're finished reading the Summary Information dialog box, click OK or press **Enter**.

FILLING OUT SUMMARY INFORMATION DIALOG BOXES

When you save a document for the first time in Word or save a file under a new file name, Word displays a Summary Information dialog box, as shown in Figure 24–6. Summary information can be used to help you

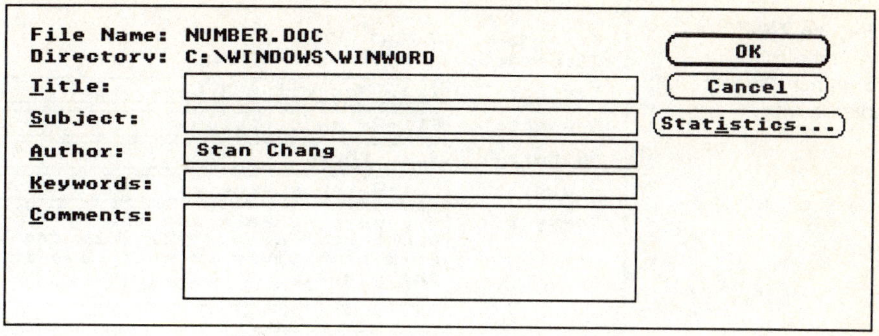

Figure 24–6.
An incomplete
Summary Information
dialog box.

```
File Name: NUMBER.DOC
Directory: C:\WINDOWS\WINWORD                    (    OK    )
Title:     [                              ]      ( Cancel  )
Subject:   [                              ]      (Statistics...)
Author:    [ Stan Chang                   ]
Keywords:  [                              ]
Comments:  [                              ]
           [                              ]
           [                              ]
```

- recall the contents of and details about a document, including when it was worked on, who worked on it, and how long the work took.

- locate a document using the document retrieval system.

You can record information about the current file that helps you identify the file at a future date. You can type the title for the file, fill in the subject and the author, add keywords and comments. If you decide that you don't want to use the Summary Information dialog box to supply additional information, you can tell Word not to automatically display the dialog box in this way:

1. Choose the Utilities Customize command.

2. Turn off the Prompt for Summary Info option.

3. Click OK or press **Enter**.

Because much of the information you use to search for documents comes from the Summary Information dialog boxes, you'll need to have a good understanding of what types of information you can enter and how you can use that information later. Figure 24–7 shows a Summary Information dialog box that has been filled out. You can type up to 255 characters in all the boxes. Here's a description of what you enter in the boxes:

In the box	Type this
Title	A descriptive title for the document.
Subject	A description of the document's contents.

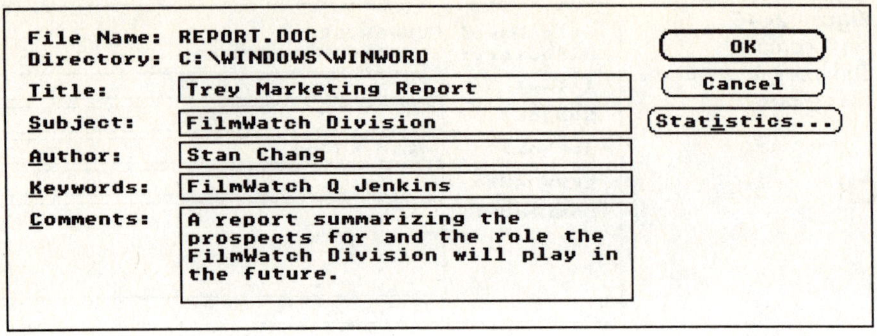

Figure 24–7.
A completed
Summary Information
dialog box.

```
File Name: REPORT.DOC                              ( OK )
Directory: C:\WINDOWS\WINWORD                       ( Cancel )
Title:     Trey Marketing Report
Subject:   FilmWatch Division                     ( Statistics... )
Author:    Stan Chang
Keywords:  FilmWatch Q Jenkins
Comments:  A report summarizing the
           prospects for and the role the
           FilmWatch Division will play in
           the future.
```

Author	The name of the person who created the document. Word suggests the name of the person who originally used the program, but you can change this if necessary.
Keywords	Words or phrases that help in identifying this document. If you want to keep track of all documents that involved a certain customer, product, legal case, or other topic, you can type the customer name, product name, legal case name, or words to identify a certain topic.
Comments	Any further information you want to add to clarify the document. For example, you might type something like "This letter responds to a query from the IRS about our fiscal year."

EDITING SUMMARY INFORMATION

When you revise a file, Word doesn't automatically display the Summary Information dialog box. If you want to edit any of the other fields or add new information, use the following procedure.

To edit the summary information for a file:

1. Choose the Edit Summary Info command. Word displays the Summary Information dialog box for the document containing the insertion point.

2. Edit or add new information to the Summary Information dialog box.

3. Click OK or press **Enter**.

CHECKING THE STATISTICS ABOUT A FILE

You can use the Edit Summary Info command to display a Statistics panel about your document, like the one shown in Figure 24–8. The Statistics panel lists:

- the file's name and directory

- the template name (if any) and title (if any) of the file

- the creation date

- the date and time the file was last saved, followed by an indication of who saved it

- the revision number

- the total editing time

- the date and time the file was last printed

- number of pages in the file at the last save

- number of words in the file at the last save

- number of characters in the file at the last save

To check the statistics for a document:

1. Choose the Edit Summary Info command.

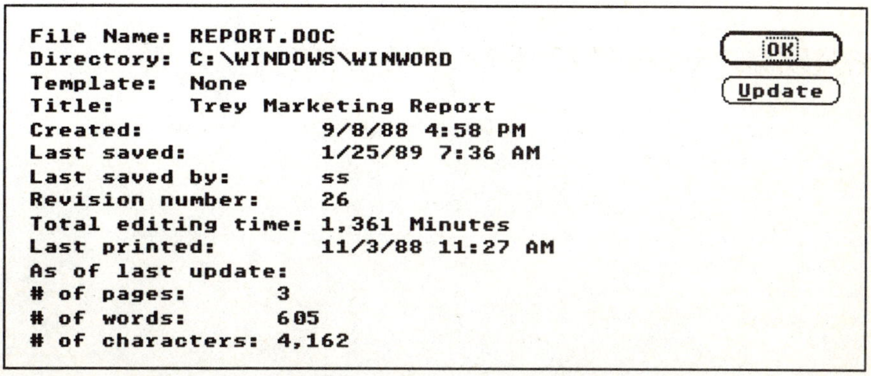

Figure 24–8.
A Statistics panel.

```
File Name: REPORT.DOC                              ( OK )
Directory: C:\WINDOWS\WINWORD
Template:  None                                    ( Update )
Title:     Trey Marketing Report
Created:            9/8/88 4:58 PM
Last saved:         1/25/89 7:36 AM
Last saved by:      ss
Revision number:    26
Total editing time: 1,361 Minutes
Last printed:       11/3/88 11:27 AM
As of last update:
# of pages:      3
# of words:      605
# of characters: 4,162
```

2. Choose Statistics.

3. To make sure the statistics are up to date, choose Update. Word repaginates the document, counts the words, and updates the statistics.

Part VI

CUSTOMIZING WORD

If you don't like the current default settings Word uses, you can change many of the aspects of Word to make it fit the way you work. This part of the book shows you how.

Chapter 25 introduces you to Word's macros. You'll see how to write your own macros to make Word do your repetitive tasks for you. It's as easy as recording a tape.

In Chapter 26, you'll see how you can change the default units of measurement Word uses, as well as many other default settings. You'll see how to add and subtract commands from menus, how to assign commands to keys, and how to change the Word screen to your liking.

Using Macros

Have you ever wished that you could automate word-processing tasks that you repeat frequently? For example, you may format bulleted lists often in your documents, entering the correct ANSI or IBM PC character code for bullets, then formatting the paragraphs and setting tabs to produce hanging indents. With Word, you can record these actions one time as a macro—and for all subsequent bulleted lists you can click a mouse button or press a key combination, then sit back and watch Word do all of the steps for you.

A *macro* is a set of commands, keystrokes, and other instructions that automate repetitive or complex Word tasks. As a matter of fact, Word's commands are all macros. You can easily record your own macros to do exactly what you want. Macros can perform very simple actions, like inserting a specific set of characters, or they can contain complex instructions with programming elements such as structure and control statements and variables.

If you want your macro to be easily accessible, you can add it to a menu so you can choose it like any other command. If you're a dedicated keyboard user, you can assign a key combination to the macro so you can run it without taking your fingers off the keys.

You can create a macro to do almost anything in Word. You are limited only by your imagination. This chapter shows how to

- plan macros.

- record macros.

- run macros.

- assign macros to menus and keys.

- troubleshoot and correct macros.

- rename macros.

- delete macros.

CREATING YOUR OWN MACROS

There are two ways to create a macro:

- by recording keystrokes and commands

- by typing representations for keystrokes, commands, and instructions, using Word's macro language

Because recording a macro is much easier than using the macro language, this chapter concentrates on the recording method. (As a matter of fact, the easiest way to learn the macro language is to record several steps, then check the macro text using the procedure in Troubleshooting and Correcting Macros later in this chapter. You can also check your Word *Technical Reference* guide for more information about using the macro language.)

Recording macros is as easy as recording an audio or VCR tape. Here are the basic steps you use to create your macro.

1. Plan the steps that you want the macro to perform and choose a name for your macro.

2. Turn on the macro recorder and name the macro, perform the steps, then turn off the macro recorder.

3. Test the macro to see if it works.

4. If necessary, record the macro again or edit a written copy of it.

Planning a Macro

Before you record a macro, you should think about what you want the macro to do. Keep in mind that every action you perform is recorded. Doing a little planning up front saves time, because you improve your odds of recording the macro right the first time, instead of having to edit and re-record later.

Here are some general guidelines for planning macros:

- Don't use the mouse to select text or scroll in a macro. (When you use the macro on the next document, the macro can't know where you want to begin or end your selection.)

- It's okay to use key combinations to select or scroll if the keys select specific blocks of text (such as a paragraph or the whole document) or if they scroll to a definite location that remains the same in every document, such as the beginning or end of a document. In general, though, you'll probably find it's easier if you plan to select text before running a macro that affects it.

- Don't plan for the macro to begin a time-consuming process, such as printing or merging form letters. This takes control out of your hands. Instead, make the last step in the macro display the appropriate dialog box. Then you can turn on the printer, check other settings, and begin the process when you're ready.

You might want to write a short description of the steps you want the macro to perform, creating a script you can follow. It's also a good idea to rehearse the steps you've planned for your macro before you begin recording, just to make sure you haven't left anything out. Here are some examples of planning steps for macros:

Example: Steps for a Macro That Formats an Item in a Bulleted List

1. Use the Format Paragraph command to set the following indents for the selected paragraph:

Left indent:	1 inch
Right indent:	1 inch
First line indent	−.5 inch

2. Insert a bullet character (using the ANSI character code Alt+0183 on the numeric keypad) and a tab character in front of the selected paragraph.

Example: Steps for a Macro That Sets Up a File to Print Three Double-Spaced Copies

1. Press **Ctrl+5** on the numeric keypad to select the entire document.

2. Press **Ctrl+2** to double-space the text.

3. Choose the File Print command.

4. Type **3** in the Copies box.

Example: Steps for a Macro that Sets Up a File to Print on Letterhead Stationery That Inserts a Sheet at a Time

1. Choose the Format Document command and type **2.5in** in the Top Margin box.

2. Choose the File Printer Setup command.

3. Choose Setup, then choose Manual from the Paper Feed box.

4. Click OK or press **Enter** to return to the Printer Setup dialog box.

5. Click OK or press **Enter** to close the Printer Setup dialog box.

6. Choose the File Print command.

These are just a few very short examples of what you might plan for a macro to do. A macro can be very complex. Say, for example, you have a consistent page format you like to use from time to time: legal-size paper, 2-inch margins top and bottom, 1-inch side margins, a running head that puts the page number in italic in the middle of the top margin, and a running foot that centers the date in the bottom margin. You could record all the necessary formatting actions, then just use the mouse or press a couple of keys to make the macro format your document. Magic!

As well as deciding on the steps you want your macro to perform, you should decide on a name. The name should be descriptive so that you can remember what the macro does. Macro names must begin with a letter and can contain up to 33 characters consisting of letters and numbers (no punctuation, spaces, or formatting). Here are some examples of macro names: bulletitem, print2copies, bolditalic, letter-inverts, docformat.

Macro names must be unique, so you may want to display the Macro Run dialog box to check the list of macros in your template to make sure the name hasn't already been used. If you accidentally try to save a macro with the same name as another, Word tells you that the name has already been used.

Recording a Macro

Recording a macro is just like making a videotape of your actions—whatever you do is recorded, in exactly the same way you do it. After you've recorded the macro, you can run it to reproduce your actions, just like you would play a videotape. Word responds to the macro just as if you were performing the actions yourself.

To record a macro:

1. Choose the Macro Record command. Word displays the dialog box shown in Figure 25–1.

2. Type a name for the macro.

3. In the Context box, choose one of these options:

Choose	To
Global	Save the macro in the NORMAL.DOT template, making it available to all documents.
Template	Save the macro in the template you're using.

4. In the Description box, type a short description of the macro to remind you of what the macro does.

5. Click OK or press **Enter** to begin recording. Word displays REC in the status bar to remind you that the recorder is on.

6. Perform the actions you want to record. There's no hurry. The recorder records only when you press the keys or use the mouse, so take the time you need to think or refer to your notes.

7. When you've performed all the steps, choose the Macro Stop Recorder command.

Next, you'll want to run your macro to test it.

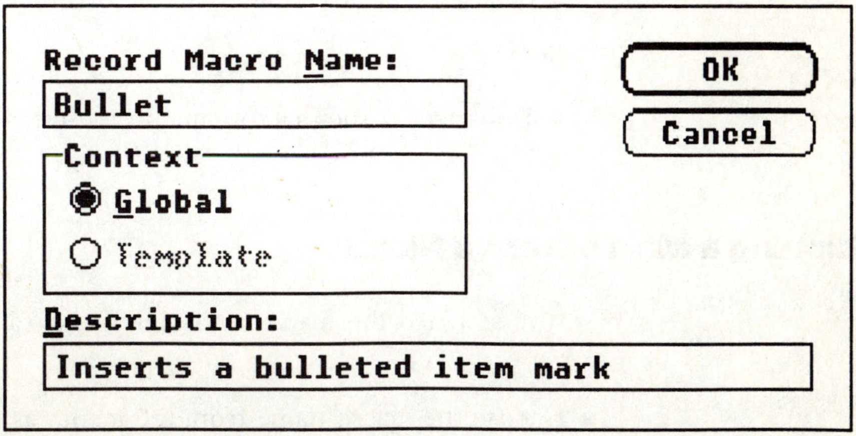

Figure 25–1.
The Macro Record dialog box.

RUNNING A MACRO

To run a macro, you can use three different procedures, depending on whether you've assigned the macro to a menu or to a key combination. The macro instructions are carried out at the insertion point, so be sure to move the insertion point or select text as necessary before you start the macro.

Helpful Hint

If you're running a macro for the first time to test it, be sure to save your document first (as a matter of fact, it's *always* a good safety measure to save your work before you run a macro). That way, if the macro does something unexpected that garbles the text, you can close the document without saving it, discarding the changes made by the macro. You could also create a test document to use for macro-testing purposes.

Choosing a Macro from a List

When you haven't assigned a macro to a menu or to a key combination, you can run it by selecting it in this way:

1. Choose the Macro Run command.

2. Do one of the following:

   ■ Select the macro name from the list, then press **Enter**.

   or

   ■ Double-click the macro name in the list.

Running a Macro from a Menu

If you've assigned the macro to a menu, you can run the macro in this way:

   ■ Choose the macro name from the menu, as in Figure 25–2.

Figure 25-2.
Running a macro
assigned to a menu.

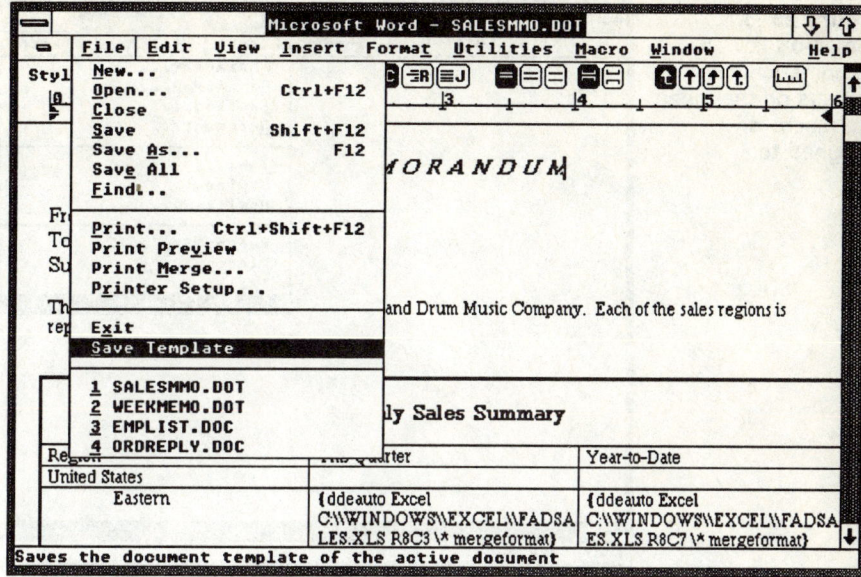

Running a Macro Using Its Key Combination

If the macro you want to run has an assigned key combination, you can run the macro without choosing a command first. If the macro is also assigned to a menu, its key combination is displayed along with its name on the menu, as shown in Figure 25-3.

To run a macro when you know its key combination:

1. Move the insertion point or select text as necessary.

2. Press the key combination.

INTERRUPTING OR CANCELING A MACRO

If you need to interrupt or cancel a macro after you've started it:

1. Press **Esc**. Word displays the message Macro Interrupted.

2. Click OK or press **Enter**.

ASSIGNING MACROS TO KEYS OR MENUS

After you've created and tested your macro, you can assign it to a menu and/or to a key combination. You don't *have* to do either of

Figure 25–3.
A macro's key
combination also
appears on the menu
the macro is
assigned to.

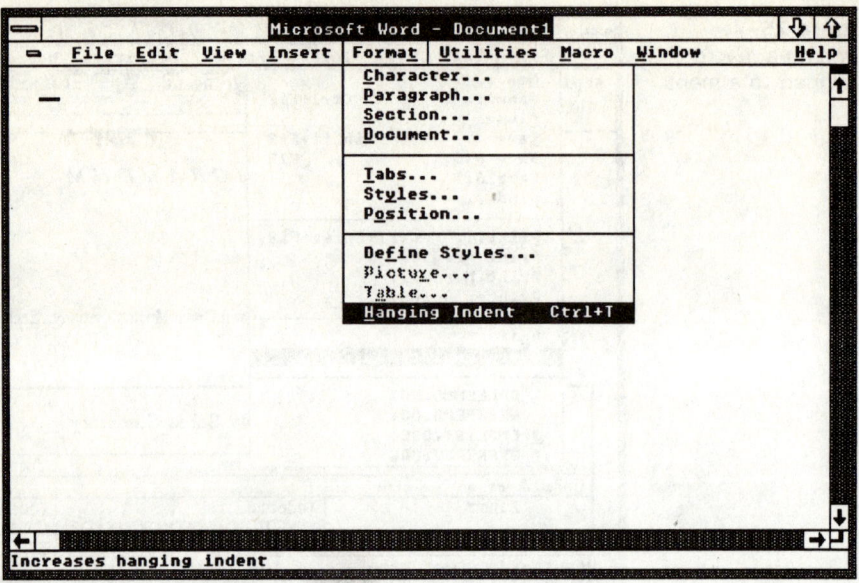

these steps, however, because you can always run macros by selecting
the macro name in the Macro Run list box.

Assigning Macros to Menus

When you assign a macro to a menu, it displays and behaves just like
a Word command.

Every command on a Word menu has an underlined letter that you
can use to choose the command from the keyboard. When you assign
a macro to a menu, you need to designate the letter in the macro
name that you want to use in this way. Word initially suggests the letter
by placing an ampersand (&) in front of a letter in the name (see the
Menu Text box in Figure 25–4). The ampersand causes an underline
to appear under the following letter when the name appears on a
menu (for example, &Zap creates the menu command Zap). You can
change the underlined letter by putting the ampersand in front of any
other letter in the macro name. Make sure, though, it doesn't conflict
with the underlined letter in any other command on that menu.

To assign a macro to a menu:

1. Choose the Macro Assign to Menu command. Word displays the
   dialog box shown in Figure 25–4.

Figure 25–4.
Adding a macro to
the Format menu.

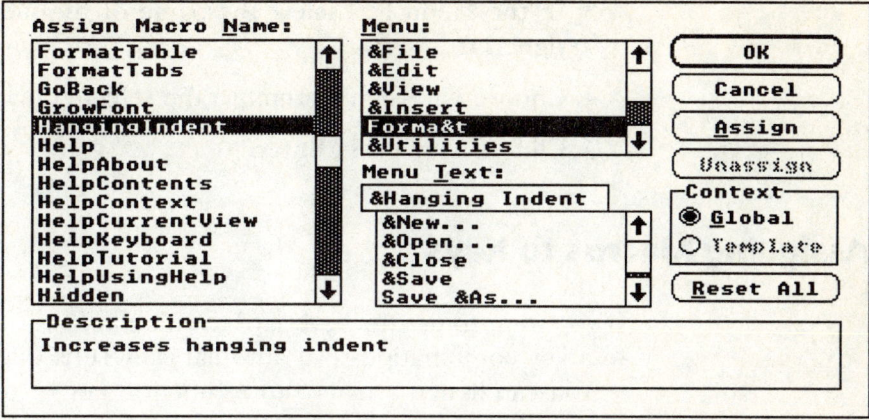

2. Select the macro name from the Assign Macro Name list.

3. Select a menu name from the Menu list.

4. In the Menu Text box, type the name that you want to appear on the menu. (Because menus have limited space, you may want to use a name that is shorter than the original name you gave to the macro.)

5. Choose one of the following options in the Context box:

Choose	To
Global	Save the assignment in the NORMAL.DOT template to make it available to all documents.
Template	Save the assignment in the template file you're using now.

6. Choose Assign to add the macro to the menu.

7. Click OK or press **Enter**.

Figure 25–4 illustrates adding a macro named Hanging Indent to the Format menu.

You can take a macro off a menu as easily as you added it. To remove a macro from a menu:

1. Choose the Macro Assign to Menu command.

2. In the Assign Macro Name list, select the macro you want to remove from a menu.

3. In the Menu list, select the name of the menu the macro is assigned to.

4. Choose Unassign to remove the selected macro from the menu.

5. Click OK or press **Enter**.

Assigning Macros to Keys

If you want to use the keyboard to run macros, you can assign a macro to a key combination so it automatically runs that macro.

You can assign a macro to a function key or to a Ctrl+*key* combination. Because each macro's key combination must be unique, you must choose a combination of keys that is currently "unassigned." The best way to do this is through trial and error using the following procedure—Word tells you if a key combination is already assigned to something else. To improve your chances of picking a unique combination, we suggest using one of the following combinations:

- Ctrl+Shift+another key

- Ctrl+number key (either from top keyboard row or from numeric keypad with NumLock on)

To assign a macro to keys:

1. Choose the Macro Assign to Key command. Word displays the dialog box shown in Figure 25–5.

2. Select the macro name from the list. Word lists any current key assignments in the Current Keys box.

3. Press the function key or the Ctrl+key combination you want to assign to your macro. The keys you press appear in the Key box (see Figure 25–5).

   If the key combination you typed is currently assigned, Word lists the command it's assigned to. If the key combination is not currently in use, Word displays [currently unassigned] in the Key box.

4. Repeat step 3 until you see [currently unassigned] in the Key box.

5. Choose Assign to assign the key combination to the macro.

6. Click OK or press **Enter**.

Figure 25–5.
Assigning a macro to keys.

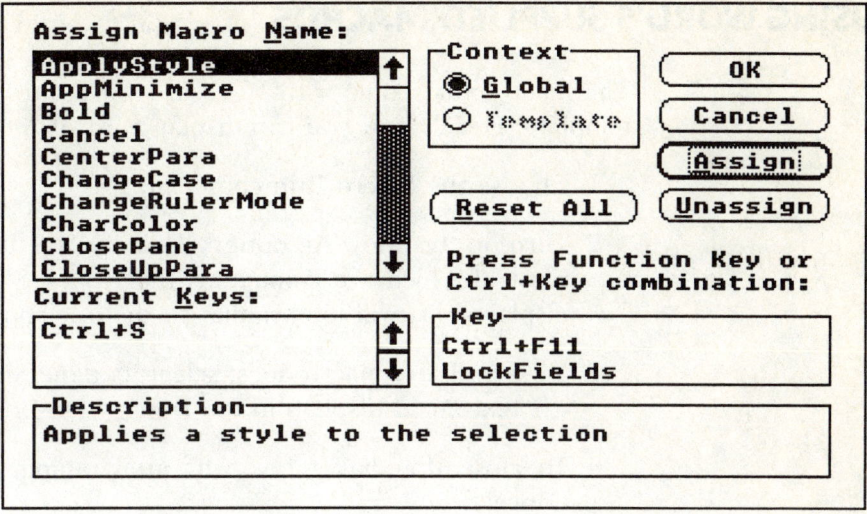

You can check key assignments at any time by selecting the macro name in the Macro Assign to Key dialog box. If the macro is also assigned to a menu, the keys appear alongside the name on the menu.

Just like almost everything else in Word, key assignments are not necessarily permanent. If you change your mind, you can always "unassign" a key assignment in this way:

1. Choose the Macro Assign to Key command.

2. Select the macro name.

3. If there's more than one key combination in the Current Keys box, select the key combination you want to "unassign."

4. Choose Unassign.

5. Click OK or press **Enter**.

If key assignments have gotten so confusing that you'd like to return to using Word's default assignments, you can use the following procedure to restore key combinations to the original Word settings:

1. Choose the Macro Assign to Key command.

2. Choose Reset All.

3. Click OK or press **Enter**.

USING WORD'S SUPPLIED MACROS

The macros that come with Word are stored in the NORMAL.DOT template. Here's how you can display a list of these macros:

1. Choose the Macro Run command.

2. Turn on the Show All option. This displays all of Word's macros, most of which are commands that you see on the menus. The displayed list will look similar to the one shown in Figure 25–6.

3. To see what a macro does, select its name in the list, then read the text Word displays in the Description box.

4. To close the dialog box without running the macro, choose Cancel.

You can run Word's supplied macros as is, or assign them to different menus or keys using the procedures described earlier in this chapter.

TROUBLESHOOTING AND CORRECTING MACROS

If your macro is fairly simple, but you've made a mistake in recording, the easiest way to fix it is to record the macro again.

If you've recorded a complex macro and it's not working properly, you can use the procedures in this section to step through the macro instructions in various ways to see just what's wrong and then correct the macro text.

Figure 25–6.
Macros supplied with Word.

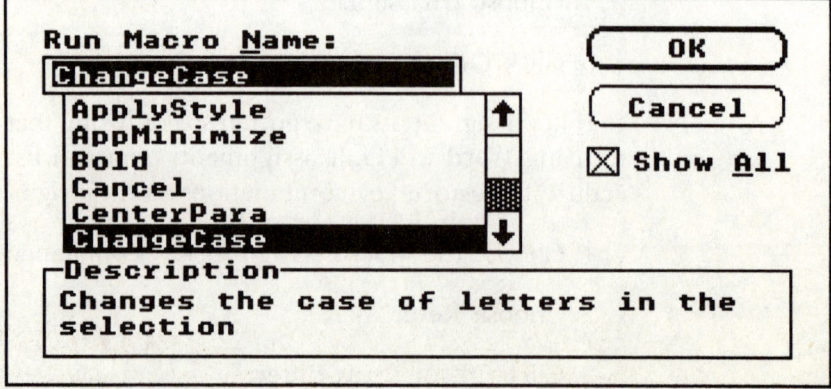

To step through a macro:

1. Choose the Macro Edit command.

2. Do one of the following:

   ■ Select the name of the macro from the list, then press **Enter**.

   or

   ■ Double-click the macro name in the list.

   Word displays the macro text in the Macro Edit window, as shown in Figure 25–7.

3. If you want to step through the instructions in the macro, choose one of the buttons in the edit bar at the top of the window:

Choose	To
Start/ Continue	Run the active macro or continue running after a pause.
Step	Run each macro instruction as a single step, stopping after each instruction.

Figure 25–7.
Troubleshooting a macro in the Macro Edit window.

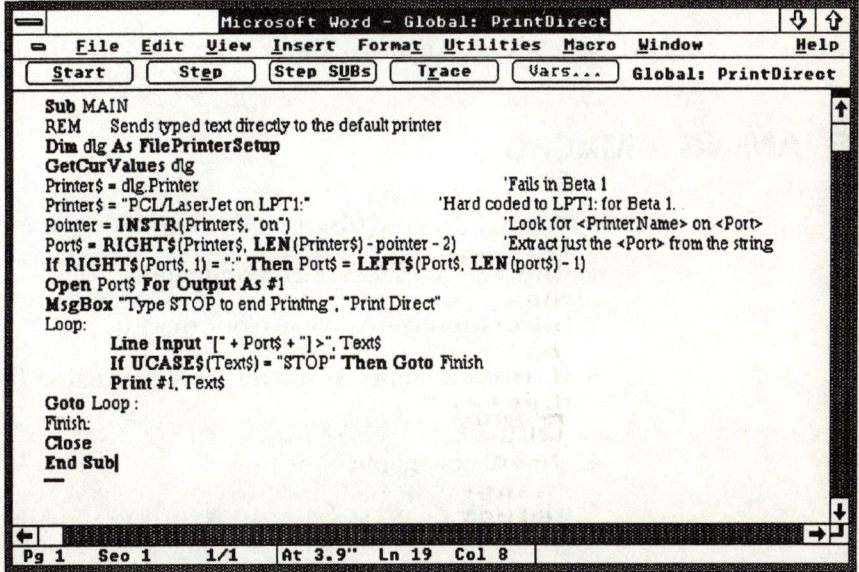

Step SUBS (subroutine)	Run each macro instruction as a single step, stopping after each instruction, unless the instruction is a macro (subroutine), which will be run in its entirety before stopping.
Trace	Highlight each instruction as the macro is running.
Var	Display the macro variables.

4. Edit the macro text as necessary to correct it. (See the Word *Technical Reference* for more information about the macro language.)

5. When you're finished, choose Document Control Close (**Ctrl+F4**) to close the Macro Edit window.

CHANGING A MACRO'S DESCRIPTION

When you want to change the name or description of a macro that you created without changing the macro instructions, do this:

1. Choose the Macro Edit command.

2. Change the description text in the dialog box.

3. Choose Set.

4. Click OK or press **Enter**.

RENAMING A MACRO

To change the name of a macro that you created:

1. Choose the Macro Edit command.

2. Select the macro name from the list.

3. Choose Rename. Word displays the dialog box shown in Figure 25–8.

4. Type a new name.

5. Click OK or press **Enter** to return to the Macro Edit dialog box.

6. Click OK or press **Enter**.

Figure 25–8.
Renaming a macro.

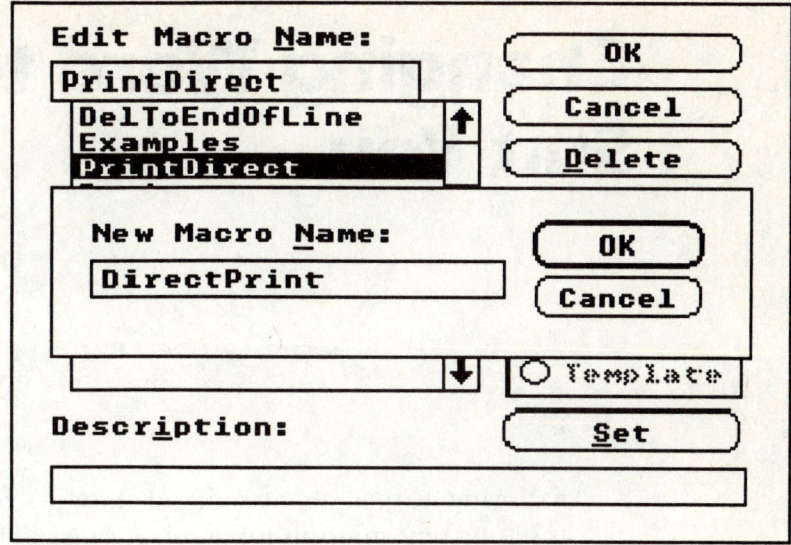

Edit Macro **N**ame:

OK

PrintDirect

Cancel

DelToEndOfLine

Delete

Examples
PrintDirect

New Macro **N**ame:

OK

DirectPrint

Cancel

○ Template

Descr**i**ption:

Set

DELETING A MACRO

When you no longer need a macro that you created, you can get rid of it to free up disk space and computer memory.

Note: If you're using the Macro Edit window to correct a macro when you decide to delete it, close the Macro Edit window before you use the following procedure.

To delete a macro:

1. Choose the Macro Edit command.

2. Choose the name of the macro from the Edit Macro Name list box.

3. Choose Delete.

4. Click OK or press **Enter**.

## Chapter Twenty-Six

Changing Word to Suit You

You've already learned about some of the ways to customize Word, such as setting time intervals for automatic saves, changing the default tab width, turning on background pagination, and creating your own macros. In this chapter, you'll see that you can customize Word even further by rearranging menus and key assignments. So you don't use a command on a menu? Get rid of it! Do you wish that a dialog box option appeared on a menu? Put it there! You say you want to assign key combinations that are easy to remember? You can customize Word's command structure to reflect the way you like to work.

If you don't like Word's default settings, you can change many of them, too. Want to measure with centimeters instead of inches? Want to use a comma instead of a period as the decimal character? Go ahead—you can now make Word use the default settings you want. This chapter shows how you change the way Word treats the monitor and the way it treats your documents. It describes how to

- add or delete commands and dialog box options from menus.

- assign keys to commands and dialog box options.

- change the default unit of measurement and other default settings.

- change the colors of the Word screen.

- customize the help system.

- return all Word options to their original settings.

ASSIGNING COMMANDS AND DIALOG BOX OPTIONS TO NEW MENUS AND KEYS

You can use the Macro menu to add commands and dialog box options to menus, delete them from menus, or assign them to different keys. However, there is one big disadvantage to rearranging and reassigning commands that you should consider before you make drastic changes. When you move commands, the program no longer exactly matches the documentation (or this book!), so it may be more confusing to learn new tasks.

All of Word's commands and dialog box options are stored as macros in the NORMAL.DOT template. For example, the Utilities Sort command is stored as the UtilSort macro; the Bold option in the Format Character dialog box is stored as the Bold macro; the Centered option in the Format Paragraph dialog box is stored as the CenterPara macro. To add these options to menus or assign them to keys, you just assign the appropriate macro to a menu or to a key combination.

Finding Out What a Command or Dialog Box Option Does

If you don't know the function of a macro in the Assign Macro Name list, you can easily ask Word to display a description of that macro.

To see a description of a macro in the list:

1. Choose the Macro Assign to Menu command. Word displays the dialog box shown in Figure 26–1.

Figure 26–1.
The Macro Assign to Menu list box displays a description when you select a macro from the list.

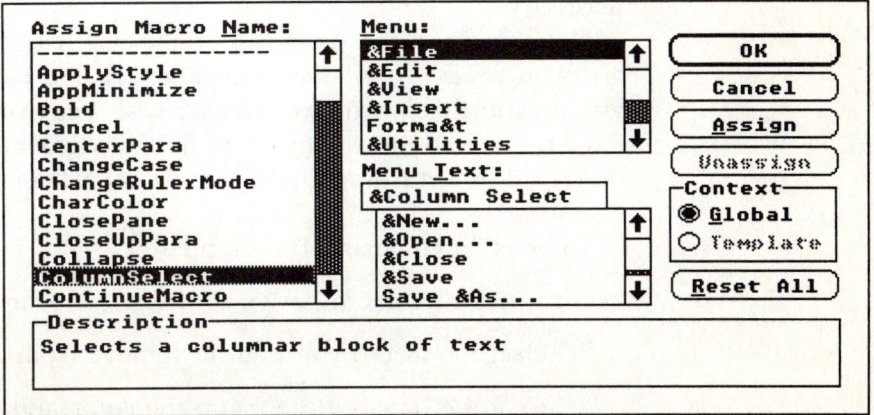

2. Select the macro in the list.

3. Read the description of the macro in the Description box.

4. Choose Cancel to close the dialog box without making any changes.

Printing a List of Assignments

You can always print a list of all of Word's commands with their current key assignments and descriptions in this way:

1. Choose the File Print command.

2. Select Key Assignments from the drop-down Print list.

3. Click OK or press **Enter** to begin printing. It may take a few minutes for Word to compile the list and print it, so be patient.

This list makes a handy reference guide, especially when you've customized your system. You can also return commands to their original assignments at any time. You learn how to do all these tasks in the following sections.

Deleting a Command from a Menu

If you think that a menu is too long or you want to move a command to a new menu, you can easily delete a command from a menu. Commands that you delete from menus remain in the list of macros, so you can always return them to their original menu locations if necessary.

Note: Because the Assign to Menu and Assign to Key commands give you access to all the commands, dialog box options, and key assignments that Word uses, it's *not* a wise idea to delete either of them from the Macro menu. If you do this by accident, use the procedure described in Returning Options to Original Assignments later in this chapter.

To delete a command from a menu:

1. Choose the Macro Assign to Menu command.

2. Select the macro you want to remove from a menu.

3. Select the name of the menu the command is assigned to.

4. Select the menu text.

5. Choose Unassign to remove the selected command from its menu.

6. Click OK or press **Enter**. The next time you pull down the menu, you'll see that the command is gone.

Adding a Command to a Menu

If you find that you're constantly opening a dialog box to use the same option, you might want to turn that option into a command on a menu so you can use it more quickly. When you assign a macro to a menu, it appears and behaves just like any other Word command.

Every command on a Word menu has an underlined letter that you can use to choose the command from the keyboard. When you assign a macro to a menu, you need to designate the letter in the macro name that you want to use in this way. Word initially suggests the letter by placing an ampersand (&) in front of a letter in the name (see the Menu Text box in Figure 26–1). The ampersand causes an underline to appear under the following letter when the name appears on a menu. You can change the underlined letter by moving the ampersand in front of any other letter in the macro name. Make sure, though, it doesn't conflict with the underlined letter in any other name on that menu.

To assign a macro to a menu:

1. Choose the Macro Assign to Menu command. Word displays the dialog box shown in Figure 26–1.

2. Select the macro name from the Assign Macro Name list.

3. Select a menu name from the Menu list.

4. In the Menu Text box, type the name that you want to appear on the menu. (Because menus have limited space, you may want to use a name that is shorter than the original name you gave to the macro.)

5. Choose one of the following options:

Choose	To
Global	Save the assignment in the NORMAL.DOT template to make it available to all documents.

Template   Save the assignment in the template file you're using now.

6. Choose Assign to add the macro to the menu.

7. Click OK or press **Enter**.

Figure 26–2 shows the Format menu after the Bold macro has been added to it.

◣ **EXAMPLE: Adding an Option to a Menu**

Say that you like to use overtype mode to type over existing text, but you can never remember the keys to press to turn overtype on. You decide you want to add the overtype macro to the Edit menu. Here's what you'd do:

1. Choose the Macro Assign to Menu command.

2. Select Overtype from the Assign Macro Name list.

3. Select Edit from the Menu list. Word proposes Overtype as the command name. That's short enough to list on a menu, so you accept it.

4. Choose Global to save the assignment in the NORMAL.DOT template to make it available to all documents.

Figure 26–2.
The Bold dialog box option added to the Format menu.

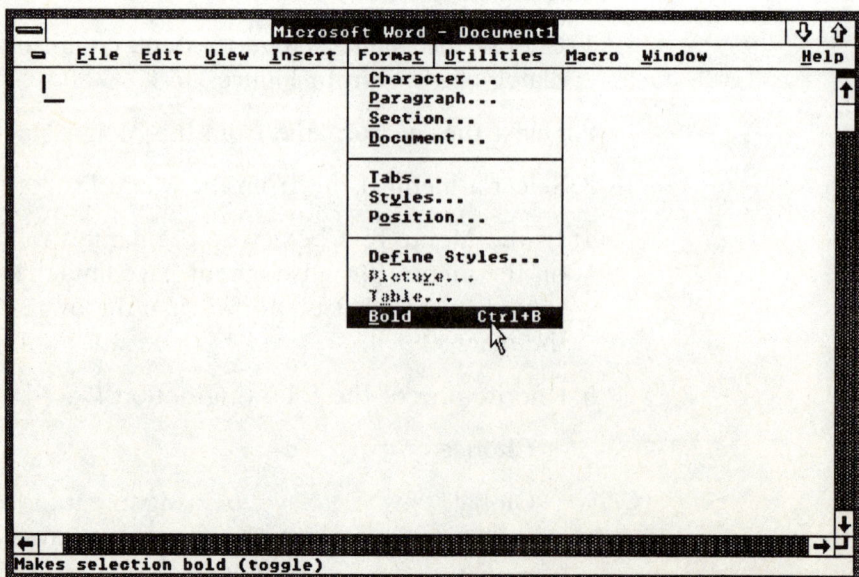

5. Choose Assign to add the macro to the menu.

6. Click OK or press **Enter**.

The next time you pull down the Edit menu, you see the new Overtype command. Just choose it to toggle overtype on or off.

Assigning Commands to Keys

If you want to use the keyboard to choose commands, you can assign a command or dialog box option to a single function key or a Ctrl key combination so you simply press those keys to run the appropriate macro.

You can assign a macro to a function key or to a Ctrl+*key* combination. Because each macro's key combination must be unique, you must choose a combination of keys that is currently "unassigned." The best way to do this is through trial and error using the following procedure—Word tells you if a key combination is already assigned to something else. To improve your chances of picking a unique combination, we suggest using one of the following combinations:

- Ctrl+Shift+another key

- Ctrl+number key (either from top keyboard row or from numeric keypad with NumLock on)

To assign a command or dialog box option to keys:

1. Choose the Macro Assign to Key command. Word displays the dialog box shown in Figure 26–3.

2. Select the macro name from the list. Word displays any current key assignments in the Current Keys box.

3. Press the function key or the Ctrl+*key* combination you want to assign to your macro. The keys you press appear in the Key box.

   If the key combination you typed is currently assigned, Word lists the command the key is assigned to. If the key combination is not currently in use, Word displays [currently unassigned] in the Key box.

4. Repeat step 3 until you see [currently unassigned] in the Key box.

Figure 26-3.
Assigning a macro to keys.

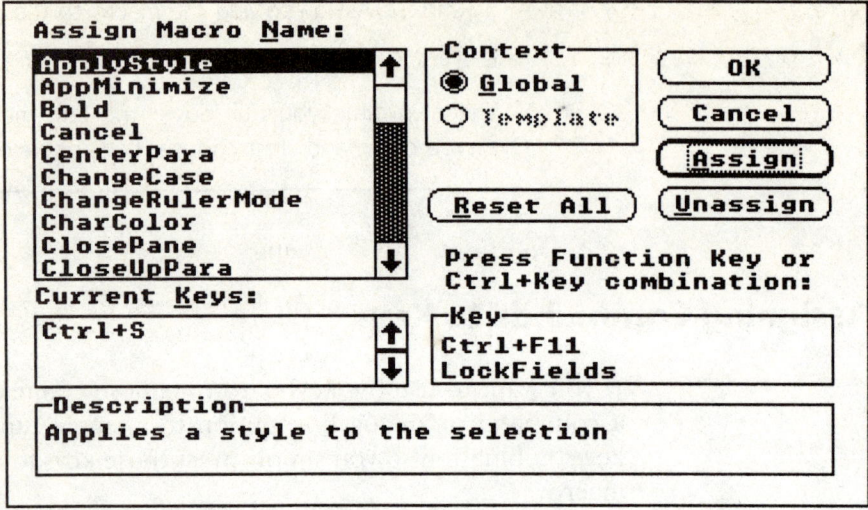

5. Choose Assign to assign the key combination to the macro.

6. Click OK or press **Enter**.

You can check key assignments at any time by selecting the macro name in the Macro Assign to Key dialog box. If the macro is also assigned to a menu, the keys appear alongside the name on the menu.

Removing Key Assignments from Commands

Just like almost everything else in Word, key assignments are not necessarily permanent. If you change your mind, you can always "unassign" a key assignment in this way:

1. Choose the Macro Assign to Key command.

2. Select the macro name.

3. If there's more than one key combination in the Current Keys box, select the key combination you want to "unassign."

4. Choose Unassign.

5. Click OK or press **Enter**.

Returning Commands and Dialog Box Options to Their Original Assignments

If menus and key assignments have gotten so confusing that you'd like to return to using Word's default assignments, you can restore key combinations as they were when Word was shipped in this way:

1. Do one of the following:

   ■ Choose the Macro Assign to Key command to restore key assignments.

   or

   ■ Choose the Macro Assign to Menu command to restore menu assignments.

2. Choose Reset All.

3. Click OK or press **Enter**.

CHANGING THE DEFAULT UNIT OF MEASUREMENT

Word uses inches as its default unit of measurement, but you can change this to centimeters, points, or picas. Word then uses the new unit of measurement in text boxes and in the ruler.

To change the default unit of measurement:

1. Choose the Utilities Customize command. Word displays the dialog box shown in Figure 26–4.

2. Select a new unit of measurement from one of the options.

3. Click OK or press **Enter**. Word changes the units on the ruler and in dialog boxes that use measurements.

SETTING SCREEN-DISPLAY PREFERENCES

The View Preferences command controls the way text is displayed in the Word window. You can choose options to see special characters and other options that are invisible by default. All of the options in the View Preferences dialog box are toggles. To turn on the options, just choose them to place an X in the accompanying check boxes. To

Figure 26–4.
The Utilities
Customize command
controls many
default settings.

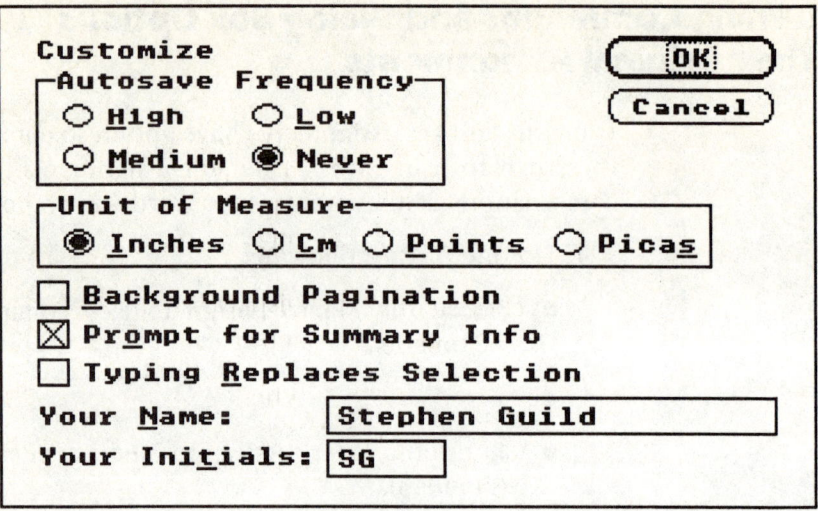

Figure 26–5.
The View Preferences
dialog box.

turn them off, choose them again to make the X disappear. Word saves
your choices in the WINWORD.INI file.

To adjust the window display:

1. Choose the View Preferences command. Word displays the dialog
box shown in Figure 26–5.

2. Choose options to turn them on; choose them again to turn them
off. Word displays an X to indicate that an option is "on."

3. Choose OK or press **Enter**.

The options include:

Option	Description
Tabs	Displays or removes tab characters (→).
Spaces	Displays or removes space characters (·).

Paragraph Marks	Displays or removes paragraph marks (¶).
Optional Hyphens	When turned on, optional hyphens appear as logical NOT symbols, and nonbreaking hyphens appear as extra long hyphens. When turned off, all types of hyphens look alike.
Hidden Text	Displays or removes text formatted as hidden text.
Show All	When on, displays all of the above, as well as field codes, table gridlines, and text boundaries.
Display as Printed	When on, displays text and graphics exactly as they appear when printed on your printer. Turning this on limits the use of certain fonts and point sizes on the monitor.
Pictures	Displays pictures when turned on, displays blank boxes in place of pictures when turned off. Turning this option off can speed up redrawing the screen after scrolling and other operations.
Text Boundaries	Displays or removes the nonprinting dotted boxes around headers, footers, and fixed-positioned objects.
Horizontal Scroll Bar	Displays or removes the scroll bar at the bottom of document windows.
Vertical Scroll Bar	Displays or removes the scroll bar on the right side of document windows.
Table Gridlines	Displays or removes the nonprinting dotted lines and cell text markers around cell borders in tables.

You can also type a measurement in the Style Area Width box to choose how wide you want the style name area—the portion of the window that contains the name of each style assigned to a paragraph.

CUSTOMIZING THE HELP SYSTEM

You can customize Word's help system by adding bookmarks to make it easier for you to use. This section shows you how.

Recall that bookmarks are names that you assign to selected text in a file. Once you've assigned a bookmark to a help topic, you can use the bookmark name to quickly jump to the "bookmarked" topic, by-passing all the jump terms you normally have to use.

To add a bookmark to a help topic:

1. Display the help topic you want to assign a bookmark to.

2. Choose the Bookmark Define command. Help usually proposes the topic's name as the bookmark, as shown in Figure 26–6. If you don't want to accept this name or if no name is proposed, type the term you want to use as a bookmark.

3. Click OK or press **Enter**. Word assigns the bookmark name to the help topic.

When you want to jump to your "bookmarked" help topic:

■ Choose the bookmark name from the Bookmark menu in the Help window.

To remove a bookmark from a help topic:

Figure 26–6.
Adding a bookmark
to a help topic.

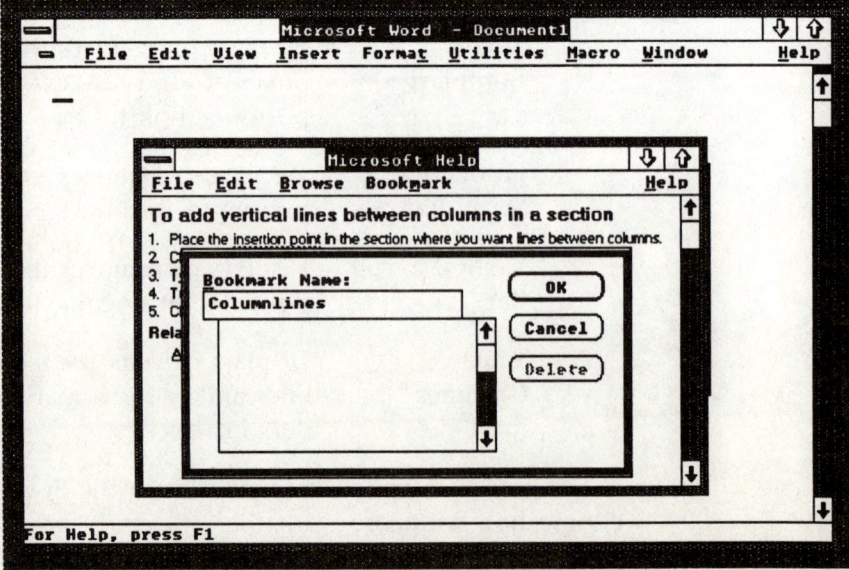

1. Choose the Bookmark Define command in the Help window.

2. Select the bookmark name you want to delete.

3. Choose Delete.

CHANGING THE FORMATS OF NUMBERS, DATES, AND TIMES

Because Word was created in the United States, it uses U.S. settings by default for dates and numbers. For example, Americans normally write 1/30/89 when they mean January 30, 1989. However, in most other countries of the world, this date would be written as 30/1/89. Another U.S.-specific standard is using a comma as a separator between thousands and hundreds, when many other parts of the world use periods instead. And although 24-hour time format is normally used only by the military in the United States (we prefer to say 3 P.M. instead of 1500 hours), the 24-hour system is the standard in most other places.

If you want to change these country-specific settings (as well as others), you can use the Windows Control Panel like this:

1. In Word, choose the Run command from the Word Control menu (**Alt, Spacebar, U**).

2. Choose Control Panel from the dialog box that appears, then choose OK. This displays the Control Panel window, shown in Figure 26–7.

3. Choose the Country Settings command from the Preferences menu. This displays the dialog box shown in Figure 26–8.

4. Change the options as necessary. If you want to switch all the settings to match the standards for a specific country, just select the country from the list.

5. Click OK or press **Enter**.

6. Choose the Close command from the Control Panel menu (**Alt+F4**) to close the window and return to Word.

Changes you make using the Control Panel are stored in the WIN.INI file.

Figure 26–7.
The Windows Control
Panel window.

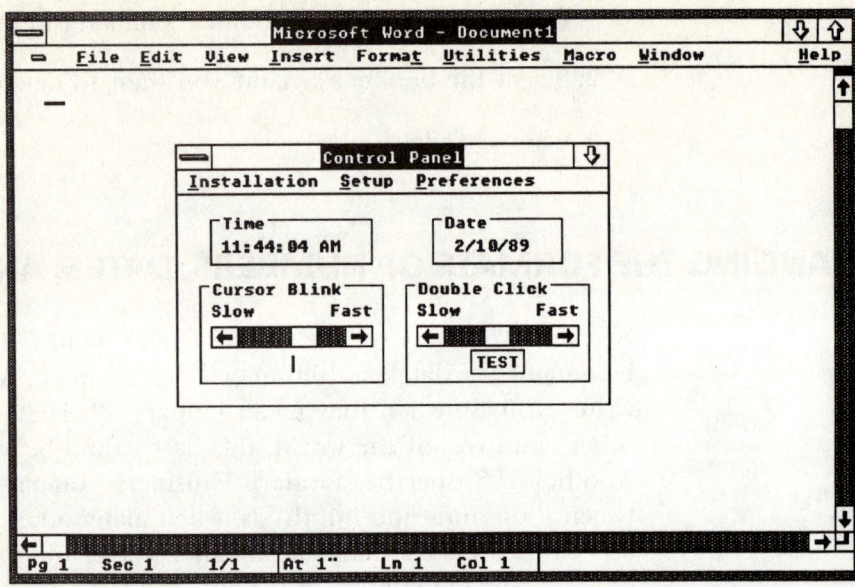

Figure 26–8.
Changing country-
specific settings with
the Control Panel.

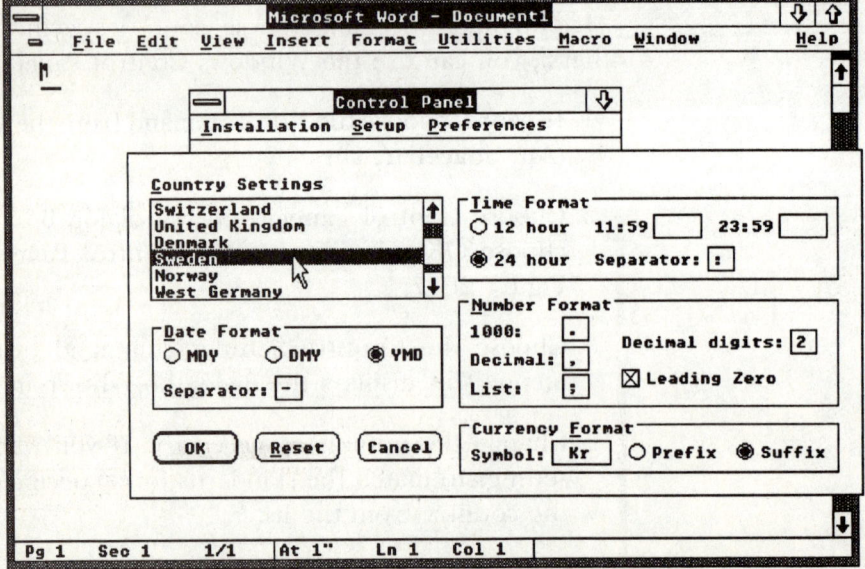

CHANGING THE COLORS OF THE WORD SCREEN

Just like any other Windows program, you can use the Control Panel
to change the colors of the Word screen. Here's how:

1. In Word, choose the Run command from the Word Control menu (**Alt, Spacebar, U**).

2. Choose Control Panel from the dialog box that appears, then choose OK. This displays the Control Panel window, shown in Figure 26–7.

3. Choose the Screen Colors command from the Preferences menu. This displays the dialog box shown in Figure 26–9.

4. In the Screen Colors list, select the part of the screen you want to change. For example, if you want to change the color of the menu bar, select Menu Bar.

5. Use the mouse or the arrow keys to move the boxes in the Hue, Bright, and Color slider bars. As you change the slider bars, you see the appropriate part of the screen change color in the Sample screen at the right. If you want to cancel your changes and start over, choose Reset.

6. Repeat steps 4 and 5 to change any other parts of the screen you want.

7. Click OK or press **Enter** when you've changed the colors to your satisfaction.

Figure 26–9.
Changing screen colors with the Control Panel.

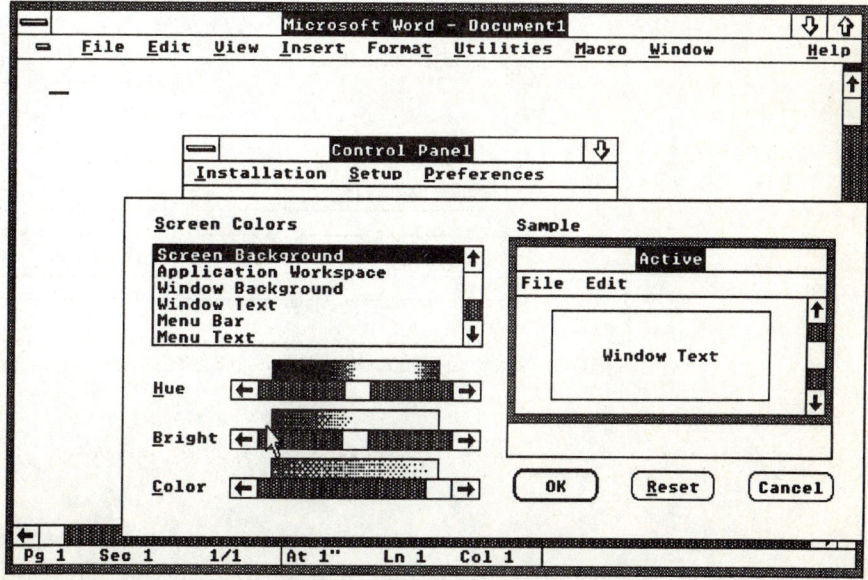

8. Choose the Close command from the Control Panel menu (**Alt+F4**) to close the window and return to Word.

Changes you make with the Control Panel are stored in the WIN.INI file.

CHANGING ALL OPTIONS BACK TO THEIR ORIGINAL SETTINGS

Word keeps all the changes you make to the Word program in a file named WINWORD.INI. If you ever want to restore Word settings to the way they were the first time the software was used, here's how:

■ Delete the WINWORD.INI file. (Use the operating system DEL command or the File Delete command in the MS-DOS Executive.)

Deleting the WINWORD.INI file deletes all the changes you've made to customize the program. This has no effect whatsoever on the files you've created with Word. When you run Word for Windows again, Word prompts you for your name and initials, just like it did the very first time you used the program. Then Word creates a new WINWORD.INI file to store new settings.

Deleting WINWORD.INI causes Word to switch back to short menus, so the very first thing you may want to do is choose View Full Menus to display the complete set of commands.

Index